INTRODUCTION TO
SOCIOLOGY

INTRODUCTION TO
SOCIOLOGY

An Alternate Approach

General Editor
J. Paul Grayson

gage PUBLISHING LIMITED
TORONTO ONTARIO CANADA

Canadian Cataloguing in Publication Data

Main entry under title:
Introduction to sociology: an alternate approach

Bibliography: p.
ISBN 0-7715-5792-2

1. Sociology—Addresses, essays, lectures.
I. Grayson, J. Paul (John Paul), 1944-

HM51.I57   301   C83-094187-8

Co-ordinating Editors: Joan Kerr, Kathy Austin

Editors: Geraldine Kikuta, Susan Yates

Designer: Susan Weiss

Cover Design: Susan Weiss

2 3 4 5 WC 87 86 85 84

Written, Printed and Bound in Canada

More Gage Books in Sociology

CANADIAN SOCIETY
Growth and Dualism—Roderic Beaujot and Kevin
  McQuillan
Canadian Society—Bernard R. Blishen, Frank E. Jones,
  Kaspar D. Naegele, and John Porter
Prophecy and Protest—Samuel D. Clark, J. Paul
  Grayson and Linda M. Grayson
The Measure of Canadian Society—John Porter

THE FAMILY
Courtship, Marriage and the Family in Canada—G. N.
  Ramu
Families in Canada Today—M. Eichler
The Canadian Family—K. Ishwaran

SEX AND SEX ROLES
Secret Oppression—Constance Backhouse and Leah
  Cohen
The Sexes—R. N. Whitehurst and G. V. Booth

MINORITIES AND RACISM
Ethnicity and Human Rights in Canada—Evelyn Kallen

DEVIANCE AND CRIMINOLOGY
Police Command—Brian A. Grosman
Policing in Canada—William Kelly and Nora Kelly
Crime and You—A. M. Kirkpatrick and W. T. McGrath
Crime and Its Treatment in Canada—W. T. McGrath
Hookers, Rounders & Desk Clerks—Robert Prus and
  Styllianoss Irini
Roadhustler—Robert C. Prus and C. R. D. Sharper
Policeman—Claude L. Vincent

EDUCATION
Education, Change and Society—Richard A. Carlton,
  Louise A. Colley, and Neil J. MacKinnon

CONTRIBUTORS

Bernd Baldus
University of Toronto
Toronto, ON

E. J. Bennett
Osgoode Law School
York University
Downsview, ON

Carl J. Cuneo
McMaster University
Hamilton, ON

John R. Hofley
University of Winnipeg
Winnipeg, MB

J. Paul Grayson
York University
Downsview, ON

John D. Jackson
Concordia University
Montreal, PQ

John Alan Lee
University of Toronto
Toronto, ON

Graham S. Lowe
University of Alberta
Edmonton, AB

Greg M. Nielsen
Université de Montréal
Montreal, PQ

D. A. Nock
Lakehead University
Thunder Bay, ON

M. Ornstein
York University
Downsview, ON

R. James Sacouman
Acadia University
Wolfville, NS

Dorothy E. Smith
Ontario Institute for
Studies in Education
Toronto, ON

Roz Usiskin
University of Winnipeg
Winnipeg, MB

Henry Veltmeyer
Saint Mary's University
Halifax, NS

W. G. West
Ontario Institute for
Studies in Education
Toronto, ON

Dennis William Wilcox-Magill
University of Toronto
Toronto, ON

CONTENTS

PREFACE

Objectives

This book has two objectives. The first is to introduce the reader to the main ideas of a certain kind of sociology. The second is to use these ideas in explaining the society in which the reader lives.

The type of sociology found in this volume can be described as materialist. In general, materialism is a way of looking at the world that "highlights the central role played in history by the productive activities of mankind, and that therefore locates a principal motive for historical change in the struggle among social classes over their respective shares in the fruits of production" (Heilbroner 1980:21). If the meaning of this passage is not immediately clear, hopefully it will become so after the reader has examined the following chapters. All of them are written from a materialist perspective.

To identify a perspective as materialist is not enough. There are several variants of materialism. It will soon be apparent to the reader of this book that a type of materialism called Marxism is a major thread that weaves the chapters together. Some of the major figures in this tradition include Marx and Engels, Gramsci, Althusser and Poulantzas. Readers will also detect in many instances the influence of what is called the Canadian political economy tradition. Names prominent in this school include Innis, Lower, and Fowke.

It should be stated at the outset that some scholars view these two orientations—Marxism and Canadian political economy—as incompatible. Others see them as capable of important cross-fertilization. Wallace Clement is among the latter. "The revival of both Marxism and political economy," Clement writes, "marks an invigoration of social science in Canada, an invigoration which combines an awareness of contemporary issues in Canadian society and a desire to do something about the Canadian condition" (1978:iii). Many of the authors of this text would agree with Clement. Some would not. Differences aside, all would agree on the validity of many Marxist concepts and ideas.

It will become clear from a reading of the text that the authors of this book believe that there is a close relationship between the two objectives stated above—that in order to fully understand what is going on in Canada one needs a materialist perspective; that in order to understand the materialist perspective it is necessary to examine actual societies. Furthermore, they reject the idea found in many other sociology texts that the first goal of sociology is to find universal laws of human behavior. They would agree with S.D. Clark when he writes:

> Sociologists in Canada have tended to take too seriously what was said in the first chapter of the introductory textbook in sociology or what they had been told by their American sociology teachers. Sociology is a science in search of universal principles of social organization and social behavior. It knows no national boundaries. If a sociological principle has validity, it has such whether the form of social behavior is to be found in Pakistan, in West Africa, or the Arctic regions of Canada.
>
> There can be no quarrel with such a statement of the ends of sociology. What the first chapter of the introductory textbook fails to point out, however, is the fact that in an effort to formulate general principles of social organization and social behavior the sociologist must study society, and it is to the examination of his own society that he very largely turns. There is nothing strange nor undesirable about this. A sociology that is worth its own salt is a sociology that develops out of a deep concern about the problems of society. The nearer one is to those problems the greater is the concern (1976:127).

About the Book

It will be clear from the way in which they write that the authors of this book are critical of many aspects of Canadian society. Their concerns include the dehumanization that occurs in many workplaces; the subordination of women in the family; the way in which the state serves the interests of some classes and not others; the way in which education perpetuates inequalities; the underdevelopment of some areas of Canada, and so on.

It must not be assumed that because of these criticisms the authors view other existing societies, such as the Soviet Union and/or China, as preferable places in which to live. Most would argue that the forms of political oppression experienced in places like the Soviet Union may be just as unbearable as in many capitalist societies. At the same time, when compared to a number of capitalist societies like El Salvador, Honduras, and so on, the current record of the Soviet Union with regard to political freedom looks rather good. The critique of existing societies that is either implicitly or explicitly embodied in the authors' analysis derives from the belief that it is possible to build a better society than the one in which we live. Most would start their building process by forging close links with the Canadian working class.

By definition, the authors of this book are critical of the way in which sociology, and particularly introductory sociology, is usually taught. Most share Clark's view that the first step on the path to sociological knowledge involves the understanding of one's society and one's place in it. It is not surprising, therefore, that many of the authors have been involved in the "Canadianization movement' in sociology. They have been concerned that the type of sociology taught deal with Canadian problems and that it recognize the peculiarities of the Canadian circumstance. Given this interest it is not surprising that some—but not all—of them have also engaged in activities centered on altering the general economic, political and cultural subordination of Canada to the United States. All have been concerned with making Canada a better place in which to live.

How to Read the Book

The text begins with a general introduction to the various ways in which Canada has been studied. It then moves to an examination of some of the general ideas of Marxism, one of the major threads of the text. Many of the ideas of this chapter are then taken up in the discussion of specific social phenomena such as class, the family, culture, education, and so on. The book concludes with a chapter on research and writing in the social sciences.

There are two ways in which the book can be read. The reader can start at the beginning and go through to the end. This type of reading will take the reader systematically through general approaches to the study of society and Canadian society, the main ideas of Marxism, and some important social phenomena. But the reader can also be eclectic. Each chapter contains sufficient introductory material such that the reader should be able to understand it without having to know what was discussed in the previous chapters.

In essence, it is possible to have your cake and eat it too. Those who prefer to start with a general orientation and then examine how the orientation can be used in the study of concrete phenomena should start at the beginning and work through. Those who would rather examine specific phenomena and then look at the way in which common threads can be found in many if not all phenomena should begin their reading with the chapters on specific aspects of society. They can then return to the more theoretical chapters. Whatever the route taken, it is hoped that after finishing the text the reader will have a deeper insight into him(her)self, sociology, and Canadian society.

J. Paul Grayson
Atkinson College
York University

Theoretical Approaches

PARADIGMS AND SOCIAL SCIENCE IN ENGLISH CANADA

Dennis William Wilcox-Magill

Introduction

The untrained mind views the social world as a maze of confused and unrelated events. The social scientific mind views the world through a framework or gestalt. It weaves fragmented events together within a systematic frame of reference. This framework is called a paradigm.

More broadly defined, a paradigm is *a set of mental images* shared by a number of individuals within an academic discipline. As Ritzer notes, a paradigm is "...a fundamental image of the subject matter within a science. It serves to define what should be studied, what questions should be asked, how they should be asked, and what rules should be followed in interpreting the answers obtained. The paradigm is the broadest unit of consensus within a science and serves to differentiate one scientific community (or subcommunity) from another" (1975:7. See also, Kuhn 1970a; 1970b; 1977 and Eckberg and Hill 1979). Thus, a paradigm facilitates communications among individuals who share the same vocabulary.

The continuity of a paradigm over generations is assured through the introduction of new recruits into a discipline, which most frequently occurs within universities. In these institutions students study specialized fields of knowledge. They also learn disciplinary ways of providing technical solutions to problems and mental images to interpret these solutions. This process takes place through laboratory experiments, reading textbooks and research papers, the writing of research papers, and examinations. Each student who reads this text and reflects about the materialist paradigm is being introduced to a specific mode of intellectual consciousness.

Not all university professors agree on the basic paradigm in their discipline. Using questionnaire data collected from eighty university graduate departments, Lodahl and Gorden (1972) documented that physicists and chemists had greater agreement over discipline content than did sociologists and political scientists. Thus, it can be asserted that the physical sciences have greater paradigmatic development than do the social sciences. Indeed, no paradigm in sociology has been able to maintain pre-eminence over an extended period.

Paradigms and the Social Sciences in English Canada

Despite the low level of paradigmatic development in the social sciences, the concept of paradigm can be used in identifying various theoretical approaches to the study of society. At a very general level, it isolates a set of mental images shared by a group of individuals. In this chapter four paradigms that have emerged in English Canada will be considered. They are the ecological, the fabian, the staple, and the frontier-social change. Each will be examined by focussing on (1) the Canadian social scientists who played a central role in the institutionalization of the paradigms; (2) the intellectual influences on their ideas; (3) their major publications and core ideas; and (4) their legacy. Chapter six will discuss perspectives for analysing society that have emerged in Quebec.

It must be stressed at the outset that the paradigms discussed here are not all inclusive of those that have been applied in English Canada and elsewhere. For example, no representatives of what are called the symbolic interactionist and functional approaches can be found among the group selected for analysis. Many other textbooks give places of prominence to such individuals. Likewise, they pay considerable attention to the European theorists such as Emile Durkheim (1858-1917) and Max Weber (1864-1920).

The symbolic interactionist and functional approaches have been ignored because their impact on the development of a sociology of Canada has been minimal. Durkheim and Weber, on the other hand, are given less attention than in other texts because it is the intent of this book to present a materialist approach to the study of society. As a consequence, Karl Marx (1818-1883) receives a great deal of attention. The ideas of other relevant classical theorists are raised if the subject matter warrants their inclusion.

Many contemporary writings on Canada reflect the influence of American practitioners rather than the Canadians represented in this chapter. This is the result of the rapid expansion of sociology departments in the 1960s. A large number of university positions in English Canada were filled by Americans trained in the United States and these individuals tended to favor ideas and images more appropriate to the study of the United States than Canada.

The Canadian founders of sociology considered in this chapter adopted a broad outlook toward the features of Canadian society. They were generally concerned with "macro" considerations such as the development of cities, regions, or the entire country. This macro concern was not always shared by the large number of sociologists who entered English Canadian universities in the 1960s.

H.A. Innis, a political economist rather than a sociologist, is included in this chapter because of the impact his ideas have had on many young Canadian sociologists. Although a controversial viewpoint, some academics see a blending of Canadian political economy and Marxism as a major rejuvenating force for the social sciences in Canada.

HIGHLIGHT

1. Paradigms are sets of mental images shared by individuals or a particular discipline that define what is to be studied, what questions are to be asked, how they should be asked, and how the answers should be interpreted.
2. There is less agreement over paradigms in the social sciences than in the physical sciences.
3. Four general paradigms that have been applied to the macro study of Canada are the ecological, the fabian, the staple, and the frontier-social change.
4. As a consequence of the influx of academics from the United States in the 1960s, aspects of the paradigms of the Canadian founders of sociology in English Canada have been overlooked in contemporary writings.

THE ECOLOGICAL PARADIGM

The ecological paradigm was introduced into Canadian intellectual life by Carl Addington Dawson (1887-1964). Dawson was the founder of sociology in English Canada.

Biography. Two of the important influences of Dawson's formative years were his religious family background and growing up in a rural Prince Edward Island community. Of Scottish descent, Dawson's great-grandfather immigrated from the North of Ireland to Prince Edward Island in 1812. He was the first Methodist minister to settle in the province. Dawson's father was a farmer in Augustine Cove, a small community of twenty-five families. In later years, Dawson's childhood experiences in rural Prince Edward Island communities contributed to his insightful sociological analysis of pioneer community organization in Western Canada.

In 1911, after teaching for three years in his native province, Dawson entered the Sophomore class of Acadia University. This was a Baptist-affiliated institution in Nova Scotia with an enrolment of 200 students. After graduation in 1912, he accepted a pastoral position at the Baptist Church in Lockeport, Nova Scotia. He moved to Chicago in 1916 to pursue a Bachelor of Divinity at the University of Chicago. This move had significant consequences for his career and the history of Canadian sociology.

Contrasted with life in small Prince Edward Island and Nova Scotia communities, Chicago was an enriching and stimulating experience for twenty-seven-year-old Dawson. The city was a complex metropolitan environment. It had experienced large-scale immigration of Poles, Swedes, Bohemians, Norwegians, Dutch, Danes, Croations, Lithuanians, and Greeks. Also, there was steady migration of Blacks from the South. The Chicago urban environment and its ethnic diversity had a tremendous impact on Dawson. During his later teaching career, "Immigration" became one of his favorite courses.

Intellectual Influences.   At the University of Chicago the Divinity School and the Department of Sociology were closely associated. Dawson was greatly influenced by Robert E. Park (1864-1944), the most dynamic individual of the "Chicago School of Sociology."

Park's most original sociological contribution was his association with the development of human ecology. This theoretical approach borrowed Darwinian ideas about the interdependence of plant and animal life within zones whose boundaries were defined by observation. This approach was defined by R.D. McKenzie (1925:63-64) as:

> ...[the] study of the spatial and temporal relations of human beings as affected by the selective, distributive, and accommodative forces of the environment. Human ecology is fundamentally interested in the effect of position, in both time and space, upon institutions and human behavior....These spatial relationships of human beings are the products of competition and selection, and are continuously in the process of change as new factors enter to disturb the competitive relations or to facilitate mobility. Human institutions and human nature itself become accommodated to certain spatial relationships of human beings. As these spatial relationships change, the physical basis of social relations is altered, thereby producing social and political problems.

Two of Park's central concepts were "natural histories" and "natural areas." Natural histories referred to an abstract procedure of analysing and categorizing social processes. They involved the construction of "ideal type" representations. Specific social realities were thus studied not to isolate a unique historical phenomenon. Instead, they were to reveal common patterns of change or typical ecological stages or "cycles" of institutional development.

Natural areas were "subcultures" which emerged as the result of social processes. These areas go through typical stages of development and have their own character and moral climate. One goal of sociology, according to Park, was to study these stages of development and through observation portray the subjective values, perceptions, and code of conduct of the inhabitants.

A former newspaper reporter, Park emphasized in his lectures the importance of exploring these natural areas as an objective observer.

Chicago was viewed as a social laboratory. Graduate students were encouraged "...to explore the city on foot—to walk around various neighbourhoods, occasionally talking to people they met and recording their observations afterward in detail. The purpose was to get a feel for what was out there." (Carey 1975:178)

Examples of the natural area studies are the classic Chicago sociological studies including: *The Hobo: The Sociology of Homeless Men* (Anderson 1923); *The Ghetto*, (Wirth 1928); and *The Gold Coast and the Slum* (Zorbaugh 1929).

From Park, Dawson learned: (1) the importance of studying the city as a sociological laboratory; (2) the relevance of investigating natural histories and natural areas, particularly those of ethnic groups; and (3) the ecological paradigm. Human ecology then became the theoretical approach Dawson taught to generations of Canadian sociology students.

Academic Career.   While studying at Chicago, Dawson worked as an assistant pastor at Englewood Baptist Church. His studies were interrupted in 1918 by a telegram requesting his services in the army. For the next eighteen months he served as an honorary Captain on the Y.M.C.A. trans-Atlantic staff.

In 1919, he returned to Chicago as an instructor in the Sociology Department at the University of Chicago. From 1921 to 1922, he was head of the Department of Sociology, at Y.M.C.A. College in Chicago. On September 1, 1922, he was awarded a Ph.D. sociology degree, for a thesis entitled, "The Social Basis of Knowledge."

In June 1922, Dawson accepted an offer from McGill University as assistant professor of Social Sciences and director of the School of Social Workers. In 1925, he was appointed associate professor and, under his chairmanship, a separate Department of Sociology was established with a Master of Arts program.

Recognizing the dearth of Canadian sociological publications, Dawson organized the McGill sociology curriculum around what he perceived to be important sociological issues in Canada: immigration, the city, the frontier, and the social organization of ethnic groups.

In 1927, Dawson was joined by Everett C. Hughes (1897-1983), a Chicago-trained sociologist and a student of Robert Park. Within several years, they had developed a miniature Chicago school of sociology at McGill. At the graduate level, students were expected to undertake extensive fieldwork research. Most frequently the research was based on concepts derived from the human ecology paradigm. In 1939, Hughes left Canada to assume a position at the University of Chicago. Four years later, Hughes' seminal book was published—*French Canada in Transition* (1943).

Carl Dawson retired from McGill in 1952. He died at the age of seventy-seven on January 16, 1964. During his lifetime he had received continued academic recognition. He was president of the Canadian Political Science Association, a fellow of the Royal Society of Canada, chairman of the Canadian Social Science Research Council, and his alma mater (Acadia) awarded him an L.L.D.

Major Publications and Core Ideas.   Dawson's publications dealt with urban life, ecological processes, and frontier settlement of the Canadian west. In a 1926 article describing the social organization of Montreal, he borrowed the ecological ideas of the Canadian born University of Chicago sociologist, E.W. Burgess (1886-1966). The expansion of the urban environment was "... viewed as a selective process which distributes individuals into occupations, and sifts groups into areas of residence" (Dawson 1926:4). Cities, Dawson argued, grew from the center in a series of successive concentric zones:

Zone One: Central Business District. The central financial, cultural and political area characterized by high rent values and great mobility of the population.

Zone Two: Zone of Transition. A previous area of residence that has been invaded by light-manufacturing and business. While sites are held speculatively for sale as future business use, the residences are allowed to deteriorate. Rents are relatively low. The area becomes a slum with a shifting population. It is an area where immigrants first settle and usually houses several immigrant colonies. It is also, to use Dawson's term, the "city bad-lands" (the home of vice and crime).

Zone Three: Working Men's Homes. An area occupied by skilled and unskilled factory workers. Also, "... this third zone is the place of second residence for immigrant groups. They have succeeded economically; they have been disturbed by further deterioration in the area of first residence; they have been pushed out by newer immigrants and they have moved to a more stable and wholesome community. While the sudden entry of many immigrants speeds up the junking process of the second circle, it also seriously affects the social adjustment in each succeeding circle" (Dawson 1926:5-6). This population movement is called ecological invasion and succession.

Zone Four: Residential. An area of exclusive residents with single-family dwellings and high-class apartments.

Zone Five: Commuters' Zone. The area comprised of the suburbs and satellite cities within thirty to sixty minutes from the central business district.

Dawson noted that Montreal expanded from the center (Zone 1). However, as the city had been squeezed between the river and the mountain, it grew into a series of concentric kidney shapes.

Figure 1 illustrates the ecological process called succession. That is, as the city expanded, there was a strong tendency for each inner zone to extend its boundaries by invading its immediate surrounding outer zone.

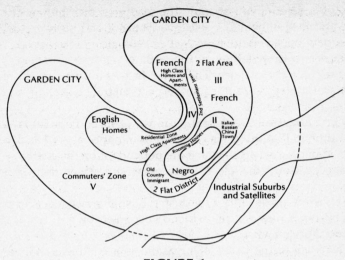

FIGURE 1
Dawson's 1926 Ecological View of Montreal

SOURCE: Dawson 1926:7.

In Dawson's view, the city was not a fragmented world of isolated parts; it was an organism of structural interdependence.

This pattern of concentric zones also accounts for Dawson's description of the city's social organization. Within these zones there existed a vast collection of natural areas. They were characterized by population types in respect to such factors as race, age, sex ratio, and standards of living. Each natural area had its unique social organizations, customs, group traditions, and sentiments.

Dawson's students learned these basic ecological concepts and investigated the natural histories (cycles of development) of natural areas. They also documented their internal social organization. Specifically, Montreal's ethnic mosaic was researched by graduate students working under Dawson's supervision. Immigrant studies were completed on the British (Reynolds 1933), the Ukrainian (Mamchur 1934), the Italian (Bayley 1939), and the Jewish (Seidel 1939) communities. Other studies were completed on such topics as the French invasion of the Eastern townships (Hunter 1939) and the human ecology of the St. John River Valley (Lewis 1939).

One of Dawson's major intellectual contributions was *An Introduction to Sociology* co-authored with Warner E. Gettys (1891-1973). The text was first published in 1929 and revised in 1935 and 1948. Rated among the ten best-selling introductory sociology texts in North America, it became the "bible" for several generations of McGill undergraduate sociology students. Drawing from a wide range of primary sources, the text explained the basic concepts of human ecology. Competition was viewed as a determinant shaping the territorial distribution of human groups and institutions. The selective distribution which resulted from this competition was influenced by five ecological processes:

(1) **Concentration** defined as the settling of a large number of individuals in a given space. The prime factors influencing this process were strategic positions in respect to transportation and great natural resources.

(2) **Centralization–Decentralization** a form of population concentration in that there is a center of dominance as well as decentralized peripheral areas which are dependent on the center.

(3) **Segregation** is the selective process whereby well-defined population types cluster together.

(4) **Invasion** or the entry of industry, business, residence, or population types into an area which is occupied by a different type of social organization.

(5) **Succession,** the result of invasion, is a complete change of the existing form of distribution.

Through the interconnection of these five social processes, "...the ecological order with its characteristic distribution of human tasks takes on its patterned formation" (Dawson and Gettys 1929:219).

When distributed, this ecological order was modified by the social processes of conflict, accommodation, and assimilation. To quote Dawson and Gettys (1929:556-57):

> Through competition, man discovers his place in the community and in his occupation. The institutions that guide his efforts are subject to the play of forces in the selective process. The product is an ecological order in which the different elements remain in a state of equilibrium until some force disturbs it. Selective activity in human communities is partially controlled by the social processes of conflict, accommodation, and assimilation.
>
> Conflict is the political process. Persons and groups become aware of their competitors. Issues arise which are settled by force of arms, a surplus of votes, a battle of tongues, or a barrage of looks. If the defeat is accepted, both parties to the conflict release their tensions and modify their organized activities to meet the new situation. We remember the host of readjustments that have followed in the wake of the World War. Social relationships are being reestablished in the folkways and mores of a new social order. Society is a network of such accommodations which each new generation takes over and supplements. It is through the process of accommodation that social organization takes form. Assimilation is the fundamental cultural process. Tensions fade out and the social order is established in a body of common memoires. This structural stability is threatened constantly by forces which are never under complete social control.

It was the interaction among these social processes which produced the "environing social order."

The 1935 edition of the text gave more consideration to cultural areas and patterns. These were topics of specific interest to Dawson who in 1929 had started to teach a course on culture areas in Canada. Another important addition was a study manual which provided outlines to guide student research projects in six areas: community, family, ethnic groups, strikes, organized social movements, and the individual. These outlines involved collecting data from a variety of sources such as census publications, newspapers, interviews, and life histories.

The research emphasis of this study manual provided the basis of teaching sociology at McGill. First-year students were sent into the city to observe natural areas and ecological processes. They completed a sociological analysis of their family, or wrote individual life histories. These assignments were the direct result of Dawson's belief that one learned sociology by "doing it." He was committed to the idea that it was necessary to do more than study abstract concepts. It was also essential to complete first-hand observation and analyse the data using concepts from the text.

Dawson's major research project was a comprehensive study of frontier settlement of the Canadian west. Initiated in 1929 under a grant from the Social Science Research Council, New York, the project involved some of the major Canadian scholars of the day: W.A. Mackintosh (1895-1970), A.R.M. Lower (b.1889), and Harold Innis (1894-1952).

To complete the field work, Dawson spent part of the summer of 1929 and all of the summer of 1930 with his research assistants in western Canada. He visited the communities under study and interviewed key informants. A number of his research assistants, who interviewed the pioneer families and studied the social organization of ethnic groups, were McGill sociology graduate students who wrote their theses under Dawson's direction (Tuttle 1931; Craig 1933; and Younge 1933).

From this research, Dawson published three of the eight volumes in the Canadian Frontiers of Settlement Series (1934; 1936; Dawson and Younge, 1940). His three volumes implicitly and explicitly employed an ecological paradigm. One of the volumes (1934) focused on the Peace River Country, an area of approximately 47 000 000 acres in northwestern Alberta and northeastern British Columbia. Population distribution and the nature of social organization were interpreted in terms of how typical agricultural regions passed through successive stages of settlements: the outpost; isolated agricultural areas; the integration of agricultural areas; and the period of centralization and regional autonomy. These were successive stages. Each linked in an organic manner to the previous and prepared the way for its successor. Using the ecological processes of segregation, assimilation, invasion and succession, another volume compared the group settlement of five ethnic communities in western Canada: the Doukhobors, Mennonites, and Mormons who settled in farm villages; and the German catholics and French Canadians who settled on scattered farmsteads in segregated areas (Dawson 1936).

The Legacy.   The sociology department that Dawson founded trained most of the next generation of Canadian-educated sociologists. Many of those individuals were his students. A number of them adopted the ecological paradigm. One of his students, Rex Lucus (1924-1978), who published a book on one-industry Canadian communities highlighted Dawson's influence with the following dedication: "To the memory of Carl Addington Dawson, 1887-1964 pioneer Canadian sociologist, and the teacher who introduced me to Canadian Communities" (Lucus 1971). The dedication speaks for itself. One of the greatest legacies that can be left by a scholar is his intellectual influence.

HIGHLIGHT

1. C.A. Dawson can be regarded as the founder of sociology in English Canada. His approach to the study of society, learned at the University of Chicago, can be described as human ecology.
2. Human ecology is a paradigm in which it is assumed that the spacial distribution of groups of individuals is a consequence of inter-related ecological processes.
3. In the 1920s, 1930s, and 1940s, an entire generation of sociologists at McGill University were weaned on human ecology.
4. Dawson's major works on Canada from the human ecology perspective focussed on patterns of settlement in the prairies. However, both he and his students conducted extensive inquiries into the social composition of Montreal.

THE FABIAN PARADIGM

The fabian approach is exemplified by the careers of Leonard Marsh (1906-1982) and John Porter (1921-1979). The former was an architect of the Canadian welfare state. The latter was Canada's pre-eminent macro-sociologist.

Leonard Charles Marsh: A Canadian Fabian

Biography.   The youngest son of a British lower middle-class family, Leonard Marsh was born in 1906. He spent his childhood in a London suburb. An outstanding student, he was offered scholarships by both Oxford and the University of London, and in 1925 he enrolled in the London School of Economics. This experience molded his economic and sociological ideas. It likewise generated his interest in studying structured inequality, and fostered his life-long commitment to changing society through rational social planning.

Intellectual Influences.   The origins of the London School of Economics is part of the history of the British fabians. They were a small group of socialist idealists whose goal was social reform along collectivist lines. The essence of fabianism is represented by Sidney Webb (1859-1947) and Beatrice Webb (1859-1943).

In 1894, the Fabian Society received a bequest of ten thousand pounds to be spent "... within ten years to the propaganda and other purposes of the said society and its Socialism" (Caine 1963:18). Sidney Webb as chairman of the trust fund urged that it be used to establish a School of Economics. The school opened in 1895 and five years later became part of the newly organized University of London. The school became the favorite child of the Webbs who left their imprint on its curriculum and organization.

"Lying a foundation of facts" was the Webbs' scientific approach to the study of society. In their view, a scientific sociology would emerge through the precise observation and collection of actual facts about the life history of social institutions, such as the trade union movement. As Beatrice Webb recorded in her diary on February 20, 1900:

> We have always claimed that the study of the structure and function of society was as much a science as the study of any other form of life, and ought to be pursued by the scientific methods used in other organic sciences. Hypotheses ought to be used, not as the unquestioned premise from which to deduce an unquestioned conclusion, but as an order of thought to be verified by observation and experiment. Such history as will be taught at the School will be the history of social institutions discovered from documents, statistics and the observation of the actual structure and working of living organizations (Caine 1963:74).

It was through social research into "facts" that scientifically valid policies would be formulated by an educated élite. Thus, the London School of Economics would not be just the first British university devoted to the study of the social sciences, it would also educate an élite who would lead the country to the promised land of collectivism. On the basis of this belief, the Webbs patronized the careers of two young men who were later to influence Marsh's intellectual development. They were William Beveridge (1879-1963) and H. Llewellyn Smith (1864-1945). From them, Marsh learned the empirical social science tradition. They generated his interest in studying social inequality, and fostered his belief in welfare policy as a mechanism to reduce social inequalities.

In 1919, Beveridge, who later became the architect of the British welfare state, was appointed Director of the London School of Economics. By following two of the Webbs' intellectual aims, he built the school into an internationally known institution for the study of the social sciences. First, the social sciences were to be based on observation and analysis of facts, rather than on the analysis of concepts; and second, the school would be interdisciplinary rather than narrowly specialized. Its curriculum was to include economics, political science, statistics, geography, sociology, anthropology, and law. Accordingly, ideas could be exchanged and criticized from a variety of social science perspectives.

A former civil servant, H. Llewellyn Smith, joined the London School of Economics in 1928. He assumed the directorship of the New Survey of London Life and Labour. This was a research project funded in large part by the Laura Spelman Rockefeller Foundation Memorial. The original classic London Life and Labour study (1886-1903) had been launched by Charles Booth (1840-1916), a successful British businessman (Simey and Simey 1960). The new survey was to compare the conditions with the facts in the original Booth study.

Leonard Marsh enrolled in the London School of Economics in 1925. It was the school's multi-disciplinary intellectual milieu and his research apprenticeship with the new survey study that shaped the destinative feature of his later work. Indeed, his years at the school led to the making of a Canadian fabian.

Although Marsh read the work of theoretical social scientists, the books and articles by the Fabians made a deeper impression. His later publications reveal the impact of the fabian fact finding approach, a tradition that stressed the systematic collection of data rather than the formulation of theoretical deductions to explain human behavior. From the fabians, he accepted the assumption that legislation for social change should be based on scientific premises. This assumption was reinforced by studying with Beveridge who believed in "...the almost unlimited possibility of 'social engineering' or rational social planning" (Harris 1977:106).

After graduating with first-class honors from the London School of Economics, Marsh accepted the position of assistant secretary for the new survey. His apprenticeship with H. Llewellyn Smith, had taught him the importance of systematic fact collection and how to interpret their relation to the formulation of social policy. The first volume of the study, *Forty Years of Change*, was published in 1930. Marsh collaborated on four chapters: "Cost of Living," "Wages of Labour and Earnings," "House Rents and Overcrowding," and "Unemployment and Its Treatment." The stage had been set, so to speak, for his later Canadian research.

Academic Career.   In 1930, McGill University received a grant of $110 000 from the Rockefeller Foundation to study unemployment in Montreal. The project was to involve faculty from McGill's Departments of Sociology, Psychology, Education, Public Health, and Law. In his search for a project director, McGill's principal, Sir William Currie, wrote to William Beveridge who recommended Leonard Marsh.

Marsh accepted the appointment as director of the first Canadian interdisciplinary social science research program and lecturer in the Department of Economics. He taught courses on industrial fluctuations and social legislation. Further to his research tasks, he wrote a doctoral thesis for McGill's School of Economics. In 1941, Marsh left McGill to become research advisor to the federal government's Post-War Reconstruction Committee. After four years of wartime service in Ottawa, Marsh worked as welfare advisor and, later, information officer for the United Nations Relief and Rehabilitation Administration. Returning to Canada in 1947, he was appointed the director of research at the School of Social Work, University of British Columbia. In 1965, the university appointed him a professor of educational sociology.

Marsh retired in 1973. In recognition of his intellectual contribution, he was awarded honorary degrees from York University and from McMaster University. In 1980, the Canadian Sociology and Anthropology Association elected him an honorary president.

Major Publications and Core Ideas. Strictly speaking, there is no well-defined fabian paradigm with a set of interrelated concepts. However, there were four mental images that guided fabian research.

(1) A belief in the social philosophy of utilitarianism, "the greatest happiness of the greater number." The utilitarianism goal was that there should be a national minimum of incomes, standards, and housing. No individual should be allowed to fall below these national minima.

(2) There should be equality in the conditions of opportunity. However, given the institutionalized nature of inequality, structural modifications in the institutions underlying the class structure were necessary to assure equality of opportunity.

(3) These modifications would emerge from a foundation of facts. The proposals for change would result from a detailed factual analysis of the nature and extent of social inequality.

(4) The modifications were to be implemented following Sidney Webb's assumption of "the inevitability of gradualness." That is, peaceful parliamentary changes through piecemeal legislation and administrative reorganization. This model of social change is rooted in an unyielding belief in rational bureaucratic planning and social engineering.

All of these images are reflected in Marsh's 1940 classic study, *Canadians In and Out of Work: A Survey of Economic Classes and Their Relation to the Labour Market.* This book focussed on structured inequality in Canadian society. Social class was measured by social divisions or status groups based on the occupational structure. Using data from the census, the analysis portrayed the social class distribution on the basis of occupational status of the Canadian population in 1931. Among the dimensions considered were: (1) distribution of inequality; (2) self-perpetuating mechanisms; (3) institutional linkages; and (4) structural modification of the institutions underlying the class structure.

Marsh's detailed cross-classification revealed that Canada, a nation in 1931 with a population of about eleven million, was a society with vast social inequalities which varied along sex, regional, and ethnic lines.

TABLE 1
Social Classes In Canada
Estimated Distribution of Families*

Class	Number	Percentage
Well-to-do†	*10,500*	*0.6*
Middle Classes	*492,000*	*25.7*
Business operators or owners (small and medium scale)	121,700	6.4
Professional, technical, managerial, commercial	178,200	9.3
White-collar workers, n.e.s.	110,700	5.8
Responsible and independent industrial workers	81,400	4.2
Working Classes	*815,000*	*42.5*
Skilled workers	257,300	13.4
Intermediate workers	213,900	11.2
Unskilled and manual workers	343,800	17.9
Farm Classes	*598,700*	*31.2*
Farmers, fishermen, etc.	516,800	27.0
Farm workers, etc.	81,900	4.2
Total	1,916,200	100

*Based on the figures for married gainfully occupied males; as at 1931.
†Including finance, industry, and professions.
SOURCE: Marsh 1940:391.

Table 1 shows the extent of this inequality. The well-to-do were less than 1 percent of the population and the overwhelming majority of Canadians were members of the working class or farmers, farm workers, and fishermen.

Inequality was reflected in the distribution of income. Most Canadians lived below a national economic level required for a decent standard of living. To quote Marsh (1940:198-199).

> What is often called an "American standard of living", enabling a liberal and varied diet, housing accommodation which includes a few domestic labour-saving devices, reasonable provision for health and recreation, etc., requires at the most frugal calculation $2,000.00; and some would put it considerably higher. This is characteristic only of managerial, professional, and higher-grade commercial and clerical families, the upper 15 per cent of wage and salary earnings; at a generous estimate, not more than a quarter of all Canadian families.

To Marsh, limited access to educational opportunities was a major determinant of the self-perpetuating nature of inequality. An individual's class position in the occupational structure was, by and large, linked to his or her educational training. However, as the average cost of four years of high school was estimated to be around $500, the financial burden tended to be prohibitive for children from the working classes.

Accordingly, there was a strong relationship between access to the opportunity structure and social class. Those who went to high school, and especially those who went to university, were a small, privileged minority.

Marsh (1940:417) observed that: "The shape of society depends on a number of minorities who have power in the crucial spheres of life...." Indirectly, his statement raises the important questions on how various classes are distributed and linked to various institutional sectors: finance, industry, the government, the civil service, and so forth. The institutional sector he selected to examine was the federal House of Commons and the Legislative assemblies of two central provinces, Ontario and Quebec. Table 2 lists the occupational class background of the elected members of these bodies.

There was a direct correlation between social class and elected membership: the higher the social class, the greater the membership. Indeed,

TABLE 2
Vocational Background of Members of
The Federal House of Commons and of
Certain Provincial Legislatures

Occupation	House of Commons 1936	1940	Candidates 1940	Provincial Legislative Assemblies Ontario	Quebec 1936	1939
Independent means	5	7	12	3	1	—
Business proprietors	23	16	42	9	6	7
Merchants.................	29	27	64	6	16	18
Salaried managers..........	6	5	23	5	1	1
Commercial agents.........	9	17	50	3	7	8
Lawyers	72	74	160	17	25	25
Doctors, dentists	18	18	47	12	13	8
Clergymen	4	6	11	—	—	—
Other older professions	4	3	6	—	—	1
Engineers, etc..............	7	6	10	—	1	1
Teachers, principals	10	8	28	—	—	1
Lesser professions	3	1	19	2	2	4
Journalists	7	2	15	—	1	1
Public officials	3	3	10	4	2	—
Farmers	33	38	96	20	9	5
Wage-earners..............	9	9	57	3	6	6
Unspecified or indeterminate............	3	5	22	6	—	—
Total.....................	245	245	672*	90	90	86

*Full list of candidates was not available when this list was compiled

SOURCE: Marsh 1940: 419. Excluded from this table is the Alberta Legislature before and after the first victory of the Social Credit Party in 1935. The 1935 election witnessed a sharp decline in farmer representation and the elimination of wage-earner members. See Marsh 417-425.

the political decision makers were primarily from professional (mainly legal) and business backgrounds. The most under-represented group were the industrial wage earners. Regretably, Marsh failed to ask two critical theoretical questions: what were the political and social reasons for this relationship between class and the state, and what were the consequences of this relationship. These questions will be dealt with later in this text from a Marxist perspective.

Marsh's portrait of Canada in 1931, before the height of the depression years, was a society with a bottom heavy class structure. Given this fact, how was equality to be achieved? Marsh suggested several structural modifications necessary for a more equitable society. They included (1) a diversity of secondary education; (2) a national scholarship program; (3) training facilities for the adolescent population; (4) a modernized federal employment service; (5) a program to dovetail employment and education experiences; (6) social insurance legislation; (7) the elimination of regressive elements of taxation; (8) the redistribution of income in the form of welfare services; and (9) public work programs.

Marsh immigrated to Canada at the beginning of the depression. During the decade from 1930 to 1940, the unemployment rate was never below ten percent of the work force. In 1933, nearly a quarter of the labor force was unemployed. Prairie farmers suffered through a lengthy drought. Unemployed Canadians were dependent on municipal relief, if it was available. Being "on the dole" was a humiliating experience. Thousands of single, homeless men built roads and bridges for the federal government for a mere twenty cents a day plus food, clothing, and lodging.

As a result of the human suffering he observed in Montreal and his deeply-rooted fabian beliefs, Marsh was drawn to a small group of individuals who had founded an organization called The League for Social Reconstruction (LSR). It was one of the first left-wing intellectual groups in Canada. Its members were "...overwhelmingly college-educated, urban, anglophone, and central Canadian" (Horn 1980:14).

Marsh was president of the LSR from 1937 to 1939. Between 1933 and 1939, he gave numerous public lectures for the league. He contributed to the 1935 multi-authored *Social Planning for Canada* (1975), and in 1938, with two other LSR members, he produced a shortened and simpler version entitled *Democracy Needs Socialism*.

Social Planning for Canada was an indictment of the system of monopoly capitalism in Canada. It rejected the competitive ethic and the profit-motive. Part one which contained the indictment focused on the end of a century of progress, the nature of the Canadian economy, the structure of Canadian industry, the mechanism of the market, agriculture, and the inefficiency of the system. Part two, "What Socialist Planning Really Means," outlined structural modifications to reconstruct society through a planned and socialized economy.

Taken as a whole, *Social Planning for Canada* is a detailed analysis which should be read in its entirety. By and large, the skeleton of the argument is contained in the League's 1932 Manifesto (Social Planning for Canada 1975:IX-XI):

The League for Social Reconstruction is an association of men and women who are working for the establishment in Canada of a social order in which the basic principle regulating production, distribution and service will be the common good rather than private profit.

The present capitalist system has shown itself unjust and inhuman, economically wasteful, and a standing threat to peace and democratic government. Over the whole world it has led to a struggle for raw materials and markets and to a consequent international competition in armaments which were among the main causes of the last great war and which constantly threaten to bring on new wars. In the advanced industrial countries it has led to the concentration of wealth in the hands of a small irresponsible minority of bankers and industrialists whose economic power constantly threatens to nullify our political democracy. The result in Canada is a society in which the interests of farmers and of wage and salaried workers—the great majority of the population—are habitually sacrificed to those of this small minority. Despite our abundant natural resources the mass of the people have not been freed from poverty and insecurity. Unregulated competitive production condemns them to alternate periods of feverish prosperity, in which the main benefits go to speculators and profiteers, and to catastrophic depression, in which the common man's normal state of insecurity and hardship is accentuated.

We are convinced that these evils are inherent in any system in which private profit is the main stimulus to economic effort. We therefore look to the establishment in Canada of a new social order which will substitute a planned and socialized economy for the existing chaotic individualism and which, by achieving an approximate economic equality among all men in place of the present glaring inequalities, will eliminate the domination of one class by another.

As essential first steps towards the realization of this new order we advocate:
1 Public ownership and operation of the public utilities connected with transportation, communications, and electric power, and of such other industries as are already approaching conditions of monopolistic control.
2 Nationalization of Banks and other financial institutions with a view to the regulation of all credit and investment operations.
3 The further development of agricultural co-operative institutions for the production and merchandising of agricultural products.
4 Social legislation to secure to the worker adequate income and leisure, freedom of association, insurance against illness, accident, old age, and unemployment, and an effective voice in the management of his industry.
5 Publicly organized health, hospital, and medical services.
6 A taxation policy emphasising steeply graduated income and inheritance taxes.
7 The creation of a National Planning Commission.

8 The vesting in Canada of the power to amend and interpret the Canadian constitution so as to give the federal government power to control the national economic development.

9 A foreign policy designed to secure international co-operation in regulating trade, industry and finance, and to promote disarmament and world peace.

Social Planning for Canada is a sophisticated example of research within the fabian paradigm. Its model of democratic socialism was "... ameliorative, gradualist, and dedicated to peaceful change through the parliamentary system" (Berger 1976:69). Needless to say, some members of the LSR were connected with the founding of the Co-operative Commonwealth Federation, the original name of the New Democratic Party.

Following the fabian tradition, structural modification was a theme Marsh returned to in 1943 when he published his *Report of Social Security For Canada* (1975). The report stressed the failure of unemployment relief programs. Based on research of standard of living budgets, "... it was estimated that a minimum subsistence budget for a family of five required an annual income of $1,134. in 1940" (Guest 1980:112). This amount placed a large number of Canadians below the poverty line.

To rectify this inequality, Marsh recommended a comprehensive system of social security and employment programs. Children's allowance, health insurance, training and guidance facilities, and a national investment of public work programs were also recommended. As a number of these recommendations later became part of the federal government's social security legislation, Marsh was one of the first architects of the Canadian welfare state.

The Legacy.   Leonard Marsh's *Canadians In and Out of Work* was a significant contribution to sociology. It was the first systematic attempt to analyse the Canadian class structure. Although it is difficult to assess the import of his innovative role as an advocate of social security policies, one fact is clear: a number of Marsh's social security recommendations are now part of the fabric of Canadian society.

John Porter: A Macrosociologist

Biography.   The son of a British immigrant working-class family, Porter was born in Vancouver on November 12, 1921. At age fifteen, before completing high school, he moved to England. There he worked at various casual jobs until he was hired as a journalist by the *Daily Sketch* of London. He joined the Canadian army in 1940 and served until the end of the war when he enrolled in the London School of Economics. He graduated in 1949 with a B.Sc.(Economics). This education laid the foundation for his later development of a Canadian macrosociology.

Intellectual Influences.   From the prestigious faculty of social scientists at the LSE, Porter learned to untangle the underlying meaning of social reality through a multi-disciplinary prism. He was particularly influenced by the work of Leonard Trelawney Hobhouse (1864-1929) who wrote about evolutionary sociology in the service of democracy and social reform (For a summary of Hobhouse's ideas, see Barnes 1948:614-53).

The task of reconstructing a war-torn world was a challenge for social science students. It was "... the period of optimism when it was felt that the social environment could be controlled, that depressions could be made a thing of the past, and distributive justice was a matter of social engineering" (Porter 1979a:10). Many of Porter's discussions with his fellow students were about problems of social inequality and colonization. Vallee (1980:14) described this vibrant environment:

> ... [the] LSE was dominated by a spirit of optimism about the chances of reconstructing a world that was badly out of joint. Social democracy was the prevailing ideology, a kind of socialism without revolution which had been advocated by two generations of Fabian scholars and writers. A vital role in the socioeconomic reconstruction was to be assumed by the sociologist through his research, the ideal form of which Porter later described as "rational enquiry guided by humanistic values." This research was to have direct bearing on social policy and its findings stated in language which laymen could understand. Very special attention was to be devoted to exposing those inequalities which derived from structural faults in the distribution of power and life-chances.

To a considerable extent, Porter's postwar academic and personal experiences shaped his sociological perspective. His future sociological work fell within the Fabian tradition.

Academic Career.   Porter returned to Canada in 1949 and accepted a position at Carleton College (now Carleton University). At that time it was a small institution which rented space in downtown Ottawa. Most of Porter's academic career was spent at Carleton. He served as chairman of the Sociology Department, director of the Faculty of Social Sciences, and academic vice-president.

While continuing his teaching, he spent fifteen years writing his monumental work, *The Vertical Mosaic: An Analysis of Class and Power in Canada* (Porter 1965). For this study, he received in 1966 both his D.Sc. from the LSE and the prestigious McIver Award from the American Sociological Association.

John Porter was Canada's pre-eminent sociologist. He was a Canadian Fellow in the International Institute for Labour Studies in Geneva (1966-1967) and occupied the Canadian Chair at Harvard (1974-1975). He was elected Fellow of the Royal Society of Canada and Honorary President of the Canadian Sociology and Anthropology Association (1972). In 1981, *The Canadian Review of Sociology and Anthropology* published a special issue about his ideas as a posthumous tribute.

Major Publications and Core Ideas.   John Porter's work is an exemplification of the fabian paradigm. At the macrosociological level, he investigated the distributive nature of structured inequality. However, his work was not purely theoretical. He was deeply concerned with both the injustices associated with the Canadian class system and how to redress these injustices. Thus, a number of his publications addressed the question: what are appropriate structural modifications to change the institutional mechanisms which underlay the social class system. These fabian leanings are evident in his books: *The Vertical Mosaic* (Porter 1965); his collected essays printed in *The Measure of Canadian Society; Education, Equality, and Opportunity* (1979); *Does Money Matter? Prospects for Higher Education in Ontario* (M. Porter, J. Porter, and B. Blishen 1973); and *Stations and Calling: Making It Through The School System* (J. Porter, M. Porter, and B. Blishen 1982).

He described the post-Marxist industrial world by asserting that: "In the nineteenth century it may have been the case that two...[social classes] classified by the criterion of owning or not owning property were sociological groups, but in the present world such classes are statistical categories and nothing more" (Porter 1965:20). Given this belief, social classes were viewed as artificial statistical groupings which had their origin in economic processes and economic differences. They were descriptive categories which predicted behavior. To quote Porter (1965:10):

> When people within a particular income range, or at a particular skill or educational level are grouped together it will be found that they behave in ways different from people grouped together in another income range or at another skill or educational level. The farther removed one class is from another the greater will be differences in behaviour. An almost universal example of such differences in industrial society is the inverse relationship between average level of income and average size of family. Other examples of differences in behaviour are: participation in various kinds of organizations and associations, child-rearing practices, deviant behaviour such as crime, suicide, and mental disorders, attitudes and prejudices, and I.Q. performances of children.

His factual argument demonstrated the clear-cut socioeconomic variations in mobility, income, and ethnic group membership. Specifically, ethnicity tended to be a barrier to equality. Indeed, it also "...served as a form of class control of the major power structures by charter ethnic groups who remain over-represented in the élite structures" (Porter 1975:294).

Besides examining social class variations, Porter, like Marsh, focused on the barriers which prevented many Canadians from equally sharing in the benefits of their society (Porter 1965:168-72). These barriers perpetuated the class-based nature of the educational system. It was the children of the privileged who, in the main, had access to upward occupational mobility through educational training. This generalization was documented by examining the class origins of high school and university students (Porter 1965:180-91).

Power was a central theme of *The Vertical Mosaic*. It was defined as "... the recognized right to make effective decisions on behalf of a group of people" (Porter 1965:201). Such power was usually wielded by elites in institutional and bureaucratic structures such as business, labor, politics, federal government, the mass media, universities and religion. It was these elite systems that Porter systematically analysed.

A major concern was the economic élite comprised of Canadian residents who held directorships in 170 dominant corporations. Their predominant social characteristics were: (1) a professional or financial background; (2) a tendency for family continuity to extend over generations; and (3) British background (only 6.7 percent were French Canadians although French Canadians made up one-third of the Canadian population). It was this small, relatively homogenous economic élite, interlocked through social networks, that dominated Canadian economic life.

Porter's analysis of social classes, elites, and power were rooted in a belief that the social scientist had a moral responsibility to society. His work combined rigorous empirical research with a commitment to social justice. In his words (1979b:2):

> Although many would like to avoid the issue, social scientists have to choose sides and to fashion their work with a clear idea of what their values are. Some may think there is a neutral position on every issue of great social importance which can be analysed objectively, but that is the position of the bureaucrat rather than the intellectual, and almost always a position taken from a power base with a prior commitment to the status quo. Some social scientists believe themselves to be neutral when in fact they have become neuterized by employing statistical accounting procedures as their major tools in the service of existing bureaucracies and power centres.
>
> To me, the major task of social science is to abstract from the confused flow of events perspectives which clarify and which permit some judgment about a society in the light of moral principles.

The Legacy.   Porter's legacy is succinctly stated by Wallace Clement: "In the annals of Canadian sociology it will be recorded that John Porter was a great egalitarian, a committed scholar, and a profound teacher for an entire generation" (Clement 1980:112). Porter's greatest contribution, *The Vertical Mosaic* laid the foundation for a macrosociology of Canadian sociology. It shattered the myth that there were no social classes in Canadian society and no barriers limiting opportunity.

His ideas have been examined and re-examined (Heap 1974). They have been criticized (Niosi 1978:127-33), and they have been retested (Clement 1975). Indeed, *The Vertical Mosaic* has become an important part of Canadian intellectual history.

HIGHLIGHT

1. The cornerstone of the Fabian approach to the study of society was that research should lay down a foundation of facts. It should not get bogged down in theoretical or conceptual debates.
2. The major institution for the dissemination of Fabian ideas in social science was the London School of Economics (LSE). It was here that Leonard Marsh acquired his interdisciplinary orientation and a commitment to eradicate inequality.
3. The influence of the LSE on Marsh is manifested in his analysis of inequality in Canada, in his support for the left-leaning League for Social Reconstruction, and in his contribution to the modern Canadian welfare state.
4. Like Leonard Marsh, John Porter was profoundly influenced by his education at the London School of Economics.
5. Whereas the social scientists of Marsh's day had been confronted by the problems of the Depression, Porter and his contemporaries were faced with the difficulties of post war reconstruction.
6. Porter, like Marsh, continued the study of inequality in Canadian society. By and large, he viewed the educational system as a major key toward the elimination of inequality.

THE STAPLES PARADIGM

The staples paradigm is the original intellectual contribution of Harold Adams Innis (1894-1952). He was Canada's foremost political economist.

Biography.   The son of a Baptist farming family, H.A. Innis was born on November 5, 1894, near Otterville, Oxford County, Ontario. His early education was in southern Ontario. He attended the then Toronto located McMaster University, from 1912 to 1916 with the exception of five months in 1915 when he was a primary school teacher in Londonville, northern Alberta.

His brief teaching appointment outside Ontario had an impact on his view of Canadian society. As his biographer noted: "He had made the acquaintance of the new West. He had learned something of the West's peculiar problems. The anxieties and vexations of high interest rates and transport problems had become familiar to him through very real examples. He brought back with him some understanding of the West's conception of its own nature, and of its attitude to the nation as a whole" (Creighton 1957:27). Innis later expressed these observations in *The History of the Canadian Pacific Railway (1923)*.

At the age of twenty, H.A. Innis graduated from McMaster and enlisted in the Canadian army. He was wounded while on active duty in France. After convalescing in England, he returned to Canada and earned his M.A. in Economics from McMaster. In 1918, he enrolled at the University of Chicago. The Chicago experience exposed him to ideas which he would later weave into an original contribution to Canadian social science.

Intellectual Influences.   Although Innis had planned a career in the legal profession, his interest in economics intensified and the die was cast. At the University of Chicago, he wrote his Ph.D. thesis which was later published in 1923 as *A History of the Canadian Pacific Railway*.

Innis was influenced by a number of Chicago economists:

> ...[He] studied with Frank Knight, who taught economic theory and statistics with such scepticism that, 'one could never again become lost in admiration of statistical compilations...'; J.M. Clark, from whom he learned of 'overhead costs,' which assumed a central importance in Innis's studies in Canadian economic history; C.S. Duncan, who emphasized in his lectures on marketing the connections 'between the physical characteristics of a commodity and the marketing structure built up in relation to it'; and Chester Wright, who taught courses on trusts and American economic history and who supervised Innis's doctoral thesis on the Canadian Pacific Railway (Berger 1976:87-88).

At Chicago, he studied the iconoclastic views of Thorstein Veblen (1857-1929) (for a critical interpretation of Veblen's ideas see Reisman, 1953). Innis admired Veblen's attack on static economics, the emphasis on the dynamics of economic change, the developmental approach to the study of economic systems and institutions, and the style of academic craftsmanship which integrated economic history and theory (Innis 1929a). Veblen also sensitized Innis to the impact of technology on societal organization.

In the formulation of the staples perspective, Innis' ideas were molded by other scholars. One of these was the Scottish political economist Adam Smith (1723-1790) who stressed the importance of commodity specialization in new countries (Smith 1976). The Canadian historian William A. Macintosh (1895-1970) who focussed on the role of staple products in Canadian history (Macintosh, 1923) was a further influence on Innis. So was the Scottish geographer Marion Newbigin (1869-1934) whose book, *Canada: The Great River, The Lands and the Men* (1926), alerted Innis to the geographical effect of the St. Lawrence River and the Pre-Cambrian Shield.

Academic Career.   In 1920, Innis accepted an appointment in the Department of Political Economy at the University of Toronto. During the next twenty-two years, he became Canada's senior academic states-man. At Toronto, he held key administrative roles. He was chairman of the Department of Political Economy and Dean of the School of Gradu-ate Studies. He was a member of the 1934 Nova Scotia commission on the province's economy and the 1949 Royal Commission on Transporta-tion. He was a driving force behind the 1940 establishment of the Canadian Social Science Research Council. Innis was elected president of four prestigious learned groups: the Canadian Political Science Asso-ciation, the Economic History Association, the Royal Society of Canada, and the American Economic Association. He was awarded honorary degrees from New Brunswick, McMaster, Laval, Manitoba, and Glas-gow.

Innis died prematurely on November 8, 1952. Twelve years later, the University of Toronto established Innis College in his honor. A quarter of a century after his death, he was still regarded as Canada's greatest economic historian. In 1977, *The Journal of Canadian Studies* published a special issue assessing his ideas.

Major Publications and Ideas.   *A History of the Canadian Pacific Railway* (1923), Innis's first book, was an exhaustive factual study of finance, debt structures, overhead costs, and speed of expansion of the Canadian Pacific Railway. The book was critical of the dominance of the West by eastern Canada.

The staples approach was outlined in three economic histories: *The Fur Trade in Canada* (1956); *Settlement and the Mining Frontier* (1936); and *The Cod Fisheries* (1978). The rationale underlying the three volumes was explained over half a century ago when Innis wrote about the teaching of economic history in Canada. He argued that a serious obstacle to research in Canadian economics and economic history was the tendency to use economic theories that applied to older industrialized nations but not to Canada. Canada, he argued, must be examined in the light of its trade patterns within an international economy (Innis 1929b:12):

> ...it would appear that Canadian economic history must be approached from the standpoint of trade with other countries, France in the beginning, later Great Britain and the United States, and finally the Orient and the world generally. Economists will be safe in following the political scientist and the historian in their studies of the relationship of Canada to other countries. Canada's development in relation to other countries meant the development of trade from the Atlantic seaboard in commodities accessi-

ble by water transport. With primitive transportation fish and furs occupied a dominant position and the exhaustion of furs was followed by lumber. Economists cannot pretend to an understanding of Canadian economic history without an adequate history of transportation. A history of transportation must be accompanied by history of trade and especially of the trade relations between Canada and old countries. Further, Canadians will find it necessary to work out the economic history of each industry, especially in technique and capital organization.

This argument contains two central interrelated themes of the staple paradigm. First, is the idea of center-margin relations. Such relations involved the process whereby the colony supplied staple commodities in the form of raw materials to the mother country. The latter used these materials in the manufacture of both a finished product and goods in demand in the colony. Second, this center-margin relation resulted in a so-called staple domination in the colony. In other words, the predominant activity of colonists was the production of the staple or the facilities that promoted its production. The economic history of the Canadian colony, then, could only be understood through an examination of the influence of a series of staples. They were fish, fur, timber, wheat, and minerals.

In general, the staple commodity—its technological nature and relation to geography—molded the character of the newly forming society. The production of the staple for the manufacturing nation shaped the colony's agricultural patterns; investment patterns; transportation growth and costs; and its industrial, financial, and political institutions. Canada was a prime example of a colonial society that had never been self-sufficient. Throughout her history Canada assumed a marginal economic relation, first with Britain, and then with the United States.

The Fur Trade exemplifies the staple paradigm. It stressed the relation between geographical, technological, and economic forces. Demand for beaver fur in Europe shaped the evolution of New France and its institutions. The fur trade affected New France's transportation patterns and costs, contact with the Indians, population settlement, agricultural policies, and military conflicts.

In the post-conquest period, the centralized Northwest Company was the dominant institution in the fur trade. By the early 1820s, its organization extended from the Atlantic to the Pacific and it laid the foundation of contemporary Canada. As Innis wrote (1956:392-93):

> It is no mere accident that the present Dominion coincides roughly with the fur trading areas of northern North America. The basis of supplies for the trade in Quebec, in western Ontario, and in British Columbia represent the agricultural areas of the present Dominion. The Northwest Company was the forerunner of the present confederation.

Canada emerged as a political entity with boundaries largely determined by the fur trade. . . . The present Dominion emerged not in spite of geography but because of it.

In describing the relation between capitalism and the staples, Innis noted how Canadian political institutions were shaped by staple production and transportation. To facilitate staple movement before Confederation, external capital investment was required for canals and railways. This investment required the development of a strong centralized government. It emerged through the Act of Union and the British North America Act (Innis 1956:396-402). Thus, the political origin of Canada was rooted in centre-margin economic relations and staple domination.

During the latter part of his life, Innis moved beyond the study of Canadian economics. His *Bias of Communication* (1951) and *Empire and Communication* (1950) focused on the technology of communication and the stability of empires.

The Legacy.   Although the staples paradigm contains a set of mental images to guide economic history, Innis never integrated the ideas into an explicit theoretical framework. Despite this lack of formal codification, Innis' ideas stamped the Toronto School of Economic History. It started from the assumption that staple commodities molded Canadian historical development and sociological organization. This premise has served as the springboard for a formally developed staple theory of economic growth (Watkins 1967) and it has been criticized (McNally 1981).

Despite the criticism, Innis' political economy tradition has stood the test of time. He is still Canada's most widely quoted economic historian. In recent years, his ideas have influenced research on the silent surrender of the Canadian economy to American multinational corporations (Levitt 1970). Innis' basic approach has also influenced many young Canadian scholars with a Marxist orientation (Watkins 1977).

HIGHLIGHT

1. H.A. Innis, the best known social scientist produced by Canada, was the founder of the Toronto School of Political Economy.
2. Innis believed that models of economic development developed elsewhere were not suitable to the study of Canada.
3. An adequate interpretation of Canada had to recognize the centre-margin dynamic in Canadian development. In other words, it had to take account of the fact that Canada had developed in response to European and later American demands for staple products such as fur, timber, fish, wheat and minerals.
4. Although Innis was not a sociologist, his ideas have had a major impact on a number of Canadian sociologists.

THE FRONTIER-SOCIAL CHANGE PARADIGM

The frontier-social change paradigm, developed by Samuel Delbert Clark, is the sociological by-product of the staple approach.

Biography. S.D. Clark was born on an Alberta farm on February 24, 1910. He grew up in a rural environment near Lloydminister on the Alberta-Saskatchewan border. This agricultural background was undoubtedly a factor shaping Clark's later research interests in agrarian protest movements.

In 1930, Clark was awarded a B.A. (honors) in history and political science from the University of Saskatchewan. The next year he earned an M.A. in history. His thesis was entitled, "Settlement in Saskatchewan with Special Reference to the Influence of Dry Farming." He moved to Toronto and from 1931-1932 was a Ph.D. student in history at the Univesity of Toronto.

The depression cut short the funding for his studies and he accepted a scholarship from the Saskatchewan committee of the Imperial Daughters of the Empire to study in England. The depression had raised questions in his mind about capitalism and because of its radical reputation he decided to study at The London School of Economics.

In 1933, Clark returned to Canada. For the next two years he completed M.A. studies in the Department of Sociology at McGill University. He studied with Carl Dawson and Everett Hughes. He wrote a second M.A. thesis on The Canadian Manufacturers' Association as a pressure group. He returned to the University of Toronto as a Ph.D. candidate in political science. From 1937-1938, he was a lecturer in political science and sociology at the University of Manitoba. He completed his Ph.D. thesis in 1938 and returned to the University of Toronto to teach sociology until his retirement in 1976.

Intellectual Influences. Early in his academic career, Clark was exposed to radical social thought. At the University of Toronto in the early 1930s, he attended meetings of The League for Social Reconstruction. At The London School of Economics, he studied Marx and the works of the Fabians. The latter argued for rational social planning to reconstruct society. Although these ideas opened new intellectual horizons and stressed the economic underpinnings of society, they did not provide the assumptions upon which Clark constructed his later sociological explanations.

Clark's biographer, Harry H. Hiller, has pointed to the multiplicity of influences in Clark's paradigm and its origins (Hiller 1982:68). Three influences, however, are predominant. The first is the frontier thesis of the American historian, Frederick Jackson Turner (1861-1932). American development, Turner argued, was related to the movement of population to the West. The frontier was the furthermost settlement in the West where social organization and government were loosely organized. The frontier itself was a process which transformed customs, institutions, and behavior. Without formal controls, individualism and democracy emerged and were shaped by the frontier (for an interpretation of Turner see Hofstadter 1968). Clark studied the frontier thesis as an undergraduate and later during graduate work at the University of Toronto. He read the work of Canadian historians such as Arthur Lower who utilized the frontier argument.

The second influence emerged from his studies at McGill of the "Chicago School of Sociology". Clark became familiar with the theory of social disorganization-reorganization as developed by W.I. Thomas (1863-1947) and Florian Znaniecki (1882-1958) in their classic study *The Polish Peasant in Europe and America* (1918-20). (For a discussion of the social disorganization paradigm see Carey 1975:95-120.) Thomas and Znaniecki pointed to disruption of life in new environments. Here existing rules of behavior had a decreasing influence on the behavior of individuals and groups. The resultant state of social disorganization, however, was temporary. It was followed by reorganized behavior and institutions.

A study of immigrant movement to the United States, *The Polish Peasant*, examined family and community disorganization. Society was viewed as a process that moved along a three-stage process from organization to disorganization to reorganization. Clark drew upon this model but with differences. As Hiller notes (1981:71):

> Clark did not focus on a particular ethnic group or discuss social life in the old world as Thomas and Znaniecki had, but he did find historical evidence for the thesis that settlement on the new Canadian frontiers was a socially disorienting experience just as it was for the Polish peasant, and he assumed then that social disorganization was evidence of the effects of residence in a new environment. . . . The major difference between Thomas and Znaniecki and Clark was that Clark stressed the context of economic expansion and new forms of economic exploitation rather than just immigration as the cause of disorganization, and in this way he retained the Innisian perspective. He argued that new forms of production resulted in both geographical and occupational shifts in the population leading to social breakdown. Clark took from Thomas and Znaniecki the idea that a former state of stability or organization could be taken for granted and that the disorganizing process would eventually lead to another state of equilibrium. What needed investigation then was the social change from one integrative state to another in which the interstitial period was necessarily problematic. Clark also found in the Polish peasant study a sociological legitimation for the use of personal documents (e.g., letters, diaries, biographies) as evidence of basic social processes, which appealed to his research dispositions.

Third, Clark's work was heavily indebeted to the ideas of his intellectual mentor, H.A. Innis. Clark and Innis had first met at the London School of Economics when the Canadian political economist delivered a lecture on economic materialism. Clark later studied under Innis and for over a decade they were colleagues at the University of Toronto.

Innis had noted that "... the shift to new staple invariably produced periods of crisis in which adjustments in the old structure were painfully made and a new pattern created in relation to the new staple" (Innis 1950:5). Clark built upon the staple paradigm starting with Innis' economic view of staple exploitation and examining the resultant social disruptions. Clark's work, then, is a fusion of the frontier thesis, the social disorganization-reorganization approach, and the staples paradigm.

Academic Career. Clark spent most of his thirty-eight-year academic career at the University of Toronto. When sociology split from political economy in 1963 he was made chairman of the Sociology Department, a position he held until 1969.

Clark became a dominant figure in the development of sociology in Canada. From 1944 to 1959, he was editor of the Social Credit in Alberta Series, sponsored by the Canadian Social Science Research Council through a special grant from the Rockefeller Foundation. The series produced ten books: W.L. Morton, *The Progressive Party in Canada* (1950); D.C. Masters, *The Winnipeg General Strike* (1950); Jean Burnet, *Next year country* (1951); C.B. MacPherson, *Democracy in Alberta* (1953); J.R. Mallory, *Social Credit and the Federal Party in Alberta* (1954); W.E. Mann, *Sect, Cult and Church in Alberta* (1955); V.E. Fowke, *The National Policy and the Wheat Economy* (1957); L.G. Thomas, *The Liberal Party in Canada* (1959); S.D. Clark, *Movements of Political Protest in Canada* (1959); and J.A. Irving, *The Social Credit Movement in Alberta* (1959).

In recognition of his intellectual contributions, Clark was elected a member of the Royal Society and served as president during 1975-1976. He received the Tyrrell Medal from the Royal Society of Canada in 1960. He was made an honorary president of the Canadian Sociology and Anthropology Association (1967), and Foreign Honorary Member of the American Academy of Arts and Science. He was appointed Officer, Order of Canada. He was awarded honorary degrees from the universities of Calgary, Dalhousie, and St. Mary's.

Major Publications and Core Ideas. Clark's major publications were: *The Canadian Manufacturer's Association: A Study in Collective Bargaining and Political Pressure* (1939); *The Social Development of Canada* (1942); *Church and Sect in Canada* (1948); *Movements of Political Protest in Canada, 1640-1840* (1959); *The Developing Canadian Community* (1962);

The Suburban Society (1966); *The New Urban Poor* (1978); and *Canadian Society in Historical Perspective* (1976).

In his early writings there was a set of mental images that guided Clark's study of social change in the Canadian frontier. In 1939, he suggested that a defining characteristic of Canadian social history "... has been the recurrent emergence of areas of social life involving new patterns of social re-adjustment and social life" (Clark 1939:351). Much of this social re-adjustment occurred in the frontier.

The frontier was used to refer to an area which developed *a new form of economic enterprise (staple production)*. Examples include the fur trade in New France, the fisheries in the Maritime colonies, the timber trade in Upper Canada, and mining in British Columbia and the Yukon. The frontier could also be a location which used *new techniques of economic exploitation.* In these areas there are "... special kinds of demands upon social organization, and the failure to fully meet these demands resulted in disturbances in social relationships which may be described as social problems" (Clark 1942:2). The disturbance reached its peak when economic development was at its most rapid pace.

Clark listed some of the factors which led to social disorganization: (1) distance from centres of control and supply; (2) the allocation of capital to the new economic enterprise rather than to community services; (3) the lack of school teachers, clergy, and medical practitioners; and (4) the type of individuals attracted to the frontier, such as the different age and sex compositions or the emigration of "social misfits."

Given this social disorganization, a state of normlessness in which behavior was not guided by institutionalized codes of conduct could emerge. In these circumstances, a set of reformers frequently came to the forefront. They were outside the traditional institutions and could challenge existing authority.

When the reformers' ideas articulated real and long-term social needs and dissatisfactions, "... the vague and inarticulate feelings of large numbers of people were crystallized and identified with a clear-defined goal" (Clark 1942:15). Thereafter social movements could emerge. Clark argues that, "It was the need for social expression rather than the character or motives of reformers which gave rise to reform movements" (1942:15).

These social reform movements provided a solution to individual and social needs. With time, the reform movement became institutionalized. It appointed officials and developed an ideology which was accepted by its followers. The reform movements became part of the established order and a final phase of social reorganization was reached.

This movement from disorganization to reorganization was a process which brought about a new social equilibrium. The cycle moving toward equilibrium, however, was never totally attained. New disturbances led to further problems of social organization and adjustment.

Clark used the disorganization-reorganization argument in his *Church and Sect in Canada*, a study of religious movements and social change. The basic premise of the research was that "the church has grown out of the conditions of a mature society; the sect has been the product of what might be called frontier conditions of social life" (Clark 1948:XII). In the frontier, which was associated with a particular form of economic endeavor, the traditional codes of behavior and institutions were challenged. The result was social disorganization. Through an examination of evangelical movements, Clark illustrated how sects integrated unattached frontier populations. The sect was a mechanism for reform and a social means of reorganization. With stability, however, sects took on church-like formal characteristics.

Clark did not limit his analysis to rural areas. In response to poverty and unemployment, sects arose in urban frontiers such as in the shipbuilding industry in the Maritimes. In any frontier, then, sects emerged as the consequence of social disorganization. (For a more detailed analysis of Clark's analysis of religion, see Hiller 1982:79-89.)

The same frontier social change model was less explicitly used in *Movements of Political Protest in Canada, 1640-1840* (1959). Clark was concerned with the breakdown of old established political organizations and the re-establishment of the social order with new forms of behavior and institutions. He extended his analysis by comparing political social movements in Canada and the United States. The frontier revolts succeeded in the United States. In Canada, he argued, there were forces which led to their defeat. One was the geography of the St. Lawrence which shaped a pattern of centralized authority. Another was the Canadian counter-revolutionary character which evolved as a reaction to American revolutionary movements.

Clark's last two books, *The Suburban Society* (1966) and *The New Urban Poor* (1978) studied contemporary Canadian frontiers, but the disorganization-reorganization model was not explicitly utilized.

The Legacy.   As often happens with the works of an influential scholar, Clark's ideas have been assessed and criticized (Harrison 1981; Hiller 1982). *Church and Sect in Canada* (1948) and *Movements of Political Protest in Canada* (1959) illustrated the importance of historical research to the social scientist and how any explanation of social change must be rooted in its historical realities. However, Clark's most lasting contribution may well be his attempt to link forms of social organization and disorganization to Innis' ideas on staple development.

HIGHLIGHT

1. S.D. Clark was influenced by The London School of Economics, the frontier thesis of Frederick Jackson Turner, the "Chicago School of

Sociology", and H.A. Innis. The last three of these influences are clearly evident in his work.

2. Fundamental to his early research is the idea that staple development in new areas–frontiers–leads to social disorganization. Social movements are a result. Gradually, however, order is established.

3. Throughout his career Clark influenced the development of sociology in Canada through his own writings, editorship of the Social Credit series of studies, and his chairmanship at the University of Toronto.

SOME RECENT DEVELOPMENTS

Dawson, Marsh, Porter, Innis, and Clark began their academic careers at a time when sociology was not an autonomous discipline in Canada. Carl Dawson established the first Canadian sociology department in 1925. For the next half century Canadian academics in the traditional disciplines of history, economics, and political science tended to view sociology with scepticism.

Those sociology programs that existed at Canadian universities were frequently part of prestigious disciplines such as political economy at the University of Toronto. However, the 1960s and early 1970s was a period of phenomenal growth in sociology. It resulted from a state policy to increase the size of the post-secondary educational system. Sociology undergraduate and graduate programs multiplied.

When Carl Dawson retired in 1952 there were fewer than fifty sociologists in Canada. By 1979, there were 617 who held positions at anglophone universities. The majority were recruited from outside Canada (Grayson and Magill 1981:14-33).

As an academic discipline, sociology expanded during the 1960s. It was a decade that also witnessed the eruption of economic, political, and cultural nationalism in English Canada (Resnick 1977:145-99). Influenced by the Innisian staple paradigm, many scholars rooted their nationalism in a clearcut documentation of the branch plant nature of the Canadian economy. Other concerns were American restraints on Canadian political autonomy and cultural influences from the American mass media were also seen as causes for alarm.

Nationalism was voiced by a number of sociologists. They were disturbed that the low number of Canadians in a department led to situations in which hiring practices tended to favor the employment of other foreign academics, particularly Americans. The concern initiated the 1970-1976 "Canadianization Debate in English Canada." (For a concise history of the debate see O'Hearn 1981.) The initiators of the debate intended to Canadianize sociology in anglophone universities. They would do so, in part, through the hiring of Canadian-educated Canadians and the development of an indigenous social science.

The idea of a value-free social science was rejected by those concerned with Canadianization. It was argued that sociological knowledge was shaped by its socio-cultural context and imported paradigms failed to understand the unique sociological relations of Canadian society (O'Hearn 1981:159). This position was reflected in one of the conclusions of *To Know Ourselves: The Report of the Commission on Canadian Studies* (Symons 1975:78). It stated:

> A number of leading Canadian sociologists expressed the view to the Commission that their profession was now so totally alienated from Canadian concerns and values that it was time to consider re-inventing sociology as a discipline at one or two selected universities in Canada. If this could be done, they suggested, it would provide a fresh chance to develop at least a few major centres of Canadian sociology. Having looked closely at the situation in sociology at many of our universities, and inquired carefully into a good many of the problems and circumstances described to it, the Commission understands very well the conditions that cause so many able, and often younger, Canadian sociologists to share the sentiments contained in such a suggestion. There is, indeed, a real danger that sociology, and perhaps to a lesser extent anthropology, as fields of scholarship in Canada will become so oriented to American interests, values, methodologies and research priorities that they can no longer effectively serve the academic and social interests of this country.

The issues surrounding the debate polarized faculty members in many sociology departments. They also resulted in resignations from the Canadian Sociology and Anthropology Association.

The debate, however, had positive consequences. Academic positions in sociology tended to be more frequently filled by Canadians educated in Canadian universities. It was these Canadian educated Canadian citizens who in English Canada contributed disproportionately to the study of Canada (Grayson and Magill 1981). Many had been influenced by Innis' view on Canadian dependency, Porter's macrosociological approach to the study of Canadian society, and Clark's emphasis on historical social change. The impact of these and other influences will be evident in the following chapters.

Conclusion

What has been omitted from this chapter is a fifth paradigm—Marxism. In its academic form, Marxism has not had a long history in English Canada. Recently, however, the number of works written on Canada from a Marxist perspective have mushroomed. These books and articles form the basis of this textbook.

Although an identifiable Marxist paradigm exists, not all sociologists agree on some of its subtle—and not so subtle—points. Hence, some of the following authors may approach a problem in a slightly different way than other authors. When this occurs, the differences of opinion are indicated. The reader may decide which of the interpretations seems most plausible.

SUGGESTED READINGS

General

Masters of Sociological Thought: Ideas in Historical and Social Context (second edition), Lewis A. Coser. New York: Harcourt Brace Jovanovich, Inc., 1977. A clearly written overview of the ideas of a number of leading European and American social scientists. The biography of each theorist is briefly sketched and their ideas examined within the larger intellectual and social contexts.

The Writing of Canadian History: Aspects of English-Canadian Historical Writing: 1900 to 1970, Carl Berger. Toronto: Oxford University Press, 1976. An excellent summary of the work of major Canadian-English historians. Their publications are examined within the intellectual and social contexts that influenced the ideas.

Ecology

Robert E. Park: Biography of A Sociologist, Winifred Rauschenbush. Durham: University Press, 1979. Using published and unpublished papers, letters, and interviews with family and friends, this book is a "natural history" of one of the most influential founding fathers of human ecology.

Quest for An American Sociology: Robert E. Park and the Chicago School, Fred H. Matthews. Montreal: McGill-Queens University Press, 1977. A biographical study of Robert Park which examines the personal and intellectual influences on his ideas.

Chicago Sociology 1920-1930, Robert L. Faris. Chicago: University of Chicago Press, 1970. A history of the "Chicago School of Sociology." The ideas of this School dominated American and Canadian sociology for several decades.

Fabian

The Fabians, Norman and Jeanne MacKenzie. New York: Simon and Schuster, 1977. An extraordinary story of the group of intellectuals who founded Fabianism and laid the ground for British socialism.

The League for Social Reconstruction: Intellectual Origins of the Democratic Left in Canada 1930-1942, Michiel Horn. Toronto: University of Toronto Press, 1980. A historical account of the work of a small number of individuals who founded the first Canadian left-wing intellectual organization. The League was founded during the Great Depression and its ideas are important for examining Canadian economic and social conditions during the current recession.

Staples

The Ideas File of Harold Adams Innis, William Christian (ed.). Toronto: University of Toronto Press, 1980. The staple ideas of Harold Innis are evident in *The Fur Trade*. In addition, in reviewing this classic book, it is intellectually stimulating to skim the approximately 1500 notes in Innis's Idea File which shows the inner working of a mind dedicated to research and reflection. After reading the arguments in each chapter in this text, it is recommended that they be ordered in an Idea File.

Frontier-Social Change

Society and Change: S.D. Clark and the Development of Canadian Sociology, Harry H. Hiller. Toronto: University of Toronto Press, 1982. An intellectual biography of one of the founding fathers of Canadian Sociology.

A CLASSICAL MARXIST PERSPECTIVE

Carl J. Cuneo

Introduction

What do people think of when they hear the words "Marxist" or "Communist"?—Russia? Mainland China? Vietnam? Eastern Europe? Cuba? Guerilla movements in Asia, Africa and Latin America? Airline highjackings? Terrorism? The Red Brigade in Italy? Palestinians? The association of these words with "Marxism" and "Communism" is made for us in schools and the popular press. Images of something bad and evil, dark and sinister are created in our minds. These associations and images may or may not correctly describe reality; yet they persist.

They emerge from the Cold War between the Soviet Union and the United States. The United States characterizes the Soviet Union as evil because it is "Marxist" or "Communist". The Soviet Union, in turn, portrays the United States as evil because it is capitalist. In reality, the economy and politics of the Soviet Union are not entirely communist. One principle of communism is *direct* control of factories by workers. But in the Soviet Union the Party and state bureaucracy, rather than workers, directly control the factories. The United States also deviates from several principles of capitalism. One of these is the sanctity of private ownership of property. But the American state has, at times, bailed out private corporations such as Chrysler. Such actions do not accord with the capitalist ethos of "Free enterprise", laissez-faire, and the private market.

The Cold War of words, therefore, distorts reality. To understand Marxism and capitalism, we have to go beneath this war of words to a more basic underlying reality. The reality involves the recognition of the existence of two powerful socio-economic and political systems, the United States and the Soviet Union. Each trys to extend its sphere of influence in the world at the cost of the other. The war of words masks this underlying reality.

It is necessary to separate the terms "Marxism" and "capitalism" from Cold War ideology and inquire into their scientific and sociological meanings. When this is done, we discover that *Marxism is a scientific theory and methodology and capitalism is a political and economic system.*

"Theory" and "methodology" will be discussed more extensively in the chapter by Hofley and Usiskin.

As a theory and methodology, Marxism can be used to describe and explain the central features of capitalism. Many chapters in this book attempt to do this for Canada which is organized on a capitalist basis. To understand many of these chapters, we must first examine selected features of the classical Marxist perspective. This is the purpose of the present chapter.

Marxism is a body of thought that stretches from the 1840s to the present. Marxist writers base many of their original principles on the works of Karl Marx who lived in Europe and England between 1818 and 1883.

Classical Marxism embraces the writings of Karl Marx and another socialist, Frederick Engels, who worked closely with him. This chapter is limited to selected features of their writings. Many contemporary Marxist writers are called "neo-Marxists" because they have developed Karl Marx's ideas in new directions and have begun to explore new problems in greater depth. However, they still maintain much of Marx's fundamental theory and methodology. Naturally, not all Marxist writers are in complete agreement with one another. This element of "dissensus" provides one of the great strengths of Marxism. It can be used to analyze new problems in a fresh way without losing touch with all of its founding principles. This is one of the purposes of the book. The present chapter will not discuss neo-Marxism since the approach becomes manifest in much of the rest of the volume.

The chapter is divided into several parts. In the early parts, we outline some of the basic assumptions and concepts in materialism and Karl Marx's labor theory of value. In later parts, we relate his concepts of class, ideology and the state to the labor theory of value.

In this chapter we will be concerned not only with the Marxist approach to economics and social class but also to ideology, politics, and the state. However, since economics and class form the foundation for the Marxist understanding of ideology, politics and the state, we will place most of our emphasis on the Marxist theory of economics and class. At appropriate points, we will show the ways in which ideology, politics and the state are related to economics and social class.

Materialism and Social Organization

In this section we introduce a set of concepts which form the foundation of materialism. Many of them are based on a simplified interpretation of the writings of Karl Marx. To these are added concepts such as "economic relationships and organizations", "political relationships and organizations", and "power". These further illuminate the Marxist perspective.

Many of these concepts will later be used in our discussion of class, ideology, and the state.

Materialism.   We must have food, clothes, and shelter before we read books, attend theatres, and vote in elections. If we spend almost all our energy fighting starvation, searching for warm clothes, and looking for shelter, we would not have the physical strength left for reading, theatre-going, and voting. In other words, we must first cope with the physical forces of nature before engaging in intellectual, cultural and political activities.

Sociologists adopt a materialist perspective when they look at human behavior in this way. *Materialism* is the description and explanation of human behavior that assigns a greater priority to physical and economic activities than to cultural, political, and intellectual activities (Marx and Engels 1947:3-43; Marx 1970a:20-22; Engels 1972a:603). This definition is more general than the one in the Preface and subsumes it.

A materialist perspective does not imply that ideas are not important. It merely means that in general economic and physical activities have a greater influence on ideas than ideas have on physical and economic activities. We can try to write a book, but are unlikely to be successful if we are starving. At the same time, having enough food to eat gives us the strength to write. But it will not guarantee that we will in fact write a book. Nor will it guarantee its quality. Writing books may earn us the money to buy food. But first we need sufficient food to gain the strength to write. This is why as a society we must first engage in basic economic and physical activities before going on to political, intellectual, cultural and artistic endeavors.

Economic Relationships and Organizations.   Nature confronts us in a number of different ways. Some food, such as wild cherries, are found in their natural state and do not require domestication. Other food, such as corn, requires planting, fertilizing and harvesting. Crops can be grown by hermits living alone. They do not have to co-operate with other hermits or with people from society in order to survive.

Most of us do not live this way. We need others to grow the food we eat. We have to co-operate with them in order to survive. Through time we set up regular relationships with others on whom we depend for our survival (Marx and Engels, 1947:6-9). The consumer in the city depends on the farmer in the countryside to grow food. The farmer depends on the consumer for money to buy seeds and fertilizer. Through time, farmers and consumers come to mutually depend on one another. This mutual dependence takes the form of regular and stable patterns of economic relations between them. The farmer may sell to the same consumers at the same market year after year. A social relation, based on their attempt to survive economically, is thereby set up between the farmer and consumer. This is one of the basic features of materialism: *in the process of surviving, people set up relatively stable economic relationships with one another.*

An *economic relationship* is a stable and relatively frequent set of contacts between two persons mutually dependent on one another for the production, distribution, or consumption of goods and services. As these economic relationships become more complex and involve regular contacts among such people as farmers, consumers, merchants, bankers, industrialists, and workers, they become economic organizations: farmers, bankers, industrialists, and merchants each hire others to work for them and in this way build up their business organizations. An *economic organization* is a complex formal network of social relationships among more than two people mutually dependent on one another for the production, distribution, or consumption of goods and services.

Nature.   Economic relationships and organizations radically transform nature into something quite different from its original state. Primitive tribesmen may kill a few animals to eat or cut a few trees to keep warm. Otherwise, they leave nature untouched.

During the Vietnam War in Southeast Asia in the 1960s and 1970s, the United States napalmed villages and vast tracts of jungle. It did not leave nature untouched. It transformed nature so radically that its original state could hardly be recognized.

The United States, with its vast military organizations, research establishments, and industrial factories, has many more complex economic relationships and organizations than peasants and primitive tribesmen. This illustrates a principle of materialism: *complex economic relationships and organizations radically transform nature more than do simple ones.* It is the mutual dependence of people on one another that transforms nature. As nature is transformed, so are economic relationships and organizations.

The destruction of the Vietnamese countryside and its peasants led to massive protests by students and other anti-war activists at home in the United States. These protests contributed eventually to the withdrawal of the United States from Vietnam. The technological war waged by the United States may have resulted in a transformation of the Vietnamese countryside, but in the process the United States itself was to some extent transformed. One principle of materialism is that, as people attempt to survive, they transform the nature that confronts them. Their relationship to nature, in turn, transforms their own economic relationships and organization. As Marx and Engels point out, *women transform nature, and in the process transform themselves. Man transforms nature, and in the process transforms himself* (Marx and Engels, 1947:7).

Means of Production.   In order to survive, people must produce goods and services to satisfy their wants. There are a number of means they employ to do this. Land is a basic requirement. Tools, such as hammers, are the means carpenters use to build tables, chairs and houses. In factories, more sophisticated means are required. Large pieces of machinery, such as presses, stamping machines, and even automated assembly lines, are essential. Large warehouses and buildings are required. Other means, such as raw materials, are also necessary before we can start producing goods. Wood is required for making tables, yarn for making coats, and various metal alloys for making cars. All these items are the means by which further goods are produced. The *means of production* are the land, buildings, raw materials, semi-processed materials, tools, machinery, light, fuel and other material elements necessary for the production of goods and services (Marx 1967a:199; 1970a:20-1; Mills 1962:82-3).

The staples discussed in the previous chapter by Dennis Magill are one type of means of production. Without the means of production, goods and services cannot be produced. It is therefore essential that these means be assembled before further production begins. However, the stock of these means can be replenished from time to time after production has begun. *Forces of production* is a somewhat broader concept: it includes the means of production as well as the technical division of labor, skills, the social division of labor, and markets.

Power. Power is the capacity of a person or organization to force others to do things they would not otherwise do. Force may be exercised with or without the consent of those against whom the power is directed (Weber 1968:53; Dahrendorf 1959:165-73; Porter 1965:201-10; Clement 1975:3-4).

In Canada and several other western industrialized societies, many employees are forbidden by law to strike while they have a contract with their employers. If a three-year collective bargaining agreement has been signed, employees must wait until the end of the three years before they are in a legal position to strike. However, wildcat strikes sometimes occur during the life of a contract (Crispo and Arthurs 1968; Flood 1972). These are often staged by rank-and-file employees dissatisfied with the contract's terms.

In this case, though workers are not totally powerless, employers have greater power than their employees. This power rests in the resources they can call upon to break the strike.

These resources include the use of the courts to issue injunctions, the threat of imprisonment or fines, the use of police, and the hiring of strikebreakers. Resources, then, form an essential ingredient in the exercise of power. For power to be exercised, however, resources do not always have to be expended. The mere threat of their use is often effective. For example, employers can simply threaten to call the police. In this case, resources are not expended. But the threatened use of the police may be sufficient to intimidate workers into going back to work.

The *ultimate resource employers exercise is their control and ownership of the means of production* i.e. control over the tools etc. that workers must use in earning a living. This is the basis of the greater power of employers compared to their employees.

Political Relationships and Organizations.

Economic relationships and organizations have been looked at in terms of the production, distribution, and consumption of goods. Power is exercised in these relationships and organizations. Employers' control of the means of production determines how their employees will carry out their daily tasks. The control of markets by large economic organizations (corporations) determines the range of goods available to consumers. As well as being economic relationships, these encounters, to the degree that they involve power, are also political relationships.

A *political relationship* is a stable and relatively frequent set of contacts between two persons or organizations in which power is exercised. In such a relationship, one person or organization forces others to engage in actions which they would not otherwise consider. Employers, for example, force employees to work at a fast pace on assembly lines when they would prefer to work at a slower pace on smaller machines. In this political relationship, the control by employers of the means of production and the paycheck forces employees to obey the orders given by the foremen. Such relationships will be examined by Graham Lowe in his chapter on work.

An apparent paradox is evident in the definitions of economic and political relationships. The reason is simple. *In the production of goods in the factory, the relationship between employers and employees is both economic and political.* It is economic to the extent that goods are produced. It is political to the extent that power is exercised. This does not mean, however, that all political relationships are equally economic. The leader of the Liberal Party of Canada tells his party members when they must vote along party lines in the House of Commons. Party members who refuse to go along with such orders are sometimes expelled from the party. This is a political relationship between the leader and his party members. It is not an economic relationship, although it could have economic consequences if the leader threatened to withdraw party finances from the election campaigns of the rebellious party members.

A *political organization* is a complex formal network of social relationships, built on the basis of power, among more than two people. Most economic organizations are also political. Banks are both economic and political organizations. Not only are they organized on the basis of the ultimate economic good—money—but also their boards of directors exercise considerable power over their employees and customers. Political organizations, however, are not always economic. The Progressive

Conservative party of Canada is a political organization much more than an economic one. It is organized more on the basis of power than money, although the latter is not irrelevant to its chances of success during elections.

HIGHLIGHT

1. Marxism is a form of materialism. That is, while it does not dismiss the importance of ideas, it gives primacy to economic matters in explaining societies.
2. The theories of means of production and forces of production are central to a Marxist analysis.
3. Ownership of the means of production confers power.
4. Power exercised by employers is both economic and political.

The Productive Process

Relations of Production. In primitive societies, most tribesmen possess their own means of producing the goods for their survival. Each tribesman has his own spears, seeds for planting, and knives. The relations of each tribesman to the means of production is the same. Each owns and controls his own means of production.

The situation in Canadian society today is quite different. One of the most important means for producing goods are large buildings and the machinery contained within them. These are very costly and only a few Canadians can afford them. The majority of the population finds these means too expensive, although most of us have our own hammers and screwdrivers at home. But such tools are only for our personal use around the house. They are not the means by which we can produce cars or snowblowers at home. In Canada, therefore, unlike the situation in primitive society, there are two different relations of individuals to the means of production. A small part of the population owns and controls the most important means of production, such as heavy machinery and factories. A much greater part of the population lacks both ownership and control of such means of production. The *relations of production* describe the relation of the individual to the means of production, either in the capacity of ownership and control or in the capacity of non-ownership and non-control.

These relations are both economic and political. They are economic to the extent that they are concerned with the production, distribution, or consumption of goods and services. They are political to the extent that they are concerned with the exercise of power. The relations of production, one of the most important ideas in this book, will form the foundation for the Marxist definition of class later in this chapter.

Labor Power.   Owning and controlling the means of production are important for survival. However, if most Canadians do not have ownership or control over the means of production, how do they survive? The simplest way of answering this question is to point out that they depend for their survival on those who do own the means of production. It is therefore necessary to understand the nature of this dependence.

Most of us have been hired, at one time or another, to work for others. In return, we receive a wage or salary for a specified period of work. This is the way in which most Canadians survive. They work for employers who hire them. But this dependence on employers is not the same for all of us. Some of us are sought out by many employers so that we have little difficulty finding a job. Others have much greater difficulty finding work. In other words, we are not equally desirable in the eyes of our employers. The reason for this is that we do not have an equal capacity for work. Our capacity to work is a very complicated matter covering a wide range of physical and mental skills and qualities. Some of us are physically strong and are therefore well suited to engage in heavy manual labor. Others are much weaker and are unsuited for this kind of work. Some of us have picked up specialized skills such as carpentry, auto mechanics, and typing in school or college and are therefore suitable for more specialized jobs. Because most Canadians lack any control over the means of production, the only power they have is over their own capacity to work or to labor in return for the wage or salary they receive from employers. This is why we call this capacity our labor power. *Labor power* can be viewed as *the total physical and mental capacity people have to work* (Marx 1967a:167).

Labor Market.   In Canadian society one's labor power or capacity to work is not useful unless it can be sold to others. This act of selling is the means by which most Canadians survive. The *labor market* is the set of economic relationships, with political and cultural characteristics, in which those who lack control and ownership of the means of production sell their labor power for a wage or salary to others who have control and ownership of the means of production.

There are two exchanges that occur in the labor market: 1) Workers *sell* part of their labor-power and receive in return a wage or salary which they use to purchase food, clothing and other essential goods. 2) The employer pays the workers' wages and salaries in return for which he receives part of their labor-power. The labor-power is used to produce goods in the employers' factories or other business establishments (Marx 1967a:167-76).

The labor market is not a place where equals meet (Marx 1977:270-80). The only power employees have is their capacity to work. The great power of the employer derives from his ownership and control of the means of production. Ownership gives him power over his workers.

Employees need to work for their employer in order to earn money to buy food and clothes. If employees refuse to work they either starve or try to obtain welfare from the government. Either prospect is undesirable. *Control and ownership of the means of production, then, is the source of the power of employers over workers and of the inequality in the economic and political relationships in the labor market.*

The inequality between employers and employees in the labor market changes from time to time. Employees try to increase their power. Employers try to reduce even further the power of their employees. One of the things that affects the inequality in this economic and political relationship is the number of jobs available. If there are more workers than the number of jobs available, the employer is freer to choose the workers he wants to hire. If he is dissatisfied with the workers he has hired, he can replace them with others who do not have a job and who are looking for work. In this situation, employers increase their power over workers.

When unemployment is high, the power of workers in the labor market usually weakens. During such times, employers are relatively successful in refusing demands for large wage increases or in reducing the wages of their workers. On the other hand, if there are more jobs than workers with the required skill, the employer is forced to hire whatever workers are available. If he is dissatisfied with their work, he may not want to fire them in case he is unable to replace them. *When unemployment is low, the power of the employer in the labor market weakens and the power of the employee increases.* Employees have more success during such times in winning wage increases from their employers (Smith 1972;1976; Ashenfelter and Johnson 1967; Snyder 1977). But the power of the workers does not increase to the extent that they challenge the employers' control of the means of production. This is an entirely different matter that will be discussed later.

Changes in the labor market are also affected by the formation of economic and political organizations. Such organizations can be formed by either employers or employees. Employers in the same line of business have often formed organizations to protect and advance their interests. In Canada, manufacturers have formed the Canadian Manufacturers Association; mine owners have organized the Canadian Mining Association; bankers have formed the Canadian Bankers Association. These organizations reinforce the inequality between employers and employees in the labor market.

One way this is accomplished is through the effort expended by these organizations to maintain a uniform level of wages. Organizations such as the Canadian Mining Association may agree on maximum wages which mine owners should pay their workers. Where such agreements are made, mine workers find it difficult to play one mine owner off against another. It is therefore to the advantage of employers to co-operate with one another in dealing with their employees. This illustrates a principle operating in the labor market: *the formation of common economic and political organizations among employers increases their power in the labor market and weakens the power of their employees.*

A similar situation exists among employees. Where workers face employers on their own without the protection of an association of other workers, their power is considerably weakened. Employers can pay whatever wages they wish. The individual employees do not have an organization of workers to protect their interests. *The formation of common political and economic organizations such as trade unions among workers considerably increases their power in the labor market.* Trade unions, such as the Canadian Union of Public Employees or the United Steelworkers of America, can bargain with employers for wage increases. If employers refuse to grant significant increases, unions can back their demands with the threat of a strike.

The inequality between employers and employees in the labor market shifts as their respective economic and political organizations grow stronger or become weaker. However, despite the formation of such organizations among workers, in the long run, employers, because of their control and ownership of the means of production, still retain power over their employees. It is only when employees, in an occupation of a plant, take over control of the means of production that they are able to fundamentally challenge the greater power of employers in the labor market and shift the balance of power in their favor. The main point to remember is that the *labor market is an economic and political relationship between employers and employees and that the balance of power constantly shifts with changes in the availability of jobs and the strength of economic and political organizations.*

Contradiction Versus Conflict.   In discussing the labor market, we have seen that the interests of employers and employees are not the same. This difference is not only one of dissimilarity, but also of opposition. It is in the interest of employers to restrain wage increases in order to keep their costs under control. It is in the interests of employees to increase wages so that they may earn more money to buy food, clothing, and the other necessities of life.

This tension or antagonism between employers and employees may simply exist without the formation of separate economic and political organizations to express their opposing interests. *Contradiction* or antagonism is opposition *without* its visible expression through the mobilization of economic and political organizations. The mere fact of opposing interests over wages on the part of employers and employees constitutes a contradiction. The social psychological aspects of such contradictions will be discussed by Bernd Baldus in a later chapter.

When these contradictions become visibly expressed in the clash of competing relationships and organizations such as strikes, a situation of conflict has arisen. *Conflict* or struggle is opposition that becomes visibly expressed through the mobilization of economic and political relationships and organizations (Marx 1954;1970a:21;1969;1972; Mao Tse-Tung 1954; Althusser 1970:94-8; Dahrendorf 1959). The clash of the Canadian Labor Congress and the Canadian Manufacturers Association over wages is one kind of conflict between employers and employees.

Ideologies.   Workers may have different ideas about their lack of control and ownership of the means of production. One group of workers may not recognize their lack of ownership and control. They may believe that the means of production are controlled and owned by "society", and that employers and employees receive their just returns from production according to their contributions. Workers contribute their labor to production, and employers their money. However, this belief does not accurately reflect the relations of production in which workers lack ownership and control. It is a belief which supports the interests of employers.

If employees believe that the means of production are controlled and owned by "society", they will never challenge the privileged private ownership and control enjoyed by employers. Nor will they question the unequal power between them. This false belief is contrary to the interests of workers. As long as they hold this false belief, their dependence on employers for their livelihood in the form of wages and salaries will be maintained.

It is incorrect, however, to think that a set of beliefs is unimportant if it does not accurately reflect the economic and political relationships between employers and employees. In the employee-employer relationship, for example, such a set of beliefs guides the behavior of the employees. To this extent, the set of beliefs is important and must be taken into account by sociologists studying employees' lives.

A second group of workers may hold a different set of ideas. They may believe that they lack ownership and control of the means of production. These workers may think that they will be forever dependent on employers for their livelihood and permanently reduced to a powerless position unless they challenge their employers' private ownership and control. This group of workers holds a set of beliefs that correctly reflects the objective relations of employees and employers to the means of production. These beliefs are important in a way that is different from the beliefs held in the first group of workers.

The second set of beliefs has a greater potential of convincing workers to start a radical transformation in the relations of production, and to introduce a new society having greater equality than currently exists. These beliefs, then, are more in the interests of workers and less in the interests of employers.

We call both sets of beliefs *ideologies*. These are sets of ideas, attitudes, beliefs and opinions on the basis of which people live out their lives. Ideologies may either accurately reflect or distort the relations of individuals to the means of production. Whatever their nature, people have faith and trust in their own beliefs and, on this basis, live, work, and act them out. Ideologies may support the interests of employers or employees. They have profound implications for the maintenance or transformation of society. Ideologies, whether true or false, are therefore to be taken seriously. In a later chapter by Grayson, the idea of ideology will be refined further.

In 1846, Marx and Engels (1947:13-4) viewed ideology as consisting of "ideas, of conceptions, of consciousness" which are "directly interwoven with the material activity and the material intercourse of men . . .". Later, in 1859, Marx (1970a:21) elevated ideology into a superstructure encompassing "legal, political, religious, artistic, or philosophic" forms. These forms are viewed as analytically separable from "the economic foundation (which) lead sooner or later to the transformation of the whole immense super-structure." Louis Althusser, a neo-Marxist, appears to have two theories of ideology. One locates ideology in a superstructure elevated above, and relatively autonomous from, the "economic foundation". The other locates ideology within "material existence" (cf. Althusser 1971:129-31, 152-65; Hirst 1979).

HIGHLIGHT

1. Since workers do not own their means of production, they are compelled to sell their labor-power to survive. If the supply of labor is high, wages are low. Frequently, the owners stand together to enforce low wages in an industry. Workers organize through unions in attempts to raise wages.
2. Ideologies are sets of ideas that try to explain to individuals why things are the way they are. Usually they simply confuse the true nature of dominance in society.

Value

Commodity.   So far we have been discussing the economic and political relations of production between employers and employees. In these relations, goods such as cars, tables, and food are produced. Most of these goods are exchanged for money in the market. We may produce other goods at home and use them ourselves rather than selling them in the market. Some of us may know how to make a dress. We may work on this at home at night and on weekends. On completion, we may decide not to sell it but to wear it. Similar dresses may be made by women workers in a garment factory. Their employer may have invested money in the production of these dresses. His purpose may not have been to have the women workers wear the dresses, but to exchange them in the market for money.

We have, then, two types of goods. One is consumed by its producer without being exchanged for money in the market. This is called a *product*. The other is called a *commodity*. It is produced and exchanged in the market for an amount of money (Marx 1967a:40-41). Workers produce commodities in factories to be sold in the marketplace.

Earlier in this chapter we stated that labor-power is bought and sold in the labor market. Employees sell their capacity to work to employers who give them wages. *Labor-power, then, is a commodity.* It is produced and exchanged for money in a market. But it is a commodity that is different from cars and furniture. Its production does not occur in the economic and political relations of production in the factory, but in other relations. Labor-power is produced in homes and schools.

Previously, we pointed out that labor-power includes the physical and mental capacities of workers. Physical capacity embraces bodily growth and development. Food is essential for this. When a mother prepares meals for her child, she is helping to produce the child's labor-power for later in life when her child becomes a worker and sells her/his labor-power in the labor market. When a wife prepares meals for her husband, she is helping to renew his exhausted labor-power which he sells for a wage on the labor market. The domestic labor of women as it relates to the work process will be examined in greater detail in the chapter by Dorothy Smith.

The mental capacity of labor-power is produced not only at home, but also in schools. When a mother teaches her child the importance of work, she instils an ideology that becomes part of the child's mental capacity. Such an ideology will be important for the child's motivation to obtain a job later in life. When a teacher at school drills students in the importance of obedience to authority figures (such as the prime minister, priest or rabbi, and corporation president), the student learns an ideology of obedience important later in life in his or her relations with employers. The production of the commodity labor-power, then, occurs outside the factory at home and in schools. This labor-power is repeatedly exchanged for a wage in the labor market. David Nock will give more evidence of this dynamic in his chapter on education.

Value.   Selling and buying in markets must be based on some standard of the equivalence of commodities. One way of establishing the equivalence of commodities is by looking at their price expressed by money. The exchange of money for food in a supermarket must be based on some standard of the worth of food. Storeowners likely will think that bread and milk are worth more than what their customers are willing to pay. Similarly, there must be some standard for the exchange of labor-power in the labor market. Workers will think that their labor-power is worth more than what their employers are willing to pay.

If a toy doll and a toy truck are each priced at $11.73, we say that they are worth the same. Instead of exchanging money, we could exchange the doll for the truck without feeling cheated. However, next week the doll may be priced at $12.50 and the truck at $17.80. Are they no longer of equal worth? The price of the truck may have risen faster because there was a greater demand for the truck than for the doll. On the other hand, there may have been two manufacturers of the truck and eighteen manufacturers of the doll. The two manufacturers of the truck may have gotten together to arbitrarily raise the price of the truck since they knew they had no competitors who could sell below their price. It would have been much more difficult for the doll manufacturers to do this since there would have been much more competition among all eighteen of them. Because the money price of commodities is exposed to influences, such as this, which has little to do with their 'true value,' we may not want to use price as a measure of value.

A different way to determine the value of commodities is to ask what common characteristic they take on as they are being produced. We saw previously that employers, in order to produce commodities, purchase labor-power. The labor of employees goes into the production of commodities. *One characteristic which all commodities have in common is labor.*

Each worker labors for a certain length of time on the production of a commodity. In the above example, workers may have put seventeen hours of labor into the production of the doll and twenty-one hours into the truck. We say therefore that the truck has a greater value, measured in labor time, than the doll. The *value* of a commodity is the amount of labor that goes into its production. The greater the amount of labor in a commodity, the higher its value (Marx 1967a:35-41). Price in the form of money may or may not coincide with the value of a commodity.

Labor is put into a commodity at different stages of its production. There are two types of labor that go into the production of a chair. The first occurs when workers in a furniture factory put their labor into the manufacture of the chair. This process may consist of sawing and planing the wood, setting the joints, and applying a protective coat of varnish. This is the active labor that workers apply to the chair. For this reason, it is called *living labor* or the amount of labor put into a commodity during its actual production.

The second type of labor occurred before the wood arrived at the furniture factory gates. Timbermen cut the trees. Truckers transported the trees to sawmills. Workers at sawmills cut the trees into planks and truckers then transported the planks to the furniture factory.

The wood used in the furniture factory was part of the raw materials which earlier in this chapter we included in the means of production (along with machinery, land, buildings, tools, fuel, etc.). We call the labor in these means of production *dead labor*. This is the amount of labor previously put into commodities that now form the means of production used in the process of making further commodities. This labor is frozen in such commodities as the wood on which the furniture factory employees work. It is not the active, living labor of the furniture workers. For this reason it is called dead. The total value of commodities consists of the sum of living labor and dead labor.

Since labor-power is a commodity, it can be argued that its value is equal to the amount of labor required to produce it. The value of the labor-power of a welder, for example, consists of three parts. As Dorothy Smith later points out, one part consists of unpaid domestic labor. The welder's mother labored to raise him from childhood to adolescence. She fed and clothed him, she washed his clothes, and taught him such ideologies as obedience to authority, co-operation, and competition among his friends. His wife now feeds him on a daily basis, does the shopping, and washes the floors and his clothes. The labor of mother and wife is not paid directly except for the money given to them by their husbands (unless they have their own jobs outside the home). This domestic work is living labor since it is actively put into the commodity labor-power by the mother and wife.

A second part of the value of the welder's labor-power is contained in the commodities bought on the market and consumed by him. The food which his wife buys at the supermarket contains a value consisting of the labor put into it by wage-earning farmworkers and employees in canning factories. Similarly, there is value in the house inhabited by the welder and his family. This value consists partly of the labor of construction workers who built the house. These commodities form dead labor since the workers (farmworkers, canning factory workers, construction workers) do not put their own labor directly into the welder's labor-power, but only into the commodities (food, home) which he consumes.

The third part of the value of the welder's labor-power consists of the labor of his teachers in the elementary and secondary schools he attended and in the technical college where he learned his trade. This is living labor since it is put directly into the welder's labor-power. The value of the welder's labor-power, then, consists of the living labor of unpaid family members (mother and wife); the dead labor of the workers who produce commodities which he consumes; and, the living labor of the teachers at the various schools he attended. Labor-power, like other commodities such as chairs, dolls, trucks, and food, can be viewed as having a value partly determined by the amount of labor put into its production. In all cases, the value of a commodity is equal to the total labor (both living and dead) that went into its production.

Use-Value. The usefulness of the previously considered toy doll and truck may not be the same. A child may receive five years' use out of the truck but only two years out of the doll before it falls apart. The *use-value* of a commodity is its utility in satisfying the needs of the person who consumes it (Marx 1967a:35-41). Some commodities have a greater utility than others.

Use-value is not the same as value. The *concrete quality* of a commodity and the degree to which it satisfies the needs of a consumer expresses its use-value. The *abstract quantity* of labor-time required to produce a commodity expresses its value. An atomic bomb is a commodity with a low use-value because it destroys human life, but it has a high value because a great amount of labor went into its development and production. A book on love-making is a commodity with a high use-value because it aids thousands of couples in the production of many new lives, but it has a low value because it requires only a small amount of labor by a few people to produce it.

Labor-power, as a commodity, also has both use-value and value. A chemical manufacturer may have hired a theoretical chemist, with a Ph.D. degree in both chemistry and physics, to develop a synthetic bullet proof plastic vest. Because of the thousands of hours of labor-time that went into this chemist's training, the value of his labor-power is very high. But he may have been trained in such advanced chemical theory that he cannot apply his theory to the practical problem of vest development. His use-value to the manufacturer is therefore not great, despite the high value of his labor-power. As in the case of other commodities, use-value and value of labor-power are not the same.

Labor Process.   Use-value and values are produced simultaneously when cars roll off the assembly line. In this situation labor is applied to raw materials and machinery. As a consequence a physical transformation of the material ingredients of the cars occurs as they move along the assembly line.

There are three parts to this process. One includes the *activity* of the laborers themselves, such as welding, setting dies, hammering bolts, and putting on doors. A second part consists of the *instruments* of labor or tools and machinery, such as hammers, torches, presses, and assembly lines. The third part includes the *subject* or the raw and semi-processed *materials*, such as aluminum, steel, rubber, and plastic, to which the labor activity is applied. The *labor process* is the application of the activity of the worker, with the help of instruments of labor, to raw and semi-processed materials (Marx 1967a:177-85). In the labor process, value is produced as a quantity of abstract labor-time applied to the commodities being produced. *At the same time*, concrete useful qualities and hence use-values are being produced. The labor process therefore is a dual process: it is the production of both use-value and value. The labor-process will be extensively analyzed in the chapter on work by Lowe.

HIGHLIGHT

1. The value of a commodity can be determined by the amount of labor that went into its production. Such labor can be classified as "living" and "dead".
2. Commodities have both a value and a use-value. The former is determined by the amount of labor required to produce it; the latter by the degree to which it satisfies human needs.

Capital and Labor

Capital Accumulation.   The wealth of Canadian society is produced through the labor-process. Money is invested by employers in the means of production and labor-power before the production of commodities can begin. Once production starts, the labor process is set in motion. Workers apply their skill and strength to the transformation of commodities. At the end of production, new commodities, with a different physical form and added value, are sold in the market. The employer receives from this sale a sum of money greater than the amount he invested at the onset of production. His wealth has therefore increased. He invests his money in order to increase it. *Capital* is money which is invested in the means of production and labor-power for the purpose of increasing it (Marx 1967a:146-55).

A mother, in contrast, may buy a package of carrots at the local grocery store. She invests her money in carrots, but does not increase it. The carrots are bought solely for their use-value—for the purpose of satisfying the physical needs of her family. This illustrates the distinction between money as 'money' and money as 'capital'.

Money as 'money' is spent, not to increase it, but solely to satisfy human needs. Money as 'capital' is spent both to increase money and to satisfy human needs. The search by the employer for greater wealth is satisfied temporarily by the increased return he receives from his investment. But this increased return does not permanently satisfy his appetite for greater wealth. After each return, he re-invests his money in order to obtain an ever greater increase. The process by which people constantly invest and re-invest their capital to increase their wealth is called *capital accumulation* (Marx 1967a:612-712). The employer accumulates wealth; the housewife, seeking to feed her family, does not accumulate wealth. She merely tries to survive. Capital accumulation, as will be seen later, leads to uneven regional development, both at the national and international levels.

Constant Capital.   *Constant capital* is the capital employers invest in the means of production (Marx 1967a:209) such as raw materials. It is called constant because its value (dead labor) does not increase throughout the process of production. This does not mean that constant capital is not important for accumulating wealth. It merely means that constant capital by itself cannot explain increases in wealth. Surplus labor, which will be discussed shortly, is the source of increased wealth.

One part of the final value of commodities is transferred from the means of production—machinery, raw materials, etc.—to the commodity itself. It must be stressed, however, that not all of the value of the means of production enters the commodity. An auto assembly line contains value, but each time a car is produced, the total value of the line does not pass into the car. If this were the case, the car manufacturer would be receiving the value of an assembly line each time a car is produced. Rather, each year one part of value remains fixed in the assembly line and the other part circulates to the cars being produced. In an assembly line that lasts for ten years, one-tenth of its value passes each year into the cars that roll off the line. At the end of the first year, one-tenth of value circulates and nine-tenths remains fixed. At the end of ten years, the total value of the assembly line has passed into all the cars produced in this period. The part of the value of machinery that circulates is called *depreciation.*

Means of production have different rates of depreciation. Machinery, tools, buildings, and land have slow rates of depreciation. However, almost the total value of fuel, light, raw and semi-processed materials circulates in each year of production. *Fixed constant capital* is the value of the means of production that is *not* transferred to commodities in a specific period of production. *Circulating constant capital* is the part of the value of the means of production that is transferred to commodities in a specific period of production (Marx 1967b:157-82).

Necessary Labor.   A press operator may earn $10 per hour or $400 per 40-hour week. After deductions for income tax, unemployment insurance, Canada Pension, union dues, and a health plan, he takes home $310 per week. From this, he and his wife must pay for their accommodation, food, hydro, heat, and clothes for themselves and their two children. Since his wife cannot find a job outside the home, the wages he receives are the only means by which the family subsists.

For most people employed by others, the *means of subsistence* are the average wages and salaries they receive. These means enable the production and, through time, reproduction of the press operator's labor-power. They enable his wife to feed and clothe him so that he can go to work on a daily and weekly basis. His wages must also pay for the means of subsistence of the other three family members. The labor that the press operator performs at work is therefore necessary to pay the cost of the means of subsistence of himself and his family.

Necessary labor is the amount of labor essential to pay the cost of the means of subsistence of workers and their dependents. It is equivalent to the average cost of reproducing their labor-power (Marx 1967a:216-17).

In monetary terms, wages may be a more or less exact expression of the value of labor-power.

Surplus Labor and Surplus Value. We have already seen that the value of the means of production does not increase from the beginning to the end of production and that the means of production cannot by themselves account for capital accumulation or the increase in wealth. Capital accumulation must be based therefore on the only other commodity, labor-power, in which the employer invests capital. The application of labor-power to production is living labor. Living labor must be the basis on which wealth is created. The workers' wages *appear* to cover the entire working day. But things are not what they appear to be.

Employees earn for the employer in a few hours what he pays them for the whole day. In one sense, they work the rest of the day free.

One paid part of the working day is necessary labor. It is the part that pays the cost of the worker's means of subsistence. If employees must work five hours to earn a sufficient amount to pay for their means of subsistence, the necessary labor equals five hours. However, if the working day is eight hours, employees labor three hours without being paid. Such labor is surplus to the amount of labor employees must perform to exist.

Surplus labor is the amount of labor workers perform without being paid (Marx 1967a:217). This extra, free labor, is the amount of labor, above necessary labor, added to commodities from the beginning to the end of production. The amount of labor in a commodity at the end of production may be 100 hours or, in money terms, $900. The total cost to the employer of dead labor in the means of production and living labor transferred to the commodity in production may only have been 67 hours or $600. The difference is 33 hours of labor, or $300. This is surplus labor. Translated into value terms, this is *surplus value* or the extra value workers produce and add to commodities in the process of production over and above the value of circulating constant capital and necessary labor (Marx 1967a:212-20). Surplus value is capital accumulation or the extent to which capital increases from the beginning to the end of production.

Variable Capital. We can now consider the capital which employers invest in labor-power. Since the value of commodities increases as a result of the application of labor-power, the capital invested in it is not called constant. Instead, it is called variable: it enables the value of commodities to vary, or increase. *Variable capital*, then, is the capital invested in labor-power that takes on the money expression of wages (Marx 1967a:209). The total wage bill of employers is equal to the total variable capital they invest.

Rate of Surplus Value.   Owners of a shoe factory in one year may invest $870 000 in variable capital to pay the wages of the labor performed by their employees. The value of capital invested in the means of production, which is transferred to the shoes as they pass through production, may come to $1 000 000. Therefore, the total value of necessary labor and the means of production transferred to the shoes is $1 870 000. The value of the shoes when sold at the end of one year's production may be $2 000 000. A surplus value of $130 000 has thereby been added to the shoes through the employees' labor. This is the amount by which employers of the shoe company *exploit* their workers. The extraction of this wealth is called *exploitation* because it represents an amount of money which employers have taken away from their workers without giving it back to them in wages.

To find out the *rate* at which employers exploit their workers, we divide surplus value by variable capital, or $130 000 by $870 000. This works out to 15 percent. The ratio of surplus value produced by labor to variable capital invested in their wages is called the *rate of surplus value* (Marx 1967a:212-20). The higher this rate, the more employers exploit their workers. The lower this rate, the less employers exploit their workers. It is the most important aspect of the relations of production between employers and employees as it represents the transfer of wealth from employees to employers. It is also a political relationship of the power of employers over their employees. This relation is one of *contradiction* to the extent that there is not a mobilization of organizations of employees and employers that clash over the rate of surplus value. Such a situation of contradiction exists in both unionized and non-unionized factories. On the other hand, once workers mobilize through unions or other means to demand an increase in wages, this contradictory relation is transformed into one of *conflict*. If all other factors remain constant, an increase in wages decreases the rate of surplus value and therefore the rate at which employers exploit their workers.

Marx thought that, as capitalism developed, the rate of surplus value would generally increase. However, he did not rule out the possibility of decreases in the rate of surplus value over short periods of time. Between 1793 and 1913, as capitalism spread throughout the world, the rate of surplus value generally increased (Mandel 1975:130-32). However, in some capitalist countries, especially Canada, the United States, Great Britain, Germany, Italy, and Japan, the rate of surplus value fluctuated between the two great World Wars.

In the wake of the Bolshevik revolution in Russia in 1917, and widespread labor protests in the West at the end of World War I, the rate of surplus value decreased between 1918 and 1923. Demands for wage increases and spreading unionization resulted in workers winning back some of the surplus value extracted from them during the war. However, between 1923 and 1929, the West experienced an almost unprecedented period of prosperity. During this period, workers' wages did not increase significantly and trade union organizations stagnated. Not surprisingly, the rate of surplus value dramatically increased. This came to a halt during the Great Depression between 1929 and 1935. Markets stagnated, many factories closed down while others reduced their work force. Unemployment increased dramatically. The rate of surplus value during this period declined sharply.

The period between 1935 and 1939 was marked by a hesitant and uncertain recovery because the effects of the Depression were still being felt. Similarly, the rate of surplus value began to increase in a very slow and reluctant manner. Capitalist economies needed a sudden stimulus in order to raise the rate of surplus value to unprecedented levels. This was provided by World War II, 1939-45.

By 1943, armament production was booming. Trade union organization and wages were held in check by governments, and the rate of surplus value began to increase dramatically. This increase continued throughout the entire post-war period between 1945 and 1966. During these years inflation did not rise dramatically. Trade union organizations spread slowly, and only modest wage gains were granted to workers. This acceleration in the rate of surplus value came to a halt in 1967.

Between 1967 and today, the rate of surplus value has stagnated (Mandel 1975; 1978; 1980; Cuneo 1978a; 1982b). The stagnation reflects the economic crises which the western capitalist countries have experienced. Increases in labor productivity have fallen off, inflation has increased enormously, unemployment has accelerated, and trade union organizations have spread to new sectors of the economy such as white-collar employment and the state. With stronger economic and political organizations among workers, the wages of unionized workers have increased. Even though Marx predicted that the rate of surplus value would increase with the development of capitalism, it now appears that when capitalism enters a period of crisis, the rate of surplus value either stagnates or declines. If such a situation were to persist indefinitely, capitalism itself would enter a period of breakdown and transformation.

HIGHLIGHT

1. Money becomes capital when it is spent in such a way as to make more money.
2. In the process of production, the value of the means of production, such as raw materials, tools, and machinery, remains constant. Part of their value is transferred to the commodity being produced.
3. Necessary labor is the amount of paid labor necessary for the worker to sustain him/herself and his/her family.
4. Surplus labor is labor the worker is not paid for. It is the basis of the profit of the owner of the means of production.

5. Surplus value is the extra value workers put into commodities over and above the value of dead and necessary labor.
6. Marx's prediction of a general rise in the rate of surplus value interrupted by temporary periods of stagnation and decline is true when applied to Canada and other advanced capitalist countries.

Production and Circulation

Spheres of Production and Circulation.   Surplus value is produced through the physical transformation of commodities in the labor-process. The combination of all aspects of business in which surplus value is produced is called the *sphere of production* (Marx 1967b:63-85, 238-47). In Canada, the sphere of production consists of business establishments in such areas as manufacturing, agri-business, forestry, lumbering, mining, fishing, oil and gas production, utilities, services, and transportation. *The exploitation of laborers by their employers, and the generation of wealth and surplus value, occurs only in the sphere of production. Therefore, the rate of surplus value can be discussed only for this sphere.* You will see from other chapters of this book that some authors deal with this matter in a slightly different way.

The sphere of production, however, cannot live an isolated existence. For production to continue, goods and services must be sold in the market, either to other business establishments or to individual consumers. If commodities are not sold, they are stockpiled in factory warehouses. Production is then cut back, employees are thrown out of work, and the sphere of production enters a crisis, such as during the Great Depression between 1929 and 1935, or in the North American auto industry since 1980. The sphere of production, then, is dependent on repeated selling and buying in the marketplace.

The combination of all exchanges of buying and selling in a society is known as the *sphere of circulation* (Marx 1967b:23-62, 86-99, 121-28). Money, physical commodities, and services can be traded. In Canada, such business establishments as banks, trust and mortgage companies, life insurance companies, retail and wholesale stores, and corporations make up the sphere of circulation.

This sphere cannot exist in isolation. It is dependent on the sphere of production. If goods and services are not produced, they cannot be sold and bought. The dependence, however, runs even deeper than this. As noted previously, wealth is produced through the exploitation of labor by employers. As commodities are produced through the labor-process, surplus value is extracted from labor. This extraction is expressed in the rate of surplus value. *Wealth is not produced in the sphere of circulation. It is only realized in this sphere through the exchange of commodities.*

Because of this fact, the spheres of production and circulation are not equal. The sphere of circulation has a greater dependence on the sphere of production (Marx 1973:88-100). The wealth earned in the sphere of circulation must first be generated in the sphere of production. For example, the interest which the Canadian Imperial Bank of Commerce (sphere of circulation) receives from its bank loans to the Massey-Ferguson tractor company (sphere of production) comes from the surplus value produced by the employees of Massey-Ferguson. In fact, the wealth earned in the sphere of production can *never* be generated first in the sphere of circulation. The profits of Massey-Ferguson do not come from the labor of bank tellers in the Canadian Imperial Bank of Commerce. The dependence of circulation on production is expressed through productive and unproductive labor.

Productive and Unproductive Labor.   An assembly-line worker employed by Massey-Ferguson may work an eight-hour shift. In the first five hours, he may perform all the labor that is necessary to pay his living expenses. For this necessary labor he is paid wages. In the other three hours, he may perform for Massey-Ferguson what amounts to free surplus labor. This adds extra labor to raw materials and transforms them into tractors. In value terms, this labor adds value to tractors over and above the cost of the assembly-line worker's wages and materials. Thus, he adds surplus value to tractors.

The teller in the Canadian Imperial Bank of Commerce may also work an eight-hour day. She may be similarly paid in the first five hours for her necessary labor which covers her living expenses. During the other three hours she performs free surplus labor. Such labor may be arranging Bank documents for a $500 000 loan to Massey-Ferguson. This does *not* add value to commodities, such as tractors. They are produced in the factories of Massey-Ferguson, not in the buildings of the Bank. The teller's surplus labor merely allows the Bank to arrange the loan to Massey-Ferguson, and to realize interest on this loan. The interest the Bank receives from the loan is part of the surplus value generated by Massey-Ferguson's assembly-line workers.

Out of this interest the Bank pays the wages of its tellers and other employees. The surplus labor of its employees enables the Bank to keep for itself part of the surplus value generated in companies in the sphere of production. Thus, the surplus labor of its employees allows the Bank to make a profit, but this profit does not come from any surplus value produced by its own employees (they do not produce surplus value). Besides its wages, the Bank pays its other expenses out of such interest on loans. What is left over becomes its total profits.

Productive labor directly produces surplus value. It is found only in the sphere of production, such as in Massey-Ferguson. *Unproductive labor* does not produce surplus value but only allows it to be realized or shared by employers through their employees' surplus labor. Labor in the sphere of circulation, such as in the Canadian Imperial Bank of Commerce, is unproductive. The wages of unproductive labor in the sphere of circulation are paid out of the surplus value generated by productive labor in the sphere of production (Marx 1977:1038-49; 1963a:152-304; Gough 1972; O'Connor 1975; Braverman 1974:410-23; Cuneo 1978a:286; 1978b:139-41; 1979a:6-7; 1980a:241-47; 1982b).

HIGHLIGHT

1. The sphere of production includes all activities associated with producing commodities and surplus value. The sphere of circulation includes all activities connected with the sale of commodities. Wealth is never generated in the sphere of circulation, but only in the sphere of production.
2. Productive labor is that which produces surplus value in the sphere of production. Unproductive labor facilitates the realization of surplus value in trading activities but does not itself produce surplus value.

The State Mode of Production and Historical Materialism

The State.   Earlier in this chapter, we defined power, political relationships, and political organizations. They were seen as an integral part of the relations of production between employers and employees. However, we should not assume that all instances of power, and political relationships and organizations, are found in the immediate relations of production. They can also exist *outside* these relations. Nowhere is this more evident than in the *state* which is the most complex set of political relationships and organizations existing in a society.

While not all Marxists agree on their ideas of the state, one view is that it is a complex political institution consisting of the government (central executive or cabinet), administration (civil service), legislature (Parliament), education, the courts, prisons, police, and military at the federal, provincial and municipal levels (Miliband 1973:50-1; Althusser, 1971). In Canada, part of the mass media, such as the C.B.C., is also included in the state. The central purpose of the state is the exercise of power to maintain order and stability in society, and to assist in the accumulation of capital.

Although the maintenance of order might be seen as advantageous to all citizens in a society, state decisions usually benefit one part of the population more than another. This is most evident in state intervention in the relations of production. Although the state exists formally outside the immediate relations of production in the private sector, it passes laws empowering it to intervene in this sector. One example is collective bargaining legislation regulating the relations between unions and management. When a dispute between these parties cannot be settled, the state often appoints an arbitrator to settle it. However, the settlement often goes against the interests of employees. They may have demanded a thirty percent wage increase over three years to cope with an expected inflation rate of forty percent. The arbitrator may have forced upon them an eighteen percent increase. Despite their dissatisfaction with the settlement, the employees, feeling that their demands and interests have been betrayed, are ordered back to work.

Employers may also feel that their interests have been betrayed. They would rather not give their employees any wage increase at all. But the settlement assures that the employees will work without striking for the duration of the three-year contract. A no-strike provision has been included in the contract backed up by the force of law and supported by threats of fines and imprisonment for violation. It thus appears that the state has acted more on behalf of management than the union.

Two general principles emerge out of this discussion: (a) the state appears to act on behalf of all citizens, but usually makes decisions more beneficial to one part of the population than another; (b) although the state exists formally outside the immediate relations of production, it intervenes in these relations and thereby becomes an integral part of them. We will return to a discussion of the state at several points throughout the rest of the chapter.

Mode of Production.   People employed in garment factories in Canada are stationed at hundreds of sewing machines. Each person is given the task of sewing one piece of a dress together. One sews on the sleeves, another puts on the collar, and a third sews the hem. This is the method, or mode, by which dresses are made today. This mode of producing dresses consists mainly of economic relationships and organizations, such as the economic production of dresses, their distribution for sale in stores, the payment of the women's wages, and the organization of machinery and yarn (means of production) before production can begin.

This example illustrates the *narrow view of the mode of production* or the view that the mode of production only consists of the economic aspects of production (Marx 1970a:20-1; Hindess and Hirst 1975:9). This view excludes from the definition of mode of production the ideologies or ideas of workers and management, the political aspects of the relations between them, and the intervention by the state in the immediate relations of production. *The narrow view of mode of production may be defined as the economic combination of the relations and forces of production between which exists both compatibility and contradiction.*

There is also a *broad view of the mode of production* which incorporates ideology, political relationships and organizations, and the state within the mode of production (Marx 1967a:Chapter 10; 1969; 1972). From this viewpoint, the power struggle between garment factory workers and their employers, their beliefs about this struggle, and the intervention by the state in this conflict would be an integral part of the broad view of the mode of production. *The broad view of mode of production may be defined as the economic, political, and ideological combination of the relations and forces of production between which exists both compatibility and contradiction.* We might ask why social scientists place any importance on this broad view. After all, is not the mode of production *only* an economic phenomenon? The broad perspective maintains that an artificial separation among the economic, ideological and political aspects of mode of production cannot be made. They are all an integral part of the way goods and services are produced, distributed, sold and consumed. Historical changes in a society are thus viewed broadly in terms of the integration, contradictions and conflicts, among the economic, ideological, and political aspects of mode of production.

The mode of production is not necessarily the same in different historical periods. In early nineteenth century Canada, dresses were not made by people employed in factories. Rather, they were often made by women who lived on farms and who did not work for a wage. The clothes they made were for themselves, their husbands, and their children. Rarely did they sell clothes on the open market. In other words, they consumed what they produced. Sewing was not divided among several women. The same woman by herself made the entire dress. For women, and men, the mode of production is different depending on whether they lived on farms in the nineteenth century or were employed in garment factories in the twentieth century.

The study of the economic aspects of the mode of production shows how societies undergo change. This is especially true for the materialist perspective as outlined at the beginning of the chapter. According to this perspective, ideologies and political relationships change *more or less* in response to changes in the economic mode of production. Ideologies and politics can bring about changes in the economic mode of production, but this happens less frequently.

Historical Materialism.   As will be seen in a later chapter by Veltmeyer, in the first half of the nineteenth century, the farmers of Ontario shipped large quantities of wheat to the merchants of Montreal. They, in turn, sent the wheat on to England. Britain charged lower tariffs on Canadian wheat than on wheat from other countries outside its empire. The higher tariffs against other countries meant altogether higher prices for wheat for British laborers. Since wheat was a major part of their daily diet, high tariffs thereby raised the cost of the laborers' means of subsistence. In response, they demanded higher wages from their employers. The latter resisted, and an economic and political conflict erupted between them. Laborers joined the Chartist movement which demanded radical political reforms in the British state. In order to reduce the intensity of conflict, manufacturing employers pressured the state to remove the tariffs on wheat. Such action would cheapen wheat and ease the upward pressure on wages, and this was done in 1846.

The effect on Canada was disastrous. The farmers and merchants of Canada no longer enjoyed protection in the British market. They now had to compete on equal terms with other countries. As a result, the merchants of Montreal, who depended on the wheat trade for their livelihood, suffered an economic collapse. They lost their capital in the wheat trade, and many of them went bankrupt. To cope with a capital shortage, they appealed to the United States to invest capital in Canadian business establishments (Cuneo 1982a).

By 1860, United States corporations began to invest heavily in Canadian industrial businesses. However, if these businesses were to grow and prosper, they needed a large supply of labor. This supply was to come from the farms and from immigrants flowing into Canada. Increasingly, a greater part of the population ceased to have an independent existence on farms and started to work for wages in factories. Assisting this transition in the mode of production from self-subsistence in agriculture to a wage subsistence in factories, the Canadian state passed laws that facilitated American investment in the Canadian economy.

The method of analyzing these changes illustrates *historical materialism*. Contradictions and conflicts in the economic mode of production (especially in the forces of production) bring about, sooner or later, further changes in the forces and relations of production and in ideology and politics (Marx 1970a:20-2; Engels 1969:10; 1972b:14; 1972a:603-4). In the above case, the contradiction in Britain between the value of labor-power and the level of wages (wages were below value) helped to bring about disintegration in the self-subsistence of Canadian farmers and the rise of new relations of production in factories set up with the help of American capital. As a result of these changes in the economic mode of production, the British state lost a considerable amount of control over Canada. Moreover, the same events led to an eventual transformation of the Canadian state, and the introduction of measures facilitating American investment. The ideologies of Canadians also began to change— from the attitude of protecting one's small piece of land on Canadian farms to ideas of conflict between employers and employees in Canadian factories.

The above analysis is an example of the method of historical materialism. *Historical materialism* is a method by which economic, political and ideological changes over time are studied by affirming the primacy of economic factors and changes. The agents of change are the contradictions and conflicts that occur within the economic mode of production. They also include conflicts and contradictions between the economic mode and its ideological and political aspects. Contradictions and conflicts are not the passive objects of history, but instead involve the active stimulation of human intervention. This occurs through the organization of people into *social classes* and the *conflict* or *struggle* between classes. It is to this subject that we now turn.

HIGHLIGHT

1. The state usually acts in the interests of a particular class, those owning and controlling the means of production.
2. The narrow view of the mode of production confines it to the strictly economic aspects of production. The broad view includes ideological and political factors as well.
3. Historical materialism is a method of studying change that gives primacy to the role of economic factors.

Definitions of Class

Karl Marx used three essential ideas to define class. These are 'means of production,' 'labor-power', and 'conflict' or 'struggle'. All three terms were defined in earlier sections of the chapter.

Marx discussed two main classes in capitalist societies—the bourgeoisie and proletariat—and eight other classes or parts of classes. These were landowners, serfs, peasants, rural laborers, petty bourgeoisie, intelligentsia, lumpenproletariat, and the ruling class (Ollman 1968). Veltmeyer and Ornstein will examine the neo-Marxist evolution of a number of these classes in the following chapters.

In this chapter, we will only be concerned with the classical definitions of class in the writings of Marx and Engels. It must be noted that not all authors fully agree on the nature and number of classes in a given historical period. It is important therefore that the reader understand the particular treatment given to class if he/she is to get the most out of the chapters of this book. Differences aside, all authors agree that ownership or non-ownership of the means of production is the crucial factor in defining class.

Bourgeoisie and Proletariat. Marx argued that there were two major classes in capitalist societies (but see Marx 1967c:885-6 where he argued that landowners also form one of the main classes in capitalist society). The *bourgeoisie* or *capitalist class* owns the means of production and purchases labor-power from others for a wage to work in their business. The *proletariat* or *working class* does not own the means of production but sells its labor-power to capitalists in order to earn a wage to support itself in the form of food, clothing and shelter. The ownership of the means of production gives the bourgeoisie the power to determine what is produced and who will receive benefits from production. The lack of ownership of the means of production by the working class excludes it from this kind of power. Therefore, it must rely on its labor-power to survive. The wages it receives from the sale of labor-power are used to purchase food, clothing, and housing. These items of subsistence replenish the capacity of the workers to return to work on a daily basis.

Marx saw both a contradiction and a conflict of interests between classes. This is expressed by each class wanting to increase its share in the *distribution of wealth* between them. Part of this distribution takes the form of wages paid to workers by the capitalists. When wages go up, workers usually increase their share of the wealth, and capitalists decrease their share. The latter will try therefore to keep wages low or to prevent them from rising too dramatically. This brings them into *conflict* with the working class. Such conflict often takes the form of strikes and lockouts in factories.

Since the distribution of wealth is largely determined by who owns the means of production, it is not surprising that workers and capitalists often come into conflict over *who owns and controls the means of production*. Workers have often tried to take control of factories while capitalists have tried to prevent them. Such conflicts often spill over the factory walls into the society at large. They can take a *political* form in which capitalists will support one political party and workers will support a different party. The party supported by capitalists is usually a conservative or liberal one that believes in private ownership of the means of production by the capitalists. Workers will more often support a socialist party that aims at gaining control of the state in order to abolish private capitalist ownership of the means of production. Class develops to its highest form when conflict involves open and violent confrontation between workers and capitalists in the political arena of society.

Marx viewed the conflict between the bourgeoisie and proletariat as the catalyst that would bring about a transition from capitalist society to socialist society. In capitalist society there is private ownership of the means of production and the existence of classes. A socialist society would have neither private ownership of the means of production nor, as classes are defined in terms of ownership of the means of production, the existence of classes.

The other eight classes that Marx defined exist at different stages in history. We will therefore have to broaden our perspective to include a society that existed before the rise of capitalist society. This society is usually called "feudalism". Many, but not all, of the other eight classes Marx talked about are found in the period of transition from feudal society to capitalist society. This period of transition is sometimes called "simple, commodity production" because most people, owning their own means of production and hiring little or no wage-labor, consumed much of what they produced. We can now focus on the nature of these classes.

Landowners formed the dominant class in feudal society. They owned vast amounts of land which was the most important means of production. Landowners did not directly work their land. Others, called serfs, occupied their land and paid the landowners a rent. This rent formed the basis of the wealth of landowners.

Serfs were one of the classes that occupied the land in feudal societies. They paid the landowners a rent in the form of cash, in the form of crops they grew, or in the form of labor they performed on the landowner's estate. Even though serfs did not legally own the land which they farmed, they had much control over how they farmed the land. Since they did not work for the landowners for a wage they maintained some independence.

Peasants were small owners of land (in contrast to the big landowners). They contributed their own labor to the land. Peasants did not have serfs occupying their land, and therefore did not collect rent from them. Nor did they hire for a wage rural laborers, the next class we will consider. Peasants were relatively independent, and consumed much of what they produced. They were numerous during the era of petty commodity production in the transition from feudalism to capitalism.

Rural laborers were a class that lived off the land in the transition from feudalism to capitalism, and in capitalism itself. They were in a different position than the serfs and peasants. Rural laborers worked for a wage paid to them in either produce or money. When they were hired by either peasants or landowners, the latter two classes were transformed into capitalist farmers. Rural laborers had no ownership in or control over the land and, consequently, they were one of the poorest classes in feudal society.

In feudal society, and in the transition to capitalism, there were many conflicts among landowners, serfs, peasants and rural laborers. Much of this conflict was over the distribution of wealth. Landowners would try to raise the amount of rent they charged the serfs while the serfs would resist. Similarly, rural laborers would ask for a greater share of the wealth which capitalist farmers resisted. These conflicts eventually led to a mass movement of serfs, peasants, and rural laborers from the countryside to the towns. This was one of the first signs that feudal society was beginning to decline and capitalist production was beginning to emerge.

Marx also talked about a number of classes found in the towns and cities of feudal Europe. These survived in a different form in simple commodity and capitalist societies. One of these classes was the *petty bourgeoisie* to which Marx gave great attention. It consisted of small shopkeepers and craftsmen and women who owned their own businesses or means of production. They were not employed by other classes for a wage. They contributed their own labor to their own businesses. The petty bourgeoisie usually did not hire others to work for them, although as their businesses grew in size they started to do this.

We should be clear about the differences between the petty bourgeoisie and the bourgeoisie. The latter do not contribute their own labor in producing goods and services in their own businesses while the former do. Regarding other people's labor, the bourgeoisie hires the labor of the working class for a wage while the petty bourgeoisie usually does not do this. Therefore, the bourgeoisie exploits workers and extracts surplus value from them, but the petty bourgeoisie does not engage in this activity.

With the beginnings of capitalism, the petty bourgeoisie found themselves in a peculiar position in relation to the bourgeoisie and the proletariat. They shared with the bourgeoisie the characteristic of owning their means of production. But they also shared with workers the characteristic of having to labor to earn a means of livelihood; however, they labored for themselves rather than for other classes. Because of their peculiar position the petty bourgeoisie had shifting alliances and conflicts with both the bourgeoisie and the proletariat (Marx 1969).

At times, the petty bourgeoisie supported the bourgeoisie and came into conflict with the proletariat. This was especially true over the price of commodities. Both the bourgeoisie and the petty bourgeoisie were interested in maintaining high prices for the commodities they sold. But since the proletariat were the consumers of many of these commodities, they were interested in lowering the price of goods. They consequently came into conflict with both the petty bourgeoisie and the bourgeoisie.

On other issues the petty bourgeoisie established alliances with the proletariat and came into conflict with the bourgeoisie. This often occurred over the question of debt. The homes of the proletariat and the businesses of the petty bourgeoisie were often mortgaged to members of the bourgeoisie. When times were bad, the proletariat and the petty bourgeoisie had difficulty in paying their debts to the bourgeoisie. As a result, they both came into conflict with the bourgeoisie.

The debts suffered by the petty bourgeoisie and the difficulty they had in competing with the larger bourgeoisie often resulted in the bourgeoisie taking over the businesses of the petty bourgeoisie and integrating them into larger businesses. With the decline of feudalism and simple commodity production, and the emergence of capitalism, the petty bourgeoisie as a class began to decline. Although some members of this class did grow into large businesses and became members of the bourgeoisie, Marx thought that many of them would fall into the proletariat. This would increase the size of the proletariat and intensify the conflict between the proletariat and the bourgeoisie. The petty bourgeoisie, even in fairly advanced stages of capitalist societies, has not completely disappeared.

A class that has some characteristics similar to the petty bourgeoisie is the *intelligentsia*. This consists of such people as lawyers, writers, journalists, and artists. They have characteristics that lead some other authors in this book to define them as members of a class called the new petty bourgeoisie. They own their own means of production and usually do not hire members of the working class to work for them. The main difference between the intelligentsia and the petty bourgeoisie concerns *ideology*, a term introduced in an earlier part of the chapter.

Ideology is often used to support the interest of one class against those of one or more other classes. As we saw above, both the bourgeoisie and the proletariat have an interest in increasing their own share in the distribution of wealth. A set of ideas justifying an increase in profits is an ideology supporting the interests of the bourgeoisie. The argument that wages must increase to stay ahead of inflation is an ideology supporting the interests of the working class. Karl Marx argued that the intelligentsia specialized in the production and sale of ideology while the petty bourgeoisie specialized in the production and sale of *material* commodities such as food, shoes and clothes.

The ideas produced by the intelligentsia can support its own class interests or the interests of other classes. When lawyers develop legal arguments justifying private ownership of property, they are producing an ideology supporting the interests of the bourgeoisie. On the other hand, when labor lawyers hired by trade unions develop legal arguments justifying wage increases, they are producing an ideology supporting the interests of the working class. In these ways, the production of ideology by the intelligentsia plays a role in class conflict. Ideas are produced supporting the interests of one class against another class.

At times ideology can have the opposite effect. The intelligentsia can produce ideas which weaken the intensity of conflict among classes. Marx argued that such ideas are in the interests of the bourgeoisie. The ideas contained within religion, brotherhood, fraternity, and nation direct the attention of the working class away from its conflict with the bourgeoisie and towards issues on which it is likely to identify with the bourgeoisie. When workers go to church and are told that "the poor shall inherit the earth", they are less likely to complain about their poverty. Quite often workers and capitalists belong to the same church and identify with the same religious ideas, rather than coming into conflict with one another over their share in the distribution of wealth, or over who owns and controls the means of production.

An additional class that assumes some importance with the growth of capitalist societies is the *lumpenproletariat.* As its title suggests, it shares certain characteristics with the proletariat. Both classes lack ownership of the means of production. But the lumpenproletariat is also different from the proletariat. While the proletariat is employed in wage labor by capitalists, the lumpenproletariat is often outside this wage relationship. It does not work full time for capitalists. It is quite often unemployed or is involved in some "deviant" type of activity such as prostitution, crime, or begging. At one point Marx (1972:75) argued that the lumpenproletariat consisted of such diverse groups as "...vagabonds, discharged soldiers, discharged jailbirds, escaped galley slaves, swindlers, montebanks, lazzaroni, pick-pockets, tricksters, gamblers, maquereaus (procurers), brothel keepers, porters, literati, organ-grinders, ragpickers, knife grinders, tinkers, beggars...".

The lumpenproletariat is most significant because of its potential role in class conflict. It is a class that is *used* by other classes to advance their own interests in their conflict with other classes. When members of the working class go on strike, the lumpenproletariat, in the form of unemployed workers, are often used by capitalists as strike-breakers. They are used to break up picket lines and disorganize the strikers. This use of the lumpenproletariat usually increases the level of violence in the conflict between the bourgeoisie and the proletariat. The practice can also weaken the unity of the working class by pitting the lumpenproletariat against full-time workers. For these reasons, Marx called the lumpenproletariat the "dangerous" class.

The final class discussed by Marx is the *ruling class*. It is different from all the other classes because it is defined by the political rule of a particular class (landowners or the bourgeoisie) in an institution—the state—which is formally outside the structure of classes.

Marx looked upon the relation between the state and the dominant economic class in two different ways (Miliband 1965:283-5). His *primary* view was that the modern state is dominated by the bourgeoisie. This perspective is summed up in a famous passage from *The Communist Manifesto*: "The executive of the modern state is but a committee for managing the common affairs of the whole bourgeoisie" (Marx 1954:18). This is the best known of Marx's views on the relation between the bourgeoisie and the state.

There is also a *secondary* view evident in *The Eighteenth Brumaire of Louis Bonaparte*. According to this perspective, the state can in exceptional circumstances become independent of the bourgeoisie and assert its authority over all classes. Louis Bonaparte did this in his coup d'etat in France in 1851. Bonaparte sought to place himself in the position as the representative of both the peasants and the lumpenproletariat. This gave him a power base against the bourgeoisie and the proletariat. Perhaps paradoxically, bourgeois interests were safeguarded in the Bonapartist state. In taking power away from the bourgeoisie, Bonaparte acted on their behalf, although not at their behest.

These two views illustrate the potentially different internal structures of the ruling class. In both perspectives, the class owning the major means of production (landlords in feudalism and the bourgeoisie in capitalism) rule politically. This means that their economic power becomes translated into political power. In the *primary* view, class rule takes the form of *direct participation* by either landlords or the bourgeoisie in the councils of the state. In the *secondary* view, the political rule of the landlords or the bourgeoisie is assured, not by their direct participation in the state, but by the overwhelming economic power they exercise in society through their ownership and control of the means of production.

For example, the Canadian bourgeoisie can apply political pressure on the state by crippling the economy on which the state relies for its tax revenues. Large corporations can do this by refusing to explore for new oil and gas, or by raising interest rates so high that small businesses go bankrupt and workers lose their homes through excessively high mortgage rates. The *ruling class* then, is the economically dominant class which exercises either direct or indirect political power over the state.

The connection between the state and the economically dominant class is important in class conflict. Depending upon the period, the class interests of either the landowners or the bourgeoisie are expressed through the state. Marx argued that the state better expresses and supports the interests of the bourgeoisie than any other class in capitalist society. For this reason, the conflict between the working class and the bourgeoisie ultimately takes the form of a proletarian revolution against the state. This occurred in the 1917 Bolshevik revolution in Russia.

We should not think that working class interests are never expressed through the state. Especially within the secondary view above, Marxism suggests that the state will grant minor concessions to the working class in order to prevent a working class revolution. This is one of the central arguments used by Marxism to explain the rise of the welfare state in the 20th century. The distribution of relief funds and unemployment assistance to the Canadian working class during the Great Depression of the early 1930s discouraged it from engaging in radical protests against the state and the bourgeois class (Cuneo 1979b; 1980b).

HIGHLIGHT

1. The major determinant of class is ownership or non-ownership of the means of production.
2. In total, Marx talked about 10 classes. Two of these, the bourgeoisie and proletariat, are products of capitalism. The others are found in feudalism, or in the transition to capitalism.
3. The ruling class can be viewed as the class involved in direct or indirect political rule. (landlords in feudalism and the bourgeoisie in capitalism).

Production and Circulation Revisited

In the discussion of Marx's labor theory of value and the ten classes mention was made of the production of wealth and its distribution to those immediately involved in its production. The bourgeoisie distributes part of its wealth in the form of wages to the working class directly involved in its production, and keeps the rest. But the distribution of wealth depends not only on the production of goods but also on their sale. If goods are not sold, neither the bourgeoisie nor the working class can claim their respective share in the distribution of wealth. To handle this problem Marx distinguished between the sphere of production and the sphere of circulation defined earlier. It will now be seen that there are two activities involved in the sphere of circulation—commercial and financial.

Commercial activities refer to the buying and selling of commodities such as clothes, food and furniture. *Financial activities* refer to the buying and selling of money in bank accounts, loans, and mortgages. As noted previously, wealth is produced in the sphere of production but is only realized in the sphere of circulation. Marx used these ideas to introduce divisions within the bourgeoisie and within the working class which he called *class fractions*. To understand the nature of these fractions, it is necessary to further develop his theory of production and circulation.

Labor as Source of Wealth.   Marx's theory of class is based on the idea that the source of all wealth is labor. The accumulation of wealth by the bourgeoisie is possible *only* because they hire wage-workers in the spheres of production and circulation. For Marx, the bourgeoisie cannot exist without the working class since the latter is the source of bourgeois wealth. The working class needs the bourgeoisie since, before the overthrow of capitalist production, the working class must earn a wage to support itself. This can be done only by going to work for the bourgeoisie.

Marx (1967a; 1967b; 1967c) outlined a systematic theory of production and circulation. It can be depicted as follows:

$$M-C\underset{MP}{\overset{L}{\ldots}}P\ldots C'-M'$$

M represents money. C stands for commodities which come in two forms: L or the labor-power of the working class, and MP or the means of production. P represents the sphere of production. The two dashes (M—C and C'—M') represent the sphere of circulation. Initially the capitalist starts off with M money. He then purchases (M—L and M—MP) two types of commodities in the sphere of circulation. The first is labor-power from the working class for which he pays wages. The second are the means of production such as machinery, land, buildings, and tools. Thus, before the capitalist can begin production, he must transform his money into labor power and means of production. These then enter the sphere of production symbolized by "...P...". Once production is completed, the capitalist can bring his commodities (e.g. automobiles and furniture) to the market and sell them in the sphere of circulation (C'—M'). The C' at the end of production is greater than the C at the beginning of production. Similarly, the M', which the capitalist has after producing and selling his commodities, is greater than the M he invested at the beginning of production. Since the capitalist owns the means of production and the labor-power purchased from the working class, the increase in wealth (M' minus M) at the end of production all ends up in his hands rather than in the pockets of the working class.

The central question for Marx was *how* production increases wealth. As noted previously, he argued that the value of the means of production does not increase during production. Their value is simply transferred from the raw materials and machinery at the beginning of production to the commodities (e.g. automobiles) at the end of production. It is labor-power which is the source of the increase in wealth at the end of production. To explain this increase, Marx argued that the wages paid to workers represent only the amount necessary to replenish their labor-power so they can return to work the next day. There is an extra amount of labor workers do each day for which they are not paid. This unpaid labor is the basis of the increase in the wealth of the bourgeoisie at the end of production.

In an earlier section, we noted that Marx called this increase in wealth *surplus value*. It is equivalent to the total value of commodities at the end of production minus the value of the means of production (circulating constant capital) and labor-power (C' minus C, or M' minus M). When surplus value is divided by the wages of productive labor, it is called the *rate of surplus value* or *class exploitation*. This represents the rate at which the bourgeois class extracts wealth from the labor of the working class in the sphere of production. It is the central class relationship in the Marxian theory of conflict.

Class Fractions.   It was on the basis of this theory of production and circulation that Marx created divisions or fractions within the bourgeoisie and the working class. There are three fractions within the bourgeois class and two fractions within the working class. These are shown in Chart 1. The three fractions within the bourgeoisie are industrial capitalists, financial capitalists, and commercial capitalists.

Industrial capitalists operate in the sphere of production. They own the means of production in which goods and services are produced (such as the Steel Company of Canada). Financial and commercial capitalists operate in the sphere of circulation. *Financial capitalists* own businesses that specialize in the buying and selling of money such as banks, trust companies, loan companies, and life insurance companies. *Commercial capitalists* own businesses that specialize in the buying and selling of commodities such as food, furniture and clothing, as in supermarkets or department stores.

All three types of capitalists hire members of the working class for a wage. But the labor the working class performs for each of them is different and this forms the basis for dividing the working class into two fractions. As noted previously productive laborers produce surplus value in the sphere of production. They are hired by industrial capitalists. Unproductive laborers do not produce surplus value, as noted earlier. They only perform labor that assists the realization of wealth in the sphere of circulation. They are hired by financial and commercial capi-

CHART 1
Class Fractions in the Distribution of Surplus Value

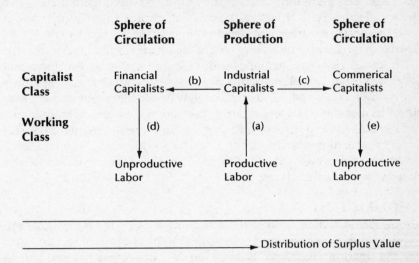

talists in the sphere of circulation. Bank tellers and store cashiers are two kinds of unproductive laborers.

We now have two basic relationships between the working class and the bourgeoisie. The one is between industrial capitalists and productive laborers. This is the relationship in which the wealth of the entire bourgeoisie is produced. The other class relationship is between financial and commercial capitalists on the one hand and unproductive laborers on the other. Surplus value is not produced in this relationship but is only realized through the buying and selling of commodities and money. The labor of the unproductive fraction of the working class is concerned with the circulation of commodities and money rather than with the production of goods and services.

Distribution of Wealth. We are now in a position to extend our understanding of the distribution of wealth between the working class and the capitalist class. Productive laborers within the working class produce the surplus value for the industrial bourgeoisie, for which they are paid. This is indicated by arrow (a) in Chart 1. Industrial capitalists depend on commercial capitalists to sell their commodities and on financial capitalists to supply them with money to purchase labor-power and the means of production. For these 'services', the industrial capitalist must share with commercial and financial capitalists part of the surplus value he extracts from his own productive workers. Thus, part of the surplus value of industrial capitalists is distributed to commercial and financial capitalists. This is indicated by arrows (b) and (c) in Chart 1. In turn, commercial and financial capitalists do not keep the entire surplus value distributed to them. They must hire unproductive laborers to perform tasks (such as keeping records of sales). The wages of unproductive laborers are deducted from the surplus value of commercial and financial capitalists. Therefore, part of the surplus value of commercial and financial capitalists is distributed to their unproductive laborers in the form of wages. This is symbolized by arrows (d) and (e) in Chart 1.

In the division of activities among class fractions, the industrial capitalist often cannot realize his surplus value until financial capitalists extend him credit and commercial capitalists sell his commodities. Thus, industrial, commercial and financial capitalists are dependent upon one another. More importantly, all three are ultimately dependent on productive and unproductive laborers. Marx's outline of the interdependence of production and circulation is thus also a theory of the interdependence of class fractions.

HIGHLIGHT

1. Classes can be divided into fractions depending upon their place in the productive process. The bourgeoisie has industrial, commercial, and financial fractions. The working class has productive and unproductive fractions.
2. Ultimately, all class fractions depend on the productive sector of the working class: the surplus value produced by this fraction is, through various mechanisms, distributed among other class fractions.

Class Organization

At one point Marx (1963b:172-5) distinguished between *class-in-itself* and *class-for-itself*. A *class-in-itself* is simply a number of individuals who share a common relationship to the means of production. These persons do not collectively organize to defend and promote the interests that emerge out of their relationship to the means of production.

The most concrete reference for class-in-itself is in Marx's writings on the French peasantry in the middle of the nineteenth century. He likened the peasantry to a "sack of potatoes" consisting of numerous individuals and their families, separated from one another in their economic and social endeavors, who displayed little sense of community and identification with one another as a peasant class (Marx 1967; 1972).

A *class-for-itself* is a class that organizes itself socially and politically, in terms of its interests, in the production and circulation of commodities. Class-for-itself is the transformation of class-in-itself into a collectivity organized on the basis of a consciousness of its economic, social, and political interests. In capitalist societies, workers or capitalists who do not have a sense of collective organization and opposition to one another express the characteristics of a class-in-itself. Class-for-itself is the transformation of these individualized relations into collective conflict over the production and distribution of wealth, the ownership of the means of production, and/or the control of the political state. Marx expended considerable effort in his concrete analysis of historical societies, especially France, to show that the actions and organizations of classes are contingent on numerous economic, political, and ideological conditions.

Marx thought that three economic conditions brought the working class to act on its own interests against the bourgeoisie. These were the growth of modern industry, the concentration of workers at the workplace, and the sudden eruption of industrial and commercial crises which galvanize workers to take collective political action (Marx 1969; 1972; 1963b:171-3). There were also two political conditions which Marx referred to as affecting the organization of classes. These are parliamentary democracy and the universal franchise (or the vote).

Parliamentary democracy is an instrument through which the separate fractions of the ruling class combine politically against threats of working class revolution. In mid-nineteenth century France, the parliamentary republic became an institution which organized the separate interests of the landowners, the financial aristocracy, and the large industrialists as "the common rule of the bourgeoisie" (Marx 1969; 1972:56, 96-7). At the same time, the universal franchise affected the political organization of the working class by providing an instrument through which workers' collective economic, social and political interests could be expressed. On the other hand, Marx and Engels noted that the franchise was also an instrument through which the bourgeoisie could integrate the working class into the goals of a bourgeois-dominated state. To the extent that this occurred, the franchise was seen as an instrument for defeating the organization of the working class on behalf of bourgeois interests.

Turning to ideological conditions that affect the transformation of class-in-itself into class-for-itself, we noted in the discussion of Marx's ten classes that the intelligentsia generates ideologies that play a role in class conflict. This class can produce ideologies that defend the interests of certain classes against the interests of other classes. One area in which many members of the intelligentsia produce ideologies is the mass media, which will be discussed in later chapters. Through the media, the intelligentsia disseminate the ideas of brotherhood, fraternity, and nationalism. All of these ideas encourage the working class to identify with the interests of the "public will". However, the economic interests behind the "public will" are those of the bourgeoisie. The acceptance of such ideas by the working class functions to suppress its own class interests and to promote the interests of the bourgeoisie.

The ruling class owns and controls the major means of production in the society. It is this fact which makes the bourgeoisie the ruling ideological force in the society. This was powerfully expressed by Marx and Engels (1947:39) in the following passage:

> The ideas of the ruling class are in every epoch the ruling ideas: i.e. the class, which is the ruling material force of society, is at the same time its ruling intellectual force. The class which has the means of material production at its disposal, has control at the same time over the means of mental production, so that thereby, generally speaking, the ideas of those who lack the means of mental production are subject to it. The ruling ideas are nothing more than the ideal expression of the dominant material relationships, the dominant material relationships grasped as ideas; hence of the relationships which make the one class the ruling one, therefore the ideas of its dominance. The individuals composing the ruling class possess among other things consciousness, and therefore think. In so far, therefore, as they rule as a class and determine the extent and compass of an epoch, it is self-evident that they do this in their whole range, hence among other things rule also as thinkers, as producers of ideas, and regulate the production and distribution of the ideas of their age: thus their ideas are the ruling ideas of the epoch.

It must be emphasized however that there is not an automatic relation between material forces and their ideological expression. The ideological organization of the bourgeoisie into a class-for-itself is not automatic. It is contingent on a number of conditions. Similarly, the ideological subjection of the working class to the bourgeoisie is also not automatic. It becomes possible during certain crises in history. It is during such crises (e.g. Russia between 1905 and 1917) that the working class develops an alternative ideological consciousness as a revolutionary force and prepares itself for transforming the economic structures of society.

HIGHLIGHT

1. Marx distinguished between a "class-in-itself"and a "class-for-itself." The former is simply defined as the type of relationship a number of individuals have to the means of production. The latter is an organized group that is conscious of the role it plays in the productive process.
2. The development of consciousness or the formation of a class-for-itself is not automatic. It depends on a number of economic, political and ideological developments.

The Main Line of Class Conflict

The logic of Marx's entire work on political economy from the 1840s to the 1850s leads to four somewhat different propositions about the main lines or axes of class conflict in capitalist societies. First, as a general proposition, Marx argued that as capitalist production developed, the conflict between bourgeoisie and proletarians would intensify, and culminate in the overthrow of the bourgeoisie by the proletarians. This would be followed by a transition period of the dictatorship of the proletariat during which the last vestiges of bourgeois opposition would be eliminated. The final step would be the ushering in of a classless communist society (Marx 1954; 1963b:166-175; 1970b).

Second, in his mature work on political economy in *Das Kapital* Marx expected, implicitly if not explicitly, that the main line of class conflict would emerge from the relationship between one fraction of the bourgeoisie—the industrial capitalists—and what we previously called one fraction of the working class—productive laborers. This is the relationship in which surplus value or the wealth of the entire bourgeoisie is generated. It is this fraction of the working class that Marx saw as exploited by the industrial bourgeoisie. This exploitation increases with mechanization.

Machines allow the productivity of labor to increase. Productivity (not to be confused with the term "productive labor") is measured by the degree to which goods are produced on the basis of an increasingly smaller amount of labor provided by technological aids. As productivity increases, the amount of surplus value that is generated by productive labor also increases. Therefore, the productive laborer is increasingly exploited. The logic of this argument leads us to expect the leadership of a working class revolution to emerge out of the ranks of productive workers.

Third, the logic of Marx's work on political economy also leads us to a conclusion quite different from the second proposition. With the advance of capitalism, the increasing use of technology expands labor productivity. At the same time the resulting increased output saturates the commodity markets. Excess commodities cannot be sold. Production must be cut back. Inventories are stockpiled. Factories are shut down, and workers lose their jobs. This increases the size of the unemployed, or what Marx called *floating and stagnant reserve labor.* The impoverishment of large sections of the working class follows (Marx 1967a:Ch. 25). Such developments might lead us to expect revolution from the impoverished or reserve labor section of the working class. Marx, however, did not develop a systematic theory along these lines.

As a fourth proposition about the main line of class conflict, Marx pointed to intense conflict between a general revolutionary working class and the state. The latter is the embodiment of the particular interests of the different bourgeois class fractions. This proposition is somewhat similar to the first proposition—except that the emphasis has changed to conflict between the working class and the state rather than between the working class and the bourgeois class. In this proposition, because the state is the embodiment of the bourgeoisie, the working class would have "to smash the state" before it could usher in a classless communist society (Marx 1954; 1970b; Lenin 1965).

HIGHLIGHT

1. In different writings, Marx referred to a total of four main lines of class conflict in capitalist society. All lines of conflict were to create a dynamic that would end in the destruction of capitalism and the emergence of a classless society.

Conclusions

This chapter has provided a simplified interpretation of classical Marxism through a selection of writings from Karl Marx and Frederick Engels, the fathers of modern-day Marxism and neo-Marxism. Many of the other chapters of the book will discuss various topics from neo-Marxist perspectives.

There is a great deal of diversity in neo-Marxism. Several varieties have centered on the Third World. Some writers have been concerned with the underdevelopment of the Third World as a consequence of its domination by the developed capitalist West (Frank 1967; 1969; 1978; 1981; Amin 1974; 1977; 1980; Emmanuel 1972; Kay 1975). Western and Eastern European writers have been broadly concerned with the relation between reformist and revolutionary Marxism and the role of workers in trade unions and in parliamentary democracy (e.g. Kolakowski 1978). There has also been a concern in neo-Marxism with more narrowly defined areas, such as women's domestic labor, the organizational structure of the state (Therborn 1978), the welfare state (Gough 1979), medicine (Navarro 1978), and education (Bowles and Gintis 1976). Some of these ideas will become manifest in later chapters.

Canadian political economy, a topic which permeates the book, covers not only the varieties of classical Marxism and neo-Marxism, but also schools of thought and research lying totally outside the Marxist perspective. The student will then quite justifiably ask, "What are the unifying themes underlying Canadian Marxist and non-Marxist political economy?"

Two unifying themes appear to stand out from all other possible ones. First, both Marxist and non-Marxist Canadian political economies analyze social, political and ideological structures and changes in terms of economic processes. This was called "materialism" in the preface to the book. Such analyses allow political economy to incorporate perspectives from a wide variety of disciplines. They include sociology, economics, political science, history, anthropology and industrial relations. Therefore, it is not as restrictive in its perspective as traditional sociology which erects rigid barriers against other disciplines. In a sense, from the narrow perspective of the single discipline of sociology, a new kind of Canadian sociology is being born. It promises to develop a variety of interesting insights and research findings in the future.

Second, both Marxist and non-Marxist Canadian political economies implicitly, if not explicitly, adopt a critical stance toward status quo economic, political and ideological structures. Hence, it adopts a value-relevant position that is anything *but* conservative. Some conventional sociologists have used this value-relevance to dismiss outright our alternative approach to sociology. They have contrasted such value-relevance with their own "value-neutrality" and "scientific objectivity". But behind such labels lies a conservative value-relevant perspective. For example, to argue, as functional sociologists do, that societies are inherently stable and that crises are minor and self-correcting is to adopt a sociology that supports the conservative status-quo. Is *this* not a value-relevant position? Such a position is often used, not only to advance these conventional brands of sociology, but also to fetter the alternative approach to sociology as developed in this book.

SUGGESTED READINGS

The Eighteenth Brumaire of Louis Bonaparte, Karl Marx. New York: International Publishers, 1972. A concrete study of the "independence of the state" manifested in Louis Bonaparte's coup d'etat in mid-nineteenth century France.

The Class Struggles in France, 1848-50, Karl Marx. New York: International Publishers, 1969. A concrete study by Marx of the reasons for the failure and defeat of the Parisian worker's revolution in June of 1848.

Capital. Vols. 1-3. Karl Marx. New York: International Publishers, 1967. An exposition of the general laws of capitalist development, focussing on the labor theory of value and the breakdown of capitalism as a socio-economic system.

The German Ideology, Karl Marx and Frederick Engels. Edited with an introduction by R. Pascal. New York: International Publishers, 1947. One of the first statements by Marx and Engels of historical materialism and their view of the relations among the economic, political and intellectual activities of man.

The Communist Manifesto. Introduced by Stephan T. Possony, Karl Marx. Chicago: Henry Regnery, 1948. Written by Marx with the collaboration of Engels at the request of the Communist League for a political doctrine, this pamphlet sets out some of Marx's first insights into the historical development and nature of capitalism and its eventual breakdown and transition to socialism.

THE DEVELOPMENT OF CAPITALISM AND THE CAPITALIST WORLD SYSTEM

Henry Veltmeyer

Introduction

The essence of the sociological perspective is to place the behavior, problems, and experiences of the individual in a wide context, and to analyse them in relation to the 'social structure'. Usually, what concerns the individual as a unique experience or personal problem is, in fact, part of a much larger pattern. It is shared by others in the same position in society. In this book, the basic context within which such experiences and so on are analysed is Canada.

However, it is both possible and necessary to place the analysis in a wider context yet: a complex of relationships and conditions that binds Canada with many of the world's nations into one economic system. As we will see in this chapter, capitalism, especially in its present monopoly phase, transcends national boundaries and has become increasingly global in scope. Neither the development of Canada as a whole, nor some of its more serious problems such as unemployment, inflation, widespread poverty, erosion of living standards, economic dependence and de-industrialization, can be properly understood, if at all, without taking into account the nature of the capitalist system in its world-wide dimension. In this chapter we will take a closer look at the historical development of capitalism, the world-capitalist system, and Canada's place within it. In doing so we will build on some of the ideas put forward in the previous chapter.

Perspectives on Social Development

To place the analysis of Canadian society in a global perspective, it is essential, first of all, to establish the conditions under which capitalism was born and the basis of its world-wide development. There are, however, a number of theoretical perspectives on such questions which emphasize different elements in the rise and development of the modern world system. Four of these perspectives are particularly important. They provide the foundation for most sociological and historical studies on this subject. Within each perspective a different theory of the rise and development of modern industrial capitalist societies, such as Canada's, is advanced. We will briefly identify the basic elements of each theory.

Modernization Theory.   Until the mid 1970s a widespread approach to the study of societal development was based on 'modernization theory'.[1] The theory rests on the notion that there are two fundamental types of society, traditional and modern. Such societies are characterized by the core values that underlie their major institutions.

Within this perspective it is assumed that the development of an economically advanced 'industrial society' is essentially a question of transforming the basic institutions of traditional or pre-modern societies. These institutions are re-oriented in accordance with what are regarded as modern values such as achievement, individualism, universalism, and functional specificity.[2] In other words, the basic process in the development of industrial society involved a change not at the level of society's mode of production (from feudalism to capitalism) as described in the last chapter, but at the level of its basic values (from traditionalism to modernism).

Modernization, it is argued, involves the development of economic, social, and political institutions that are highly specialized in their basic functions, and that can produce a society of highly mobile, achievement-oriented individuals. These people are able to freely choose their occupation in life and to rise to a social position that corresponds to their capacities, motivations and interests.[3]

In some cases, the essential conditions of such a development (open and universal education, a large middle class, political democracy, free enterprise, modern technology, entrepreneurship, sufficient capital, etc.) can be generated spontaneously within a given society. In other cases, the obstacles to development, such as powerful traditions, are too great. As a consequence the society remains stuck in the quagmire of economic, social, and political backwardness. This, it is assumed, is the situation today with many Third World countries. Their only escape from backwardness and poverty is dependent on foreign aid, support from the industrialized economies of 'Western' society, and acceptance of modern values.[4]

This modernization theory has been used not only to explain the economic backwardness of many countries in the 'Third World'. It also has been used, for instance, to explain the depressing poverty and social problems that afflict so many of Canada's native peoples. From this perspective these problems are rooted in the internal structure of traditional (i.e. native) society. Because native peoples are oriented to the old (i.e. traditional) values, they are unable to adapt to the requirements of Canada's modern industrial society. They are equally unable to take advantage of its inherent opportunities.

The absence of traditional values can also explain Canada's birth and early development through variations of a 'frontier thesis' (Lower 1958 inter alia). This thesis, as shown in the chapter by Magill, basically assumes that an open frontier in the colonies of North America fostered the development of modern values. It also embodies the notion that the conditions for later industrial development were directly related to the ability of a frontier people to escape the fettering traditions of a backward-looking semi-feudal European civilization. The 'frontier-thesis' similarly provides an historical explanation of the delayed transition to industrial society in Quebec.[5]

Dependency Theory.   Throughout the 1970s, and into the 1980s, the modernization approach to the study of societal development has become increasingly displaced by what has been called 'dependency theory'.[6] The basic proposition and underlying assumptions of this theory are directly at odds with modernization theory. In the first place, it rejects the concept of two different types of society, one producing the conditions of economic development, the other those of underdevelopment. In opposition to this dualist conception of societal development, dependency theorists argue that development and underdevelopment are the simultaneous products of one and the same system: capitalism operating on a world-scale.

The theory expounds that the wealthy and advanced industrial development of some parts of the world (the rich countries of Western Europe and North America) is based largely on the exploitation of other parts (the poor underdeveloped countries of the Third World). Historically, the latter were dominated economically as well as politically by the former. They were, as a consequence, reduced to colonial appendages and economic satellites. Within the so-called metropolis-satellite structure of this system, the colonized areas generated a vast economic surplus of wealth and capital. This was then expropriated and siphoned off by various means into the metropolitan centres. The consequence was impoverishment of the satellite and enrichment of the metropolis. This exploitative relationship, as the following quotation suggests, also applies to underdeveloped areas within a country. It is also applicable to the relationship between urban centres and the surrounding countryside.

> However competitive the economic structure of the metropolis may have been in any given stage of its development, the structure of the world capitalist system as a whole, as well as that of its peripheral satellites, has been highly monopolistic throughout the history of capitalist development. Accordingly, external monopoly has always resulted in the expropriation...of a significant part of the economic surplus produced in [the satellites] and its appropriation by another part of the world capitalist system...it is this exploitative relation which in chain-like fashion extends the capitalist link between the capitalist world and national metropolises

to the regional centers, and so on to large landowners or merchants who expropriate surplus from small peasants or tenants, and sometimes even from these latter to landless laborers exploited by them in turn. At each step along the way, the relatively few capitalists above exercise monopoly power over the many below, expropriating some or all of their economic surplus and, to the extent that they are not expropriated in turn by the still fewer above them, appropriating it for their own use.[6a]

This is the basic proposition of dependency theory. Another important proposition is that the economic backwardness of the Third World results from its dependency on the international market system which favors industrialized countries. The latter control the capital, technology, and markets essential for growth (Baran 1957; Wallerstein 1974).

There are three important consequences of this dependent status. One is that it leads to an international division of productive activities and labor which is geared to the needs of the metropolitan centres of the system. Essentially, it means a division which, as Marx pointed out, 'converts one part of the globe into a chiefly agricultural field of production, for supplying the other part which remains a chiefly industrial field' (*Capital*, I:451). The effects of this division of labor, as it relates to Canada, will be discussed below.

Another consequence of dependent status within the world market is *unequal exchange*. This term refers to the capacity of metropolitan capitalists to sell their products at a monopoly price while, at the same time, paying the producers of raw materials and staple goods in colonized areas much less than their products are worth. Because the labor embodied in these products is under-valued, raw material exports from the economic satellites work as a hidden means of transferring economic surplus into the metropolitan centres of the system. We will illustrate below the workings of this system. It applies particularly well to the relationship that existed between the Hudson Bay Company and the native peoples engaged in the fur trade in Canada's early history. It also applies more generally to the relationship between industry and agriculture, town and country, and between developed and underdeveloped regions within Canada (Archibald 1971 and Cambell 1978).

A third consequence of colonial status is the interlocking of economic and political interests, and increasing interdependence, between the local merchants maintained in the colony by trade, and the foreign bourgeoisie on which it is dependent. The conditions of this class alliance and its impact on developments in Canada will be examined later.

Staple Theory.   Another theory that has particular relevance to Canada, and indeed is distinctively Canadian in its origin and many applications, is the staple theory[7] discussed in detail in chapter 1. The theory has various formulations but essentially states that much of Canada's development has been shaped by the production of staple goods for metropolitan markets. The staples that have had the greatest impact on Canadian society are successively cod, fur, timber, and wheat. According to those who extend staple theory into the twentieth century, hydroelectricity, oil, and other sources of energy can be added to the list.[8]

The conditions leading to staple development have been both internal and external to Canada. The most important 'internal' factors emphasized by the staple theory are geographic and technological. These terms refer to conditions which both allow and limit the capacity to exploit and develop a given natural resource. However, more important than these conditions of staple production, are the conditions of economic, and political, dependence involved in the mercantilist trading system. It was within this framework that much of Canada's early development took place; that is, within a system which converted Canada into a resource hinterland for the benefit of a metropolitan centre.

Consistent with the idea of a metropolis-hinterland relationship, Arthur Lower, a well-known Canadian historian, has described Canada's history as a series of movements "from colony to colony". We will make further reference to this colonial development below. At this juncture, it is sufficient to note that staple theory overlaps with dependency theory. However, dependency theory is more conscious of the capitalist nature of the system involved in development. Nonetheless, both theories work from the conception of international trade as a 'world system' with a dominant core (or metropolitan centre) and a periphery (or hinterland) in which the economies are reduced to satellites. Both theories draw attention to, and emphasize, the effects of dependent status on a nation's development, and conditions that subordinate developments in the dependent economy, and society, to metropolitan requirements.

The Theory of Imperialism.   Another theory of particular relevance to an analysis of the world capitalist economy is the Marxist theory of imperialism.[9] Unlike dependency theory, which also works from general Marxist principles, this theory of imperialism is based on, and works closely with, Marx's general theory of capitalist development—a theory of the laws that govern the functioning of the capitalist mode of production.[10] This theory assumes that the basis of capitalist development is the national economy but under certain conditions—at a certain stage in its development—capital is forced to go 'international'. It is required to spread overseas in search of cheaper raw materials, low cost labor, and markets for its surplus capital and manufactured goods.

Marxists have generally turned to a theory advanced by Lenin to explain the conditions of capitalist expansion. According to Lenin, as capitalism exhausts its capacity to expand production within national societies, it develops the following characteristics:

(1) "the concentration of production and capital . . . developed to such a high stage that it [creates] monopolies which play a decisive role in economic life;

(2) the merging of bank capital with individual capital, and the creation . . . of a financial oligarchy;

(3) the export of capital as distinguished from the export of commodities acquires exceptional importance;

(4) the formation of international monopolist capitalist associations which share the world among themselves; and

(5) the territorial division of the whole world among the biggest capitalist powers is completed" (Lenin 1965).

Because of the assumed tendency to expand into, and exploit cheaper sources of raw materials, and to subjugate their colonies both economically and politically to their own interests, this theory overlaps with dependency theory. However, in opposition to dependency theory, the major exponents of the imperialism theory (excluding Luxemburg) do not believe that capitalist development in the most advanced industrialized economies derives from the economic surplus accumulated in peripheral social formations. Rather, they believe that this development is based mainly on exploitation of workers within capitalist societies. In other words, underdevelopment is not regarded as the product of capitalism per se. Instead, it results from 'an insufficiency of capitalist development' (i.e. a lack of wage-labor exploitation).

Theorists of imperialism also believe that in its expansion, capitalism creates many of the same conditions that prevail in its country of origin. It breaks down pre-capitalist modes of production and progressively converts people into wage-laborers. Such individuals become subjected to capitalist exploitation, and the ultimate results will be the same as those found in capitalist countries.

What does the theory of imperialism imply? For one thing, it implies that the world capitalist system should be analysed in terms of all the countries where the capitalist mode of production is established, rather than in terms of the international market. In other words, greater attention should be paid to class relations within given social formations of the world system and to class struggle as the driving force behind economic development. This is, in effect, the major guide to analysis provided by the theory of imperialism. This directive provides a useful point of departure for an analysis of the world capitalist system. It is particularly useful for tracing out the important stages of capitalist development in any particular country in the world economy. We will, in fact, rely on the theory of imperialism in this regard. It will become evident that the authors of some other chapters do not necessarily share this view.

HIGHLIGHT

1. Many features of Canadian society can only be understood if Canada is seen in its relations to other societies, especially in terms of a capitalist world system.
2. There are four basic theories of social development: modernization theory; dependency theory; staple theory; and the theory of imperialism.
3. Some Marxists analyse social development from a dependency perspective; others from the perspective of imperialism. In Canada, a number of Marxists incorporate some of the insights of staple theory into their analyses.

Metropolitan Capitalism and the World System

It is clear that Canada today is part of a world system dominated by the capitalist mode of production. What is not so clear are the stages involved in the development of this system. Nevertheless, at a very general level, it is possible to identify at least three major stages:

1. Commercial capitalism or mercantilism (1500-1800).
2. Industrial or competitive capitalism (1800-1890).
3. Monopoly capitalism or imperialism (since 1890).

Each stage involves a qualitative development in society's forces of production and a corresponding form of imperialism.

Commercial Capitalism or Mercantilism

The origins of the contemporary world capitalist system can be traced back to the mid-fifteenth century. This period saw the rise of a vast commercial network that radiated from a number of points in Western Europe into the Mediterranean, the coastal regions of West Africa and the Indian ocean, the Americas, Eastern Europe, parts of the Indonesian archipelago, the Phillipines, and, ultimately, even parts of coastal China. (Wallerstein 1974:Chapter 2). At first, this giant commercial network bore resemblance to the large trade empires found in previous historic epochs. However, subsequent developments show that the trading network formed in the wake of this European expansion was different in a number of important respects.

For one thing, all of the other trade empires eventually collapsed under the weight of supporting large armies in foreign territories. Such armies were necessary to oversee the collection of tribute and to maintain political control. In all of these empires, commerce was secondary to the extraction of tribute and obedience. Expansion in these cases invariably took the form of political conquest and was organized by a state elite composed of soldiers, glory-seeking emperors, and learned, but anti-business, religious officials. In contrast, the European expansion of the fifteenth century, and beyond, was propelled largely by an incipient capitalist class of merchants, financiers, and manufacturers. This class was concerned with the search for profits derived from various types of commercial and business enterprise.

At first, these capitalists lent or contributed money for the ventures of monarchs and religious officials seeking to extend their domain by conquest. But the motivation of the financial backers was profit for the sake of profit. Both long-distance trade and the search for bullion in the Americas were major forms of capitalist enterprise during this period. As such, commerce was also a primary source of what is called *primitive accumulation*[11]. This term refers to capital used to expand productive capacity and eventually to industrialize the European economies.

The economic bonds between the central states of western Europe and other societies proved far more durable than the bonds of classical empire. The effects of this commercial network spread inland from the coasts, and outward from the mines and plantations established in the Americas. They spread into all parts of the world. They destroyed or fundamentally altered all societies except for a handful of isolated and remote peoples. By 1900, almost the entire world had been brought into this giant economic system. Only Japan managed to escape Western domination.

The development of commerce into a world-wide system was centuries in the making. It involved a protracted process in which the two foundations of the capitalist mode of production—money wealth and the proletariat—were slowly being formed. The process of this formation (primitive accumulation) involved a number of developments that extended from the fifth century to the Industrial Revolution in the late eighteenth century. By the latter date capitalism had emerged as the dominant mode of production.

The first development in primitive accumulation was in the sphere of commerce itself—in the evolution of what is called the *mercantilist system* of world trade. This system evolved in two discernible phases. The first phase was "that of overt theft, of the plunder and enslavement of, Amerindians for work in the mines" and "the era of publicly sponsored piracy as other nations who lacked Iberia's direct access to New World gold and silver sought their share of the spoils in other ways" (Naylor 1980:16). In other words, it was the age in which Europeans 'discovered' the Americas, and sacrificed and subjugated the native people to their rapacious quest for bullion.

The bullion was used to pay for the Asian trade in spices and luxury goods, and as a general medium of exchange within Europe. The massive increase of bullion in circulation had important long-term effects on the various economies of small European nation states. Besides causing a tremendous inflation in the prices of agricultural and manufactured goods, the plundered gold and silver created conditions that led to the stagnation of the Spanish and Portuguese economies, the weakening and partial destruction of the feudal nobility all over Europe, and the economic expansion and relative prosperity of North-Western Europe. Most gold and silver filtered into North-Western Europe through the purchase of manufactured goods. It thereby stimulated the development of industry in these economies and provided merchants with the capital to set up large overseas trading companies. The resulting commercial conglomerates were charged by the European monarchs with governmental and colonizing responsibilities.

The formation of these state-chartered trading companies in the early 1600s signalled a new era in European capitalist expansion: that of merchant's capital or *mercantilism*. The working of this mercantilist system was fairly simple in principle. However, it was exceedingly complex in detail.

Starting with a small technological advantage and a capitalist (profit-oriented) form of enterprise, the states of North-Western Europe (especially Holland and England, in chronological order of dominance) engaged in commerce throughout the world. They took raw materials and cheaply produced agricultural goods in return for their efficiently produced, manufactured goods. They used their superior fleets and military technology to keep trade routes open and their business organizations to expand markets. In peripheral areas, particularly in Eastern Europe, they linked their commercial interests with the interests of local landlords. These landlords, in turn, extracted an agricultural surplus out of their population in order to have goods for commerce with the West. The result of these practices was a 'second serfdom' for the peasantry.

In some relatively unpopulated areas, especially on the North Atlantic coast of the Americas, various European states, notably France and England, encouraged the development of agricultural settlements. Besides enabling their colonies to support themselves in terms of food production, these settlements protected the territorial claims of the European powers. They also extracted fish, fur, and other staple products for metropolitan markets. The indigenous populations in these territories were killed or removed from their lands. In some parts of the Americas, Indians were enslaved to work in the mines, or to otherwise support the small Spanish settlements. Europeans brought African slaves (purchased on the coast of Africa from Africans who collected slaves for exchange with European products) to the Caribbean and Brazil. Such individuals worked the plantations producing tropical agricultural staples, chiefly tobacco, sugar, and cotton.

The traffic in black African slaves over the next few centuries reached gigantic proportions. Estimates of the number of African slaves imported into the Americas range from 900 000 in the sixteenth century, 2.75 million in the seventeenth century, 7 million in the eighteenth century, to 4 million in the nineteenth century (Fage 1962:83; Sheridan 1969:13).

These estimates, however, did not account for the many millions that either died in the slave wars, during their transport to and confinement on the African coast, or on the 'middle passage' across the Atlantic. Total estimates of Africans actually forced to leave their homes in the course of the slave trade reach as high as 100 million (Frank 1978:22).

The slave trade was the keystone in what became the largest trading network within the mercantilist system: the Atlantic triangle. The significance of this trade for the capitalist development of Europe is brought out very clearly in the following quote from a historian who would later become Prime Minister of Trinidad and Tobago:

> In this triangular trade England—France and colonial America equally—supplied the exports and the ships; Africa *the human merchandise*; the plantations *the colonial raw materials*. The slave ships sailed from the home country with a cargo of manufactured goods. These were exchanged at a profit on the coast of Africa for Negroes, who were traded on the plantations, at another profit, in exchange for a cargo of colonial produce to be taken back to the home country. As the volume of trade increased, the triangular trade was supplemented, but never supplanted, by direct trade between home country and the West Indies (or other colonialized regions), exchanging home (and Oriental) manufacturers directly for colonial produce. The triangular trade thereby gave a triple stimulus to British industry. The Negroes were purchased with British (and Oriental) manufacturers; transported to the plantations, they produced sugar, cotton, indigo, molasses, and other tropical products, the processing of which created new industries in England; while the maintenance of the Negroes and their owners on the plantations provided another market for British industry, New England agriculture and the Newfoundland fisheries. By 1750 there was hardly a trading or manufacturing town in England which was not in some way connected with the triangular or direct colonial trade. The profits obtained provided one of the main streams of that accumulation of capital in England which financed the industrial Revolution (Eric Williams 1966:51-2).

The mercantilist system was a major source of capital accumulation in Europe. As such, it was a necessary condition for the emergence of industrial capitalism. The historic conditions of this primitive accumulation—centuries of colonial plunder and trade—is summed up eloquently by Marx:

> The modern history of capital dates from the creation in the 16th century of a world-embracing commerce and a world-embracing market. . . . The colonies secured a market for the budding manufactures, and, through the monopoly of the market, an increasing accumulation. The treasures captured outside Europe by undisguised looting, enslavement, and murder, floated back to the mother-country and were turned into capital. . . . As a matter of fact, the method of primitive accumulation is anything but idyllic. . . . In actual history it is notorious that conquest, enslavement, robbery, murder, briefly force, play the great part. . . .

The discovery of gold and silver in America, the extirpation, enslavement and entombment in mines of the aboriginal population, the beginning of the conquest and looting of the East Indies, the turning of Africa into a warren for the commercial hunting of black-skins, signalized the rosy dawn of the era of capitalist production. These idyllic proceedings are the chief momenta of primitive accumulation. On their heels treads the commercial war of the European nations, with the globe for its theatre.... Liverpool waxed fat on the slave trade. This was its method of primitive accumulation.... In fact, the veiled slavery of the wage workers in Europe needed, for its pedestal, slavery pure and simple in the new world.... Capital comes [into the world] dripping from head to foot, from every pore, with blood and dirt (*Capital* I, 715, 146, 753-4, 714, 751, 759-60).

The money accumulated by merchants is but one side of the complex process leading to modern capitalism. In itself, Marx notes, money is not capital. "What enables money—wealth—to become capital is the encounter, on one side, with free workers; and on the other side, with the necessaries and materials, etc. which previously were in one way or another the property of the masses who have now become propertyless and are also *free* and purchaseable...[it is the] exchange [of] money for the *living labor* of the workers who have been set free...which enables money to transform itself into capital" (1973:505-7).

In other words, capitalism requires both a concentration of money wealth (capital) and an available supply of 'free' wage labor. As seen in the last chapter the latter is supplied by a class of individuals compelled by their lack of property to sell their labor to the capitalists. Marx exposes the 'secret' of the 'so-called primitive accumulation' in the following terms:

The capitalist system presupposes the complete separation of the laborers from all property in the means by which they realize their labor. As soon as capitalist production is on its own legs, it not only maintains this separation, but reproduces it on a continually extending scale. The process, therefore, that clears the way for the capitalist system, can be none other than the process which takes away from the laborers the possession of his means of production; a process that transforms...the immediate producers into wage-laborers...so-called primitive accumulation...is nothing else than the historical process of divorcing the producer from the means of production (*Capital*, I:714, 875).[11a]

It is in this historical process of expropriation that we have the second major development in the pre-history of capitalism: the *formation of a proletariat*. As with the expansion of trade and commerce, this development was both diversified and complex. In Europe, it involved a protracted process of transition from feudalism to capitalism. The process took from the fourteenth century to the late eighteenth century. By the latter date the two 'poles' of the capitalist system (money wealth and the proletariat) were finally brought together in a series of revolutionary developments of an economic, political, and intellectual nature.

Until this time, the money amassed by the commercial bourgeoisie of Atlantic Western Europe did not constitute capitalism as such. In fact, it was no different from the wealth accumulated in pre-capitalist trade in the Roman Empire, the Arab world, the Italian and Hanseatic towns, the Islamised Savannah area of Africa, or the seaport areas of Southern China. It was merely a monopolistic extortion of surplus slave labor at one end and feudal rent at the other.

What changed all this, and converted various concentrations of commercial wealth (based on slave labor, serfdom, monopoly trade, outright plunder and other methods of extortion) into capital, was the formation of a class for hire. It was comprised of individuals who sold their labor-power for a wage. The formation of such a proletariat was a lengthy process. It began with the dissolution of feudalism, an economic system which reached its height and dominated Europe in the twelfth and thirteenth centuries.

Feudalism was characterized by a landholding aristocracy who extracted, usually in kind and in labor services, a surplus from the peasant serfs who resided on their manors. Under this system, the landlords lived off the labor of the peasant. The peasant, however, was guaranteed access to land. Moreover, as a member of a village community he could not be driven away or proletarianized. (In this respect, serfs were unlike slaves who were simply property to be bought and sold at will. If the lord transferred possession of the manor to another nobleman, the serf simply had another lord.) However, by the end of the fourteenth century, serfdom substantially declined. Lords found it necessary, or advantageous, to transform labor obligations and dues in kind into fixed money rents, or to hire wage labor to work their land.

Some lords attempted to solve their revenue problems by intensifying rather than commuting labor services. This practice ultimately led to both the flight of many serfs to the towns and to open peasant revolts (Hilton 1962, 1969: Hilton and Fagan 1950). Over the centuries the combination of these and other factors (population growth, the expansion of trade and commerce, etc.) dissolved the feudal system. Peasants were freed both from serfdom and their ties to the land.

Many former serfs came close to being independent small businessmen. They would rent the land from the lord, sell the produce to cover the rents, and retain the remaining revenues. This system gave peasants a greater incentive to produce and thereby increased their marketing surplus. Increased marketing surpluses led to more payments in lieu of services, more subsequent marketings, and so forth. The cumulative effect was a very gradual breakdown of feudal custom and tradition, and a substitution of the market, and the search for profits, as the organizing principle of production. By the middle of the fourteenth century, money rents generally exceeded the value of labor services (Lazonick 1974:8-17).

Despite this development, the majority of people still depended on access to land for subsistence well into the fifteenth century. And, in the atypical case of England, two-thirds of the landholding population retained customary rights to work strips of arable land in the common openfields (Tawney 1912:24). It was this population that formed the social base of England's industrial revolution in the late 1700s.

This landholding population was converted into a proletariat by the enclosure of the common fields on which they, together with a substantial class of squatters, cottagers, and agricultural laborers, were totally or partially dependent. These enclosed lands were used by the landed nobility, in ever-increasing need of cash, to graze sheep in order to satisfy the booming textile industries' demand for English wool.

The enclosure movement was already quite advanced by the sixteenth century. In some areas, by this date, as many as seventy-five to ninety percent of the tenants were forced out of the countryside into the cities in efforts to support themselves. These enclosures, together with a naturally increasing population, further destroyed remaining feudal ties. The result was the creation of a large, new labor force—a labor force without land, without any tools or instruments of production, and with only their labor-power to sell. The migration to the cities meant more labor for capitalist industries, more men for the armies and navies, more people to colonize new lands, and more potential consumers, or buyers of products.

Much of the new labor force was absorbed in a growing manufacturing system based on wage labor. In feudal society, manufacturing or industrial production was monopolized by closed guilds of craftsmen. They owned their workshop, tools, and raw materials, and functioned as independent, small-scale entrepreneurs. By the sixteenth century, this handicraft type of industry had been largely replaced in the export sector by what is called a capitalist *putting out system.*

In the earliest period of this system, the merchant capitalist would furnish an independent craftsman with raw materials and pay him a fee to work them into finished products. Thus, the capitalist owned the product throughout all stages of production although the work was done in independent workshops. With the growth of a 'free' labor supply, the putting out system of manufacturing evolved into a system in which the merchant-capitalist owned the tools and machinery, and often the building in which production took place. He hired workers to use these tools, furnished them with the raw materials, and took the finished products.

The worker in this system no longer sold a finished product to the merchant. He sold only his labor-power to the capitalist who was in the process of being converted from a merchant into a manufacturer, or industrialist (in direct control of the productive process). The manufacturer then had to sell the product of the worker's labor at a price high enough to pay wages and other costs, and still make a profit. In essence, he acquired surplus value as described in the chapter by Cuneo. The merchant who bought the product from the manufacturer had to make a further profit in the course of transporting and marketing the product.

This putting out system first developed in the textile industries but throughout the sixteenth and seventeenth centuries it was extended until it was common in most types of manufacturing. Although it was not yet the modern type of factory production, the system's increased degree of specialization led to significant increases in productivity and the accumulation of a vast pool of capital. The mass of functioning capital accumulated in the putting out system of industry over the years (from the mid-1500s to the late 1700s) was enormous.

The vast accumulation of capital was reflected in the tremendous inflationary spiral of the sixteenth and seventeenth centuries. Throughout the period, the prices of manufactured goods, relative to both rents and real wages, rose dramatically. The greatest beneficiary of this 'price revolution' was the incipient class of industrial capitalists. They paid lower real wages, bought materials that appreciated in value and received larger and larger profits. Needless to say, the merchants who monopolized the international marketing of these goods made handsome profits as well. By one estimate (Mandel 1970:443-5), during 1760-80, profits from India and the West Indies more than doubled the accumulation money available in Europe.

While the rapid growth of the world market increased the demand for manufactured goods and stimulated the development of capitalist industry, the necessary supply of wage labor was being created. The means of this supply was provided by the continuing enclosure of common fields. In the eighteenth century, however, the enclosure movement involved much more than the conversion of arable land to pasture by a commercially-oriented landed gentry in need of cash. It was elevated to the level of national policy.

Having passed the first private Enclosure Act in 1710, the British parliament passed one hundred such Acts between 1720 and 1750, a further one hundred and thirty-nine in the following decade, and, at an ever accelerating pace, another nine hundred or so, in the crucial years 1764-80 (Mantoux 1964:141-2). By 1810, with the Industrial Revolution well under way, over three thousand Acts of Enclosure had been passed. These affected most common fields. The impact of these enclosures and their role in the emergence of industrial capitalism in Britain is summed up clearly by the historian Mantoux:

> ...the enclosures and the engrossing of farms ultimately resulted in placing at the disposal of industry resources in labor and energy which made it possible for the factory system to develop. Industry was becoming, as it were, a new land in the very midst of the country, another America attracting immigrants by the thousands—with this difference: that instead

of being a discovery it was a creation...many of the small yeomen and farmers, reduced to the condition of wage-earners, shared the fate of the laborers, who came to the towns, in search of work. They possessed nothing, and could offer nothing but their labor. These were to form the working population, the anonymous multitude in the factories—the army of the industrial revolution.... There is, therefore, an intimate connection between the movement by which English agriculture was transformed and the rise of the factory system (Mantoux, 1964:165-84).

HIGHLIGHT

1. The world capitalist system evolved in three stages: commercial capitalism or mercantilism; industrial or competitive capitalism; monopoly capitalism or imperialism.
2. Commercial capitalism was the era in which primitive accumulation occurred; the period in which the initial capital for industrialization was acquired.
3. During the period of commercial capitalism, mercantilist policies resulted in the extraction of goods and people—slaves—from African, Asian, and American societies for the benefit of European societies.
4. The period of commercial capitalism was one in which a working class started to develop in Europe. This class sold its labor to employers in order to gain its means of existence. By and large, it was comprised of individuals who had been driven off their lands by landlords in the enclosure movement.

Industrial or Competitive Capitalism

The Industrial Revolution of the late 1700s in England marks the emergence of capitalism as the dominant mode of production. Although its basic requirements of accumulated money wealth and a mass of exploited labor, had gradually formed in the preceding mercantilist era, and it had already appeared in embryonic form in agriculture and in manufacturing, capitalism did not mature until late 1700s. It was at this time that the new steam and machine technology revolutionized the nature of industrial production. With these developments, Marx observed, the Age of Modern Industry began.

The Industrial Revolution, first in Britain and later in other metropolitan countries, involved extensive transformations of the polity, society, and culture, as well as the economy. The changes in metropolitan countries which are associated with the development of capitalism into a world system are now examined.

Capitalism became dominant when the relationship that existed between capitalists and workers in the sixteenth century export industries was extended to other areas of production. Beginning with textiles, the capitalist relation of wage-labor spread from industry to industry.

Finally, it dominated the entire economy of England and other European countries. The only exception was in the realm of agriculture. Here independent production was based on family labor.

In England, capitalism was already quite advanced by the start of the nineteenth century. It was virtually completed soon thereafter. Other metropolitan countries, to varying degrees, were caught up in the same industrializing process. Indeed, it appears that once the capitalist mode of production is rooted in the economy, it tends to reproduce itself on an ever-increasing scale with the creation of both more workers and more capitalists.

By the mid-1800s, the social structure of England and many cities of Western Europe revolved around the wage-labor system. The industrial bourgeoisie had in most cases captured political power and was influencing the economy. At the same time, an increasing proportion of the population was becoming proletarianized—i.e. dependent on wage-labor for livelihood. The growth of this proletariat and its transformation into an industrial working class is one of the most striking developments and characteristic features of capitalism in metropolitan societies.

The central institution of modern industry is the factory. It is an industrial organization based on the technical division of work between a workshop, in which workers work with machines, and an office, where the administrative side of production is concentrated. This organization was markedly different from earlier forms of industry in which the manual and mental operations involved in production were not separated.

At first, workers operated the machines used to manufacture raw materials into commodities (saleable goods). In later developments of the factory system, production was increasingly broken down to specialized operations and functionally specific tasks. Each of these tasks was assigned to one worker. This development went hand-in-hand with important advances in technology designed to increase productivity to unprecedented levels and radically transform the nature of work. These issues will be given full treatment in a later chapter on work.

The factory system grew steadily throughout the nineteenth century. Its progress was fueled by an expanding army of dispossessed peasants and other proletarians. However, to create a class of proletarians and then to bring them together in the factory was only the first set of problems faced, and solved by, the capitalists. Another problem was in the transformation of these proletarians to an industrial working class accustomed to the regularity and discipline of factory-work.

The workers who made the transition from the domestic workshop or the farm to the factory, entered an entirely new system of work and culture. Work in this context was no longer scheduled in accordance with the rhythm of seasonal conditions or the needs of workers. It was regulated by time and machines. Needless to say, workers at first strongly resisted being treated as appendages of the machines they were paid to operate often for 12 or more hours a day. They developed various forms of resistance including deliberate destruction of machinery, absenteeism, quitting on pay days, idleness, refusal to work, socializing on the job, and, in the case of child laborers, play.

The history of industrial relations in the nineteenth century is replete with reference to such problems. Factory owners dealt with, and eventually solved, such difficulties through a combination of incentives, sanctions, and the creation of a new work ethos (see Kealey, 1973 for a review of this problem in Canada). The process of moulding rural migrants and proletarians into factory workers was painful and long. Ultimately, however, the appropriate capitalist institutions and culture were developed and the factory system became self-supporting, and able to establish itself in the leading sectors of the economy.

A particularly important feature of the new era of industrial capitalism was a change in metropolitan economic policy from monopoly and protectionism to competition and free trade. This policy arose from the victorious economic and political struggle of a growing industrial bourgeoisie against the relatively declining agrarian and mercantile interests. This policy change was designed to open up the world market to goods manufactured in England. More importantly, it was intended to secure a source of cheap foodstuffs and raw materials.

The policy of free trade, symbolized in North America by the repeal of the Corn Laws in 1846, worked against the interests of both British landowners and the mercantile bourgeoisie. Formerly, they had been able to sell colonial products in Britain at monopoly prices. The repeal of both the Corn Laws and other mechanisms of monopoly pricing had a dramatic direct effect on the price of basic foodstuffs, and an indirect effect on the wages that the industrialists had to pay their workers. The dismantling of the mercantile system also allowed the new industrialists to lower their costs of production by securing cheaper sources of raw materials. In 1849 the final blow was struck at the mercantilist system. In this year several Navigation Acts set up in the seventeenth century to promote British capital overseas and to protect British industry were replaced. At this point, the industrial bourgeoisie had essentially won its battle to institute free trade and, thereafter, to elevate it into a natural scientific law.

Free trade had an accelerating effect on the volume of trade and led to an explosive growth of foreign trade. Ferrer (1967:83) estimates that international trade tripled between 1700 and 1820, quintupled between 1820 and 1870, and soared after that. This growth of trade and commerce institutionalized the international divisions of labor that had formed within the mercantilist system.

In this division, the metropolitan centres of Europe and America became suppliers of manufactured goods. The countries and colonies on the periphery supplied raw materials and foodstuffs. In effect, the countries on the periphery, whatever their political status, were converted into economic colonies, geared towards, and dependent on, the requirements of the metropolis. There are significant long-term consequences of this colonial dependency. One of these is the failure to develop a 'home market', a prerequisite essential for the development of an independent, mature industrial-capitalist economy.

HIGHLIGHT

1. The two basic characteristics of competitive capitalism are widespread proletarianization and the development of the factory system.
2. Workers frequently resisted the new form of discipline that was imposed on them by the factory through various means.
3. During the period of competitive capitalism, state protection, which was important in the earlier process of primitive capital accumulation, was withdrawn from the monopolies.

Monopoly Capitalism or Imperialism

The next stage in the development of capitalism began with the crash of 1873 and the ensuing Great Depression which lasted into the 1890s. This depression, which affected every country where capitalism had taken hold or had penetrated through trade, was rooted in the nature of competitive capitalism itself.

All capitalist economies suffer from a fundamental contradiction. On the one hand, capitalist production is oriented towards, and based on, private profit-making. On the other hand, as Marx noted, under capitalism there is an inherent tendency for the average rate of profit to fall. This tendency results in cyclical crises. Production successively contracts, expands, and again contracts, as capitalists attempt to maintain the rate of profit.

A major depression in this cycle occurred in 1873 in all capitalist economies, including Canada. Cut-throat competition between capitalist firms had brought down prices to unprofitable levels and investment was cut back everywhere. In many cases production ground to a virtual halt. The huge reservoir of productive capacity that had been built up over the preceding fifty years was effectively drained.

Capitalists developed a number of 'solutions' to the crisis, which, by the onset of the First World War in 1914 had wrought a fundamental transformation in the structure of the capitalist system and the world economy. The first structural response was for capitalists to buy out their competitors or force them out of business. If they were successful, they could establish a monopoly in the marketing of given lines of production. By the turn of the century, this process was quite advanced in most capitalist economies in Western Europe and North America. The downward pressure on prices created by excessive competition was in these cases reversed when giant monopolies in the major industries were formed. The concentration and centralization of capital and production was accompanied by a second major development: the merger of bank capital with industrial capital.

The growth of large-scale industry and the emergence of cartels, syndicates, trusts and other forms of monopoly were largely based on the capital of the largest banks. These bankers were the major financiers of an emerging complex of giant industrial corporations. Some of this finance took the form of interest-bearing loans. Most of it, however, involved the purchase of shares in the capital stock of the corporate monopolies formed in the period. In order to meet their expanding requirements for capital, industrial enterprises sponsored by the banks and other institutions of financial capital were formed into limited-liability public corporations. The largest of these came to be dominated by finance-capitalists. These were a newly formed class or financial oligarchy representing the fusion of bank with industrial capital.

The third structural response to the 1873 crisis was to lower the cost of capitalist production and to offset the tendency for falling profits at the centre by drawing on the periphery for cheaper sources of raw materials and foodstuffs. Thus the period 1873-1914 was characterized above all by a new round of imperialism—the forcible expansion overseas into sources of cheap raw materials and foodstuffs. To facilitate this process, the most advanced capitalist economies like England increased their exports of capital (in the form of interest-bearing loans and portfolio investments such as bonds and securities) to the point that they exceeded the export of commodities. The exported capital was largely invested in railways, utilities, government finance, and other infrastructural supports of world trade and commerce. To protect these investments, and to guarantee access to the world's resources, the imperialist powers formed international monopolist capitalist associations and divided the entire world among themselves.

By 1914, these developments had largely run their course. Within the economies of the imperialist powers the newly formed class of finance capitalists had established the basic institutions of monopoly capital. These institutions formed the basis of industrial development throughout the twentieth century. The rest of the world, especially the less developed and underdeveloped countries of today's Third World, had been carved up, subjugated politically, and reduced to economic colonies. Great Britain had established an economic empire of unparalleled proportions. It was the undisputed centre of a world capitalist system.

The next thirty years (1915-1944) saw a momentous evolution of this system as well as a number of changes. By 1945 they would result in a new world order dominated by the United States. The new order had its origins just after the American war of 1812. The end of the war corresponded to the displacement by the nascent industrial bourgeoisie of the old commercial oligarchy. By the end of the 1850s a network of railways in the United States had created a large national market. At the same time, national firms integrated horizontally across the country.

As the civil war expansion gave way to the depression of the 1870s and 1880s, new corporate giants began to emerge, to expand and attempt to control their supply of raw material resources (Naylor 1980:18). With a general revival of industry in the 1890s (the Golden Age of Manufacturing throughout North America) the American firm began its international expansion in the form of the multi-divisional corporation. This entity was integrated vertically and horizontally over a multitude of production lines. It soon began to challenge the old European powers in their traditional export markets abroad.

The years before the First World War saw the modest beginnings of the instrument of metropolitan expansion that would in a few decades come to dominate the world economy: *the multi- or trans-national corporation.* Initially, the movement abroad by these corporations in the form of direct investment was small and largely restricted to Mexico and Canada. Investment in these two countries was a natural spill-over of the internal growth of American capital.

Prior to 1914, the United States was a net debtor to Britain, and the number and scale of its industrial corporations with multi-national operations was limited. The world economy was largely the preserve of European, especially British, finance capital. All this changed with World War I and the economic chaos of the post-war recession. These two events weakened the entire world structure.

The Second World War launched a second major upheaval in the imperialist system. It left the European rival powers economically devastated, finally ended the British Empire, and established American hegemony over the new capitalist order. The basis of this order was an agreement in 1944 among the major capitalist countries to use the American dollar, backed by the unsurpassed productive capacity of American industry, as the standard currency of world trade. With American hegemony unchallenged, the U.S.-based multi-national corporations spread globally. The resulting empire enveloped most of the non-capitalist world creating conditions that will be discussed in chapter 4.

HIGHLIGHT

1. The period of monopoly capitalism is characterized by the emergence of a few giant corporations in many areas of production and the fusion of finance and industrial capital.
2. The early years of monopoly capitalism saw the imperialist powers divide the world into colonies and spheres of influence.

3. Whereas Britain had been the primary capitalist power in the era of competitive capitalism, in the era of monopoly capitalism the role was increasingly assumed by the United States.

Capitalism in Canada: Hinterland or Centre?

In broad outline, we have reviewed the major structural transformations of the world capitalist system. The major structure of this system is the division between the rich and developed countries of Western Europe, Japan, and North America, and the poor and less developed countries of Asia, Africa, and Latin America. A number of countries, especially what are called European settler states like Canada and Australia, are notoriously difficult to place in this division. They tend to combine the structural characteristics of the rich, developed countries at the centre of the world capitalist system and those of the poor, underdeveloped countries on the periphery.

On the one hand, Canada's national income, industrial structure, and the foreign investments of its own capitalists, point toward a small economy of the developed metropolitan type. On the other hand, the economic importance of Canada's staple exports, the derivative and dependent nature of its industrial structure, and the overwhelming volume of foreign, especially American investment in, and ownership of, its major industries, points in a different direction. They suggest a view of Canada as a remarkably large and wealthy variant of the colonial type economy. Indeed, in this connection Canada has been termed 'the richest colony' (Williams 1976). To place this problem in perspective and to better understand both the present structure of the world system and Canada's place in it, it is necessary to trace the major stages of capitalist development in Canada.

Mercantilism I: Fish, Fur, and French Rule (1600-1763)

The economic history of Canada began in the early sixteenth century as an unanticipated off-shoot of the European scramble for New World bullion. From the beginning, throughout the seventeenth century, and well into the eighteenth century, Canada grew very slowly as a base for fishing and fur-trading for European, especially British and French, merchants. Both fish and fur well suited the logic of European overseas expansion in its primary phase. They provided a quick and ready source of large profits, with little work beyond the simple and seasonal looting of an immediate resource base (Naylor 1980:19).

The fisheries, cultivated by the English in particular, provided both a profitable source of trade and seasonal employment for thousands of fishermen. However, for many years little remained in Canada, except some small outports to service the annual return of the British fleet.

Agriculture, the basis of any self-sufficient and substantial settlement, was actively discouraged. In the case of Newfoundland, it was actually prohibited unless directly connected to the fishery. By the mid-seventeenth century, however, a resident fishery had begun to develop not only in Newfoundland, the major focal point of the British dominated fishing effort, but also along the shore of the St. Lawrence and at various points along the Atlantic seaboard.

This fishing effort was largely managed and financed by British merchants. They operated under the protected trade arrangements of various Navigation Acts. Within these arrangements, different relations of fish production were developed.

Most typically, merchants furnished capital in the form of commercial credit, which was extended to the resident fishermen in advance of the catch. There were a number of important consequences of this so-called 'trucking system'. Primarily, the fishermen were generally placed in a position of dependence vis-à-vis the merchant, often locking them into a chain of debt-bondage (Ommer 1981). Also, until Newfoundland became an official colony in 1824, the powerful interests of the British fish merchants prevented large-scale settlement and industrial development. With all available capital deployed in the lucrative fish trade, little was left for independent economic development or spin-off industries. Newfoundland was locked into a staple-trap, producing for and dependent on, the metropolitan market.

The French fur trade, especially in its early years, also fitted into the logic of European expansion in its mercantilist phase. In the early seventeenth century, the French established a number of settlements along the St. Lawrence claimed for France by Cartier in 1540 to supply the European market with beaver pelts. Eventually, in the 1590s and further in 1604, the French monarch granted to various companies of merchants monopoly rights over the fur trade. He also gave them governmental and colonizing responsibilities. These chartered companies established fur-gathering outposts first in Acadia, and then along the St. Lawrence and further inland. Such establishments included the first permanent settlement in 1608 at what is now Quebec City.

While the English concentrated on Newfoundland and the eastern seaboard, the French expanded inland. They set up an extensive trade network with Indians in the Great Lakes region. In this network, the fur pelts were collected by Indian trappers and either brought to the company's trading posts or picked up at certain collection-points by middlemen (coureurs-de-bois). It was these individuals who sold furs on commission to company agents in Quebec and Montreal.

The company in turn would transport pelts to Europe. There they would be manufactured into hats and other luxury items. The profitability of this trade for the French merchants who sponsored it was such that during the years 1675 to 1760, seventy-seven percent of all fur revenue ended up in France. Five percent of it went directly to the Crown and the rest to the metropolitan monopoly. Of the remainder, fourteen percent was appropriated by the New France fur merchants (twenty or so families), while nine percent was spread more widely in the colony. Only a very small part of the 9 percent returned to the actual trapper (Hamlin 1969:55).

Like the fisheries, the fur trade also discouraged the development of agriculture and colonial settlement. However, by 1663, New France was declared a Royal Colony. Now a more extensive settlement was encouraged. French officials granted *seigneuries* (large estates) to military personnel and other favorites. They sent to France for indentured servants and women to work the land under feudal tenure. Eventually, they created in the valley of St. Lawrence a loose replica of French society.

The structure of this society can be presented in the form of a pyramid with a hierarchy of classes. At the top of this hierarchy was found a small clique of government and church officials who in the name of the Crown and the Church, constituted the ruling class. Immediately below this clique were the owners of property, the landholding *seigneurs* and the large merchants. On a social level, these individuals ranked with church officials in a parallel religious hierarchy. Below this class were the colonists, the tenant farmers and artisans who formed the producing and working classes.

This picture, is, of course, an oversimplification. Within this class structure and social hierarchy there were people who were not rulers, owners, producers or workers. Not directly involved in either the feudal regime or the fur trade, these people constituted a 'middle class' of lesser merchants, professionals, and independent farmers, as well as adventurers of various sorts. However, prior to the conquest of New France, this class was a relatively insignificant element of the social structure.

Mercantilism II: Fur, Timber and British Rule (1763-1850)

With the conquest of New France in 1760, and the conclusion of hostilities between France and England three years later, Canada entered its second, and most important, period of primitive accumulation. The developments over the next eighty years, or so, would lay the foundation of industrial capitalism in North America. At the beginning of these developments in 1763, the colonies that now make up Canada were part of a large and diverse British Empire. Included in this empire were the plantation economies of the Caribbean Islands and the Southern colonies; the largely self-sufficient middle-colonies of New York, Pennsylvania and New Jersey that occupied a privileged position in the North Atlantic re-export trade; and New England, the major entrepot in the British Caribbean trade.

Together, the northernmost colonies (now Canada) constituted less than five percent of the two and one-quarter million people in Britain's North American Empire (Pomfret 1981:17-8). Newfoundland and Nova Scotia were small colonies, important to Britain for fish. But, they were a heavy drain on both capital and revenues, particularly with respect to military expenditures in Nova Scotia. Quebec, on the other hand, continued to be a major source of wealth. The bulk of it was appropriated by mercantile monopolies in England and a handful, six hundred or so, merchants that had followed the British army into Montreal.

Although most British North American colonies at the time were engaged in agriculture, the economy still revolved around the fur trade. A large part of this activity was conducted by the Hudson Bay Company. This company of British merchants had been granted a royal charter in 1670. After establishing trading posts around James Bay, the Company acquired exclusive rights to the shores of the Hudson Bay, and to Rupert's Land, the large land mass west of the Great Lakes region.

Despite the use of Hudson Bay to the north as a trading route, the St. Lawrence remained, by far, the most important route for North American fur exports. By 1763, when New France officially ceded to Britain, ending a century and a half of rivalry over colonial hegemony, British fur traders operating out of Montreal had taken over the French network. A fierce conflict ensued over the control of the Northwest fur trade. It ended in 1821 when the Hudson Bay Company absorbed the operations of the Montreal traders.

By the 1800s, the fur trade had been displaced in economic importance by a number of developments. In its wake, the American Revolution had brought the immigration of thousands of Empire loyalists. These were settled with land grants in Nova Scotia, New Brunswick and the Southern region of the Great Lakes. The massive immigration not only led in 1791 to the division of Quebec into Upper and Lower Canada, but also to the rapid growth of an agricultural economy which became more self-sufficient in food than the rest of British North America.

By 1821, this rapidly growing agricultural community formed the basis of an industrial economy in the Toronto-Hamilton area. Although still small in terms of employment, this industrial complex was already an important sector of the Canadian economy. Together with the surrounding agricultural frontier, it absorbed the greatest part of a massive influx of European immigrants throughout the first half of the nineteenth century.

Another development which diminished the economic importance of the fur trade were the activities of merchants in Montreal, and various ports in the Maritimes. They displaced the control exercised by the seaboard ex-colonies in the United States of British North American trade. By 1808, the number of ships landing in British North American ports exceeded the number landing in U.S. ports (Pomfret, 21). With preferential access to the large British market, many Montreal merchants grew wealthy on American goods exported via Canada. So did merchants in Nova Scotia, with respect to the British West Indies trade. In terms of exports to Britain, timber had replaced fur as the dominant export staple. With a growing demand in Britain for timber during, and after, the Napoleonic Wars, a flourishing export trade in timber developed in Quebec City and Saint John.

The growth of the staple trade based on timber, early in the nineteenth century, brought about a number of distinct developments for the history of Canada. Each of these was the source of some 'Great Fortunes', that together provided the necessary ingredients of industrial capitalism.

The first development concerned the continuing extraction of huge profits by the Hudson Bay Company out of the trapping activities of native peoples both in the Hudson Bay area and in Rupert's Land. Within this large territory, the Company had exclusive rights to own land, levy taxes, administer justice, keep troops, and, most importantly, to maintain a commercial monopoly. Under these conditions, the fur trade was based on the hyper-exploitation of the Indian population. These people had become thoroughly dependent on the sale of fur for gun powder, and other necessities, at a rate of exchange increasingly unfavorable to Indians. The more furs that were brought in caused lower prices to be paid, and thus, the search for more furs to maintain the supplies of powder became harder. The lower prices meant the merchant—and the Company—became even richer.

Over the years, the fur trade built the personal fortunes of a succession of governors who represented both King and Company. Some of these fortunes were invested in land, banks, and steamships. A number found their way into the largest, and most significant, capitalist enterprise of the nineteenth century: the Canadian Pacific Railroad.[12]

Another set of developments that contributed to the rise of industrial production arose out of the conquest of New France. The merchants who had followed the British army into Montreal after the conquest made a financial "killing" from manipulation of French currency (See Naylor, 1973). Also, these merchants, together with the clique that had installed itself as representatives of the British Crown, granted themselves, or acquired by various means, huge tracts of land and other productive assets. Through their control over the Executive Council, this amalgam of English petty nobility (the chateau clique), shipping merchants and wholesale traders, managed to concentrate in their own hands seventy-five percent of all the productive resources accumulated in Montreal. At the same time, the Montreal merchants were in a position to advance, and pursue, their interests in directing the trade of continental North America along the St. Lawrence river by rebuilding the commercial empire of the St. Lawrence.

In Upper Canada, as in Quebec, a ruling group of government officials, officers and other elements of an English petty nobility, had created a new class of landed proprietors. However, the policy of free land grants to Empire loyalists, and the general availability of land on the market, led to the formation of a vigorous class of independent farmers. Such individuals provided both a source of foodstuffs for growing urban centres like Hamilton, Toronto, and Kingston, and a market for consumer goods traditionally imported from Britain but increasingly manufactured in these urban centres.

In the area northwest of Lake Ontario, a complex of manufacturing industries, and various urban communities, had developed as early as the 1820s. These industries were generally based on the factory system and employed wage-labor. By the 1870s the Industrial Revolution had reached Canada.

The existence of a nucleus of capitalist enterprise had been reflected in the rebellion of 1837-38 in which an incipient industrial bourgeoisie allied with farmers and other elements of the petty bourgeoisie in a struggle against the Family Compact. The latter were an amalgam of mercantile and agrarian interests who had, in the words of Judge Thorpe, 'gorged themselves on the plunder of every Department and squeezed every dollar out of the wretched inhabitants' (Myers, 1972:70).[13]

In the Maritimes, there were a number of important developments in the first half of the nineteenth century. With independence of the United States, Nova Scotia cast itself in the role of Britain's junior partner in Empire. It soon achieved the privileged position in the British West Indies trade earlier occupied by New England. In this trade, a number of wholesale merchants made large fortunes that were invested in shipbuilding, and a range of consumer goods industries including grist mills, tanneries and distilleries, land speculation and banking. Such investments yielded large returns. Similar fortunes were made in various adventures on the high seas, such as piracy.

Beyond these developments, the Nova Scotian economy was, by mid-nineteenth century, still heavily geared to the production of, and trade in, staple commodities. There was some manufacturing, but it too was dominated by staple-processing and commerce-serving industries, like saw-milling and shipbuilding. Together, these industries accounted for over sixty percent of the total value of manufacturing in 1861 (McCann 1981:30). A number of consumer goods industries developed in Halifax, but most manufactured products were imported from Britain, or the United States. To all intents and purposes, by mid-century, Nova Scotia still had a largely mercantilist economy.

In Prince Edward Island a new class of landed proprietors was created by colonial fiat. Such a class had formed in each British colony through the colonial administration's control over crown lands. But in Prince Edward Island (P.E.I.) it was created virtually overnight. In one day in

1767, the Island of St. John (P.E.I.) was divided into 67 lots. These were granted—by lottery—to private proprietors in return for promises to promote settlement and other responsibilities (Bumsted 1981). Soon after, in a period lasting from about 1780 to the mid-1790s, local officials, through various manoeuvres, managed to transfer much of the land into their own hands. As a result, by 1830, the Island had developed a resident class of landed proprietors as well as a half dozen, or so, absentee landlords. The latter held estates of 100 000 acres each.

This monopoly of land held by absentee landlords effectively blocked the early development of an independent class of working proprietors, or family farmers. Two-thirds of the population (22 000 people) were tenants. They were described by officials as 'the dregs of the poor houses of England, the lowest description of Irish and the scum of Newfoundland' (Bird, 40). The conflict between these tenants and the proprietors throughout the first half of the nineteenth century overshadowed the colony's participation in mercantile trade.

Perhaps the most significant development in the Maritimes in the nineteenth century was related to the timber trade conducted, for the most part, out of Quebec City and Saint John. The strong British demand for timber resulted in the development of New Brunswick as a 'timber colony'. Up to three-quarters of the population was directly or indirectly dependent on the timber trade (Wynn 1981). Saint John not only became one of the largest ports in the world, but, like Halifax, it became a focal point for a range of new industries stimulated by the timber trade. A number of these industries, although generally small, tended to employ wage-labor. By mid-century, Saint John, Halifax, and several other urban centres in the Maritimes had developed a nucleus of capitalist enterprise in the manufacturing sector. By the time of Confederation, 1867, there was already a strong base of capitalist industry supported by a network of local banks in cities throughout the Maritimes.

The timber trade contributed to the development of capitalist industry in other ways as well. As we have seen, by the beginning of the nineteenth century, there were various accumulations of money capital in Canada. But these did not lead to a system of industrial capitalism until around 1850. Various explanations for this have been given.

The economic historian, Tom Naylor (1972), has argued that the delayed introduction and eventual weakness of industrial capitalism in Canada was the direct result of the prolonged dominance of mercantile capitalists. The conservative, low-risk orientation of this class, in its search for safe short-term ventures, resulted in a disinclination to invest in risky, long-term industrial ventures. A better explanation, however, has been proffered by Claire Pentland (1960).

According to Pentland, the real issue in the development of industrial capitalism in Canada was the availability of a supply of free wage-labor—a class of individuals compelled to sell their labor-power in exchange for a wage. It was in the formation of a class of wage laborers that the timber trade contributed most to the development of industrial capitalism in Canada. The source of this capitalist labor market was the mass of impoverished Irish farmers and other elements of surplus population created by centuries of plunder, extortion and exploitation.

Because the timber merchants had trouble filling their ships on the return voyage from Europe, a cheap means of transporting immigrants was made available. Throughout the 1820s, 1830s and 1840s, thousands of immigrants arrived in these ships. From 1815 to 1830, a total of 168 615 immigrants arrived at the Port of Quebec alone. Altogether it has been estimated that by 1850 the timber ships brought 800 000 immigrants from the British Isles to Canada (Pentland 1959). Most of these ended up in the industrial centres and farms of Upper Canada, as well as settling in Lower Canada, Nova Scotia and New Brunswick (Pomfret 1981:26). It was the combination of this proletariat, and the money accumulated in mercantilist trade, or extorted through various other means, that by mid-century helped launch the system of industrial capitalism in Canada.

The Age of Industry, 1846-1900

Industrial capitalism in Canada is traced by some scholars to 1846. This year saw the repeal of the Corn Laws which symbolized the defeat of mercantile interests by industrial interests in Britain. This 'bourgeois revolution' which took place all over Europe in the nineteenth century, broke the power of the landholding-mercantile oligarchy and led to the formation of a new ruling class, an industrial railroad oligarchy. The growing power of this new class in Canada is reflected in various Acts of Parliament. The Guarantee Act of 1849 provided massive subsidies from the public treasury to build a railway. In 1854 feudal tenure in Quebec was abolished. By 1858, protective tariffs were instituted for Canadian manufacturing. These tariffs, incorporated in various plans for Confederation, ultimately became a key element of the National Policy pursued by the first post-Confederation governments.

The scheme of Confederation and the National Policy of the Macdonald government have given rise to much debate. Some see in such measures the prolonged dominance of the mercantile capitalist class. This group, cut adrift by Britain, attempted to reassert its position through policies that would open up a new staple trade and, with it, the old dream of a commercial empire along the St. Lawrence (Naylor 1972).

This interpretation of Confederation and Macdonald's National Policy has been disputed. According to Ryerson (1976) and others, Confederation and the National Policy do not express a mercantile strategy. They represent the interests of the industrial sector of the capitalist class. This class was concerned above all with the protection of domestic industry and the expansion of the market.

Thus, the Western extension of the railroad worked, and was advanced, as a mechanism of industrialization. It expanded the domestic market for Eastern manufacturing industries, which were protected by tariffs, as well as stimulating the growth of local manufacturing. The Canadian Pacific Railroad was not only the largest capitalist enterprise of the nineteenth century in Canada. It was also an absolutely critical factor in the development of capitalist industry.

In the period 1850-70, the railway boom, the development of local manufacturing, the influx of immigrant labor, and the diminution of available new land[14] combined to launch the 'Age of Industry' in Canada. The extension of the railway from sixty-six to two thousand miles in the decade 1850-60 was directly responsible for the steady growth of local manufacturing in a number of urban centres. In this decade, exports turned from wheat to flour, and from timber to lumber and ships. Imports increasingly took the form of capital rather than consumer goods. By the 1870s, consumer goods industries had developed in most Canadian cities. They supplied the countryside with shoes, clothing, beer, whiskey, furniture, etc. All such products were manufactured with the help of machine-based technology. The factory system had in most cases already displaced domestic handicrafts.

In addition, heavy industry developed in a number of urban centres. The number of steel mills increased in the 1850s from one hundred and fifty-eight to over three thousand. Railway shops were set up in Montreal, Kingston, Toronto, and Hamilton. By the 1860s they were producing locomotives, sleeping cars, boilers, etc. Flour mills and sugar refineries were established, as well as iron forges and rolling mills, and farm machine manufacturers. Over the decade, industrial employment had risen from 71 000 to 145 000.

Confederation and the National Policy of the Macdonald government stimulated the further development of industry. In the period between 1870 and 1890, the number of manufacturing establishments in Canada increased from 41 000 to 75 000. At the same time the number of workers increased from 187 000 to 369 000. The capital (re-invested profits) employed in these enterprises increased from $77 million to $353 million (Clarke, 6). This growth of capitalist manufacturing continued even through the recession years (1873-96) before exploding in what has become known as the 'Golden Age of Manufacturing' (1896-1910). In this period, there was an especially strong expansion of capital goods industries like primary iron and steel, finished iron and steel and their products, structural steel, and railway stock. Well before 1910, many communities in Ontario, Quebec, and the Maritimes had successfully completed the transition from mercantile to industrial capitalism (McCann 1981).

The Emergence and Consolidation of Monopoly Capitalism, 1900-44

The inherent tendency of capitalism towards concentration and monopoly manifested itself very early in Canada, both in banking and in industry. By the turn of the century, three corporations (the Canadian Pacific, Canadian Northern and the Grand Trunk Railroads) controlled almost all the railroad lines in Canada. Thirty-nine large firms (with sales over one million dollars) already accounted for fifteen percent of the value of all manufacturing output. Each had close to monopoly control over their respective markets. By 1911, after a wave of mergers, one hundred and fifty large corporations accounted for thirty-one percent of all manufacturing output.

The years 1900-13 were marked by mergers in the heavy industry sector. The result was the formation of giant corporations like Canada Cement, Amalgamated Asbestos, Canadian Car and Foundry, Dominion Steel Corporation and Steel Company of Canada. Important mergers took place among producers of iron and steel, textiles, tobacco, brewing, milling and paper. In each case, these activities resulted either in monopoly or an oligopoly (Epp 1973:102-75).

From the years 1909 to 1911 forty-one industrial corporations were formed through the merger of one hundred and ninety-six companies. As a result, by 1917, the number of manufacturing establishments had been reduced from 75 000 in 1890 to 21 000. At the same time the number of employees increased from 369 000 to over 600 000. The volume of invested capital had risen to over two billion dollars (Clarke 8).

In banking the same pattern of merger was evident. In 1867, there were thirty-three chartered banks. By 1914, only twenty-two remained. The five largest accounted for fifty percent of the assets of all commercial banks in Canada (Neufeld 1972:78-9, 99).

The tendency to concentration and monopoly deepened throughout World War I and the post-war period. Another spectacular wave of mergers occurred in the years 1925-30. During this time another five hundred and fifty firms were consolidated through one hundred and twenty mergers. As a result, the average capital per establishment increased from $4000 in 1890 to $178 000 in 1930.

By 1930, economic activity in most industries was accounted for by four or fewer firms. As a partial consequence the federal government in 1935 established a Royal Commission on Price Spreads. However, despite the attack of this Commission on unfair trade practices, monopoly pricing and other 'evils' of 'imperfect competition' in many sectors of the economy, by 1945 *all* major industries were monopolistic. Indeed, in a 1947 study (McCollum) it was discovered that 86.9% of the gross assets of all industrial corporations were accounted for by 100 conglomerates. These corporations, in turn, were dominated by '50 big shots', almost all of whom were finance capitalists (banker-industrialists). Various pools of industrial capital had been created, but none so large as that amassed by the five big banks. These formed the keystone and economic centre of the system of corporate or monopoly capitalism.

Canada: Imperialist Power or Colony?

The development of an advanced form of monopoly capitalism in Canada raises the question: can Canada best be viewed as a developed economy of the metropolitan type, and as an imperialist power: or is it best seen as an underdeveloped hinterland economy of the colonial type? The answer is not clear.

On the one hand, as we have seen, Canada's history involves a succession of colonial relationships. The first of these involved France and the second Britain. It has been argued that since 1867 Canada has retained a form of dependent colonial status with respect first to British capital, and more recently (since perhaps the 1920s) to American capital. This so-called neo-colonial status is based on two conditions of economic dependence: 1) the continued orientation of the Canadian economy within the world division of labor towards the export of staple goods for metropolitan markets; and 2) the high degree of foreign investment of capital in the Canadian economy, especially in the productive sectors of resource extraction and manufacturing. Both of these conditions are highly characteristic of underdeveloped colonial type economies within the world capitalist system.

On the other hand, Canada shares the industrial structure and productive capacities of the most advanced capitalist countries. Since 1867, foreign investments have never exceeded the scale of domestic capital. Until the contemporary period, most of these investments took the form of portfolio loan capital. It does not involve direct control over Canadian industry. Furthermore, Canada in its development, has exhibited all of the characteristic features of advanced capitalism or imperialism. One of the conditions of imperialism as noted earlier in this chapter is:

> the concentration of production and capital...developed to such a high stage that it [creates] monopolies which play a decisive role in economic life.

There is clearly no question about this type of development in Canada.

The institutions of monopoly capitalism emerged in the last decades of the nineteenth century and were consolidated by 1945. The course taken by this process closely follows developments in the most advanced capitalist countries. Indeed, throughout the twentieth century, Canada has exhibited higher levels of concentration and greater degrees of monopoly than the United States. Until recently the U.S. was the undisputed centre of the world capitalist system (Clement 1977:138-41).

A second characteristic of imperialism outlined previously was "the merging of bank capital with industrial capital, and the creation of a financial oligarchy". As in Western Europe and the United States, the concentration of production and capital in Canada in the 1870-1914 period was accompanied, indeed, based on, the fusion of bank capital and industrial capital. The biggest banks were heavily involved from the very beginning in financing industrial development (see, for example, the case study by Frost, 1978). The consolidation of capital and production at the turn of the century, and beyond, was based almost exclusively on the activities of the new financial oligarchy formed in the period.

This belief can be seen in the 1913 Grain Grower's Guide, 'Who Owns Canada?'. The guide identified forty-two leading 'plutocrats' who together controlled the directorates of the largest banks, utilities, and enterprises in transportation and manufacturing. The list included DOSCO, the largest manufacturing concern in Canada, the Canadian Pacific Railroad and the Hudson Bay Company (Epp 1973:177-96).

There is no question that the plutocrats identified in the Grain Grower's Guide represented the leading elements of finance capitalism. Over two-thirds held bank directorates, and about half of these were directors of the Bank of Montreal and the Bank of Commerce. Also included were eight of the Bank of Montreal's twelve directors; four of the Imperial Bank's eleven directors; three of the Molson Bank's seven directors; and three of the Dominion Bank's nine directors. The Royal Bank and the Metropolitan Bank were each represented by its president. The Bank of Nova Scotia was represented by two directors, and the Bank of Toronto was represented by Stephen Meighen, a member of a prominent political family.

Furthermore, at least four-fifths of the corporate mergers during 1909-13 were arranged by these plutocrats without having to sell shares to raise capital. Those mergers that did require 'outside' financing brought into the core group of finance capitalists another generation of financiers and promoters (Epp 1973, ch. viii, x; Anthony 1979). By 1914, there was a substantial measure of finance capitalism in the Canadian economy. Most of it predated the first merger movement.

The additional observations concerning imperialism referred to earlier include the following:

the export of capital as distinguished from the export of commodities acquired exceptional importance; the formation of international monopolist capitalist associations which share the world among themselves, and the territorial division of the whole world among the biggest capitalist powers is completed.

Even before Confederation, a number of home-grown capitalists made their fortunes on the basis of exploitation in Latin America. By the 1920s, these and other capitalists were investing in the West Indies, Mexico, Brazil, British Guiana, and the West coast of Africa. By 1930, the total of these investments had reached 1.2 billion dollars. By 1945, they reached over two billion dollars, making Canada the fifth largest exporter of capital in the world (Souza 1977:52). Also, there are innumerable examples of Canadian corporations, as well as U.S. subsidiaries operating out of Canada, participating in international cartels and price-fixing arrangements.

Even though Canada never acquired colonies of its own, its leading capitalists fully participated in the territorial division of the world by imperialist powers. They did this either in alliance with U.S. capitalists or on their own. In this division, Canadian capital cornered, or was allowed, a good slice of the investment, or exploitation, 'opportunities' existing in the Caribbean (Chodos 1977). Also, the capital of some of Canada's major utilities was formed in Latin America. It was then used to set up similar monopolies in Brazil, Mexico and elsewhere in the Caribbean and Latin America. These countries also provided useful tax havens for Canadian monopoly capital.

In short, it would appear that Canada has developed historically both as a colony, an under-developed resource hinterland for metropolitan capital, and as an imperialist power; a junior partner in monopoly capitalism's global reach. It must be stressed, however, that not all authors of this book would accept this analysis in its entirety. To appreciate fully the nature and historic legacy of this dual status, it is necessary to update some important developments in the world system since 1944 and to reconstruct Canada's place in this system. This will be done and the consequences explored in the following chapter.

HIGHLIGHT

1. Original development in Canada was an offshoot of the trade in staples—fish and fur—by Britain and France.
2. After the conquest of New France by Britain, staple production remained the leading sector of the economy. Gradually, however, small industries developed to supply local markets.
3. In the last quarter of the nineteenth century, modern manufacturing in Canada involved the establishment of factories, the use of machine technology, and the growth of a sizeable working class.

Conclusion

One of the most difficult problems in social science is to understand how societies change and evolve over long periods of time. In the study of this problem it is possible to distinguish two quite different approaches. There is an approach that analyses societal development in terms of the values that underlie society's key institutions. These are the values to which members of society are either committed or oriented in their roles. In this approach, societal development is primarily a matter of reorienting behavior and institutions away from traditional values towards modern values. The emphasis on modernization characterizes the general framework of social science.

Also, there is a general approach that emphasizes changes and developments at the level of society's mode of production. Within this perspective the study of societal developments is primarily a matter of establishing the conditions under which capitalism emerged and developed into a world system.

These specific theories have been advanced within this perspective. First, there is the *dependency theory* of underdevelopment. This theory, based on Marxist principles, argues that the capitalist development of some parts of the world is based on the exploitation of others. Second, there is the *staples theory* of economic growth. It arises from, and is applied to, a particular set of conditions found only in some countries like Canada with a high land/people ratio. The theory argues basically that the development of Canada (and perhaps other countries in Canada's position) is shaped by the opportunities and requirements of a succession of export trades in basic (relatively unprocessed) staple goods. A third theory builds from a Marxist analysis of the capitalist system. It argues that *imperialism* is a consequence of the development of capitalism.

With reference to these theories, capitalist societies develop through three basic stages: a stage of primitive accumulation in which the foundations of the capitalist system are laid; a stage in which the capitalist mode of industrial production comes to dominate the economy, with corresponding developments at other levels of society; and a stage in which the internal contradictions of competitive capitalism lead to the development of large corporations that monopolize the markets of the world system. A specific form of expansion, and a particular organization of the world system corresponds to each stage of development. In this organization, Canada has developed both as an economic colony and as an imperialist power. The conditions of this dual status, in relation to the latest phase of capitalism in its world-wide development, will be explored further in the next chapter.

NOTES

[1]This theory has taken many forms. A highly representative selection of studies based on the theory can be found in Etzioni and Etzioni (1964) and Finkle and Gamble (1971). For a devastating critique of the assumptions underlying modernization theory see Frank, 1971.

[2]This formulation is based on a widely used but now largely defunct model developed by Talcott Parsons (1968). In this model, the roles that individuals play within any and all social institutions are prescribed by society and these prescriptions vary along the following value dimensions: ascription—achievement, particularism—universalism, collectivity orientation—individualism and functional diffuseness—specificity. According to Parsons, the institutions of modern society are oriented towards the second of each paired value (pattern variable).

[3]This is perhaps the central proposition of the theory of modern society. Its classical formulation can be found in Davis and Moore (1945).

[4]This proposition that societal development is essentially a matter of diffusing capital, values, technology, and modern institutions form the developed societies of the modern world is another cornerstone of modernization theory. Examples of this diffusion model of societal development are legion. See in particular the readings collected by Etzioni and Etzioni (1964) and Finkle and Gamble (1971) and the general review by Chilcote and Edelstein (1974:3-25).

[5]See Forbes (1978) and Cross (1970).

[6]Major exponents of this theory include Frank (1966, 1967), Dos Santos (1973), Wallerstein (1974), Jalee (1968), and Amin (1974, 1976, 1977). In Canada, dependency theory has provided an essential cornerstone of a recently reviewed political economy approach, as reflected in the works of Levitt (1970), Watkins (1977a), Laxer (1973), and Clement (1977), and Naylor (1980) among others. For further details and reference to further studies about this theory see Davis (1971), D.E.C. (1974), and Veltmeyer (1980).

[6a]Copyright © 1967, 1969 by André Gunder Frank. Reprinted by permission of Monthly Review Press.

[7]This theory takes various forms but as far as recent social science is concerned derives primarily from the works of Harold Innis as extended and reformulated by Mel Watkins (1977b). In this form, the theory has had numerous applications, especially over the last decade with a pronounced revival of a political economy tradition (see Drache, 1978). Studies in this tradition include Drache (1977), Watkins (1977b), Hutchenson (1978), among many others. An alternative approach can be found in the works of S.D. Clark, who, it has been said, made Innis dance to a Sociological tune. On this question see Harrison (1982).

[8]There is quite a debate on this question. Many scholars accept the staples thesis as it relates to Canada's early history. Some, like Pentland (1980), argue its decreased relevance after 1820. Others, however, extend it well into the nineteenth century, with the development of export trades based on timber and then wheat (Fowke 1957). Also, Canada's general reliance on the export of relatively unprocessed material resources in the twentieth century has given rise to further extensions of the theory (see Drache, 1978).

[9]The classics of this theory are Hilferding (1910), Luxemburg (1913), Bukharin (1915) and Lenin (1916). Over the years, however, the theory has been extended and reformulated many times. For reference to, and an excellent discussion of these studies, see Brewer (1980) as well as several Suggested Readings.

[10]Of the various laws specified by Marx, the most important refers to the tendency towards a falling rate of average profit. This process has been described in the previous chapter by

Cuneo. On the basis of this theory, Marx postulated a tendency toward the development of large monopolies and the forcible expansion of the system into cheaper sources of raw materials and new markets.

[11]The word 'primitive' here is used in the sense of 'belonging to the first age, period, or stage' not in the common sense of 'simple, rude, or rough' and in a technical sense to mean 'original' or 'primary' rather than derivative. In this sense, 'primitive accumulation' refers to the period in which the preconditions of capitalist accumulation are established.

[11a]From *Grundrisse: Foundations of the Critique of Political Economy*, by Karl Marx, translated by Martin Nicolaus. © 1973 Random House, Inc.

[12]See Chodos (1973).

[13]See Ryerson (1968) and Myers (1972).

[14]On land as a critical factor of capitalist development see Teeple (1972).

SUGGESTED READINGS

Development Education Centre, Underdevelopment in Canada: Notes towards an Analytical Framework (1974). This pamphlet provides a clear and succinct outline of the major concepts used in a Dependency perspective on social development. A useful introduction to an understanding of some of Canada's most critical problems.

Sociology of Development and Underdevelopments of Sociology, A. G. Frank. London: Pluto Press, 1971. A major critique of Modernisation theory in its major forms. Worthwhile reading for a close and critical examination of the misplaced premises of the sociological study of societal development.

How Europe Underdeveloped Africa, Walter Rodney. A highly readable account of the process by which the capitalist development of Europe was based on and caused the underdevelopment of Africa. Parallels the earlier classical study of Latin America underdevelopment by A.F. Frank (1967).

Imperialism: The Hebert Stage of Capitalism , V. I. Lenin. Peking: Foreign Languages Press, 1965. This text remains the major reference point for a Marxist analysis of the necessity for Imperialism at the highest stage of capitalist development. It applied particularly to the age of European Imperialism in the late 19th century.

Unequal Development, Samir Amin. New York: Monthly Review Press, 1976. In the 20th century the accumulation of capital on a world scale has produced new forms of imperialism, especially after WW II. This analysis of these forms of imperialism is by one of the foremost internationally renowned economists. Not easy reading, but worthwhile for a basic understanding of the world capitalist system today. For a more readable account of the consequences of this unequal world-wide development read Harrison (1981).

LATE CAPITALISM, CORPORATE POWER, AND IMPERIALISM

Henry Veltmeyer

Introduction

In chapter 3 we traced the evolution of the capitalist system and its inherent tendency toward imperialist expansion. It was seen that the world order set up at each stage of capitalist development provided an important source of capital as well as a means of offsetting capitalism's basic tendency toward crisis and conflict. By 1945, this tendency had already resulted in a major world-wide depression and two world wars. It had also spawned the development of socialism and various colonial movements for national liberation. Despite these developments, however, the capitalist system as a whole managed to avert the conditions of a severe and prolonged crisis from which it could not recover. Once again it did so by restructuring on a world scale. It set up a world system that would provide the basis for a new round of capitalist expansion. This system, established in 1944 at Bretton Woods by the major capitalist powers, is essentially still in place today. It continues despite various cracks and strains and, more recently, the onset of another prolonged crisis.

The current world system is also the source of some of the most serious problems experienced today at some level by most Canadians and at a deeper level by many people all over the world. This chapter will give us a closer look at the system that produced, and continues to produce, these difficulties. We will, first of all, examine the basic structure of the contemporary world system. Second, we will examine Canada's position within this structure. And third, we will examine some of the major forces gathering within the world system. Such forces are leading to structural transformation and perhaps the collapse of the entire system.

LATE CAPITALISM AND THE WORLD SYSTEM

The Multinational Corporation and the New Imperialism

From the sixteenth to the eighteenth century, the major instrument of capitalist expansion was the chartered company of European merchants.

114

The operation of these companies created a European-centred world market for agricultural products and other staples. The profits derived from the privileged position of the strong states of Western Europe and some of the English-speaking North American colonies was a major factor in the industrial takeoff of the period.

As seen in the last chapter, from the late nineteenth century to the second world war, a major structural change developed in the world economy. It was no longer characterized primarily by the international exchange of commodities. Although the international exchange of raw materials and staple products for manufactured goods persisted and was even reinforced in this period, the internationalization of money capital was more characteristic of the world economy. Internationalization involved, in this case, the export of capital from the European core of the system to its underdeveloped periphery. This pattern of capital exports occurred on a massive scale. It led to the formation of export enclaves in peripheral economies and to the pillage of their resources by various means, especially trade.

By the second world war, the world system had undergone further changes of fundamental importance. The United States had replaced Britain as the major source of international capital, and the form of this capital had changed. No longer was it based on the portfolio investments of individual capitalists and institutions. It now involved direct investment (purchase of stock) by the large industrial corporations. In general such organizations experienced a dramatic increase in size and productive capacity as a result of the same war which devastated Europe and brought about the final collapse of the British Empire. These multinational corporations first emerged in the late nineteenth century. Ever since then they have been growing and expanding.

Under the new international trade and monetary system established at Bretton Woods[1], the leading capitalist states recommenced their global reach and embarked on an expansion of unprecedented proportions. The largest corporations and banks, most of which were based in the United States, soon took a commanding position in the world economy. They dominated both the supply of resources for the third world and the markets of the advanced capitalist economies. This dominance was felt especially by those nations of western Europe which were rebuilt with Marshall Plan dollars.

To appreciate the importance of multinational corporations (MNCs) in the world economy, we need only compare them in size and scope with the economies of the nation states. Table 1 ranks the top 100 economies in the world system in 1970. Thirty-seven of these were MNCs. The financial transactions of each of the top ten exceeded the GNP of over 153 countries, and stormed ahead at two or three times the pace of the world's nations (*New Internationalist* 37 March 1976:2). The largest concentration of these corporations was in the United States. Until recently the United States tended to dominate the post-war world

TABLE 1
Top 100 Countries and Companies in 1976
Ranked by Gross National Product and Worldwide Company Sales[2]

Rank '76	'70	Name Country/Company	Amount GNP/Sales (Billion $US)	Company Headquarters
1	1	· United States	1,694.9	
2	2	· USSR	717.5	
3	3	· Japan	573.9	
4	4	· Federal Republic of Germany (West)	461.8	
5	5	· France	356.0	
6	6	· People's Republic of China	307.0	
7	7	· United Kingdom	233.5	
8	9	· Canada	182.5	
9	8	· Italy	180.6	
10	12	· Brazil	143.0	
11	16	· Spain	107.2	
12	11	· Poland	99.1	
13	15	· Australia	97.3	
14	19	· Netherlands	91.6	
15	10	· India	87.8	
16	13	· German Democratic Republic (East)	75.8	
17	18	Sweden	74.2	
18	39	*Iran	69.2	
19	20	· Belgium	68.9	
21	23	· Switzerland	58.1	
22	17	Czechoslovakia	56.5	

Rank '76	'70	Name Country/Company	Amount GNP/Sales (Billion $US)	Company Headquarters
51		*Algeria	16.7	
52	61	Gulf Oil	16.4	US
53	47	· IBM	16.3	US
54	52	Thailand	16.3	
55	—	· Portugal	16.1	
56	—	*Iraq	16.0	
57	51	Unilever	15.8	Netherlands/UK
58	44	· General Electric	15.7	US
59	49	Colombia	15.7	
60	50	Chrysler	15.5	US
61	—	*Libya	15.1	
62	—	*Kuwait	14.4	
63	58	Peru	13.4	
64	26	Pakistan	13.1	
65	19	New Zealand	13.1	
66	53	· ITT	11.8	US
67	75	· Standard Oil (Indiana)	11.5	US
68	67	· Philips'	11.5	Netherlands
69	46	Chile	10.9	
70	81	Democratic People's Republic of Korea (No)	10.8	
71	55	Egypt	10.7	
72	71	Malaysia	10.6	

Rank		Name	Value	Country
23	29	· Exxon'	48.6	US
24	24	· General Motors	47.2	US
25	33	Austria	42.2	
26	45	Turkey	41.3	
27	—	*Saudi Arabia	40.9	
28	22	Argentina	40.7	
29	30	· Denmark	39.0	
30	25	Yugoslavia	37.7	
31	36	· Royal Dutch/Shell Group	36.1	Netherlands/UK
32	32	*Indonesia	36.1	
33	27	South Africa	33.7	
34	35	· Norway	31.4	
35	37	*Venezuela	31.3	
36	—	*Nigeria	30.9	
37	21	Romania	30.0	
38	31	· Ford Motor	28.8	US
39	33	Finland	27.8	
40	54	· Texaco	26.4	US
41	43	· Mobil	26.1	US
42	43	South Korea	25.3	
43	—	Hungary	24.8	
44	42	Greece	23.6	
45	34	Bulgaria	21.6	
46	—	National Iranian Oil	19.7	Iran
47	66	· Standard Oil of California	19.4	US
48	69	· British Petroleum	19.1	UK
49	40	Philippines	18.0	
50	60	Taiwan	17.1	
73	—	· ENI	10.0	Italy
74	—	*United Arab Emirates	10.0	
75	—	· Francaise des Petroles	9.9	France
76	59	Hong King	9.9	
77	—	Israel	9.7	
78	89	· Renault	9.4	France
79	95	· Hoechst	9.3	W. Germany
80	—	BASF	9.2	W. Germany
81	91	Petroleos de Venezuela	9.1	Venezuela
82	84	· Daimler-Benz	9.0	W. Germany
83	63	Morocco	8.9	
84	64	· US Steel	8.6	US
85	77	· Volkswagenwerk	8.5	W. Germany
86	—	· Atlantic Richfield	8.5	US
87	72	· E.I. Du Pont	8.4	US
88	—	Bayer	8.3	W. Germany
89	72	· Ireland	8.3	
90	70	· Nippon Steel	8.1	Japan
91	86	· Siemens	8.1	W. Germany
92	—	· Continental Oil	8.0	US
93	93	Cuba	8.0	
94	—	· August Thyssen-Hutte	7.9	W. Germany
95	—	· Toyota Motor	7.7	Japan
96	—	Viet Nam	7.7	
97	—	Nestle	7.6	Switzerland
98	79	· ELF-Acquitaine	7.5	France
99	—	· Imperial Chemical Industries (ICI)	7.4	UK
100	—	Puerto Rico	7.4	

· Members of Trilateral Commission
*Members of OPEC

SOURCE: 1978 World Bank Atlas; 1977 Fortune 500.

capitalist system. By 1971, 298 of the largest American corporations accounted for 26 percent of world trade and 75 percent of total foreign investments. Given the form of this capital investment (direct investment), a large and increasing proportion of world trade was and is based on transnational production facilities.

Even by conservative estimates, the value of internationalized production now exceeds the value of international trade. Moreover, much of what is treated as international trade is to a considerable and increasing extent composed of shipments among branches and affiliates of MNCs (Rowthorn 1971). Such parent-to-affiliate or intrafirm transfers account for about 25 percent of all British exports and imports and an estimated 33 percent of American manufacturing exports. The intrafirm shipments of MNCs based in the United States alone represented about 11 percent of total world exports in 1970 (Fitt et al. 442 N8-9). Indications are that this percentage has increased, particularly with respect to Canada whose resource-based and manufacturing industries are to a considerable extent owned outright by these American corporations. By 1970, over 60 percent of Canada's exports and 68.7 percent of its imports were with the United States. The bulk of this trade involved parent-to-affiliate transfers (see *Gray Report* 1972, discussed by Clement 1977:23-24).

The important feature of this new transnationalized economy is not only its size and its growing share of the world economy, but the high and unprecedented concentration of raw economic power. This power derives from a number of characteristics of the MNC. With an annual turnover that dwarfs the GNP or revenues of many countries, these corporations are able to mobilize sufficient resources to penetrate most economies at will and to dictate their own terms.

A second characteristic of MNCs giving rise to power is the widespread nature of their activities, both over product lines and over countries. One study (Vernon 1971:285), indicated that of 187 selected MNCs based in the United States, the median corporation was involved in twenty-two production lines and operated in eleven countries. Such diversified international production means tremendous flexibility for management. It frees corporate finances from dependence on any one product or country. It also increases the capacity of the corporation to artificially manipulate transfer prices. Such a possibility results in lower taxes and higher profits for the corporation, lower revenues for the host government, and higher prices for consumers everywhere.[3]

Third, MNCs operate on the frontiers of technology and dominate research and development. In fact, their capacity to monopolize the development of new technologies and their consequent industrial applications are the keys to the dominance of the MNC in the world economy. It also helps explain their relative power vis-à-vis many nation states (on the conditions of this dominance and power see Fitt et al. 1980:XI-XII).

Development of new technology also accounts for the continued dominance of the world economy by American MNCs. They still, for example, manage to control four-fifths of the computer industry at the cutting edge of new technological developments (*New York Times* 1982 01 02). Since the Second World War these corporations have increasingly shifted their investments into the manufacturing industries of other countries, especially those with advanced technology. Even though American corporations account for less than 10 percent of manufacturing output in western Europe, they own, and otherwise to a considerable extent control, many of its high technology industries. The same applies to American direct investments in Canadian manufacturing, more than 50 percent of which has been foreign-owned since 1957. American capital and ownership is highly concentrated in precisely those industries which are characterized by the most advanced technology.

Most research and development of new technology takes place in corporate headquarters. As a result, many countries are placed in a position of dependence on the MNC with respect to economic and industrial development. Technological dependence is also reflected in the balance of international payments of many countries. These are increasingly in deficit because of royalty charges, patent costs, and bank loans needed to cover the purchase of technology.

A fourth characteristic giving rise to the power of the MNC is the centralization of decision making. All studies on this question (see especially Marchak 1979) agree on one finding. Power relative to overall decision making is concentrated in a small group of senior executives at corporate headquarters. Recent listings by *Fortune* of the top fifty MNCs (Table 1) show that these headquarters are increasingly spread across all advanced capitalist countries—the core of the present world system. Nonetheless, 25 percent are still located in the United States. This number includes seven of the top ten ranked by sales.

The major effects of the centralization of corporate decision making are technological and financial control and the weakening of economic, political, and cultural sovereignty in the countries that host the corporate branch plants. As a consequence, large areas of the world are increasingly subject to the interests and decisions of a small number of corporate owners and managers. Such individuals constitute the major elements of an international capitalist class.[4]

Finally, power in the world capitalist system derives from the collective characteristics of MNCs. In any one industry, for instance, production tends to be dominated by a small number of giant corporations. The consequence is an enormous world scale oligopolistic market power. And since corporations in any industry almost always fix their prices in sympathy with one another, oligopoly in form becomes monopoly in fact. Thus, the world supply and price of major commodities are generally controlled by price-fixing cartels or monopoly associations. These divide the world market among themselves.

The formation of monopolies in key sectors of the world economy must also be seen in conjunction with the speed and frequency of mergers which produce giant world conglomerates. On the basis of present trends it has been estimated (Hymer, quoted in Evans 1971:25, 676) that within the present decade, 300 of these conglomerates control 60 percent to 70 percent of the world's industrial output. In addition, they will account for four-fifths of the productive assets of the non-communist world.

The New International Division of Labor

The conclusion is clear. The integration of the world economy is increasingly based on the MNC rather than on the nation state. This does not mean, however, that the nation state is no longer a significant factor in the world economy. The giant corporations that roam the world in search of profit all have a national base. More importantly, they are both regulated and supported by their respective governments in the national interest.

In actual fact, MNCs have tended to function as the shock-troops of modern imperialism. They are a means of extending American domination over the world system. More recently, with the relative decline of American hegemony vis-à-vis Japan and West Germany in particular, the MNCs, together with a handful of powerful international banks, have created an economic system that supersedes the control of the most powerful states in the capitalist world. As suggested by various studies collected by Sklar (1980), this world system is co-ordinated and run by a small number of industrialists, bankers, and their representatives in the central capitalist states.

The formation of large international corporations and banks has had a significant impact on the structure of the post-war world economy. For one thing, it has broken down the old British-led imperialist division of labor. It had been based on a small core of heavily industrialized capitalist countries trading with a large number of raw material-supplying countries on the periphery. The transnational operations of the largest banks and industrial corporations have replaced this international division with a single world system based on national differences in the price of industrial labor.

With the entire world as their field of operations, the capitalists behind the world's large MNCs naturally seek out the cheapest source of labor. In the process they pit one country against another. With average wage rates between one-sixth to one-twentieth of those that prevail in the advanced capitalist countries, the third world countries of Asia, Africa, and Latin America, have been the obvious targets of international capitalists. Such countries have become the inevitable "beneficiaries" of MNCs' investments and activities.

The immediate result of this development is a dramatic expansion of Third World industrialization since World War II. This increased industrialization is directly related to the foreign operations of the MNCs and the world's largest banks. The role and increasing importance of these banks is reflected in the dramatic increase since World War II of overseas subsidiaries. In the case of those banks based in the United States, the number of overseas subsidiaries has risen from 95 in 1959 to 460 in 1969, and to 874 in 1975 (Munoz 1981:77).

As with the MNCs the banks derive a large and increasing share of their total profits from their operations in the Third World. This explains why so many subsidiaries of large American-based international banks can be found in Latin America—49 in 1959, 235 in 1969, and 529 in 1975. The extra profitability of these branch-plant banking operations is such that a substantial measure of the new wave of third world industrialization is actually financed by local capital. A number of studies point to this. Muller (1973) shows that most of the new capital used to set up or take over manufacturing industries in the Third World (or in Canada for that matter) originates there either as retained earnings or domestic savings. Indeed, the citizens of these countries in effect pay to have foreigners take over their industries.

The internationalization of both capital and the supply of labor has not destroyed the basic metropolis-satellite (centre-periphery) structure of the world economy. Indeed, notwithstanding some important modifications, it may even have reinforced it.

First, the bulk of the Third World's new manufacturing industries, output, and exports are highly concentrated. In fact, by 1973, just two countries, Hong Kong and Korea, accounted for 38.7 percent of all the Third World's manufacturing exports to twenty-one leading developed countries. If one adds to these two countries of the Asian semi-periphery, Brazil, and Mexico, then four countries account for more than half of the Third World's manufacturing output and exports to the advanced capitalist countries.

The 'semi-periphery' countries of the world capitalist system are characterized by relatively high levels of economic growth, industrialization, and middle levels of average income. As for the other so-called "developing countries", all but seven have raw materials as more than half their exports, seventy-six have over 85 percent of their exports as raw materials, and nineteen have almost 100 percent of their exports as raw materials (CWDE 1981:sheet #1). Given that every year raw materials represent a smaller percentage of world trade, and given a strong tendency for the prices of these commodities to deteriorate relative to manufactured products, this heavy dependence on the sale of raw materials and staple goods has meant increasing disparities of income. It has also resulted in a decline of living standards, and high levels of poverty in much of the Third World (North-South CWDE:1980).

Second, most of the new industrialization is geared to the requirements of the large corporations based in the advanced capitalist countries. It is in fact part of the world-wide operations of such companies. Within these operations industry in the Third World and the semi-periphery takes two principal forms.

In the European fringe (Greece, Ireland, Spain, and Turkey) and some countries in Latin America (Brazil, Argentina, and Mexico) industrial production, as in Canada, is largely based on the operations of the MNCs' affiliates and wholly-owned subsidiaries. On the basis of this branch-plant structure, the MNCs gain direct access to important new markets as well as supplies of raw materials, resources, and low-cost labor. Furthermore, their branch-plants allow the MNCs to establish industrial enclaves and export platforms under conditions that are highly favorable for capitalist enterprise. Such conditions include a developed economic infrastructure (public works, transportation and communication, utilities, schools, etc.), a docile, non-unionized workforce, tax concessions, and a "favorable business climate."

In other parts of the Third World, especially in the semi-peripheral economies of the Pacific Rim (Hong Kong, Korea, Singapore, Taiwan, Malaysia), a different industrial structure has developed. Here, the labor intensive lines of industrial production are generally sub-contracted to "independent" firms. Many of them employ fewer than ten or even five individuals. Within this international subcontracting system, the MNCs generally retain control over research and final marketing. They also provide the basic source of technical assistance, management expertise, loan capital, technology, and, in some cases, even physical equipment (Froebel et al. 1980).

The advantages of this international subcontracting strategy for the MNC are obvious. Effective control over production and marketing is retained with minimal or no investment in the firm itself. And it allows the MNC to draw on vast reserves of cheap labor without having to bear the costs, responsibilities, and problems of direct employment. These are largely borne by the growing army of third world subcontractors. Recent studies (Bromley and Gerry 1979) show that such individuals or companies employ up to one-half of the economically active population in many third world cities.

The Class Structure of the Imperialist System

Even allowing for the high-growth, medium income areas of the semi-periphery, the basic structure of the world capitalist system is built on one basic division. A core of rich, highly-industrialized countries in

Western Europe, North America, Japan, Australia and New Zealand is on one side. The under-developed countries of Asia, Africa, and Latin America are on the other side. All indications are that since the end of World War II, despite the political independence of most former colonies, this divide[5] has deepened. The result is progressively greater discrepancies in the quality of life.

The bulk of the world's poor, the vast mass of exploited producers and workers, is found in the Third World. By way of contrast, a disproportionate share of the non-communist world's accumulated wealth is concentrated in the imperialist centres of the capitalist system. The latter, accounting for 27 percent of the world's economically active population in 1975 disposed of 83 percent of the world's total income! The remaining 17 percent was distributed very unevenly among a billion individuals and their families in the dominated peripheral areas of the Third World.

Although per capita income is a very crude indicator of wealth and quality of life, it is, nonetheless, very revealing. At one pole of the world economy, we find societies that represent one-quarter of the world's population. These dispose of at least three-quarters of the accumulated and newly produced wealth and income. They eat 80 percent of its proteins, consume 85 percent of its energy supplies, and receive 80 percent of the world's gross international production of goods and services (Lean 1978). At the other end of the pole, there are more than 800 million people, representing 40 percent of the Third World, living in a state of absolute poverty (*World Development Report* 1978). They want for adequate food, shelter, education, and health care. More than a third are malnourished to the point of physical or mental impairment (Moyes 1981). Besides these "absolutely poor," most of whom live in the under-developed countries of Asia and Africa, many more people do not have access to essential public services such as potable water or education.

The MNCs that dominate the world capitalist system are largely responsible for these conditions. There is, first of all, a historical dimension to the poverty and misery of many people in the Third World. Centuries of colonial plunder and exploitation have exacted their toll. The economies of many countries in Latin America, Africa, and Asia have been seriously underdeveloped and impoverished by the same process that developed and enriched the countries at the centre of the imperialist system (Frank 1967; Magdoff 1969; Rodney *inter alia*). There can be little question about this. However, the contemporary world system is also designed to perpetuate and reproduce the conditions of this underdevelopment.

The international division of production of labor tends to block the autonomous development of third world countries. In addition, there are clear indications that countries in the Third World are still being systematically drained of their wealth and potential capital. The capital investment and aid introduced into the Third World by MNCs work primarily as a pump to drain off larger amounts of capital in the form of repatriated profits, dividends paid to metropolitan shareholders, royalty and patent charges on transferred technology, or management fees.

Vast amounts of capital are also siphoned by the large international banks as interest on loans. In fact, payment and servicing of such loans for many third world countries now consumes a third of all export revenues. Even the substantial revenues derived from Mexico's massive oil reserves do not cover that country's huge foreign debt. In 1980 it exceeded a staggering $60 billion.[6] If one adds to this drain the surplus extracted from third world countries in the form of intrafirm transfer pricing and trade, the drain of capital assumes the proportion of a massive haemorrhage. The economist Samir Amin (1976:133-45) has calculated that third world countries lose at least $22 billion per year in unequal exchange (i.e. underpricing of its commodity exports). This is more than twice what they receive in foreign investment and aid.

When these sums are added to the more direct forms of surplus transfer, the Third World over the years has been a massive exporter of much-needed capital. Such capital inevitably ends up in the metropolitan centres. To be more precise, it falls into the hands (holding companies and banks) of their capitalist classes. Under these conditions, there should be little wonder about the failure of third world countries to escape the vicious circle of underdevelopment.

HIGHLIGHT

1. Since World War II, the United States has clearly occupied a place of prominence in the world capitalist system formerly dominated by Britain.
2. During the same period, multinational corporations have managed to transfer great masses of wealth from peripheral societies to metropolitan societies.
3. The ability of the multinational to dominate world markets is based on its ability to command high technology, its size, its diversity in terms of product lines, its centralization of decision making and its monopoly practices.
4. Since World War II, branch plants of metropolitan centred banks also have become a characteristic feature of imperialism.
5. Although some third world societies, such as Hong Kong and Korea, export a high percentage of manufactured commodities, the majority continue to be suppliers of raw materials.
6. The activities of multinationals in third world societies create a prosperous class of national bourgeoisie. The vast majority, however, dwell in abject poverty. In fact, their position has been declining in recent years.

CANADA AND THE CONTEMPORARY WORLD SYSTEM

How does Canada fit into the basic metropolis-satellite or centre-periphery structure of the contemporary world imperialist system? This question, as noted in Chapter 3, has been the source of much controversy and remains unsettled. On the one hand, as an integral part of the North American capitalist domain, Canada has experienced levels of growth and development characteristic of metropolitan economies. To some extent it has shared in the spoils of empire. On the other hand, Canada is a dependent part of this domain. In a number of respects it has been placed in a similar position to many third world countries. As a result, Canada has experienced some conditions of underdevelopment—capital drain, over-reliance on staple production, and loss of sovereignty.

Canada as a Branch Plant

As we saw in Chapter 3, the roots of this underdevelopment are to some extent historical. Specifically, they can be traced back to the penetration of, and eventual dependence on, American industrial capital. The first instance of such penetration occurred in the latter half of the nineteenth century. British and Canadian capitalists displayed a preference for relatively safe investment outlets in the nonindustrial sectors of the economy. Not surprisingly, a number of American corporations jumped the tariff wall of the Macdonald government's National Policy and began to fill the void by investing in Canadian industry. They also set up branch plants. By 1926, these branch plants had already accounted for 30 percent of Canada's manufacturing assets, 32 percent of those in mining and smelting, 3 percent of railway assets, and 20 percent of all other utilities (Clement 1977:91).

Table 2 indicates that this penetration of the Canadian economy was associated with a shift in the structure and primary source of international capital. In the early years of the twentieth century, around 90 percent of all capital exports took the form of portfolio investments. These originated largely in Great Britain. By the 1960s, this proportion had fallen to one-fifth of total investments. The concomitant expansion of direct investments is associated with the growth of the large multinational corporation, and is the form of investment characteristic of advanced industrial capitalism.

As Table 3 indicates, Canada has been the chief recipient of this growth. It accounts for a high and fairly constant share of all American direct investment. At first, the major outlets of this investment were in resource development and transportation. However, manufacturing in

TABLE 2
Foreign Capital Invested in Canada, Selected Year Ends

(Book value of assets in millions of Canadian dollars)

	1867	1900	1913	1926	1939	1946	1952	1960	1964	1965
U.K. direct	—	65	200	336	336	335	544	1,535	1,944	2,013
portfolio	185	1,000	2,618	2,301	2,110	1,333	1,340	1,824	1,519	1,485
Total	185	1,065	2,818	2,637	2,476	1,668	1,884	3,359	3,463	3,498
U.S. direct	15	175	520	1,403	1,881	2,428	4,532	10,549	12,901	13,940
portfolio	—	30	315	1,793	2,270	2,729	3,466	6,169	8,542	9,365
Total	15	205	835	3,196	4,151	5,157	7,998	16,718	21,443	23,305
Other direct	—	—	50	43	49	63	144	788	1,044	1,255
portfolio	—	35	147	127	237	290	358	1,349	1,404	1,449
Total	—	35	197	170	286	353	502	2,137	2,448	2,704
All direct	15	240	770	1,782	2,296	2,826	5,220	12,872	15,889	17,208
All portfolio	185	1,065	3,080	4,221	4,617	4,352	5,164	9,342	11,465	12,299
GRAND TOTAL	200	1,305	3,850	6,003	6,913	7,179	10,384	22,214	27,354	29,507
Direct as percentage of total foreign investment	7.5	18.5	20.0	30.0	33.5	39.0	50.0	58.0	58.0	58.3
U.S. as percentage of total foreign investment	7.5	15.5	21.5	53.0	60.0	72.0	77.0	75.0	78.5	79.0

SOURCE: Dominion Bureau of Statistics, The Canadian Balance of International Payments, 1963, 1964 and 1965 and International Investment Position, p. 126, and Quarterly Estimates of the Canadian Balance of International Payments, Third Quarter 1968, p. 17. Computations and tabulation by Levitt (1970:67).

Canada already accounted for 40 percent of American direct investments in 1935. The figure was a result largely of the broadening of the United States market to include Canada. It was likewise a means of overcoming the tariffs and other barriers to free trade erected in Canada, especially in the 1930s. After the Second World War, however, American corporations increasingly turned their investments toward manufacturing and the production of oil as part of their global strategy.

In 1929, less than 40 percent of American direct investment abroad was in manufacturing and petroleum. By 1950, the share of manufacturing and petroleum had risen to 61 percent. There was a particularly strong upsurge of direct investment in these activities in the late 1950s and the 1960s. The lion's share of this new investment went to Canada.

From 1958 to 1966, the book value of all accumulated direct investments in Canada from the United States increased from $27 billion to $55 billion. Seventy percent was concentrated in manufacturing and petroleum. The scale of these investments is staggering.

In 1966, 31 percent of the assets of all United States' foreign affiliates were located in a country—Canada—with a population of only twenty million. Canada was host to 47 percent of all mining and smelting subsidiaries, 35 percent of the manufacturing subsidiaries, and 22 percent of all petroleum extracting and refining subsidiaries (Levitt 1970:164).

The most immediate impact of this foreign investment has been on the ownership of industry and the structure of trade in Canada. In spite of various changes in the pattern of American direct investment, *Canada*

TABLE 3
Geographic Distribution of U.S. Direct Investment, 1897-1966

	1897	1914	1924	1935	1958	1964	1966
	Book value in millions of U.S. $						
Europe	131.0	573.0	921.0	1,369.0	4,382	12,100	16,200
Canada	159.7	618.4	1,080.5	1,692.4	8,939	13,800	16,840
Mexico	200.2	587.1	735.4	651.7			
Latin America	59.1	413.7	1,090.6	1,878.2	8,700	8,000	9,854
All other countries	84.5	460.8	1,560.9	1,627.3	5,034	9,500	11,668
TOTAL	634.5	2,653.0	5,388.7	7,219.2	27,075	44,300	54,562
	in percentages						
Europe	20.6	21.7	17.4	19.0	16.2	27.0	29.6
Canada	25.3	23.4	20.0	23.5	32.0	31.0	31.0
Mexico	31.5	22.3	13.7	9.0			
Latin America	9.3	15.7	20.2	26.0	32.2	20.0	18.1
All other countries	13.3	17.0	28.7	21.5	18.6	22.0	21.3
TOTAL	100.0	100.0	100.0	100.0	100.0	100.0	100.0

SOURCE: Levitt 1970:160-61.

TABLE 4
Foreign Direct Investment in Canada by Sector[1], 1926-78

Sector	Percentage of foreign-owned assets in each sector in:							
	1926	1948	1957	1959	1962	1972	1974	1978
Manufacturing	38	42	50	51	54	56	57	53
Petroleum and gas	.	.	64	62	63	79	99[2]	73[3]
Mining and smelting	37	.	56	59	.	65	60	47[3]
Railways	55	.	30	.	.	.	.	.
Other Utilities	32	.	15	.	.	.	.	.

SOURCES: Porter (1965:267); Safarian (1966:14); Calura (1972, 1974, 1978).

(1) Except for the early years only the productive sectors of the economy are listed with statistics based on the total number of corporations classified by ownership. The other sectors (construction, utilities, trade, and services) are largely Canadian owned. Thus, for the economy as a whole, 29 percent of all assets are foreign controlled. 66 percent of the total assets are, in fact, accounted for by 500 corporations, almost one half of which are foreign controlled.

(2) Only petroleum and coal products here included. To this point, industry consisted almost entirely of large foreign MNCs.

(3) The significant decline in foreign control of the petroleum, gas, and mining sectors (8 percent drop from 1977 level) is largely the result of a dramatic increase in the capitalisation of Petro-Canada Exploration Inc., a subsidiary of Petro-Canada, which in 1978 more than doubled its assets and increased its equity more than ten-fold.

has more foreign ownership than all of the other industrialized countries combined. It is by far the largest branch-plant economy in the world. No other country comes close to Canada in the share of its major industries owned and therefore controlled by foreign enterprises.

Table 4 shows that this foreign ownership is especially pronounced in resource extraction and manufacturing. In the resource sector, foreign ownership of assets in some industries (petroleum and coal production) goes as high as 92 percent. Likewise in the manufacturing sector, foreign (largely American) ownership is particularly pronounced in the most concentrated, high technology industries. These include primary metals, petroleum and coal, rubber, chemicals, machinery, and transport equipment. Altogether, by 1975, 423 manufacturing firms, 1.5 percent of the total, accounted for 69.5 percent of all assets, 61.3 percent of all sales, and 69.1 percent of all profits in manufacturing. Of these 423 firms, 66 percent were foreign-owned. This number included six of the top ten industrials, all of which are subsidiaries of American corporations. Indeed they are, for the most part, the very same corporations that dominate the world economy.

The Consequences of Foreign Ownership

The impact of this foreign ownership on Canadian society is enormous. Not only is it evident in economic dependence, but it is reflected in various patterns of political and cultural dependence as well as in our structural underdevelopment.[7] This economic dependence particularly affects Canada's industry and trade policies. These, in turn, determine Canada's position in the world system within which Canadians generally have to live and work.

Capital Drain.   The dependent structure of Canada's industry and trade is reflected, first of all, in a clear pattern of capital drain from Canada into the United States. The process has been in evidence throughout the imperialist phase of capitalist development. In the first place, a number of studies have found that less than 10 percent of American investments in, and takeovers of, Canadian industry involved an actual inflow of capital (Pattison 1978).[8] Most of these listed investments were derived from retained earnings or money borrowed from Canadian banks. Table 5 illustrates this pattern for various years from 1963 to 1976.

Not only does foreign investment in Canadian industry involve little actual capital inflow, but also the capital that is imported from the United

TABLE 5
Sources of Capital for American-owned Subsidiaries Located
Outside the United States
(Annual Averages)

	Total Investment ($ millions)	Reinvested profits	Capital from the United States	Domestic sources (loans, depreciation, amortization, etc.)
	(in percentages)			
Canada				
1963-1965	42.4		11.4	46.2(17.9)*
All Countries				
1966-1968	$1,778.0	66.8	4.6	28.6
1969-1971	2,813.3	48.4	13.6	38.0
Canada				
1972	30.0		6.0	64.0(19.0)*
Latin America				
1972	2.0		26.0	72.0(33.0)*
Other Third World Countries				
1972	15.0		12.0	73.0(39.0)*
Europe				
1972	18.0		9.0	73.0(30.0)*
All Countries				
1972-1974	6,987.0	47.8	−28.0	80.2
1975-1976	7,127.0	46.5	23.4	30.1

*Figures in parentheses refer to the percentage of capital in the form of domestic loans.

SOURCES: Levitt (1970:180-81); Fitt et al. (1980:38); U.S. Department of Commerce (1979).

States is used largely to take over existing profitable Canadian firms and to generate a substantial surplus. The foreign operations of American-controlled corporations are so profitable that their annual remittances of dividends, royalties, licence fees, rentals, and management charges substantially exceed the annual outflow of American capital. This has been so for every single year since 1900. The sole exception is the depression period between 1928-1931. In these years American corporations used available financial resources to purchase bankrupt businesses in foreign countries (Levitt 1970:164). However, even in these years, American corporations reaped returns from their Canadian investments five times greater than new capital deployed.

In the post war period, the total inflow of short- and long-term investments into Canada from all foreign sources was $20.3 billion. Hurtig (1976:11) estimates that this investment cost Canada $40.9 billion—$24.4 billion in remitted dividends and interests and $16.5 billion in service charges. Table 6, which breaks down the capital income account of the United States by geographic regions and industries, shows

TABLE 6
Capital Income Accounts According to Industrial and Geographic Sectors, 1950-1964
(in millions of U.S. dollars)

	Western Europe	Canada	America	All other Countries	Total
PETROLEUM					
Outflow U.S. Capital	−2,474	−2,401	−1,272	−1,818	−7,265
Income to U.S.	+971	+595	+5,951	+9,758	+17,275
Balance	−1,503	−1,806	+4,679	+7,940	+9,310
MANUFACTURING					
Outflow U.S. Capital	−2,945	−1,429	−1,114	−616	−6,104
Income to U.S.	+3,687	+3,261	+1,227	+1,119	+9,294
Balance	+742	+1,832	+113	+503	+3,190
TRADE					
Outflow U.S. Capital	−1,093	−972	−631	−356	−3,052
Income to U.S.	+1,413	+1,385	+2,220	+1,001	+6,013
Balance	+320	+413	+1,589	+645	+2,967
MINING AND SMELTING					
Outflow U.S. Capital	—	−1,105	−610	−261	−1,976
Income to U.S.	—	+673	+1,610	+521	+2,804
Balance	—	−432	+1,000	+260	+828
ALL INDUSTRIES					
Total Outflow U.S. Capital	−6,512	−5,907	−3,627	−3,051	−19,097
Total Income to U.S.	+6,071	+5,914	+11,008	+12,399	+35,392
BALANCE	−441	+7	+7,381	+9,345	+16,295

SOURCE: Compiled by Levitt (1970:166) from United States Department of Commerce, *Balance of Payments Statistical Supplement*, 1963, and *Survey of Current Business*, various issues.

that Canadian manufacturing was a particularly important source of capital income for American corporations.

Over the critical period of expansion (1960-64), the Canadian manufacturing subsidiaries of these corporations contributed $1.8 billion, or almost two-thirds of America's favorable balance on its capital-income account. Levitt (1970:105) notes that this large outflow of Canadian capital occurred in spite of relatively low profit ratios and high rates of profit retention in manufacturing. The explanation offered is that many of these American subsidiaries were established so long ago that the value of their assets had increased manifold with constant ploughing back of profits. In fact, Daniel Drache (1975:9), by taking into account these retained earnings, found that the $37 billion invested by American capitalists in Canada over the whole period 1900-67 had realized total profits of $130 billion. A handsome dividend indeed!

A brief glimpse at the most recently available data shows no change in this basic pattern. In 1980, the subsidiaries of American corporations remitted $19 billion in profits and interest (representing an 18.4 percent return on capital) and $5.7 billion in royalties and fees. They reinvested $17 billion in retained earnings for further expansion (*Survey of Current Business* August 1981). The actual outflow of new capital was a mere $1.5 billion, the lowest since 1959. The relatively low outflow resulted in a favorable balance on the capital income account of an astounding $24 billion (including an $8.2 billion adjustment in assets). Canada, by itself, contributed almost 28 percent ($6.7 billion) of this total.

Industrial Underdevelopment.   The direct transfer of capital as dividends, interests, rents, and service charges is one of the more obvious consequences of direct foreign investment and ownership. As noted earlier, dependency theorists generally argue that this capital drain is a major cause of economic underdevelopment. Some economists, however, argue that it is an acceptable cost of attracting the investment capital, technology, and entrepreneurship necessary to develop a country's economy. These economists emphasize the positive aspects of foreign direct investment in the development of Canada's resource and manufacturing industries. Indeed, Canada's high levels of per capita income and other indicators of economic growth and social development are largely attributed by these economists to the advantages of being a resource-rich hinterland of American industry. As an extension and an integrated part of the American economy, it is argued, Canada has benefited from direct access to its superior financial resources, technological developments, and large markets.

What this position fails to consider, however, are the structural sources of underdevelopment inherent in a branch-plant economy. For one thing, as an essential appendage of American capital, the Canadian economy is locked into a division of production and labor that inhibits, distorts, or otherwise unbalances its industrial development. This is perhaps most readily apparent in the structure of Canada's external trade.

First, like that of most third world countries, Canada's economy is disproportionate to and dependent on export markets. In 1968, when exports made up only 4 percent of the GNP of the United States, the Canadian GNP comprised 24 percent in exports (*Fortune* 84 1971:144-49; in Clement 1977:35). Throughout the 1970s this ratio of exports to GNP was held fairly constant.

Second, Canada's external trade is largely with one country. In 1976, 67.1 percent of Canada's exports and 68.7 percent of its imports were with the United States. While this trade dependence has long been characteristic of Canada, its intensity has increased rapidly since World War II. Writing at the beginning of the 1960s, Aitken (1961:7) noted: "Since Canada became a nation in 1867, the value of Canadian-American trade has increased some eighty-fold [while]...total world trade... increased only about twenty times." Various data compiled by Clement (1977:86) show that the volume of this trade has continued to grow, and with it the density of Canada's trade relationship with the United States.

Third, the strong dependence on trade with the United States throughout the twentieth century does not mean that over the years little has changed in Canada's economic relations with the United States. In actual fact, the nature of these relations in the post-war era has changed in an important way from earlier relations at the turn of the century. Then, trade between the United States and Canada was largely conducted by separate firms. Capitalists in Canada bought from and sold their goods to capitalists in the United States. Now, however, after the massive onslaught of direct American investment in Canada, around 75 percent of all trading by foreign-controlled companies in Canada involves intracompany transfers. These occur within one corporation that straddles the American boundary (Clement 1977:86-87). What proportion of total Canadian trade this involves is unknown. However, as Clement points out, "the fact that most of the key exporting activities are foreign-controlled suggests that the proportion is high" (1977:87).

This intrafirm structure of trade has important consequences. For one thing, it provides a mechanism for the hidden transfer of surplus value and capital income. By selling their Canadian subsidiaries component parts at inflated prices and charging them excessive rates for the use of technology, management fees, and other services, the parent company is able to substantially lower the level of declared taxable profits in Canada. Various studies (see for example Levitt 1970:164-68) suggest that this practice is employed extensively in both Latin America and Canada. It is a significant factor in the capital-income accounts of the largest American-based transnational corporations.

Another and perhaps more important consequence of Canada's

branch-plant economy is reflected in the types of goods that are exported and imported. With respect to Canadian exports, one study found that (excluding automobiles and auto parts) only 15 percent involved completely manufactured goods. This compared with 51.9 percent for West Germany, 51.4 percent for the United States, 39.2 percent for Denmark, 29.3 percent for Norway, 57.1 percent for Japan, 71.4 percent for Hong Kong, and 51.1 percent for South America (Williams 1976:29). With manufacturing exports in recent years averaging less than 15 percent of all its commodity exports, and less than 2 percent of its GNP, Canada tends to perform near the very bottom of the industrially advanced capitalist countries.

As for the other side of trade, Canada imports more manufactured goods per capita than any of the above countries. It imports twice the European average and four times that of the United States (Clement 1977:86). In 1975, Canada imported $10 billion more manufactured end products than it exported. Of these 85 percent came from the United States. The resulting deficit in Canada's manufacturing trade is absolutely staggering. In 1966, it was already $3.4 billion. By 1977 it had climbed to $11.1 billion. This sum translates into almost $500 for every Canadian (Laxer and Laxer 1977:33). This massive deficit did not result in the collapse of Canada's economy only because of the enormous exports of Canadian industrial raw materials to the United States.

By the end of the 1950s, over 70 percent of Canada's exports to the United States comprised raw materials and resources (Aitken 1961:74-75). Since then Canada has continued to function largely as a resource base for American industry. In 1972-1973, nearly one-third of American imports of industrial raw materials, fuels, and lubricants came from Canada (Teeple 1977:28). Clearly this trade pattern and the economic structure that lies behind it are extensively shaped by the priorities and requirements of American corporations.

To appreciate fully the consequences of foreign ownership on the Canadian economy, it is necessary to take a close look at the structure of Canada's merchandise trade with the United States. Not only is it characterized by an exchange of raw materials for manufactured goods—a classic pattern of the old imperialism—but there is an obvious and important difference between the type of manufactured goods that Canada exports and those that it imports. The most significant distinction is the high knowledge (i.e., technology and skilled labor) involved in the manufactured imports. Table 7 illustrates this very clearly with respect to 1970 and 1975.

These imports are produced by precisely those industries that are expanding in the world economy. They include the strategic sector of highly productive manufacturing industries that are based on the most advanced technological research. The marked dependence of the Canadian economy on manufacturing imports of this type reflects a basic

TABLE 7
Balance Of Trade In Higher Technology
Manufacturing By Principal Industrial Groups
(in $million)

	1970		Year Ended 1975 09 30		Year Ended 1975 09 10 Compared with 1970 Effect on Balance of Payments
	Net Exports	Net Imports	Net Exports	Net Imports	
1) Manmade Fibres	—	19.8	—	28.8	−9.0
2) Chemicals	—	175.2	—	466.1	−290.0
3) Petroleum & Coal Products	—	115.0	292.2	—	+407.0
4) Industrial Machinery	—	278.9	—	703.2	−424.3
5) Mechanical Handling Equipment	—	57.3	—	229.8	−108.9
6) Other Industrial Machinery	—	656.6	—	1279.0	−622.4
7) Agricultural Machinery	—	132.2	—	690.8	−558.5
8) Rail Locomotives & Rolling Stock	—	12.7	—	51.8	−39.1
9) Road Transport Equipment	295.4	—	—	1763.3	−2058.7
10) Aircraft & Parts	46.1	—	—	219.8	−265.9
11) Other Vehicles	—	6.9	—	33.0	−26.1
12) Communications Equipment	—	129.3	—	481.7	−352.4
13) Heating, Refrigeration, Air Conditioning Equipment	—	78.6	—	183.5	−104.9
14) Misc. Domestic & Comm'l Appliances	—	322.9	—	675.3	−352.4
15) Measuring & Control Equipment	—	177.3	—	318.4	−141.1
16) Tools	—	54.1	—	142.5	−88.4
17) Office machinery	—	182.3	—	348.6	−166.3
18) Pharmaceutical Supplies	—	124.8	—	289.4	−164.6
19) Photographic Goods	—	136.3	—	312.8	−176.5
TOTAL	—	2318.9	—	7925.9	−5607.0

SOURCE: Information supplied by Statistics Canada
Trade Analysis Branch (G. Dines 18/11/75)

problem with its branch-plant industrial structure. Technological research and development is largely done elsewhere, generally the United States.

Technological dependence, a major feature of all branch-plant economies, is reflected particularly in the very low rate of technological research and innovation undertaken in Canadian industry. A 1969 study by OECD that compared technological research and development activity among the ten most advanced industrialized countries placed Canada ninth on one index and tenth on three others (Bourgault 1972). In the same vein, a more recent study found that the ratio of research and development to GNP in Canada over the last decade has been only 25 percent to 40 percent of that in the other industrialized countries. It was further found that this ratio has declined from 1.24 in 1970 to 1.03 in 1976 (McMillan 1978:45).

The significance of technological dependence for Canada is brought out in two studies commissioned by the Science Council of Canada. Both studies (Cordell 1971 and Bourgault 1972) are concerned with explaining the basic weakness and the dramatic decline of Canadian manufacturing over the last two decades. The extent of this decline can be traced out in a study by Richard Starke (1978).

The Starke study shows a relative decline in the manufacturing sector of the Canadian economy, in terms of the value of total production, share of total employment, and, as we have already noted, in the manufacturing content of Canada's exports. The decline had reached such critical proportions by the mid-1970s that social scientists began to talk widely of a process of de-industrialization (Laxer 1973; Drache 1977; inter alia). As the Cordell and Bourgeault studies make clear, this de-industrialization or relative decline of manufacturing has nothing to do with access to or failure to attract foreign capital. To the contrary. It is linked to certain structural trends in the world economy and a strategic dependence on the multinational corporations. These dominate key sectors of the Canadian economy.

For one thing, technical research and development by MNCs are highly centralized. For another, as Bourgeault argues, the crisis of Canadian manufacturing arises out of a situation which forces Canadian firms to compete on the domestic market with affiliates of foreign firms. The latter have direct access to the parent company's superior technology and reserves of capital. As a result, Canadian manufacturing is caught in a double-squeeze. On the one hand, the more labor-intensive or resource-based manufacturing industries come under increasing pressure from third world countries in the new international division of labor. On the other hand, with so much of its economy controlled by foreign capital, Canada is in no position to compete with other industrialized nations for the development of science-intensive industries.

Is Canada an Imperialist Power?

Canada is the largest recipient of foreign investment of any country in the world—$47 billion by 1977. Along with this foreign capital Canada has acquired all of the problems associated with a branch-plant econ-

omy, including the weakening of economic, political, and cultural sovereignty. However, Canada is not just on the receiving end of these
problems. As suggested earlier, throughout much of the twentieth century, it has been the fifth or sixth largest exporter of investment capital in
the capitalist world. Indeed, in 1960 it was the third largest.

On a per capita basis, the volume of exported capital up to the Second
World War was substantial. But what of the contemporary period in
which a significant part of the Canadian economy has been reduced to
an appendage of American industrial capital? Tables 8 and 9 tell the tale.
They indicate very clearly that Canada has continued its dual role as a
resource market for American industrial capital and as an important
source of investment capital. It is both a colony and an imperialist power.
Indeed, despite its increasing dependence on American capital in the
1960s and early 1970s, since 1975 Canada has exported more capital in
the form of direct investment than it received.

Table 8 shows a direct investment outflow of over $8.8 billion between
1975 and 1980. With an inflow of $2.2 billion, the net outflow is a
startling $6.6 billion. In keeping with the strategy of multinational
corporations, most of this Canadian investment is located in the rich
market areas of the United States, England and West Germany. However, over the period 1973-1977, Canadian direct investment in developing countries increased by over 70 percent. According to a study by the
Organization for Economic Co-operation and Development (OECD), the

TABLE 8
Direct Investment Flows, 1970-1980
($ millions)

Year	INTO CANADA (+)	OUT OF CANADA (−)	BALANCE (surplus +, or deficit −)
1970	905	315	+590
1971	925	230	+695
1972	620	400	+220
1973	830	770	−60
1974	845	810	+35
1975	725	915	−190
1976	−300*	590	−890
1977	475	740	−265
1978	85	2,010	−1,925
1979	675	1,945	−1,270
1980	535	2,675	−2,140

*A negative figure in the inflow column represents the net of this year's direct
investment inflow and the sale of foreign-owned assets in Canada to Canadians or
Canadian governments.

SOURCE: Statistics Canada, *Quarterly Estimates of the Canadian Balance of
International Payments* (various years). Compiled by LAWG letter, vii. 1/2
(1981), p. 3.

TABLE 9
Canadian Investment Abroad By Location Of Investment,
Selected Years And Countries
($ millions)

	1960	1965	1970	1973	1975	1977
United States	1,632	2,041	3,251	3,926	5,559	7,027
United Kingdom	257	482	586	798	1,019	1,410
Other Europe	90	198	489	652	846	1,250
Australia	71	141	246	397	453	442
Asia	32	65	134	201	317	559
(of which) Japan				72	74	61
Africa	68	72	134	125	167	198
(of which) South Africa			73	104	126	123
Latin America and Caribbean	331	470	1,328	1,700	2,133	2,519
Bahamas			151	178	147	148
Bermuda			136	351	462	408
Jamaica			109	115	118	112
Trinidad and Tobago					24	29
Other Caribbean			67	104	108	154
Mexico			45	54	75	65
Venezuela			12	12	19	22
Brazil					1,039	1,403
Argentina			808	891	39	57
Other Latin America					102	121
Total All Countries	2,481	3,469	6,188	7,835	10,526	13,443
Total Developed Countries		2,915	4,675	5,953	8,070	10,243
Total Developing Countries		554	1,513	1,882	2,456	3,200
as % of all countries		16.0%	24.3%	24.0%	23.3%	23.8%

SOURCE: Dominion Bureau of Statistics and Statistics Canada, *"Canada's international investment position"* (various years).
Compiled by LAWG, letter vii, 1/2 (1981) p. 4.

share of total Canadian direct investment flows allocated to the Third World increased from 17 percent in the 1969-1970 two-year period, to 61 percent in the 1975-1976 period (Paris: OECD 1978; in LAWG letter 1981:3). As indicated in Table 9 most of this investment is concentrated in Latin America, and especially in the Caribbean islands where Canada has long been the principal agent of economic imperialism.

According to Statistics Canada (1980), close to 70 percent of all Canadian foreign investment is accounted for by just twenty-two corporations. Of these, fifteen corporations control 168 of the 270 Canadian subsidiaries found in Latin America (LAWG letter 1981:8). The key question is: who owns or controls these companies incorporated in Canada?

Given the foreign control of so much of Canada's economy it might be supposed that Canada's foreign investments represent a form of "subimperialism," i.e., a means of channelling ownership and investment in the Third World through Canada. This is evidently the case for Falconbridge

Nickel Mines Ltd. It is listed as Canadian by the criteria of stock ownership (at least 51 percent is held in Canada). However, it is effectively controlled by the Superior Oil Company of Houston, Texas. There are further indications that foreign-controlled Canadian firms are much more inclined to invest in the Third World than their controlled-in-Canada counterparts.

Despite these indications of subimperialism, many corporations, for example, Seagrams, Brascan, Noranda, Massey-Ferguson, Molson's, and the Moore Corporation, are overwhelmingly Canadian. Statistics Canada, moreover, reports that in 1977 Canadian-controlled corporations accounted for 85 percent of Canada's foreign investment. The proportion is even higher if investment in the Third World is analysed by itself (LAWG letter 1981:4-5).

Since Canada is presently ranked as the sixth or seventh largest foreign investor in the capitalist world, the conclusion is fairly clear. Canada continues to play a dual role in the world capitalist order. Hence, Canada both depends on, and participates in, the foreign investment that contributes to the underdevelopment of third world countries. As long as capitalism prevails in the world economy, Canada will not likely escape the double consequences of this position.

HIGHLIGHT

1. In the twentieth century, British portfolio investment in Canada has been replaced increasingly by direct investment in manufacturing by the United States.
2. Canada has a greater degree of foreign ownership of its economy than all other industrialized countries combined.
3. The consequences of foreign ownership include a drain of capital and underdevelopment. Indeed, in recent years, Canada has experienced what is called de-industrialization. In other words, Canada has become more and more dependent on the production of raw materials for export, rather than on the export of manufactured goods.
4. Although Canada in many ways has a branch-plant economy, Canadian-based corporations also invest in third world countries. While in some cases this is a form of subimperialism, much of this investment emanates from bona fide Canadian-owned corporations. Hence, Canada both depends on and participates in the foreign investment that contributes to the underdevelopment of third world countries.

CRISIS AND CHANGE IN THE WORLD IMPERIALIST SYSTEM

The rate of economic growth and the pace of industrial development after the Second World War was unprecedented in the history of capitalism. As a result many political and economic leaders in capitalist countries argued that capitalism had finally overcome its internal contradictions detected by Marx a century earlier. These pronouncements aside, subsequent developments indicate very clearly that capitalism has not changed its nature in the least. It is as crisis-ridden as ever. Indeed, after a number of minor recessions (downturns in industrial production and economic growth) spanning several years, all of the advanced capitalist countries, to varying degrees, have been hit by the worst structural crisis since the 1930s.

For the capitalist world overall, statistics for the 1973-1976 period reflect a decline of 1 percent in the GNP, an 8.8 percent increase in the cost of living, a miniscule increase (0.6 percent) in the level of industrial production, a 23.6 percent increase in the rate of unemployment, a 10 percent decline in the level of industrial profits, a 5 percent decline (adjusted for inflation) in sales, a 20 percent decline in housing starts, and a 3 percent decline in general purchasing power.

The fact that nearly a decade later none of the capitalist countries has been able to shake off fully the effects of this crisis indicates a disturbance much more serious than a mere fluctuation in an ordinary business cycle. In fact, the emergence of stagflation (combined stagnation and inflation) in the mid-1970s and its persistence into the 1980s suggest that the entire capitalist system is in the throes of its most severe structural crisis to date.

What are the elements of this crisis? Various studies suggest four major dimensions: (1) a declining rate of average profit at the centre of the system; (2) a resurgence of interimperialist rivalry; (3) an energy crisis triggered by the formation of OPEC (a cartel of oil producing countries) and the dramatic increase since 1973 of the world price of oil; and (4) the resurgence of economic nationalism. Economic nationalism is a response to the power and metropolitan interests of the MNCs that dominate the world economy and to the nation states that support them.

The Falling Rate of Profit

According to Marx, the propensity of capitalism toward crisis is based on its inherent tendency toward a falling rate of average profit. In retrospect, it is possible to see how the capitalist system was able to offset this tendency throughout the boom period of 1948-1967. In the first place, massive exports of investment capital were used to exploit large reserves of cheap labor and to pillage the Third World of its energy and mineral resources. This pillage was based on the monopoly structure of international trade. By broadening the gap between the prices of products manufactured in the metropolitan centres of the system and commodities produced on the periphery, the metropolitan-based multinational corporations increased their yield of surplus value. In the process they reduced two-thirds of humanity to ruin and poverty. In Latin America alone, the drain of surplus value increased a deficit of working capital from $10 billion to $60 billion in a few years.

A second factor offsetting the tendency toward a falling rate of profit was the rapid scientific and technological development in the post-war period (Vigier 1980). As Marx had theorized for an earlier period, an accelerated pace of technological improvements has a contradictory effect on capitalist development. On the one hand, it substantially increases the productivity of labor. It thus offsets pressure on profits to decline. This increased productivity was a major factor in the economic expansion and prosperity of the 1950s and 1960s in metropolitan countries. On the other hand, general technological progress considerably shortens the time in which a particular corporation can take advantage of its market position. As a result, investments must be renewed faster and faster. Consequently, the organic composition of capital (c/v) tends to increase. The net result is a tendency for the average rate of profit to fall.

Vigier (1980:120) points out that a declining rate of profit was redressed by larger and more frequent injections of investment capital. Capital infusion explains why, after a sudden rise, from 5 percent in 1945 to 20 percent in the 1950s, the average rate of profit in advanced capitalist economies gradually declined. It fell to 10 percent in 1965 and to less than 5 percent by 1973.

Interimperialist Rivalry

History has been punctuated by periods of acute rivalry and of relative peace among capitalist countries. Those of peace are distinguished by long waves of economic growth that coincide with a fairly well-coordinated system of production, a stable division of labor, and, as a rule, a firmly established hierarchy of nations with one hegemonic power (Amin 1981:33). Periods of acute rivalry, on the other hand, are distinguished by:

> long waves of relatively slow growth associated with an increasingly unstable structure of the world capitalist system: the social and class alliances that helped maintain the preceding stability began to break up; international competition intensifies; the preceding hierarchial arrangements among nations is challenged; and consequently international alliances and the international division of labor are subject to change. . . . These features . . . are signs of a deep crisis, very different from the typical business-cycle decline (Amin 1981:33-34).

There is little question that the world capitalist system is presently in another phase of general crisis. This one is similar to the twenty-year period between the First and the Second World Wars. Then Germany and the United States struggled for succession to Great Britain as the hegemonic power. The United States emerged from the Second World

War as the stronger power. For a time its clear dominance ended inter-imperialist rivalry.

By the late 1960s, the United States had fallen victim to the very forces it had set in motion. For one thing, it had lost its overwhelming advantage in world markets over its competitors, especially Japan and Germany. The domestic industries of these two countries had developed a competitive edge. In addition, they were steadily increasing their share of the world's industrial production. The relative decline of the less productive American economy and the loss of its hegemony since the mid-1960s is evident in newspapers and in a number of recent studies. Among other things, these studies show a sharp decline in exports of manufactured products: from about 30 percent of total world exports in 1953 to 16 percent in 1976 (*MR* 33/5 1981:12).

The loss of hegemony involves more than interimperialist rivalry. It also reflects the trend toward a new international division of industrial labor. That is, the relative decline of the American economy in the world capitalist system is the inevitable result of the rapid expansion of the large MNCs. Increasingly, these corporations are no longer tied to the expansion of a national economy. Indeed, the capital of a particular country embodied in these corporations can be relatively strong and expansive while the national economy is relatively weak or in decline. This is certainly the case for Great Britain. And it is equally the case for the United States. By 1974, according to the Paris-based organization for Economic Co-operation and Development (OECD), the United States "is and will remain the most depressed of all major countries" (Heron, 46).

Why is this the case when the American corporations that dominate the world economy are doing so well? As indicated in the August 1980 issue of *Fortune*, the world's fifty largest corporations are generally exempt from the recession which has set in and is working its way through each industrialized country. American corporations are not governed by nationalist policies. They are ruled by laws of international competition and profit maximization. "Even American Imperialism," as Moore and Wills note, "is subject to the laws governing the world imperialist system" (1977:46).

This general point can be easily illustrated by automobile production. It involves three of the top ten multinationals and employs close to one out of every six American workers. In the United States this industry has been in a state of perpetual and deepening crisis since the early 1970s. One result has been massive layoffs in major cities. However, the three corporations that dominate this industry, throughout the same period of disinvestment and layoffs at home, were heavily involved in expanded production overseas. The policy of these automobile companies was necessarily determined by a need to maximize profits, not by American nationalism. This same policy applies to the other large MNCs, the top 100 of which in 1974 already accounted for more than half of all manufacturing assets and income in the United States. Constrained by laws of capital accumulation that have begun to operate on a global scale, these MNCs themselves are largely responsible for the structural crisis in the American economy (see Harrington 1980).

The Energy Crisis and Economic Nationalism

By 1970, the tendency for a falling rate of profit clearly had surfaced. It led to a drastic decline in investment and industrial production in the major capitalist countries. For several years, however, this decline was masked by a proportional expansion of credit extended by the large international banks. While the resulting accumulation of huge debt in each country kept the wheels of industry turning, it also fueled a strong inflationary tendency. By 1973, this tendency had worked itself through each capitalist economy. It drastically reduced the purchasing capacity of consumers. Then OPEC struck.

Overnight, the price of oil, the most critical source of energy for the industrial economies of the western world, increased four-fold. The effect on capitalist economy was almost instantaneous. Within a year the economies of western Europe and Japan were thrown into the worst recession since the 1930s. No country was immune. Even the United States' economy which had gone into recession earlier, and was not as directly affected by the OPEC action, moved more deeply into recession. By November 1972, there were already 4.3 million unemployed in the United States. Within a year this number climbed to 7 million. The industries in the forefront of technological advance were worse hit (Fitt et al. 1980:156). In the other industrialized countries the story was substantially the same.

This generalized crisis of the capitalist system has provoked a number of responses from the nation states involved. One of the responses has been economic nationalism (Girvan 1980).

In the Third World, the excessive power of the MNCs, mono-export dependence, and the imperialism of aid and trade have been long-standing issues. However, in the context of a world recession and the cartelization of oil production, economic nationalism was given an added impetus.

This was especially true for countries producing strategic and important sources of primary commodities such as bauxite, phosphate, copper, tin, and coffee. In order for these countries to gain greater control over their resource-based economies, and to arrest or reverse the deteriorating terms of their trade, they have increasingly insisted on state participation in corporate ventures and ownership. They have explored or formed themselves into OPEC-like producing cartels. More generally they have made a collective call for a New International Economic Order (NIEC). However, despite various sources of leverage (interimperialist rivalry, the rise of a non-aligned movement, the expansion of the socialist bloc, and the development in the Third World of state capitalism) this resurgence of economic nationalism has had little impact so far on the basic situation of third world countries.

In countries like Australia and Canada, that have the structural characteristics of a developed economy but predominantly foreign ownership in their manufacturing and resource industries, economic nationalism has taken a different form. Here, the issue has been posed in terms of the limited effectiveness of traditional techniques of economic control and regulation in the context of a branch-plant economy. This was very clearly expressed by Herb Gray, Canada's minister of regional and industrial development:

> The considerable and growing extent to which Canada's economic activity is foreign- and especially U.S.-dominated has led to the emergence in the country of an industrial structure which reflects mainly the growth priorities of foreign firms. Many of these firms have invested in Canada in order to extend the market for their manufactured products. As a result Canada finds itself imprisoned in a system of technological development and innovation which is remote-controlled from abroad. Other enterprises have invested in Canada in order to extract natural resources which will be consumed in the firms' country of origin. In both cases, to the extent that these enterprises are influenced by their home environment, their investment decisions reflect the priorities of foreign economic systems or governments. In turn, this evolution has contributed to the *integration of Canada into the world economy* in a way which may make it difficult for the country to achieve its own growth and employment targets.
>
> Another aspect of this foreign domination is the apparition of *truncated* enterprises, many of whose most important functions are carried out abroad, in the parent company, with the result that fewer such functions are being carried out in Canada and the country's ability to carry them out has been reduced. All these phenomena have made it more difficult for the Government to keep control of the national environment; they have also affected the social, cultural and political atmosphere of Canada.
>
> The ever-growing internationalization of many important sectors of industry and the expansion of multinational companies—the institutional consequences of the scale of direct foreign investment—contribute further to the complex of factors which limit the Government's ability to control the national economic environment. For instance, although many U.S. companies began their international operations in Canada, they now have subsidiaries in several other countries. The control they exercise over productive enterprises situated in various countries augments the power and flexibility they can call upon in their dealings with the Canadian Government. Furthermore, this aggravates the problems posed by the truncation of Canadian firms, in that it reduces the likelihood that the multinationals will localize more of their functions in Canada; foreign Governments do not hesitate to intervene directly to control enterprises belonging to non-residents established on their territory. The agreements

reached by other governments with the multinationals may well have harmful consequences for Canada, especially if this country has no negotiation mechanism available or chooses not to use it (quoted in Fitt 1980:44-5).

As we saw earlier, the issue posed here remains unresolved. In countries like Canada and Austraila, the nation state is generally caught between the powerful pull from the MNCs to adapt to the requirements of transnationalized capital (by accepting some reduction in sovereignty) and pressures from opposing national groups and classes who see the nation state as the last means of defending their interests. The often noted failure of both Canada and Australia to develop a coherent industrial strategy and to escape the worst effects of the world crisis must be placed and understood in this context.

The issue of economic nationalism has even emerged in the United States, the home base of the greatest number of multinational corporations. There, however, economic nationalism is largely a matter of restoring American hegemony over the world system and exporting to its rivals its own problems of structural unemployment and runaway inflation.

The first moves in this direction were made by Richard Nixon in 1973 when the monetary and trade agreements which had governed the world system since 1944 were unilaterally abandoned by the United States. Nixon's first "shock treatment" was to float the dollar. Its fall, relative to the currency of its leading competitors, was deliberately accelerated by selling off large quantities of gold. The intent was to boost exports and thus reduce the United States' huge balance of payments deficit. Second, the Nixon administration consciously rejected any attempts to bring down the price of oil. Indeed, there are indications that it actually engineered the dramatic increase in the price of oil as a means of striking at its rivals (Europe and Japan) and as part of a broader strategy of boosting the competitive position of its export industries.

By the end of 1975, the United States, to some extent, had managed to redress its position vis-à-vis its western European and Japanese rivals. Its balance of payments had markedly improved. Imports were reduced. At the same time, the fall in the value of the dollar, combined with increased sales of armaments and agricultural products, boosted exports, especially to Asia and the oil-producing states. However, the other industrial countries, plunged into crisis somewhat later than the United States, soon began to take similar steps. As a result, the developed countries in the capitalist system turned a $27 billion collective deficit in 1974 into a $7 billion surplus by 1975.

The other half of metropolitan capitalist development was a radical deterioration of the Third World's economic position. Since 1975, apart from the oil producers, there really have no longer been any "developing" countries. Certain nations on the semi-periphery of the world system are continuing to expand in industrial terms. But this expansion only benefits the large multinationals, the local business classes, and the reactionary regimes generally connected to them. The economic position of the majority of the population in most cases has worsened.

Take the case of Brazil, easily the Third World's most favored recipient of multinational investment capital. Throughout the 1960s and the 1970s economic growth rates were so high that it was hailed an "economic miracle." However, over the same period real wages declined by 40 percent (Amin 1981:30). Behind the economic miracle of high growth lies the abject poverty of over forty million people. Most of the wealth generated in the high growth period of 1960-1977 that was not siphoned off by the MNCs and international banks (viz., national deficit of over $60 billion in 1980) went to the richest 10 percent of the population. They raised their share of total income from 39.6 percent to 51 percent (*Latin America* March 28, 1980:6). At the same time, the richest 1 percent took their share from 11.9 percent to 18.3 percent. Thus, they received more than the poorest 50 percent. Their share of total income had fallen from 17.4 percent to 13.1 percent (ibid.).

The case of Brazil illustrates a general pattern. In other third world countries favored by foreign investment and multinational enterprise the story is substantially the same. By recent estimates, the gap in per capita incomes between the rich and the poor in these countries has increased by 10 percent a year for each year in the 1970s (Fitt et al. 1980:163).

It would appear that at a general level the leading capitalist countries have closed ranks against the Third World. Once again the metropolitan countries have been groping toward a new alignment. They have established a stable hierarchy of relations among themselves on the basis of extra profits extracted from third world countries. Nevertheless, the capitalist countries have not been able to stave off the effects of crisis. This was not true of previous slumps.

Normally, cyclical downturns in industrial production tend to bottom out in about three years. But, even a casual look at the international data shows that after six years of "recovery," world capitalism, far from enjoying prosperity, has entered a period of growing stagnation. Well into the recovery period, unemployment in almost all capitalist countries is at record levels in the 1980s. Inflation is rising from an already historically high plateau, industrial production is lagging, and investment is weak.

It hardly need be said that under these conditions, third world countries pursuing an export-led industrialization strategy, or branch-plant economies like Canada, will find it increasingly difficult to maintain overall production and export levels. As a result, they will experience an even larger decline in living standards and increased doses of inflation, unemployment, and other problems of capitalism. And, unless the interimperialist or intraimperialist class struggles—or yet again, the antagonism between the socialist and capitalist camps—lead to another world war, these problems will be a reflection of mounting class struggles all over the Third World and a more general political struggle between countries on both sides of the north-south divide. All that one can hope for with respect to this difficult and stormy period ahead is that these various struggles will eventually do away with imperialism and class rule in the international arena. On the basis of recent history, however, the prognosis is not favorable.

HIGHLIGHT

1. Capitalist societies are currently undergoing the most serious crisis since the 1930s.
2. The current crisis is the result of a falling rate of profit, interimperialist rivalry, and the energy crisis.
3. Nationalism has been an important response of countries to these events. Through nationalist policies, many countries hope to protect themselves from the trends inherent in the world capitalist system.

Conclusion

The contemporary world capitalist system was set up toward the end of World War II. In the context of a general collapse of the British Empire, it was designed by the major capitalist powers as a means of countering the challenge of a growing international socialist movement and various colonial wars of national liberation. Settling for a realignment of power among themselves, the major capitalist states worked out a system that allowed them to expand into the Third World's sources of energy and cheap labor. Such decisions resulted in the opening up of a new wave of capitalist expansion, and a new form of imperialism.

The vehicle for capitalist expansion was the multinational corporation—an organization through which capital could be accumulated on a world scale. A characteristic feature of MNCs is power, both economical and political. Within the framework of the new world system this power is so encompassing that the MNCs have come to dominate the new international division of labor and the markets associated with it. Thus the world economy is effectively run by a new international class of monopoly capitalists.

As in earlier stages of capitalist development, Canada has had a dual role to play within this world system. On the one hand, it has participated in the new imperialism. It has done so both by itself and in association with American capitalists. On the other hand, in relation to the United States, as the world's largest branch-plant economy, Canada has been converted into a resource-hinterland for American industry. The consequences of this neo-colonial dependence are many. They include foreign control over key sectors of the economy, a truncated and dependent industrial structure, and some loss of cultural independence and sovereignty.

As in earlier forms of development, the internal contradictions of the capitalist system, increasingly manifest on a global scale, have generated a structural crisis. At present the system is in the midst of one of its most severe and protracted crises. Whether the system as a whole, or in its various parts, can once again restructure itself and stave off the conditions of this crisis remains to be seen. Indications are that the imperialist system is beginning to exhaust its capacity to expand production on a world-wide capitalist basis. Although they are not yet properly understood, there are various forces of revolutionary change gathering in some parts of the world. The conditions under which these forces will push the imperialist system to its limits have not yet been established. Some of them will be discussed in different contexts in other chapters.

NOTES

[1]Major elements of this agreement included: (a) fixed international exchange rates between currencies; (b) the replacement of the British pound with the American dollar as the basic medium of international commodity exchange; and (c) relation of a fixed dollar price for gold. Two institutions were created to manage this plan; the International Monetary Fund (IMF) and the World Bank.

[2]When the list of the world's economies is extended to 130, one-half are MNCs. Other GNP comparisons in 1976: Guatemala 4.4; Burma 3.8; Kenya 3.5; Bolivia 3.0; Panama 2.0; Jordan 1.8; Sierra Leone 0.6; Somalia 0.4.

[3]At its simplest, transfer pricing involves firms over-invoicing imports and under-invoicing exports in order to move profits surreptitiously from one country to another. On this procedure see in particular Vaitsos (1974) and Murray (1981).

[4]On the early formation of this class see Shoup and Mintes (1977), a masterful account of the American sector as it operated through the Council of Foreign Relations (a private but powerful policy-planning group) to secretly plan the policies of modern-day imperialism and then to introduce them into the American government. For the later extension of this policy-making group into the Trilateral Commission see various studies collected together by Sklar (1980).

[5]Another way of understanding the world system is to group together the industrialized developed countries in both the capitalist and communist worlds and to divide these from the mass of poor and underdeveloped nations of the Third World found largely in the southern hemisphere. In this conception of a north-south divide the differences between the communist and capitalist systems are seen to be less important than differences in the level of industrial development and the distribution of the world's resources and wealth.

[6]The increasing scope of this problem of debt servicing is evident in the following statistics on the external public debt as a percentage of GNP for selected third world countries.

	1970	1976		1970	1976
Zaire	17.3	63.8	South Korea	22.8	26.7
India	14.8	14.6	Nicaragua	19.4	37.8
Pakistan	30.5	45.1	Peru	14.8	31.8
Tanzania	18.1	35.7	Chile	24.0	39.1

| Egypt | 23.7 | 48.1 | Jamaica | 10.3 | 36.6 |
| Zambia | 32.0 | 53.7 | Mexico | 9.8 | 20.8 |

(Source: World Bank 1978:Table 11)

To appreciate the immensity of the problem involved in these statistics consider Mexico's public external debt which in 1976 was $15.5 billion, climbing by 1980 to $60 billion. Brazil's external debt was even larger.

[7]There are many studies on these conditions of dependence. See Clement and Drache (1978) for a useful compilation.

[8]Indications are that foreign capital is increasingly used to take over existing and successful companies rather than establish new enterprises. A 1973 study commissioned by the United Nations on the methods by which MNCs based in the United States purchased a host company found that in the typical case of Canada, acquisitions (purchases of companies previously under local control) increased from 29.5 percent of total affiliates set up by 1946 to 45.2 percent over the 1946-47 period and 57.9 percent in the 1958-67 period.

SUGGESTED READINGS

Of Dust and Time and Dreams and Agonies, Pat Bird. Toronto: The Canadian News Synthesis Project, 1975. A highly readable summary account of Canada's history. Emphasizing developments that are generally ignored in high school history texts, it should be read with Bergeron's (1971) history of Quebec as an introduction to a more critical understanding of Canada's social development.

Unequal Union, Stanley Ryerson. New York: International Publishing, 1968. A systematic detailed analysis of class relations and conflicts in the period preceding Confederation by one of Canada's foremost historians. An indispensable source for understanding a crucial period of Canada's history that brings into sharp analytical focus capitalism in Canada.

A History of Canadian Wealth, Gustavos Myers. Toronto: James Lewis & Samuel, 1972. Largely ignored until recently, this text, written early in the 20th century, provides a wealth of detail on the conditions under which Canada's first capitalists accumulated their fortunes.

Continental Corporate Power, Wallace Clement. Toronto: McClelland & Stewart, 1977. A sociological study of corporate capitalism in Canada. The central focus of the study is on the power structure located in the dominant corporations of the North American economy. The corporate elites in Canada and the United States are compared as to their organisation, relative power, and class relations.

REGIONAL UNEVEN DEVELOPMENT, REGIONALISM AND STRUGGLE

R. James Sacouman

Introduction

Capitalist inequality becomes manifest in many different ways. Carl Cuneo has shown how class inequality is at the heart of the capitalist system. In the last two chapters Veltmeyer showed how the enrichment of capitalist 'core' or 'metropolitan' societies resulted in part from the impoverishment of the rest of the world. In a later chapter Dorothy Smith will demonstrate how the subordination of women, while not unique to capitalism, is shaped by it. In this chapter the relation between capitalism and regional underdevelopment will be examined. It will be seen that regionalism and the 'national question' are but two sides of the same coin.

Usually, one of three perspectives is used to account for regionalism. In the first, the *idealist*, emphasis is placed on cultural and/or psychological matters. For example, 'Newfie Jokes' embody the notion that people from that part of the world are dumb and/or culturally naive and that their underdevelopment can be explained by reference to these factors. The second explanation for regional underdevelopment, the *economistic*, views all regional differences as the mechanical result of the natural operation of the economic system. The third perspective, the *reformist* one, embodies the idea that regionalism results from inappropriate governmental policies.

As will be seen later, each of these approaches has its limitations and tends to obscure the nature of regionalism. In addition, each contains ideas as to how the problem of regionalism can be solved. However, before turning to matters such as these, it makes sense to provide some definitions and state the fundamental assumptions of this chapter.

As the term regionalism is used in many different ways, in order to understand what in this chapter will be called uneven development and regionalism, it is essential to define key terms. *Regional uneven development* denotes a spatial distribution of structured inequality. *Regionalisms*, or regional cultures, are variations in ways of living associated with inhabiting a particular place in a country. Regionalism is best viewed as a relatively creative, but also often contradictory, class-rooted response to regional uneven development.

The main argument of this chapter is that regionalism in the less developed, or peripheral, regions of Canada and the world has been, and is, a central component of *class struggle*. This premise will be explored through analysis of unequal development, the theories and theorists of idealism, economism, and reformism, and an application of Marxist theory to the Canadian case.

HIGHLIGHT

1. The national question cannot be understood independent of the regional question in Canada.
2. The nature of this relationship is frequently obscured by the idealist, economistic, and reformist perspectives taken by analysts.
3. Uneven regional development and/or regionalism occur with the development of capitalism.

Regional Inequality in Canada: Some Selected Indicators

The likelihood of having any job, let alone a 'good' job, varies across Canada and over time. A first indication of the variation can be gleaned from the official unemployment rates by province.

Among other things, Table 1 demonstrates that an employable person is at least three times as likely to be unemployed in Newfoundland than in either Saskatchewan or Alberta. Such a person is twice as likely to be unemployed in Prince Edward Island, Nova Scotia, New Brunswick, and Quebec than in Saskatchewan and Alberta. Ontario, Manitoba and British Columbia have middle range unemployment rates.

TABLE 1
Unemployment rates (%), by province, 1972-78*

Year	Province									
	Nfld	**PEI**	**NS**	**NB**	**Que**	**Ont**	**Man**	**Sask**	**Alta**	**BC**
1972	9.2	10.8	7.0	7.0	7.5	5.0	5.4	4.4	5.6	7.8
1973	10.0	....	6.6	7.7	6.8	4.3	4.6	3.5	5.3	6.7
1974	13.0	....	6.8	7.5	6.6	4.4	3.6	2.8	3.5	6.2
1975	14.0	8.0	7.7	9.8	8.1	6.3	4.5	2.9	4.1	8.5
1976	13.4	9.6	9.5	11.0	8.7	6.2	4.7	3.9	4.0	8.6
1977	15.6	9.9	10.6	13.2	10.3	7.0	5.9	4.5	4.5	8.5
1978	16.4	9.9	10.6	12.6	10.9	7.2	6.5	4.9	4.7	8.3

*SOURCE: Statistics Canada, 1981:270.

One immediate reason for the variations in official unemployment is confirmed in Table 2. There are simply fewer jobs of any sort, including casual, part-time, seasonal and temporary jobs available in areas like the Maritimes.

TABLE 2

Job vacancies, all categories[1], by province, annual averages 1973-78, and job vacancies (thousands), and vacancy rates[2] per 1,000 jobs, by quarter 1978*

Item and year	Nfld	NS	NB	Que	Ont	Man	Sask	Alta	BC	Canada[3]
Job vacancies										
Annual average										
1973	1.5	2.0	2.2	22.6	33.1	4.2	2.1	8.0	9.4	85.8
1974	1.4	2.4	2.2	21.4	41.0	5.7	4.1	13.1	9.8	101.7
1975	1.0	1.5	1.8	15.3	23.0	4.1	3.5	8.1	4.5	63.3
1976	0.6	1.1	1.2	11.9	17.6	2.9	2.5	9.2	4.1	51.4
1977	0.5	0.9	0.8	9.5	17.5	2.0	1.7	7.2	4.0	44.4
1978	0.5	1.1	0.7	9.3	17.1	1.9	1.5	7.8	4.1	44.5
By quarter 1978										
1st quarter	0.4	1.0	0.6	8.1	14.6	1.4	1.2	6.9	3.5	37.9
2nd quarter	0.6	1.2	0.9	10.0	16.9	2.2	1.6	7.1	4.8	45.6
3rd quarter	0.4	1.4	0.9	10.5	18.3	2.2	1.6	9.8	4.6	50.0
4th quarter	0.4	1.0	0.7	8.8	18.8	1.9	1.4	7.3	3.8	44.3
Vacancy rates										
By quarter 1978										
1st quarter	3	4	3	4	4	4	4	9	4	4
2nd quarter	4	4	4	4	5	6	6	9	5	5
3rd quarter	3	5	4	4	5	6	5	12	4	5
4th quarter	3	3	3	4	5	5	5	9	4	5

[1] Includes full-time, casual, part-time, seasonal and temporary jobs.
[2] A rate is obtained by expressing the number of vacancies per 1,000 existing jobs in all industries, except agriculture, fishing and trapping, domestic service and the non-civilian component of public administration and defence.
[3] Includes Prince Edward Island, Yukon and Northwest Territories.

*SOURCE: Statistics Canada, 1981:273.

Official unemployment rates only include previously employed persons who have sought work in the previous four weeks. They do not take into consideration the "hidden" unemployed, those previously employed persons who are reported by Statistics Canada to have given up searching for jobs. Clearly, the variations by province in unemployment rates would increase when discouraged workers are counted as unemployed.

The true unemployment rates *and* the variations would be greater if the following were counted: a) those who have part-time work but would prefer full-time work; b) those in government sponsored training programs who are single parents and heads of households, or those who receive social assistance, and who would be listed as employable if suitable jobs and day-care were available; c) students who would prefer to work, if jobs were available; d) those who are 55 years and over, who have been forced into early retirement; and f) those who have never officially worked, or who have not officially worked in a very long time (see Gonick 1978:21 and 22).

Since 1978, unemployment has risen even further than indicated in the tables. Sometimes, the official rates of *increase* in unemployment, *not* the actual rates of unemployment, have risen faster in the areas of less unemployment than in the areas with the most unemployment. However, real unemployment rates in areas of high unemployment remain staggeringly higher than in areas of less unemployment.

Jobs are where most people, but not capitalists, derive their earnings. Since fewer women work for income in depressed regions, family incomes tend to vary in an inverse relationship to unemployment rates. This is indicated in Tables 3 and 4.

In many cases the gaps in family income by province have not closed since 1961. The Atlantic provinces, the region with the greatest unemployment rates *and* the largest average family size, has the largest percentage of poor families.

As Tables 5 and 6 confirm, many aspects of health and welfare vary by region. Except when the figures inflate as a consequence of the inclusion of Native and Inuit peoples in the North and the Prairies, the Atlantic region is most deprived. Not having running water, a household bath or shower, or a household flush toilet, is over three times as likely in the Atlantic region than in Canada as a whole.

Cuneo (1978b) has presented further indicators of regional inequality. He arranges provinces into core, semi-peripheral and peripheral regions. When large-scale manufacturing is used as the key criterion, the lack of sizable manufacturing in Saskatchewan and Manitoba allow these provinces to join the Atlantic region in the periphery of Canada. The 'periphery', by this criterion, receives fewer interprovincial migrants. It also contains far fewer people who think their region is more powerful than other regions, or that their region is better off than other regions. Similarly many indicate that they would rather live elsewhere.

TABLE 3
Average income of families in current and constant dollars by region, selected years, 1961-78*

Region	1961	1967	1971	1973	1975	1977	1978
Current dollars							
Atlantic provinces	4,156	5,767	7,936	9,965	13,474	16,590	17,064
Quebec	5,294	7,404	9,919	12,024	15,446	19,056	20,261
Ontario	5,773	8,438	11,483	13,912	18,047	21,600	22,628
Prairie provinces	4,836	6,908	9,309	11,760	16,177	19,712	21,242
British Columbia	5,491	7,829	11,212	13,942	17,746	21,040	23,327
CANADA	5,317	7,602	10,368	12,716	16,613	20,101	21,346
Constant (1971) dollars							
Atlantic provinces	5,544	6,667	7,936	8,839	9,728	10,319	9,744
Quebec	7,062	8,559	9,919	10,665	11,152	11,853	11,569
Ontario	7,701	9,754	11,483	12,340	13,030	13,435	12,921
Prairie provinces	6,451	7,986	9,309	10,431	11,680	12,261	12,129
British Columbia	7,325	9,050	11,212	12,367	12,813	13,087	13,320
CANADA	7,093	8,788	10,368	11,279	11,994	12,503	12,189

*SOURCE: Statistics Canada, 1981:290.

TABLE 4
Percentage distribution of families by income group, by region, 1978*

Year and income group	Atlantic provinces	Quebec	Ontario	Prairie provinces	British Columbia	Canada
1978						
Under $3,000	2.3	1.5	1.3	2.6	1.8	1.7
$3,000-$4,999	4.3	3.6	3.2	3.3	1.8	3.3
5,000- 6,999	10.3	6.8	5.0	4.9	2.8	5.7
7,000- 8,999	9.4	5.7	4.2	6.9	7.1	5.8
9,000-10,999	7.2	5.6	4.5	6.0	4.0	5.2
11,000-11,999	4.6	2.8	2.6	2.3	2.0	2.7
12,000-12,999	3.8	3.5	2.0	2.7	2.9	2.8
13,000-13,999	2.9	2.9	3.4	3.1	2.5	3.1
14,000-14,999	3.8	3.8	3.5	3.0	3.3	3.5
15,000-15,999	4.6	3.8	3.2	3.0	3.6	3.5
16,000-16,999	3.4	3.6	2.8	3.4	2.3	3.1
17,000-17,999	4.0	4.3	3.1	3.7	3.7	3.7
18,000-19,999	6.2	7.1	7.0	6.7	7.2	6.9
20,000-21,999	5.9	7.7	7.7	6.2	7.3	7.2
22,000-24,999	7.5	8.8	11.3	10.5	9.5	10.0
25,000-29,999	8.4	11.5	13.1	11.9	11.0	11.8
30,000-34,999	5.0	7.8	8.8	7.9	11.6	8.4
35,000 and over	6.4	9.2	13.3	12.1	15.5	11.6
Total	100.0	100.0	100.0	100.0	100.0	100.0
Average income	17,064	20,261	22,628	21,242	23,327	21,346
Median income	15,304	18,592	21,105	19,567	21,345	19,717
Sample size	1,330	1,785	2,014	1,514	726	7,369

*SOURCE: Statistics Canada, 1981:291.

TABLE 5
A few further indicators of regional inequality by province, 1974*

	Ratio of active physicians to population	Ratio of licensed dentists to population by province of licensure	Percent of occupied dwellings with 1.0 or more persons per room
Newfoundland	1:836	1:8,667	
Prince Edward Island	1:1,035	1:2,878	23.8
Nova Scotia	1:552	1:3,466	
New Brunswick	1:923	1:4,891	
Quebec	1:558	1:3,235	21.8
Ontario	1:568	1:2,309	13.5
Manitoba	1:561	1:2,864	
Saskatchewan	1:727	1:3,563	15.7
Alberta	1:634	1:2,380	
British Columbia	1:562	1:1,999	12.2
Yukon	1:870	—	
Northwest Territories	1:1,121	—	
CANADA	1:586	1:2,670	16.8

*SOURCE: Statistics Canada, 1978: 83, 84, 262.

TABLE 6
Percentage of occupied dwellings *without* amenities, 1971*

	Piped running water	Exclusive use of bath or shower	Exclusive use of flush toilets
Atlantic	9.6	27.1	17.5
Quebec	0.3	5.8	0.6
Ontario	1.1	3.6	2.4
Prairies	8.0	12.3	12.0
British Columbia	1.3	3.3	2.2
CANADA	2.7	7.4	4.6

*SOURCE: Statistics Canada, 1974: 215.

TABLE 7
Still more aspects of regional inequality in Canada*

	Core (Ontario)	Semi-periphery (B.C., Alberta, Quebec)	Periphery (Atlantic, Sask., Man.)
1. Average number of employees per manufacturing establishment, 1971.	56	44	27
2. Percentage distribution of manufacturing establishments with 1,000 or more employees, 1971.	59	36	5
3. Percentage of 1966 to 1971 interprovincial migrants residing in region.	30	48	22
4. Percentage of a 1965 national sample thinking region *more powerful* than other regions.	32	19	2
5. Percentage of a 1965 national sample thinking region *better off* than other regions.	51	21	1
6. Percentage of a 1965 national sample stating *would like to live in* region.	37	24	4

*SOURCE: Cuneo, 1978: 151.

The success of Ontario as the manufacturing core and province of opportunity resulted from the relative economic advantages derived from the influx of U.S. manufacturing capital. The results of this development are shown in Table 8.

American controlled manufacturing capital is much less evenly distributed than Canadian controlled manufacturing capital. Consequently Ontario workers are the major losers when U.S. capital returns home in times of crisis. Ontario is also the base for indigenous big capitalists. Ontario's premier position has recently been eroded as a result of the increase in the prosperity of Alberta in particular.

HIGHLIGHT

1. Uneven regional development can be seen in: (a) localized higher unemployment and lower living standards; (b) the historic location of industry in central Canada; and (c) the attitudes of the residents of some regions.

Misunderstanding Regionalization and Regionalism in Canada

An Example of Idealist Theory: the World of S.D. Clark.   Perhaps no sociologist in Canada has written so much on the social development of Canada and on regional social movements as Samuel Delbert Clark. Certainly no sociologist writing in these areas can claim the esteem of S.D. Clark. Clark's major works (1942; 1959; 1968; 1978) consistently develop a non-Marxist classless theory.

In *The Social Development of Canada* we can find statements that clearly bear on the general questions of unequal development and regionalism. Here, as elsewhere, what we have called regionalism is examined in the framework of frontier and more established parts of the country.

Early in the book Clark indicates that: "An emphasis...has been placed upon the particular problem of the relationship of frontier economic expansion in Canada, or more strictly the opening up of new areas or fields of economic exploitation, to the development of social organization" (1942:1). The stress here is on the novelty of economic expansion by capital brought from outside of the frontier and on the obtaining of social organization or equilibrium in a new area of settlement. For Clark, equilibrium occurs when the frontier economy matures and state controlled social organization adjusts (1942:2-4).

For Clark, contrary to the perspective adopted in this book, exploitation of workers is not seen as primarily rooted in social production. It is viewed as merely geographical. The metropolis versus the hinterland; urban versus rural; or areas of stable versus unstable staple resources, e.g., farming versus furs. All of these are regional divisions and are viewed as providing antagonistic "sets of cultural values" (1942:21, 27 and 104).

Individuals and entire populations in frontier areas are seen as inherently unstable, especially under conditions of rapid frontier development. They consequently need to have organizational controls such as the mounted police imposed through state-run organizations (1942:3

and 4). The character of the population is nonconformist and the people are often misfits who have been least socially accommodated. Moreover, they are open to the enthusiasm generated by reform movements if the leadership seems to provide a solution to the social crises inherent in a "situation of anomie" (1942:4-18; 1959:72). Frontier individuals or those who are on the periphery, are thus viewed as reactive, not creative. Protest movements that frequently arise on the frontier, are also seen as fundamentally reactive. They are composed of misfits and are led by organizers for their own interests.

An interpretation of Clark's *Movements of Political Protest in Canada: 1640-1840* reinforces the idea that his principles and focus of analysis are the antithesis to those of Marx. In this work, Clark seeks to place the Social Credit movement in Alberta (a profoundly conservative movement) in a historical perspective by focussing on the pervasiveness of the frontier experience in the broad North American continental system (1959:vii).

For Clark, North America, like Asia, has been a breeding ground for "Utopian movements". It has also spawned "political discontent". Such developments in both North America and Asia result from both continents' large land mass and the resulting difficulty of establishing centralized control (1959:4).

Both the U.S. and Canadian frontier experience were essentially the same for Clark. The exception is that, in Canada, liberal democratic movements (and their desire for local autonomy), which naturally sprang from the frontier experience, were successfully suppressed by vested, counter-revolutionary interests. Such movements threatened establishment control of the Canadian community (1959:6, 9). This suppression has led to a spirit of "responsible" compromise in the Canadian community. At the same time it has held in check the 'natural' push of the "masses" of the Canadian people to the implementation of liberal ideas. It has also retarded capitalist growth (1959:10; 1968:242, 248 and 249).

For Clark, all major North American "movements for independence" between 1640 and 1840 are viewed as American led and fortified, and Canadian supported. Even the War of 1812 and the Rebellions of 1837 are viewed as American liberation efforts. Both north and south of the Canadian border such movements resulted from frontier circumstances and intended to free all the continental system from British control (1959:129 and 255).

Clark sees the frontier experience and its value system as continental and borderless (1968:234). At the same time, whereas he views all frontier protest to be reactive (coming from "irresponsible misfits") no matter how democratic, the Canadian frontier people are seen as doubly reactive—supportive of a U.S. led liberation which itself is viewed as only a result of frontier conditions.

The indigenous Patriote movement of 1837 as described in the chapter in this volume on Quebec was for Clark only a rebellion or a resistance movement, requiring the later U.S.-based leadership to become more creatively revolutionary (1959:305, 330). The thrust of all these American liberations of Canada died after the 1830s largely because of "the strengthening of more responsible elements in American political life" (1959:440).

For Clark, real political change occurs through the efforts of "uncompromising and often irresponsible" reformers. These individuals set the conditions for compromise by more "tolerant" leaders (1959:505). All movements of reform, whether religious or political, are seen by Clark as movements of moral reform which are products of economic expansion (1940:203; see also 1948). The point is that reform, when it occurs, is moral reform, not social reform. Moral reform is really the product of sober responsible leadership.

Clark's own statement of his historical method and theory is contained in a collection of essays entitled *The Developing Canadian Community*. Quite correctly, Clark summarized his early interest in Canadian development as being guided by "the conviction that sociology had much to gain from the study of the society of the past and that the sensible place for the Canadian sociologist to begin, was with the study of his own society" (1968:xi). He was adamantly against "any effort on the part of the sociologist to fit history into a tight, preconceived, theoretical scheme" such as he asserts was done by the nineteenth century philosophers of history, such as Marx (1968:vi, 270).

Clark had previously seen all, or most, liberal democratic reform as being U.S. sponsored. Also, because he interpreted Marx only as "Utopian", he denied the existence of a Marxist theory of social change. The consequence was the construction of Clark's ideas of change along idealist lines (1968:279, 295-301). His treatment of frontiers and settled parts of the country reflects this orientation. The fundamental differences between the two are described in cultural terms.

An Example of the Economistic Theory: the Works of H.A. Innis.

S.D. Clark's works are a major example of the idealist perspective. The works of H.A. Innis (e.g., 1936; 1956; 1970; 1978), the contribution they have made to the understanding of Canadian development notwithstanding, are the best classical example in Canadian social science of the non-Marxist economistic theory in understanding regionalization and regionalism. It must be stressed though, that some other authors of this book would dispute this claim.

H.A. Innis, 'the father of anglophone Canadian social science' and S.D. Clark's teacher, examined in great historical detail the economic history of regionalized staples dependence, i.e. the reliance of a region on one product such as wheat. However, in none of his works did Innis ever codify his approach. He preferred to overwhelm the reader with empirical detail. Fortunately, later pro-Innisian analysts (especially Watkins, 1967; 1977) have systematized his writings so that a brief examination of his key concepts and propositions is possible.

Central to Innis' approach is the materialist understanding of the economic nature, geographical distribution, and effects of the exploitation of particular raw materials, or semi-finished products. Different staples—fur, fish, iron ore, timber, etc.—require different degrees of on-site or near-site processing. Since any particular staple is usually not spread throughout the nation-state, its particular geographical location relative to markets and transportation routes, together with its inherent nature, determines its local or regional development potential. Together, the nature of the staple and its geographical location determine the association the region will have with other regions.

In his examination of the salt-cod trade on the Canadian east coast (1978), Innis argues that the nature of the highly perishable staple, cod, its coastal location and its low-capital technological requirements for 'curing', resulted in the development of many small, fishing villages. Recent scholarship (e.g., Alexander 1977; Ommer 1981) has implicitly and explicitly criticized Innis' economistic emphasis in *The Cod Fisheries*.

While a number of serious social analysts have tried to link Innis' staples approach to Marxism (see, esp., Watkins, 1977), others question such an association. McNally (1981), for example, links Innis' materialism, his economic-geographical determinism, and his technological emphasis to the very same "commodity fetishism" that Marx attacked in *Capital* and other places over a hundred years ago. McNally writes that:

> In Innis' staple theory of Canadian history it is the staple commodities themselves that dictate the patterns of historical development and social organization. . . . By ascribing the creative role in the historical process to the primary commodity itself, Innis' staple theory systematically ignored the role of the social relations of production in shaping and reproducing society. . . . As Carl Berger [1976:98] has pointed out, Innis' history of Canada was history "dehumanized"—the making of history by human beings, albeit in conditions not of their own choosing, plays no role in his works (1981:46 and 47).

Fundamentally, like all other economistic approaches, Innis' staple theory is inadequate to the social understanding of regionalization and regionalism in Canada. It makes regionalization natural and thus, inevitable. Regionalization is intrinsic to development based on staple production. The struggles of human beings against unequal development are therefore declared irrational. Whereas S.D. Clark's approach soars idealistically to account for regional "character", H.A. Innis' approach cannot see human beings through the veil of a particular brand of materialism.

An Example of the Reformist Theory: the Works of Vernon C. Fowke.
The works of Vernon C. Fowke (1947; 1957) provide the best, and a classical attempt, to combine Innis' emphasis on staples with

Clark's focus on centralized expansion. Fowke provides this synthesis in his political-economic history of wheat in the Canadian prairies. Unlike Innis, Fowke argues that the wheat economy and the development of single staple dependence in the Prairies was not simply a consequence of reliance on the wheat staple. Rather, it was the result of a series of conscious policy decisions taken by the federal state. These eventually led to the rapid populating of a fragile, dependent region. Unlike Clark, Fowke sides with those who lived in the hinterland, as opposed to the centre.

In his most important work, *The National Policy and the Wheat Economy* (1957), Fowke argues that immigration, settlement, transportation and tariff policies—in combination these measures were called the National Policy—both required, and resulted in, the development in the Prairies of a "bread-basket" relationship with the urban areas of Canada. The Prairies would also provide a captive market for central Canadian manufacturers. For Fowke, "a wheat economy became functional, yet subordinate to the industrialization and urbanization of the central provinces" (Knuttila and McCrorie 1980:263).

Some analysts have consciously extended Fowke's "hinterland perspective" to an attack on the internal colonialism of the Canadian state's regionalization policy (e.g., Phillips 1978). As we shall see in a later section, many current "hinterland" supporters accept Fowke's central argument that bad policy decisions, not capitalism, have caused regional dependencies. Many of these current hinterland advocates also accept Fowke's argument that fairer policies would solve the disparities. In essence, the wrongs of capitalism can be righted with fairer deals.

Fowke's analysis, like the analyses of many current hinterland supporters, is reformist. This is true not because it documents the need for reforms, but because it assumes that mere reforms are adequate, and all that are possible. As Knuttila and McCrorie (1980) point out, and as will be developed in the rest of this chapter, this reformist stance is embedded in a failure to analyse social relations of production and emergent class struggles.

As we have seen, each approach attempts to reduce the regional problem to either the cultural, the economic, or the political aspect. None recognize that capitalist production is a social whole. It involves the interrelated social production and reproduction over time and space of 'the economy', 'culture' and 'the political system'. None recognize that humans make the world through, especially, class struggle, though not under conditions of their own choosing.

HIGHLIGHT

1. The idealist interpretation of uneven development and regionalism, as put forward by Clark in his analyses of frontiers, focuses on cultural explanations.
2. H.A. Innis, a major exponent of economistic explanations of Cana-

dian regionalism, concentrates on the consequences of staple production for national and regional development.
3. The reformist approach to regionalism, as articulated by Fowke, sees regionalism as the result of state policy. As such it can be corrected by state policy.

Understanding Regional Uneven Development: From Marx to Canada

Karl Marx's theory of capitalism was developed in order to document both the necessity and possibility of socialist revolution in the world. In other words, at least from the "Manifesto" onwards, all of Marx's work should be understood as an attempt to contribute to workers' revolution, which he viewed as the first fully creative revolutionary struggle in global human history (Marx 1973a; 1973b; 1973c; 1975; 1976; 1978; 1981).

Marx wanted to understand, explain and transform capitalism. He therefore chose to examine the classic development of capitalism in western Europe. He often took England as the classic case.

Marx did *not* develop a full-fledged theory of regional uneven development. Nor did Marx ever develop a full-fledged theory of any of the inequalities of capitalism except for class formation and class conflict in social production. Nonetheless, his focus on the social relations of social production allows us to select some key aspects of what a theory of regional uneven development must include.

As seen in earlier chapters by Cuneo and Veltmeyer, the origins of modern capitalism can be found in a period of so-called primitive capital accumulation. This term refers to the period in which laborers were separated from their own means of production and were required to work with means of production owned by others. Over time, this state of affairs became self-sustaining.

Primitive accumulation required economic coercion. It also involved intense state violence. As Marx states, the classic history of the expropriation of small property holders in England, "is written in the annals of mankind in letters of blood and fire" (1976:875). At the same time he affirms that: "The history of this expropriation assumes different aspects in different countries, and runs through its various phases in different orders of succession, and at different historical epochs. Only in England, which we therefore take as our example, has it the classic form" (1976:876). Thus, while Marx fully expected most primitive accumulation to be a bloody battle lost by the small property holders, he did recognize its spatial-temporal differences.

After the period of primitive accumulation, the central social relationship in so-called expanded capitalist reproduction, is the class conflict over the rate of exploitation. In one of Veltmeyer's chapters this was symbolized by s/v. The rate of exploitation as a whole can be increased in two ways: 1) surplus value appropriated from creative labor-power 's' must be increased above the rate of increase of wages; or 2) the total wage packet 'v' must be decreased relative to the surplus value expropriated.

Marx primarily focused on the increasing of surplus value through the extension and intensification of the working day. He also documented historic class struggles between capital and the state, and the workers. Such struggles centred on attempts to increase exploitation. He saw the development of a reserve army of labor resulting from this increasing exploitation and redundancy.

The expansion of a reserve army of labor often deflects, for Marx, the struggle between labor and capitalist to the struggle between worker and worker, or employed and unemployed. Also, except in times of crisis, the state is often free to act as if it were relatively autonomous from the capital-labor relation. All the time, however, it contributes to maintaining the division between the 'reserve army' of labor and the regulars. Socialism requires the refocussing of struggle to the real conflict between capitalist and laborer.

Finally, and most importantly, the increase of a relative surplus population was crucial to social contradiction in capitalism as Marx perceived it. The so-called "absolute general law of capital accumulation" (Marx 1976:762-870), referred to the increasing distance between the vast majority of workers and the small capitalist class which exploited them. At the same time, the capitalists depend on workers to act as consumers in order for capitalists to realize profits. This increasing distance was the specific barrier to everlasting capitalism and the clear basis for the necessity of revolution (see Lebowitz, 1982).

Just as the process of primitive accumulation occurred in different ways in different places, the continuation of capitalism often affects regions in particular ways. In some areas, efforts to extract profits may lead to the exploitation of large numbers of agricultural petty producers. Such was the case in the Canadian West. In other areas, profits may derive from the direct exploitation of workers in factories, forests, and mines. Sometimes, this process, as noted above, is accompanied by the development of a large pool of reserve labor that is not re-absorbed into the productive process. Such was the case in the Maritime provinces.

The Marxist Theory of Regional Uneven Development in Canada

A thoroughly Marxist theory of regional uneven development in Canada has really only developed since the mid-1970s. Earlier, Marxist views had tended to reduce the Canadian situation either to an oversimplified labor-capital relationship (Pentland 1981) or to reduce the regional question to the single-class, single-staple dependence of petty commodity producers (e.g., Macpherson 1953). The latter group assumed that regionalism resulted from, for example, the exploitation by a Toronto-Montreal based bourgeoisie of primarily western based farmers.

Their weaknesses aside, the Canadian classical approaches were more adequate in their historical detail than the *initial* attempts by a number of leftist analysts in the 1970s to theorize regionalism. The latter group viewed regionalism as: 1) a product of external control (e.g., Archibald 1971); 2) a product of capitalist centralization, or corporate elite location (e.g., Clement 1978); or 3) a product of capital concentration and the capitalist-working class economic relationship (e.g., Cuneo 1978b).

More recent analyses of the actual variety of class formations and class conflicts in various regions have been increasingly fruitful. They have viewed such conflicts as results of the historically uneven development of capitalism in Canada. More importantly, they have recognized that regionalism cannot be explained simply in terms of an oversimplified labor-capital relationship, or the exploitation of petty producers. Rather, they have focussed on the ways in which a variety of different classes in conflict with one another produce regionalism.

Probably because these analyses have been undertaken in two of the historically most underdeveloped regions of Canada, they have not reduced capitalist development to the strictly capitalist-working class relationship. Prairie farmers, for example, are *not* proletarians. Moreover, they are much more varied in their social relationships to the means of production—land and equipment—than simplistic analyses would reveal.

In the Maritimes, a large reserve of surplus population can be found. Many individuals who form this reserve are semi-proletarianized. That is, they are employed part-time in wage labor. In some cases, it is possible to characterize entire families as semi-proletarianized. Such individuals and families have engaged in a variety of class struggles (see Sacouman, 1980; Brym and Sacouman, 1979).

Analyses of regional uneven development undertaken from the perspective of those in the disadvantaged region reveal the limitations of economistic reductionism, i.e. the tendency to view all behavior as emanating directly from economic motives, practiced by some Marxists. Such analyses also associate the state with capitalist social production. This approach contrasts with the 'relative autonomy of the state' position examined and adopted by some other authors in this book.

More precisely, analyses of periods of class conflict demonstrate the active, if uneven, participation of all branches of the state in smashing major strikes, and in maiming and occasionally murdering workers. They also show the essentially coercive role of the courts, the legislatures and government commissions in response to militant struggle. It has been necessary for Marxist intellectuals to develop an approach which places state and state-civil society relations more thoroughly within the lived experience of coercion.

HIGHLIGHT

1. Marx did not develop a theory of uneven development or regionalism. However, his ideas can be used in examinations of these phenomena.
2. The process of primitive capital accumulation whereby the worker is first separated from the means of production, has occurred in different ways in different places. Similarly, the subsequent development of capitalism has taken on peculiarities specific to time and place. A recognition of these possibilities underlies an examination of regionalism from a Marxist perspective. Sometimes, for example, those occupying a disadvantaged class position also tend to inhabit a particular part of the country.
3. Early Marxist attempts to explain Canadian regionalism were too simplistic. Recently, a number of cogent analyses have emerged. They take into account the complexity of class struggle as it becomes manifested in regionalism.

A Critical Evaluation of Some Recent Analyses of Regionalism

Canadian politicians unquestionably use regionalism for their own purposes. Those in the provinces tend to proclaim it, while federal politicians bemoan it. Usually the requisite class dimension of regionalism is omitted in expressions of concern for 'all' in their region or 'all' in their country.

Canadian social scientists also tend to be either complainers or proclaimers. However, the better analysts at least recognize the class dimension. Usually, though, this recognition is buried in a non-Marxist mode of analysis.

In a short overview, Swainson (1980) describes three recent books by the former group, the complainers: Stevenson (1979), Bell and Tepperman (1979), and Marsden and Harvey (1979). Each work especially decries the growth of political regionalism in Canada because it purportedly leads to a situation of 'divide and conquer'.

All three works share with some current 'Marxist' approaches the idealistic view that if regionalism would only go away, national politics would be more fair and creative. Stevenson sees regionalism as aiding elite accommodation, i.e., the making of deals between regional based elites that purportedly hold the country together. He similarly sees regionalism as an impediment to ridding Canada of other inequalities, such as the oppression of women and of native peoples. Bell and Tepperman see regionalism as underpinning a lack of creative ideals in Canadian political culture. Marsden and Harvey see regionalism as fracturing class consciousness and diluting the potential for national change.

There is, of course, some degree of concrete reality behind analyses such as the foregoing. Politicians in particular, and representatives of the capitalist state in general, do regularly use regionalism to hide class exploitation. These politicians and state representatives, and those social scientists who follow them, attack regionalism. But they do so in the name of an ideal classless "national interest". In reality, it is difficult to argue that a national interest exists independent of the interests of particular classes.

While the bemoaners tend to substitute a mythically classless nationalism for vulgar regionalism, contemporary non-Marxist proclaimers of regionalism carry on Vernon Fowke's classical reformism. They see uneven development as fundamentally a political problem of incorrect policy. Three such reformists are: Forbes (1979) who writes on the Maritimes; House (1981) who discusses Newfoundland and Labrador; and Richards and Pratt (1979) who describe the "New West" of Alberta and Saskatchewan.

Forbes' work, probably the strongest of the three empirically, is an examination of the Maritime Rights Movement, 1918-1927. The Maritime Rights Movement was a political/lobbying movement set up by businessmen and professionals to attain a better deal for Maritime business and better parliamentary representation with Confederation (see Forbes 1979). For Forbes, *despite* its leadership and programme, the Maritime Rights Movement was a beyond-class and classless regionalist grouping of progressive Maritimers.

Forbes essentially accepts the Movement's analysis of Maritime grievances. They were a result of bad federal policies; they did not derive from the uneven development of capitalism. Because he strives to present the image of the progressive Maritimer, as opposed to the common stereotype of Maritime conservatism, Forbes cannot see that his entire book is filled with data for a solid class analysis of the Maritime Rights Movement. He does not critically investigate the non-policy roots of regional underdevelopment, and therefore remains locked into calling for a fairer deal, despite the utter failure of the reformist group he was studying.

J.D. House's article (1981) focusses on the current and potential impact of oil exploration in coastal Labrador. It is a major example of much that is merely ideological and anti-Marxist in the reformist approach to regionalism. Reformism is the only way to redress regional ills, asserts House, because: 1) "messianic" revolution is "utopian"; 2) the people of coastal Labrador have been incorporated into the major institutions of

Newfoundland society; and 3) a "welfare dependency" has been built up, that supposedly cannot be removed. House therefore proposes a "moderate dependency theory" which calls upon the paternalistic "sensitive intervention" of the Newfoundland government and calls for the "political will" of the provincial state segment to develop a sensitive interprovincial regional policy. House's hope is that a reformist provincial government can move coastal Labrador from underdevelopment and "chronic undevelopment" to "dependent development" based on oil.

The class basis for House's reformism has been ably criticized by Overton (1979) in an article on the emergence in Newfoundland of a new middle class of neo-nationalist bureaucrats and academics. Both of these groups are seen as pursuing a class strategy of aggrandizement. House's article tends to mere anti-Marxist ideology because, as he admits, his own data so far support the increasing alienation, not incorporation, of coastal Labradorians from oil interests and the provincial government. House never shows why it is anything but utopian to hope for an all-class sensitivity from the Peckford neo-nationalist class segment, or how "political will" can control oil for the benefit of "the little people".

A more subtle reformism is found in Richards' and Pratt's important volume, *Prairie Capitalism* (1979). The authors trace the economic development of the new staples of potash, oil and natural gas in Saskatchewan and Alberta. They also document the impact of these staples on the former agricultural base, classes and politics of these two provinces.

Their central argument is that a move away from "dependent capitalism" has been engineered by an emerging "new middle class". It is comprised of provincial state officials and bureaucrats in concert with a rising indigenous corporate elite (see Richards and Pratt 1979). The authors support what they see to be a growth in the "relative autonomy" of the province from American and central Canadian monopoly capital. Such autonomy is deserving of support both in its social democratic guise in Saskatchewan and its conservative dress in Alberta.

Again, like the previous reformist works discussed, Richards and Pratt's reformism is problematic because: 1) it underestimates the degree of economic power of multinational monopoly capital while overestimating the importance of the provincial political will; 2) it neglects the class dimension involved in the linkage between the provincial state and multinational and indigenous capital; and 3) it provides a solely political solution to a profoundly political-economic-social-cultural process of uneven capitalist development.

HIGHLIGHT

1. Politicians and academics either proclaim or bemoan the phenomenon of regionalism. The former believe that policies should be intro-

duced that would mitigate the negative effects of regionalism. The latter maintain that regional orientations mitigate against the development of national unity.

Regionalism and Class Struggle: Some Concluding Notes

There exists *no* adequate analysis, yet, of regionalism in Canada. However, a number of steps have been taken in the right direction.

Regionalism in relatively advanced capitalist countries is one central political-cultural expression of the profoundly uneven socio-economic development of capitalism both globally and nationally. Samir Amin (1980:113 and 114) has best captured the process of regionalism within any relatively advanced capitalist country:

> Development has always been unequal in all class societies. Due to the character of the alliances-compromises made in the course of its evolution, the bourgeois revolution itself engendered subsequent inequalities in the development of capitalism. These inequalities developed on several planes simultaneously. Internally (within a national or multi-national state) they took the form of regional inequalities, which sometimes coincided with national conflicts. Internationally they took the form of unequal paces in the accumulation of capital from one country to the other within the group of central capitalist formation on a world scale. Beginning at the end of the nineteenth century, the division of the planet into dominant imperialist formations and dominated, incomplete colonial or semicolonial capitalist formations assumed its definitive, contemporary shape.
>
> The absolutely general character of unequal development can lead to confusion. If the analysis is too vague, if it equates all manifestations of unequal development regardless of context (inequality between center and periphery or between centers, or within a center) and reasons by analogy, it will miss the particular features of each case.[1]

An adequate understanding of Canadian regionalisms must *begin* with a Marxist analysis of the regional uneven development of capitalism in Canada. Regionalism cannot be wished away because it splits the working class and because it is not nationalist. It must be understood, not as the reactive strategy of some sort of false class consciousness, but as a creative strategy for class struggle through which the wants, needs and desires of particular class segments are consciously expressed, organized, and fought for.

NOTES

[1] © 1980 by Monthly Review Press. Reprinted by permission of Monthly Review Press.

SUGGESTED READINGS

Canadian Review of Sociology and Anthropology, Murray K. Knuttila and James N. McCrorie, 1980. Volume 17, No. 3. A special issue on dependency, underdevelopment and regionalism.

Review of Radical Political Economics, 1978. Volume 10, No. 3. A special issue on uneven regional development.

Studies in Political Economy: A Socialist Review, David McNally, 1981. Number 6. A special issue on rethinking Canadian political economy.

Prairie Capitalism: Power and Influence in the New West, John Richards and Larry Pratt. Toronto: McClelland and Stewart, 1979. The strongest example of the reformist position.

Underdevelopment and Social Movements in Atlantic Canada, Robert J. Brym and R. James Sacouman (eds.). Toronto: New Hogtown Press. A Marxist set of analyses from the east coast.

Quebec Society

THE DEVELOPMENT OF QUEBEC: CLASS AND NATION

Greg M. Nielsen
John D. Jackson

Introduction

Contact between peoples occurs in different ways. Cultural diffusion, conquest, forced and voluntary migration are all examples. A typology by Stanley Lieberson (1961) is a useful device in classifying such situations. In his first type of contact, an indigenous ethnic, national or racial group subordinates migrating peoples. Such was the case when, at the turn of the century, hundreds of thousands of Eastern Europeans came to the Canadian West. The second type of contact is a situation in which an indigenous population is subordinated by an incoming population. The subordination of Amerindians and Inuit by Europeans is an example of this second type.

The social organization which follows contact will vary according to the type of situation. In Canada, the conquest and subordination of New France by England was contact of the second type. The clash was between fully or partially developed societies and the outcome was such that one society displaced the other within a new political-economic framework. The subsequent relations between the two societies were relations of conflict and accommodation, of negotiations, alliances and enmities.

In contrast, the first type of contact usually involves individual or family migration. Whole societies do not come into contact. Rather, voluntary migrants adjust to a "host society". The end result is some form of adjustment to the chosen place of migration. It is not a peace that is negotiated among antagonists.

Many English Canadians persist in viewing the development of Quebec and French-English relations within the context of ethnicity and the first type of contact situation. However, the fact remains that the relations between French and English, and the processes which have determined the various links between social class and nationalism in Quebec, result from the second type of contact (Jackson 1977:64-5).

It is important to keep this in mind in an analysis of Quebec. We are not speaking about ethnic groups and immigrants when we refer to French and English Quebecers or to French and English Canada. We are talking about social classes and nationalisms and how the latter *world views* weave in and out of class struggle.

Nationalism is a world view—a way in which people envisage themselves and interpret their worlds. As such, a world view is a combination of ideas, values and experiences from which emerges actual practices, including the way in which argument, or *discourse* is carried out and positions are stated. Thus does nationalism as a world view carry political, economic, religious, etc. argument and expression. Accordingly, the concept of world view is much broader than the concept of ideology as used in other chapters. It permits us to attend to the manner in which the elements of political, economic and religious discourse emerge from nationalism to intersect with social class.

It is also important to keep in mind that what occurred in New France, then in British North America and, finally, in Canada was part of a global system, not merely a set of local events. This point was emphasized in the chapters by Veltmeyer. Imperialism and colonialism were the handmaidens of capitalism; French-English conflict in Canada and the subsequent emergence of the two nationalisms were parts of this process.

Québécois sociologists have been addressing these issues for generations. Indeed, the problems of the analysis of world views and their manifestations in various forms remains a central area of debate. For this reason, the first section of this chapter will review the major debates which have occurred over the years within Québécois sociology. Such an examination will also provide some insight into the major differences between Québécois and English-Canadian sociology as discussed in the chapter by Magill. In the remaining parts of this chapter the theme of class and nation will be developed. The major interest will be in the relation between social class and nationalism in its various forms. We will trace these forms as they emerge, assume a dominant position, and then decline.

The Origins and Development of Québécois Sociology[1]

The treatment of the development of sociology in Quebec will stress the pivotal points around which debates in the discipline revolved and out of which, from time to time, a transitory synthesis emerged. The discipline first appeared on the scene, as it did elsewhere in North America, in the late 1800s. The first sociologist in Quebec was Léon Gérin (1863-1951).

Since its beginnings, it might be said that in contrast with sociology in English Canada, French sociology in Quebec has had a dual tendency. In the first place, as John Porter remarked, there is a tendency towards more macro-sociological subjects (1965:507-8). In the second place, the Québécois sociologist has been more politically engaged than his English-Canadian counterpart. Indeed, the definition of the Québécois collectively as an ethnic group, a nation, a society, a social formation or a region is both a theoretical and political act (Fournier and Houle 1980:22).[2] Of course, the same would hold for English-Canadian sociology. But English-Canadian sociologists have been, until recently, largely insensitive to the political implications of their theoretical constructs.

Despite the work of Gérin (1863-1951), Edmond de Nevers (1862-1906), Errol Bouchette (1863-1912), Etienne Parent (1802-1874), and other pioneering sociologists, the discipline remained fairly marginal in francophone universities. Apart from the interest of a few civil servants, it was hardly visible. Jean-Charles Falardeau referred to this time during which sociology was of little importance as a period of "proto-sociology". It was a phase during which the intellectual foundations of the discipline were outlined. It was not until after the Second World War that sociology was guaranteed a future in Quebec universities and research centres. It was also during this period that interesting ideological divisions first appeared among Québécois sociologists. In part, these divisions stemmed from the difference in orientations found in Europe and the United States.

Many will argue that the 'Chicago School' orientation exemplified by Everett Hughes at McGill University during the 1930s created the first generation of modern Quebec sociologists. Jean-Charles Falardeau, Jacques Brazeau and Hubert Guindon are included among the French-Canadian students of Hughes. Others will argue that those who went to Paris following the Second World War had a much stronger impact on sociology's first generation in modern Quebec. Fernand Dumont, Marcel Rioux, and Pierre Elliott Trudeau are among those who first attended courses given by Gurvitch and other French sociologists (Duchastel 1981).

Whichever version one chooses to support regarding the origin of modern Québécois sociology, the unique emergence of European and American orientations within the same institutions remains an outstanding fact. It is not uncommon today, for example, to have as required undergraduate courses both epistemology and quantitative methods, along with reading lists in both French and English.

Today's Québécois sociologists occupy a privileged position in this unique fusion of anglo-franco traditions though this position is not without its difficulties. The fusion of radically different orientations requires an effort to overcome the inherent tensions within such a duality. As Jacques Dofny has pointed out, this duality creates a triple effect: 1) the sociologist must assimilate two types of sociology; 2) he must overcome the inherent tensions; and 3) he must apply the resulting theoretical schema and methodological techniques to a rapidly changing society (1975:307).

It is not uncommon for Québécois graduate students who go to American, British or English-Canadian graduate schools to have a stronger background in European theory than their fellow North American and British students. At the same time, Québécois students in Europe would have a stronger background in American sociology than their fellow European students. One would expect this to lead to a very promising and original synthesis. Generally speaking, this is not the case inasmuch as there is no one approach to sociology in Quebec. In this sense, it is not different from anywhere else. Nevertheless, what has tended to hold the field together and display quality and originality, has been the tendency to apply diverse approaches to Quebec phenomena. It is this continual and recurring aspect in the history of Québécois sociology which stands out. Keeping these preliminary remarks in mind, we can proceed to outline the major debates or divisions among modern Québécois sociologists concerning the construction of their object of study; namely, Quebec society.

Debates of the 1950s: The Rural-Urban Continuum.   The first modern period of sociology in Quebec, as indicated above, was largely marked by the influence of the 'Chicago School'. The work of Everett Hughes and Horace Miner was, in turn, influenced by the earlier work of Léon Gérin and others. The first wave of sociologists in the 1950s, Marcel Rioux, Fernand Dumont, Guy Rocher, Jacques Brazeau, Jean-Charles Falardeau, Léon Dion, and Hubert Guindon all managed to develop differing interpretations of their predecessors' works.

One of the central debates which emerged during this period and one which remains unresolved, concerns the interpretation of the overall historical, political and social development of Quebec society since its founding. Much of the debate in the 1950s took place around the hypothesis of the rural/urban continuum. This hypothesis had been posed by the Chicago anthropologist Robert Redfield in his essays on "folk" societies (1930). The hypothesis holds that the development of Quebec society can be explained by its transition from an essentially rural or "folk society" to an industrial society. In effect, it is a variety of cultural determinism. In response to this hypothesis emerged a variety of articles, books, dissertations and monographs. They ranged from avid support to outright rejection.

One of the phenomena sociologists attempted to explain, based on the rural/urban continuum, was the late industrial development of Quebec and the absence of the French-Canadian entrepreneur in the industrial sector. In contrast, Albert Faucher and Maurice Lamontagne argued in 1953 that the late development of Quebec was really nothing more than "the simple regional manifestation of the general economic evolution of the North American continent and that it could not be considered in any fashion as the result of cultural environment" (Durocher and Linteau 1980:38).

On the other hand, Norman Taylor, relying more on the Chicago School hypothesis, went into factories and conducted extensive interviews with workers, managers and owners in order to better understand the production process. According to Taylor, the absence of the French-Canadian entrepreneur is explained in large measure by a conservative traditional cultural environment. Such a milieu is characterized by a set of values stressing close ties between family and church in the rural community. It is held that the traditionalism of the French habitant (peasant-farmer) retarded the modernization process of Quebec. Faucher and Lamontagne, according to Taylor, simply dismiss this explanation of "Quebec along with the importance of cultural influences altogether" (Rioux and Martin 1969:272).

The *political-economy* theme adopted by Faucher and Lamontagne reappears in the sixties and seventies in a variety of forms. So does the *cultural determinism* theme of the Chicago School. A notable criticism of the cultural determinism inherent in the rural/urban thesis came from Phillip Garigue (1960:181-200).

Garigue's criticism was directed toward the work of Gérin and its later developments as seen in Hughes, Redfield, Miner, Falardeau, Rioux and Guindon. He makes three points. First, he is critical of the absence of an overall historical analysis, a not uncommon failing of the Chicago School. This leads to an uncritical acceptance of Gérin's original hypothesis regarding the feudal nature of New France. It similarly results in the historical interpretation of Quebec as an essentially rural society in contrast to the rest of urban North America.

The second part of Garigue's critique concerns the absence of adequate methods and concepts to explain the complex nature of Quebec society. Finally, according to Garigue, Quebec has never been an "essentially rural society" bound together by a set of feudal relations. Quebec has always been, since the early days of New France, an urban society with urban relations. "Neither the word 'traditional' nor the word 'rural' means homogeneous in the province of Quebec." In other words, the rural/urban continuum thesis, dating back to Gérin, is considered by Garigue to be essentially mystical, "with no more empirical foundation in it than most myths" (Garigue, 1960:192).

Unfortunately, Garigue does not develop his general critique of the Chicago School apart from a limited follow-up in St. Justine on the social and historical development of the rural community in Quebec (1960). The response to the criticisms of Garigue acknowledged the problems of the concept of "folk society". There was, nonetheless, a refusal to abandon the basic hypothesis of the rural/urban continuum. As far as Guindon and Rioux are concerned, Garigue does not offer an adequate alternative hypothesis that can deal with the problems of peasant culture. Nor can he deal with the transformation of rural to urban social structures.

The important difference between Garigue and his colleagues is really bound up in the overall historical analysis of the origins of French Canada. According to Rioux, "it seems very premature to talk about towns in New France, since the colony numbered only eight hundred inhabitants in 1658, of whom only two hundred were born on this continent" (Rioux and Martin 1969:165). Thus, through the fifties the theme of the historical interpretation of Quebec society remained the centre of discussion and controversy among Québécois sociologists.

Debates of the 1960s: Class and Nation.   The early period of the quiet revolution in Quebec opened the universities to new ideas and challenges. The activities of these institutions had been severely curtailed by the conservative Duplessis regime of the 1940s and 1950s. Never before had debate and political action been so prevalent among Québécois sociologists. It was during this period that a strong Marxist influence began to solidify within Quebec social science departments. In 1961, Jacques Dofny and Marcel Rioux presented a paper at Carleton University on the analysis of social classes in Quebec. Their English Canadian colleagues were astounded by the new concept of "ethnic class" which their paper proposed. As Dofny remarked, "We were really struck, Rioux and I, by the extreme reaction expressed on the part of our English colleagues regarding this concept" (Dofny 1975:307).

The concept of "ethnic class" contains a twofold proposition. On the one hand, Dofny and Rioux argue that there is a uniquely Canadian working class. On the other, they argue that French-Canadian society is also a unique social class which has suffered an unequel economic and social development since the English conquest of 1763. Social class within Quebec then takes a double form. First, Quebec is a social class within Canada. Second, there are class levels or structures within Quebec itself. Dofny and Rioux term this proposition the "double class structure of Quebec".

For the first time a clear articulation of the subordinate position of Quebec society, relative to Canada as a whole, was translated into modern sociological vocabulary. In this sense the shock expressed by their English Canadian counterparts is not especially surprising. The proposition of the "double class structure of Quebec" is further refined by Rioux and continues to be of central importance to his scholarly approach (1978). Dofny has also recently clarified his position concerning the "ethnic class" concept, stating that:

> Class analysis in Quebec necessitates recourse to a double system of stratification, which has led to the use of the concept of 'ethnic class' and to show how the actors in such a situation participate in class struggle and historical change at different levels of social reality (1978:87-102).

It was during the early 1960s that Québécois sociologists were sur-rounded by European scholars who had been invited to the University of Montréal. F. Isambert (sociology of religion), M. Mendras (rural sociol-ogy), E. Morin and V. Morin (sociology of mass communications), A. Touraine (sociology of work and social movements), Lucien Goldmann (sociology of culture) and S. Mallet (sociology of the working class) were among those invited as visiting professors. The tendency to invite European rather than American scholars had a significant impact on Quebec's second generation of sociologists who were coming of age toward the end of the 1960s.

Nicole Laurin-Frenette, Gilles Bourque, and others, once students of Dofny and Rioux, were to be influenced by the French communist philosopher Louis Althusser and his student Nicos Poulantzas. The somewhat more orthodox interpretations of the French version of Marx-ism lead Laurin-Frenette and Bourque to a radical critique of the old concept of "ethnic class". The substance of their criticism was that "ethnic class" is the result of a fundamentally idealist approach which sees social reality as the result of consciousness, rather than the other way around. This premise leads to a view of the 'nation' not as resting "on a collection of scientifically analysable objective facts, but as result-ing from the pure subjectivity of the individuals who are a part of it" (Bourque and Laurin-Frenette 1972:187). They go on to argue that Rioux's and Dofny's view of the history of Quebec is a history of 'representations' of appearances which exist only at the level of cons-ciousness.

There is also a political implication of the Bourque-Laurin-Frenette critique. Whereas Rioux, Dofny and Dumont are fairly sympathetic to the independentist and social democratic aspirations of the Parti Québécois, Bourque and Laurin-Frenette reject their nationalism as an ideological expression of the interests of the Quebec francophone mid-dle-class (petty bourgeoisie). As they suggest:

> We believe that the theoretical foundations developed by these sociologists (Dumont, Rioux and Dofny) underlies all those political positions that favour joining the Parti Québécois and encourage tactical support for the bourgeoisie, without upholding the need for a specifically working class organization (Bourque and Laurin-Frenette 1972:186).

In other words, for these new working class theorists "the concepts of 'ethnic class' and 'ethnic consciousness' are scientifically doubtful and politically suspect" (Bourque and Laurin-Frenette 1972:186).

Debates of the 1970s and Beyond: The National Question, Socialist Formulations.
The late sixties and early seventies were marked by a new political alliance in Quebec—the Parti Québécois. The founding of the party and subsequent events have had a definite impact

on sociologists during the 1970s. The Parti Québécois was formed in 1968 as the result of intense debates among the nationalist groups of the sixties. We will explore the actual developments leading to the formation of the party later. For the moment we will only mention the general kinds of reactions to the party's rise to power and the importance of its presence for the development of the left in sociology.

The founding of the Parti Québécois was the beginning of what some sociologists would call the 'institutionalisation of a social movement' (Guindon 1978:212-46; 1981). For others, the Parti Québécois represents the only legitimate guardian of Quebec's interests (Rioux 1978; 1980). For still others, as we have seen, it simply represented the interests of the Quebec petty bourgeoisie (Bourque and Laurin-Frenette 1972).

In any case, in 1970, the Parti Québécois won 23.1 percent of the popular vote, 30.2 percent by 1973, and in 1976 it was elected with 41.4 percent. It was re-elected in 1981 with 49.2 percent of the popular vote. Whatever the interpretation of the Parti Québécois significance, it is clear that it is a political and social reality which is likely to remain at the centre of debate, not only among sociologists, but among Quebec intellectuals as a whole.

For Gilles Bourque and a new generation of political-economy oriented Marxists, including Pierre Fournier, Anne Legaré, Jorge Niosi, Arnaud Sales, Denis Monière and others, the nationalist question in Quebec is seen as the ideological expression of the capitalist mode of production. Historically, the capitalist mode of production has tended to expand quickly into non-capitalist areas i.e., in peripheral societies where industrial development was either non-existent or at a low level. The capitalist mode of production requires growth in order to survive. The accumulation of capital and the reproduction of the accumulation necessitates an expansion into new markets in order to develop new profits from the exploitation of primary and secondary resources. The expansion process simultaneously produces and reproduces the relations of production, which is to say, social classes.

The process of expansion required by the capitalist mode of production is characteristically imperialist. As seen earlier, it takes the general form of a centre comprised of a series of industrialized states that occupy specific geographical areas, and the peripheral non-capitalist and semi-capitalist societies. The exploitation and domination of the capitalist centre over the periphery results in what is termed 'unequal exchange'.

For Bourque, Monière, Fournier, et al., there is a direct relation between the process of imperialism and nationalism. The nature of this relation results from the development of the nation state. Essentially the role of the state in the capitalist mode of production is to guarantee that the conditions of production, including class relations, technical, intellectual, ideological, and cultural capacities, are in fact in place. The state through its repressive agencies (police, courts, bureaucracy, etc.) and its ideological agencies (family, media, education, etc.) maintains the conditions for production but guarantees the overall dominance of the upper classes.

Nationalism is produced and disseminated through the state apparatus, and, as such, is directly related to the capitalist process of production. According to Bourque, nationalism has a double effect within the capitalist social formation. The nationalistic economic policy of the bourgeois state determines the interior market and its requirements for expansion. The state is therefore the absolute centre of the social formation which surrounds it. At the same time it serves as the exterior link to other nation states (Bourque 1977:68).

Bourque and Legaré (1979) continue to outline the history of Quebec in terms of the more or less direct relation between the development of class and nation in Quebec. Others have amassed empirical studies concerning class structure within Quebec and its relations to Canadian, American, and European capital. To give a few examples, Arnaud Sales (1979) traces the history of the Québécois bourgeoisie in *La Bourgeoisie industrielle au Québec*; Jorge Niosi (1978) places the Québécois bourgeoisie within the Canadian context in *La contrôle financier du capitalisme Canadien*; Pierre Fournier et al. (1978) study various questions related to the production process and the reproduction of social classes in *Le capitalism au Québec*; and Denis Roch (1979) examines the working class structure within Quebec in *Luttes de classes et question nationale au Québec: 1948-1968*. Each of these studies more or less follows the theory of nationalism as interpreted from a classical Marxist perspective.

One lone attempt at a criticism of Bourque, et al. (outside of the occasional polemical rejection of the political-economy Marxists by some of the sociologists from the fifties and sixties) comes from Nicole Laurin-Frenette's *Production de l'Etat et formes de la nation* (1978). The book is actually an extended essay in which the author attempts to re-define a theoretical approach to the study of the production of nationalism by the state. In the process of this reconstruction the author distances herself from the earlier position she had developed with Bourque (Bourque and Laurin-Frenette 1972).

Her criticism of Bourque's position is that his consideration of nationalism makes no distinction between the nation and ideology. Bourque, according to Laurin-Frenette, sees nationalism as being a mirror reflection of the nation state. In other words "the national territory, the national market, the national language etc." are nothing more than manifest illusions which result from the nation state (Laurin-Frenette 1978:30). The national form of the capitalist social formation, for Bourque et al., determines not only social classes but also the nature of struggle and conflict between social classes.

This position, as taken by Bourque, suggests that social classes are the only valid groups to study within a social formation: "The nation—the ensemble, the community, the various national groups," are all simply imaginary reflections of the capitalist mode of production (Laurin-Frenete 1978:30). As they are not forms of class consciousness, they are not valid forms of consciousness at all. Where they are defined as forms of class consciousness, community, nation, etc. are referred to as imaginary ideological constructions associated with the petty bourgeoisie. In contrast, for Laurin-Frenette,

> classes are not aggregates, groups or categories of people. They are rather ensembles and sub-ensembles of people which are formed in specific situations and combinations of situations within the entire process of the social formation (Laurin-Frenette 1978:30).

Although the rupture between Bourque et al. and Laurin-Frenette is often subtle, the importance of the criticism should not be underestimated. The implications of Laurin-Frenette's argument not only suggests differences at the conceptual level, but also at the level of analysis.

The principle data used to support concepts and theories in the studies by Sales, Niosi, Fournier, Bourque, Legaré, and Fournier are for the most part quantitative. They are taken largely from government census and other survey material. Laurin-Frenette suggests a return to the more qualitative community studies of the earlier period of Quebec sociology. Such an approach would avoid the more mechanistic tendency of the more orthodox political economy tradition. It would also facilitate the detection of the subtle nuances that often exist between social groups, classes, the state and the production of nationalism. Laurin-Frenette rejects the theoretical validity of the approaches of Rioux, Garigue, Guindon, as well as the older Chicago School proponents. At the same time she is among the first of the new generation of Québécois sociologists to insist on the rich sociological contents of all of these peoples' work. According to Laurin-Frenette, a reconstruction of the earlier monographs on French communities is of great importance in coming to grips with problems of the historical development of social class and nationalism in Quebec (Laurin-Frenette 1978:102-3).

Dumont, Rioux, Rocher, and others are today perhaps much closer to the political aspirations of the Parti Québécois than their younger colleagues. This is expressed in the differing orientations each group has developed. It is also found in the political divisions inside and outside the Parti Québécois. These divisions have only recently become visible.

An analysis of Quebec society requires reference to both the contemporary debates among sociologists as well as to the debates which occurred in the earlier periods of sociology in Quebec. Without this information the analysis could slip into either the cultural determinism of the earlier period or the mechanistic Marxism of the later period.

The important fact about sociology in Quebec is that Quebec society has been, and remains, the principal object of study. The debate has not centred on whether or not to study one's own society as it has in English Canada, but on the nature of that society. The debates of the last several decades, as outlined above, have centred around a quest for the social realities of one's own milieu. Thus has each new synthesis represented a definition of that reality.

In the following sections we will analyse the interaction between social classes and nationalism in the political and economic domains. It would be useful to keep in mind that ideologies are not systematically organized concepts and propositions. Instead they are loosely structured views of the world in which residual, emergent and dominant elements are present.

HIGHLIGHT

1. Historically, the conquest must be viewed as a situation in which one society subordinated another. A new political-economic framework was the outcome.
2. Sociology in Quebec has tended towards macro-sociological subjects and the Québécois sociologist has been more politically engaged than his English-Canadian counterpart.
3. Québécois sociology manifests the influence of both European and American orientations within the discipline.
4. Several debates have surfaced in Quebec sociology. They have centred in the rural-urban continuum, class and nation, and nationalism and the capitalist mode of production.
5. In Quebec, unlike the rest of Canada, there has always been an emphasis on holistic analyses of Quebec society.

Class and Nation: From New France to Confederation

The first phases of European settlement in the new world began in response to "the demands of European metropolitan centres for fish, fur and lumber" (Easterbrook and Aitken 1956:21). Trade in these and other staples provided the necessities for home consumption in Europe. As trade goods, they also provided the capital for expansion and industrialization. The colonization of North America proceeded hand in hand with the emergence of capitalism and the establishment of nation states in Europe. In the latter a merchant class rapidly succeeded a landed aristocracy, and mercantilism was in the process of becoming the prevailing economic practice. Mercantilism focussed on the "internal economic consolidation and/or expansion of the state" (Naylor 1975a:5). At the global level, the major mercantile states, Spain, Portugal, Holland, France and England, met in North America and elsewhere as each sought to increase its wealth. The struggles within each of these societies between new emerging classes and old classes were no less intense than the struggles between the states themselves.

It is under these circumstances that Quebec was settled. These circumstances, in turn, governed the class structure, the alliances and enmities, and the corresponding ideologies of the colony. It was a time during which feudal society gave way to capitalist society. This is not to suggest a point in time at which one mode stops and the other begins, but a period of time in which the elements of the old are combining with the elements of the new in different ways in different places. In this process, merchant capital, the forerunner of industrial capital, accumulated through the exploitation of territories peripheral to the metropolitan centres.The colonial system tied periphery to centre in order to:

> (1) secure the safety and property of merchants engaged in the colonial trade (primarily monopolistic trading companies); (2) to exclude the competition of foreign merchants; and (3) to regulate the terms of trade between the [centre] and the [periphery] in such a way as to ensure that the lions share of the benefit would accrue to the former (Sweezy 1968:297).

The French Regime: Mercantilism, State and Church.   Fish and fur were the first trade goods exploited by merchant capital in New France. Both England and France were involved with these commodities in the northern half of the Americas from the sixteenth century onward. Clashes between the two were constant in response to local, as well as to global, conflicts of interests. For France the exploitation of neither fish nor fur led to colonization on a large scale. With some variation according to the type of fishery conducted, "the fishery did not itself lead to any large-scale colonizing effort" (Ryerson 1963:77). What settlement did take place was limited to coastal outposts set up to dry and cure fish, and to protect the equipment needed through the winters (Innis 1956:27-42). However, the constant search for a Northwest passage and the lucrative fur trade pushed settlement up the St. Lawrence, northward along the Ottawa River, and westward to the Great Lakes. The resulting settlements, of which Montreal was one, were mainly commercial and military outposts. They were part of the colonial infrastructure designed to funnel wealth from hinterland to metropolitan centre.

Resistance to settlement. New forces in the making would eventually turn the tide toward settlement. The process of forcefully separating producers from the means of production, i.e., of separating labor from property, throughout western Europe, released thousands of people from the ties which bound them to an older mode of production (Marx 1967:713-6). The dispossessed, who were products of this separation, in the countryside, in the towns, and in the cities provided a population for migration and colonization. The dominant classes and the state could rid themselves of a dangerously idle population. At the same time they could ensure the settlement of new lands. Trading companies, however, worked against settlement. They felt that it would, in a number of ways, lead to a reduction in their profits.

The resistance of the trading companies took place in spite of the requirements to establish settlements written into the charters granting trading monopolies to companies of French merchants. From the merchants' point of view, settlers would drain off profits with demands for services and protection. In addition, they would tend to enter the fur trade as small scale entrepreneurs, thus interfering with monopoly rights. These objections notwithstanding, settlement did proceed, but at a much slower pace than in New England. By 1621, thirteen years after the founding of the settlement at Quebec and fourteen years after the founding of Jamestown in Virginia, eleven settlers were recorded in New France. By 1627, seventy-six settlers were to be found around Quebec. In total they cultivated 18 to 20 arpents of land. The year Montreal was founded, the colony boasted 300 settlers. In contrast, 10 000 were located in New Holland on the Hudson and some 25 000 were reported in the Massachusetts colony (Ryerson 1963:85-6). By the time New France was declared a Royal Colony in 1663, 2500 people were settled along the St. Lawrence.

Petty producers and local merchants. The conflicting positions and ideologies of the dominant classes revolved around the settlement question. The class structure was a composite of coalitions, alliances and antagonisms. It tied together a feudal aristocracy, the clergy, merchants and state administrators. Subordinate to these were the majority of the people, the habitants. Feudal interests, represented by the church and the seigneurs, tended to favor settlement. The merchants, and at times, the state, tended to favor the development of trade. Sometimes, however, the state found itself in alliance with the church and seigneurs on the settlement issue.

The establishment of a Royal Colony in 1663 increased the presence and the influence of the state apparatus. Settlement did occur and with it came craftsmen, entrepreneurs and farmers. A new class was in formation. This new class, a class of petty producers, or independent commodity producers, played a crucial role in New France following the conquest. As Denis Monière points out, petty production is not a capitalist mode, but is often grafted on to capitalism as well as to other modes of production (1981:33).

The activity of artisans and the family farm best illustrate petty production. This mode was to occupy a prominent position in post-conquest Quebec. Its base was located in the craftsmen and habitants of the colony.

The principal structural characteristic of independent commodity production is that worker and owner are one. The producer or laborer is also the owner of the means of production. The emphasis is on *use* rather than on *exchange* values, and there is little capital accumulation for its own sake.

Another new development after the mid-1600s was the appearance of an indigenous, or Canadian, merchant class. The development of this class was indicated in the form of the Compagnie des Habitants in 1645 (Ryerson 1963:122). The local population was beginning to refer to itself as "Canadois" and, in 1647, the inhabitants of Quebec, Three Rivers and Montreal were granted the right to elect spokesmen to the governing council. This latter move signalled the increasing importance of local merchants and petty producers.

At the same time, the lower orders were gaining a reputation for being most unruly. They resisted the imposition of church tithes, avoided the clergy and, in the towns, expressed their dissatisfaction through demonstrations and riots. The common people of New France possessed that same independence of spirit as the people of New England. This commonality, however, was never to be realized politically.

Colonial world views. The world views and accompanying forms of discourse woven into this newly developing society were complex. At one level was the absolutism of the monarchy. It was bound to both the gallicism of state and certain segments of church and the ultramontanism of other segments. Absolutism found a ready alliance with gallicism which held that in temporal matters the king was subject to himself and not to church authority. Gallicism, not unlike the Anglicanism of England, aimed to transfer political power from church to state. Ultramontanism, by comparison, placed absolute power in the church and held to the principle of popular sovereignty. At another level, the economic doctrine of mercantilism was tied to an evangelism insofar as colonization was regarded as both economic exploitation and the search for religious converts. These various positions were played out in New France through church and clergy, the seigneurial class, merchants, and state administrators.

The habitant, as independent commodity producer and as one who could produce for his own subsistence and that of his family without selling his labor, was not bound to accept the views of the dominant classes. He did not even feel their effects during this period. According to Jean Pierre Wallot:

> The seignorial system produced a new social type whose interests were united in it: the independent habitant, exempt from personal taxes, owning his land, highly mobile because of the fur trade and the abundance of land, released from seignorial statute labour, and on a footing with the seigneur in community relations (1969:375).

In contrast the Canadian seigneurs were not usually of noble origin, nor was their status tied to their titles. They were mainly town residents and part of "a developing bourgeoisie made up of landowners, merchants, soldiers and administrators" (Monière 1981:42).

This was the structure which was intact when the British entered the colony in 1760. It was a European colony somewhat in the image of the France of the day. However, it had already broken the bonds of the old order and "because of local circumstances and the peculiarities of the colonial situation, absolutism did not achieve expression as a state despotism" (Monière 1981:43-4). Most certainly it was not a traditional peasant society with an urban core. It was an extension of metropolitan France. It was this society that was to come face to face with its English counterpart.

The wars of colonization and empire building had been going on for some time. England and France had clashed in New France in the early days of Champlain's first settlement at Quebec and had continued to do so. These were the wars of merchants and monopolies for domination of the New World trade routes.

By the mid-eighteenth century the shift from mercantile to industrial capital was underway and at varying stages of development in France, England, New France and New England. Slowly, a class of "free" laborers emerged in the colony. They were a creation not only of construction projects (the construction of defences at Louisbourg employed hundreds of workers), but also of shipyards, ironworks and other forms of manufacturing. It is interesting to note that in 1741 when workers in the Quebec city shipyard went on strike, labor was imported from France to break the strike. But these men too walked off the job in support of local labor (Ryerson 1963:154). These events were hardly characteristic of peasant societies.

The Conquest: Stage I.   It is important to appreciate the fact that the Conquest, and subsequent events, were a microcosm of the imperial wars of European powers. The Conquest also involved the meeting of *two societies* in which modes of production were differentially related. The implications for the class structure which was to follow must be examined closely in order to understand the emergence and meaning of the two nationalisms—English and French.

The meeting of two class structures. There are two major interpretations of the consequences of the Conquest. One, usually referred to as the "Quebec school", is based on an argument, generally playing down the effects of the Conquest:

> presenting it as a blessing for the Canadians and, by encouraging the belief that it brought with it freedom and prosperity, veiling the reality of British colonial rule and the domination of the clerical-middle-class élite (Monière 1981:55).

The other is referred to as the "Montreal school". It builds its interpretation around the fact of imperialism and the consequences of colonial domination.

What then were the immediate effects of the Conquest? The colony's economic structure remained the same. It continued to be largely based on trade goods with some manufacturing. The political arrangements remained the same, except, of course, that French was replaced by English authority. The fact of two societies, one victorious and dominant and the other vanquished and subordinate, introduced a new dimension to New France, now a part of British North America. It was the dimension of *nationalism*. Two nations faced each other within a single body politic. Mercantilism maintained its dominant position but with variations tied to the peculiarities of class contradictions at play in each society at the time of Conquest.

During the three years following the capitulation of Quebec and Montreal, French administrators, merchants, and some of the wealthiest families departed. Left behind were the lower classes of town and country, the less wealthy among the merchants and seigneurs, and the clergy. Among this collection of people were the petty producers of farm and city.

British military personnel replaced French administrators. In addition British merchants from England and the colonies to the south rushed in to take advantage of the lucrative French commercial empire. The French merchants found themselves with no choice but to act as agents for the new English merchant class. Lacking both credit and capital they found themselves acting as intermediaries for British trade. In effect, the secular side of French authority had been destroyed. So had the power of the Canadian merchants. It remained for the Church and the seigneurial class to work out an accommodation with the new rulers. Moreover, and this is a point of some importance for future events, the new colonial administrators were sympathetic to the goals of the clergy. As one historian has noted, "the English ruling class, of which were composed practically all military officers and governmental officials, was Tory and feudal" (Lower 1958:96).

The beginnings of nationalism. Structurally, early governors and officials were agents of British mercantilism. Ideologically, they were not as intent on developing a commercial empire as the merchants of New France had been. Indeed, they found themselves in open conflict with their own commercial class, the English merchants. The first governor of British Quebec referred to this group as "a set of licentious fanatics" (Lower 1958:98-9). New political parties reflecting these divisions soon emerged. The conflicts they became involved in represented a self-conscious clash of nationalisms; two nationalisms intertwined with a complex class structure.

English merchants were inclined to share with the French petty producers and working class a distaste for feudal constraints on capital accumulation and associated political freedoms. The Church, the seignorial class, and British administrators were in opposition to these groups. At the same time, neither English nor Canadian merchants could afford to totally oppose the ruling group. Their support was required for protection and legitimization.

The Canadian petty producers were in a different position, and this is a point of some importance. Independent though they were, as a consequence of the Conquest, they were cut off from their habitual ties to French merchants and administrators. Their recourse was to retreat to the countryside. However, in the small towns and villages they found themselves under the domination of clergy and seigneur in a setting that was far more feudal than any arrangement experienced under the French regime. It was *after the Conquest* that the residual elements of feudalism dominated. The seigneurs, like the Canadian merchants, could no longer profit from the fur trade and related activities. Accordingly, their income was to come from feudal rents and dues. These were now collected and legitimated under a British authority.

Such were the arrangements emerging from the union of the Canadian and English societies. As might be expected, almost all of the inhabitants of British Quebec were French in language and Roman Catholic in religion. Such facts left the British with a sense of disquiet. To add to these worries of the British was their awareness of the possibility of revolt in the colonies to the south.

The accommodation between British and French yielded two class structures. Each identified with a particular *national* group. One structure, that was associated with the Canadians, was based on a petty producer mode of production. The other, associated with the English, was based on a capitalist mode of production. The way in which the former was grafted onto the latter was also the way in which the Canadian nation was grafted onto British nationhood. The Quebec Act of 1774 legitimated these and other new arrangements. As Ryerson pointed out, "This measure simply carried forward and codified the terms of the class alliance that Murray and Carleton had forged" (1963:206). Feudal obligations were returned and enforced. French civil and English criminal law were to prevail, and elective institutions were denied. This denial was a safeguard against the possibility of French control of the colony. It also assured that the demands of the English merchants, many of whom were commoners with potentially revolutionary ideas from New England, would have limited effects.

New world views. Ideologically, a new element had been added to the colony. There were not only the democratic discourse of merchants and commoners, a lingering absolutism among the British ruling class despite a constitutional monarchy, and the ultramontanism of the Roman Church. There was also the embryo of a new world view.

Nationalism was expressed by the Canadians in a defensive manner aimed at cultural preservation. The English expressed it in an offensive manner. In contrast to the French their goals were to be achieved through policies of *assimilation*. Assimilation was clearly the intent of the proclamation of 1763 which established the Province of Quebec under British rule (Wade 1955:54). Partly to establish a line of defense against the signs of revolt in New England and partly to hold back the demands from various quarters for a legislative assembly, the Quebec Act of 1774 was drawn up later to seal the hegemony of church, seigneur and British administrator. In addition, it was intended to indicate the success of a conciliation-co-operation position over the earlier assimilation policies. There was a fear that the "inhabitants of Canada were united 'in common principle and wish' with the inhabitants of the other colonies" to the south (Clark 1962:44).

This fear was well grounded. Mass democracy was supported by the French-speaking habitants and petty producers of town and country. It was, in effect, the emergent element resting on resistance to the new English/Canadian alliance of élites (Monière 1981:69). Following Brunet (1969:54-5), Monière notes a general passive resistance towards the new ruling class and a distrust of both clergy and seigneur (1981:69). This same mass democracy carried the seeds of later resistance to colonial rule on the part of Canadian petty producers. It was to meld with the popular democracy of the New England rebels, an ideology which was to some extent already implanted among the merchant class.

The Conquest: Stage II. By the time the New England colonies openly rebelled against domination from London, the situation in Canada was a complex one. It was complex because one mode of production (capitalist) moved to succeed another (petty commodity production), and because two nationalisms were associated. As a consequence, it was possible to interpret one's daily life in terms of nationalism and to neglect the realities of class struggle. The new Canadian élite of clergy and administrators were to make good use of this possibility. They used it to secure a modicum of loyalty toward the new colonial masters. For the clergy, loyalty was to preserve one's language and religion against the onslaught of the universalizing trends of democracy.

The American Revolution: a restructuring of Quebec. In the fall of 1775 hostilities began between the thirteen colonies to the south and England. The conflict suggested a failure of one of the assumptions implicit in the Quebec Act: that the habitants could be counted upon to demonstrate a loyalty to the English Crown. Several members of the merchant class (English and French alike) aided the advancing revolutionary army, preparing the way for an occupation of Montreal. Parish after parish welcomed the revolutionary forces as they advanced through the Lake Champlain district and up the Richelieu. Many Canadians joined the advancing army. This was indeed a North American revolution. The Province of Quebec as a colony in British North America was part of that revolution.

For various reasons, the dominance of the clerical-seigneurial élite combined with the military strength of England in the St. Lawrence held fast. The revolutionary forces withdrew from Montreal leaving Quebec. As a consequence Canada emerged as the centre for conservative forces in North America. The possibility of union with the United States arose again in 1812 and during the rebellions of 1836-37.

A new dimension was added to the national issue following the revolutionary war. Americans loyal to the Crown migrated to the townships east of Montreal. They also went to what was to become Upper Canada and later Ontario, and to the Maritimes. Nationalism took on a new significance. The French-speaking citizens of the colony were, for the first time, faced with a sizeable number of English-speaking and Protestant settlers. These newcomers, though loyal to the monarchy, brought with them the popular democracy of the English colonies. They therefore added their voices to the chorus demanding an elective assembly.

The legitimation of the two nationalisms. The next significant constitutional event occurred fifteen years after the revolutionary wars. It was the Constitutional Act of 1791 which divided the Province into two political, territorial, and national communities, Upper (Ontario) and Lower (Quebec) Canada. Each had a legislative assembly. This move provided the political instrument in Quebec for the ascendancy of a French-Canadian petty bourgeoisie and its now nationalist-liberal world view. It also sealed the existence of two nations in British North America. The events which led to, and followed, the Constitutional Act are extremely important in Canadian history. The year 1791 should be viewed therefore as a pivotal point.

At a global level the imperial wars continued. The British North American colonies were a part of this system. It was a system in which industrial capital was moving into a dominant position eclipsing the remnants of feudalism and mercantile capitalism. This was certainly the case in England and in the United States.

The continuing conflict between England and the United States was, on the one hand, a struggle between two factions of industrial capital for dominance in North America, and on the high seas. On the other hand, English objectives were "unmistakably. . . counter-revolutionary" (Ryerson 1963:269). At the same time the United States was moving away from its national revolutionary ideals to the consolidation and expansion of industrial capital.

Within this setting Quebec found itself largely dependent upon a continuing English dominated mercantile capitalism. Industrial capital was developing but not as rapidly as in the United States. The slow, and never complete, development of industrial capital in Canada was based on the role it was to play in British and then United States industrial development.

Merchant capital provided a part of the investment required to fuel industrial development in England. Indirectly, it also facilitated the production of low cost foodstuffs and lumber for Britain in order to offset the costs of reproduction. This was the colonial relation at its best.

In the Canadas, the fur trade declined rapidly during this period. It was replaced by the timber and lumber trade and increased exports of agricultural products. These exports indicate a commercialization of agriculture, a process from which the new English-speaking farmers in the Eastern Townships would be the first beneficiaries. Later their "cousins" in Upper Canada would also benefit (Bernier 1976:425).

The petty producers of the St. Lawrence Valley parishes also specialized and experienced some financial gain. The benefits, however, were short lived. French-Canadians were excluded from the Eastern Townships since it was colonial policy not to grant new seigneuries. The immediate result was that land, especially good land, unexhausted from years of tilling, was scarce. Problems were in the making.

Between 1784 and 1831, "there was 234 percent rise in population on the seigneurial lands, while the acreage under cultivation grew by only 138 percent" (Monière 1981:84). Hemmed in by a colonial policy which, in effect, opened new lands only to migrating American farmers, and enforced seigneurial obligations on Canadian farmers, and by a commercial class dominated by English merchants, the ability of the petty producer mode of production to reproduce itself was severely curtailed.

The petty bourgeoisie and the 'double structure'. Many French speaking Canadians migrated to the towns and to the United States. They provided a ready labor supply for the new textile mills and for the rapidly expanding timber and lumber trade. Over the same period, members of this class had moved into the professions to serve the needs of farms and villages. Others developed small industries related to farm products. This new class, a petty bourgeoisie, was also confined by the colonial relation. This relation was *at once* a domination by another class and another nation. The French-Canadian professionals and small industrialists were prevented from entering the many posts in the colonial administration because they were open only to the English. They were also unable to gain capital to expand their operations. As a consequence, they had no choice but to ally themselves with the impoverished French-Canadian rural class in common cause against colonial domination. The nationalism and liberalism of the petty bourgeoisie opposed the assimilationist brand of English nationalism and the Tory control of the colonial elite. The Constitutional Act provided this class with the means for political advancement.

By 1810 it is possible to identify distinct classes within the population: 1) English large scale commercial capitalists, dominated by the English commercial middle class; 2) English administrators at higher levels; and

3) a relatively successful collection of English farmers settled in the Eastern Townships. On the other side, as it were, there were: 1) an ascendent French-speaking petty bourgeoisie; 2) a landowning class in decline; and 3) the clergy still in a dominant position. At the bottom there was a rural class subsisting on farms and a growing laboring class.

The petty bourgeoisie opposed the clergy and the colonial regime. Its interests combined with the rural population and the laboring class. With this social base it sought, and gained, leadership through the Assembly and the rapid development of a free press.

The peculiarity of the position of the petty bourgeoisie, a peculiarity which fostered its particular world view, was that it could not tie its political liberalism to its appropriate economic base, that of the expansion of trade and industry. English capital prevented it from doing so. At the same time, it could not, as Monière has pointed out, accept the hegemony of the English merchant class. The latter was the class which constrained its development along normal lines (1981:87). Consequently, it fell back on its own people on the farms and in the villages for support. With a nationalist world view as an organizing principle, the political liberalism of the French speaking petty bourgeoisie, detached from its true economic base, could only be realized by separating from the colonial master. Such an end could be achieved through a national revolution or through annexation to the United States.

The Conquest: Stage III.   While the 1791 Constitution Act provided the framework for two distinct societies—French Lower Canada and English Upper Canada—it also provided the framework for continuing French-English conflict within Lower Canada. Emerging from these conflicts were two nationalist world views and corresponding political and economic discourses.

The Constitution Act gave representative but not responsible governments to the colonies. Elected representatives in the assembly were constrained by an appointed executive authority. To some extent, this united the interests of French Canadian with English Canadian. Segments of both groups demanded full, responsible government. However, from a national perspective, six percent of the population was English and yet 32 percent of the assembly seats in Lower Canada were held by this group. The English also dominated the appointed executive councils. Thus conflicts over taxes, finances, and language followed the national cleavage.

Underlying the national cleavage was the criss-crossing within and between class alliances and enmities. The French-Canadian petty bourgeoisie, who had the support of the general population, dominated the assembly. In opposition stood an English-Canadian bourgeoisie in control of the Executive and Legislative Councils. Ironically, the English-Canadian bourgeoisie found themselves "deprived of the assembly as a vehicle for its class interests" and, in the main, forced into an alliance with colonial administrators (Monière 1981:88). This alliance provided the only route through which the English-Canadian bourgeoisie could gain control of the state apparatus.

Nationalism and the quest for state control. In effect, conflicts during the period between the 1791 Constitution Act and the Union Act of 1840 revolved around a three-way struggle to gain control of the state apparatus. There were the old clergy-seignorial-colonial administrator alliance, the English-Canadian (largely of British and American origin) bourgeoisie, and the French-Canadian petty bourgeoisie. Most issues brought the first two groups into alliance against the third.

A conservative nationalism slowly emerged from among the French-Canadians in the first group. This nationalism was to combine with an English-Canadian colonial world view to oppose the radical nationalism of the third group. It is important not to forget that it was this radical nationalism which embodied ideas of the "new order". The concepts of democracy, freedom and popular control were, in Lower Canada, carried by the French-Canadian petty bourgeoisie.

The "Canadian Party" was founded to represent the political and economic objectives of the French-Canadian petty bourgeoisie. This political instrument along with a new press—*Le Canadien* and, later, *La Minerve*—provided the tools for building a nationalist cause together with demands for a democratic social and political order.

It was not until the nineteenth century that French-Canadian nationalism became more than episodic and with it came a new awareness of common class interests between the petty bourgeoisie and the common people (Monière 1981:90). The process took root within the framework of a largely French assembly and colony (Lower Canada). And it took place at the same time as similar movements toward self-determination were in process in Europe (Serbs, Greeks and Belgians) and in South America (Monière 1981:91).

As a consequence of a "double domination", the struggles of the petty bourgeoisie pointed in two directions. In one direction the petty bourgeoisie "was trying to establish industries based on the transformation of agricultural products, such as breweries, distilleries, etc." (Bernier 1976:426). To accomplish this objective, it was necessary to locate larger markets free of the constraints of seignorial rights. This necessity placed the petty bourgeoisie in opposition to seignorial rights and the clergy-seignorial alliance.

In the other direction, in the move toward the new political freedoms, the petty bourgeoisie found itself in opposition to a strong assimilation policy fostered by the colonial administration and the English speaking merchants. The latter group also drained off public funds for its canal and railway schemes further frustrating the economic objectives of the petty bourgeoisie. That the petty bourgeoisie found common interest with the mass of the French-Canadian population and that its nationalist world view was expressed through a discourse of political democracy was not an accident of history.

Impasse and rebellion. The specific issues around which these struggles took place were many. By 1809, Governor Craig had made a move not unlike the War Measures Act of 1970: "the *Canadien* printing press was seized and its printer jailed, soldiers filled the streets and the postal service was suspended" (Monière 1981:93). The assimilation policies of the colonial government became most obvious during the debates over immigration. Between 1830 and 1850 several hundred thousand immigrants, mostly Irish, arrived from Britain to settle in Montreal, the Eastern Townships south of Montreal, and in Upper Canada. The Canadian Party in the Assembly refused to recognize the Eastern Townships as part of Lower Canada. Therefore they did not qualify for public funds. The same Party also refused to release funds for the canal building schemes of British and English-Canadian capitalists.

An impasse had been reached. It led to demands from English-Canadian capital for a union of the colonies under one assembly and executive. This was resisted by the Canadian Party. The rebellions of 1837-38 under the leadership of Papineau and the patriots of the Canadian Party arose from this impasse.

On the one hand, the rebels opposed the entrenched power of colonial administrator, clergy, seigneur. On the other they opposed the English-Canadian bourgeoisie, its control of the appointed councils, and its schemes for capital expansion. Now two variations on the French-Canadian nationalist theme, which were to remain a part of subsequent struggles in Quebec, were visible.

One was a conservative type. It limited its programme to administrative reforms and espoused co-operation with English Canada. In so doing, French Canadian society was defined in cultural terms (specifically language and religion) rather than in political and economic terms. The other, the nationalism of the 'patriots', as they were called, was democratic, republican, secular and anti-clerical. It was indeed the voice of modernism in a wilderness of French and English conservatism. It was a voice which called for a French-Canadian republic and, at times, seriously considered annexation to the United States.

The defeat of the forces of rebellion and the imposition of the Act of Union in 1840 was seen as a second conquest. In the words of the moderate Lafontaine, the leader of the new Lower Canadian Reform Party, the 1840 union was:

> an act of injustice and despotism in that it is imposed upon us without our consent, in that it deprives Lower Canada of the legitimate number of its representatives in that it deprives us of the use of our language in the proceedings of the legislature (Wade 1955:230).[2a]

Here then was the defeat of the forces of liberalism and republicanism, and a victory for clerical control and the English-Canadian commercial bourgeoisie. The petty bourgeoisie of French-Canada now had no option but to cast its lot with capital expansion. The conservative nationalist world view under clerical control became dominant.

To Confederation.   The Act of Union joined Upper and Lower Canada. They were now to be referred to as Canada East (Quebec) and Canada West (Ontario). Responsible government, however, remained as remote as it was in 1791. Control continued to rest in appointed councils and a governor general. French Canada, it appeared, had also lost representative government. Seats in the assembly were equally distributed between the two colonies while one, Canada East, had some 200 000 more people within its borders than did the other. Furthermore, English was designated as the only language of the assembly, and, initially, French-Canadians were excluded from the appointed councils. The assimilationist policies of the colonial administration were quite explicit in the new Act. This assimilationist stand was part of the discourse associated with the colonial administrators and factions of the English-Canadian bourgeoisie.

English and French nationalisms. There was emerging at the same time a new variety of English-Canadian nationalism. It had its roots in the reaction to the Upper Canadian rebellions led by Mackenzie. The nationalism was a view based on a concept of duality: two peoples, two cultures and two languages. It suited well the now dominant conservative nationalism of French Canada. It found its political base in the Baldwin-Lafontaine government of the new assembly—a union of Upper and Lower Canadian reform parties. Both parties found common cause in their opposition to the entrenched power of the colonial executive councils. Though colonialism, as such, was accepted, reform was directed toward obtaining control of local affairs, markets and the economic infrastructure. Underlying this mild administrative reformism was the economic ascendency of Canada West in agriculture and forestry (Monière 1981:122).

The parti-démocratique or Les Rouges, as they were popularly known, opposed the reformism of Lafontaine's party in Canada East. Les Rouges carried the political discourse of the 1837-38 rebels. Its members were committed to republican principles, representation by population, and elective offices for all branches of government. They were also inclined toward annexation to the United States (Wade 1955:262).

The pressure of this latter faction, combined with the more moderate demand for responsible government by the reform parties, led to a defensive consolidation of the colonial administrator-clergy link (though by mid-century seignorial rights had been abolished). Indeed, the colonial office was inclined to respond favorably to the *cultural* demands of French Canada thereby retaining clergy loyalty against the more radical *political* and *economic* demands of the democrats. This position is well expressed in a letter from Governor Elgin to the British colonial office in 1848:

> The sentiment of French-Canadian nationality which Papineau endeavors to pervert to purposes of faction, may yet...if properly improved furnish the best remaining security against annexation to the States (Wade, 1955:260).

A more virulent form of English-Canadian nationalism nearly ended the life of Governor Elgin. In 1849 an anglophone mob sacked and burned the parliament buildings in Montreal. They were outraged against cultural concessions granted the French, the Lower Canadian Rebellion Losses Act, and a perceived "French Parliament."

While the two nationalisms occupied popular attention, the government of the Canadas was unambiguously a tool in the hands of those supporting capital expansion. The public funding of canals and railways dominated political discussions and at the same time, Canada West was gradually moving into the economic orbit of the United States. Canada East was mainly excluded from the benefits of this development. However, its "treasury" paid dearly to save bankrupt Canada West from total economic disaster.

New forms of colonial domination. Monière notes that the period after 1840 was an important turning point in the development of ideologies in Quebec. The defeat of the patriote movement was the defeat of modernism in Canada. It also signaled new forms of colonial domination interwoven with rigid social relations that were to take over (1981:129).

The conservative liberals of La Fontaine were the proponents of a cultural nationalism. This nationalism proved its worth in the success of the dual government in the assembly, the return of French-Canadians to the executive councils, the return of the use of French in the assembly, and in the winning of a degree of responsible government. The opening of markets, contracts and offices to the petty bourgeoisie tended to bring a large segment of this class over to a more moderate view and win their support for programs of capital expansion.

Les Rouges continued to carry the radical liberalism of the pre-rebellion period. The faction was composed of a limited number of petty bourgeoisie. They maintained an alliance with the farming population and refused to ally with the conservative liberals and the English-Canadian bourgeoisie (Monière 1981:132). Liberal, nationalist and anti-clerical, Les Rouges opposed Church and English commercial domination alike. They favored mass education, improvement in farming techniques, a republican style of government, and dozens of minor reforms. All were anathema to the clergy and the English-Canadian commercial class.

As for the Church, it championed an ultramontanism which eschewed all modern freedoms and any kind of reconciliation with liberalism. It saw church and state as one. Thus politics and religion both fell under the control of the clergy. By adopting a conservative nationalism, as Monière points out, the ultramontanists were able to maintain an alliance of sorts with the reform government. At the same time, they could resort to a "back to the land", return to the old days movement and a general retreat from the contemporary world. Such measures were the best means of survival for French-Canada under clerical domination. The small, clerically dominated French-Canadian village devoted to family and church, and populated by a happy and simple people, is the stereotype produced by the clerical world view. However, this view never quite matched reality.

By the time confederation was a point of discussion, the dominant elements in the world view of French Canada were a combination of the conservative liberalism of the reformists and the conservative nationalism of the ultramontanists of the Roman Catholic Church. In opposition, and as emergent elements, stood the weaker vision of the radical liberals. A Canada devoted to a commercial capitalism in support of industrial development in Britain and the United States had won the day.

HIGHLIGHT

1. Initial settlement in New France was connected with the exploitation of staple products for European markets.
2. Prior to the Conquest, the Quebec class structure was one in which there was an attempt to duplicate the French feudal structure. The attempt, however, had a limited success.
3. As a consequence of the Conquest, the French withdrew from commerce—their place was taken by British and American merchants—and the French independent commodity producers mode of production was grafted onto a British capitalist mode. These modes were to become the basis of two nationalisms.
4. The division of Canada into what are now called Ontario and Quebec followed the migration of English-speaking settlers after the American Revolution. The ideas of such individuals were consistent with those of Quebecers demanding elective institutions.
5. The rebellions of 1837 were in Quebec a conflict between a liberal French-speaking petty bourgeoisie with habitant support; and an alliance of English-speaking merchants and the clergy.
6. After the Act of Union, 1840, cleavages in Quebec between, on the one side the petty bourgeoisie and the habitants, and, on the other side the English-speaking merchants and clergy, found organizational embodiment in Les Rouges and a conservative coalition, respectively.

Post Confederation Quebec

The radical-liberal variety of nationalism displayed in the actions of the
Patriotes of 1837 was defeated by the repressive apparatus of the British
colonial rulers in combination with the conservative-liberal nationalisms
of the reform parties. The movement for independence ended with the
hanging of twelve of the most important leaders, and the deportation to
Australia of fifty-eight others (Ryerson 1968:437-45). In the processes
leading to the Act of Union and finally to Confederation, the display of
the "iron fist" of British hegemony during the patriot rebellions would
prove to have been decisive. In effect, British/English-Canadian
interests had succeeded in setting back the independence movement in
Quebec by at least one hundred years. The enormous ideological implications of the destruction of such a social movement should not be
underestimated. As Rioux has commented: "From the ideological point
of view, this is the most significant period until the end of the 1950s"
(1976:54).

The petty bourgeoisie of Quebec were seduced into confederation
under a set of conditions which were less than desirable. The middle
class was composed of a relatively uneducated first generation descen-
dants of peasant stock. They were a minority in a majority situation.
They suffered both the repression of the British conquest and now the
defeat of the Patriots. The social and political conditions inherited by the
Canada East negotiators at the time of Confederation were not favorable. Under these conditions of negotiation the Canada East voters, forty-
eight in all, were divided. There were twenty-six in favor of confederation and twenty-two opposed. Of the sixty-seven votes from Canada
West (Ontario), sixty-five were in favor. The Quebec voters who voted
"no" were primarily concerned about eventual English domination over
their cultural and economic activities. On the other hand, those who
voted "yes" were fearful of possible American invasion, and represented
the conservative interests of the clergy. There was no clear consensus
among the Canada East voters. After all, the idea of confederation was
not theirs:

> The British North America Act [was] a law of the British parliament. It was
> not an expression of the will of the people of Canada: it expressed the
> desire of Canada's middle class to lay hold of a state (Monière 1981:153).

What then underlies the purpose of the federated state? Whose economic and political interests would this state serve? What were the social
and ideological results of the new institutional order which formed
following confederation? In short, what were the forms of nationalist
discourse inside Quebec over the last century and what relation did these
forms have with social classes and the state?

Industrialization and Monopoly Capitalism. "From the middle of the 19th century to the middle of the 20th century capitalism (in Quebec) reproduced itself in a medieval language" (Laurin-Frenette 1978:82). In Quebec, the language or discourse of feudalism combined a set of relations between the family, the church, and the land. Its mode of production was rapidly penetrated by British and American capital. Until the middle of the nineteenth century the habitant (petty producer) mode of production was essentially self-sufficient. Large families were able to supply their own labor force. Trading was principally between neighbors in town markets. The penetration of outside investment capital raised by the Canadian state for the railroads, and a growing population, forced out an old set of social relations and ushered in a new set. In short, Quebec was entering the monopoly phase of world capitalist expansion.

The exclusion of French Quebec. The self-sufficient mode of production of the French habitant was actually becoming outdated by the beginning of the nineteenth century. The increasing population made it more and more impossible to continue this type of production. Often there would be up to thirty people, involving three generations, in one household. The absence of industry meant that the only mobility for the young was through the extended family. As no more land could be developed for the extended family, emigration to the United States and Ontario became the solution for many. Between 1830 and 1930 over 800 000 Québécois emigrated, mostly to the United States. Ironically, if this population had emigrated to western Canada, it is quite likely that the western population would be French-speaking today. In any case, despite enormous external and internal pressures, in 1851, 80 percent of a population of one million was rural (Monière 1981:146).

Industry was based in Montreal and Quebec City. The entrepreneurs, markets, techniques, and capital all came from outside.

The end of the nineteenth and the beginning of the twentieth centuries saw world wide movement toward monopolization. In Canada, following Confederation, four banks out of fifty controlled 43 percent of bank capital. By 1928, there were only ten banks. In 1930, four of the ten controlled 82 percent of bank capital. This figure represented 63 percent of all capital in the country. In 1900, investments came from Britain and to a lesser extent the United States: 85 percent from the former and 15 percent from the latter. By 1930, the Americans had succeeded to the dominant position. They had 61 percent of investment to their credit. British investment accounted for 35 percent. The two provinces which served as centres for this investment were Quebec and Ontario.

The industrial base had long been shifting from Quebec to Ontario. Such development had occurred with the shift from British to American domination. At the national level, though, it was really Ontario and Quebec that dominated development. By 1918, Quebec and Ontario were the homes of 74.4 percent of the industrial establishments in Canada and by 1940 the figure reached 81 percent (Bourque and Legaré 1979:115).[3]

Resistance to proletarianization. Strictly speaking, it is difficult to see Quebec, as some have argued, as a colony of Canada. Yet there are certain systematic inequalities between the two. By 1939, for example, the net value of production was calculated at 44 percent in Ontario and 25 percent in Quebec. In Ontario, development has centred around heavy industry. In Quebec it has been mostly light or secondary industry (Bourque and Legaré 1979:120). Quebec is far from being the most underdeveloped region in Canada but it is nonetheless more underdeveloped than Ontario. Bourque and Legaré argue that this unequal development has nothing to do with an anglophone wish to develop Ontario rather than Quebec. Rather, they suggest that the solution is to be found in the late accommodation of feudal relations in Quebec and the general resistance to proletarianization on the part of Quebec petty producers. Indeed, outside of relatively small industrial centres which were developing in Quebec City and Montreal, much of the population remained rural. Between 1881 and 1911, Faucher and Lamontagne point out that "the manufacturing pattern... rests mostly on miscellaneous materials, vegetable, and animal, and especially on textile, leather, log and lumber products" (Rioux and Martin 1969:262). Ontario, at this time, was engaged more in mining and steel industries. By the end of the century, the total value of production was "estimated at $150 million. Of this, agriculture contributed 65 percent, forestry 25 percent, manufacturing four percent, fishing and mining about two percent each" (Rioux and Martin 1969:262).

The shift from sail to steam in the earlier part of the nineteenth century and the grain boom in Canada West in 1870, had a dramatic impact on the Quebec economic structure following Confederation. The former tended to create a rapid expansion of the forestry industry. The latter led to a general economic depression and an overall shift in agricultural production. Still, the essentially agricultural base could not support the increase in population, which rose from 1 488 535 in 1891 to 2 002 712 in 1911 (Rioux 1974:183). The entry into the dairy and lumber economy helped cement Quebec's dependency on internal markets, techniques and means of production. In effect, capitalist penetration of the formerly self-sufficient mode of production in Quebec was virtually complete well before the end of the nineteenth century.

The resistance breaks down. Between 1910 and 1940 rapid industrialization occurred in Quebec. Industrialization was a consequence of foreign investments largely from Britain and later from the United States. The First World War helped make Quebec more competitive in the lumber industry. Scandinavian and east European countries, Quebec's major competitors, could no longer compete. The war opened the market for agricultural goods, and there was an increasing demand for manufactured goods.

An industrial urban proletariat appeared for the first time in larger numbers than the rural peasantry. The proletarianization process was in full swing. Emigration to the United States was slowing and the working class was growing "a phenomena attributable in part to the 'active proletarianization' of Quebec women". The shift from rural to urban production went from 65 percent rural in 1900 to 12 percent in 1935. The urban population rose from "39 percent of the total in 1901 to 63 percent in 1929." During this period 172 000 people left the land for the cities (Monière 1981:178-9).

The emergence of the urban proletariat in Quebec did not coincide with the emergence of an indigenous bourgeoisie equal to a national bourgeoisie. The dominant bourgeoisie came from outside of Quebec. It represented foreign capital investment. The industrial and financial bourgeoisie was mainly composed of Americans and English-Canadians with a very small number of French-Canadian capitalists. Monière cites a report from an early Catholic labor union which indicates a reaction of workers to this overwhelming hegemonic process:

> Our natural wealth is monopolized by foreigners; our work force is exploited by the development of artificial industries, four fifths foreign owned; production is organized in lopsided and irrational ways for the benefit of big business rather than the immediate needs of the consumer....We have to face the future. Should we continue to let the Americans and English take the best of what we have, and gradually reduce us to menials? (1981:180).

The domination of foreign capital has continued throughout the history of Quebec. The Quebec petty bourgeoisie maintained its position and achieved a slow but steady growth. The ethnic division of labor, that is comprised of the essentially francophone work force on the one hand, and the essentially Anglo-Saxon owners on the other, also continued throughout the industrial epoch (Bourque and Legaré 1979:156).

The shift from British to American investment was well on its way by the 1930s. Following the Second World War, the influx of American capital overtook British investment.

The Confederation period, the economic crises of 1880, and the long industrialization process, characterize the overall structure of Quebec society between 1867 and 1960. However, to this point the discussion has been principally of an economic nature. It also includes a consideration of the penetration of capitalism and the general structure of social classes throughout the period. In order to explain the relation of nationalism to the development of social classes in Quebec we must examine its expressions within the political and ideological apparatus of the Quebec social structure.

The Traditional Alliance and the Nationalist World View of Survival.

The traditional alliance between clergy and colonial administration disappeared with the advent of Confederation. The petty bourgeois interests were henceforth represented in the National Assembly. In other words, a power shift had occurred forcing the clergy to make a new alliance. The ideology of the clergy had to modernize in order to meet the demands of the new order. Thus were they forced to become more overtly political. They were required to control the votes for the various competing political factions. Naturally, those factions which were most strongly allied with the clerical ideology were elected.

The role of the church. The church modified its overt activities by being more actively engaged in community activities, such as newspapers and politics and its world view was a modification of that present during the pre-confederation period. The nationalist discourse of the alliance thus carried a strong residual element. Its basic tenets were borrowed from the past but its form was relatively new.

During the British period, the aim of the clergy was to eventually evolve a French Catholic state on the banks of the St. Lawrence. This aim now could have the support of a recognized political power. In addition, a new wave of catholic revival was taking place in Europe and the Quebec clergy easily gained strong support from the Vatican. The world view of the clergy which came into position following Confederation retained the ultramontanist position.

The ultramontanist world view should not be seen as an all-encompassing view of Quebec, although it would certainly seem to have been the dominant one. Indeed, there were several 'cracks in the monolith'. Despite the anti-liberal, anti-union and anti-socialist tenets of ultramontanism, each of these elements appear at one time or another and required compromises with the church.

Ultramontanism controlled the legitimized internal relations of class and power. It also provided resistance to the liberalism which accompanied capitalist penetration. The church provided the ideological legitimization for the basically conservative political apparatus. In turn, the church was guaranteed jurisdiction over education and culture. It was the church which produced the nationalist discourse of this epoch (Laurin-Frenette 1978:97).

Quebec nationalism and the absence of control. This form of nationalism cannot be understood without referring to the internal conditions. In other words, the absence of any real control of the means of production either by the petty bourgeoisie or the clergy meant their real role as the dominant social class in Quebec was to provide social control of its population. This was the result of colonial domination.

The power of the dominant class depended on economic investments from outside. Neither the clergy nor the petty bourgeoisie had any real input into the economic planning of their own society. As a consequence French Catholic nationalism did not have to define itself in terms of the necessity of industrial development and the entrenchment of an indigenous French bourgeoisie. "Rather, it was defined in terms of the entrenchment of its class role as official intermediary in the structure of dependence" (Monière 1981:176).

On survival. The conservative nature of the nationalist ideology was expressed in the doctrine which the Church taught to the farmers, workers and petty bourgeoisie of the day. To be close to the land, to have large, extended families, and of course, to be devoutly Catholic. Only through the careful following of the church's catechism could the French-Canadian race survive on a continent of Anglo-Saxon protestantism. Survival was the key.

A number of events supported this general belief. The Riel affair in Manitoba and later in Saskatchewan; Canadian involvement in the Boer War; the Manitoba School Act; Regulation 17 in Ontario, which reduced the use of French in the schools; and the conscription crises of the First and Second World Wars all added fuel to French-Canadian nationalism.

Politically, Quebec had been manipulated by the clergy, to support conservative governments. The trend continued on both the provincial and federal levels until the election of Laurier in 1896. The Quebec political scene between 1867 and 1896 was dominated by two individuals: Jules-Paul Tardivel and Honoré Mercier. The former can be considered the father of contemporary separatist thinking in Quebec. The latter was the leader of the first nationalist party in Quebec. Both were sanctioned by the clergy and both were ultramontanists. The clergy continued to place liberals on its sinners' list until the end of the century when Vatican intervention prohibited a direct role in politics.

Since the end of the nineteenth century, Quebec has voted liberal federally. There has been only one exception. Provincially, however, it elected liberal governments until the Duplessis conservative regime began in 1936.

The banishing of the clergy from active politics was a minor but significant set-back for them. The Church and the political apparatus were closer to being on equal grounds. It would take another sixty years before the political apparatus would take over the various educational and cultural institutions of Quebec society.

The nationalist political discourse, although it was often *independantist or separatist*, as in the case of Mercier's nationalist party in Quebec, took on a very different tenor at the federal level. Laurier argued a 'pan-Canadian nationalism'. This position placed the political apparatus above nationalism and carried the older liberal conservative notion of duality and equality with respect to French and English Canada. Meanwhile the Church accommodated the new petty bourgeoisie by altering its own hierarchy and forging a new alliance with the players in the political apparatus. Such developments signify a modification of the ultramontanist world view, but not an abandonment of it.

The church and the reproduction of labor. The family structure of the French-Canadian community was tightly bound to the church. "The sacred functions for the large family are explicit in the roman catholic doctrine" (Miner 1974:65). The church, during the period of industrialization, controlled family beliefs, values, and norms. It accomplished this end through education and religious functions and by forming alliances with the petty bourgeoisie. As a result the Church, during the industrialization period, served as the principal apparatus of the reproduction of the conditions of production.

The discourse of reproduction, at least at the provincial level, was expressed in terms of political autonomy. The Church also argued for an independent Quebec economy with an indigenous bourgeoisie. However, the fundamental ultramontanist world view of the Church became more and more out of step with the industrialization process. What was at one time active was now becoming a static view of the world.

The Duplessis Regime.   Politics and the Church experienced their final alliance during the Duplessis era. This period began when Maurice Duplessis, authoritarian and French Catholic, champion of Quebec autonomy, took power in 1936. He did so at the head of the Union National party. He was defeated in 1939 but swept back to power in 1944. He remained there until his death in 1959 (Quinn 1963; Boismenu 1981). Most liberal thinkers of the day saw this as the period of the "grande noirceur" (great darkness). For the liberal petty bourgeoisie, it was as if the political apparatus had returned to the ultramontanism of the turn of the century. The Duplessis regime represented the interests of the non-monopoly, mostly rural, petty bourgeoisie. For the first time the division between fractions within the petty bourgeoisie clearly emerged.

The origins of class divisions in Quebec society are rooted in the differing alliances each class fraction formed with the bourgeoisie (largely English-Canadian and American) that controlled it. The liberals, from Laurier onward, allied themselves with the managerial class. It represented the interests of the British, and later American, investors. Duplessis and the conservative Union National party allied itself with the rural merchant class. Traditionally, this group had been controlled by the church. The nationalist discourse produced by the political apparatus took on the same form as it had following Confederation. However, no matter how authoritarian the Duplessis regime became, there was always a liberal opposition in the shadows.

Duplessis came to power in the middle of the Great Depression. By 1936 there was almost thirty percent unemployment with more than 100 000 people on relief. His message was simple and effective: a return to the old values would eventually restore stability and, therefore, prosperity. The old values were rural values, religious values, the values of more than three centuries of French-Canadian ruralism and Catholicism. As Duplessis himself put it: "Agriculture is an element of economic stability and social order. We must maintain and protect our rural base" (Bourque and Legaré 1979:141).

For Duplessis, spiritual values came first. There was, as a consequence, a revival of the fears of industrialization, urbanization, and social change. He took power in the middle of a general "back to the land" movement, itself a reaction against the industrialization processes which had been building for some time. During this particular period (1931-41) there was an increase of 13.7 percent of the number of farms in Quebec and a 4 percent increase in cultivated land. Duplessis encouraged the "back to the land" movement between 1936 and 1939. Consequently, between 1944 and 1959 "he continued his policy of supporting agriculture" (Bourque and Legaré 1979:143-4). He also supported agriculture because of the distribution of seats in favor of rural constituencies.

The autonomy and the agricultural policy of Duplessis were given a huge boost by the conscription crisis of 1942. Elsewhere in Canada there was pressure on the federal government of Mackenzie King to legislate mandatory conscription into the armed forces.

For the most part Quebec wanted nothing to do with a war fought on European soil and certainly felt no affinity toward Britain. English Canada tended to favor conscription. As a consequence, it viewed French Canadians as traitors. In a national referendum on the issue, French Canadians voted overwhelmingly against conscription. English Canadians voted in favor by a large majority. As in the Boer War and the First World War, French Canadians were once again forced to participate in a war they did not accept as theirs. In 1942 conscription was law.

In 1942 the 'anti-conscriptionists' founded the Bloc Populaire. It grew out of the League for the Defense of Canada (the 'no' campaign in the conscription crisis). Its platform stressed provincial autonomy and anti-monopoly measures. It argued that all previous governments had allowed the monopolies a free hand in Quebec. Now there must be strong state-intervention to offset this influence. Hence the 'Bloc' platform was a curious mixture of traditionalist and progressive policies. Following the war, and a return to prosperity, the party was disbanded. It had, however, succeeded in raising feelings of autonomy in the province. Duplessis, re-elected in 1944, cashed in on the autonomy and traditional elements in the platform and ignored the progressive elements (Quinn 1963:48-72; Milner and Milner 1973:105-73).

Duplessis' autonomous leanings did not hinder the penetration of capital, especially capital from the United States following the Second World War. If anything, Duplessis fully endorsed the free entry of massive American capital (Boismenu 1981:41).

The Union National party of the traditional rural petty bourgeoisie, oriented its policy toward the creation of regional markets. It is not surprising, therefore, that it assisted American capital by tax concessions and the building of regional infrastructures such as roads, hospitals, and other services (Bourque and Legaré 1979:193-4). In 1955, 37 percent of the provincial budget was tied up in transportation, communications, and natural resource projects. "In the period 1953-1961, the total American investment nearly doubled from $2,305 million to $4,320 million, or 74 percent of direct capital investment" (Monière 1981:229). The ownership of the means of production by French Canadians was 10 to 15 percent (Monière 1981:229).

In the wake of the inflow of foreign capital Duplessis saw Quebec as a reservoir of cheap labor. The task of the political apparatus would be to control this labor force, not to develop the rich natural resources. This would be left to others. Duplessis' "approach to economic reality was simplistic, demagogic, uncomprehending of the complex industrial world in its monopoly phase" (Monière 1981:238).

The ultramontanist world view of the Duplessis regime led to a whole series of repressive and reactionary measures against organized labor. For Duplessis, and the traditional petty bourgeoisie, unions were organizations for christian charity. They should not oppose capital. Duplessis employed legislation to oppose industrial discontent. He also kept wages as low as possible, and diffused the power of the catholic unions once they began to turn increasingly radical. He passed Bills 19 and 20. These allowed his government to intervene in collective contract agreements and re-set wage scales. Bill 5 gave him the power to decertify any union which had any communist membership (Quinn 1963:94). Police were used as strike breakers in Asbestos in 1949, Louisville in 1952, and Murdochville in 1956. Welfare, unemployment insurance, universal health insurance, or any other social programs were opposed by Duplessis. Education was a process to teach the young the values of an 'older society'.

The ideological opposition to the Duplessis regime came from a variety of organizations. They were, for the most part, liberal in orientation and belief. Many of the newspapers and political organizations such as Action Libéral, Bloc Populaire and Action Nationale, supported the autonomous principles of Duplessis, but attacked his economic policy. *Le Devoir* and *Cité Libre* attacked all aspects of the regime. Some of the more central figures of *Cité Libre* were Jean Marchand, Gerard Pelletier, and Pierre Elliot Trudeau.

The opposition was inspired by the increasing gap between cultural and economic realities in Quebec. French Canadians were comparing their standard of living and cultural habits with other industrialized nations. In so doing they discovered they had fallen behind. The old idea of survival was becoming vastly outmoded in the eyes of an emerging group of unionists, journalists, artists, students and intellectuals. The opposition ideology of the day expressed a desire to "bridge the gap between Quebec culture and Quebec society". It thereby represented technical, economic and urban industrialization. As Rioux states: "the opponents of the regime...were inspired not only by [the idea] of confrontation but more fundamentally by [the idea] of catching up" (1978:70).

HIGHLIGHT

1. Although the capitalist mode of production was in the process of penetrating the infrastructure of Quebec society in the period following confederation, for the most part the day to day relations remained pre-capitalist. Reproduction of the conditions of production was carried out in a medieval discourse.
2. During this epoch the double class structure continued. Nationally Quebec was underdeveloped and internally, francophones occupied the lower class positions while the anglophone bosses of British and then American corporations forged an alliance with the fractions of the rural based petty bourgeoisie.
3. Despite an increased industrialization of Quebec, until the 1960s, the conservative nationalism of the church and the Duplessis regime remained dominant. In the 1950s the opposition to the conservationism which came to be seen as an obstacle to Quebec's industrialization process was expressed in a discourse of *rattrapage* rooted in a liberal world view.

New Class Alliances and the Emergence of the Left

Maurice Duplessis, the last demi-god of the traditional rural alliance between clergy and petty bourgeoisie, died in 1959. Less than a year later the liberal reformist government of Jean Lesage came to power. It marked the beginning of the quiet revolution.

A new, modern petty bourgeoisie was rising to a position of political and economic power. It was doing so without the mandatory alliance with the church.

The traditional alliance was no longer capable of coping with the exploitation of foreign capital. It could no longer keep external cultural and political realities from penetrating the French Canadian milieu. In effect, the imperialist cycle which had been developing since the sixteenth century was launching Quebec into the modern workings of the capitalist world system.

The political apparatus must provide new services which meet the new demands of capital. At the same time, cultural relations which define the meanings of a society must also change. During this period the nationalist world view does not disappear along with the traditional alliances. Instead, it emerges in a variety of forms which correspond to the new alliances and cultural changes.

The Quiet Revolution. Although it has been interpreted from a variety of different viewpoints, the quiet revolution is considered to have been first and foremost a cultural revolution. As Rioux put it: "The quiet revolution was more a mental revolution, a development of critical attitudes towards men [and women] and affairs than it was a revolution-ary action per se" (1978:75). Social groups, social classes and fractions of social classes, which had been previously represented by the clergy, were re-organizing themselves. They began to articulate their sense of inferi-ority and domination not only under the traditional alliance within Quebec but also within the North American continent. French Canadi-ans in Quebec, from this point on, would refer to themselves as Québécois.

The political apparatus, under the Lesage liberals, "reaffirmed the political hegemony of the Canadian monopoly bourgeoisie" within Quebec (Bourque and Legaré 1979:178). For Monière, "the expression 'quiet revolution'...encompasses the reforms carried out under liberal administrators," and not a fundamental re-structuring of political and economic power (1981:251). The cultural revolution did not extend far beyond the political apparatus nor did it last for more than six years.

During the Quiet Revolution, the political apparatus replaced the services the church had offered for more than three hundred years. One of the first acts of the Lesage government was to take over education. Bill 60 created the education ministry. As a result, in ten years enrolment rose 100 percent in secondary schools, 82 percent in colleges, and 169 percent in universities. The government priorities in this period were social welfare, health, education, and the creation of Crown corporations to assist small businesses.

The Parti Québécois and the Crystallization of the Left. Nation-alist political discourse, since the defeat of the Patriotes in the nineteenth century, was expressed as provincial autonomy for Quebec. Few people, with perhaps the exception of Mercier, Bouchette, and a few others who argued for economic independence as early as 1904, saw the Quebec state as being able to support an independent Quebec (Tremblay 1977:9-47). However, the advent of the quiet revolution, the almost total demise of clerical power, the new streamlined political apparatus, and the general cultural renaissance, produced a new nationalist discourse. The tone of the discourse shifted from survival to 'catching up' and from autonomy to independence. Indeed, the 1960s saw an explosion of independence groups ranging from the far left to the far right.

Among the *independantist* groups which took 8 percent of the vote in 1966, were included: the Rassemblement pour l'Indépendence Nationale

(RIN), the Alliance Laurentienne, Action Socialiste pour l'Indépendance Nationale, Parti Républican du Québec, Ralliement Nationale, and, later, the Mouvement Souveraineté Association. The latter group was formed in 1967 under the leadership of René Levesque, a former cabinet minister with the Lesage government.

One year later the Parti Québécois was born. Its founding was marked by a series of compromises between the left and right wing nationalist parties. Levesque, and Parizeau (now Minister of Finance) gave the party an air of respectability. The party represented a crystallization of political aspirations regarding the future independence of Quebec. Its members ranged from a socialist wing led by the Parti-Pris group, to the left wing social democrats of the R.I.N., to the right of centre groups which emerged from the older rural alliances of the Union National and the Social Credit parties.

The Parti Québécois, whose original membership came largely from the new petty bourgeoisie, "teachers and students, civil servants, and highly trained professionals", was considerably softer in its tone than the socialist wing of the party or even the R.I.N. (Monière 1981:267). The P.Q. retained the political platform of independence. But it did not advocate a separate independent Quebec. Rather, the P.Q. tried to soften such a political shock by shifting the platform to political sovereignty with economic association. The objective of the P.Q. has been to slowly and democratically convince its population of the necessity of such a transformation. There are two streams of thought within its ranks. One stream emphasizes a technocratic form of efficiency. It advocates a rational, and functional management of society by the state. The other stream emphasizes a decentralization of the state bureaucracies in order to reconcile efficiency with participatory democracy.

Following the founding of the Parti Québécois, and coinciding with a rise of a socialist world view and increasingly radicalized unions, a series of small terrorist groups under the name of the Front de Libération du Québec (F.L.Q.) intensified their activity. In 1970 they kidnapped a high-ranking government official, Pierre Laporte, and a British diplomat, James Cross. For this militant group, Quebec independence was possible only through the process of violent revolution. What was required was a total re-structuring of Quebec society. This form of nationalism and its terrorist application were met with the iron fist of the Canadian military through the War Measures Act in October of 1970. The whole affair lasted almost six weeks, and would not be forgotten by the Quebec population.

In a sense, the events of the 'October Crisis' helped to solidify the P.Q. alliance. The P.Q. was penetrated by R.C.M.P. agents. Its members were arrested and questioned. In the end, it emerged as an untainted democratic, peaceful organization. Its public image was intact and the pressure from the militant left temporarily delayed. In the elections which followed (1973 and 1976) the P.Q.'s strategy leaned more toward getting the vote than educating the Quebec population about sovereignty-associa- tion. In this sense, the P.Q. became more and more a party reacting to public opinion polls in hopes of achieving power, rather than stimulating a social movement. Guindon argues that the loss of the referendum on sovereignty association in June 1980, was largely due to the 'political marketing' strategy of the P.Q. rather than a strategy of 'political mobili- zation'. In the former strategy the emphasis is placed on "playing up to the consumers' preferences". In the latter, the emphasis is placed on "political action". The fact that this strategy was chosen is a result of the over-institutionalization of a national movement. Guindon explains:

> A movement capitalizes on unrest that it spreads. Institutions, on the contrary, adapt to their environment as constituted. As a movemeent succeeds, its legitimacy as well as its membership and resources increases; its degree of conflict with things as they are decreases. This process of increasing accommodation is called, in sociological jargon, the institution- alization of a movement (Guindon 1981:20).[4]

Crisis and Disintegration.   Levesque, president of the Party with 300 000 card-carrying members, and premier of Quebec, held the alli- ance together for a convincing victory in the election of 1981. The loss of the referendum in 1980, however, put the Parti Québécois in an awk- ward position. In fact, without the promise of independence the P.Q. platform moved one giant step closer to that of the Quebec Liberal Party.

In 1976 the election of the P.Q. was seen as a popular victory. This established the hegemony of the Parti Quebecois over the nationalist movement. The legislation of Bill 101, a law restricting the use of English on public signs and access to English schools, while it shocked anglo- Quebeckers, at the same time it has been strongly supported by the majority francophone population. The prospect of the referendum in the first term of office, the outraged reaction from Ottawa, and the clear-cut class interests of the Canadian bourgeoisie which penetrated the pro- Canada (anti-P.Q.) movement, all acted as elements holding the P.Q. alliance together. The actual demise, or disintegration, of the alliance began around 1978. The issue was the debate over the wording of the referendum question.

The alliance of the Parti Pris socialist group, the R.I.N. social demo- crats, and the Liberal and Union National elements, lasted almost ten years before the splits in the party developed into outright oppositional movements. It is difficult to comprehend how the selection of some one hundred words for a referendum could create such a disturbance. On the one hand, the left wing of the party had long advocated the outright independence, or sovereignty, approach. On the other hand, the centre and right wing of the party wanted economic association with Canada. In other words, one side expressed socialist economic planning for a future independent socialist Quebec state. The other side expressed a gradual *étapisme*, or step by step plan leading to a future democratic Quebec nation with a mixed economy and close ties with English Canada.

Although these are the extreme positions leaving considerable room in between, they characterize the division among the party's rank and file. Evidence of the break resurfaced recently in a purge of the party's militant left. It was occasioned by an internal referendum re-establishing the hegemony of Levesque and his closest cabinet ministers over the party. As a result of this purge, a number of militant socialist riding representatives have resigned.

At times it is difficult to establish how ministers within the party actually align themselves, given that the alliance may change depending on circumstances. Nonetheless, the report of the *comité des 11* (eleven government ministers) concerning a review of the budget policy for 1981-82 clearly denounced government policy as favoring private enterprise (Fournier 1982:61). The resignation of a series of left wing ministers (Burns, Payette, Couture, O'Neil), the purge of the left wing riding representatives, and the growing dissatisfaction expressed in the report of the *comité des 11*, marked a clear shift to the right within the party.

The shift to the right within the P.Q. did not necessarily suggest that the independence issue was about to disappear. Nationalist discourse has been, and continues to remain at the centre of both right wing and left wing groups throughout Quebec history. The questions are: will the objective antagonisms between the state and progressive forces in Quebec outweigh the necessary alliance that must be forged in order to bring about a sovereign nation? Will the party survive the present world fiscal crisis which has forced the state into a period of economic *décroissance* or decline?

Quebec, in 1982, faced a possible $3 billion deficit, the likelihood of the federal government withholding transfer payments of millions of dollars, and a staggering interest rate. In the presence of this fiscal crisis, the provincial state had one of two options. It could borrow the money on the open market. This solution would increase the already crushing burden of the deficit. Alternately, it could cut back on spending in education, medicare, and other social services. At the same time it could institute hard-line policies against labor union demands.

The P.Q. implemented aspects of both these options. Education budgets were slashed, or held to no growth. There was talk of holding civil servant, and other wage demands, within the public service to no increase or, in some cases, actually reducing wages. In the meantime, unemployment increased steadily. In some areas it reached 40 percent.

Economic and social crisis is deeply rooted in today's capitalist world system and as such the Quebec experience is not atypical compared with many other societies. In effect, nation states are in a period of intense reconstruction all over the world. The national question in Quebec is very much a part of this process. In this respect, the position of the Parti Québécois is roughly similar to the nationalist governments of Mercier and Duplessis.

All three governments faced growing opposition movements on their left flank during times of economic and social crisis. Such was the case despite a general consensus regarding provincial autonomy. For Mercier, the opposition was from pan-Canadian liberalism finally expressing itself in Laurier's brand of federalism. For Duplessis, it was from a similar liberalism, but with a modernist (catching up) twist.

For the P.Q. the opposition is coming from its own left flank in the form of a growing militant socialism. There is also a continuation of the pan-Canadian liberalism which confronted both Mercier and Duplessis. What is strikingly different between the P.Q. and the previous nationalist governments is the importance of socialist ideology. We will examine in the section below the forms of socialist ideology that have appeared in the last few years. They have coincided with the disintegration of the P.Q. alliance.

Forms of Socialist Discourse in Contemporary Quebec

For years, there has been talk in Quebec of forming a socialist party. Yet events since the Quiet Revolution have tended to absorb the various interest groups who might have otherwise established it. Recent events in Quebec, events which do not usually appear in the mass media, would seem to indicate a general movement towards the forming of such a party. At the very least they suggest the development of a strong lobby to influence P.Q. policies. The events referred to are the development, over the last few years, of an alternative press, and the recent popular summit meetings launching several socialist movements. François Fournier cites the recent appearance of the following journals which voice feminist, socialist and/or counter-cultural forms of criticisms against established powers: *Temps Fou*, *Des Cahiers du Socialisme*, *Possibles*, *Zone Libre*, *Interventions Critiques*, *Presse Libre*, and *Conjoncture Politique*. In addition to the alternative press, five social movements have been founded: "Le Mouvement socialiste (M.S.), le Regroupement pour le socialisme (R.P.S.), l'Organisation des jeunes indépendantistes pour un Québec communautaire (L.O.G.I.Q.C.), le Coloque unitaire de la gauche" and the anglophone Black Rock Group (Fournier 1982A:53).

The mixture of socialism and independence is not new in Quebec. According to Fournier, we have seen the Parti Pris group in the sixties, its assimilation into the P.Q. during the seventies, and now a third wave of it in the eighties (1982:53). A combination of ecology groups, feminists, *autogestionaires* or workers' management groups, and a variety of co-operatives and socialists seem to have one major point in common: the independence of Quebec. These groups do not represent the extreme left wing in Quebec (the communist party of Quebec has a tentative alliance with a faction of the P.Q.) as we shall see below. Nor are all of these groups directly related to specific working class organizations. However, each maintains a certain degree of interaction and communication with other such organizations. Finally, to a lesser or greater degree, these groups tend to see the P.Q. as growing increasingly ineffective regarding the completion of the independence project. They also criticize the ways in which the P.Q. has been dealing with labor problems, the women's question, the environmental crisis, and minority problems within Quebec.

Le Mouvement socialiste was founded in the autumn of 1981 with the publication of its manifesto: *Manifeste du mouvement pour un Québec socialiste, indépendant, démocratique et pour l'égalité entre les hommes et les femmes*: Le *Comité des cent.*[5] Within one month 8000 copies were distributed. The document calls for a break from capitalism, the equality of men and women, and a pledge to work democratically toward socialist goals. It denounces authoritarian and bureaucratic forms of socialism. It insists that an ideal model for a socialist society does not exist. It argues that the Quebec people must construct their own socialist society. The means by which this new society is to be constructed include the nationalization of the means of production, a radical decentralization of the state, the abolition of private decision making, and the destruction of the sexual division of labor.

Le Regroupement pour le socialisme dates back to 1978. Then groups of militants from Montreal, Quebec, and Rimouski met to co-ordinate their activities in various regions of the province. The group considers itself to be a continuation of the new left groups which appeared in Quebec between 1968 and 1973. It identifies with certain international struggles championed by this faction of the left such as the student riots in Paris of 1968 and anti-imperialist conflicts in Africa, Chili, and now in El Salvador. Like le Mouvement socialiste, the R.P.S. sees itself as a militant group fighting for unions, women, and the solidarity of the different regions within Quebec (Fournier 1982B:230).

Le Colloque unitaire de la gauche, or the colloquium for the uniting of the left, included some two hundred participants and took place in November 1981. An eighteen-member committee organized the meeting including eight members of the Communist Party of Quebec, and a number of P.Q. members (Fournier 1982A:55). As Fournier reports, the discussion largely centred around four principles: "1) the condemnation of monopolies and multi-nationals, 2) the increase of the state intervention in the economy, 3) the development of a greater political and economic democracy, and 4) the right of Quebec to self-determination" (1982b:55). Of these four principles the major emphasis of the discussions focussed on the development of an economic strategy. The alliance of the Parti Québécois faction with the Communist Party of Quebec dates back to the referendum when the communists threw their support into the *oui* campaign at the last minute in order to reaffirm their relations with the left of the P.Q. The meeting adjourned with a promise to meet again in the spring of 1982, and to organize a larger turnout. *Le Québec indépendant et communautaire* was first formed during the referendum as a student movement for the *oui* side of the campaign. The group defines itself as being autonomous from all political parties. Its aim is to serve as a pressure group among youth organizations distributing information and promoting dialogue regarding the independence of Quebec. Its criticisms of the P.Q. are threefold: 1) The P.Q. has become overly bureaucratized and reduced to a simple electoral machine; 2) It is no longer progressive in that it cannot change the structural inequalities in Quebec; and 3) The P.Q. has diluted the "independantist project" by its gradualist approach to such a point as to render it impotent (Fournier 1982A:60). At the same time, however, the group condemns extreme left wing factions which seek immediate and radical change within Quebec. In this sense, it seeks gradual changes. In fact it qualifies its project as "reformist". The movement is strongly allied with the left factions of the P.Q. It maintains the position that the state must play a strong role in the future of the development of the Quebec economy and social structure.

The Black Rock Group also launched its manifesto and declared itself as a social movement in the fall of 1981. It is essentially anglophone in makeup and working-class in background. It takes its name from a huge black rock at the base of the Victoria Bridge in Montreal. The Black Rock memorial stone "honors the 6000 Irish immigrants that died of typhoid fever in 1847."[6]

The group sees itself as being caught between the exodus of the English-Canadian bourgeoisie, who traditionally protected what working-class jobs there were for them, and the new waves of Québécois nationalism. The latter have not included them in their battles against hegemonic powers. Although the group has a strong base in the anglo-working-class communities of Montreal, it draws on a cross-section of communities and sub-communities, poets, playwrights, students, unemployed, under-employed, and other sub-proletarians. The loyalty to its working-class origins and its marginality within Quebec is eloquently expressed in the following excerpt from its manifesto:

> Working class neighbourhoods are supposed to produce hockey players, not poets or playwrights. . . . Nothing is supposed to come from us. Certainly not art. . . . This is no longer a statement—this is a threat. Our class shall no longer be your convenience. We, the sons and daughters of those who died on strange beaches so Redpath Crescent [one of the richest streets in Montreal] would survive, will have our say. I am sorry it is not only the French who threaten you. We shall reverse the disease. We will create in these troubled times. . . . The Black Rock is not the myth of

Sisyphus. We have pushed it up the hill and into your factories. It is washed with blood and now it shall be washed with the creative energies of a new generation.[7]

It is obviously very difficult for us to predict whether or not these socialist movements will find one another. Even if they do, it is not clear that they would be able to form an effective alliance. There is, however, a definite political vacuum which has been increasing in intensity since the disintegration of the P.Q. alliance began. It is being filled by these social movements. The outlook for the left in Quebec looks remarkably optimistic in this light, even though so much would seem to depend on forces and events which exist outside Quebec.

HIGHLIGHT
1. The Quiet Revolution ushered in under the Lesage provincial Liberals in the 1960s, represented an important ideological change in Quebec.
2. The discourse of separatism took on new meanings in the aftermath of the Quiet Revolution.
3. In the late 1960s, separatist groups coalesced under the Parti Québécois (P.Q.). Its founding, in 1968, was marked by compromises between left and right wing nationalist parties.
4. With the evolution of a rightest position within the Parti Québécois marked by the resignation of left wing ministers, the purge of left wing riding representatives, and the dissatisfaction of government ministers, the P.Q. ceased to represent the interests which originally formed the P.Q. alliance. Consequently, the possibility for the formation of a socialist party is greater than ever.

Conclusion: Social Class and Nationalism

This chapter has focussed on the manner in which struggles occur in concrete historical conditions. We have examined these struggles in terms of the world views (nationalist, ultramontanist, liberal, conservative, socialist, etc.) and the various discourses emerging from these views (political, religious, economic, etc.). These have served as mediating structures for social groups and social classes within Quebec society. Moreover, we have located the historical struggles of the Quebec people within the overall context of the capitalist world system.

The act of defining areas of study within Quebec society is both political and theoretical. For generations, Québécois sociologists have engaged in rich debates regarding the theoretical and political implications of the sociology of their own society. Many of these debates concern the problem of the national question. Some are bound up in problems of historical interpretation. Others are more concerned with the dialectical relation among culture, politics, and economics. The approach developed in this chapter has tended to focus on the latter of these concerns. However, we have tried to borrow from each tradition.

In *The Development of Quebec: Class and Nation*, we have seen a variety of forms of activity all colored by the nationalist world view. Nationalism has served both the left and the right, reactionary classes as well as progressive ones. Without coming to grips with this point, a consideration of social change in Quebec society can be only partial. Our intention has been to provide a holistic analysis of the manner in which ideologies and forms of activity in the economic, political and social realms are interwoven in daily class struggles.

NOTES

[1] In outlining this section we relied extensively on three articles which have appeared recently: Fournier and Houle 1980:21-44; Legaré 1980:61-84; and Laurin-Frenette 1981:1-34.

[2] Translations from the French are by the authors.

[2a] Mason Wade, *The French Canadians* (London: Macmillan Press Ltd.), 1955.

[3] For a more complete discussion of the structure of foreign domination of the Canadian economy see: Kari Levitt 1970; Robert Laxer et al., 1973; and Arnold Sales 1979.

[4] On the other hand, Guindon (1981), like Rioux (1980), sees the referendum loss as a result of scare tactics on the part of the massive federal liberal propoganda machine which entered the final key phase of the campaign. For an analysis of the period prior to the referendum see Monière 1979.

[5] An English translation of the manifesto appears in *The Canadian Journal of Political and Social Thought* (1982:109-138), edited by Arthur Kroker.

[6] "Black Rock Manifesto," in *The Canadian Journal of Political and Social Theory*, Volume 6, No. 1 and 2, 1982, pp. 139-143.

[7] ibid.

SUGGESTED READINGS

French Canada in Transition, Everett Hughes. Chicago: University of Chicago Press, 1943. A classic study in the effects of industrialisation, social class, institutions, and French/English relations in a Quebec community during the 1930s. Although the main argument has to do with the rural-urban continuum, as developed by the Chicago School of Sociology, it is richly documented and provides an in depth description of Quebec society frozen in a particular period of time.

French Canadian Society, Marcel Rioux and Yves Martin. Toronto: McClelland and Stewart, 1965. This is a collection of articles, all written before 1965, on Quebec society. It includes sections on institutions, populations, ecology, economic structures, social class and cultural change. It is also an excellent source for the debates in the social science of the day.

Ideologies in Quebec: The historical development, Denis Monière. Toronto: University of Toronto Press, 1981. The first complete survey, based on secondary materials, of ideology in Quebec over the last four centuries. It approaches the subject from a Marxist political economy perspective. Even though it suffers from such a broad objective it is filled with information and guides to contemporary debates.

Quebec: Social Change and Political Crisis, Kenneth McRoberts and Dale Posgate. Toronto: McClelland and Stewart, 1980. The authors approach the history of Quebec from a modernization stance rather than a developmentalist one. They particularly accent recent social and political change providing a detailed outline of events since 1960. It compensates for absences in Monière's book even though the two approaches differ.

Deux Pays Pour Vivre: Un Plaidoyer, Marcel Rioux and Susan Crean. Montréal: Editions Coopératives Albert Saint-Martin, 1980. For the ambitious students who wish to practice their French and impress their professor this is a unique book. It is the only critical work available that outlines the independence project for both Anglo-Canada and Quebec at the same time. It pleas for two independent, sovereign nations to be achieved through a mutual struggle against American cultural domination.

THE DEVELOPMENT OF CLASS IN CANADA
Michael D. Ornstein

Introduction

The authors of this book share the idea that class is to be understood in terms of ownership of the means of production. On a number of specific issues, however, researchers who accept this general perspective differ. There is no consensus on the class structure of advanced capitalist societies. The difficulty arises from developments in the economic structure of capitalism which result in only a minority of employed workers being engaged in productive labor.

The central issue is whether or not the working class should include all, or any part, of the white collar work force, managers at various levels, supervisory personnel, the police and armed forces, government employees, and workers in wholesale and retail trade. Equally fundamental is the problem of understanding the class positions of unpaid domestic workers and the unemployed and discouraged workers who form what is often called the "reserve army of the unemployed". Because of these questions, the following discussion of the Canadian class structure cannot proceed without taking sides. The first section of this chapter will describe the contemporary Canadian class structure and show where there is disagreement over who belongs to which social class.

The points at issue involve more than simply assigning individuals to one of a number of social classes, for classes themselves may be internally divided. Theorists and historical students of class structure can be arranged on a continuum from those (such as Nicos Poulantzas) whose definition of the working class is very narrow, to others (such as Leo Johnson) who include more or less all employed workers in the working class. The analysis presented here takes the "inclusive" position but stresses the extent of divisions within the working class.

Erik Olin Wright criticizes Poulantzas's theory of class because it includes only about one-quarter of the labor force in the working class. Wright argues "It is hard to imagine a viable socialist movement developing in an advanced capitalist country in which less than one in five people are workers" (1976:23). In fact, the socialist movements that have taken power (for example in China, Cuba, and the Soviet Union) have done so in nations where the working class was a small minority.[1] Class analysis should not seek to achieve some numerical goal in distributing workers among classes. Instead, it should first provide a basis for understanding the economic and political factors at work in the evolution of the Canadian social formation and, second, provide a framework for examining institutions such as the educational system, the law, the family, and culture.

Using data gathered in a variety of surveys of the Canadian population and businesses, the first section of this chapter gives estimates of the numbers in the various classes and fractions. Knowing the approximate numbers in social classes is important to economic and political analysis. Discussions of the rise of the labor movement or of prairie populism, for example, require some knowledge of the number of workers, or of farmers.

Any modern class analysis encounters a number of "boundary problems" at which there appears to be no precise way to specify the line between two classes. When does a craftsman working in a small shop employ enough labor-power to change from an independent commodity producer into a capitalist? There is no precise point. It is not worth debating the question of whether independent commodity producers constitute, say, five instead of six percent of the labor force. Far more important are historical *changes* in the sizes of social classes.

From the decennial censuses and a variety of other publications, mostly by the Federal Government, the second section of this chapter examines the Canadian class structure over the past century. Although the best available, these data have gaps; they were not gathered with the objective of providing the basis for a class analysis of Canada. Still, by combining data from a number of sources it is possible to show the main factors at work in shaping the Canadian class structure.

A full understanding of class in Canada requires both an historical and an international context. The Canadian censuses and other records provide the basis for an examination of the origins of the modern class structure in nineteenth century Canada. It is frequently argued that Canada has a distinctive class structure that reflects our past (and sometimes, it is said, present) colonial relation to other nations. To address this issue, the last section of this chapter will compare the class structure of Canada to that of other advanced capitalist nations.

This chapter focusses essentially on class *structure*, rather than individuals' consciousness of their class positions. That many Canadians are unaware of their class positions, at least in the sense of taking a class view of the state and politics, is both a manifestation of a central feature of many advanced capitalist societies and an important theoretical and political problem. The relation between class structure and political consciousness appears more clear in the past, perhaps partly by benefit of hindsight. As Block (1977) argues, there is a reciprocal relation between class structure and politics. The structure of the capitalist economy tends to produce political reactions (such as the formation of unions); in turn, political organization (in unions, parties, community organizations, etc.) pushes the economy and hence the class structure in certain directions. These linkages are conditioned by a variety of factors including the world economy, nationality and culture, religion, the family, and inequality between women and men.

This chapter does not address the question of how individuals come to occupy their class positions. Instead, it concentrates on how the structure of class positions evolves over time. Numerous studies have dealt with the first concern: they have shown the fairly strong impact of gender, race, social origin and education on careers.[2] The areas of "social mobility" and "social stratification" in sociology are concerned with these issues.

Transformations of the class structure are partly responsible for what is often termed "structural mobility". For example, there are simply not enough farms remaining for all the children of farmers to remain in farming; expanding class positions, on the other hand, must draw on individuals from other class backgrounds. Beyond this mobility, educational institutions and the almost complete separation of workers from their means of production (and hence little need for most workers to inherit or acquire capital) provide opportunities for mobility. Because of socialization patterns, tracking in the schools, the inheritance of wealth and other factors only a part of the possible mobility is actually realized. Research suggests that advanced capitalist societies are relatively similar in terms of the extent of occupational mobility.[3] Women, and racial and ethnic minorities have historically been concentrated in certain class positions which usually compare unfavorably to the positions occupied by white, Anglo-Saxon men.[4] This chapter concentrates on describing changes in the class structure, as understood in terms of positions, but not the characteristics, of their occupants.

The Class Structure of Contemporary Canada

Class Distributions.   The production and distribution of commodities takes place in a "social formation" that unites independent commodity production and the capitalist mode of production. The term social formation is taken here in the narrow sense to describe *co-existing modes of production.* Contemporary Canada could only be described as capitalist, since capitalist production dominates the economy. But, while the capitalist mode of production dominates, it is not exclusive. It co-exists with independent commodity production by artisans, farmers, fishermen, and other small-scale producers. The distinction separates what is often called "small business" from companies in which the proprietors do not play the major role in the actual process of production, even if they direct it and own the capital. One distinctive feature of modern capitalism is that an increasing proportion of life's necessities produced *outside* (and often substituting for their former production *inside*) the home never take a commodity form, including most social welfare services, education, public utilities. Still other necessities are produced as commodities but are purchased by the state. These include buildings, road construction, day-care, building maintenance, and computer services.

Table 1 shows the approximate proportions of the employed labor force in these categories. About six percent of the employed are capitalists, about 13 percent are petty bourgeois, and four-fifths of the employed labor force are, if it is very broadly defined, in the working class. These figures should be taken as rough approximations only. The discussion below will show why and will make clear the assumptions on which these numbers are based.

A sizeable minority of the adult population is not engaged in production and distribution of commodities or government service. They include the unemployed, now about thirteen percent of the work force.

TABLE 1
Approximate Distribution Of Social Classes And Other Social Categories For Canada, 1981

	Specification/fraction	Percent of employed labour force	Percent of population 18-64 years
Capitalist class	all owners and part owners of companies with five or more workers	6	4
Petty bourgeoisie	all self-employed excluding above	13	8
Working class	employed by capital	56	34
	employed by crown corporations	5	3
	employed in direct government service	20	11
The unemployed	by official definition		3
	'discouraged workers'		(1) (included below)
Housewives			25
Students			4
Disabled			1
Retired			7
Total		100	100

SOURCE: Quality of Life 1981 national survey, sample size=2950

Another two or three percent are discouraged workers who are not counted as unemployed by the official definition because they are not actively seeking work, believing their chances of finding it are too remote. About twenty-five percent of the adult population are house-wives, four percent are students, one percent are disabled, and seven percent are retired.

These groups are not completely outside the class structure. They take part in the reproduction of the social formation and relationships with the employed. Housewives reproduce the class structure by raising children and caring for the households of the employed. Students grow up in families with positions in the class structure and, when their education is completed, occupy class positions themselves. The disabled may have been injured in the course of work. And the retired live from income that largely reflects their class positions as workers before retirement.[5]

Capitalists, especially the minority of them who control corporations of even moderate size, constitute a tiny proportion of the population. Less than one percent of the population effectively controls the majority of the nation's productive capacity. Table 2 shows the distribution of wealth as measured in a sample survey of the population. The units of analysis are families, with unattached individuals counted separately, ordered in terms of total wealth.

In 1977, 30.9 percent of the population had equity under $5000 and together they held only 1.5 percent of all equity in business, farms, and professional practices, 2.2 percent of stocks in public traded corpora-tions, and 2.5 percent of miscellaneous financial assets (such as privately held mortgages). At the other end of the scale the 1.7 percent of family units with $300 000 or more in assets controlled 49.9 percent of business equity, 44 percent of stocks, and 63 percent of miscellaneous financial assets! Virtually all of the very rich were wealthy by virtue of their ownership of businesses. While only 2.1 percent of all household units with less than $5000 had any equity in a business, farm or professional practice, 67.7 percent of wealth holders in the $150 000 to $300 000 category had some business equity—the average was $121 185 worth—and fully 89.7 percent of the units with $300 000 or more wealth had some business equity—the average amount was $343 877. The obverse of the class structure defined in the world of production and distribution is thus a very unequal distribution of personal wealth and income and hence of the comforts they buy. In 1977 dollars, 65 percent of the top wealth-holders had incomes of $25 000 or more and 51 percent had incomes of $35 000 or more—the average income was $50 316 (Statistics Canada, 1979:71). The structure of inequality in Canadian society is thus deeply rooted in the ownership of large corporations by a class that constitutes a tiny minority of the population.

In the Canadian social formation, capitalism and independent com-

TABLE 2
Distribution Of Equity In Business, Stock, And Miscellaneous Financial Assets, 1977 For Families And Unattached Individuals

Amount of wealth	Percentage of families and unattached individuals	Equity in Business, Farms and Professional Interest			Stocks			Miscellaneous Financial Assets (excluding RRSPs, stocks)		
		Percent with any	Mean Value for Owners (dollars)	Percent of Assets	Percent with any	Mean Holding for those with any (dollars)	Percent of Assets	Percent with any	Mean Holding for those with any (dollars)	Percent of Assets
Under $5,000	30.9	2.1*	2317*	1.5*	1.0*	648*	2.2*	2.5*	629*	2.5*
$5,000-9,999	7.6	5.1	5774	0.2	3.6	1898	0.5	4.6	2829	0.5
$10,000-14,999	5.7	5.5	10650	0.3	11.0	1695	1.2	4.5	3072	0.5
$15,000-29,999	13.0	10.9	10567	1.4	6.3	2364	2.0	5.7	5455	2.0
$30,000-49,999	14.8	12.1	16031	2.7	8.3	2685	3.5	6.8	5827	2.9
$50,000-99,999	17.4	16.3	32368	8.7	13.8	4496	11.6	9.7	11000	9.1
$100,000-149,999	5.8	33.1	55265	10.1	22.0	9844	13.5	19.1	16793	9.1
$150,000-299,999	3.2	67.7	121185	25.0	26.5	23538	21.5	26.1	25305	10.4
$300,000 and up	1.7	89.7	343877	49.9	31.4	76553	44.0	35.3	214321	63.0
Total	100.0	13.0	80763	99.8	8.5	10946	100.0	7.6	26808	100.0

*estimates
SOURCE: The Distribution of Income and Wealth in Canada 1977, (Ottawa: Statistics Canada).

modity production are not combined abstractly. The two modes of production have a direct relationship in the marketplace. In some spheres of production, commodities can be efficiently produced on a small or a large scale, for example luxury furniture and clothing, residential construction such as plumbing and electrical wiring, and restaurant food. In the sphere of distribution, certain commodities may be purchased from both small, retail stores and large chain, or department stores. Capitalists also buy from and sell to independent commodity producers. Farmers purchase seed, fertilizer, farm machinery, and transportation, and obtain credit from capitalists. Conflict over the prices of these commodities has been the source of continuing political battles on the prairies and sometimes other regions of Canada.

The antagonism of the petty bourgeoisie to big capital reflects both the generally greater economic power of capital and the dependence of the petty bourgeoisie on big capital for commodities and services, especially transportation, banking, and marketing. One alternative is for small producers to develop their own collective services, such as marketing cooperatives. They may also force government regulation of the prices charged, such as the Crow's Nest Pass Agreement for grain transportation by rail from the West.

Independent Commodity Production.   Independent commodity production involves only one class of producers, often called the petty bourgeoisie. Four fractions of this class may be distinguished: primary producers in agriculture, fishing and hunting; craft manufacturers and tradesmen engaged in small-scale production in shops and on construction sites; shop-keepers in retail trade and sales agents in wholesale trade; and independent professionals in medicine, law, engineering and other areas. These fractions have historically different relations to the larger class structure.

As noted above, primary producers come into conflict with big capital because of their dependence on it for supplies, transportation, sales and financing. For the most part, however, they are not in direct competition with big capital, corporate farming is not yet the most important element in agriculture. Inshore fishermen in the Atlantic region, however, compete with deep sea fishing carried out by large corporations. Similarly, craft manufacturers and tradesmen are often in direct competition with capitalist producers. Changes in technology that have rendered small-scale production inefficient have eliminated the petty bourgeoisie from one industry after another. In the construction trades, however, the unsteadiness of work has provided less incentive for large capital to move in, since it would have to bear the cost of idle time. In retail and wholesale trade the rapid, recent development of franchising represents a means of partial control by large capitalist enterprises.

Professionals generally do not have antagonistic relations to big capital. Some groups, such as lawyers and doctors, have developed special relations with the state which licences them. These arrangements generally work to the financial advantage of professionals. The law profession, or at least its most influential elements, has allied itself with big capital. It defends capital directly in legal proceedings, arranging loans, mergers and takeovers. Still, conflicts between professions and capital may develop. For example, attempts by physicians to raise their fees may arouse opposition from businessmen who don't want to pay higher taxes for medical care. In practice, the state is put in the position of directly confronting the physicians on behalf of business interests and workers.

The independent commodity producers in primary production are concentrated in the prairie and Atlantic provinces and the large corporations on which they are dependent are headquartered in central Canada. As a result, economic conflict between the primary producers and big capital has important regional dimensions. Furthermore, the Federal Government, which is put in the position of regulating regional conflict, has a central Canadian base. Especially in the West, the traditional domination of the provinces' entire economies by primary production draws provincial governments into the regional conflict as well. The conflict reflects the uneven development of the capitalist social formation and can be viewed as deriving from the capital accumulation process. Sacouman deals with this dynamic in an earlier chapter.

Capitalist Production. Capitalists and workers are the two great classes of the capitalist mode of production. Capitalists are distinct from the petty bourgeoisie in that they live from the surplus value produced by the workers. Capitalists expropriate surplus value *directly* by purchasing the labor power of workers in productive industry (including transportation) or *indirectly* by providing services to productive capital in commerce (retail and wholesale) and banking.

Active capitalists should be distinguished from ordinary stockholders. The former take part in the management of existing businesses and plan the development of new ones; the latter live off the proceeds of what is often inherited wealth.[6]

Landowners may constitute a distinct class who come into conflict with capital (in the feudal or capitalist modes of production). But, in modern times, landowners are, at most, a fraction of the capitalist class. The capitalist class is also divided in terms of the amounts of capital controlled. The boundary separating capitalists from the petty bourgeoisie cannot be fixed with certainty. Nonetheless, a vast gap, at both the levels of economics and consciousness, separates the craftsperson with one or two helpers and the manager who takes no role in actual production. There is, however, no corresponding upper boundary to the capitalist class. In modern capitalist nations a moderate size meeting room would be sufficient to assemble the people who control at least one quarter of the entire economy.

The rise of the modern corporation is not exactly news; however, the extent of domination by big capital is not well known. The Corporations and Labour Unions Returns Act, passed by Parliament in 1960, requires the collection of data on foreign ownership in Canada—which was the impetus for its passage—and also on corporate concentration. A very high level of intercorporate ownership has rendered the corporation, which is the conventional unit for analysis of corporate concentration, partly obsolete. These concentration figures in Table 3 are based on "enterprises"; that is, on groups of corporations linked by chains of ownership. The largest 25 non-financial enterprises in Canada constitute only a tiny fraction of the total of 304 339 enterprises (.0082 percent), but account for a startling 21.2 percent of all sales, 30.3 percent of all assets, and 28.2 percent of profits! The largest 100 enterprises account for 37.3 percent of all sales, 48.5 percent of assets and 48.2 percent of profits.

In the financial sector concentration is even greater. Of the $350.1

TABLE 3
Major Characteristics Of Non-Financial Corporations By Size Of Controlling Enterprise (as ranked by sales), 1979

Enterprise Characteristic	25 leading enterprises	26th to 100th leading enterprises	101st to 500th leading enterprises	All remaining enterprises	Total
Number of enterprises	25	75	400	303,839	304,339
Number of corporations controlled	552	788	1,927	307,431	310,698
Financial Averages ($ million)					
Sales	4087	1033	196.6	.735	1.583
Assets	4914	929	170.7	.462	1.332
Profits	429.2	102.9	17.7	.041	.125
Percentage Distribution					
Enterprises	.0082	.0246	.1314	99.84	100.0
Corporations	.17	.25	.62	98.95	100.0
Sales	21.2	16.1	16.3	46.4	100.0
Assets	30.3	18.2	16.8	34.7	100.0
Profits	28.2	20.2	18.6	41.6	100.0
Ratio of profits/assets	.087	.105	.103	.089	.094

SOURCE: *Corporations and Labour Unions Returns Act: Report for 1979*, Part I— Corporations. (Ottawa: Statistics Canada), p. 40.

billion in assets controlled by Canadian banks as of October 1981, 92.2 percent is controlled by the five "big banks". The largest, The Royal Bank, accounts for $87.5 billion or 25.0 percent; the Canadian Imperial Bank of Commerce for $66.8 billion or 19.1 percent; and the Bank of Montreal for $63.8 billion or 18.2 percent. A similar level of concentration also exists among insurance companies in Canada.[7]

Concentration in retail trade is more difficult to measure but appears to be lower than in manufacturing or banking. In 1980 chain stores accounted for $35.4 billion in retail sales, compared to $48.5 billion for independent stores (*Retail Trade* Dec. 1980). About one third of the independent's sales are automobiles. So, eliminating autos, retail trade is split about evenly between chain stores and independents. Food ($11.1 billion in sales) and department stores ($9.4 billion in sales) account for the greater part (58 percent) of sales by chain stores.

As Table 4 indicates, the manufacturing sector is dominated by the capitalist mode of production. This concentration, and the domination of capitalist production is apparent from the distributions of employees, value of shipments and value added in production. The 0.46 percent of firms with 1000 or more employees employ 17.5 percent of workers in manufacturing. These employees carry out approximately twenty-five percent of all production. The 26.5 percent of all establishments with fewer than five employees employ only about one percent of employees and account for less than one percent of all production.

The last three columns of Table 4 demonstrate three important features of the development of capitalist production. First, larger firms have higher rates of pay. Second, larger firms are much less likely to include their owners among the people actively engaged in production. Third, the proportion of non-production employees engaged in supervision and control, record keeping, and sales grows from 5.7 percent for the smallest manufacturers to about one in three for establishments with 200 or more employees.

Monopoly Capitalism. One important question is whether the dominant mode of production should be characterized as "monopoly capitalist", rather than capitalist. The answer depends on the meaning attached to the term "monopoly". If it is taken to mean that the economy is dominated by large firms, then we need proceed no further. But monopoly may be better defined in two more precise ways: as the description of a market in which consumers find no price competition; or as a description of an industry in which profits are artificially elevated by restricting output, preventing the entry of new producers, or manipulating prices. Although when an industry is monopolized it tends to fit *both* these definitions, they have quite different implications for understanding capitalism.

The existence of monopoly in terms of the second definition of

TABLE 4
Manufacturing Activity By Size Of Establishment, 1978

Number of employees	Number of Establishments	Percentage Distribution				Average hourly wage for production workers	Average number of working owners and partners per establishment	Number of non-production workers per worker in production
		Establishments	Employees	Value of shipments of own production	Value added in production			
Less than 5	8481	26.5	1.08	0.76	0.71	5.17	.516	.057
5-9	5288	16.5	2.38	1.26	1.20	5.19	.224	.100
10-19	5429	17.0	4.8	2.9	3.0	5.34	.056	.195
20-49	6148	19.2	11.9	8.3	8.6	5.48	.020	.241
50-99	2962	9.3	12.3	10.1	10.4	5.68	.002	.283
100-199	2004	6.3	17.3	16.4	16.3	6.15	.005	.291
200-499	1174	3.7	20.3	21.8	21.4	6.60	.021	.327
500-999	330	1.03	12.4	14.6	15.0	7.49	.000	.351
1000 or more	147	0.46	17.5	23.8	23.4	8.36	.000	.341
Total	31,963	100.0	100.0	100.0	100.0	6.50	.189	.296
Total	31,963		1,310,524	$129,019 mil	$51,679 mil			

SOURCE: *Manufacturing Industries of Canada: National and Provincial Areas 1978*. (Ottawa: Statistics Canada), pp. 190-1.

artificially elevated *profits* would suggest that monopoly capitalism is a distinct mode of production. This is because competition between capitalists for higher profits is the fundamental market mechanism which Marx identifies as responsible for the constantly changing character of capitalism. The capitalist economy is transformed by the "migration" of capital into spheres of production that offer above average rates of profit.[8] However, it is not always possible for capital to "escape" from low profit industries. The capital embodied in a low-profit railway or a large manufacturing plant, for example, is immobilized because it takes the form of fixed capital. A capitalist owner will find it difficult to get a good price for a money-losing business. Systematic underinvestment is a strategy to get around this. A good example is the long term strategy adopted by the Canadian Pacific Railway. It increasingly took profits from the passenger rail business and invested them in a huge variety of other profitable enterprises. Not surprisingly, this corporation's new name is simply Canadian Pacific Ltd.

Since some sectors of the economy (such as steelmaking, the shoe industry and textiles) are competitive and there is evidence that new investments are made in spheres of production offering high profits, the question is whether the economy can be divided into two sectors one of which is monopolistic and the other competitive. Various labels have been attached to the two sectors. For example, Galbraith (1971) calls them the planning and market systems; the terms "core" and "periphery" are also used. The monopoly sector is understood by economists to be dominated by large corporations, uses large-scale, rapidly developing technology, yields high profits because the corporations limit price competition, and offers workers good pay and benefits since these can be passed on to buyers in the form of higher prices. In the competitive sector production is on a small scale, profits are low, and workers are poorly paid.

Not surprisingly William Averitt's (1968) important early formulation of this theory was titled *The Dual Economy*. Doeringer and Piore (1971) then made the important link between this core-periphery division among capitalist enterprises and the low wages of racial and ethnic minorities and women. They argued that discrimination confined some groups of workers to the competitive sector where they received lower wages. Sometimes a third economic sector, usually government (see O'Connor 1973), is added to the economic scheme. Models of this type may be generally termed "segmentation" theories. The implications of segmentation theory for the analysis of work is discussed in detail in the following chapter.

Table 5 is again based on the 1979 CALURA report and provides the basis for a brief consideration of the validity of dualist arguments about the Canadian economy. The 130 696 companies surveyed have been divided into thirty-three broad industrial categories and arranged in

TABLE 5
Characteristics Of 33 Major Industries, 1979

Industry	Percent of industry sales		Number of corporations	Total assets (millions of dollars)	Mean assets	Ratio of sales to assets	Ratio of before tax profits to assets	June 1979 Average weekly earnings for all employees	Percent women employees
	Top 4 enterprises	Top 8 enterprises							
Tobacco Products	90.8	99.6	17	1146	67.41	.98	.122	345	37.6
Communications	68.9	78.8	841	17573	20.90	.38	.069	326	37.8
Transportation equipment	67.4	72.9	1266	11391	9.00	2.40	.094	359	11.6
Petroleum and coal products	66.6	88.3	52	19787	380.52	1.05	.136	441	19.9
Rubber products	61.5	83.3	112	1708	15.25	1.51	.104	313	18.1
Storage	60.3	68.4	536	1738	3.24	.47	.053	321	14.2
Primary metals	58.3	72.5	426	10873	25.52	1.02	.115	372	7.2
Metal mining	50.1	68.1	121	17159	141.81	.53	.175	401	5.7
Public utilities	48.9	65.7	1064	55415	52.08	.25	.032	398	14.8
Transportation	48.2	52.6	15108	30399	2.01	.77	.059	332	10.2
Beverages	41.3	64.3	336	2876	8.56	1.02	.101	350	12.5
Textile mills	39.9	47.0	913	3033	3.32	1.52	.115	258	36.9
Paper and allied industries	36.5	50.8	591	15279	25.85	1.03	.106	375	12.6
Mineral fuels	36.4	57.1	930	31119	33.45	.53	.160	442	16.4
Electrical products	34.4	45.9	1035	6108	5.90	1.38	.089	300	33.4
Non-metallic minerals	30.1	43.2	1447	5502	3.80	.54	.069	348	12.7
Machinery	29.6	37.4	1599	5179	3.24	1.57	.106	331	12.6
Chemicals & chemical products	26.2	38.5	939	8904	9.48	1.21	.122	344	24.6
Other mining	23.2	33.5	3558	7472	2.10	.56	.094	390*	6.0*
Printing, publishing and allied industries	20.3	30.3	4500	3277	.73	1.53	.138	295	35.3

Miscellaneous manufacturing	20.1	26.4	3970	3759	.95	1.67	.105	257	38.6
Wood industries	19.0	25.4	2740	5414	1.98	1.36	.161	306	8.7
Food	18.7	28.5	3348	9460	2.83	2.55	.092	273	29.7
Furniture industries	16.6	21.9	1917	1253	.65	1.67	.091	247	20.8
Knitting mills	16.4	25.4	286	464	1.62	1.77	.086	194	66.8
Leather products	15.2	27.4	406	619	1.53	1.85	.115	197	58.3
Metal fabricating	13.2	20.1	426	10873	25.52	1.02	.115	321	14.8
Retail trade	13.0	21.8	60813	27809	.42	2.71	.118	190	40.4
Clothing industries	8.9	12.1	2357	1889	.80	2.03	.109	191	76.0
Services	8.8	12.3	81463	27261	.34	1.04	.093	195	43.3
Wholesale trade	7.7	12.0	41392	39118	.95	2.32	.076	285	24.8
Agriculture, forestry & fishing	6.0	8.2	16179	5978	.37	.96	.088	—	—
Construction	2.8	4.6	48990	18790	.38	1.46	.062	425	6.1
Total			310696	405301	1.30	1.19	.094		

*estimates

SOURCE: *Corporations and Labour Unions Returns Act*, Report of 1979 Part I—Corporations. (Ottawa: Statistics Canada, 1981). *Employment, Earnings and Hours*, July 1979.

order of concentration, which is measured by the percent of all sales in the industry accounted for by the largest four enterprises. An enterprise is defined as a group of companies controlled by a single corporation.

There is enormous variation in this measure. The most concentrated industry is "tobacco products" where the four largest enterprises account for 90.8 percent of sales and the eight largest for 99.6 percent of sales. In communications, the second most concentrated industry, the corresponding percentages are 68.9 percent and 78.8 percent. The remaining thirty-one industries are quite evenly distributed down to the construction industry in which the top four enterprises account for only 2.8 percent of sales and the top eight for 4.6 percent. The continuity of the concentration figures suggests that dividing the economy into a small number of sectors will obscure some of its important features.

Nevertheless, it is still worth pursuing the question of whether firms in more concentrated industries tend to provide higher profits, to pay higher wages, etc. Column 5 of the table shows, not surprisingly, that enterprises in the most concentrated industries have, on average, greater assets than those in less concentrated industries. The relationship is, however, not very strong. The ratio of sales to assets bears almost no relation to concentration. This is surprising in view of the prediction that only large firms are prepared to make the long-term investments required by some industries.

Still more surprising is the finding, in the next column, that concentration has very little relation to rates of profit. The last two columns show, as predicted, that concentrated industries and those in which the average firm is larger tend to pay higher wages and to employ smaller numbers of women workers. In particular, note that the three manufacturing industries with the greatest proportion of women workers (knitting mills, leather products, and clothing industries) pay lower average wages than any other manufacturing industries. The other two very low paying industries (retail trade and services) also employ large proportions of women.

From the above we can see that dual economy theory provides a poor explanation of the distribution of profits in the economy, but a good explanation of wage differentials. The tendency of the industrial structure is thus to build barriers between groups of workers by dividing them into different wage strata. Furthermore, women are both divided from, and disadvantaged in comparison to men.

The Working Class.   The most important current dispute about class structure concerns the working class, not the capitalist class or petty bourgeoisie. Once the owners of means of production are eliminated, we are left with workers in a bewildering variety of occupations who definitely do not own their own means of production. This variety finds its roots in the structure of the modern capitalist economy. Divisions in the working class result from the following:

a. Some workers do productive labor, that is they produce surplus value in the form of commodities; other workers in commerce and banking are paid a part of the total surplus by their capitalist employers; still other workers are employed by government and so are paid from the portion of the total surplus collected as taxes.

b. The complex authority structures required for modern business place many workers in positions of authority over other workers. Long chains of authority may leave only a minority of workers with authority over no other worker.

c. Related to authority relations are great variations in personal autonomy, from almost none for workers on assembly lines to a great deal for workers in some highly skilled occupations.

d. Great variations in levels of pay are attributable to the types of industry and corporate size.

Table 6 shows the distribution of employed workers among a number of these categories, again on the basis of a 1981 sample survey.

Even allowing for some exaggeration, this table shows that only a minority of workers are in the closely supervised work situations traditionally associated with the "working class". These results should not be taken as evidence that the employees of modern capitalism have become their own bosses. But they do show the differences in authority and privilege that help to prevent workers from realizing and protesting their positions as employees who do not own or control the business (or governmental organizations) where they work.

These divisions are important consequences. For some groups of workers, their conditions of work produce conflict in the workplace, struggles to organize trade unions, and political radicalism in some groups of workers; other groups of workers exhibit little sign of political organization. These differences in activism are related to the distribution of racial and ethnic minorities and women workers among places of work and occupations. Workers with supervisory authority, higher pay, more personal autonomy, and who do not engage in productive labor, are more likely to be politically conservative.

A number of theorists explain the political disunity of the working class by theoretical arguments that some classes of employed workers are actually outside the working class. Nicos Poulantzas (1974) takes the most extreme position. He includes only productive workers engaged in production of *material* commodities (i.e. he excludes workers employed in all the service industries) in the working class. Poulantzas classifies these workers in a new class he calls the "new petty bourgeoisie". This class becomes larger as capitalism develops. It includes the following: workers who do "mental" as opposed to manual labor in the production

TABLE 6
Various Characteristics Of Employed Workers

Characteristic	Category	Percentage
Proportion of work time spent supervising other workers	None	53
	Less than one quarter	13
	About one quarter	13
	About one half	9
	More than one half	4
	Nearly all the time	8
Number of other workers supervised	None	53
	One or two	14
	Three to five	14
	Six to nine	7
	Ten to nineteen	7
	Twenty to forty-nine	2
	Fifty or more	3
Any time spent planning future activities of firm or organization	No	71
	Yes, section of organization	24
	Yes, for entire organization	5
Involved in planning major expenditures	No	89
	Yes	11
Proportion of work time spent on planning	None	71
	Less than one quarter	12
	About one quarter	11
	About one half	4
	More than one half	2
Speed of work regulated by equipment	No	84
	Yes	16
Worker required to produce a quota	No	76
	Yes	24
Able to leave job to do minor errands	No	40
	Yes, at breaks	17
	Yes, any time	43
Frequency of supervision by superior	Several times a day	10
	Once or twice a day	15
	Two or three times a week	8
	Less often	53
	No supervisor	14

SOURCE: Quality of Life 1981 national survey.

of material commodities, including the operators of complex machinery; draughtsmen, clerks, and computer programmers; technicians whose work involves the monitoring and control of production; producers of non-material commodities, such as the employees of a private, profit-making school; and all workers in commerce and banking (they do not do productive labor).

Marx's own work does not refer to the class of productive worker but to the class of *wage-laborers*. With capitalists and land-owners, wage laborers make up "the three big classes of modern society based upon the capitalist mode of production" (1959:885). Writing only in the 1860's Marx describes the process of production in modern factories and the disappearance of small factories whose owners directly supervised production. He writes:

> The *real lever* of the overall labour process is increasingly not the individual workers. Instead, *labour-power socially combined* and the various competing labour-powers which together form the entire production machine participate in very different ways in the process of making commodities...some work better with their hands, others with their heads, one as a manager, engineer, technologists, etc., the other as overseer, the third as manual labourer... An ever increasing number of types of labour are included in the immediate concept of *productive labour*, and those who perform it are classified as *productive workers*, workers directly exploited by capital and *subordinated* to its process of production and expansion. If we consider the aggregate *worker*, i.e. if we take all the members comprising the workshop together, then we see that their *combined activity* results materially in an aggregate product...the activity of this aggregate labour-power is its immediate productive consumption by capital, i.e. it is the self-valorization process of capital....[8a]

In Marx's terminology a group of workers who co-operate in a complex manufacturing process constitute the 'collective worker'. But we need to consider the special positions of supervisors and of public sector employees. The supervisors have dual roles in the work process. They co-ordinate production by the "collective worker" while maintaining capitalist relations of production by making sure that work is carried out at the pace and in the way that maximizes the surplus value. The first is productive labor (at least when employed in the manufacture of commodities); the second is not.   In modern production direct supervision, which was once carried out by the capitalist is specialized into an occupation that does not include the capitalist's other role of directing investment. We should note that supervisors are employees. They sell their labor-power to the capitalist in the same way as the workers they oversee. In contemporary capitalism, of course, the same can be said of corporate executives, since their pay is also largely in the form of salary, which may be supplemented by a bonus based on profits. But executives differ from supervisors in that the very high levels of executive salaries largely reflect their role of serving capitalist business owners, not the cost of reproducing their labor-power.

The situation of state employees is much more complex. They can be broken into a number of categories. First we can distinguish the employees of corporations in industries that produce value which are owned by the state. In Canada these include the provincial electrical utilities, some of the telephone companies, the Canada Development Corporation, Air Canada and the Canadian National Railway, Petro Canada, Canada Post, many local surface transportation companies in metropolitan areas, and approximately half the Saskatchewan potash industry, etc., etc.

Some of these corporations are profit-making and others receive large subsidies. Their workers receive wages and are subject to the same discipline as the employees of private corporations. The corporations also bargain with their employers (at least when permitted to do so by law) in the same way as in the private sector. These state enterprises may be dealt with in the same way as private corporations. Their executives are a part (and potentially a fraction) of the capitalist class and their workers are a part of the working class.[9]

Other sectors of the state do not produce commodities. They include central administrative structures, social service agencies, schools, hospitals, universities, the police and armed forces, and public works departments charged with supplying water, road repair, public recreational facilities, etc. These state employees are paid wages out of the surplus value collected by the state through the taxation of workers and business. Poulantzas and Carchedi consider all such workers are part of the "new middle class" while Wright assigns most to the working class.

The class into which these government workers are placed depends on how the contradiction between two aspects of their situation is resolved. On the one hand, the social relations of production in government organizations are like those in capitalist enterprises. Any illusions that might have existed on this score have surely been destroyed by the past five years of cutbacks in government services and the now established pattern of collective bargaining in the public service. On the other hand, the labor-power of government workers is paid for out of "revenue" and not with capital, as is true for productive workers in corporations. Following the argument concerning the unproductive employees of commercial and banking establishments, government workers are then assigned to the working class. But they are distinguished as a fraction of that class.

What about the managers of government services, including high level civil servants and elected politicians? The temptation is to incorporate them into the capitalist class on the grounds they are charged with the administration of a capitalist state. This would be a mistake. The political latitude permitted state managers is limited and in relation to their employees they play the capitalist role of constantly intensifying the labor process while bargaining to minimize wages. On the other hand, the state must be institutionally distinguished from the capitalist class because its objective is the reproduction of the social formation *as a whole*, rather than the reproduction of an individual capital. These two objectives are complementary but distinct. For this reason we assign state managers to a category distinct from the capitalist and working classes.

HIGHLIGHT

1. Marxist theorists agree on some general principles but not on the nature or number of classes in capitalist societies.

2. In contemporary Canada, a very small minority of the population controls the majority of capital.

3. The various fractions of the petty bourgeoisie have different relationships to the bourgeoisie. Some, like farmers, have antagonistic relationships. Others, like professionals, have complementary relationships.

4. In production, distribution and finance, the Canadian economy is very concentrated.

5. Capitalism in Canada may be described as competitive, in that corporations compete to produce higher profits and new investment is heaviest in industries with above average rates of profit. In terms of wage levels the economy is differentiated along a continuum, not segmented into just the monopoly and competitive sectors. Highly concentrated industries tend to pay higher wages and to employ smaller proportions of women and minority groups.

6. Divisions in the working class are based on differences between productive and non-productive labor, authority, personal autonomy, and pay levels.

A Century of Change

Outlines of the Canadian Class Structure. The most important force behind the development of social classes is the struggle between capital and labor over wages and control of the work process. The constant effort to increase profits leads capitalists to reshape the labor process to minimize the labor time required to produce each commodity. The result is a reduction of the skills required in work, intensification of supervision, development of production processes in which the pace of work is mechanically regulated, and the centralization of production in large factories. This transformation of work and particularly because of increasingly large-scale factory production, leads to a change of the class structure itself.

The impetus to innovation in capitalism results from competition between capitalists. They constantly attempt to lower costs of production since the commodities they produced must be priced at market levels when sold. Otherwise, there is no guarantee they will be sold at all. Since there are physical limits to how hard people will work (termed by Marx the "intensification of labour"), the introduction of labor-saving machinery is required to lower costs and raise profits. Given a decisive technological advantage, the capitalist can hope for more than higher profits. He can hope to drive competitors out of business. For example, the failure of the American computer maker Univac to rapidly incorporate semi-conductors into its computers led to its fall from almost complete domination of the market. IBM's successful adoption of the invention allowed it to take Univac's place. The flow of capital into new activities (often termed "spheres of production") also is motivated by competition between capitalists. Capitalists compete to discover areas of investment giving the greatest profit, irrespective of the particular kinds of commodities produced.

Thus capitalists may produce luxury goods in quantity while failing to provide enough or adequate housing and food for the population. This simply indicates that greater profits are being made from the production of luxuries than from necessities. Thus capitalist economies are unplanned in the sense that the drive for profit, rather than an assessment of the peoples' basic needs, guides production. Of course, political pressure and the fear of disorder drive the state to meet some unfulfilled needs, for example in the form of public housing.

The adoption of innovations in manufacturing carries with it a tendency towards large-scale production which reduces the amount of labor time required to produce a given commodity. At least since the industrial revolution, labor saving machinery has required increases in the scale of production. The tendency, however, is not irreversible, and there are examples of inventions reducing the scale of efficient production. For example, the recent development of microcomputers allows some computation which formerly took place on large computers to be decentralized. Still, the major impact of microcomputers is to cut down the labor time required for clerical workers to type documents, keep files, and carry out accounting procedures.

The tendency towards large-scale production also leads to the decline of independent commodity production and the increasing domination of capitalist production within the Canadian social formation. Within the capitalist mode of production the smaller capitalists are constantly under pressure from big capital.

Beyond the tendency for production to take place on a larger scale, with the development of the capitalist mode of production, Marx sees a tendency for the proportion of living labor in the value of commodities to fall (in relation to the proportions of the value of raw materials and "wear and tear" on productive machinery) (1959:III). As a result Marx predicts the rate of profit will fall and economic crises result. At first glance, the falling proportion of living labor in the productive process would appear to be a necessary consequence of production on an increased scale. But the matter is far more complex.

Although the physical bulk of raw materials and machinery have increased, their *value, in terms of labor time,* is continually decreased by technological advances in the spheres of production that produce the raw materials and productive machinery. Furthermore, the growth of new labor intensive spheres of production (particularly the service industries) may counterbalance the tendency in older spheres (particularly manufacturing) for production to become automated. Because the link between this issue and the Marxist theory of economic crisis, the question of the changing composition of capital is an important subject of empirical analysis.[10]

The discussion to this point has been phrased in rather general terms of "tendencies" in the development of capitalism. The rest of this section uses historical data to describe the actual development of capitalism in Canada. Unfortunately these data do not provide a straightforward description of how classes changed. Very good data are available on farming in Canada because of the long-standing concern of governments with agricultural production, but serious problems arise in describing the growth of capitalist production. Much research work remains to be done in these areas. It will require an understanding of the economic process of capital accumulation and of changes in the occupational and organizational character of firms.

Capitalist Development in Canada. Table 7 contains estimates of the composition of the gross national product (GNP) for 1870 to 1920. Statistics of this kind are part of what is known as "national accounts", a system devised by economists to describe the workings of modern capitalist economies.[11]

The years after Confederation saw a decline in the role of agriculture in the national economy. This affected the independent farmers who have historically formed the most important element of the petty bourgeoisie. Agriculture's share of the GNP fell from one-third of the total in 1870 to just less than one-fifth by 1920. This *relative* decline began at a time when the dollar value of agricultural production was still growing rapidly. Adjusting prices to 1900 dollars, agricultural production rose rapidly from $125 million in 1870 to $430 million in 1910. It then declined to $373 million in 1920.

A number of other broad trends are apparent in Table 7. The proportion of the GNP due to manufacturing grows by 3.6 percent between 1880 and 1890, but shows no further rise until 1920. Forest operations declined as timber became depleted. They fell from 9.6 percent of the total GNP in 1870 to only 3.8 percent in 1920. Interest and dividends paid to foreigners rose from 0.9 percent in 1870 to 2.7 percent in 1880, then showed no further increase. This does not necessarily mean that foreign investment played approximately the same role in the economy over the 1880 to 1920 period. Changes in the form of investment (i.e. portfolio versus direct) and in the policies of firms regarding payouts of their shareholders influenced the outflow of funds.

Production of services almost doubled in the period under discussion. It rose from 20.9 percent to 35.3 percent of the GNP. The process of the large-scale introduction of machines in factories is known as "industrialization". In Canada no dramatic increase in the proportion of manufacturing in the GNP actually took place. This pattern is a distinctive feature of the Canadian economy. Its interpretation, however, is the subject of some dispute. The last section of this chapter will examine the issue in more detail.

It is clear nonetheless that the years after 1870 witnessed a decisive

TABLE 7
Gross National Product, Percentage Distribution Among Components, By Year, 1870-1920

	1870	1880	1890	1900	1910	1920
Agriculture	33.3	32.0	27.0	26.7	22.8	19.4
Fishing and trapping	1.1	1.9	1.6	1.6	0.9	0.9
Mining	0.9	1.0	1.4	3.3	2.6	2.5
Forest Operations	9.6	8.6	6.6	4.9	3.9	3.8
Manufacturing	19.0	18.9	23.5	21.1	22.7	24.2
Construction	3.0	3.8	4.6	3.9	5.1	5.5
Services	20.9	22.4	26.7	29.4	33.7	35.3
Rent	9.4	10.0	8.6	8.5	8.1	6.5
Net interest and dividends paid abroad	-0.9	-2.7	-3.7	-3.0	-3.7	-3.0
Indirect taxes less subsidies	3.7	4.1	3.7	3.6	3.9	4.9
Total	100.0	100.0	100.0	100.0	100.0	100.0
Gross National Product ($ millions)	459	581	803	1057	2235	5529
Gross National Product adjusted to constant dollars	375	509	777	1057	1886	1923
Gross National Product per capita, in constant dollars	102	118	161	197	262	219

SOURCE: M. C. Urquhart and K. A. H. Buckley, *Historical Statistics of Canada.* (Toronto: Macmillan, 1965), pp. 141, 291, 14.

TABLE 8
Percentage Distribution Of Net National Income At Factor Cost, 1926-1980

Year	Wages and Salaries+	Corporations before taxes	Dividends paid to non-residents	Interest and miscellaneous investment income	Net income of farm operators from farming	Net farm income of unincorporated business including rents	Inventory valuation adjustment	Total	Net National Income at Factor Cost Total (millions)	Price Adjusted Total (millions)	Per Capita
				Percentage Distribution							
1926	58.1	10.3	-2.3	2.3	14.8	15.7	1.1	100.0	4,129	3213	340
1930	64.3	7.4	-4.1	3.1	7.9	15.9	5.5	100.0	4,399	3945	386
1935	68.4	11.7	-3.9	3.1	7.2	14.2	-0.7	100.0	3,099	3283	303
1940	63.2	17.0	-3.6	2.3	9.5	14.0	-2.4	100.0	5,063	4688	412
1945	64.7	13.1	-1.5	2.4	9.4	12.3	-0.4	100.0	9,665	7316	606
1950	62.9	17.9	-2.8	2.7	9.0	12.9	-2.6	100.0	14,553	6891	503
1955	65.6	15.9	-1.8	3.5	5.1	12.5	-0.8	100.0	21,908	10008	638
1960	69.8	13.4	-1.7	3.9	3.6	11.1	-0.1	100.0	28,837	12489	699
1965	70.1	15.3	-2.0	4.6	3.4	9.4	-0.8	100.0	41,219	15933	811
1970	74.1	12.0	-1.5	5.4	1.9	8.4	-0.3	100.0	64,235	23897	1122
1975	73.1	15.2	-1.4	6.6	3.1	5.7	-2.3	100.0	129,824	26801	1181
1980	71.4	16.4	-1.4	9.7	2.1	4.9	-3.0	100.0	227,498	30886*	1292*

*estimated
+includes supplementary labour income and military pay and allowances
SOURCES: National Income and Expenditure Accounts, Vol. 1, 1926-1974 (Ottawa: Statistics Canada, 1976).
Economic Review, April 1979 and April 1981 (Ottawa: Department of Finance).

turning away from primary production towards manufacturing and services. In 1870 the primary industries accounted for 44.9 percent of the GNP, compared to 26.6 percent in 1920. Over the same period manufacturing, construction, and services rose from 42.9 to 65 percent. From 1870 the relative share of the GNP for the agricultural fraction of the petty bourgeoisie declined. In addition, the rising manufacturing, service, and construction industries are dominated by capitalist production.

The second to last row of figures in Table 7 for 1910 shows the rapid expansion of the overall economy during this period. Removing the effect of price changes, gross national product increased from $375 million (1900 dollars) to $1923 million, an increase of 413 percent. Half of this increase is attributable to increased population. *Per capita* GNP approximately doubled over the 1870-1920 period.

Table 8 continues these data until 1980, on a far more certain basis than is available in the earlier data. The last columns show the continuing and dramatic increases in both the value of NNP adjusted for inflation and per capita NNP. Net National Product is equal to Net National Income as shown in Table 8; it is very similar to GNP, but excludes the effects of indirect taxes, government subsidies, and capital consumption allowances (which measure depreciation in businesses). The price adjusted NNP increased by a factor of more than eight, while the per capita value rises from $340 dollars (1935-39 base) to $1181. After 1970 there appears to be an abrupt end to a long period of growth in per capita NNP—a sign of the decline of the capitalist economies in the nineteen seventies.[12]

The rise of the capitalist mode of production and decline of independent commodity production is evident in the declines of both the proportion of NNP for the income of farm operators and in the "net non-farm income of unincorporated business including rents" which falls from 15.7 percent of the total in 1926 to only 4.9 percent in 1980. The two categories associated with capitalist production, "wages and salaries" and "corporate profits before taxes" increase over these approximately fifty years, by 1980 reaching a total of 87.8 percent of net national income. Finally, note the rapid increase in the category "interest and miscellaneous investment income" after 1960. This income does not accrue to a single class for it includes the interest paid on savings of workers, interest on corporate bank deposits, etc. Nevertheless, the rapid increase (to almost ten percent of net national income of 1980) obviously works to the advantage of people and businesses with large savings—thereby redistributing income from the poor to the rich.

The occupational distributions in Tables 9 and 10 supplement the national accounts data.[13] First, note the decline after 1931 in the absolute number of workers in agriculture. It reflects the onset of a period of drought and poor harvests. Table 8 shows that absolute farm income had peaked about twenty years earlier. The nineteen thirties initiated an

TABLE 9
Occupation By Class For Canada, 1851-1941

Class of Occupation*	1851	1861	1871	1881	1891	1901	1911	1921	1931	1941
Number in thousands										
Agriculture	165	325	480	663	735	717	934	1042	1132	1084
Industrial	71	145	213	287	383	460	663	685	849	1026
Commercial	18	45	75	108	149	182	381	493	642	682
Domestic	35	42	60	75	126	148	206	207	357	433
Professional	12	20	39	53	60	74	99	170	221	275
Labourers	149	172	125	166	105	123	324	307	444	264
Other unclassified			18	39	58	79	117	269	282	432
Total	450	749	1010	1391	1616	1783	2724	3173	3927	4196
Population	1842	3091	3486	4325	4833	5371	7207	8788	10376	11507
Percentage Distribution										
Agriculture	36.7	43.4	47.5	47.7	45.5	40.2	34.3	32.8	28.8	25.8
Industrial	15.8	19.4	21.1	20.6	23.7	25.8	24.4	21.5	21.6	24.5
Commercial	4.0	6.0	7.4	7.8	9.2	10.1	14.0	15.6	16.4	16.3
Domestic	7.8	5.6	5.9	5.4	7.8	8.4	7.5	6.5	9.1	10.3
Professional	2.6	2.6	3.9	3.8	3.7	4.2	3.6	5.4	5.6	6.5
Labourers	33.1	23.0	12.4	11.9	6.5	6.9	11.9	9.7	11.3	6.3
Other unclassified			1.8	2.8	3.6	4.4	4.3	8.5	7.2	10.3
Total	100.0	100.0	100.0	100.0	100.0	100.0	100.0	100.0	100.0	100.0

*Commercial class includes occupations in accounting, retail and wholesale trade.
Domestic class includes occupations in personal service, hotel keeping, etc.
Professional class includes lawyers, physicians, engineers, police, municipal employees, teachers and professors, artists of all types.

SOURCE: François-Albert Angers and Patrick Allen, *Evolution de la Structure des Emplois au Canada* (Montréal: Ecole des Hautes Etudes Commerciales, 1954).

TABLE 10

Percentage Distribution Of Occupations Of The Labour Force Aged 15 Or Over, 1901–1981[a]

Occupation	1901[b]	1911	1921	1931	1941[c]	1951	1961	1971	1981[d]
White collar occupations									
Proprietary and managerial	4.3	4.7	7.3	5.6	5.4	7.4	7.8	9.5	7.4
Professional	4.6	3.8	5.4	6.1	6.7	7.3	9.8	12.7	14.6
Clerical	3.2	3.8	6.9	6.7	7.2	10.7	12.7	14.8	17.4
Commercial	3.1	4.4	5.1	5.4	5.4	6.0	6.8	6.9	9.7
Financial		0.3	0.6	0.7	0.6	0.6	0.8	—[e]	—[e]
Blue collar occupations									
Manufacturing and mechanical	15.9	13.6	11.4	11.6	16.1	17.2	16.1	17.2	{ 16.4
Labourers (except in primary industries)	7.2	11.9	9.7	11.3	6.3	6.6	5.3	5.1	
Construction	4.7	4.8	4.7	4.7	4.7	5.5	5.2	6.8	6.7
Primary Occupations									
Agricultural	40.3	34.4	32.6	28.6	25.7	15.7	10.0	7.4	5.1
Fishing, hunting and trapping	1.5	1.3	0.9	1.2	1.2	1.0	0.6	0.4	0.4
Logging	0.9	1.5	1.2	1.1	1.9	1.9	1.2	0.7	0.7
Mining and quarrying	1.6	2.3	1.5	1.5	1.7	1.2	1.0	0.7	0.7
Transporation and Communication	4.4	5.6	5.5	6.3	6.4	7.8	7.7	5.4	6.3
Personal service	7.8	7.3	5.8	8.2	9.3	7.2	9.1	{ 12.4	{ 13.8
All other service	0.4	0.3	1.2	1.1	1.2	2.6	3.3		
Not stated	0.0	0.0	0.2	0.0	0.2	1.2	2.6	0.0	0.8
Total	100.0	100.0	100.0	100.0	100.0	100.0	100.0	100.0	100.0

a. excluding Yukon and Northwest Territories
b. ten years and over
c. excluding active duty military personnel
d. estimated
e. included in other categories.

SOURCE: Sylvia Ostry, *The Occupational Composition of the Canadian Labour Force*. (Ottawa: Dominion Bureau of Statistics, 1967). *The Labour Force* (Ottawa: Statistics Canada), Sept. 1971 and July 1981. Col. 1 adds to 99.9; Col. 4 adds to 100.1; Col. 6 adds to 99.9.

absolute decline of agriculture (and so of a class fraction) in the social formation.

The tendency for capitalist production to require increasingly larger resources to be devoted to the commercial and banking activities constituting the sphere of circulation is readily apparent from these occupational data. In 1851 commercial workers constituted a mere four percent of the labor force, by 1900 it was about ten percent, and by 1941 16.3 percent. The somewhat different classification in Table 10 also demonstrates such a trend. Despite the increasing size of businesses and corresponding fall in the number of direct proprietors the "proprietary and managerial" category also grows, showing the general increase in the number of managers. Professionals, broadly defined in these tables to include all teachers, also increase their share of the workforce. Transportation and communications workers increase somewhat from 4.4 percent of all workers in 1901 to 63 percent in 1981. Other categories do not change very much, including personal service and construction.

The Development of Manufacturing.   Unfortunately, no single, consistent series of data is available to show the change in the size of manufacturing establishments. Table 11 summarizes two series, one for 1870 to 1957; the second for 1957 to 1978. As the common measures for 1957 show, the change in the calculation of the series produces a small decrease in the number of eligible establishments and employees in the survey.

Before considering these series, it is worth taking a closer look at the state of manufacturing in Canada before large scale industrialization. The 1871 Census of Canada is the first "modern" census, in the sense that its data and producers are comparable to what became the norm in later censuses. The most valuable innovations over previous efforts are the coverage in identical format of Ontario, Quebec, Nova Scotia, and New Brunswick, and the extensive census of industrial establishments.

The industrial census of 1871 covers 40 735 establishments. Together they employed 187 942 "hands". This number represented only 5.4 percent of the population at the time. Each establishment averaged only 4.6 employees. Clearly only a tiny part of the economy can be said to have entered the capitalist mode of production.

Most manufacturing was carried out in small shops whose proprietors were in positions where the petty bourgeoisie, as a class, merges into the capitalist class. In 1871, many forms of production which are today unimaginable in anything but large enterprises were carried out on virtually a craft scale. For example, the average number of employees of agricultural implement makers was only 10.1, foundries and machine working shops 16.5, oil refineries 8.6, distilleries 23.2, and so on. Still smaller shops accounted for most manufacturing of carriages (average size 3.0), boots and shoes (4.5), furniture (5.1), and beer (6.3). It is unlikely that more than twenty factories in all four provinces employed as many as one hundred workers each. Large companies were concentrated in a handful of industries including glass works, rolling mills, sewing machine factories, cotton mills, and sugar refineries.

At what point did manufacturing change from the early capitalist form described in the data for 1871 to something resembling modern capitalist production? The data in Table 11 show a dramatic increase in the *amount* of manufacturing between 1870 and 1890. The number of establishments rose from 39 000 to 70 000 (3.0 percent per year) and the number of employees from 182 000 to 351 000 (3.3 percent per year). However, the average number of employees per establishment did not change. Then, between 1895 and 1905, the average number of employees per establishment approximately quintupled, from 5.0 to 25.2, with hardly any change in the total number of employees. The rapidity of technological change is evident in the 48 percent increase in value added per employee (after prices are adjusted to constant dollars).

The number of employees in manufacturing and the average size of factories did not change appreciably between 1910 and 1940. Still the value added per employee rose by about seventy percent over the three decades. Establishment size increased from 29.9 employees to 38.5 between 1940 and 1945. This increase reflects the impact of war production—then falls almost to pre-war levels. The next important jump occurs between 1960 and 1975. The process of development in manufacturing, it would appear, is very uneven. Periods of rapid growth alternate with near stagnation.

The increasing role of supervisory and office employees in the process of production is visible from the first available measure for 1905 (remember these data are restricted to manufacturing; see also the occupational data in Tables 9 and 10). The proportion of supervisory and office workers rises from less than one in ten at the turn of the century to just over one in four from 1965 onward. In contrast, an average of only 0.3 percent of the people engaged in manufacturing are working owners or partners. This pattern shows the sharpness of the division between workers and capitalists in modern times.

Agricultural Production.   We conclude this discussion of the development of class with a brief examination of changes in agricultural production, and of the fraction of the petty bourgeoisie in farming. The number of farms increased steadily from 1871 until 1931; began to decline after 1941; and declined very steeply from 1951 to 1971. Between 1941 and 1971 half of all farms disappeared. At the same time the average size of all farms approximately doubled from 236.8 to 463.4 acres. In the same period, the farm population fell dramatically from 31.7 percent to only 6.9 percent of the total for Canada.

Compared to manufacturing, changes in farm size are quite steady.

TABLE 11

Summary Statistics Of Manufacturing Industries, Canada, 1917-1978

Year	Number of establishments	Number of employees	Mean employees per establishment	Supervisory and office employees as a percent of all employees	Value added per employee (prices adjusted 1935-1939 100)	Working owners and partners a percent of all employees
OLD SERIES*						
1870	38,898	181,679	4.7	—	657	
1880	47,079	248,042	5.3	—	718	
1895	69,716	351,139	5.0	—	870	
1900	—	422,824	—	—	935	
1905	15,197	382,702	25.2	9.2	—	
1910	—	509,977	—	8.4	1386	
1917	22,043	571,866	26.6	10.7	1370	
1920	22,376	576,417	25.8	13.4	1307	
1925	20,956	522,661	24.9	13.6	1672	
1930	22,586	614,348	27.2	13.8	2160	
1935	24,000	556,363	23.2	17.6	2195	
1940	25,471	761,639	29.9	17.8	2360	
1945	28,979	1,118,015	38.5	17.0	2411	
1950	35,942	1,183,297	32.9	19.5	2378	
1955	38,182	1,298,461	34.0	22.1	3107	
1957	37,875	1,359,061	35.9	23.1	3050	
NEW SERIES*						
1957	33,551	1,340,948	40.0	22.8	3953	—
1960	32,852	1,275,476	38.8	23.8	4623	0.9
1965	33,310	1,570,299	47.1	28.9	5342	0.7
1970	31,928	1,637,001	51.3	28.7	5998	0.4
1975	30,100	1,741,159	57.8	27.0	5775	0.3
1978	31,963	1,790,618	56.0	26.8	7030	

SOURCES: Old Series: M. C. Urquhart and K. A. H. Buckley, *Historical Statistics of Canada.* (Toronto: Macmillan, 1965), pp. 462-3, 294-5.
New Series: *Manufacturing Industries of Canada: National and Provincial Areas.* (Ottawa: Statistics Canada).
*as the two sets of values for 1957 show, the basis of the series changes to eliminate some small employers

TABLE 12
Farm Characteristics By Year

Farm Characteristic	1871	1881	1891+	1901	1911	1921	1931	1941	1951	1961	1971	1976*
Number of farms	367,862	464,025	620,486	511,073	682,329	711,090	728,623	732,832	623,091	480,903	366,128	369,000
Size of farm (percentages)												
1-4 acres	11.0	16.2	30.9	7.7	6.4	3.0	2.7	1.6	1.5	2.0	2.0	2.1
5-10 acres				3.6	3.6	3.2	3.3	2.9	3.4	2.5	2.8	3.1
11-50 acres	21.4	20.1	14.2	15.9	13.0	11.6	11.0	10.5	9.5	7.1	7.3	8.4
51-100 acres	38.4	33.8	25.4	30.7	24.1	22.3	20.4	21.8	19.8	14.1	12.2	12.4
101-200 acres	22.3	22.0	21.0	29.5	33.4	32.3	32.0	31.5	27.9	24.2	21.8	21.3
201-300 acres	6.9	7.9	8.5	12.6	19.5	27.6	4.9	5.1	6.3	7.9	8.0	7.8
301-479 acres							14.2	14.1	15.1	16.0	15.7	14.9
480-639 acres							5.0	5.3	6.4	8.0	8.2	7.6
640 acres or more							6.5	7.2	10.1	18.2	22.0	22.4
Total	100.0	100.0	100.0	100.0	100.0	100.0	100.0	100.0	100.0	100.0	100.0	100.0
Total area (1000's acres)	36,046	45,358	60,288	63,422	108,966	140,887	163,114	173,563	174,047	172,551	169,668	175,500
Mean area	98.0	97.7	97.2	124.1	159.7	198.2	223.9	236.8	279.3	358.8	463.4	475
Farm population (1000's)								3,152	2,912	2,128	1,489	
Farm population (% of Canada)								31.7	20.8	11.7	6.9	

*estimated to 1971 basis
SOURCE: Canadian Census, Volumes on Agriculture 1871-1976
         Economic Review April 1979 (Ottawa: Dept. of Finance), p. 180.

+includes farms under 1 acre not in figures of other years. Removing these small farms would yield 510,000 farms with a mean area of about 112 acres and the size distribution: 1-10 acres 13%, 11-50 acres 18%, 51-100 acres 32%, 101-200 acres 26%, and 201 acres or more 11%.

Farms became larger in all but two decades over the past century, 1871-1881 (when number of farms and total acreage still increased by one quarter) and 1931-41 (the depression). The decline of farmers as the historically most important fraction of the petty bourgeoisie represents, first, their unequal struggle with other classes. This conflict is manifested most clearly in the decline of farmers' share of the national income relative to farm numbers and population and in farm prices. The second aspect of the decline is the obvious impact of competition among farmers which has accelerated the introduction of new technology and thereby decreased the number of farm operators. At the same time the total area under cultivation has shown no appreciable change since 1931.

The Process of Capitalist Development

The increasing size of corporations reflects changes in technology, the adoption of technology by capitalists attempting to lower their labor costs, and bankruptcies and takeovers of small firms. A number of conflicts shape the development of capitalism. What is classically characterized as the "class struggle", pits workers against their capitalist employers. The balance of power, represented in the ratio of wages and salaries to corporate profits, is one outcome of this struggle. The legal rights of trade unions, government regulations specifying hours of work and other employee rights, and health and safety legislation are other outcomes. These legal gains exist in the context of extensive legislated and unlegislated employer rights. Indeed, the formalization of workers' rights often proceeds in tandem with the granting of powers to management. Nevertheless, workers have made enormous gains since 1872 when trade unions were granted legal status. Until that year trade unions were illegal and their members could be charged with seditious conspiracy (see Logan, 1948).

The most visible aspect of class conflict is the long record of strikes in Canada. Numerous demonstrations, such as those in opposition to the imposition of wage controls in 1975, marches of the unemployed during the Depression, and earlier struggles to limit the length of the working day are further manifestations of class conflict. A less visible aspect of conflict is the constant negotiating, sometimes in contract discussions and other times in less formal bargaining, of the conditions of work. Still less visible is the constant conflict over authority in the workplace that is part of everyday life in capitalism.

How does class conflict affect the class structure? There is a reciprocal relationship between them. The length of the working day and the intensity of labor, both of which are affected by actions like strikes, combine with the wage level to determine the relation between variable and constant capital in the process of capitalist production. Competition and the effort to maximize profits drives capitalists in two directions which affect the class structure. First, they attempt to maximize the intensity of labor. One step in this process is the development of a stratum of workers who supervise and control others. The organization of work is also altered, with the same objective. Second, new technology is adopted. This decreases the labor time required to produce commodities. Thus technological development is used by capitalists to fight the increased bargaining power of workers in trade unions. Paradoxically, struggles by workers play a role in continuing the revolution in technology of modern capitalism. The new technology tends to force small capitalists out of business (since the new machinery is expensive) and reinforces the positions of large, monopolistic firms.

A second impact of the class struggle relates to the state. There are numerous examples of intervention in labor disputes by local and provincial police, the RCMP, and the armed forces (see Jamieson 1968). In the twentieth century, the few spectacular uses of force, such as in the suppression of the Winnipeg General Strike, have been far overshadowed by the less obvious role of the state in regulating labor relations. It has developed mechanisms to institutionalize conflicts between capital and labor. The objective is to eliminate the use of force and to replace demands for control of the work process with monetary demands. To meet the continuing pressure of unemployment, always present in the capitalist economy, capitalist states including Canada have instituted unemployment insurance, job creation programs and retraining schemes. These, in turn, require the hiring of state workers for their management.

A third impact of the class struggle concerns the position of Canada in the capitalist world system. As seen in an earlier chapter, workers in some industries now live under the threat that their wage demands will lead their employers to remove manufacturing to a low wage country. They may also lose their jobs because of increased imports. Thus international differences in wage levels and working conditions are among the factors determining the character of the world system. The mobility of capital and commodities produces constant readjustments as the accumulation of capital takes place on a world scale.

As was emphasized in the discussion of firm size, competition among capitalists plays a power role in concentrating capital in fewer and fewer hands. Bankruptcies and the (less noticeable) closing down of small businesses also play a role. Such events are far more numerous in times of economic downturn. In these periods the already powerful forces towards monopolization are accelerated.

Mergers and takeovers have played a major role in concentrating power in the hands of a small capitalist class since the nineteenth century. Some of the largest Canadian firms were created in one of several waves of mergers. Smucker (1980:86) notes that between 1909 and 1913 smaller companies were merged to form a number of very large oligopolistic corporations, including Canada Cement, Amalgamated Asbestos, Canada Car and Foundry, Dominion Steel Corporation, and the Steel Company of Canada. The initial mergers of competing companies in the same industry have given way in recent years to "vertical" integration, whereby firms take over other corporations who are their suppliers and customers. From the 1960s on, conglomerate takeovers have expanded the field to include takeovers of firms in completely unrelated industries. Power Corporation, Argus, and the Thomson holdings are among the largest examples. This concentration has gone on with no important opposition from the Canadian state.[14]

HIGHLIGHT

1. In efforts to remain competitive, capitalists rely on the increasing use of technology to lower their labor costs.
2. Twentieth century Canada has been characterized by: (1) a decrease in the numbers of petty bourgeoisie; (2) an increase in the number of salaried and wage earning workers; and (3) an increase in the number of professionals.
3. In the twentieth century, the total number of manufacturing enterprises increased. So did the total number of people employed and the average size of business enterprises. At the same time, the average size of farms increased while the number and proportion of farmers in the population fell dramatically.
4. These trends in the class structure arise from the constant conflict of classes in Canada and the larger process of capital accumulation in the world system.

The Canadian Class Structure in International Perspective

As the Vietnamese war escalated, many people in the advanced capitalist nations developed an increasing awareness of the militaristic aspect of imperialism and of the system of international inequality. Canada appeared to occupy a curious intermediary position in this system characterized by Kari Levitt (1970:127) as a "rich, industrialized, underdeveloped economy". On the one hand Canada enjoyed the material privilege of the developed capitalist world. However, it was a resource dependent economy, with a much higher level of foreign investment and a lower level of research and development than other developed nations.

In a series of publications beginning about 1970, English-Canadian social scientists have elaborated a colonial theory of Canadian development. At times they drew on an existing tradition in Canadian political economy called staple theory. The best known scholar in this school, as mentioned earlier, is Harold Innis.

The following quotations summarize the main arguments made from the colonial perspective:

From the beginning the national bourgeoisie directs its efforts towards activities of the intermediary type. The basis of its strength is found in its aptitude for trade and small business enterprises, and in securing commissions... In protecting the massive inflows of American funds, the Canadian bourgeoisie realized their historic mission as an intermediary... Owing their primary commitment to foreign benefactors, they put the needs of capital before the needs of the Canadian people. (Drache 1970:20-1)

In Canada, the process of penetration by direct investment has been aided considerably by the legacy of merchant capital, an overdeveloped transportation and financial infrastructure which drains funds away from industry. The tightly cartelized banking system cannot provide long-term risk capital, but is concerned primarily with liquidity... Indigenous industrial capitalism was historically a weak force, stultified by the domination of merchant capital and (the) branch plant industry... The Canadian industrial bourgeoisie has thus been relegated to the position of managing branch plants for foreign masters... Control of the Canadian economy lies overwhelmingly with the branch plant group (Naylor 1972:30-2).

The Canadian indigenous elite is boxed in by its own past, in which most of the productive areas of the economy—manufacturing and resources— were given up to foreign capitalists. Meanwhile this elite has stayed safely away from industrialization while enriching itself through interest on capital, provision of support services such as transportation and utilities, and the buying or selling of existing companies (Clement 1977:290).

A note of pessimism runs through research from which the quotations derive. George Grant titled his work on the subject *Lament for a Nation* (1965). Levitt (1970) argues,

After twenty-five years of heavy American direct investment Canada's freedom of action has been progressively restricted to the point where it is doubtful whether it can be regained. (1970:116)

The implication of these theoretical arguments, which advance what might be termed a colonial model of the Canadian class structure, is that Canada is fundamentally different from other advanced capitalist nations. We will address the legitimacy of the colonial model by looking at certain aspects of the structure of *contemporary* Canada. These theorists argue that colonial development has produced a social formation that is distinctively different from that of nations which experienced autonomous (or "autocentric") development.

Two avenues of research will be suggested as tests of the contemporary results of colonial development. First, we will examine the class structure of Canada as a whole to see whether it provides evidence of "distortion". Second, we will focus specifically on the Canadian capitalist class, to see whether it is actually dominated by "mercantile" or "commercial" interests. We will proceed largely on the basis of comparisons between Canada and other advanced capitalist nations.

There is some question as to what constitute the appropriate bases for comparisons of this kind. It is common to compare Canada unfavorably to the United States, the richest and most powerful capitalist nation, then to conclude that underdevelopment exists. More appropriate bases of comparison are provided by Australia, the Scandinavian countries, and some of the smaller European capitalist nations.

It is not yet possible to make precise comparisons among the class structures of advanced capitalist nations. However, studies are currently being undertaken by Wright and a number of international collaborators on these matters. In the absence of direct data, comparisons must be based on industrial and occupational distributions. Some of these are shown in Tables 13 and 14. Another aspect of the colonial model, the degree to which Canadian development has been structured by merchant capital, will be examined later.

As the colonial model would predict, among the ten nations shown, Canada has the smallest proportion of workers in manufacturing. But the differences between Canada and the United States and Australia are very small. Canada also has the highest numbers of workers in the category of "community, social, and personal services" and in "mining and quarrying". In the remaining industrial categories, Canada is within the range of the remaining nine countries. Especially when we compare the Canadian and Australian industrial structures (Australia also has a British colonial legacy and a history of white settlement in a large and still sparsely populated land) to that of the United States, it is difficult to argue for Canadian distinctiveness. The data on occupations tell a similar story (unfortunately data are not available for some of the nations for which industrial distributions are in Table 13). Again, Canada is found to have the lowest proportion in the combined category of "production and related workers, transport equipment operators and labourers", but Canada's occupational structure is not remarkably dissimilar from other nations.

The reader should be alerted to the fact that other contributors to this volume may not believe that examining the class structure in the way I propose is the best way of either validating or invalidating the colonial model. In addition, I will argue that the comparative differences in class structure are minimal. However, the Science Council of Canada argues that these differences, small though they are, distinguish Canada from other industrial societies.

Wallace Clement, an advocate of the colonial model, argues that what he regards as the distinctive Canadian class structure also affects opportunities for social mobility, "The result is a highly structured economy with few avenues through which the lower class can rise" (1977:293). A number of empirical studies have addressed this issue (Turrittin 1974; Ornstein 1981) but none finds any evidence of lower mobility in Canada as compared to the U.S., Britain, Australia, and the Scandinavian countries.

TABLE 13
Percentage Distribution Of Employed Workers By Occupation For Canada And Seven Other Advanced Capitalist Nations

Occupation	Canada (1981)	Australia (1980)	Austria (1980)	Fed. Rep. of Germany (1980)	Japan (1980)	Netherlands (1977)	Sweden (1980)	United States (1980)
Professional, technical, and related workers	15.9	14.0	3.6	14.0	9.2	17.5	25.8	15.4
Administrative and managerial workers	8.2	6.6	} 20.2	3.0	4.9	2.5	2.3	10.8
Clerical and related workers	17.7	16.9		20.2	17.7	19.0	12.0	18.4
Sales workers	10.2	9.2	9.1	8.8	14.1	10.6	8.0	6.2
Service workers	13.5	9.8	17.0	11.2	8.4	10.7	13.2*	13.6
Agriculture, animal husbandry, forestry workers, fishermen and hunters	5.8	7.1	10.4	5.5	10.8	6.1	5.4	2.7
Production and related workers transport equipment operators and labourers	28.6	36.4	39.7	37.3	34.9	33.6	33.3	32.9
Total	100.0	100.0	100.0	100.0	100.0	100.0	100.0	100.0
Number employed	10,699	62,378	3,088	26,470	55,547	4,687	4,318	103,867*

*includes sport and recreation
SOURCE: *Year Book of Labour Statistics 1981* (Geneva: International Labour Organization).

TABLE 14
Percentage Distribution Of Employed Persons By Industry For Canada And Nine Other Market Economy Nations

Industry	Canada (1981)	Australia (1979)	France (1980)	Fed. Rep. of Germany (1980)	Italy (1980)	Japan (1980)	Netherlands (1979)	Sweden (1980)	United Kingdom (1980)	United States (1980)
Agriculture, hunting, fishing, forestry	5.3	6.6	8.8	5.9	⎱14.4	10.4	5.8	5.6	2.7	3.5
Mining, quarrying	1.8	1.3	0.7	1.3	⎰	0.2	0.2	0.3	1.4	1.0
Manufacturing	19.5	⎱22.2	25.7	35.1	26.9	24.8	22.0	24.2	28.4	22.7
Electricity, gas, water	1.2	⎰	0.9	0.9	1.1	0.5	0.9	0.9	1.4	1.4
Construction	5.4	7.7	8.6	7.6	10.1	9.9	10.5	6.8	6.9	6.6
Wholesale, retail trade, restaurants, hotels	17.0	20.3	15.9	14.6	18.8	22.7	16.8	13.7	17.3	20.4
Transport, storage, communication	7.1	7.8	6.3	5.8	5.6	6.3	6.7	7.0	6.5	5.1
Finance, insurance, real estate, business service	5.4	8.0	7.3	5.6	2.6	5.7	7.8	6.7	6.4	8.2
Community, social and Personal services	37.3	26.1	25.8	23.2	20.5	19.5	29.3	34.8	29.0	31.1
Total	100.0	100.0	100.0	100.0	100.0	100.0	100.0	100.0	100.0	100.0
Number employed (000's)	10,699	6,401	21,190*	25,948*	20,385*	55,230	4,834*	4,232	24,366*	103,867*

*excludes Armed Forces and persons with activities not adequately defined
SOURCE: *Year Book of Labour Statistics* 1981 and 1982 Ch. 1, Table 2a (Geneva: © International Labour Organization).

An examination of the Canadian class structure as a whole provides weak support for the colonial model of the Canadian class structure. The Canadian structure is not quantitatively different from that of other capitalist nations. Differences that do exist are small when taken in the context of the world economy. Any comparison between Canada and other nations leaves Canada decisively in the camp of the most privileged *and* developed nations. (See, for additional comparative figures the World Bank's annual *World Development Report*.) Amin's comment regarding divisions in the advanced capitalist nations seems an appropriate summary of the above results:

> Industrialization really does bring wealth: the level of consumption of manufactured goods depends on the level of local production of these goods. The only apparent exception, offered by rich countries that are large importers of manufactured goods (the "White Dominions," Denmark, etc.) is not really an exception, because they not only have a substantial industrial production of their own but also obtain a considerable supplement of manufactured goods, thanks to their rich and specialized agriculture (1974:70).[15]

Merchant Dominance. The second aspect of colonial theory is the argument that the Canadian capitalist class has a distinctively "mercantile" structure. The capitalist class is seen to be dominated by a coalition between Canadian capital in the banking, commercial and utilities industries and foreign capital in resources and manufacturing. Some theorists argue that underlying this is a fundamental conflict between "mercantile" interests and manufacturing.   The domination of Canadian mercantile interests, whose orientation is towards the export of staples, has resulted in Canada's failure to become a modern industrial economy. Among the symptoms of this failure are slow economic growth, high unemployment, and regional inequality. The manufacturing sector, which has surrendered to foreign capital, often produces on too small and inefficient a scale (the "miniature replica" effect). It also imports raw materials and parts even when they could be purchased domestically. Moreover, the manufacturing sector places little emphasis on exports, and carries out little research and development in Canada. There is strong evidence of these characteristics in the behavior of foreign branch plants. But that evidence alone does not constitute proof of the preceding arguments.

The characterization of Canadian capital as mercantile is particularly misleading. As Macdonald (1975) and Ryerson (1976) argue, two fundamental theoretical errors underlie this line of thinking. First, part of the capital that is characterized as "mercantile," in transportation and utilities is actually industrial. Railways and hydro-electric power production, for example, both involve industrial development in their construction and serve as necessary elements in an industrial economy. Both, in

Marxist terms, produce value by exploitation of productive labor.   Second, however the mercantile sector is defined, it is difficult to find an economic basis for the supposed conflict between mercantile and industrial capital. Marx devotes considerable space in the third volume of *Capital* (see Part IV; and Part III for background) to a discussion of the relations among industrial, commercial, and money-dealing (i.e. banking) capital. He points out that commercial and money-dealing capital perform functions indispensible to the accumulation of capital in industry. Commercial capital facilitates the circulation of commodities so that new production does not require the industrialist to wait for all the production to be sold. Banking also facilitates production by providing credit for the purchase of productive machinery and by generally facilitating the sale of the commodities produced by industry.

At a more concrete level, Macdonald casts doubt on whether merchants and industrialists in the nineteenth century constituted distinct, antagonistic groups of capitalists. He cites a number of instances where individual capitalists owned businesses in both production and trade. He also identifies instances of amicable business relations between capitalists in the two sectors.

A contemporary study of Canadian capitalism reaches a similar conclusion on the basis of an analysis of the memberships of the boards of directors of the largest Canadian firms. Taking the presence of an individual on the boards of two different companies as an indication of a relation between the firms, Carroll, Fox, and Ornstein (1982) analyze the network of relations among the one hundred largest Canadian firms. They find that the network has a dense centre of tightly interlocked firms with a periphery of less connected firms. The centre of the network is occupied by the largest Canadian financial *and industrial* firms. The foreign owned firms tend to be found in the periphery. It is precisely this strong relationship between Canadian finance and industry (which Lenin characterizes with the term "finance capital") that marks the Canadian capitalist class as a distinct national bourgeoisie. The shortcoming of this line of argument that simply opposes the colonial model is that it does not account for the evident distinctiveness of the Canadian economy, particularly the high level of foreign investment in manufacturing and its negative consequences, such as a low level of research and development.

What appears to be required in a theory of Canadian development is a balance between the particularities of Canadian capitalism and the process of capitalist accumulation that occurs in many different countries. This, however, is a difficult task. It is often difficult to identify the causes of particular developments. For example, regional development and underdevelopment in Canada (see Clement, 1979, Cuneo, 1978b) is frequently viewed as a result of both failures on the part of Canadian capital to provide for even development and from high levels of foreign investment. The basis of these conclusions is usually an analysis of foreign dominated industries and their investment patterns. But, regional inequality is found in all capitalist nations. So its presence in Canada cannot be explained by reference to foreign ownership alone.

A similar problem arises with regard to staple exports in the past and to the wide range of raw material and food exports at present. These exports are not, by themselves, a negative feature of the Canadian economy. Nor is it clear that they *cause* industrial underdevelopment. Indeed, the contrast between Canadian economic historians, phrases "export led growth" and "staple trap" captures this lack of a necessary relation between the export of staples and capitalist development.

The Canadian class structure is not remarkably different from those of other advanced capitalist nations. Nevertheless, a number of features of the economy suggest that the extraordinarily high level of foreign investment has limited the development of Canadian industry. Unfortunately, so far, no historical analysis provides comparisons with other nations nor examines the roles foreign investment and staples in relation to the accumulation process of Canadian capital. Such studies are needed before the issues raised here can be resolved.

The history of capitalism has seen a continual rearrangement of nation states. The current eclipse of British and decline of American capitalism are cases in point. Vastly increased international trade and foreign investment and the growth of the multinational corporation as the instrument of accumulation have dramatically increased the speed of these developments. Recent work, furthermore, (see Warren, 1980) suggests that some "third world" nations are rapidly becoming industrialized. The present crisis of the world economy promises continuing rivalries among capitalist nations. Canada's position *is* threatened, even if the class structure and structure of our capitalist class are not fundamentally different from those of other advanced capitalist nations.

HIGHLIGHT

1. Analyses of Canadian development can be divided into those based on the colonial model and those based on the assumption that Canadian development is fundamentally similar to that of other capitalist societies though it has distinctive features.

Conclusion

In the past century the Canadian class structure has become simpler in some respects and more complex in others. At the time of Confederation the petty bourgeoisie was economically dominant in the sense that this class carried out the greatest part of production and distribution in Canada. The petty bourgeoisie was not, however, politically dominant.

Political control was vested in the landowners, capitalists, and officials and professionals dependent on them. Amin writes:

> The simple commodity mode of production is marked in its pure form by the equality of free petty-producers and the organization of commodity exchanges among them. No society has ever been based on the predominance of this mode of production, which remains purely ideal (p. 141). The capitalist mode of production tends to become exclusive, that is, to destroy other modes of production (1974:139).[16]

The capitalist mode of production has become totally ascendant. Only a small proportion of manufacturing is carried out in small shops. The number of farmers has declined numerically from a peak in 1941 to a point where the number of farms in all of Canada is now approximately the number in the four provinces at the time of Confederation. In proportional terms the decline is much greater. Retail trade and the service industries are also subject to the forces that have brought one sphere of manufacturing after another into the realm of capitalist production. Of course, the large number of state employees are not, for the most part engaged in capitalist production. But domination by the capitalist mode of production is precisely what leads to the growth of the state. Furthermore, the organization of work in state institutions reflects the hierarchy and class domination of work directly in capitalist production and circulation.

The simplification of the class structure resulting from the domination of capitalist production is accompanied by the development of a complex and internally divided working class. The complexity arises first from differences among capitalist enterprises. Different industries and companies of different size are differentiated in their occupational structures and pay rates. Within firms, there is a wide range in wages and fringe benefits, work autonomy, authority, and types of work. This differentiation is a serious barrier to political unity of the working class.

NOTES

[1] I thank Leo Johnson for bringing this point to my attention in a personal conversation.

[2] For references to Canadian work in this area see Boyd (1982).

[3] Among the international comparisons are those in Jones (1971), Ornstein (1981), Pontinen and Uusitalo (1975), Svalastoga and Rishoj (1966) and Turrittin (1974).

[4] For discussion of the occupational position and pay of women in the labor force, see Armstrong and Armstrong (1975), Boyd (1982), Connolly (1978); for ethnic differences, see Darroch (1979) and Ornstein (1981).

[5] See Fox (1980).

[6] A long debate, initiated by Berle and Means (1933) classic study, concerns whether the separation of ownership from management in the large modern corporations affects their

behavior, either in terms of the corporations' strategy (particularly the willingness to take risks in order to achieve higher profits) or in their treatment of workers. A consensus seems to be emerging in the research literature in favor of the argument that corporate behavior is not significantly affected by the type of control.

[7]For monthly data on bank assets see the supplements to the *Canada Gazette* titled "Statement of assets and liabilities chartered banks of Canada"; the annual *Financial Post* supplement on the largest Canadian firms covers insurance companies, as well as all the other types of firms.

[8]The basic discussion of the equalization of the rate of profit is Marx (1959:Ch. 10).

[8a]From *Capital*, Vol. 1, A Critique of Political Economy by Karl Marx, translated by Ben Fowkes, Copyright © 1976. Reprinted by permission of Random House, Inc.

[9]Up to this point, the argument follows Carchedi (1976).

[10]The falling rate of profit is considered in Marx (1959:Part 3); two modern discussions are by Bell (1977) and Wright (1977).

[11]Descriptions of national accounts statistics, including definitions of components of gross national income and product, may be found in virtually any conventional introductory economics text.

[12]Interesting reading on this subject is Gamble and Walton (1976) and Mandel (1980).

[13]It is important to note the distinction between occupations and social classes in this discussion: the occupational data are used because no historical data on classes of comparable completeness is available.

[14]See Rosenbluth (1957) and Stanbury (1977).

[15]©1974 by Monthly Review Press. Reprinted by permission of Monthly Review Press.

[16]©1974 by Monthly Review Press. Reprinted by permission of Monthly Review Press.

SUGGESTED READINGS

Labour and Capital in Canada, 1650-1860, H. Clare Pentland. Toronto: Lorimer, 1981. Edited and with an introduction by Paul Phillips. A classic study of the development of capitalism. Beginning with a discussion of slavery and feudalism in Canada, Pentland traces the growth of the capitalist labor market in the nineteenth century as waves of new immigrants provided a basis for the first growth of the Canadian working class.

Economic and Social History of Quebec, 1760-1850: Structure and Conjunctures, Fernand Ouellet. Toronto: Gage, 1980. One of the finest pieces of Canadian historical writing. Ouellet brings history to life in this wonderful study of the struggle of social classes and the transformation of Quebec society. The historical issues raised in this book, published originally in French in 1966, are still unresolved, but Ouellet's perspective continues to be essential to current debates.

Class in Capitalist Society: A Study of Contemporary Britain, John Westergard and Henrietta Resler. Harmondsworth, Middlesex: Penguin, 1976. An excellent analysis of class in a contemporary capitalist society. This book is a model for the application of the concept of class to the study of modern society. Unfortunately, there is no study of this quality of Canadian society.

Passages from Antiquity to Feudalism, Perry Anderson. London: New Left Books, 1974. A fine analysis of the decline of slavery in Western Europe and the development of feudalism. Anderson brings a remarkable grasp of history and theory to this exciting survey of European history. In the process, he shows the roots of the differences between Eastern and Western Europe that persist to this day.

Classes in Contemporary Capitalism, Nicos Poulantzas. London: New Left Books, 1974. Poulantzas's most accessible work. In the course of discussing the classes in capitalist society he speaks to the central issues that must be resolved in the understanding of social classes in contemporary society.

THE NATURE OF WORK AND THE PRODUCTIVE PROCESS

Graham S. Lowe

Introduction

How many people do you know who always talk about their jobs in glowing terms? Probably very few. For most of us our jobs offer much less than we would like. This is an important observation, for the work we do directly affects virtually all other aspects of our lives. We may dislike our job because it is mindless and unrewarding, or because our boss is authoritarian. Whatever the problem, we take it home with us and our relationships with family and friends are likely to suffer. Going beyond these personal concerns, the occupational system is the major determinant of one's class position. A good job, as we all know, is the route to what society defines as 'success'. Indeed, work is the most fundamental of all human endeavors. Many of us take it for granted, but the inescapable fact is that productive activity is necessary for human survival.

Perspectives and Issues.   Industrial sociology studies the impact of industrialization on the nature of work: how it is organized, how workers experience this organization, and the links between the workplace and the larger society. Much of industrial sociology has a conservative slant. It assumes that workers and capitalists share common orientations and interests. This *value consensus*, so the argument goes, unites various social groups in pursuit of common goals, thereby ensuring order in society. Critics claim that these 'order' assumptions accept the prevailing distribution of power and rewards in industry. Industrial sociology has consequently been labelled 'management sociology', given its contribution to maintaining the status quo in the workplace.

This chapter, in presenting an alternative to orthodox industrial sociology, will utilize what C. Wright Mills (1959) calls the *sociological imagination* to examine the nature of work and the productive process. According to Mills the sociological imagination helps us analyze how our personal circumstances intersect with the flow of historical events. We can understand how people with similar 'biographies'—who, for instance, have the same social class background and occupation—are treated the same way by the institutions of society. A worker who is unemployed or who feels 'useless' because of the trivial tasks he or she performs may personally assume the blame for this plight. The sociological imagination transforms this personal trouble into a larger public issue, showing that many employees face common problems because of how the economy operates.

This chapter will accept the notion that work necessarily involves relationships of power (T. Johnson 1980:335). Inequalities in power define employer-employee relations. Conflicts result over the distribution of rewards and who controls production. The following questions that result from these considerations will guide the discussion:

1. How has the development of an advanced capitalist economy in Canada since the turn of the century transformed the type of work people do?

2. How is work organized under capitalism, and what are the effects of work 'structures' on the worker?

3. How have employers attempted to mold a disciplined and efficient workforce, and in what ways have workers resisted this?

4. What are the social values, or ideologies, which justify and therefore perpetuate existing work arrangements? To what extent do workers accept or reject these ideologies?

Work and Society.   Most employees would agree that changes for the better could be made in their jobs. The basic premise of this chapter is that a critical analysis of the labor process is the starting point for significant changes in the workplace. The *labor process* itself can be defined as *the application of labor, assisted by technology, to raw materials in order to create socially useful products. Throughout human history individuals have co-operated in productive activity in order to adapt nature to their needs. Work, then, shapes our relationships to each other and, in turn, influences the formation of social and economic institutions.* In each historical era the application of human labor to raw materials has created a distinct set of institutions. This social organization of production— whether it involves master-slave, lord-peasant, or employer-employee relationships—is referred to as a *mode of production.* Technology is important in determining the level of economic activity, but the mode of production is much more than this. Marx emphasized how a mode of production can be identified by first, the way in which the productive apparatus of society is owned and, second, how workers are drawn into social relationships because of their positions in the productive system.

For Marx, work is the basis for society. Societies are organized around different types of productive systems. This is true of Feudal, caste, slave or class societies. Each of these types of social organization reflects a particular economic base or way in which people make a living.

From the Marxist perspective, "history is a process of the continuous creation, satisfaction and recreation of human needs. This is what distinguishes men from animals, whose needs are fixed and unchanging. This is why labor, *the creative interchange between man and their social environment*, is the foundation of human society" (Giddens 1971:22). What sets human society above other forms of animal species is the ability to consciously direct and adapt our labor. In doing so, we create social and cultural conditions which facilitate even wider applications and greater productivity (Braverman 1974:56).

It is essential to grasp the objective conditions (the materials, skills and technology) which shape the work people do. But equally important, we must delve into the minds of workers to determine how they subjectively experience their jobs. Throughout history work has been a topic of much philosophical discussion as people have contemplated its meaning. Because no agreement has ever been reached on the issue, it is possible to identify three contradictory meanings, each reflecting a particular stage of economic development:

1. the view, found in antiquity, of work as a 'necessary evil' which dampens the human spirit;

2. the Protestant work ethic, upholding work as inherently good and meaningful; and

3. the humanistic view, developed by Marx and Engels, of work as liberating and fulfilling but perverted by capitalism.[1]

The ancient Greeks' ideas about work stand directly opposite to the modern view. Work was shunned by the wealthy. It was thought to dull the mind and detract from the nobler pursuits of beauty and happiness. This belief provided the ideological justification for slavery (Anthony 1977:20). Not until the Protestant reformation and the emergence of capitalism was work considered inherently good and liberating. Previously, the Old Testament outlook prevailed: ". . . physical labor is a curse imposed on man as a punishment for his sins and that the sensible man labors solely in order to keep himself alive, or if he is fortunate, in order to make a sufficient surplus to enable him to do the things he really likes" (Brown 1954:186).

Martin Luther established the doctrine that work is "the base and key to life" (Mills 1956:216). Hard work was a sure way of serving God and, therefore, improving one's chances of entering God's kingdom. A group known as Calvinists, however, qualified the implication of Luther's dictim that work could legitimately result in profits. Instead, as Max Weber (1958) documents, Calvinists believed in both the virtues of hard work and a rejection of worldly pleasures. The latter was not implied in Luther's beliefs. Nonetheless, an increase in the capital of Calvinists was the unintended consequence of their religious beliefs that prohibited consumption. It is not surprising that merchants and others engaged in related forms of economic activity were persuaded of the truth of Calvinist doctrine.

Following the convergence of economic activity and religious doctrine represented in Calvinism, English political economists went on to argue that work was the basis of the wealth and prosperity of nations (Smith 1976). Labor was seen as the source of individual property ownership and the key which unlocked all economic value. The concept of private property acquired through individual effort lies at the core of modern liberal political and economic theory.

There is also a humanistic perspective on work, based on the Renaissance notion of 'man the creator'. Human potential and creative powers could be liberated and expressed through labor. This position was later elaborated by Marx (1844). However, while Marx shared the optimism of Renaissance thinkers, he argued that capitalist production stifled the development of human potential. He felt that work increasingly becomes an alienating experience. According to Marx's reasoning, existing economic relations must be transformed to eliminate alienated labor.

The Reality of Alienation and the Ideal of Craftsmanship.   The compulsion underlying work today is not religious beliefs but economic necessity. The vast majority of people now in the labor force are employees who must sell their labor in return for a wage, or risk destitution. By tacitly agreeing to obey managerial authority, they surrender control over their own labor. *Alienation* is the resulting *condition of powerlessness* (Rinehart 1975:17; Blauner 1964:15). At the root of powerlessness are workplace relations "which give the few the ability to direct and shape production to their own ends" (Rinehart 1975:21). This alienation, asserts Rinehart, is 'normal' for the majority of Canadian workers. Given the lack of alternative forms of work, the best that most employees can expect to do is adapt and adjust.

Observing factory conditions in Britain and Europe in the mid-nineteenth century, Marx noted a tendency for everyone and everything in the capitalist marketplace to be treated as a commodity. Even human labor was devalued to the status of a commodity. It was just another 'input' for the productive system. Despite rapidly increasing wealth, the workers' relative share declined. Control over the productive process, as well as the end products, slipped from their grip. In the context of these changes in the labor process Marx identified four aspects of alienation (see Giddens 1971:12-3):

1. Workers lack control over what happens to their products; what they produce belongs to the capitalist.
2. Workers become alienated through the work process itself, for intrinsic satisfactions necessary to develop the human potential are lacking.
3. Workers become alienated from co-workers as social relationships are debased into economic relationships through the market.
4. Individuals become alienated from the essential character of the human species as our relationship with nature is transformed from active to passive adaptation.

Craftsmanship lies at the opposite end of the spectrum to alienated labor. According to Mills (1956:220) the craftsmanship of nineteenth century trades represents an ideal state in which work is fully gratifying. We can all think of a few contemporary individuals—perhaps some musicians, artists, scientists or professionals—who work independently and derive great pride and accomplishment by creating a finished product from scratch, or providing a socially useful service. Mills (1956:220) portrays the ideal of craftsmanship in terms of six job characteristics. How have your jobs measured up to these criteria?:

> There is no ulterior motive in work other than the product being made and the process of its creation. The details of daily work are meaningful because they are not detached in the worker's mind from the product of work.
> The worker is free to control his own working action.
> The craftsman is thus able to learn from his work; and to use and develop his skills in prosecution. There is no split of work and play, or work and culture. The craftsman's way of livelihood determines and infuses his entire mode of living.

In sum, the ideal of craftsmanship is a model of what work should be when investigating alienation and other contemporary work problems.

Work and Social Values.   If work is not meaningful or rewarding, why do we still want to do it? The most obvious answer is because we have to out of economic need. But this ignores the importance of social values in shoring up our commitment to the virtue of hard work. *Values* are dominant beliefs and ideas which define for members of a society what is good, desirable and ought to be. Work values serve the function of providing higher justifications for engaging in regular, disciplined wage labor.

Smucker (1980) argues that the early capitalists espoused the values of freedom and equality to justify their ascent to power. The autonomy of the individual to freely engage in market relations, choosing among employers and seeking out opportunities to rise to the top also are at the heart of the modern work ethic. But these values are highly ideological. That is, they present a world view which legitimizes the superior position of the capitalist. At the same time they help individual workers explain their daily experiences. The work ethic, for example, accounts for the success of the few by pointing to their superior abilities. And it also explains the relative lack of success for everyone else in terms of missed opportunities, personal deficiencies or laziness. Workers are, of course, always free to quit and seek work elsewhere if their jobs become intolerable.

Smucker goes on to say that the daily experiences of workers give a hollow ring to these work values. The rigid authority structures in enterprises limit freedom of choice and opportunities to 'get ahead' are seldom available for most. This discrepancy between dominant ideology and everyday reality could conceivably undermine workers' commitment to the economic system. Yet however much Canadian workers complain about specific job problems they continue to have a strongly ingrained work ethic (Burstein et al. 1975).

This persistence of the work ethic is largely explained by the dominance of individualism. In both work and non-work activities, the overriding emphasis in our society is on individual actions. Political theorist C.B. Macpherson (1962) asserts that the notion of *possessive individualism* is central to the liberal democratic tradition. According to this view, the individual is the proprietor of his or her own person and can freely enter into contractual obligations with others. Society thus consists of a series of 'market relationships' among relatively autonomous individuals. But this emphasis on the primacy of individual actions, as will be seen in the chapter on Culture, Ideology and Society, masks the reality of class rule. The political potential of a collectively organized working class is thereby diminished. The dominant ideology thus protects the economic system from serious political challenges. Despite this, workers invariably construct counter-value systems which more accurately reflect their experiences and protect their interests. Thus, in any workplace we will find at least two definitions of what constitutes 'fair and equitable' conditions of employment: the capitalists' definition and the workers' definition (Hyman and Brough, 1975). The discrepancy between these definitions reflects the unequal social positions of employers and employees, paving the way for industrial conflict.

HIGHLIGHT

1. There are two basic approaches to industrial sociology: (a) the conservative approach that stresses common interests among workers and employers; (b) an approach that examines work in terms of power relations.
2. The nature of all societies to a large degree can be characterized by the way in which their members go about making a living.
3. There are three basic orientations to work: (a) work as a necessary evil; (b) the Protestant ethic; (c) the humanist ethic.
4. Despite the potential of work to be a fulfilling experience, in modern capitalist society it most frequently is alienating.
5. Despite the alienating nature of work under capitalism, workers continue to accept employment because of economic necessity.

Capitalist Development and the Transformation of Work

Because capitalist industrialization establishes the basic framework in which work is performed, it deserves careful scrutiny. There are two major models outlining the process of industrialization: 1) the logic of industrialism thesis; and 2) the Marxist theory of capitalist development.

The Logic of Industrialism Model. This model highlights the large-scale changes accompanying the process of industrialization. Proponents of the model argue that similar changes occur in the economic and social institutions of any society progressing from an agricultural to an industrial base. A mature industrial society can be distinguished from a pre-industrial society by its small agricultural labor force and large urban white-collar population concentrated in the service sector. Industrialization tends to shift economic activity out of agriculture, into manufacturing then towards service occupations. The thesis postulates that "industrialization has an 'inherent logic' that dominates much of the activity in any industrializing society" (Dunlop et al., 1975:41; also see Kerr et al., 1960; Faunce and Form, 1969). In the long-term, industrial societies are expected to exhibit similar class structures and socioeconomic institutions.

The logic of industrialism model has a number of apparent weaknesses. It hypothesizes a 'convergent' pattern of development by stressing the uniform and homogenizing effects of industrialization. However, convergence fails to account for important national variations. Canada is an obvious case in point, as seen in an earlier chapter. Another problem with the model is the prediction that industrial development leads to a 'flattening' of the class hierarchy: the rise of a large, urban, white-collar middle class supposedly creates a bulge in the middle of the class structure. The middle class is thought to owe its existence to the benefits of industrialization: rising affluence, greater upward mobility and higher educational levels.

For some analysts, the growth of this new middle class of white-collar employees signals the 'end of ideology'. Bell (1973) who uses this concept, claims that post-World War II North American society has entered a post-industrial phase. Class-based conflicts have been displaced by the rise of knowledge as the new medium for wealth and power. In Bell's view, the dominance of service industries that characterizes post-industrial society marks the ascent of a new elite of scientific and technical workers as property ownership is supplanted by knowledge as the basis of power.

The 'logic of industrialism' thesis also overemphasizes the role of technology. This results from equating the *industrial revolution* with the rise of capitalism. The industrial revolution is defined as the substitution of machines for human skills and inanimate power for human power which precipitated the transition from simple handicraft to manufacturing production (Landes, 1969:1).

There can be little disagreement that technological innovation fuelled industrialization. The steam engine and the internal combustion engine are two elementary examples which attest to this. Yet it is misleading to view technological advances as the direct cause of social and economic changes. To do so is to fall into the trap of *technological determinism*, presenting technology as an independent force which controls the actions of individuals. Technology is more accurately understood as the product of human decisions and actions.

The Marxian Model.   Marx provides an alternative to the 'logic of industrialism' thesis. He demonstrates that the industrial revolution was more than a combination of purely technological break-throughs. New machines and techniques were necessary for manufacturing to evolve, but Marx sees their application as the result of entrepreneurial activities by capitalists to expand production and reap profits. Industrial capitalism, then, has a technical side represented by factories and production machinery. But we must recognize its social side as well. Technology is a 'social force' which is used by capitalists to control the labor process. As many early factory owners discovered, there is no better way to discipline a work force than through the regimentation imposed on a worker by the continuous operation of a machine.

The worker-boss relationship is central to Marx's analysis of how the capitalist economy operated (see Zeitlin, 1967 for an overview). He linked it directly to capital accumulation, the process of procuring and reinvesting ever greater profits as a vehicle for economic development. In turn, the secret of capital accumulation is found in the unique character of human labor-power. Briefly, the value of the worker's labor-power, expressed as a wage or salary, is always less than the selling price of whatever goods or services the worker produces. The difference corresponds to the capitalist's profit and, as such, measures the rate of capital accumulation. The capitalist strives to keep wages down by implementing new technologies, reorganizing the labor process or speeding up production in order to increase the profit margin. This process, it will be remembered, was discussed in more detail in chapter 2. Seen in this light, technological innovations which subordinate and regulate work activities form part of a conscious strategy by capitalists to further the accumulation process (Marglin 1976).

All capitalist societies have in common the mode of production described by Marx. But within each the timing and pace of economic change, the nature of the elites directing industrialization, and the internal and external factors influencing this process differ. Recall that Canada experienced a unique pattern of industrialization which distinguished it from other advanced capitalist societies. Differences in national experience notwithstanding, it is possible to identify a number of developments that have preceded industrial capitalism:

1. The rise of a new social class—the capitalists and their hired managers—who engage in entrepreneurial activity, guided by the principle of capital accumulation.
2. Rapidly expanding markets for a growing array of products and services.

3. The development and application of machine technology to the productive process.

4. The creation of a wage labor market in which labor is bought and sold much like a commodity.

5. The concentration of workers into single enterprises, where labor is organized into a collective activity directed by managers.

These points should be borne in mind when the industrialization process in Canada is examined.

Resources and Employment.   Canada's colonial role as a supplier of raw materials or staple goods to more developed nations is largely responsible for the distinctive form of capitalism in place today. Innis documented how the early staple industries of fish, fur and timber shaped Canada's social, political and economic institutions. Each staple had its own system of production, and the shift to a new staple forced adjustments in socio-economic structures. These changes were especially accentuated in the sphere of employment.

During the seventeenth and eighteenth centuries the fur trade dominated all other forms of economic activity. The beaver, the birch bark canoe and the coureurs-des-bois are vivid symbols of Canada's colonial past. What these popular images of the fur trade hide are the complex business dealings and organizational structures required to mount trading expeditions.

Prior to the 'Conquest' of 1759, voyageurs were drawn from the agricultural population of New France. Their participation in the fur trade undermined the viability of colonial agriculture. Each spring about 15 percent of the entire labor force would leave from Montreal with the canoe brigades (Cross 1974:14-9). The fleet of about fifty canoes would be loaded with goods to be traded with the Indians in return for pelts. The large canoes were 36 feet long and six feet wide, and were capable of carrying four tons of supplies or pelts as well as eight to ten men.

Pentland (1981:29) describes how "engagés were placed in the canoes and paid according to their skill, an arrangement that provided both a status system and a training program..." The men in the expedition split up at Lake Superior, some spending only the winter in the hinterland while the others stayed several years to work with Indians preparing pelts for shipment to market. There were approximately thirteen hundred men employed in the trade in the early nineteenth century (Cross 1974). These workers suffered countless hardships as they opened up trading routes across the west. Along with the workers in other staple industries, they "were the real builders of Canada" (Morton and Copp 1980:1).

The Transition to Capitalism.   Economic activity in early nineteenth century Canada was largely confined to agriculture and the staple trades. While the industrial revolution had taken hold in Britain, the manufacturing industries which sprung up in its wake were virtually absent in Canada. Most of the population were engaged in subsistence agriculture.

The family was the basic unit of production. Each member old enough to work helped in clearing and cultivating land, constructing buildings, making tools, and providing essential household goods and food. Johnson (1974) characterizes this era as the 'toiler society'. Family labor, unlike that found in the modern factory or office, was not paced by the clock or geared to profit margins and productivity quotas. Instead, the long, hard hours of toil were regulated by necessity and the patterns of nature. But the uncertainties of weather and harvests meant farmers constantly risked hardship. The one consolation was the element of independence possible after the family farm was operating and free of debts.

The iron forges at St. Maurice, Quebec, are the one important exception to the lack of industry in early nineteenth century Canada. Established in 1730 and operating for about one hundred and fifty years, the St. Maurice forges spanned pre-capitalist and capitalist modes of production (Pentland 1981:34-46). By examining the working conditions at the forges, it is possible to learn more about the paternalistic form of employment relations existing prior to the rise of capitalism.

The forges were the major domestic iron producer until the mid-nineteenth century. Skilled craftsmen, bookkeepers, carpenters and other permanent employees lived in what was perhaps the first 'company town' in North America. Workers sometimes protested against poor living and working conditions, but few left for jobs elsewhere. Part of the reason was the strong family and community ties which resulted from intermarriage with local women. But more important was the dearth of opportunities for industrial employment. Similarly, the lack of a readily available pool of labor meant the forge owners were equally dependent on the employees. In short, the fact that industrial development and a wage labor market did not exist during most of the forges' history created a mutual interdependence between employer and employee. This is the most distinctive aspect of paternalistic employment relations.

The stage for industrialization was set during the 1850s. Canal and railway construction, the depletion of accessible arable land, increased efficiency in agricultural production, and the accumulation of local merchant capital available for investment in industry all contributed to the emergence of industrial capitalism. The framework of an industrial economy—a wage labor market, the factory system of production and attendant technological changes—slowly took form, assisted by a growing domestic market for goods and services.

Hamilton, Ontario, was one of the first Canadian cities to experience the industrial revolution. In the 1850s the city boasted steam powered shops, mechanized iron, wool and steel industries, and manufacturers of railway cars, foundry products and domestic consumer goods. Although

13 percent of the nation's work force was employed in manufacturing and handicraft industries at the time of Confederation, the population was still 80 percent rural and agricultural.

The plight of the early, unskilled, industrial worker was typified by impoverishment and often brutal treatment metted out by employers. Until 1877 the Masters and Servants Act allowed courts to send unruly or absent workers to jail at an employer's request (Morton and Copp 1980:4). Testimonies before the 1889 Royal Commission on the Relations of Labor and Capital (Kealey 1973) document abuses of child and female labor in addition to hazardous health and safety conditions in factories and shops. Some of the worst excesses were committed in a Montreal cigar factory where the employer mistreated child laborers: "...in this factory apprentices were prisoned in a 'black hole' for hours at a time. Occasionally the incarceration would stretch beyond the working hours, and a special visit would be made to the factory to release the poor little fellows. A special constable, who still wore his constable's badge, was employed to overawe and strike terror into the hearts of the juvenile offenders..." (Kealey 1973:42).

Factories expanded tremendously after 1900, with the result that employment relations grew more formal and work became fragmented and routinized. Yet a sizable number of firms were small, personally owned and operated enterprises. Worker and owner shared a sense of mutual obligation. Employment conditions were settled informally with a handshake. These vestiges of nineteenth century paternalism were swept aside by the rise of large corporations and increasingly bureaucratized working conditions. With the separation of ownership and control, specialists in the new 'science' of management were hired to run these corporations. By the onset of the 1920s the economy had undergone a transformation which marked the triumph of industrial capitalism.

Resource Work Under Capitalism.   Canada is now largely a 'service society' with the majority of workers performing white-collar jobs in service industries. Yet staple industries are still the mainstay of several provincial economies: fishing in Newfoundland; mining and hydro-electric in Quebec; wheat and other grains in Saskatchewan; oil and gas in Alberta; and forestry in British Columbia. The employment relations characterizing these modern staple industries can be juxtaposed against those in the fur trade, outlined above, as a way of illuminating the differences between pre-capitalist and capitalist production relations.

The single industry community is a distinctive trait of Canada's resource-based economy.[2] The geographic location of key resources has necessitated the creation of remote towns where life is dominated by the presence of a single employer. Lucas (1971), in his study of single industry towns built around the railroad, mining or forestry, clearly portrays the feelings of isolation and domination by 'the company' among inhabitants. Anyone living in a company town was recruited by the firm, lives in a company home, uses company recreation facilities—in short, is socially and economically dependent on the company. A corporate decision to diversify or a slump in world markets can sound the death knell for such communities.

The forerunners to the mine, mill and rail towns of today were the construction camps of the railway building era. Bradwin (1974:ch. 3), in a participant-observer account of work camp conditions, notes that between 1903 and 1914 there were upwards of 3000 camps employing about 200 000 men, or about five percent of the entire adult male labor force. Camp workers, according to Bradwin, suffered from three major problems: isolation; excessive charges made by often unscrupulous contractors for supplies and other necessities; and misrepresentation of employment conditions by private agencies in the business of sending recent immigrants out to the camps.

Many workers were under contracts that involved charges for transportation to the camp, medical care, blankets, food and other services. Consequently, workers ran up considerable debts even before beginning work. Moreover, upon arrival at the camps workers found their bunkhouse homes lacking even the most rudimentary sanitation. Few men could withstand the squalor of the bunkhouses, concluded Bradwin (1974:85), and not suffer ill health. The camp work gangs were clearly part of a wage labor system, exemplified by the contracts they signed binding them to an employer. However, because construction work is labor intensive the camps escaped the full thrust of capitalist production relations.

Work in staple industries today is often highly mechanized and tightly regulated by management. In her study of living and working conditions in British Columbia forestry communities, Marchak (1979a) documents recent changes in the labor process. Cyclical fluctuations in the forestry industry create boom-bust phases which create economic instability. Workers live with the uncertainty of possible layoffs or unemployment. The strategy adapted by the companies has been to protect and expand market positions through mechanization of production. Jobs thus become more routinized, fragmented and less skilled. Ultimately, the workforce will be reduced in size. The rugged lumberjack may soon be relegated to the pages of history books. Marchak (1979:15) describes a tree harvesting machine, for example, which allows "operators to perform a range of tasks formerly requiring fallers, buckers, loaders, and numerous other specialized woodsmen. One faller and a skidder, together with a shearer or snipper machine, can now cut, delimb, and land 500 trees in a single day."

Clement's (1981) study of INCO, the world's largest nickel producer, describes how independent commodity production as defined in Chapter 2 gave way to capitalist production in mining. Traditionally, miners worked as independent prospectors on a small claim using little equipment. As mining operations moved underground, more workers were required and equipment costs soared. The turn-of-the-century capitalists who financed mining operations usually contracted out the actual tasks to teams of miners on a piece-work basis. These teams had considerable freedom to determine how the work was to be carried out. A strong sense of group identification developed. This camaraderie was reinforced by hazardous conditions and contributed to union militancy. The mining team remained a central part of production until the 1960s. Facing persistent difficulties recruiting skilled labor, keener competition and rising production costs, INCO countered with a program of mechanization and automation which resulted in a decreased demand for skilled labor but increased productivity. With the erosion of miners' skills, the semi-autonomous team lost its dominant role in production.

HIGHLIGHT

1. There are two basic models of industrial development: (a) the logic of industrialism model; (b) the Marxian model. The latter more realistically accounts for the development of industrial capitalism.
2. Prior to the development of industrial capitalism in Canada, economic activity centred on the production and distribution of raw materials or staple products such as fish, fur, and timber.
3. The transition to industrial capitalism in Canada did not occur until the 1850s, although a harbinger of industrial production could be found in the St. Maurice forges founded in 1730.
4. In Canada, the transition to industrial capitalism led to the degradation of many workers.
5. Work in staple industries continues to be important and is characterized by many of the same processes—mechanization, automation—found in manufacturing.

Jobs and the Labor Market

Basic to a capitalist economy is a market in which commodities are bought and sold. Labor, too, becomes a commodity and is subjected to market forces. A labor market in which workers are recruited by employers to fill vacant jobs is a prerequisite for the emergence and growth of capitalism. Following Edwards (1975:5) a *labor market* will be defined as encompassing "those specific mechanisms and institutions through which the purchase and sale of labor power is arranged." In short, it is the vehicle for allocating workers to specific jobs. Ideally, this allocative process matches a worker's experience, skills and education with the requirements of a vacant job. However, in reality the labor market operates to perpetuate existing social inequalities (see Johnson 1977).

Internal and External Labor Markets.   It is useful to distinguish between two kinds of labor markets: *external markets*, which exist outside organizations; and *internal markets* which operate within the confines of large bureaucratic organizations. External markets operate through the classified job ads in newspapers and employment agencies, for example. Internal markets, on the other hand, are found in large corporations or state bureaucracies where vacancies above a certain level are filled from within by existing employees. These organizations have specified 'ports of entry', usually at the bottom of the job hierarchy. A principal characteristic of internal markets is the *job ladder*. This refers to: orderly and predictable career progression; job postings and a bidding system for filling vacancies internally; an emphasis on individual merit in hiring and promotion; and training and development programs designed to tap the 'human potential' of employees in the hope they will make a long-term commitment to the organization.

Katherine Stone (1974) has examined the origins of internal labor markets in major U.S. steel companies. Contemporary job structures emerged during the 1890 to 1920 period. During these years, a new system of employee administration was implemented, based on three facets: wage incentive schemes, such as bonus payments; promotion hierarchies so workers could have some degree of upward mobility within the firm; and welfare programs to look after the non-monetary needs of workers. These changes brought some improvements in working conditions. But according to Stone, their more fundamental aims were to increase worker productivity and prevent collective opposition to managerial authority. Stone explains that "to solve the labor problem, employers developed strategies to break down the basis for a unity of interests amongst workers, and to convince them that, as individuals, their interests were identical with those of their company." (1974:128). The new payment and promotion systems, for instance, rewarded individual effort. This encouraged workers to be 'out for themselves', seeking individual solutions to work problems.

In examining the creation of the external labor market, it is necessary to begin with the transitional period leading up to capitalism. Looking at pre-confederation Canada, Pentland (1959; 1981) examines how workers were induced to flow into a formal labor market and, once there, how they were prevented from leaving. In the discussion of the St. Maurice forges it was seen that a pre-capitalist economy is typified by a shortage of both wage laborers and industrial jobs—a situation that fosters paternalistic arrangements between industrial employers and employees. In industrial operations, this personal employment relationship prevailed prior to the 1850s.

On one hand, the scarcity of wage labor inhibited industrialization. But on the other hand, it can be noted with some irony that conditions were ripe for the creation of a capitalist labor market in the Canadas by the 1840s (Teeple, 1972). By that time, a lack of cheap, arable land swelled the ranks of the propertyless unemployed. But because wage work was scarce, many migrated to the U.S. where either peasant farming or factory employment were viable alternatives.

Railway construction during the 1850s, coupled with massive inflows of Irish peasants who were too poor to acquire farm land, helped amass the first permanent labor pool. The railways also attracted skilled artisans (a group already committed to wage work) from England. Increased agricultural productivity, land shortages and immigration—all of which swelled the ranks of urban working class—aided the creation of a labor market and an 'industrial reserve army'. This army, which included the underemployed as well as the unemployed, assured expanding enterprises of a steady labor supply.

Labor Market Segmentation.   According to labor economists, the labor market is essentially one massive pool of individuals who are shunted in and out of jobs by the forces of supply and demand. The only things differentiating workers are varying skill, educational and experience levels, as well as geographic location. Workers supposedly make 'rational' choices, attempting to maximize their economic gains given their bargaining power. In sum, this view of the market emphasizes how supply and demand for labor tend towards an equilibrium in which workers and jobs are well matched (see Ostry and Zaidi 1971).

During the last decade a radical alternative to this perspective has been proposed. Known as *segmentation theory* or *dual labor market theory*, this approach is more sociological. The image of a homogenous labor market is rejected as being, among other things, too simplistic. The market is reconceptualized as composed of a number of unequal and relatively impermeable segments. These segments reflect inequalities among workers and are linked directly to the labor process within firms.

Segmentation theory assumes that the advance of corporate capitalism since 1900 has fragmented a once fairly uniform working class. By rationalizing the labor process within firms, and by breaking down tasks into simplified parts, capitalists have divided the labor market according to distinct occupational characteristics, employee behaviors, and working conditions. Workers in one segment tend to compete among themselves, not with those in other segments, for jobs. Occupations at the bottom of the job ladder, or in small firms in highly competitive industries, demand fewer skills and less commitment from the employee than do upper level technical or professional jobs. Discrete markets are thus created for each type of worker. Individuals in each segment tend to have similar characteristics. Thus one finds different sub-markets containing, for example, educated white males, ethnic minorities or women. Employers use these worker traits to determine suitability for a given job (see Gordon 1972; Edwards et al. 1975; Edwards 1979; Clairmont et al. 1981).

The different experiences of men and women in the workplace attest to the existence of unequal labor market segments. In Canadian society, women historically have been concentrated in a handful of unrewarding occupations mainly in the sales, service and clerical areas. Strong barriers to employment of women in male dominated managerial and professional jobs have only recently begun to weaken. Even so, the structure of the labor market militates against equality of earnings and opportunities for men and women.

Sex-based inequalities are not the product of a 'free market' in labor. On the contrary, they are a direct result of how employers have built into the organization of the labor process sex-linked characteristics which specify whether a male or female is most appropriate for a given job. These issues will be examined in more detail below and in the chapter on the family and the productive process.

Segmentation theory makes a further distinction between *core* and *periphery* firms. Core firms are the large corporations which dominate key resource, manufacturing and service industries. Examples include multinational oil companies and Canadian chartered banks. The sheer size, market dominance and profitability of these corporations allow them to create employment conditions which foster employment stability. Through internal labor markets, attractive job conditions are provided to create a stable work force. Firms in the competitive and labor intensive industries, described as periphery firms, cannot afford to pay the price, in terms of high wages and generous benefits, for a stable work force. Moreover, they often do not require a skilled and stable work force because much of the work itself is unskilled and routine.

Researchers at Dalhousie University in Halifax use a segmentation model to explain how poverty is linked to the operations of the labor market in the Maritimes (Clairmont et al., 1981). A large portion of poor families in the Maritimes are headed by individuals who are employed for at least part of the year. Their poverty stems from lack of access to well paying jobs. Social inequality, then, can be seen as a direct result of the prevalence of low-wage work in a region.

The researchers extend the core and periphery concepts to include occupations, in addition to establishments. This broader approach is captured in their use of the terms *marginal work world* and *central work world*. Workers in the marginal work world find it very difficult, if not impossible, to enter the central work world. The marginal work world includes occupations and places of employment which provide "for a majority of their work force or membership, employment packages characterized by low wages, limited fringe benefits, little job security and restricted internal advancement opportunities..." (Clairmont et al.

1981:290). Small, labor intensive firms and unorganized self-employed groups which serve a limited market fall into this category. Examples include textile plants, taxi drivers, sawmills and food processing plants. Even though some of these firms may be owned by giant corporations, their poor employment conditions confirm their marginal status.

In contrast, central work world establishments offer "high wages, extensive fringe benefits, internal career ladders, and job security provisions." Both employers and employees in this category are powerful. Firms are able to meet demands for improved wages and working conditions because of their dominant market position. Employees have sufficient bargaining power to extract these conditions through their trade unions or professional associations. Included in this sector are government and large, private corporations such as coal mines, petroleum refineries, auto assembly plants, pulp and paper operations, as well as self-employed professionals and unionized skilled craftsworkers.

Clairmont and his colleagues argue that the inequalities identified by their model are 'normal' under capitalism. They originate because of differences in economic power between workers and their employers. However, the key distinction between working conditions in the marginal and central work worlds concerns employment stability. Central work world firms, because of their control of the product market, can offer attractive employment conditions which foster stability. In contrast, marginal firms are unable to do this because of the largely seasonal or fluctuating nature of their activity, low training costs and the resulting ease of replacing workers or low capital investment.

HIGHLIGHT

1. Labor markets can be divided into internal and external ones. The former refer to patterns of promotion, recruitment, and so on, that take place within an organization; the latter to recruitment to an organization from outside sources.
2. The labor market can be seen as composed of various segments. Each has distinct characteristics and mobility among segments is rare.
3. Work situations can be defined as marginal or central. Marginal work situations display characteristics such as instability, low pay, and employment in small enterprises. Central work situations possess the opposite characteristics.

Labor Force Trends

An overview of historical changes in the composition of the labor force provides a solid empirical foundation for studying transformations in the labor process. Using data from the decennial censuses it is possible to trace the spread of wage labor, the growth or decline of major occupational groups, and shifts in the labor force among industries.

Occupational Changes.   As capitalism develops, labor moves from agriculture to manufacturing and, especially since World War II, towards service industries. In Canada, the working population engaged in agri- culture has steadily declined from 50 percent in 1871 to 4.7 percent by 1978. Part of the shift away from agriculture has been absorbed by manufacturing. In 1871, only 13.1 percent of the work force was engaged in industry (Smucker 1980:78). By 1951 this figure had almost doubled, even though Table 1 indicates that manufacturing registered a 6.9 percent decline between 1951 and 1978.

This more recent decline in manufacturing can be attributed to techno- logical advances which have permitted fewer workers to produce greater quantities of goods. At the same time, increased leisure time and greater affluence have contributed to a booming demand for various types of services. As Table 1 demonstrates, the greatest increases in employment in the post World War II period have occurred in services, public administration, trade and finance. This signifies the development of a service society.

The changing industrial distribution of the labor force is clearly revealed through its occupational composition. The growth in service industries just noted indicates that more and more people have been entering white-collar employment. Table 2 suggests that a dramatic shift

TABLE 1
Changes in the Distribution of the Total Labor Force, by Major Industries, Canada, 1951 and 1978

INDUSTRY	1951	1978	Percentage Change 1951 to 1978
Agriculture	18.4%	4.7%	−13.7%
Forestry	2.3	0.8	− 1.5
Fishing and trapping	0.6	0.2	− .4
Mining	1.5	1.6	+ .1
Manufacturing	26.5	19.6	− 6.9
Construction	6.8	6.3	− .5
Transportation, communications and other utilities	8.8	8.6	− .2
Trade	14.1	17.4	+ 3.3
Finance, insurance and real estate	3.0	5.5	+ 2.5
Service	18.0	28.2	+10.2
Public administration	....	7.1	+ 7.1
TOTAL	100.0	100.0	
Total number employed in Canada (in thousands)	5,097	9,972	

SOURCE: Computed from *Perspectives Canada III* (1980), Table 5.12, p. 92.

TABLE 2
Changes in the Distribution of the Total Labor Force, by Major Occupational Groups, Canada, 1901 and 1961

OCCUPATIONAL GROUP	1901	1961	Percentage Change, 1901 to 1961
All Occupations	100.0%	100.0%	
White-collar	15.2	38.6	+23.4%
Proprietary and managerial	4.3	7.9	+ 3.6
Professional	4.6	10.0	+ 5.4
Clerical	3.2	12.9	+ 9.7
Commercial and financial	3.1	7.8	+ 4.7
Manual	32.2	34.9	+ 2.7
Manufacturing and mechanical	15.9	16.4	+ .5
Construction	4.7	5.3	+ .6
Labour	7.2	5.4	− 1.8
Transporation and communication	4.4	7.8	+ 3.4
Service	8.2	10.8	+ 2.6
Personal	7.8	9.3	+ 1.5
Protective and other	0.4	1.5	+ .9
Primary	44.4	13.1	−31.3
Agriculture	40.3	10.2	−30.1
Fishing, trapping	1.6	0.6	− 1.0
Logging	0.9	1.3	+ .4
Mining, quarrying	1.6	1.0	− .6
Not Stated	—	2.6	+ 2.6

SOURCE: Computed from Meltz, (1969), Table A.1, p. 58.

has occurred since 1901. The decline in manual or blue-collar work has been more than offset by a growth in white-collar or 'mental' labor.

The growth of white-collar employment is associated with many significant social changes. Generally it denotes the emergence of a large urban middle class. For some observers, white-collar work may also signal an upgrading of job conditions. Certainly the number of professional, technical, scientific and managerial jobs has mushroomed. And many of these jobs are challenging and rewarding. But just because white-collar work is mental rather than menial does not mean that alienation no longer exists. In fact, for the average white-collar worker the rewards are meagre and the work monotonous. Clerical work is now the largest occupational group, employing over 15 percent of all workers in 1971. Most clerical jobs involve highly automated or mechanized routines for processing information, thus falling far short of the ideal of non-alienating labor described earlier.

Finally, we should make note of the extension of wage labor since 1900. Independent farmers, small businessmen and housewives have been increasingly drawn into wage employment (Johnson 1980). This process is defined as 'proletarianization' and is a natural consequence of capitalist development.

If we examine the agricultural sector, we discover that the proportion of owner-operators has declined from 72.6 percent in 1911 to 50.4 percent by 1971 (Johnson 1980:94). In terms of the total labor force, the proportion of self-employed workers dropped from 11.6 percent in 1957 to 5.4 percent in 1976 (Canada 1977:116). This trend can be interpreted as an erosion of the opportunities for self-directed labor.

Women and Work. Perhaps the most noteworthy change in the character of the labor force since 1900 has been the rising participation rate of women. In 1901 the female labor force participation rate stood at 16.1 percent.[3] This participation rate moved steadily upwards, spurred by labor shortages which women helped alleviate during both world wars, to 40.9 percent by 1975 (Canada 1977:112). Presently just over 50 percent of all adult women are gainfully employed. This trend reflects the tendency for greater numbers of wives to return to paid work after raising a family.[4]

Historically, women have performed a critical role, albeit unrecognized, in the economy. For example, Indian women directly contributed to the success of the fur trade by providing traders with a link between European and Indian cultures. Native women acted as interpreters, prepared food and cleaned pelts for shipment to markets (Van Kirk 1977). Little wonder that fur traders took Indian women as wives. Similarly, pioneer women performed essential chores in the toiler society of pre-Confederation Canada. While the males worked the fields, the women of a family performed all domestic tasks from childrearing, to tending the livestock and garden, to spinning yarn for cloths. The death of a wife was a great economic blow to the subsistence farmer, making quick remarriage an act of survival (Johnson 1974:16-7).

Beginning in the late nineteenth century women and children were recruited into the industrial workforce as cheap, unskilled labor. The 1891 census, the first to break down occupational data by sex, reports only 11.4 percent of the female population over the age of ten as gainfully employed. This percentage comprised 12.6 percent of the entire labor force (Lowe 1980a:363). The concentration of women into a handful of unrewarding, dead-end occupations has been characteristic of female employment since the 1890s. These occupations are referred to as female *job ghettos.*

Table 3 documents that in 1901 most women worked as domestic servants, teachers, dressmakers, seamstresses or office workers. The picture of female employment is somewhat different in 1979. Domestic work has been replaced by clerical work as the largest female occupation. Women are less concentrated within manufacturing and increasingly employed in the service sector. While the latter trend reflects

TABLE 3
Major Female Occupations, 1901 and 1971

Occupation	Percentage of Female Work Force in Occupation	Females as a Percentage of Total Work Force in Occupation
1901		
1. Dressmakers and seamstresses	13.5%	100.0%
2. Servants	34.2	83.7
3. Housekeepers	3.2	87.0
4. Teachers	13.0	78.0
5. Milliners	1.8	99.4
6. Paperbox and bag makers	0.1	70.8
7. Nurses	0.1	100.0
8. Office employees (not elsewhere classified)	3.7	79.6
TOTAL	69.6	
1971		
1. Stenographers and typists	12.3	96.9
2. Salepersons	6.7	51.0
3. Personal service workers	3.4	93.5
4. Teachers	6.4	66.0
5. Fabricators, assemblers, and repairers of textiles, fur, and leather products	3.4	76.0
6. Graduate nurses	3.9	95.4
7. Waiters and bartenders	4.1	76.6
8. Nursing assistants, aides and orderlies	2.9	79.2
9. Telephone operators	1.2	95.9
10. Janitors, charworkers and cleaners	2.1	32.4
TOTAL	46.4	

SOURCE: For 1901—Connelly (1978), Table 4.3, p. 88.
 For 1971—Armstrong and Armstrong (1978), Table 7, p. 3.

changes in the total labor force, it is more pronounced for women: 71 percent of female employees compared with 50.8 percent of male employees worked in service industries in 1971. However, within services women are typically employed in the least desirable jobs—just as they were 80 years ago. Over one-third of all working women, including many female university graduates, occupy clerical positions.[5]

The current occupational distribution of males and females is presented in Table 4. The data show the effects of sex-based occupational segregation. Sex-specific job definitions and requirements channel women into certain jobs and restrict their entry into others. For example, there are few women in mining, trapping, forestry, fishing, construction, engineering, scientific, agricultural, managerial or professional jobs, all of which are widely accepted as 'men's work'. In contrast, women predominate in clerical, service, teaching, and medicine and health fields, areas traditionally considered appropriate female pursuits.[6]

TABLE 4
Women as a Percentage of the Total Labor Force and Percentage Distribution of Women and Men, by Occupation, Canada, 1979

Occupation	Women as a percentage of total employed in each occupational category	Percentage distribution Women	Men
	%	%	%
Managerial and administrative	25.4	5.0	9.3
Natural sciences, engineering and mathematics	12.1	1.1	5.1
Social sciences	49.7	1.8	1.2
Religion			0.4
Teaching	56.3	6.1	3.0
Medicine and health	76.4	8.7	1.7
Artistic and recreational occupations	34.7	1.2	1.5
Clerical	77.1	34.0	6.4
Sales	39.9	10.7	10.3
Service	53.9	17.9	9.7
Agriculture	22.4	2.9	6.3
Fishing, hunting and trapping	—	—	0.4
Forestry and logging	—	—	0.9
Mining and quarrying	—	—	0.9
Processing	18.1	1.8	5.1
Machining	5.7	0.4	4.2
Product fabricating, assembling and repairing	23.5	5.6	11.6
Construction trades	1.4	0.2	10.3
Transport equipment operation	5.3	0.6	6.4
Materials handling	18.9	1.2	3.3
Other crafts and equipment operating	16.9	0.6	1.8
All occupational categories	38.8	100.0	100.0

SOURCE: 1978-1979 *Women in the Labor Force*, Part I, Participation (Labor Canada, 1980) Table 9b, p. 33.

One major effect of occupational sex segregation is that women earn less money than men, even when they perform the same work. Table 5 documents the sex-based wage differentials for major occupational groups in 1977. The average earned income of women workers was 57.8 percent that of males. This is only a slight improvement over the 54.6 percent wage gap between the sexes in 1972. Turning to specific occupations, we find that the wage gap in 1977 ranged from over 60 percent in professional and clerical jobs to 43.1 percent in primary jobs. This wage spread has been fairly stable since the turn of the century. In clerical work, for example, women earned 53 percent of the average male wage in 1901 (Lowe 1980a:366). Labor market segmentation theory, discussed above, is an insightful way of viewing sexual inequalities in the workplace.

Over time, gender-specific characteristics became part of the job

TABLE 5
Difference Between Women's and Men's Earnings, Canada, 1977

Occupation	Ratio of average female earnings to average male earnings	Difference between male and female earnings	
	%	$	%
Managerial	58.1	8 754	72.2
Professional	60.8	7 482	64.6
Clerical	63.7	4 934	56.9
Sales	46.9	7 860	113.0
Service	48.3	6 487	107.1
Farming, logging, fishing, etc.	43.1	5 575	131.8
Processing and machining	59.3	6 063	68.7
Product fabrication	54.2	6 693	84.5
Transportation, communication, etc.	58.0	5 942	72.4

SOURCE: *Women in the Labor Force*, 1977 Edition, Part II, Earnings of Men and Women (Labor Canada, 1980), Table 8B, p. 45.

requirements through the process of *sex labelling.* Entry into a particular occupation could, as a consequence, be limited to either men or women. Many of the jobs created in the wake of twentieth century industrial expansion were quickly labelled as women's work. Teaching, nursing and social work had traditionally been sex labelled because women's maternal instincts were thought appropriate for jobs devoted to caring for the sick, young and needy. When typing emerged as a new occupation in the late nineteenth century, male office workers had little interest in acquiring the necessary skills. Within a short time female stereotypes—a delicate touch, attention to detail, manual dexterity—were attached to typing jobs opening the way for women to enter. Likewise, by requiring unbroken career paths, geographic mobility or physical exertion employers could effectively limit applicants for managerial jobs to men.

It is mainly through this process of affixing sex-specific labels to jobs that discrimination operates in the labor market. The notion of a free market efficiently allocating workers to jobs solely on the basis of qualifications is a myth. Once a job is defined as female-only, the label tends to stick. The channelling of women into unchallenging, low paying, dead-end jobs thus creates rigid institutional barriers for sexual equality in the world of work (See Armstrong and Armstrong 1978; Freedman, 1976; Kanter, 1977; Lowe, 1980a; Madden, 1973; Kessler-Harris, 1975).

The 1970s witnessed a liberalization of sex role attitudes as the ideas of the women's liberation movement gained acceptance. At the same time, great numbers of married women were streaming into the labor force. Despite these trends, the labor market remains stratified on the basis of sex. Nowhere is this more apparent than in the office. The male office manager and the female secretary is the prototype of the male-female work relationship. In a word, males dominate.

Since the turn of the century women have flooded into office jobs only to end up performing the most tedious and routinized administrative tasks. Men, on the other hand, are usually recruited at the higher level of management trainee.[7] The working conditions of a secretary compare very favorably to most other clerical jobs. Yet despite its higher status and rewards, the job is infused with elements of the wife-mother role. Kanter (1977:89) describes the secretary as the 'office wife' who performs personal favors for the boss, such as taking in laundry, making coffee and buying his family's birthday gifts. This patriarchical type of relationship is also found between male clients and female sales persons, clerks or waitresses.

The ideology of patriarchy assumes that men have a pre-ordained right to dominate over women. This view is still deeply entrenched in western culture. It makes it difficult for many women to stand up and challenge the authority of a male boss—either individually or collectively through unionization (Lowe:1980b). It is indeed paradoxical that society espouses the principle of equality between the sexes. While, at the same time, women are limited by unequal opportunities in the economic sphere. Wilensky refers to this paradox (1968:243) as "the odd combination of emancipation and bondage."

Unfortunately, academic sociology has been of little help in critically analyzing sexual inequalities, for sociology has been mainly concerned with the study of male society (Acker 1978:134). Male work behavior is seen as resulting from the organization of industry and the worker's experiences on the job. But in the case of women, this sociological approach lapses into a discussion of motivation based on distinctive female traits. Feldberg and Glenn (1979) call for a new perspective which examines both men and women workers using the same conceptual framework. Contrary to conventional wisdom, the subordinate position of women in the job market does not result from their low job commitment, lack of ambition, unreliability or maternal attachment to the home. Rather, these alleged personal traits are in fact a product of, and a response to, the poor working conditions most women face.

Segmented Labor Markets and Ethnic Workers.   Women are not the only group in society discriminated against in the labor market. The segmentation model also accurately portrays the labor market experiences of many immigrant groups. Negative stereotypes have been applied to restrict the access of certain ethnic minorities to good jobs. A ready pool of labor to perform society's 'dirty work'—undesirable jobs such as dishwasher, building cleaner or chambermaid—is thus assured. Like gender, ethnicity is an ascribed trait over which individuals have no control. The more visible an ascribed characteristic, as in the case of sex or race, the easier it is for an employer to discriminate when hiring or making promotions.

John Porter's (1965) image of Canadian society as a *vertical mosaic* indicates how class position and ethnicity are intertwined. Porter uses the concept of 'entrance status' to show how immigrants enter the job market at the bottom in order to secure a niche in their new homeland. Certainly not all immigrant groups begin in such low positions, and many individual immigrants have experienced upward mobility. British engineers and technicians and American academics are obvious examples of successful immigrants. Most often, it is the immigrant from the underdeveloped countries of South-East Asia, the Caribbean or even southern Europe who, attempting to escape poverty at home, becomes trapped in a low 'entrance status' in Canada.

One measure of whether the labor market discriminates against ethnic minorities is to examine the representation of individuals from ethnic backgrounds in the country's top jobs. Clement's (1975) study of the economic elite—individuals holding directorships in one of the major corporations—revealed that these powerful decision-makers were predominantly of British stock. Francophone Canadians, who comprised 28.6 percent of the population, held only 8.4 percent of the elite posts in 1972. Other ethnic groups, making up 26.7 percent of the population, were represented in only 5.6 percent of the directorships studied (Clement 1975:231). The anglo-British were disproportionately represented in the elite. They constituted only 44.7 percent of the population yet occupied 86 percent of the elite places. For true equality of opportunity to exist, each ethnic group (or sex) would have to be represented in the elite in the same proportion as their numbers in the total population. But as Clement (1975:231) concludes: "In Canada, as in many modern societies built on conquest and immigration, ethnicity is interwoven into the class system so that it provides advantages to the conquerers while keeping the conquered and newly arrived at the bottom of the so-called 'opportunity structure'." A WASP elite thus retains a tight grasp on the reigns of economic power by admitting to their echelon only those with similar class and ethnic backgrounds.

Government immigration policy has been instrumental in creating an unequal ethnic division of labor. Immigration policy has historically responded to the labor requirements of an expanding economy. For example, in the late nineteenth century, the government explicitly encouraged the settlement of 'stalwart peasants in sheepskin coats' on the prairies in order to build an agricultural economy. Avery's (1979) research documents that after 1896 immigration policy was reformulated to serve the requirements of a growing capitalist labor market. Railways, mining and forestry companies joined industrialists to actively lobby for an 'open door' immigration policy that would provide a steady flow of cheap labor. Today's immigration policy is based on a point system which assesses the eligibility of an immigrant mainly on the basis of skills and education. The stated motive behind the policy is to match the qualifications of immigrants with job openings. Critics claim, however, that the effects are racist, with the point system heavily weighted in favor of white, educated, Western Europeans.

Any discussion of Canada's ethnic division of labor must include the relative economic positions of French and English in Quebec. Politically dominant since the conquest in 1759, anglophones have had the best opportunities and therefore occupied the most rewarding jobs in Quebec. Everett Hughes' classic study, *French Canada in Transition* (1943) describes how the process of industrialization was controlled by British and American corporations. Based on fieldwork in a Quebec textile town during the 1930s, the study focuses on the movement of Quebecois from rural, agricultural backgrounds into the new urban, industrial society. However, work in the textile factories was sharply segmented along ethnic lines. English workers held supervisory, technical and managerial positions, while French Canadians never rose above the rank of foreman.[8]

Ensuing decades have witnessed a reduction of the disparities portrayed by Hughes. The Quiet Revolution, the federal government's bilingualism policies, the rise of Quebec nationalism, and a more interventionist economic role for the provincial government have helped break down some of the barriers to equal francophone participation in the work world. A growing Quebecois business class and a large, upwardly mobile, professional, middle class now exist. Indicative of these changes is the Parti Quebecois' recent Bill 101 legislating French as the official language of work in the province.

HIGHLIGHT

1. Over the past eight decades, the number of individuals involved in white-collar occupations has increased while the numbers of blue-collar workers, farmers, and small businessmen have decreased.
2. Not only have women been restricted to specific jobs such as medical and clerical occupations, but even when they perform the same work as men they are paid much less.
3. The restriction of women to specific occupations has been legitimized through the development of stereotypes employing the "feminine" quality of females.
4. It is possible to examine the labor market in terms of ethnic segmentation as well as sexual segmentation. In Canada, individuals of various ethnic groups can be found in disproportionate numbers in certain lower-level occupations. However, the top of the occupational hierarchy is dominated by white, Anglo-Saxon, Protestants.

The Design of Work

Industrialization requires efficient forms of work organization in order to progress. Historically, in Britain, a simple workshop employing several craftsmen, each creating a finished product out of raw materials, gave way to a large factory where workers performed specialized tasks under the scrutiny of management. As Braverman (1974:59) points out, "industrial capitalism begins when a significant number of workers is employed by a single capitalist." The capitalist transformation of work organizations—whether an office, factory, mine or laboratory—involved a specialized division of labor and a hierarchial, or pyramid-shaped, arrangement of jobs within a rigid system of authority. Hierarchy and a detailed division of labor, then, are the cornerstones of modern workplace organizational design.

The Division of Labor.   A major step along the road to industrialization was the subdivision of the complex job of the craftsman into simpler components. Each of these minute tasks could then be performed more cheaply by unskilled laborers. But once all the various stages in a craftsman's job had been fragmented, simplified, and assigned to less skilled workers, co-ordinating and integrating these tasks became a problem. This in part accounts for the importance of the manager who, since the late nineteenth century, has been delegated the responsibility for unifying diverse tasks into an efficient production system. The rise of managers and other new occupational groups signifies how a proliferation of specialized jobs is central to industrialization. How this division of labor developed, and why it is so important for capitalist production can now be considered.

All human societies, regardless of how primitive, display a basic division of roles which facilitate economic activity. Often the roles are assigned according to age or sex. Economic progress expands and proliferates these roles, making them increasingly interdependent. Tasks also grow more specialized. In agricultural economies, for instance, once farmers produce a surplus of food they are able to exchange it for goods which previously they had to make themselves.

Adam Smith (1976, originally published in 1776) was first to explore the economic implications of role specialization. In his *Wealth of Nations*, Smith sought to explain the reasons for the rising productivity and growing wealth of industrializing societies. He postulated that the division of labor was largely responsible for these trends. Once a certain scale of production had been achieved, it was more efficient to break down complex jobs into simple tasks to be delegated to individual workers. Smith's famous illustration came from his observations in an English pin factory. Each worker performed one stage in pin making, from cutting the wire, straightening it, pointing it, placing a head on it, and putting the pins in paper. Ten men could produce over 48 000 pins daily by this method. "But if they had all wrought separately and independently," concluded Smith (1976:9), "...they certainly could not each of them have made twenty, perhaps not one pin in a day...."

Smith's argument about the importance of subdividing and reorganizing work to achieve increased productivity later became a guiding principle of modern management. Charles Babbage translated Smith's findings into practical business terms in 1832 (see Braverman 1974:79-82). He demonstrated that a manufacturer could cut labor costs in half by hiring unskilled women and children to perform the operations in pin-making. The connection between increased productivity and reduced labor costs, as basic as it may now seem, had been brought to the fore. Managers quickly recognized they could achieve both goals by reorganizing work and appropriating from workers control over production activities.

Hierarchy.   Capitalists devised new organizational structures to handle the growing size and complexity of their businesses. The bureaucracy was the organizational form best able to co-ordinate and integrate many specialized tasks into a coherent whole. Max Weber (1964:338) has emphasized the interdependence of the bureaucratic organization with modern capitalism: "...the capitalist system has undeniably played a major role in the development of bureaucracy. Indeed, without it capitalist production could not continue...." Bureaucracy emerged as the organizational solution to the problem of how to achieve rational, collective effort from a large group of employees each of whom performed a specialized job. The modern expression of bureaucracy is the giant corporation and government department where employees are faceless minions, where clients become mired in red tape, and where consumers are bewildered by an endless stream of new products or services.

Weber presented an *ideal type* of bureaucracy. An ideal type is an analytic tool which combines all key characteristics of a real phenomenon into an exaggerated model that offers a standard against which the reality can be compared. Weber argued that no organization was a pure, or ideal bureaucracy, although he predicted that over time it would increasingly exhibit bureaucratic characteristics. The essence of a bureaucracy is rational, efficient co-ordination of economic activity. This stands in direct contrast to the 'rule-of-thumb' found in many owner-operated nineteenth century businesses. But critics point to the human costs of bureaucratic rationality. By emphasizing positions, rules and formal authority the bureaucracy dehumanizes work, turning employees into cogs in an administrative machine.

Although he never gave a concise definition, Weber used the term bureaucracy to refer to an appointed body of administrative officials.

Generally the concept applies to any type of industry organized along hierarchical, formal lines of authority. Albrow (1970:44-5) summarizes Weber's model of the ideal bureaucracy as follows:

1. The staff members are personally free, observing only the impersonal duties of their offices.
2. There is a clear hierarchy of offices.
3. The functions of the offices are clearly specified.
4. Officials are appointed on the basis of a contract.
5. They are selected on the basis of a professional qualification, ideally substantiated by a diploma gained through examination.
6. They have a money salary, and usually pension rights. The salary is graded according to position in the hierarchy. The official can always leave the post, and under certain circumstances it may also be terminated.
7. The official's post is his sole major occupation.
8. There is a career structure, and promotion is possible either by seniority or merit, and according to the judgement of superiors.
9. The official may appropriate neither the post nor the resources which go with it.
10. He is subject to a unified code of control and disciplinary system.

There are recognizable parallels between the bureaucratic model and the concept of internal labor markets discussed earlier. Indeed, segmentation theory is one of the most current attempts to recast bureaucratic theory in a more realistic and critical light.

Weber's vision of bureaucratic efficiency was founded on the assumption that employees would readily submit to managerial authority. Bureaucrats were obliged to accept, in Weber's view, the legitimacy of the existing authority structure. By virtue of holding their positions, they agreed to operate according to the rules and to obey orders from their superiors. But this assumption of broad support for organizational goals is contradicted by the realities of bureaucratic life.

Weber's critics have accused him of neglecting sources of bureaucratic inefficiency, such as inter-departmental rivalries and when workers circumvent official regulations. Or as Merton (1952) documents, officials who slavishly follow the rules can undermine the efficiency of a bureaucracy. The rules become ends in themselves, rather than means of achieving broader organizational goals. Officials acquire a 'bureaucratic personality', compulsively following procedural manuals to the last detail. Blau's (1963) research also illustrates how bureaucracies generate the causes of their own inefficiencies. His fieldwork in U.S. government agencies revealed how workers behaved according to their own unofficial rules. In doing so, they were responding directly to organizational pressure to attain certain goals, such as handling so many clients or cases in a set period. Blau directs our attention to the tension between the official rules of the bureaucracy and the workers' counter-rules. By striving to make their jobs easier, employees may erode bureaucratic efficiency.

A major deficiency in Weber's model of bureaucracy is its neglect of the issue of worker resistance. Usually resistance takes the form of workers' informal counter-systems of production. Not surprisingly, a major concern of management has been how to thwart this by gaining worker co-operation. Workers must be persuaded to accept 'organizational goals' articulated by management as their own personal goals. In all modern industrial enterprises the few command and the many obey— or at least are expected to. Top officials must somehow justify their decisions to those below them. Management *ideology* performs this function. To elaborate, management ideology refers to those justifications used by management to explain and rationalize their superior positions, their superior rewards and their right to give orders. Bendix (1974:13) explains: "All economic enterprises have in common a basic social relation between the employers who exercise authority and the workers who obey, and all ideologies of management have in common the effort to interpret the exercise of authority in a favourable light."

Organizational goals, we have noted, are established by those in positions of power. These goals are therefore 'rational' only according to management's perspective. What is rational for workers, on the other hand, reflects their own interests—higher pay, a safer work environment, or more say—and thus may run counter to management's goals. To dismiss workers' demands as something less than rational, just because they are not consistent with management's view of reality, is patently ideological.

This leads into a discussion of power in organizations. Because management acts on behalf of corporate shareholders, they have ultimate power. Simply put, they can decide whom to hire and fire, or when to expand production or shut down. Power is a major source of inequality in work relations. But we should recognize that workplace inequalities represent a microcosm of the class antagonisms in society. Bureaucracies are the product of specific capitalist relations of production. In turn, they reinforce and solidify these social relations. But in no way should bureaucracies be seen as possessing an inner dynamic of their own, independent of the actions and decisions of the people who occupy their command posts.

To summarize, task specialization and a bureaucratic organizational structure are the foundations of capitalist production. They are the central design features of modern work. Both are means by which managers obtain increased control over production activities. Marglin (1976) provides some enlightening thoughts on why in the course of industrialization producers lost control over production. He focuses on the functions of the division of labor and hierarchy. Neither, he claims, became prominent solely on the basis of its technical superiority. In other words, they did not provide more output for the same level of input. Marglin points instead to the social functions of hierarchy and division of labor. By fragmenting tasks and centralizing control in bureaucratic structures, management was able to augment the process of capital accumulation. This was all part of an elaborate 'divide and conquer' strategy to reduce worker control over production and decrease their relative share of total profits.

HIGHLIGHT

1. A division of labor is found in nearly all societies. One aspect of social development is an increase in the complexity of the division of labor. In modern capitalist societies, the division of labor has proceeded to the point where the worker has lost control over his/her work process.
2. Bureaucracy is a form of social institution that has emerged to co-ordinate the activities of a complex division of labor. Bureaucracies, however, do not operate to the advantage of all who participate in them.

Modern Management and the Quest for Control

It is now evident that the modern bureaucratic corporation was created through the policies and practices of managers. This occupational group became central players on the economic stage in the late nineteenth century. The origins of the management function, however, can be traced back to the early industrial revolution (Pollard, 1968). The appointment of trained managers and the development of cost accounting techniques[9] were two major responses of capitalists to the problems of administering increasingly large and complex enterprises. As the nineteenth century drew to a close, trained engineers were entering management positions and shifting their attention from purely technical concerns towards organizational solutions to production inefficiencies. As Chandler (1977) suggests, the classical economic notion of a free market regulated by an 'invisible hand' was replaced by the visible hand of the corporate manager. Ownership is separated from control in the modern corporation. The board of directors, representing the shareholders or 'owners', gives managers the authority to operate the business profitably and efficiently. This mandate lies behind the managerial drive to rationalize the labor process and restructure organizations.

Scientific Management.   Braverman (1974:107) claims that "control over work through control over the decisions that are made in the course of work" is the key to all modern management. It was the American engineer, Frederick W. Taylor, who turned the principle of control into a 'science' of management. By the beginning of World War I, businessmen on both sides of the border were well acquainted with Taylor's scientific management. In fact, economic efficiency promoted by Taylor and other management 'experts' precipitated an 'efficiency craze' which permeated popular culture in the U.S., and to a lesser extent Canada, during the early twentieth century (See Nelson 1980; Haber 1964).

Taylor's management creed involved three basic principles:
1. the dissociation of the labor process from the skills of the worker;
2. the separation of the conception of a task from its execution; and
3. the use of management's resulting monopoly over knowledge to control each step in production (Braverman 1974:113-4, 119).

Braverman argues that Taylor's system degraded labor, by minutely fragmenting tasks to the point of meaninglessness and by eliminating any say by workers in how their jobs would be carried out. Taylor was the best known of the so-called 'efficiency experts' who sought to transform management into a 'science'. However, these early management consultants simply borrowed scientific jargon in order to lend respectability to their claims of objectivity and fairness. Science thus provided a sound ideological basis for the extension of management control over labor.

Taylor (1919; 1947) was convinced that *worker soldiering*, or deliberate laziness, was the great evil plaguing industry. Workers, alleged Taylor, reduced productivity by consciously restricting their efforts. This was achieved by keeping bosses ignorant of how fast a job could actually be done. Taylor's solution was to 'scientifically' determine the 'one best way' of performing a job through time-study of its component parts. A base rate of pay was then tied to a production quota. If workers exceeded the quota they received a monetary 'incentive' or bonus; lazy workers unable to achieve the quota would be forced to quit because the base rate was too low to live on. Because 'a fair day's wage' was established through scientific investigation, both workers and management would have common grounds for co-operating to increase production.

Taylor assumed, of course, that workers were driven solely by economic motives; that they were 'economic men' who acted to maximize individual economic gain. This view of human nature was colored by his preoccupation as an engineer with technical efficiency. He had identified the *labor problem*—how to obtain the co-operation of workers in production and eliminate class conflict—but his proposals had a certain naïve ring to them. The solution to this twentieth century version of the problem of order required a "complete mental revolution" on the part of both management and labor. As Taylor wrote in *Industrial Canada* (April, 1913:1224-5):

> The new outlook that comes to both sides under scientific management is that both sides very soon realize that if they stop pulling apart and both push together as hard as possible in the same direction, they can make that surplus (i.e. profits) so large that there is no occasion for any quarrel over its division. Labor gets an immense increase in wages, and still leaves a large share for capital.

Taylor's package of managerial reforms was seldom adopted completely. Applications were usually piece-meal. In fact, Taylorism represented only one of the managerial strategies for rationalizing the labor process. Palmer (1975) calls this broad assault on the workplace which accompanied the rise of industrial capitalism the "thrust for efficiency." First applied to the factory around the turn of the century, by the 1920s these innovations had proved valuable and were being used to overhaul large corporate and government offices. The thrust for efficiency was in many respects an American invention. However, the branch-plant structure of the Canadian economy and, moreover, the similar productivity and labor problems experienced in all capitalist firms account for the adoption of these practices by Canadian employers (Lowe 1979).

The Human Relations Movement.   Scientific management concentrated on redesigning tasks so that control over the labor process could be wrested from workers. The problem then became how to 'adapt' workers to the more streamlined and monotonous jobs. According to Etzioni (1975), control in organizations is founded on the *compliance* of subordinate employees. By compliance he means agreement with organizational objectives as dictated by management. This can be achieved in one of three ways, in ascending order of effectiveness:
1. coercion, through penalties and harsh discipline;
2. the introduction of utilitarian measures, which assumes that the economic self-interest of the employee is the basis of the motivation to work harder; and
3. the introduction of normative measures, which is most effective because workers, seeing their own interests as harmonious with organizational goals, are self-motivated to work hard.
Normative compliance suggests that it is not enough to get workers to automatically follow orders. They must see the orders as serving their own interests and thus be internally motivated to pursue the goals of the firm. While Taylorism combines elements of coercive and utilitarian modes of compliance, normative compliance is the basis of what is called the human relations perspective.

Taylorism treated workers like machines, as if they were devoid of human feelings. By way of contrast, the human relations approach to management deals, as the name indicates, with the 'human' side of organizations. It focuses on how workers' attitudes, values, emotions, psychological needs and interpersonal relationships shape their work behavior. In practice, human relations strives to get the best 'fit' between the worker, given his personal background and psychological make-up, and the job. Emphasis is therefore placed on careful recruitment and effective training of employees.

The human relations approach originated in a series of studies conducted by Harvard Business School researchers between 1927 and 1932 at Western Electric's sprawling Hawthorne Works on the outskirts of Chicago (see Roethlisberger and Dickson 1939). In this telephone equipment plant the importance of the 'human factor' in industry was ostensibly discovered. Western Electric management was initially concerned with the effects of fatigue and monotony on production levels—the central issues in industrial psychology at the time. Through a series of studies measuring the impact of variations in rest pauses, hours of work and lighting levels on productivity, researchers inadvertently stumbled upon the importance of social ties among workers and between workers and supervisors in determining production.[10]

In the Relay Assembly Test Room study workers were placed in two separate rooms where researchers carefully recorded production while varying light intensity for one group but not the other. To the researcher's surprise, productivity in both groups increased regardless of lighting level. Only when light intensity was reduced to that of bright moonlight did productivity decline.

Several variations on this study came up with the same inconclusive findings. The puzzled researchers, searching for possible explanations, speculated that a fundamental change had occurred in the workplace. Specifically, special treatment and status had been accorded to the workers by researchers and management simply by involving them in the study. This had the unintended effect of raising the morale of the workers, for they now felt management 'cared' about them as individuals. Productivity increased as a result. This is the famous *Hawthorne effect*. It taught managers an important lesson: the humane treatment of employees improves their motivation to co-operate and be productive.

Another phase of the research involved an extensive interview program, the first direct attempt at 'employee counselling' (see Wilensky and Wilensky 1951). Through the interviews employees revealed that relations with co-workers were the basis of *informal* behavioral codes governing production. To further explore work behavior, the Bank Wiring Observation Room study was set up. For seven months, fourteen employees were closely observed as they wired telephone switching banks. Even though workers knew they were under the direct gaze of management consultants, it was discovered that their behavior was governed by four informal group norms:
1. don't be a rate buster (don't work too fast);
2. don't be a chisler (don't work too slowly);
3. don't be a squealer (don't report co-workers to supervisors for infractions of the rules); and
4. even if exercising supervisory responsibilities, don't keep a social distance or act 'officious' (Homans 1950:ch. 3).
This study exposed the underworld of the workplace, showing how workers consciously engage in practices to oppose and subvert established authority.

A key assumption of the human relations perspective is that people desire to co-operate (see Mayo 1945). Psychological needs, beliefs and attitudes are thought to strongly influence work behavior. This is an explicit rejection of the 'economic man' assumption of scientific management. In making these arguments, however, Elton Mayo (1945) and other human relations' advocates present a condescending view of the worker. Workers, claimed Mayo, are unaware of their co-operative instinct, acting instead on the basis of irrational 'sentiments' or beliefs. Because Mayo saw the survival of society depending upon co-operation, he espoused a new industrial order run by an administrative elite. As the possessors of true rationality, the elite's duty would be to provide a work environment conducive to fulfilling the co-operative instincts of employees. Co-operation could be achieved by adopting a non-authoritarian approach to leadership, involving workers in task-related decision making and through careful selection and training. Behind the human relations prescription for industrial harmony as developed by Mayo can be found an elaborate justification for management's manipulation of workers.

Human Relations Today. Human relations is practiced under the banners of job enlargement, job enrichment, job redesign, socio-technical planning, human resources and some Quality of Working Life programs. Uniting these approaches is a common ideological framework. Employees are to be treated humanely and provided with good working conditions. But beyond a few concessions in the realm of decision-making, most of the authority remains with management.

The human relations movement, so named because it has been widely influential in management circles, identifies conflict as a destructive force and co-operation and harmony as 'healthy'. The perspective also rings of elitism. The assumption is that workers' beliefs and behavior are essentially irrational, while management's actions are rational and hence superior. What is most incredible about human relations is that it rests on a very shaky foundation. The Hawthorne studies, according to Carey (1967), were poorly conceived and incompetently executed. Furthermore, the conclusions cannot be supported by the researcher's own evidence. Economic incentives and coercive supervision seem to be better explanations for productivity changes than management's attention to human relations (Carey 1967; Acker and Van Houten 1974; Franke and Kaul 1978). This is not to deny that contemporary practitioners of human relations are sincere in their intentions to treat workers as human beings. But after the rhetoric of 'neo-human relations' has been stripped away, problems of power and inequality in organizations persist. Perrow (1972:142) provides a fitting conclusion in this respect:

One may treat a slave humanely, and even ask his opinion regarding matters he is more familiar with than his master. But to transform his basic dependency and this presumption of his incompetence with regard to his own interests, there must be an institutional process or public process whereby the opportunity and capacity for legitimate self-assertion is guaranteed.

The Concept of Control.   Braverman's *Labor and Monopoly Capital* has sparked much debate and research about the nature of control in work organizations. His model of the labor process emphasizes the relentless efforts by management to assert its control over work activities. However, it is possible to infer from Braverman that workers seemed to passively accept these assaults on their skills and job autonomy. Seldom in *Labor and Monopoly Capital* can one find mention of active worker resistance to management. Subsequent authors have attempted to deal with this limitation. Their efforts have resulted in the *new industrial sociology*. The growing literature of this new approach, which gives due recognition to Braverman's contribution to the field, juxtaposes the processes of control and resistance, indicating how employer-employee relations involve a ceaseless struggle over who controls production.

It is important to recognize that *control* is a relative concept. Using money as an analogy, few people in our society totally lack money. What is of concern is their relative poverty or affluence. That is: where do they stand economically in relation to other individuals in society? Similarly, discussions of control in the workplace should not be couched in 'all or nothing' terms. Instead of compounding Braverman's oversight by asserting that managers now make all the decisions, it is more fruitful to examine the degree of power people have to direct their work.

Following Freidman (1977:82-5), a *frontier of control*, which shifts according to the outcomes of the daily skirmishes between capital and labor can be postulated. At issue is who sets the pace of work, hours of work, order of task execution, and what constitutes fair treatment and just rewards. Sometimes workers win more autonomy in these matters through union bargaining. Furthermore, management may initiate changes of its own volition which offer workers what Freidman calls *responsible autonomy*. This is a way of obtaining worker co-operation by granting them some scope for making task-related decisions. The opposite strategy frequently used by management is one of *direct control*, exemplified by scientific management, in which coercive measures and direct supervision afford workers little job autonomy.

Examples of both types of control are found in the Canadian nickel mining industry. Clement's (1981:204) study of the International Nickel Company (INCO) describes the introduction of sophisticated 'people technology' at the ultra-modern Copper Cliff Nickel refinery. INCO's plan appears progressive, emphasizing a 'one big happy family feeling', flattening the job hierarchy and implementing a new system of on-the-job training. However, the effect is to break down traditional job autonomy. The former worker-centred apprenticeship system is replaced by a 'modular' training program which takes a machine-based approach to training. Management thereby obtains direct control, largely because the workers' skill-based bargaining power has been eroded.

To grasp the significance of the change at INCO, we need to contrast it with the 'responsible autonomy' possessed by traditional work teams in the firm's underground mining operations. These small, closely-knit groups extracted ore underground by deciding among themselves how and when each phase of the mining operation would be executed. A great deal of pride and solidarity developed as miners endured hazardous working conditions in pursuit of production bonuses. In the refinery, direct control had always existed. But by implementing human relations programs and modular training, management sought added flexibility over labor requirements. Their ultimate aim was to reduce skill levels and cut the size of the work force.

Burawoy (1979) also explores control themes, except he describes how workers adapt to existing working conditions and often internalize the goals of management. Two different ways of organizing the capitalist labor process are proposed by Burawoy (1979;194): The *despotic organization of work* relies on coercive controls over labor and is found typically in smaller firms struggling to survive in a competitive product market. The *hegemonic organization of work* is restricted to large, market dominant firms where workers have come to accept their futures as tied up with the success of the firm. They do not see their own labor as a source of profits, and therefore do not experience what Marx would term exploitation (Burawoy 1979:29). In short, consent has replaced coercion as the mechanism for integrating workers into the labor process.

The hegemonic or 'consent' model operates largely on the basis of an internal labor market. Individual workers are encouraged to get ahead and attractive job conditions foster a long-term commitment. What helped make workers part of the 'system' in the machine shop studied by Burawoy was the way the bonus system of payment operated. Workers treated the attainment of production quotas and bonus payments as a game. By playing the game, they could not very well criticize the rules which, of course, had been laid down by management. Certainly conflict existed, but it centred around the outcomes of the game—who got what—rather than challenges to the rules. The game analogy should not be taken too far, however. It may only apply to workplaces which have wage incentive plans. Yet Burawoy's argument deserves serious consideration; few workers openly question the capitalist system. Instead dissatisfactions are vented against how it tends not to work to their advantage.

HIGHLIGHT

1. Taylorism, introduced at the turn of the century, aimed at maximum worker efficiency by dividing the work process into minute, easily controlled segments.
2. The human relations approach to management, that arose in the 1930s, focuses on the social and psychological needs of workers in efforts to get them to work harder.
3. The human relations approach is currently being implemented in organizations through programs such as job enrichment. In all cases, the guiding assumption is that relations between management and workers can and should be harmonious.
4. Despite managements' attempts to control the work process, their efforts are rarely totally successful. Workers' resistance often limits the degree of regulation which management can impose.

Worker Resistance

Having established that workers are not mere pawns manipulated by management, we will now explore in more depth the various ways *formal authority* is resisted and subverted. Recall that work organizations are typically hierarchical. This arrangement sets the stage for power struggles between those at the top who make the rules and give the orders and the majority below who must obey. The employment 'contract' requires employees to relinquish certain rights and freedoms, and assume a subordinate status in return for wages. But in practice employees often take issue with the scope and nature of their rights and obligations. To reiterate an earlier point, work can thus be seen as a relationship of power which generates conflict (T. Johnson 1980). The interests of employer and employee are basically at odds, each having different definitions of what is fair and equitable (see Hyman and Brough 1975).

The Nature of Resistance and Conflict.   Workers resist the imposition of management authority and react to deprivations in the work environment in a variety of ways. Some are more effective in changing the situation than others. The most basic distinction is between *unorganized* and *organized* forms of resistance. The former category covers how workers individually cope with job-related problems. Often this involves passive adaptation, acquiescence or withdrawal. If dissatisfaction reaches an intolerable level the employee's final recourse may be to quit and seek work elsewhere.

Quitting is an escape and as such does not address the source of dissatisfaction. Only through organized collective action can workers hope to bring improvements, albeit small, in the distribution of power and rewards. Organized resistance can be *formal*, when it is channelled through a trade union, or it can be *informal*, such as the 'silent bargaining' whereby work groups surreptitiously replace company rules with their own. Not all formal resistance follows the legalistic framework of collective bargaining as laid down in federal and provincial legislation and union contracts. Sometimes unionized workers spontaneously engage in unofficial actions, such as wildcat strikes. These episodes are grass-roots protests often sparked by immediate grievances such as an unjust dismissal or injury of a co-worker.

One cannot study worker resistance without being directly concerned with industrial conflict. A strike or lockout represents the most visible type of conflict. Indeed, the majority of these events are given an 'official' status insofar as they are legally recognized and recorded by the government—even though it may later intervene should the 'public interest' be deemed threatened. But there is an 'underside' in the workplace where one encounters less defined and less visible conflicts. Hidden to the casual observer, there are undercurrents of conflict in any organization. An arbitrary or capricious action by management may transform this into open conflict.

Richard Hyman (1975) neatly incorporates the various forms of conflict into his theory of industrial relations. He shuns the concern of orthodox industrial relations with the formal, legally defined 'web of rules' which regulates job behavior and codifies employer-employee relations through collective agreements. In Hyman's assessment (1975:26), such approaches ignore the fact that in "every workplace there exists an invisible frontier of control, reducing some of the formal powers of the employer: a frontier which is defined and redefined in a continuous process of pressure and counter-pressure, conflict and accommodation, overt and tacit struggle." This definition of industrial relations incorporates both the formal and informal types of collective resistance. Industrial relations, then, can be defined broadly as "the study of processes of control over work relations; and among these processes those involving collective worker organization and action are of particular concern" (Hyman 1975:12).

The popular image portrayed by the media is that industrial conflict is a 'social problem'; that it is abnormal or pathological. But there is good reason to consider conflict a normal and 'healthy' part of industrial relations in capitalist societies. Conflict is to be expected in any economic system where people compete to get a share of scarce rewards. Watson (1980:226) argues that in this sense, conflict and co-operation are two sides of the same coin. For example, unionized workers co-operate to win improved working conditions. But in so doing they may come into conflict with other groups—notably their employer and, possibly, a public inconvenienced by a strike—whose interests differ.

The industrial relations system is geared towards the resolution of conflicts. This goal is usually achieved, considering that the vast majority of union-management disputes are settled before a strike situation is reached. Presumably, it is the *threat* of a strike by the union or a lockout by the employer which brings both sides together in a settlement. In the words of one prominent industrial relations scholar, "conflict, latent or manifest, is the essence of industrial relations, but the object of industrial relations as technique is the *resolution* of conflict" (Barbash 1979:652). What Barbash overlooks, however, is that often through collective strategies involving overt conflict, workers are able to make improvements in working conditions that the employer may not have conceded in the face of less militancy.

Work Groups.   The informal work group has been under the sociological microscope ever since its influence on industrial behavior was uncovered in the Hawthorne studies. Work group relations are largely a function of how production is organized. For example, auto workers spread out along a fast-paced assembly line have fewer opportunities to develop strong social ties than do miners or firefighters engaged in team work. It is the quality of social bonds among members which determines the group's potential for unified action. The strength of the network of social ties which unites group members is referred to as *cohesiveness.* The potential for collective action facilitated by such ties is referred to as *solidarity.* The importance of group membership, then, is twofold. First, the friendly camaraderie of the group can be a source of satisfaction. Second, strong group ties can bolster collective strength in struggles with management.

Donald Roy's (1952, 1954, 1956) participant-observer study of a Chicago machine shop offers some fascinating insights regarding work group dynamics. During the mid-1940s Roy worked as a machinist in a shop which ran on a piece-work payment system. Just as in INCO's nickel mines described by Clement, monetary incentives took the form of bonus payments for production in excess of a quota established by management. Roy documents how machine operators co-operated among themselves and with other groups in the shop whose services they required. Their collective strategy was to devise 'angles', or short-cuts, which would maximize their wages while minimizing effort. This involved the operators in 'conspiracies' with other groups—workers who supplied tools, maintained the machines or delivered raw materials—to deliberately break company rules.

Operators thus substituted their own system of production without top management's knowledge. In shop jargon, this behavior was known as 'goldbricking' on 'stinker' jobs. That is, workers relaxed and enjoyed some free time on difficult jobs that could not possibly net a bonus. Or if they were fortunate to have a 'gravey job' they could 'make out'. These were easy jobs on which operators exerted themselves, exceeding the quota to receive a bonus. Any production beyond an unofficial quota was stored up in a 'kitty' to be used to boost output figures on a slow day.

Roy's research challenges the widely accepted stereotype in human relations theory that managers are more rational and efficient than workers. The co-operative work relations in the machine shop involved ingenious schemes to streamline production, albeit to the workers' own ends. In other words, the informal production system was more effective than what management officially prescribed. In Roy's (1956) opinion, the machine operators and their co-conspirators were the true possessors of the 'logic of efficiency'.[11]

Roy's research was guided by the question: 'why do workers restrict production?' This addresses a central concern of management, namely how better relations with employees, improved working conditions, open lines of communication and effective leadership can elicit more co-operative and productive worker behavior. Burawoy (1979) returned thirty years later to the same factory Roy had studied to examine a much more radical question: 'why do workers work as hard as they do; why do they push themselves for management?' Unlike Roy, Burawoy's starting point was the division of interests between management and employees and the ensuing contest for control over production. Restriction of output, viewed in this light, becomes a weapon in 'guerilla-type' class warfare punctuated by daily skirmishes in the workplace.

Burawoy's participant observation research confirmed many of Roy's initial findings within a different interpretative framework. According to Burawoy, workers tacitly agree to exert themselves because elaborate mechanisms for manufacturing consent and co-operation operate at the point of production. The reason workers are sometimes diligent is only explicable in terms of their general job orientation. As mentioned above, the machine shop employees studied by Burawoy saw their jobs in the context of a game in which they had a good chance of winning. The spoils were high monetary bonuses for exceeding established production quotas. Participation in the game of 'making out', or earning a bonus wage is essentially individualistic. The game becomes an end in itself. And as long as workers individually have a fair chance of winning they are not likely to collectively oppose the rules.

The game is entered into as a way of procuring *relative satisfactions*; that is, some relief from the powerlessness and deprivations inherent in contemporary work arrangements. Burawoy's thesis, however, may apply only to monotonous jobs, where relative satisfactions are consequently more readily sought. Or perhaps the game analogy best suits those industries with bonus payment systems. This is the most obvious way for work to be made a game with the chance of tangible winnings.

We must acknowledge these possible limitations, but they should not obscure the central point. Most workers construct their own informal group culture, achieving alternate sources of satisfaction and making the working day a little more tolerable and pleasant.

Work Cultures.   The idea that workers construct an oppositional culture on the basis of their work experiences has recently become a prominent theme in Canadian labor history. Through the writings of Greg Kealey (1980), Bryan Palmer (1979), Craig Heron (1980) and other historians of the Canadian working class, we are discovering that late nineteenth century skilled artisans participated in a vibrant culture of control directed at preserving the integrity of their crafts.[12] Artisans and their unions strongly opposed scientific management, mechanization, the reorganization of production and other attempts by management to undermine the skills and responsibilities on which their craft tradition was based. This culture of control linked work and community. The rich associational, friendship and kinship ties of working class communities helped buttress workplace confrontations as artisans defended themselves against the onslaught of industrialization. Community activities such as parades, picnics, fire companies, and educational institutes augmented the role of craft unions by moderating the ravages of economic change. But at the same time, these institutions helped the besieged artisan adapt to the new industrial system (Palmer 1979:245). The culture of control became translated into trade union rules, negotiated wage rates and work regulations codified in union contracts.

Unionization was the most effective method for the threatened craftsman to adjust to industrialization and resist its excesses. The integration of work and community provided the basis for a working class culture which gave the artisans "a conception of workplace control that allowed them a measure of autonomy in the 'dark satanic mills' of early Canadian capitalism (Palmer 1979:245).

Toronto shoemakers are a good case in point. Kealey (1980:292) details how the shoemakers organized the Knights of St. Crispin, drawing on traditional symbols of craft pride: "From medieval craft lore, the shoemakers brought forth St. Crispin as a symbol of their historic rights and their importance to the community. Building on traditions of craft pride and solidarity, Toronto shoemakers even resorted to breaking machines in their desperate attempt to maintain decent wages and conditions in the shoe industry."

This desire to maintain traditional craft control in the face of mechanization and work rationalization was the basis for numerous episodes of industrial conflict early in the twentieth century. The booming manufacturing cities of southwestern Ontario experienced hundreds of strikes between 1901 and 1914. Many were acts of 'defiance' by organized skilled workers protesting the way mechanization and scientific management were undermining their ability to regulate the labor process (Heron and Palmer 1977).

Unions and Unionization.   The 'new working class history' represented by the above illustrates the critical role unions play in defending workers' interests. A trade union is the major institution through which workers can exert countervailing pressure on management. Unions offer workers collective bargaining as a vehicle for having some say in determining employment conditions. Unions *institutionalize* worker-boss relations by setting down procedures for resolving differences, thereby injecting a measure of predictability and stability. Hyman (1980:323) observes that unions act as "managers of discontent" by channelling and regulating conflict. But viewed somewhat differently, unions are democratic institutions giving employees a voice in otherwise authoritarian work structures.

There are limits, however, to the achievement of a more democratic workplace through unions. Critics sometimes attribute limits to the conservative nature of unionism in North America. Many of the big unions in Canada and the United States practice what is called *business unionism*. That is, they focus on obtaining monetary gains to the neglect of social justice and job control issues. More than anything, this behavior underlines the ambivalent position which unions occupy in society. By striving to get a better deal for their members, they run the risk of being co-opted or 'bought off' by management. In return for high wages and good benefits, management extracts from the union a tacit acceptance of the status quo on other matters.

The growth of unions is tied to the expansion of industrial capitalism, as workers reacted to the deprivations and inequalities in their employment. As in other capitalist societies, Canadian trade union growth followed an uneven pattern. Surges in membership usually occurred during periods of economic prosperity. In 1911 only 4.9 percent of the non-agricultural labor force was unionized. By 1978 membership ranks had mushroomed to 39 percent of the non-agricultural labor force (Smucker 1980:209).

The internationals, or American-based unions, have played an influential role in shaping the Canadian labor movement. The U.S.-based craft unions, bastions of conservative business unionism, asserted their dominance at an early stage. These U.S. unions succeeded at the 1902 Canadian Trades and Labor Congress convention in expelling industrial unions and Canadian-based unions, thereby seizing the reigns of the fledgling central labor body.[13] Despite strong sentiments that they should run their own unions, by 1911 fully 90 percent of all Canadian unionists belonged to one of the U.S. internationals. It was only during the 1970s that an independence movement gained considerable ground when a number of Canadian branches broke away from their U.S. parent unions. The trend towards national unions has been further bolstered by the spread of collective bargaining in the public sector. The effects of these trends has been to reduce the proportion of union members in internationals to 47.4 percent by 1978 (Smucker 1980:212).

Union membership varies greatly by occupation. Skilled blue-collar workers, construction workers, many professional groups and miners, loggers and other resource workers are highly organized. Unfortunately, there is no reliable union membership breakdown by occupational group. We must instead use data showing the industrial distribution of union members. In 1977 union membership by industry ranged from highs of 88.4 percent in fishing and trapping and 69.1 percent in public administration to lows of 2.3 percent in finance and 0.4 percent in agriculture (Canada 1979:74).[14]

Regional variations in the industrial and occupational composition of the work force have influenced the provincial rates of unionization. Of all the provinces, British Columbia and Quebec are the most highly unionized. Union membership also varies along sex lines. Women, historically, have been less unionized than men. In 1978, 26.8 percent of all women in the work force were union members, compared with 41.1 percent of all men (Labor Canada, 1980c:11).

A major reason for the lower representation of women in unions is the poor employment conditions in female job ghettos. These conditions inhibit collective solutions to work problems. Moreover, because established unions have their membership strength in manufacturing and resource industries, where women are less likely to find work, the option of joining a union has not been available to many women. However, growing public sector unionism has recently brought women into the ranks of organized labor in unprecedented numbers. Between 1966 and 1976 the number of female unionists jumped by 160 percent compared with a 40 percent increase for males (White, 1980:27). This new trend explodes the myth that women workers are passive, apathetic and somehow not predisposed to collective action.

Laxer (1976) has identified four stormy periods of change and conflict in the development of the Canadian labor movement. The first period, during the 1870s, is when the Nine Hour Movement gained support among a small industrial working class in Ontario manufacturing centres. The movement's goal was to improve working conditions by reducing the length of the working day. The first trade union centrals emerged out of the Nine Hour Movement. These centrals were forerunners of today's district labor councils, provincial labor federations and the Canadian Labor Congress. The latter co-ordinates the activities of individual unions.

The second period consists of the wave of labor militancy and violence following the end of World War I. Wartime inflation and nationalist pressures within unions combined with political protests in Western

Canada to set the stage for the formation of the radical One Big Union. Workers across the country were agitating for improved working conditions, higher wages to cushion inflation and employer recognition of their unions. This unrest culminated in the Winnipeg General Strike of 1919 (see Bercuson 1974). The city fell under a state of siege as striking workers and returning soldiers squared off against police and employer-sponsored vigilantes. The confrontation ended in violence after mounted police charged a crowd of demonstrators.

During the third period, between 1937 and 1947, newly formed industrial unions made significant headway organizing workers in automobile, steel, rubber, chemical, electrical and other key manufacturing industries. Strikes for union recognition, such as the one in 1937 at General Motors' Oshawa plant, were common. Out of these struggles emerged the United Auto Workers, United Steel Workers and other powerful industry-wide unions. Not until the Second World War did the state, seeking labor peace in the interests of the war effort, legislate unions some basic rights. Procedures for organizing and gaining official certification as a bargaining agent were encoded in law and compulsory collective bargaining was established.

The fourth and final stage identified by Laxer is characterized by rising militancy and nationalist sentiment manifested in a wave of strikes and break-aways from international unions during the mid-1970s.

Statistics documenting steady gains in union membership since 1900 mask the tremendous obstacles workers have overcome to achieve collective bargaining. The greatest hurdle has always been the opposition of management to unions. We have already seen that many early industrial conflicts centred around the right of workers to organize unions and have them recognized by management (Pentland 1979:19; Jamieson 1971:51-2). However, the once virulent anti-unionism of employers has now softened into a grudging acceptance. Smucker's (1980:ch. 7) analysis of changes in managerial ideologies from 1901 to 1970 indicates that collective bargaining is now tolerated as a 'necessary evil'. Instead of fighting unions head-on, managers now criticize them as being unrepresentative organizations under misguided leadership.

A number of firms still engage openly in anti-union practices in defiance of legislation which purports to protect the worker's right to union representation. One fairly common tactic is strikebreaking (Zwelling 1972). This involves strike-bound firms bringing in 'scab' workers under police protection to take the place of individuals legally on strike. Furthermore, consultants run thriving businesses advising corporate executives how to stay 'union-free' (*Globe and Mail*, 19 March 1979). Sometimes the state undermines collective bargaining by granting concessions to anti-union employers. A good example of this is the Nova Scotia government's notorious Michelin Bill. It virtually insulated the tire corporation's factories from union organizing drives in return for a promise to create jobs in the province.

It is a fair generalization that the role of the state in industrial relations has been far from neutral. This point is emphasized throughout this book. State actions can promote union recognition among recalcitrant employers, but in Canada only infrequently has this been the case. Support for unions should be a matter of public policy for, as Bain (1978) points out, unions are essential in a functioning democracy.

Ironic as it may seem, Canada's contribution to industrial peace has been the construction of an elaborate legislative and administrative apparatus placing the state in the role of 'impartial umpire' in industrial conflicts (Craven 1980). The architect of this system was Mackenzie King, the first federal Minister of Labor and later Liberal Prime Minister. King's 1907 Industrial Disputes Investigation Act became the corner-stone of Canada's modern industrial relations policy. The act provided for compulsory conciliation (fact-finding) in disputes during a 'cooling off' period, a tripartite board of arbitration, and special treatment of public interest disputes involving essential services. In some instances the state used the powers of the act to legislate the end of strikes.[15] Huxley (1979) demystifies the neutrality of state involvement by showing how it has reshaped strike activity in post-World War II Canada. By limiting their use, the government has created a pattern of less frequent but much longer strikes than would have otherwise been the case. Management prefers the greater predictability this provides over more frequent and volatile work stoppages.

Unions and Class Consciousness. Do unionized workers act purely out of economic self-interest or as a unified class during industrial disputes? Students of social change have hotly debated the extent to which unions serve as catalysts for class action aimed at transforming the status quo. Marx sparked this debate when he predicted that an oppressed working class would eventually rise up against capitalism and replace it with a more egalitarian system. History has not borne this out. No industrial working class in a western capitalist society has success-fully engaged in such revolutionary actions. General strikes have crip-pled the economies of a number of countries in recent decades, but these short-lived protests have caused little more than temporary disruptions. Nonetheless, we must seriously entertain the possibility that industrial conflict will heighten class consciousness in the future, providing the precondition for revolutionary working class action.

Mann's (1970) comparative study of industrial conflict directly addresses this issue. He found that workers in France and Italy were more communist and anti-capitalist in orientation compared with their British and American counterparts who saw themselves as partners with management. But even though French and Italian unions hold out an alternative to capitalism, they fail to offer a detailed program for executing the prescribed changes. Consequently, the dominant capitalist ideology ultimately prevails among the western working class. Militancy becomes little more than a lever for winning concessions from the employer rather than a means of changing society.

Mann acknowledges that workers are alienated in their jobs. However, he claims that most do not seek to eradicate the sources of their feelings of powerlessness and meaninglessness. Instead, workers tend to develop a 'dual consciousness' as a kind of defence mechanism. In contrast to the Marxist view of class consciousness as linking in the workers' minds job exploitation with the structure of society, a dual consciousness implies that work and non-work activities and experiences are divorced from one another. Workers mentally compartmentalize their work lives and their leisure time. They develop a 'pragmatic acceptance' of their lowly position in the economic system. Satisfactions are found outside the sphere of employment.[16]

Mann (1970) examines whether strikes represent 'explosions' of class consciousness with a cumulative effect of inducing more broadly-based pressures for change. Involvement in a strike, he finds, crystalizes an individual's identification with co-workers. Furthermore, it exposes the contradictions and inequities of the system. But we have already noted that strikes are a tactical weapon. Consequently, the solidarity they generate is not carried much beyond the event. The Common Front general strike which swept Quebec in 1971 was by any measure a surge in class consciousness. The manifestos prepared by the striking unions went as far as denouncing the evils of the capitalist system (Drache 1972a). However, beyond reinforcing an already strong tradition of labor militancy in Quebec by adding the support of white-collar public sector workers, subsequent developments suggest that the Common Front did little to pave the way for concerted class-based political action.

Smith (1978:471) interprets the effects of strikes on consciousness to be uneven. Because many strikes involve the organized and therefore more affluent members of the working class, the increased wages and benefits won by strikers have "unprogressive political consequences" for unorganized workers. The outcomes of strikes may simply confirm in their minds the injustices of the system, fostering cynicism and even negative attitudes towards unions. Even though the strike may kindle a temporary rise in class consciousness among participants, the overall political consequences are regressive.

We are forced to conclude that strikes and other forms of collective protest seldom fundamentally threaten capitalism. Workers usually have more immediate and pragmatic goals in sight. Assessing the four month long Stelco strike in Hamilton, Ontario, during 1981 an official of the steel workers' union cogently summarized the relationship between unions and class consciousness: "I think it's (the strike) class antagonism, but it's expressed in individual terms. It's not that a worker goes on strike because he hates capitalism, but because one particular boss isn't treating him well" (Peter Warrian, quoted in the *Globe and Mail*, 4 December 1981).

HIGHLIGHT

1. Worker resistance can take various forms ranging from strikes to informal mechanisms at the work group level that restrict production.
2. The possible types of work groups are related to the nature of production. For example, coal mines will develop a different work group structure than assembly lines.
3. In the early years of industrialization, a working class culture was maintained through many community institutions and social relations as well as through interactions at the workplace.
4. The trade union is the main institution involved in the promotion of the rights of the working class.
5. Trade unionism in Canada has proceeded in fits and starts. The attitude of the state towards unions has been a major factor influencing unionization.
6. Despite the existence of strikes, it is not possible to argue that workers have developed political class consciousness and will renounce the capitalist system of production.

Conclusion

A rather expansive terrain has been covered in the treatment of the meaning, nature and organization of work. We will conclude by summarizing some of the dominant themes. The first theme is change. Industrialization dramatically altered the content of the labor process and the structure of the workplace. There is an organic link between economic forces and changing work relations. Power is the second theme. It constitutes a pervasive feature of work under capitalism. Work is synonymous with power relations mainly because most people today are employees who, by definition, occupy positions of relative subordination. Two final themes are found in the dialectic of control and resistance. Over the decades managers have attempted to elicit co-operative and productive work behavior. These strategies of control run the gamut from the subtle and enlightened—the 'golden handcuffs' of attractive salary and benefits packages—to the coercive and punitive—threat of dismissal for the least infraction of the 'rules'. But despite management practices, evidence exists of workers registering their dissatisfaction with job conditions.

The reader who began the chapter hopeful for the future of work may now harbor some pessimism. Rinehart (1975:ch. 6) ended his study of work alienation by critically assessing five solutions to contemporary work problems—leisure, automation, human relations, unions and workers' control. Some of these solutions deserve reconsideration in light of recent developments.

Automation, more than ever before, may appear to hold out great promise. Micro-chip technology has revolutionized information processing capabilities so tremendously that we stand on the verge of a technological breakthrough observers refer to as the 'third industrial revolution'. Automation undoubtedly has the capacity to eliminate much white-collar drudge work and increase leisure time. But these initially favorable reactions must be tempered in view of research showing a net negative impact. Menzies' (1981) study of the effects of automated office technology on female clerical employment in Canada paints a bleak scenario. While professional work will be upgraded, there will be a corresponding deskilling and displacement of lower-level clerical personnel. Menzies predicts widespread unemployment of female clerks by 1990. In short, it is dangerous to uncritically embrace the immediate benefits of new technologies.

Quality of Working Life programs are another potential solution currently receiving much attention in management quarters. Some of the efforts to humanize work are directed at undoing the excesses of Taylorism. Fragmented and meaningless tasks can be 'enriched' to provide more of a challenge. The Ontario government is actively promoting such changes through its Quality of Working Life Centre. The list of major corporations to embark upon such plans includes Shell Oil, General Foods, and Syncrude. Critics argue, however, that QWL is just a new approach to the old problem of worker motivation (Schwartz 1981). Redesigned jobs will allow workers more opportunity to use their abilities and realize their aspirations. But this usually falls short of making significant and lasting adjustments to the authority structure of the organization. Greater discretion and responsibility in task planning and execution is possible—a recognizable improvement—but the sources of worker powerlessness persist.

In many respects we find ourselves like Rinehart, calling for workers' control over production as the most viable means of enhancing the quality of working life. One need not, however, advocate the total transformation of society to accept the advantages of having enterprises co-operatively owned and run by workers. Workers' control, according to Rinehart (1975:156), aims "to dismantle the power of capitalist employers and their bureaucratic minions, replacing them not with another elite which speaks in the name of workers but with democratically organized bodies of workers."[17] There are, in fact, a small number of Canadian firms which have achieved a significant level of worker participation in management (See Nightingale, 1982).

We will end with a comment on the role of unions in democratizing the workplace. Critics of business unionism tend to dismiss North American unions as vehicles for social change. Present union leadership, they point out, has a big stake in maintaining the status quo. There are signs of change, however, which may bode well for the future. One such indication of a new direction in Canadian unions towards greater responsiveness to rank-and-file concerns was the election of Dave Patterson to the leadership of the United Steel Workers' District 6 (central and eastern Canada) (see Roberts 1981). The old guard leadership was displaced by a swell of support for a more progressive and nationalistic vision of unionism. Obviously for unions to have more influence in the course of socio-economic change they will have to recruit unorganized workers into their fold. More generally, it is clear that whether through unions or political parties workers must develop their own organizations as tools of constructive opposition and reform.

NOTES

[1]For a good overview of the philosophical meanings of work see Mills 1956:215-38; Anthony 1977:ch. 1; Watson 1980:ch. 4.

[2]See Knight (1975) for a bibliography of published materials on company towns in Canada and the U.S.

[3]The participation rate is calculated as follows: the number of persons in the labor force divided by the population or group aged 14 years of age or older.

[4]There is a male bias in the concept of a labor force, for it assumes that only individuals working for wages are employed. This neglects the economic contribution of wives performing unpaid labor inside the home.

[5]Devereaux and Rechnitzer (1980) report that next to teaching, clerical work is the most likely job for women with BA degrees. Moreover, 40 percent of women with business diplomas end up as clerks.

[6]The high percentage of women in the medicine and health category is accounted for by nurses, nurses aides, physical and occupational therapists—not medical doctors.

[7]Bossens (1976) examines the position of women in Canadian banks, showing how they tend to be clustered in the lower clerical ranks and under-represented in management. The banks admit there are problems of discrimination. The Royal Bank's internal task force on the status of women, for instance, reported in 1977 that the organization's employment policies, while formally equitable in fact discriminated against women (see Lowe, 1980b:87).

[8]The French middle class in the town predominated in commercial services, the professions and small businesses. But as Hughes points out, these traditional occupations were not central to the emerging industrial structure of the province.

[9]Cost accounting allows the capitalist to calculate how each factor of production, including labor, contributes to overall profits.

[10]This is one of the best examples of what is known as a *serendipitous* research finding; those which are unexpected but nonetheless useful in opening up research frontiers or shedding new light on old problems. For a good discussion of serendipity in research see Merton (1968:157-62).

[11]Another study by Roy (1959) shows how work groups also provide a protective social milieux which shelters the worker from the more alienating and undesirable aspects of the job. He describes how a group of four machine operators performing monotonous tasks kept from "going nuts" by engaging in simple games and horse-play.

[12]The journal *Labor/Le Travailleur* is the best source of scholarship in this area. For an overview and critique of the field see the articles by Kealey (1981) and Bercuson (1981).

[13]Craft unions represent only the better-paid and more highly skilled craftworkers, whereas industrial unions attempt to organize all workers in an industry regardless of their job. The distinction historically has political overtones, with the craft unions being more conservative. Further, it was by defeating the principle of 'dual unionism'—two unions operating in the same industry or occupation—that the internationals managed to stifle Canadian unions.

[14]Unionization levels for other industries are as follows: construction 58.2 percent; transportation, communications and utilities 52.8 percent; forestry 50 percent; manufacturing 45.7 percent; mines, quarries and oil wells 38 percent; service industries 22.3 percent; and trade 8.1 percent.

[15]The state has also intervened in the relations between labor and capital by establishing legislation governing minimum wages, employment standards and health and safety codes.

[16]White (1981) argues that for many workers performing monotonous and unrewarding work, their major interests and sources of life satisfaction are found outside the workplace in family life, leisure activities and friendships.

[17]A recent article on a U.S. agricultural co-operative provides relevant insights. Wells (1981) reports that a better quality of working life must involve more than just a higher income; greater control over production facilitated by collective ownership was found to directly decrease alienation.

SUGGESTED READINGS

Labor and Monopoly Capital, Harry Braverman. New York: Monthly Review Press, 1974. The first comprehensive Marxist analysis of the labor process, this seminal study raised many of the research issues and debates now at the centre of the new industrial sociology.

Manufacturing Consent, Michael Burawoy. Chicago: University of Chicago Press, 1979. Probably the best piece of empirical research in industrial sociology in the last decade, this study of changing social relations in a factory over a thirty year period addresses the question of why workers exert themselves and acquiesce to their own exploitation.

Hardrock Mining, Wallace Clement. Toronto: McClelland and Stewart, 1981. A case study of the International Nickel Corporation, focusing on changing technology and industrial relations.

Contested Terrain, Richard Edwards. New York: Basic Books, 1979. A major advance in labor market segmentation theory, this book hypothesizes three major labor market segments based on different techniques firms use for controlling work.

The Politics of Work and Occupations, Geoff Esland and Graeme Salaman (eds.). Toronto: University of Toronto Press, 1980. A collection of essays by British authors on the political nature of work and the effects of this on employees.

Work in the Canadian Context, Katherina L.P. Lundy and Barbara D. Warme (eds.). Toronto: Butterworths, 1981. An anthology of Canadian contributions to the study of work from a variety of perspectives centring around three themes: work and the political economy, the division of labor, and conflicts of interest.

Labor and Capital in Canada, H. Claire Pentland. Toronto: James Lorimer, 1981. For years an 'under-ground classic', this pathbreaking study combines the staples perspective with a class analysis to examine the organization of work in pre-Confederation Canada.

The Tyranny of Work, James Rinehart. Don Mills: Longman Canada, 1975. This book analyzes the origins and contemporary manifestations of the problem of worker alienation, showing this to be a normal condition in society.

Industrialization in Canada, Joseph Smucker. Scarborough: Prentice-Hall, 1980. This textbook provides a cogent sociological analysis of the industrialization process in Canada, using as the central theme the contradictions between dominant liberal values and daily experiences on the job.

The Family, Education and the Productive Process

WOMEN, THE FAMILY AND THE PRODUCTIVE PROCESS

Dorothy E. Smith

A portion of this chapter has appeared as part of "Women's Inequality and the Family," in A. Moscovitch and L. Drover (eds.), *Inequality*, Toronto: University of Toronto Press, 1981.

Introduction

In the foregoing chapter, attention focussed on the ways in which, particularly within the capitalist mode of production, various forms of work organization are imposed on employees. The ways in which employees resisted such organization were also analysed. This chapter will provide an analysis of the integration of the mode of production and the family, and the consequences of the nature of this integration upon the status of women.

In the late nineteenth and early twentieth centuries, women struggled to secure equality as citizens. They sought higher education, access to the professions, an enlarged sphere of political influence, changes in the laws governing marriage which would enable them to own property independently of their husbands, and to control their own earnings. Above all, they sought the vote as a means to express women's interests and concerns.

On the whole, however, they did not question the division of labor that defined women's spheres as the home and children, and men's the world of paid employment, business and professions—the sphere of economic action. Though working class women were employed in factories, this was for many viewed as an interlude between their childhood and, marriage and children; or as a necessary evil. Even among working class women who earned money, a large proportion did so within the domestic sphere either as domestic servants, by taking in boarders, or by doing piece-work in their own homes.

Within the dominant classes, both women and men viewed dominant class women as exercising a significant moral leadership within their own sphere. Women were actively involved in voluntary associations which policed the lives of the poor in the name of charity. They developed policies for the education of working class women and worked to advance the science of 'domestic economy.' They were active in organizations such as the 'Women's Institutes' (founded in Canada) which were devoted to the dissemination of advances in domestic technology. Women active in the women's movement of that time saw women as potentially important in the progress toward a civilized and peaceful order. Their political initiatives, including the struggle for the vote itself, were seen as a means by which the values of the domestic sphere would be felt in the public realm. But while they recognized and attacked their political powerlessness, they did not question women's position in the family and their special relation to children. In large part their political concerns arose out of, and took for granted, their situation in the domestic sphere.

The resurgence of the women's movement in the 1960s raised more fundamental questions than previously. Women had been voting for forty years, but they had not achieved political equality. If anything, their distinctive sphere of action had declined. Other and deeper lying questions also began to emerge concerning the significance of the family, as such, in creating women's inequality. Questions were raised about the extent of men's control of the ideological apparatus of society, i.e. those processes largely controlled by men which produced and distributed knowledge, symbols, images, information, ideas, etc. through which women and men could understand themselves, each other, and the world. In effect, the new women's movement disclosed a whole culture as one-sided. Masquerading as objective, culture was seen to conceal a view of the world from the particular perspective of men. Women's experience, concerns, and needs lacked ideological vehicles of expression. Their feelings and visions lacked artistic and religious form. Their encounter with the actualities of the world lacked knowledge, science, and discourse. This was the 'alienation of culture'.

Questions were also raised about women's right to control their own bodies. Formerly, women had taken for granted that their sexuality and their capacity to produce children was transferred to their husband on marriage. It had perhaps not been clear to our mothers and grandmothers that this was the deal, but they understood its conventions. They knew that adultery by a women was occasion for divorce, and that their husbands had a right to their sexual advances. This, then, was an alienation of women's bodies.

The personal subordination of women to men through work was also called into question. The responsibility women undertook for the rearing of children, for housework, for clerical and secretarial services, for the wide range of subordinate but essential work which women perform directly for men was seen as part of a division of labor in society which subordinated women to men in a pervasive manner. Oppression was built into the routine of women's lives, into the activities and relationships in which they came into being as people.

In these three areas—the alienation of culture, the alienation of control of their bodies, and in the subordination built into their work, women came to recognize problems of a different order than those of political expression. They began to challenge their lack of power at all levels of the social process. The challenge was not seen as a feature of an impersonal order. It was embedded in the interpersonal relations between women and men in the family, on the job, in trade unions, in politics, in education, in arts, literature, music, and science. The slogan 'the personal is political' expressed women's new understanding that the power relations constitutive of their inequality were embedded in the directly personal relations between women and men. At the same time, they were properties of the power relations of a whole society. 'Political', in this context, took on a new meaning. It went vastly beyond application to the institutions of the contemporary state to embrace any relation in which inequities of power were located. Such inequities were seen not as isolated interpersonal phenomena but as a general characteristic of society that could be defined as *patriarchy*. As a consequence of a recognition of patriarchy, women realized that political organization and action should address all levels of the relation between women and men from the most intimate and personal to the most public and general.

Patriarchy.   The new perspective represented a transformation of the *problematic* of the women's movement. A problematic defines the area in which the problems to be addressed by political organization and action, or to be investigated by the researcher, lie. The problematic defined by the women's movement of the late nineteenth and early twentieth centuries located the issues and questions in the political sphere. The contemporary women's movement enlarged that problematic and redefined it to encompass all levels of relations between women and men. The concept of patriarchy enunciated this problematic and gave it political expression.

As 'patriarchy' came to be used in the women's movement, it had little to do at first with anthropological and historical usages identifying a particular form of family organization. Rather, it expressed women's directly personal experience of men's domination as a general societal attribute. It expressed the distinctively female experience of oppression. As women began to organize and sought to create means of expression and political action, the concept of patriarchy came to identify the *totality of male domination* and its pervasiveness in women's lives. Politically it identified the importance for women of acting and organizing independently of men, of removing themselves from men's authority, of learning how to speak to one another outside forms imposed by men, of seeking other ways of relating sexually, of creating the beginnings of a 'community' of women within a society dominated by men. In theory and research the lineaments of patriarchy were sought in other cultures and other historical forms. As a result, the domination of men over women came to be seen as a universal pattern, present in all societies. It therefore required examination, understanding and confrontation.

In comparison to this new approach, conventional political economic analyses of women's inequality were at first incapable of embracing the specifically personal character of women's subordination to men. The boundaries of political economy were confined to the boundaries of the social relations of the economy. They stopped short at the doorway of household economic organization, where many of life's necessities are dealt with.

In the late nineteenth century, Frederich Engels wrote a major theoretical work, *The Origin of the Family, Private Property and the State*, which was the first real attempt to go beyond the limitations of conventional analysis. But while this work was of considerable theoretical importance, it also sidelined gender relations as a topic for political economy.

In Engel's view, women had always taken responsibility for the domestic sphere of labor. Prior to the emergence of private property, however, women's domestic work related them directly to society. In such societies, Engels thought, women participated as equals with men. The gender division of labor did not lead, in his view, to women's inequality. The key to their subordination lay in a change not in the division of labor, but in the social relations through which their work was tied in to the larger society. The crucial change occurred with the development of private property.

When private property was established, so were the bases of class society. Private property, vested in an individual man as head of a family, transformed the relation of women's work to society. Her labor became a personal service to the individual man. Consequently, her relation to society was mediated by him. She occupied a private, low profile and low status position. The subordination of women was thus founded in the very change which excluded them from the sphere of political economy. Engels held that women's inequality would be done away with when private property, the base of class relations, was abolished.

Engels' thinking, important as it has been, had the paradoxical effect of excluding the relations between women and men from consideration by political economists. Women's subordination to men was located in the 'private' sphere into which political economy did not intrude. According to Engels, women's subordination happened at the beginning of history, and had no special connection with capitalist social relations. Finally, his work provided theoretical justification for subsuming women's inequality under the inequalities of class. Class and private property were fundamental. Gender inequalities were derivative. The abolition of class and private property would eliminate the bases of women's inequality. Thus, in terms of possible political action, Engels' theory provided grounds for subordinating women's issues to class issues.

Patriarchy and Class. In the development of the women's movement, individuals focussing on patriarchy opposed those stressing class when attempting to explain women's situation. The concept of patriarchy focussed on both the domination of women by men and upon that domination as a widespread general characteristic of gender relations in all kinds of societies. Hence, the struggle must be women against men. In contrast, those who embraced the class analysis, linked women's emancipation to a wider struggle to transform the bases of class society. However, their analysis was rooted in a tradition of economic and political thinking quite unable, and in practice, quite unwilling, to concede anything distinctive to the situation of women. Moreover, it was totally unable to embrace the problems of men's direct personal domination over women.

Gradually, a modification began to emerge in the women's movement. For the most part, it involved attempts to incorporate the family into the conceptual systems of political economy. One way of achieving this objective was by arguing that the current division of domestic labor in the family was a relic of the earlier feudal model of production. Consequently, women's labor in the family produced only use values for its members. By way of comparison, labor incorporated into later capitalist social relations produced both use and exchange values.

A number of writers provided theoretical specifications of the ways in which women's domestic labor contributed to the creation of value or surplus value. More recently, socialist theorists in the women's movement have begun to put forward analyses of the interpenetration of patriarchy and capitalism. This chapter carries forward this type of examination.

Overall, the chapter will provide a political economic analysis of patriarchy and explore women's experience of men's domination as it is related to class. Discussion can begin by recognizing that while criticisms can be raised of Engel's work, his method is valuable. It is a method which takes an actual work process and examines the social relations which tie it into a larger social process. Engels did not see the division of labor simply as a distribution of work roles. Rather, he saw a work process as connected to more general social relations. The implication is that we can begin to understand the inner life and work of the family and the personal relations of power between husband and wife as both situated in, and determined by, the general economic and political relations of a mode of production.

Behind the personal relations of women and men in the familial context are economic and political processes providing the conditions, exigencies, opportunities, powers, and weaknesses of the interpersonal process. Class is one major social relation to which the social and economic organization of the family are connected.

Theorists of, and research into, phenomena of class have also been male biased. Both theorists and the research they do embody the same assumptions as those demarcating the sphere of the economy from that of domesticity. Moreover, in both non-Marxist and Marxist accounts of class, women are tacked onto definitions of class based on male experience. Non-Marxists treat women as members of families from which they derive their class status. When men are under discussion their class is treated as an individual matter and not as something that derives from family. Marxists sometimes treat the family as *reproducing* class and hence as existing outside class.

Class. In general, we approach class as identifying a complex of social relations organizing the exploitation of one section of society by another. In the nineteenth century, it was easy to define class in terms of *individual* ownership or non-ownership of the means of production. But in the twentieth century, ownership has developed as a much more complex issue. There is now a division of labor within ownership itself (between owners and managers), and a differentiation of the processes of control into many specialized functions. The continuity of class from one generation to the next as will be seen in Education and the Correspondence Principle (chapter 10) has also come to involve a specialized division of labor as evident in the processes of socialization and education. The social organization of class is thus much more complex now than previously.

Underlying the contemporary elaborate division of labor is exploitation. Exploitation in this usage is not a moral but a technical term. It refers to that relation (or relations) through which a dominant class appropriates the surplus labor of the class it dominates. The dominated class labors to produce what is sufficient, not only for its own subsistence, but also for the subsistence of the dominant class (or classes) and its means of dominance. In capitalist society, ownership and control of the means of production by the dominant class is the basis of its capacity to exploit the working class. Lacking ownership of the means of production, the working class must sell its labor-power to the capitalist who makes use of the worker's labor to produce value approximately equivalent to the cost of his subsistence plus value over and above that which the capitalist appropriates (surplus value).

The division of labor within ownership, the emergence of large scale, corporate forms of holding and accumulating capital—the monopoly form of capital—along with the survival of smaller competitive forms of capitalism, have complicated the class picture of our time. Not surprisingly, an extensive theoretical literature analysing contemporary class has developed.

In this chapter, a slightly broader definition than in other chapters will be given to the 'dominant class'. It will include those who can be said to control capital through the ownership of shares and those who directly manage capital as the executives and managers of corporate enterprises. It will include also those in positions of influence and power in the elaborate ruling apparatus of government and professions. That apparatus is essential in the administrative, legal, and ideological support of the exploitative relation as well as through its control of the uses of physical force. Also included will be the so-called old petty bourgeoisie. The term dominant class, however, does not correspond to the colloquial term 'middle class' when that is equated with white-collar, non-manual workers. Many of them are related to capital in essentially the same way as the manual working class. Both are exploited either directly or through the difference between their pay and the contribution they make in their work to the realization of surplus value.

The key characteristic of class in capitalism, is exploitation. But this characteristic does not become evident in any simple way. It is not a mechanical process. Constant organizational activity at many points on the part of the dominant classes is necessary to maintain a working class which must routinely sell its labor-power to survive and thereby contribute to the generation of surplus value. Class in contemporary capitalism is a complex of relations organizing and fixing the relationships of individuals as exploiters and exploited. Although it plays a different role at different levels and in different segments of the class structure, the family is an integral part of this organization.

Exploitation is a key relation in capitalism because, as mentioned earlier, it is also its central dynamic. It is through exploitation and the creation of surplus value that the accumulative and expansive dynamic of capital arises. As capital expands, the material and social forms of society are changed. In turn, expansion reorganizes relations, requires and engenders new forms of property, new technologies, new divisions of labor, new skills, new organizational forms, and new forms of control and management to ensure that the fundamental relation of exploitation remains in place. These and other innovations entail changing relations among women and men in their work places and families. The process of change is itself dynamic and at any given moment we catch only an atemporal slice of an unceasing process. Hence, we must not impose a false fixity upon it. We must try to preserve a sense of its moving character. To understand the properties, movement, and 'structure' of the present we must be able to separate the strands of development determining its character.

The changing forms of family can be located within this process. In other words, it is possible to examine the social relations of class and the way in which they affect the family. In this way, we will be able to see the origins of the present forms of women's subordination in the early development of capitalism. We will also try to understand the distinctive form taken by the family in different classes. The history of the working class family and the forms of subordination to men experienced by working class women are not the same as those of dominant-class women. For example, the type of family we have taken so much for granted, in which women are dependent upon a man who brings in the family income, is relatively new. In order to address the differences in family organization and the social relations, we will examine the history of the dominant-class family separately from that of the working class family.

HIGHLIGHT

1. In the late nineteenth and early twentieth centuries, the women's movement concentrated on winning the vote. Recently the movement has recognized the patriarchal structure of society in which male dominance is found in all areas of human endeavor.
2. In an early work on the family, Engels argued that the subordination of women started with the development of private property. Consequently, if private property were abolished, the subordination of women would disappear.
3. In terms of change, some women stress that the primary struggle is between men and women. Others feel that the class dimension is primary. This chapter is based on the idea that the two are linked.
4. In this chapter, the term dominant class will be used to describe those who participate in the organization of the extraction of surplus labor from the working class.

The Transition to Capitalism, Independent Commodity Production, and the Status of Wives

Women and Early Capitalism.   If we look at the forms of household, family, and marriage in pre-capitalistic times, and examine those classes of society out of which the early capitalist manufacturers later emerged, we find something rather different from later family structures. We find a relation between household and workshop rather like that between two halves of a single enterprise. The household provided the subsistence of those who worked in the workshop. Many, particularly the apprentices, lived-in. Those who did not were fed while they were on the job. Moreover, a wife's role was far from confined to the domestic setting. She functioned more like a manager, overseeing the workers, keeping the accounts, and assisting in the workshop. Her contribution in these ways was so important that domestic servants often were needed to release her for duties of this kind. She might also trade or carry on a craft independently of her husband. In many types of craft or trade, the enterprise was viewed as owned by husband and wife in common so that if he died she might continue, either running it herself or bringing someone in to run it. With the rise of capitalism, however, a very different relation between husband and wife emerged.

The expansion of the market and the accumulation of capital transformed both the relations between master and workmen in the workshop and the relations between husband and wife in the home. Originally, the master shared the same work as his journeymen and apprentices. Granted, he was more skilled and experienced. But he was similar to those who worked under him. He was also a man who bought labor-power and managed labor to produce for an impersonal market. With the further development of capitalism, however, the managing function rapidly became separated from the labor process. Now master and journeyman did radically different things.

At the same time, existing law was revised to accommodate the newly emerging relations which subordinated a married woman's status fully under that of her husband. He now became the exclusive representative of the family in the market place. She had no civil existence of her own. She could not own property. Her earnings were his. She could not even commit a crime (with the exception of treason and murder of her husband) because it was held that she acted under her husband's direction. Any crime she committed was by definition his.

In essence, the new situation represented an organization of marriage and family which subordinated the family resources fully to the capitalist enterprise. The husband could draw upon those resources to the ultimate to support his business. He could squeeze resources needed for subsistence, enforce the most rigorous thrift, and appropriate property his wife inherited in order to keep his enterprise going. In the early development of capitalism there were a few sources of capital outside the family, hence the significance of this kind of control.

Furthermore, the continuity of capital required the continuity of an enterprise beyond the lifetime of its founder. That is, a man must have an heir who could enter the business and become identified with it as its owner if the capital which had been accumulated in it was to be perpetuated. Women, as wives, provided the essential links in a chain among men. A man's exclusive access to his wife's sexuality therefore must be guaranteed. As a consequence, the older, laxer sexual morality disappeared and was replaced by severe restraints upon women's sexuality.

This early form of organizing the capitalist enterprise and of providing for the continuity of capital was increasingly strained as capital accumulated. It was no longer adequate to embrace the size and complexity of enterprise and organization, or to meet the capital needs emerging in the latter half of the nineteenth century. The result was that over time the individual form of ownership was progressively displaced by (though it had by no means disappeared) and lost ground to, a new form of property relation, the corporation.

The corporation is a property relation. It specifies the rights and liabilities of those who, for example, pool their capital in the form of purchases of stock in a common enterprise. The emergence of the corporation obviously meant that property and the continuity of capital no longer depended upon the family and upon the complete subordination of women as economic actors to their husbands. Hence, family relations in the dominant classes, formerly structured by a situation in which individuals rather than companies assumed the rights and obligations of property ownership, now took on a different character.

The Transition in Canada.   The transition from a pre-capitalist to a capitalist mode of production can be found relatively recently in the history of Canadian rural family organization. However, the Canadian record is less straightforward than in Europe because of the character of the Canadian economy and its relation to the two imperial powers, Britain and the United States.

As new lands were opened up by the railroad in the West, the homesteading patterns which developed the eastern farmlands a hundred years earlier were replicated (though with a somewhat different technological base). In the 1930s, homesteading patterns in Dawson Creek, British Columbia, showed a division of labor little different from that described by Susannah Moodie and Catherine Parr Traill in early nineteenth century Upper Canada (Ontario). But behind the scene in Dawson Creek were different commercial and property-holding institutions. Once the homestead of the 1930s developed beyond the subsistence level of production, it was rapidly tied in to an economic organization very different from that characterizing early nineteenth century Upper Canada. Economic institutions such as the joint stock company developed elsewhere—in Britain or the United States—had entered the Canadian economic scene full-blown. Such institutions structured the type of economic activity such as farming and mining that naturally thrived in view of Canada's resources. Similarly, the economic institutions which matured in eastern Canada organized and articulated the localized forms of enterprise developing in the western provinces.

Recognizing that behavior is structured by institutional constraints, we can contrast the experience of women in the context of a household and farm producing its own subsistence for a largely localized market—as in Upper Canada—with the internal relations of a farming family fully subordinated to the market process. The former closely resembles the pre-capitalist form. The latter represents a type of single unit, small-scale capitalist enterprise.

Nellie McClung's autobiography gives us a picture of an interdependent organization of household and enterprise in which the housewife plays a significant part. Though her parents' farm was producing for a market, it also produced most of the subsistence of the family and other workers.

> An Ontario farm, in the early '80's was a busy place, and everyone on our farm moved briskly. My father often said of my mother that she could keep forty people busy. She certainly could think of things for people to do. Maybe that was one reason for my enjoying the farmyard so much. I loved to sit on the top rail of the fence, and luxuriantly do nothing, when I was well out of the range of her vision. Mother herself worked harder than anyone. She was the first up in the morning and the last one to go to bed at night. Our teams were on the land, and the Monday morning washing on the line well ahead of the neighbours! (McClung 1964:27)

It is clear from McClung's account that her mother, in this relationship with the household, had a role going beyond that merely of laboring to produce subsistence. It was an organizational and managerial role in which the daily scheduling of work and the mobilizing of available labor resources were part of the housewife's work. Characteristically, men produced largely for a regional market. As far as possible the subsistence of family members and hired hands would be produced by the women, wives, daughters and servants. A housewife in such a household had rights in her own products so that when there was a surplus she would market it herself. So housewives brought butter, eggs, bacon, and preserves to the market place.

In the earlier period a successful homestead would develop towards the type of household-enterprise organization described by McClung. At later stages homesteading entered a very different set of economic relations. The reasons for this are as follows.

The homestead constitutes a subsistence economy. The division of labor between husband and wife, and children as they are able, produces virtually all the family needs to survive. The contribution of both husband and wife is essential. It is hard to see how issues of relative power and status arise in such a context. However, when the homestead develops to the point of producing a marketable surplus it enters economic relations already formed in which men are the economic agents. Consequently, the relation of household and enterprise is changed. The man as economic agent enters commercial and financial relations as an individual. Farm and household policies are subordinated to the exigencies of the market, loans, credit, mortgages, etc. Even before subsistence, the farm had to produce a cash crop to enable the farmer to service his debt.

In a Canadian novel based on her own experience as a school teacher boarding with a prairie farm family in the 1920s, Martha Ostenso tells the story of the tyranny of a farmer over his wife and daughters under such conditions. She also reveals the special drudgery of his wife's existence (Ostenso 1967). There are superficial similarities to the scene described by McClung, but fundamental differences. What has happened between the childhood scene of the 1880s described by McClung and that described by Ostenso in the 1920s are changes in the political economy of Canadian farming. The late nineteenth century saw a rapid expansion of railroads accompanied with land settlement policies entailing extensive immigration. The immigrants who built the wheat economy of the Canadian prairies were generally financed by mortgages of their land and bank loans for tools, seed, and other necessities for which their crop stood as collateral.

Ostenso's novel turns on the fact that survival for the farmer in this squeeze depended on the production of a cash crop, often a single cash crop. Everything had to be subordinated to that, for everything was lost if it was not produced. Subsistence must be subordinated to production for the market. Women's labor must be withdrawn from the household and substituted for hired labor in working the land. Furthermore, to the extent that she made clothes and prepared and preserved food, her labor was substituted as far as possible for labor embodied in manufactured ('storebought') commodities. Increased inputs of her labor replaced the lack of money at every possible point in the farming enterprise. Her time and energy, indeed her life, were treated as inexhaustible. She must, in addition, bear children because their labor was also essential.

The property form identified the farm with the individual male farmer. His success in accumulating above what he had to pay out in interest depended generally upon exploiting the labor of women, both in the house and on the land. This is the situation Nellie McClung presents to typify the injustices and sufferings of farm women:

> I remember once attending the funeral of a woman who had been doing the work for a family of six children and three hired men, and she had not even a baby carriage to make her work lighter. When the last baby was three days old, just in threshing time, she died. Suddenly, and without warning, the power went off, and she quit without notice. The bereaved husband was the most astonished man in the world. He had never known Jane to do a thing like that before, and he could not get over it. In threshing time, too! (McClung 1972:114)

Farm women of that period were vividly conscious of this relation and of the injustice of the laws of matrimonial property which enabled the husband to appropriate as his what the labor of both had created. In 1910, a Saskatchewan farmeress (self-styled) stated the issue as follows:

> It may not be so in every part of the province, but here it is not the bachelor who is making the most rapid progress, buying land and in every way improving the country, but it is the married men—and why? One wonders

if the women have nothing to do with this. Who does the economizing if not the women? And pray tell me what incentive a women has to work longer hours every day than her husband, if she is to have no say in the selling or mortgaging of land her hard work has helped to pay for? Is it not the women who deny themselves most when the bills come due? It is not for myself that I so much want our rights as for our unfortunate sisters who, no matter how hard they toil, can never get what they merit. Several women in this neighbourhood have land, and I do not know of one who is not anxious for the dower law and homesteads for women, and most of them for equal suffrage (Cook and Mitchinson 1976:111).

In the political economy of prairie development, women at this period, such as those described in this passage, were doing much the same kind of work as they did on the Ontario farm of the nineteenth century. Yet once again the social relations organizing their work and their relation to their husbands were very different. Rather than playing a leading managerial role in the household/enterprise as a whole, they became as the above quotation indicates, subordinated to a market and financial structure through their husband. He, as property owner, acted as economic agent. He extracted surplus labor from his wife, the results of which were allocated to the mortgage and loan system.

Fighting Back.   Women sought ways of controlling their exploitation and their vulnerable dependence upon a man's economic ability. They struggled against the availability of alcohol so that a man couldn't drink away his wife's as well as his own source of livelihood. Women also fought for the vote as a means to change the laws through which they were exploited. There were also other ways in which they could retaliate. One was the withdrawal of women's participation in the labor on the farm.

In time, the extreme situations described by Nellie McClung and Martha Ostenso, where the farmer used his wife's and daughter's labor in both the home and on the fields disappeared as farmers grew in affluence. It was possible then for women to avoid being drawn into labor on the farm by the conscious institutionalization of a division of labor confining women to household tasks. A woman in British Columbia described how her mother prevented her from acquiring the manual skills and strength which would make her useful in the farming enterprise of her future husband. Lacking strength and competence, she would be less likely to be called upon to help. A similar practice has been described on contemporary farms in Saskatchewan (Kohl 1976:70-1).

Property rights defining the man as economic actor have only recently begun to be modified. The celebrated Murdoch case drew the attention of rural women to the fact, of which many were unaware, that their labor did not entitle them to a share of the property upon dissolution of a marriage. Their situation was still very much as the Saskatchewan farmeress described it in 1910. Mrs. Murdoch had worked for twenty-five years on her husband's ranch, doing more than the domestic work (Murdoch v. Murdoch 1976). A large part of the work of cattle ranching she did herself, since in addition to what she did when her husband was there, she took over the whole enterprise for the five months of the year he took paid employment. Yet when her marriage broke down her labor did not, in the view of the courts, entitle her to a share of the property she had helped create. Even the dissenting opinion of Justice Bora Laskin did not recognize the wife's contribution of labor to the overall enterprise as giving her any claim on the property. He disagreed with the other justices only on the grounds that her contribution had been exceptional. As a general principle, he held to the traditional view that the labor of a wife gave her no equal claim to shared property.

In the farm setting there is no physical separation of household and enterprise. Women's work in and around the household—both as direct producers (gardening, tending livestock, etc.) and in processing and storing farm produce—sharply reduces the costs of maintaining the family labor force and feeding hired workers. Nevertheless, the older complementary relation of the Ontario farm in the nineteenth century had disappeared, and with it the managerial role played, for example, by Nellie McClung's mother. The organization of the farm as an economic unit is vested in the person of the husband. Now a wife is not viewed as part of the enterprise. Men view women as "helpers," and women themselves often underestimate their own indispensable contribution to the farm (Carey 1978). In addition, the man as economic actor and property owner often connects the farm to large-scale agribusiness.

For example, in some cases large farm businesses, like Purina, supply the farmer with livestock, feed and a certain amount of money. In return, the farmer supplies the land, machinery and labor. In this relation, women's domestic labor, the economies she can achieve, the productive contribution to the family's subsistence she makes, the direct help she provides to the farming operation, and sometimes her cash earnings from part-time work outside, contribute to the profits of agribusiness. Carey points out that "agribusiness corporations have indirectly admitted that they cannot pay anyone to work for them as cheaply as a farmer, his wife and children would work for a family farm" (Carey 1978).

In the setting of the Canadian rural economy we can see the change from a form of the family and household organization which is of an immediately pre-capitalist type in which women play a significant role to a form which is fully capitalist in its subordination of household and domestic labor to the requirements of an enterprise employing wage labor and fully knitted into market and financial relations. The enterprise is identified with an individual man who is its owner, and who is the sole economic agent. The wife becomes relegated to a domestic sphere distinct from the enterprise but subordinated to it. The analogous change accompanying the rise of capitalism in Britain in the late eighteenth and early nineteenth centuries, and in the first half of the nineteenth century in the United States, resulted in a family type which we know as distinctively Victorian.

HIGHLIGHT

1. In pre-capitalistic times, in the class from which manufacturers would eventually arise, women were equal to men and their work was valued as a meaningful contribution to a family enterprise. In capitalist times, in similar families, women became subordinate to men.
2. In Canada, examples of rural families in which women participate on an equal footing with men can be found. Such families produced little for an external market. Later, similar families became integrated into a larger market, and in these circumstances women became subordinated to men.
3. Women did not always accept their subordination and devised many ways of fighting back. Nonetheless, on the contemporary farm, women have not acquired the degree of equality they once had.

Corporate Capitalism and the Changing Role of Women of the Dominant Classes

Marx tells us that the rise of capitalism is a process by which formerly personalized interdependent relations among individuals are absorbed by the market. That is, the market links very large numbers of anonymous buyers and sellers in an impersonal and autonomous process. Their interdependence appears as external to individuals, i.e. imposed on them by market forces. This process which can be referred to as one of 'externalization', continues with the rise of monopoly capitalism as does the process of corporate concentration.

The concentration of capital in the corporate form developed rapidly in Canada. It began in the period just before the First World War when the number of companies actually declined as a result of the process of concentration. These developments coincided with similar ones in the United States. They were accompanied by the development of government administrative structures and legal forms essential to give substence to the corporation as an economic actor. Similar developments were slower in Canada than in the United States. In Canada, agriculture did not lose its leading position until the 1930s. But, when these processes did begin they followed essentially the same path as developments in the United States.

Over a period of time the corporate form became the legal norm for all sizes of business. Organizationally, the corporation completes the separation of family from household. The early capitalist enterprise identified with an individual, or a partnership of individuals who depended heavily for capital and for reliable managerial assistance upon extended family resources. The family of the dominant classes included more than the household. It often involved the linking of more than one privately owned enterprise, profession, or political office.

The result was that the separation of the family from the business world was blurred. Economic organization was supported and organized by kin and familial relations in a nepotic relationship. Sons, sons-in-law, cousins, and nephews, formed a network of connections united in a common loyalty to a family and to a family name on which the credit of each member depended.

Women were at the heart of the organization of the family in this broad sense. They provided the essential connections, maintained relationships, and did the 'selective work' which excluded from this loose social organization those members whose position or conduct detracted from the credibility of the family. The advancement and security of the family involved the participation of women in the regulation of the household economy, and in ensuring that the young women of the family did not make imprudent sexual decisions. Women also became involved in the processes of making enemies, of building alliances, and in maintaining an informal evaluative system of communication known as gossip.

The corporate form replaced these familial processes with its own. Those employed must owe allegiance to the organization rather than to the family. Specific competences and qualifications became of greater importance than family ties. Alliances established within business structures and networks became central as compared to alliances in a local area or within a kin network which were secondary. As the household and family were sealed off from an active relation to the economic process (other than as a consuming unit), women became isolated and the domestic world truly privatized. The locus of advancement for the individual ceased to be identified with his family connections, with the advancement of a kin constellation, and the bases and resources these provide for the economic enterprise. Rather, advancement derived from an individual's identification with the needs of the corporate enterprise. It is this commitment which became institutionalized as a career.

In turn, the domestic labor of the dominant classes was no longer subordinated to the enterprise. It was organized as a personal service to the individual man. Its relation to the business enterprise in which he was an actor was shaped by corporate demands. As far as the wife was concerned, the individual man and his career became the enterprise. The relation of appropriation through which earlier the individual capitalist was able to appropriate his wife's property and her earnings was transposed into a customary, personal appropriation of the services of the wife which facilitated his advancement. For example, when a group of eminent sociologists wrote accounts of how one of their major pieces of work was done, some described a very substantial contribution made by their wives. However, no one raised questions about the husband's appropriation of his wife's work as his or that her work contributed to her husband's advancement in his career but not to hers (Hammond 1964).

In one respect, the basic economic organization of the family now is similar for both working and dominant classes. It is a 'consuming unit', one in which a woman's domestic labor in producing the subsistence of its individual members depends upon a money income from her husband's wage or salary. As suggested above, in the dominant classes, household and family are tied to the individual man's career or business and less to an interlinking of family relations and enterprises. Household and family are "enucleated". Though broader family relations do not disappear—indeed a significant phenomenon is the presence of networks among women that focus on the domestic sphere—they become of relatively little importance to a man's career advancement. The interests of the wife are nonetheless bound up in her husband's. She is obligated in marriage to subordinate her own interests to his career. She is expected to support him morally and socially and her domestic labor ensures his physical well-being. His career pays off for her by increasing her status socially and as a consumer.

The Transmission of Class.   The reorganization of the managerial and organizational process, the advance of the professions and government, and of science and technology intimately associated with the domination of monopoly capitalism, require generalized language skills. Language and conceptual skills in particular become a generalized requirement for playing a role within what develops as a complex, though not monolithic, ruling apparatus. It is through this apparatus that the dominant classes maintains their hold.

The bases of dominant classes have changed. They are no longer primarily engaged in individual ownership of land or business enterprises. They are lodged rather in the complex relations of a highly differentiated and specialized ruling apparatus that, as seen from other chapters, includes a range of things from culture to the state. Hence, the organization of class no longer resides primarily in the transmission of property in an enterprise from an individual to his son. The transgenerational continuities of class are now mediated by an educational process in which women play a highly significant role.

The educational system comes to provide the major transgenerational continuity of class among the dominant classes. This is particularly true for professionals and managers. Children are no longer prospective actors in the moving history of family relations entwined with property and economic enterprise. Sons are no longer prospectively those who will carry on family businesses and hence provide for the continuity of capital. Daughters are no longer those who will consolidate alliances or relations linking social, economic, and political interests into a network of kin. In this new form, the child becomes the object of parental work, particularly the work of mothers, aimed at creating a definite kind of person. He must have distinct communicative skills and capacities to take advantage of the educational process. Through it, he (more frequently than she) will obtain privileged access to occupations within the division of labor of the ruling apparatus.

There is an extensive literature studying the relations among family, class and education. Almost without exception, it ignores the fact that mothering is a work process and that the school itself depends upon the complementary work done by mothers (and to a very much lesser extent by fathers). The researchers know that something is going on in the family which makes a difference to a child's school achievement. But it never occurs to them to investigate the work that women do. That work is conceptualized in ways rendering the time, skill, and effort involved invisible. It is translated into love, into parental responsibility. Alternately, it is merely treated mechanically—home is an 'influence' on school performance; the family has an 'influence' on a child's school achievement, etc. Here, for example, is a description of the type of 'home' setting which is favorable to a child's success in school.

> David is the son of professional parents who have themselves been educated in a grammar school. They provide him with facilities for doing homework in a separate room and light a fire when necessary [it is an English study]. There is, therefore little interruption from other members of the family or from television and radio. If he has trouble with his homework he can turn to either his mother or father for help, and many books of reference are available. His cultural background is constantly a help to him at school and in his homework. Mother or father may even inspect his homework regularly or occasionally (Dale and Griffith 1970:86).

The authors are properly aware of the significance of economic factors in this picture, and it is indeed contrasted with the situation of a working class boy of similar age and abilities. What is not visible to them is the work of mothering. But it can be discerned at a number of points in the account. Mother, we may imagine, has lighted the fire and also polices the other children as well as David's access to television and radio. She has, of course, done the work of providing the food, and maintaining his clothes and the setting in which he works. His cultural background is to a very considerable extent the product of her work. She has read to him, bought appropriate records, taken him to shows, movies, museums, perhaps even concerts. At a more general level, she has spent a great deal of time and work organizing the home to facilitate his work in school and in developing his non-specific but extremely important language skills.

Mothers do a wide range of work in relation to the schooling of their children. Dominant class mothers spend considerable time, thought and skill, as well as consultation with others on the development of their children. Some of this is directly complementary to the school. They train their children in responsibilities of school work, in scheduling, in 'mood' control, and in the organization of physical behavior adapting them to the classroom. Mothers may take steps to correct their children's deficiencies, help them with their work, and prevent errors, lapses, and delays from becoming visible at school and hence consequential for the child's records. In all these ways, and no doubt more, dominant class women work to ensure that their children will steer a course through the educational process giving them access to occupations and careers in the ruling apparatus.

Working class mothers also do the work of mothering in relation to their children's schooling. But they are hampered by lack of economic resources and by the lack of university or college training. A school system which does not promote co-operation between the working class parent and the school also hinders them in their efforts.

HIGHLIGHT

1. Among the dominant classes, the family formerly served as a mechanism whereby capital could be mobilized and/or passed on from generation to generation. Now the corporation plays a similar role. The result is that a woman's work in the home becomes identified as personal service to a man.
2. To the degree that they are both consuming units, the dominant class and working-class families now have one thing in common.
3. In contemporary advanced capitalist society, maintenance of class position requires the development of language skills and education. The work mothers do with children is crucial in the mastering of both. Nonetheless, the work involved in mothering is seldom fully recognized.
4. The different material conditions of mothering (the availability of means, time, energies and skills) are consequential for differences in school achievement of dominant- and working-class children.

The Gender-Neutrality of Capitalism: a Contradiction

The rise of monopoly capitalism with its vast managerial and technical division of labor, of the state at all levels with its bureaucratic forms of administration, and of professional organization, changes the bases of access to positions of power and influence. Formerly, nearly all such positions were entered on the basis of kin and family qualifications. Also, the gender division of labor was deeply ingrained in the social fabric in work process, in power relations, and in economic organization. By way of contrast, the emergence of the forms of organization culminating in the rise of monopoly capitalism created a level and type of organization which was indifferent to gender. Kinship and family ceased to be relevant. Technical skills, managerial and administrative abilities became the types of qualifications and capacities relevant to the new ruling forms. Objectified and impersonal forms of organization were in principle indifferent to the gender of the actor. In actuality, though, women were, and are, for the most part, excluded from the ruling positions in society. Thus a contradiction exists between principle and practice.

The rise of institutionalized forms of ruling leads to a struggle. On the one hand, women of the dominant classes strive to break through barriers to their participation in institutions already weakened by the advance of capitalism. The nineteenth century phase of the women's movement described earlier involved just such a struggle. Access to higher education and to the professions in particular were important objectives for women. On the other hand, however, the very weakening of the intrinsic barriers to women's full participation appears to have resulted in an active effort to establish barriers of a new kind. In large part, this has occurred through the educational process.

In the education of women, two conceptions were at war: one demanded essentially the same education for women as for men; the other specialized them for their future roles as wives and mothers. The educational process which actually developed was one which conformed more closely to the latter. Education came to provide the ideological channels through which women's potential access to a wider arena of action was closed down.

In the educational system, women of the dominant classes learned the practice and morality of their domestic confinement in the following ways. Steps were taken to exclude women from the higher levels of professional bureaucratic, and political positions. An educational system systematically differentiating boys from girls was developed. Girls were given a distinctive education ensuring that they would be disqualified in general for the kinds of advanced training giving access to the professions and higher grades of the civil service. Their course of studies prepared them to accept the authority of experts such as psychologists in childrearing.

Education for women focusses on their language abilities, on their knowledge of social science, psychology, art, and literature. Women are thereby both prepared for their potential ancillary clerical roles in management and given the language skills needed to give the 'cultural background' on which their future children's success in school will depend. They learn also to respond to the work of psychological and sociological experts, to psychiatrists, and to physicians, and to make practical use of their understanding of the new ideologies of home and child-rearing produced by such specialists.

By providing education of this nature, the male-dominated ruling apparatus developed control over the family and its internal organization. What was learned in school helped tie the private domestic sphere to the professional, bureaucratic, and managerial controls of the ruling apparatus. Education ensured that women of the dominant classes would not acquire the types of skills which would give them an undeniable claim to entry as active participants in the ruling apparatus. It also established new ideological controls, bringing what had been a private domain under the control of the ruling apparatus. Previously, what went on in the home had been a 'wild' factor, uncontrolled by the hierarchical structure of the educational process or by the other formal controls of the ruling apparatus. The production by experts of 'prescriptions' for socializing children, was complemented by a training for women that oriented them to those experts. For those in the dominant class for whom private schools were an impossibility, this organization co-ordinated the private (family) and state (school) sectors in the reproduction of the dominant class position.

So far we have examined two types of relations. First, we have looked at a type of family that subordinates women in a subcontractual relation to a ruling apparatus of government, management, and professions. Such subordination appears in the form of personal service to husband and children. Second, we have examined an educational system that prepares women for these family functions and for the essentially subordinate clerical and professional roles played by women. The experience of women in these processes is one of the dimensions of patriarchy among dominant class women.

HIGHLIGHT

1. In principle, contemporary capitalist society is one in which women have equal access to the ruling apparatus of society. In practice, however, women are excluded from such institutions. One of the factors working against their entry is the educational system that prepares women for their future roles of mother or subordinate in various sectors of activity.

The Emergence of the 'Dependent' Family in the Working Class

Dependence of married women, and particularly of women with children, on men and men's salaries or wages is characteristic of both dominant-class and working-class family relations in contemporary capitalism. Women's dependency on men arises in different ways and takes on different forms in different class settings. (It may even now be disappearing as women's participation in the labor force increases.)

We have traced the emergence of a particular form of family in the dominant class. We have examined its origin in the rise of capitalism and its completion in the emergence of the corporate form of property that separates the economic enterprise from the individual owner and subordinates and renders women in marriage dependent upon the earned income of their husbands. The history of the present family form in the working class is very different. It does not begin with women's exclusion from economic activity. Nor does it involve the formation of a property-holding unit identified with the man. However, the legal forms were the same for both dominant classes and for the working class. These gave men the right to women's earnings. But in general, the actual practice and organization of work relations and economic contributions in the working-class family rendered the matrimonial property laws and legal concepts of the civil status of the wife largely irrelevant.

The exclusive dependence of women on men's wages has only been slowly established in the working class and remains far from complete. For working-class women, dependence is directly related to the man's wage-earning capacity, and the man's status and authority in the family are grounded in his capacity to earn. Summarizing sociological studies on the effects of wives' employment outside the home on marital power relations, Moore and Sawhill state the following:

> A number of studies have found that wives who are employed exercise a greater degree of power in their marriages. Marital power is higher among women employed full-time than those working for pay part-time or not at all, and it is greatest among women with the most prestigious occupations, women who are most committed to their work, and those whose salaries exceed their husbands'. Working women have more say especially in financial decisions. This tendency for employment to enhance women's power is strongest among lower working-class couples (Moore and Sawhill 1978).

As we learn more of women's history we find that the emergence of the dependent form of the family among the working class was far from an abrupt and immediate consequence of the rise of industrial capitalism. The process leading to this dependency was a double one. Gradually women were weaned from contributing to the means of family subsistence thereby sinking into a state of dependency. On the one hand, women came into competition with men for jobs in industry. On the other hand, their labor was essential in the home, so that home and family competed with industry for women's labor. The dependence of the mother and children on the male wage earner emerged rather slowly out of change and adjustments between these two.

In the early stages of industrialization, all members of a family might work outside the home and pool their earnings. Each member contributed to a common fund out of which family needs were met. Although a relatively small proportion of married women were employed in industry until late in the nineteenth century, the pattern of women not working outside the home and not contributing actively to the household came very late. In fact, a wife who did not work and contribute directly to the means of subsistence, and who had to depend upon her husband's wage, was undesirable. Married women worked outside the home and brought money or goods into the home in all kinds of ways. Many had gardens and produced for their families. They might also sell the small surplus they produced. Women were employed in a variety of occupations such as peddling, domestic service, farm labor, scavenging, and industrial work.

Cross's study of women's work in Montreal in the latter part of the nineteenth century shows a wide variety of enterprises in which women were employed. In addition to domestic service, women worked in textile, clothing, boot and shoe, and tobacco factories. Also, "there were many small dressmakers', milliners' and tailors' shops, and seamstresses and dressmakers who worked in private homes on a daily basis" (Cross 1978:73-4).

Women also did productive work in the home. Manufacturers put work out to women at piece-rates. Sometimes manufacturers supplied machines to women working at home. The manufacture of men's clothing "was farmed out to women working in their own homes on machines that were either rented or supplied by the manufacturer. In 1892, the J.W. Mackenzie Company had 900 hands on their outside payroll, and the H. Story Company had 1400 in addition to the 130 employed in the factory" (Cross 1978:73). Other paid work done by women in the Montreal area at that period included running boarding houses and working in small businesses.

The women workers included those who were single as well as married. It is most probably married women who took work into their homes. Moreover, the very rapid response to the opening of the *salles d'asile* (day-care nurseries) established by women in religious orders in the 1850s indicates the extent of the need. The surviving records of two such *salles d'asile* show that many children were from families in which both parents went out to work (Cross 1978:74-5).

Children were also essential contributors to the household economy. They might be employed in factory work, but they also contributed through a wide variety of opportunities for employment. Before the era of telephones, for example, children earned small sums of money by running errands and taking messages. They did odd jobs around the home, sharing in housekeeping, gardening, the care of younger children, chores such as fetching water, and the like. However, as attendance at public school became mandatory towards the end of the nineteenth century, the school came into competition with the needs of the working-class family for children's labor.

The enforcement of universal education reorganized the working-class family. Children ceased to be contributors to the household economy. They were less available to assist with household chores or to substitute for the mother in childcare. The withdrawal of child labor from the household as well as from the labor force made the presence of the mother at home more essential. Indeed, the home came to be organized around the scheduling of husband's work and children's schooling so that the mother was tied down to a household routine in a way which was, in fact, new. This markedly reduced her flexibility in relation to earning opportunities outside the home. Both husband and children might come home for a midday meal.

The school imposed standards of cleanliness which represented a serious work commitment on the part of women over and above that already presented by the working conditions of her husband. When water had to be brought from the pump and heated on the stove for bathing and washing clothes, these were major chores in the household. In the school context, the child appeared as the public product of the mother's work. Her standards of cleanliness were subject to the public appraisal of the teachers through the appearance and conduct of her child in school. The working class home as a work setting began to be organized and in some sense supervised by the school. The school itself set standards for women's work as mothers and, in various ways, enforced them.

The earlier form of economic organization of the family shifted to the new enucleated family form. In character, it was very similar to the dominant-class family. In the new form neither wife nor children contributed directly to the production of the means of subsistence through earnings outside. Both depended upon the man as wage earner for the monetary means to sustain the family. This at least was the norm, though of course many husbands could not earn enough to enable the wife to withdraw completely from wage labor. Her work was represented as a personal service to him in (implicit) exchange for being supported on his earnings. The dependent form of family organization had been established.

HIGHLIGHT

1. Among the working classes, the slide of the woman into a state of dependency on the man's wage has been a recent development. Previously, women of the working class normally contributed wages to the family economy.
2. In the early days of capitalism, children also contributed to the family wage. This was brought to a halt by the spread of mandatory school attendance.
3. Over time, the working-class family became one in which the wife was subordinated to her husband and relied for her livelihood on his paycheque.

The Working-Class Form of Patriarchy

The dynamic process of capital accumulation is also one of an increasingly extensive use of machines. The use of machines makes labor more productive, displaces labor, and over time makes the productive process generally more indifferent to differentials of physical strength. This process has two implications for working-class women. One is the actual or potential broadening of the range of jobs and industrial settings in which women can work. A second is the tendency of capitalism to generate a surplus labor population—in this case, women—which cannot be absorbed into developing sectors. As a result, the surplus labor functions as a reserve army of labor. Together, these factors create a highly competitive situation. Traditional barriers between men's and women's work tend to be broken down. At the same time, particularly when the economy slows down, there are more workers seeking jobs than there are jobs for them.

The traditionally lower wages of disadvantaged groups such as women and immigrants give them an advantage in competing for jobs. Through the nineteenth and early twentieth centuries, the policies and publications of trade unions indicate that this was a recurrent theme in male working-class views concerning women in the labor force. The issue itself is two-sided. Men were concerned about women displacing them in the labor force. They also were concerned about the implications of women's work for men's status in the family. Conceivably, wages could have been enough to tempt women away from the household. Sometimes, so the argument goes, women were earning even when husbands, brothers, and sons could not.

These complementary concerns recur again and again in the attack on women workers made by leading sectors of the trade union movement from the early nineteenth century on. Even in the 1960s the American Federation of Labor refused its support to any kind of quota system which might rectify the historic inequalities experienced by blacks and women. Of the early nineteenth century, Malmgren writes:

> There was a psychological as well as an economic basis for the male workers' uneasiness, for the chance to earn a separate wage outside the home might free wives and daughters to some extent from the control of their husbands and parents. The piteous image of the sunken-cheeked factory slave must be balanced against that of the boisterous and cheeky 'fact'ry lass'. Lord Ashley, speaking on behalf of the regulation of child and female labor in factories, warned the House of Commons of the 'ferocity' of the female operatives, of their adoption of male habits—drinking, smoking, forming clubs, and using 'disgusting' language. This, he claimed, was 'a perversion of nature', likely to produce 'disorder, insubordination, and conflict in families'. (Malmgren 1978:23)

The voice here is that of the dominant class. But on this issue the working-class man and the dominant classes have often been united.

Malmgren notes that in the early nineteenth century, this view appears to have been particularly prevalent among leading artisans in the working-class movement of Britain.

It is also prevalent among similar types of workers—crafts and trades workers—who were represented in the American Federation of Labor at the turn of the century. The AFL played a leading role in the organization and institutionalization of the gender-stratified (as well as a racially-stratified) labor market as monopoly capitalism began its great rise in North America. These relations were imported into Canada as the so-called international' unions came to dominate Canadian union organization.

Industries in which both women and men worked, such as the tobacco industry, boot and shoe manufacture, textiles and clothing, printing, and so forth, established an internal stratification ensuring exclusive male access to the more highly skilled and better-paid positions. Under Gompers's leadership, the trade union movement in North America became for working women a systematic organization of weakness relative to men, and a systematic organization of preferential access to skills and benefits for men. In marked contrast to the class orientation of the Industrial Workers of the World (IWW), there was little interest in unionizing women other than as a means of controlling them. There was a fear that bringing numbers of women into a union would result in 'petticoat' government. Women's locals were sometimes given only half the voting power of men on the grounds that they could contribute only half the dues. The Canadian Trades and Labor Congress of the early twentieth century had as an avowed goal the elimination of women, particularly married women, from the work force. The failure of the 1907 Bell Telephone operators' strike in Toronto was, in part, tied to the absence of serious support by the International Brotherhood of Electrical Workers to organize the women operators, even though the operators were striking to achieve unionization (Sangster, 1978).

Struggles to restrict women's participation, and particularly married women's participation in the labor force, went on under various guises. It does not seem likely, however, that union efforts, even when supported by at least some sections of the women's movement at that period, would have been effective in reconstituting the family in a way that maintained women's dependence on men's wages, without the active intervention of the state apparatus. The corporatist ideology enunciated by Mackenzie King formulated the principles of, and legitimated, the administrative and regulatory forms through which trade union organization in Canada was connected to state mechanisms aimed at controlling and deploying the labor force in the service of monopoly capital. In these contexts the implicit alliance between state and trade unions with a common interest—stemming from very different bases—became effective in subordinating women to domestic labor and in restricting their participation in the labor force.

The emergence of national and international market and financial organizations, centralized control of production, and universalism of managerial and technical processes, necessitated a new kind of labor force. Similar needs arose in relation to the military requirements of imperialist expansion and the devastating wars resulting from the conflict of rival empires. The need was not only for technically skilled workers, but also for a labor force, stripped of regional and ethnic cultures. It would have to be fully literate, English-speaking, familiar with factory discipline and the discipline of the machine and, in relation to the military enterprise in particular, physically healthy. The role of the educational system was not only to train this labor force, but it was also to oversee its physical fitness and its moral commitment to imperialism and capitalism. In the production of this labor force, working class mothering was seen as of special importance, particularly as it pertained to the physical health of children. Thus, the dominant classes came to have a direct interest in the allocation of women's labor to the domestic setting.

In the legislation passed during this period we can see two aspects of state interest: on the one hand, a concern to restrict the ways in which industry competed with the home for women's labor; on the other, an interest in laying the legal and administrative bases for a family form in which the costs of supporting the wife and of providing for children would be borne by the wage of the man. The latter motive obviously has special attractions during periods of economic depression. In the United States during the Depression years, there was an active campaign involving government, the media, and unions to get women, and married women in particular, out of the labor market.

From the early 1900s through to the mid-1920s there were a series of legislative measures directed towards the family and women. These reorganized the legal and administrative conditions under which the working class family functioned. Laws which earlier entitled the husband and father to appropriate the earnings of his wife and children disappeared. New legislation was passed affirming their dependence upon his wage. Men were now required to support their families whether they lived with them or not. Welfare policies were developed incorporating similar principles. These have been built into the welfare practices so that, for example, a man sharing the house of a woman welfare recipient is assumed to be supporting her and her children, hence permitting the suspension of her welfare payments. Unemployment insurance and pension plans, introduced subsequently, also created an administrative organization enforcing women's dependence on men in marriage. The seemingly genial and recent legal recognition of the common-law relationship is, in fact, part of the same theme. Furthermore, the state entry into the socialization of children through the public education system provided an important source of control. Streaming patterns similar to those characterizing the experience of dominant-class women prevented working-class women from acquiring the fundamental manual and technical skills on which access to skilled and even semi-skilled work in industry came increasingly to depend. Thus, a significant part of the increased monetary cost of producing the new kind of labor force, including the costs of women's specialization in domestic labor, would be borne directly by the working man's wage (in addition to the contribution made by the working class through taxation).

In former times, the maintenance of the subsistence of men and women and their children depended on the possession of particular skills. The provision of shelter and heat, the purchase and preparation of food, the making and maintenance of clothing, the cleaning, and the overall management of wages, were what can be termed survival work and involved survival skills. When food was short, women and children went without to ensure that the man of the household got enough, or at least the most of what there was. His capacity to earn a wage was the priority.

The working-class family was an interdependent unit organized in general to maximize the survival possibilities of its members. When unemployment or low wages made it impossible to support a family on the man's wage, women with children were faced with a fearful dilemma. A woman had to choose between the care she could give her children by staying home, which meant that there would not be enough food and they would starve or suffer malnutrition, and going out to work to earn enough to feed them, thus running the risks of inadequate supervision and care. Earning a wage large enough to support children, coupled with the provision through her household labor of many of life's necessities, was for women a condition of survival for both herself and her children. Even though it entailed her personal subordination to her husband and a lifetime's drudgery and care, the alternatives were worse.

The form of the working-class family which had emerged is one in which the man is the breadwinner and the wife and children are dependent. It is a form which entails the marked personal subordination of women to men. Working class women learn a discipline which subordinates their lives to the needs and wishes of men. The man's wage is his. It is not a family wage in the sense of possession, though it is a family wage in the sense of being sufficient (in principle) to provide for the family.

Varying customs have developed around its disposal. Sometimes a form exists whereby the wife takes the whole wage and allocates its various uses, including giving the man pocket money. But it is also possible for men not to tell their wives what they earn and to give them housekeeping money, or require them to ask for money for each purchase.

The wage relation lies between the worker and his employer, not between the family and his employer. He earns his wage and the money is his. However, there is an implicit contract between husband and wife whereby he provides for her and her children on whatever conditions he can or thinks best. She provides for him in exchange the personal and household services that he demands. The household is organized in relation to his needs and wishes in regards to his meals, sex, the children, and entertainment.

This implicit contract does not make a man into a tyrant. The sustaining of the man's capacity to continue to work under conditions that are often both psychologically and physically draining is in his wife's and the children's interest. Nonetheless, it sets the man and his wage in the central place in the household with the woman subordinated to him. As wages have increased, the breadwinner's spending money has enlarged to include leisure activities which are his, rather than hers—a larger car, a motorcycle, a boat. Even a camper often proves more for him than for her, since for the wife, it may involve little more than a transfer of labor to less convenient working conditions.

The Political Dimension.   For working-class women, this relationship has a political dimension. The discipline of accepting situations over which they have no control and the authority of a man, who also in the last analysis does not control the conditions of his wage-earning capacity, are not compatible with bold and aggressive styles of political or economic action. Women's sphere of work and responsibility is defined as subordinate to and dependent on that in which men act. The children's well-being, and the managing of the home require from women a discipline of self-abrogation and service. Masculinity and male status are, in part, expressed in men's successful separation from, and subordination of, the sphere of women's activity. They are also found in the visibility of a man's success in 'controlling' his wife (what may go on behind the scenes is another matter).

Working-class men subordinate themselves in the workplace to the authority of their supervisors. A condition of their authority in the home is this daily acceptance of the authority of others. Men assume also the physical hazards of their work. They live with the ways in which capital uses them physically and discards them psychologically. They, too, undertake a lifetime discipline if they elect to marry and support a wife and children. That responsibility can be a trap for working-class men as much as for working-class women. Through that relation a man is locked into his job and into the authority relations and the uses of his labor-power it entails. His wife's subordination, her specfic personal and visible subservience, and her economic dependence attest to his achievement. Her 'nagging', her seeking paid employment, her independent political initiatives, her public challenges to his authority would signal his failure as a man. In the political context, we find a subculture prohibiting women's participation in political activity, other than in strictly ancillary roles essentially within the domestic sphere. Thus, when women organized militant action in support of the men striking the General Motors Plant at Flint, Michigan in 1937, women had to go against norms restraining them from public forms of political action.

Earlier, Malmgren's description of dominant class fear of the 'ferocity' of female operatives was cited. Lord Ashley clearly identified the subordination of women to men in the home with their political suppression. The ideology of weak and passive women, needing protection and support, and subordinated 'naturally' to the authority of men in the home, as it was adopted by working class men and working class political and economic organization, served to secure the political control of one section of the working class by another.

Where women workers had a strong tradition of paid employment after marriage, their relation to the political process showed independent strength. For example, in the cotton mill areas of Lancashire in Britain at the time of the women's suffrage movement, there was an active and vital women's suffrage movement among women cotton mill operatives. By contrast, subordinating women to a wage earning man and confining them to the household isolates women from the political process. One consequence of this situation has been the occasional opposition by housewives to strikes on the part of their husbands. Thus, the subordination of working class women to men in the family, which was progressively perfected over the latter half of the nineteenth and the first quarter of the twentieth centuries, worked in the interests of the dominant classes in their attempt to establish a corporate society. The patriarchal form of the working class family served the interests of the dominant classes in the political and economic subordination of half the working class. This was an integral piece of the political exclusion of class as a basis for working class politics in North America.

HIGHLIGHT

1. Increasing use of machines broadened the number of potential jobs available to women. However, fearing competition for jobs, men, through agencies like unions, attempted to keep women out of the workforce.
2. A series of measures by the state also aimed at keeping women out of the workforce.
3. The fact that a family largely relies on the earnings of the husband creates a situation in which the housework of the wife is regarded as a payoff for the support provided her by the husband.
4. While wives are subordinate to husbands, husbands themselves are subordinate to others in their work.

5. The subordination of women to men in the working class family has meant that working-class women's interests have not been fully represented through organizations defending working class interests (trade unions, working class parties, etc.).

Conclusion

At the outset we confronted the terms 'patriarchy' and 'class' as key terms in contrasting and opposing accounts of women's inequality in contemporary capitalist society. Resolution of this opposition has been sought in a political economic analysis of the relation between family organization and class as a basis for women's subordination to men. As we have examined the emergence of a form of the family in which women depend upon men's earnings, and the ideological and political institutions which enforce this dependency, we can recognize patriarchal forms as means through which the dominant classes maintain their domination.

Over the history of the dominant and working classes, diverging original conditions have led to general similarities in the relation of dominant and working-class women to the household and to the labor force. Those similarities, however, overlie relations which give the dominant-class family a different role in the maintenance of the dominant class than the working-class family has in relation to the working class. The dominant-class family has been organized to maintain the domination of its classes and to provide for the transgenerational continuities of access to privileged occupational positions in the ruling apparatus. The working class family, on the other hand, is in part organized by an institutional process controlled by the dominant classes. The best that the working class family can do is to secure for its members the best possible life within the political and economic limitations which ensure that workers return every day to the market to sell their labor-power and that they will bear the cost of rearing the next generation of workers (ensuring transgenerational continuities of the working class). 'Patriarchy' thus cannot be separated from the social organization through which dominant classes secure the perpetuation of the relations of exploitation in a capitalist society.

At the same time, as we have emphasized, capitalism is fundamentally a process of change, and one which continually transforms its own social relations. Over time, the labor women have contributed to the domestic production of subsistence has been increasingly displaced (though by no means done away with) by labor and skill embodied in the products of modern industry from vacuum cleaners to canned food. Increasingly, capital has reorganized the work process in the home. The result is a reduction in the domestic demand for women's labor and an increase in the demand for money to purchase labor embodied in commercial products. At some point, what women can contribute domestically in the form of labor no longer balances what she can earn and hence add to the purchasing power of the family. The wife can no longer reduce costs effectively increasing her contribution of labor to the household process.

This, and the increased demand for women's labor, lie behind the slow but consistently upward creep of the labor force participation of married women and, indeed, of women in general. The power of the domestic economy to compete with paid employment for women has declined. The demand for certain types of women's labor or what has come to be women's labor increased greatly with the rise of corporate capitalism. Clerical, sales, and service workers were needed at low cost. The 'compact' that once existed between employers and male workers restricting the employment of married women, which avoided the direct competition of paid employment with the domestic economy controlled by the husband, has been weakened and is in decline. A man's authority to refuse to allow his wife to work is weakened by the disappearance of complementary restrictions in the employment of labor. With inflation and increasing unemployment, more married women are entering the labor force. Money earnings are essential to the family, and if the man's wage or salary does not bring in enough, then a woman's responsibilities to her home and family demand that she seek employment outside the home.

The established economic bases of family organization institutionalized in the corporatist phase of corporate capitalism are being eroded. As unemployment increases, and as threats to the middle class capacity to transmit their class status to their children become more acute, patriarchal institutions take on a protectionist character, reinforcing discriminatory practices against women. Government attempts to reduce the numbers of those on unemployment rolls by using well-worn mechanisms for forcing women into dependence upon men through its UIC and welfare policies, reduction of already inadequate child care provisions, etc. But these measures now function vacuously.

The relationship of dependency characteristic of both dominant and working-class women in the family is no longer fully viable. The previous state of affairs cannot be reinstated. Consequently, the dislocations and the arbitrary character of the patriarchal forms begin to emerge. What was formerly taken for granted as the way the world worked, is no longer so. Among dominant-class women and sections of the organized working class, the women's movement advances an ideology and establishes organization through which the latent inequalities are given objective expression. They thereafter become the focus of organized action.

The interests of women in differing class positions differ as their situation differs. The organizational means available to them to express their chosen interests also differ. But whatever the differences in objectives and interests, there are common issues. Among them is the challenge to women of both classes to claim the right to speak and organize politically *as women* and to speak and organize against oppression in the family between women and men as individuals and as sexual beings. The same holds true for the workplace. The women's movement does not collapse the interests of women of one class into those of another. But it has the capacity for the first time of fully entering both into a political and organizational arena in which women can hear what women have to say, and can speak as women for women, expressing their differences as well as discovering bases for common struggle.

SUGGESTED READINGS

The Double Ghetto, Pat and Hugh Armstrong. Toronto: McClelland and Stewart, 1978. This useful study examines the gender segregation of the labor force in Canada as well as the sphere of women's domestic labor.

Women's Oppression Today: Problems of Marxist Feminist Analysis, London: Verso, 1980. This excellent book examines the specific oppression of women in capitalism. A review of theories of patriarchy and class introduces an analysis of gender relations in the context of sexuality, ideology, education, paid employment, family, class and political organization.

Last Hired, First Fired: Women and the Canadian Force, Patricia Connelly. Toronto: Women's Press, 1978. Though Connelly's use of Marx's concept of the reserve army of labor oversimplifies, her book provides a compact and very accessible account of women's participation in the Canadian labor force.

Women, Race and Class, Angela Y. Davis. New York: Random House, 1982. A very readable collection of essays presenting women's issues and the women's movement from the perspective of black women.

Feminism and Materialism: Women and Modes of Production, Annette Kuhn and AnnMarie Wolpe. London: Routledge and Kegan Paul, 1978. A collection of excellent papers on women's oppression in capitalism. Of special relevance are those examining structures of patriarchy and capitalism in the family, sociological theories of women's work, the state and women's oppression, and education and the gender division of labor.

More Than a Labour of Love: Three Generations of Women's Work in the Home, Meg Luxton. Toronto: Women's Press, 1980. A vivid and informative description of the daily lives, family relations and household work of three generations of women living in Flin Flon, Manitoba.

Women and Revolution: a Discussion of the Unhappy Marriage of Marxism and Feminism, Lydia Sargent, ed. Boston: South End Press, 1981. A collection of more or less interesting papers focussed on Heidi Hartmann's original paper on the 'unhappy marriage' arguing that capitalism incorporated existing patriarchal structures into its own.

EDUCATION AND THE CORRESPONDENCE PRINCIPLE

D.A. Nock

Introduction

It seems like an obvious point that education is a process that is intimately tied to a mode of production. And yet whether or not this is in fact true is one of the big controversies of the sociology of education. On the one hand, many scholars propose that R.W. Nelsen (1978) has dubbed the "education-as-autonomous argument". They suggest that the educational system changes the mode of production. It is thus the primary institution in shaping a society. The alternative view, and the one that will be adopted in this chapter, has been described as the "correspondence principle". In accordance with the "correspondence principle", it is assumed that the type of educational system varies with the mode of production. For example, it is unlikely that we, in an industrial-capitalist society will learn the techniques of killing polar bears, trapping or making igloos.

In Canada we live in an industrial society: a society further characterized by its dependent monopoly capitalist status. One of its basic characteristics is the use of large scale machinery in the productive process. In pre-industrial societies most people were food producers such as farmers, hunters, or fishermen. In our industrial society large scale machinery makes it possible for approximately 10 percent of the population to feed the 90 percent who are not food producers. Thus, an educational system has arisen in which we are prepared for an urban environment. Most of us are *not* taught how to grow crops or to catch fish. We assume that food will be made available for us.

Our own mode of production is a *capitalist* one. In Chapter 2 we explored the ways in which a capitalist economy is owned by, and runs for, the general benefit of those people who have a sufficient amount of capital to be able to spend it in investment rather than on consumption. A relatively small minority owns the steel companies, transportation systems, newspapers, factories, shopping centres, banks, distilling companies, retail chains and so forth. These make up our economic system. A list of those who do own and control major sections of our economy reads like the Who's Who of Canada.

Before considering the implications of this pattern of ownership, it is necessary to clarify the meaning of some terms. The first of these is *monopoly* capitalism. As recently as three decades ago, our economic system allowed for considerably more competition between companies than it does at the present time. In addition there were more small companies and small capitalists than now. Over time the larger corporations either absorbed or drove the smaller companies and investors out of business. In 1952, for example, John Porter identified 183 "dominant" companies in the Canadian economy and 985 individuals who were directors of these corporations. By the time Wallace Clement updated Porter's study using 1972 data, he found that the 183 firms had been reduced to 113, directed by a total of 946 individuals (Clement 1975).

In 1978, there were a total of 206 695 industrial/commercial enterprises in Canada. Yet just 500 of these enterprises accounted for 51 percent of sales, 59 percent of assets, and 63 percent of profits (Cheveldayoff 1978). In other words, just a quarter of one percent of enterprises accounted for more than half of the assets and almost two-thirds of total profits. Furthermore, only 50 leading firms controlled 30 percent of assets and 31 percent of profits. Consequently, these few corporations of the private sector employ proportionately large numbers of people.

What does this pattern of ownership and employment have to do with our educational system? We can best answer this question by raising another: Why do you attend school? Partly, perhaps, for the cultural enrichment which the educational experience offers. But most students (and parents!) are also concerned with what happens after graduation. Yet what you do after completing your studies is not totally determined by what you have learned in school. If you graduate from a journalism program at Western, Carleton, or Ryerson, for example, you may be hired by a newspaper controlled by the large capitalist families which control the media—the Thomsons, the Southams, or the Irvings (who own *all* of the English language daily newspapers in New Brunswick). Your university education may have done many things for you. Indirectly it has also contributed to the further profits of these major capitalist families. At the same time it is worth noting that most of the cost of preparing you for employment will have been shouldered by the taxpayers as a whole, and by you and your family. Yet substantial economic benefit deriving from your education will go to the owners of business enterprises. The same point could be made for many other programs in the university, whether engineering, business, science, law, or sociology.

Some people might argue that the university also prepares them for employment not directly controlled by large capitalists—in the civil service, for example, in health care or education. However, employment in the private sector is still the norm in Canada, even if it is true that state employment has been increasing. More importantly, one of the main functions of the public and semi-public sectors is to service, maintain, and legitimize the capitalist sector.

Let us consider the situation of a professor of psychology at a university. He or she is not employed by a capitalist business, and may even disdain the business sector. Yet one aspect of such a professor's work may be to train psychology students who will be employed as personnel managers in business, or as market consultants and researchers for business. In a similar vein, many agencies of government hand out grants, subsidies, incentives, and tax deduction schemes for business (Lewis 1972). Quite often the supposed independence of the public and semi-public sectors from the corporate business world is more mythical than real.

Further examples of the inter-penetration of the public and private spheres can be seen right on the campus. Consider the names given to universities or their buildings. McMaster was a wealthy capitalist. The names of the Beaverbrook and Dunn families (major capitalists) are conferred upon buildings at the University of New Brunswick. McGill was founded by and named after a prominent fur trader and merchant. At Lakehead University, the library is named after Chancellor Patterson, who controlled the trade of grain.

The last term we must define is *dependent* capitalism. Since the arrival of the French, Canada has never been an independent country in both a political and an economic sense. Canada was more or less directly controlled politically by Britain until the 1860s, and economically until the 1920s. In the 1920s the United States assumed economic dominance in Canada. One of the first scholars to notice the absorption of Canada into the American economic empire was Harold Innis (1894-1953). Writing in 1930, he referred to the United States' "imperialistic policy of the twentieth century" (Innis 1975 [1930]:385-6). In a later paper (1948) Innis commented that "Canada moved from colony to nation to colony" (1973:405).

In recent decades Canada's status as an economic colony has become even more apparent; today almost a third of American direct investment in the entire world is in Canada (Clement 1975:111). For example, in 1975, 280 of the country's top 500 non-financial enterprises were not Canadian. In that year the actual number of foreign enterprises (3887) was substantially smaller than the number of Canadian-owned enterprises (203 808). Thus of the 206 695 firms operating in this country only 2 percent were foreign owned. Yet that small percentage controlled 38 percent of all assets and received 48 percent of all profits. Of the top 100 leading non-financial enterprises, 60 were foreign-owned. These firms accumulated 26 percent of all the profits in that year (Cheveldayoff 1978).

Since so many of our firms are not owned by Canadians, the chances are that many Canadian graduates will find employment in foreign-owned companies. Their service in these enterprises will in varying degrees facilitate the export of capital. The fact that many Canadians will find employment in foreign-owned firms does not immediately strike one as harmful or troubling. After all, a job is a job. But we must bear in mind that foreign ownership facilitates the export of Canadian capital. The cost of training those men and women who work for Exxon, Ford or IBM is borne by Canadians as a whole. But a disproportionate amount of the economic benefit gained by an educated workforce goes to the owners of the means of production.

HIGHLIGHT

1. The hypothesis of the correspondence principle is that the education system is influenced by the prevailing mode of production in that society.
2. In Canada, the mode of production is a form of dependent, industrial, monopoly capitalism. The pattern of ownership within this system is such that over half of the assets and almost two-thirds of the total profits are controlled by just a quarter of one percent of the enterprises.
3. In such a system, it is inevitable that the large-scale enterprises will accrue the benefits of the education system. The productivity of those students who are educated at the expense of their families and the Canadian taxpayers directly contributes to the profits of the capitalist enterprises that employ them.
4. Even the productivity of those students who find employment in the public sector indirectly contributes to the generation of surplus value in capitalist business.
5. Although only 2 percent of non-financial enterprises were foreign owned, they controlled 38 percent of all assets and received 48 percent of all profits in 1975. Since foreign-owned enterprises employ so many people, many students will eventually be employed by them. Consequently, while the cost of training these potential employees is borne by Canadians as a whole, a disproportionate amount of the economic benefits is exported to foreign owners.

Education and Modes of Production

By now it should be clear that education is intimately connected to the mode of production. In the course of our history Canada has seen three modes of production. These are the tribal, the feudal, and the capitalist modes of production. The tribal mode was that engaged in by Canada's native peoples (some continue in this mode although most have abandoned it). The modified feudal mode of production functioned in Quebec until 1854. Many Canadians came to this country from Europe to escape the feudal system itself or its residual effects. For example, the feudal system remained legally entrenched in Russia until 1861, and in a legally modified form until the Russian Revolution of 1917. Such Canadians as the Doukhobor sect left Russia explicitly to reject the Russian feudal-military society. The capitalist mode is that which characterizes Canadian society at present. In order to clarify the correspondence of the educational system to the mode of production, it is necessary to look at these three modes in detail.

Tribal Society

Tribal societies are those in which no social classes exist. No one must work for any one else, and no one in the society hires the labor of others. In such a society everyone must engage in the food production process. For various reasons, such as the lack of technology or any coercive power from above, there is no large economic surplus produced which could sustain a non-food producing class. In addition, there is no substantial division of labor, except that which exists between the sexes. For example, the Ojibway or Cree tribes existed by hunting, gathering, and fishing. All men were hunters of animals such as bears, moose, deer, rabbits, etc. The women skinned animals, did the cooking, kept the lodges, raised the children, and even did some fishing.

Another characteristic of tribal societies is their small population and large territory which result in low population densities. For example, present day Cree of the Mistassini region of Quebec only number some 600 people and live in an area of 42 500 square miles. The need for a large area is dictated by the need to hunt animals as a food source. With greater dependence upon horticulture and agriculture to provide food, more people could be supported and fed on smaller areas of land.

In tribal societies there was no State, and, consquently, no bureaucracy or agent of coercive oppression. The State only arises in societies with a class system, a complex division of labor, and a high degree of economic surplus which can support a non-producing class or classes. In tribal societies everybody (normally males, but often females as well) had access to weapons. Thus the formation of coercive authority in such societies was difficult as a would-be dictator might have found himself in trouble with his tribe.

What role did education play in tribal society? Education was provided to supply the skills needed for survival within the society and therefore mainly entailed instruction in food production, preparation and preservation; in the manufacture of essential items such as tools (baskets, mallets, bows and arrows, etc.) used for food production; in the building of lodges, and in religious rituals by which the tribe sought assurance of a continuing food supply. The nature of this process was non-formal and non-institutionalized. It was based on the proximity of parent to child. The parents instructed by demonstrating. The children learned by watching and imitating.

Euro-Canadian education, that many Indian children were eventually forced to acquire, assumed a different sort of work and general mode of production than that underlying tribal education. It also was based upon different cultural assumptions concerning the nature of appropriate political systems. In addition, all instruction was in either English or French. In most cases, even where Indians were students, instruction in their native languages was forbidden. Furthermore, this instruction was given in a formalized bureaucratic setting by people with whom the children were personally unfamiliar. This practice was contradictory to the traditions of Indian society. It is hardly surprising, then, that Indians have had difficulty "fitting in".

Thus, the education received in a traditional or semi-traditional tribal mode of production is obviously related in a very direct way to the mode of production. What people learn is related to their way of life, and to the urgent requirements of food production. They learn about bears rather than bureaucracy, hunting animals rather than corporate gamesmanship, and the building of commodities rather than the selling of them.

HIGHLIGHT

1. In tribal society, there is very little surplus once basic needs are met. Consequently, there are no classes and no state. The main division of labor is on the basis of sex.
2. The social organization of tribal societies usually reflects the fact that large numbers of people cannot be sustained on what can be hunted and gathered from small geographical areas.
3. In tribal society, education centres on survival skills.
4. Instruction is received from those with whom the child has close and intimate connections.

Slave, Feudal and Post-Feudal Societies

About 5000 B.C. the first agricultural societies arose in Mesopotamia. Because of the economic surplus they produced, these societies were able to support a relatively larger population than tribal societies. More importantly, these societies emerged as full-blown class societies. The relative egalitarianism and democracy of tribal societies were *not* present. Usually an all-powerful monarch was supported by a noble class. The actual tilling of the soil was done by slaves, serfs, or peasants who were totally excluded from participation in the government of the society.

There are many differences between what can be identified as slave, feudal, and post-feudal societies. However, in all of these types of societies, there existed a dichotomy between a small land-owning class (ranging from less than one percent to five percent of the population) able to live off the rents, taxes, and labor of the food-producers, and the vast percentage of the population that did all the physical labor of food production. This dichotomy was present in the ancient civilizations of Egypt, China, India, Mesopotamia, Greece, Rome, and in the societies of Europe during the Middle Ages. The last feudal society in Europe existed in Russia where serfdom was not legally abolished until 1861. The period following feudalism and preceeding industrial capitalism, was an era in which peasants still had to work the land of landlords—as in Ireland until the early years of this century.

This period can be referred to as post-feudal or transitional. Many agrarian societies of this nature still exist in parts of Latin America and Asia. There the landowners often form economic and political coalitions with outside capitalists. (One saw this in Nicaragua, for example, before the Sandanista Revolution). In other words, agrarian societies of the slave, feudal, or post-feudal type have been the predominant mode of production for most of the last six thousand years. Industrial capitalism is an innovation of the last three centuries.

In pre-capitalist societies, there is often an elaborate stratification system within the landowning class. First, there is the royal family. Such families are able to accumulate a lion's share of wealth. Lenski says, for example,

> In eighteenth-century Prussia, the royal estates constituted 'no less than one-third of the total arable area', a figure which was matched by the royal estates in neighboring Sweden. Prior to the emancipation of the serfs, 27.4 million men and women were state peasants, whom the czars regarded as their property to dispose of as they wished (1966:213).

The aristocratic or noble class immediately below the royal family, includes landowners with hereditary titles, such as baron, count, duke, and prince. It also encompasses lower level baronets and knights. Lenski has suggested that this noble landowning class "rarely contained more than 2 percent of the population" (1966:219). In some countries, there was also a lesser landowning class, the gentry, who were distinguished by their lack of titles. They usually had much smaller estates than their noble superiors. In the case of England, Frank Musgrove has suggested that the gentry, coupled with the aristocratic ranks, comprised 5 percent of the population (1979:143).

The Church was a very important institution in many slave, feudal, and post-feudal societies. In such societies, religion played a legitimating role for the landowning upper class. The latter, a small percentage of the population, were being maintained (and in sumptuous style) by the physical exertion of the 80 to 90 percent of the population who were the food producers. There was a need, therefore, for an institution which encouraged the food producers to believe that this state of affairs was natural or ordained by God. The Church promised the food-producing peasants a heavenly reward if they endured their lot in life. Usually, the peasants accepted this message.

The Nature of Education.   The importance of class and occupational divisions was reflected in the educational system. For the food-producers at the bottom of the social hierarchy there was traditionally no formal education. Even the instruction of peasants in the basic skills of literacy was often opposed by landowners on the grounds that the peasants might start reading rebellious and revolutionary literature. As a consequence, mass education in England was not introduced until 1870. By this time the transitional or post-feudal society had passed and the industrial-capitalist was ascendent.

To some extent the education of the food-producers in an agrarian slave, feudal or post-feudal society resembled that of a tribal society. Most instruction was given by parents, kin, or neighbors. It was based on imitation and observation of the elders, and illiteracy was the norm. Furthermore, most of this informal education was related to aspects of food-production (such as crop or animal husbandry), the basic production of handicrafts, and domestic management. It also included religious instruction from the churches and folk beliefs from the villagers. As Lenski says, "The subculture of the common people was a mixture of primitive superstition and the kinds of practical information they needed in their daily lives" (1971:186).

The life of the apprentice artisan or tradesman was somewhat different. He received a course of instruction in his trade from an established practitioner and usually lived in proximity to the master and family. Thus the education received was not bureaucratic, or formalistic. Nor was it an education based on secondary relations. The apprentice might well be in a subordinate situation, but his education was received in an environment of face-to-face interaction. Master and apprentice would come to know each other well. A typical contract between an apprentice and the master might be:

> The boy covenants to dwell as an apprentice with his master for seven years, to keep his secrets and to obey his commandments. Taverns and alehouses he shall not haunt, dice, cards or any other unlawful games he shall not use, fornication with any woman he shall not contract. He shall not absent himself by night or by day without his master's leave but be a true and faithful servant. On his side, the master undertakes to teach his apprentice his art, science or occupation with moderate correction. Finding and allowing unto his said servant meat, drink, apparel, washing, lodging and all other things during the said term of seven years, and to give unto his said apprentice at the end of the said term double apparel, to wit, one suit for holidays and suit working days (Laslett 1965:2-3).

A slave, feudal, or post-feudal society was sufficiently sophisticated to require some people who can read and write. There was a need for tax collectors, lawyers, bureaucrats, civil servants, and churchmen. There was also a need for occupations for people born into classes above the food-producers, but unable to inherit landed property. In eighteenth century England, for example, the younger sons of landowners normally did not inherit the family property and so were trained for professions in the law, the church, or the army.

Thus, the growth of higher education in an agrarian society with a pre-capitalistic mode of production serves a number of useful functions. It provided alternate "respectable" careers to non-inheritors, and prepared individuals for service in the ideological and repressive state apparatuses (law, theology, arts). The study of medicine cannot be considered training in the state apparatuses but was of obvious service in maintaining the health of the gentry and other classes of the non-food-producing sector (Horn 1967:180).

As far as the landowning aristocracy was concerned, education for its own sake was not particularly desired. Certainly 'expertise' in the modern sense was discouraged. In England, much of the learning at the most exclusive "public schools" was not of the sort that was useful in job acquisition. Most of the young aristocrats in attendance had their futures already assured. The social graces were encouraged, as were such skills as debating, rhetoric, and clubsmanship. As Guttsman points out, "Only a few of the great number of aristocratic politicians who went to Oxford or Cambridge achieved great academic distinctions, but they all took part in the social life of the place. . . . If, as a rule, the older universities failed to make scholars out of the young aristocrats, they helped to develop further the tradition of gentlemanly living. The keeping of horses, hunting, riding and gambling led the young man to the style of living of the landed squirearchy" (Guttsman 1954:17-8).

Scholars of the modern industrial-capitalist educational system have pointed to the importance of what is called the "hidden curriculum"; that is, the style and form of what is learned in the classroom may be more important than the content. In post-feudal society this was obviously true for the landed classes. In discussing the elite public-schools of England, Guttsman has noted that what was important was not the curriculum but the values learned, particularly the ability to take and to give orders. The education received at these public schools was non-utilitarian because it was assumed that most of the students would not have to work for a living. Thus, they were trained for a life of leisure through emphasis on games and recreational activities (Guttsman 1954:17).

In the feudal or post-feudal mode of production, class becomes a major feature of social organization. Education similarly becomes stratified in the following ways: 1. Education for the landowning elite becomes a matter of social polish; academic content is relatively inconsequential. 2. Education for the professions becomes useful to the feudal state and its upper landowning class. 3. Apprenticeship education becomes necessary for artisans and tradespeople. Such education is not of the "classroom" variety. 4. No formal education is provided for the food-producing masses. For them skills are acquired through observation and imitation of parents, neighbors, and kin.

It should be clear from our analysis of education that the "correspondence principle" holds true. It is impossible to discuss the educational system without understanding the nature of the mode of production, and the class system it reproduces. Is it otherwise in an industrial-capitalist system? This is the interpretation suggested by many educational scholars. But in the following pages we will see how the mode of production also affects the educational system of capitalist society.

HIGHLIGHT

1. The difference between, on the one hand, tribal societies, and, on the other, slave, feudal and post-feudal societies is that the latter can generate a surplus capable of sustaining a class structure.
2. Most slave, feudal and post feudal societies had an elaborate class structure, but the majority, who lived in poverty, sustained a luxurious life style for the upper classes who comprised only five percent of the population.
3. In general, religion legitimizes the status quo in slave, feudal, and post-feudal societies.
4. Education for the mass of the population in slave, feudal, and post-feudal societies was similar to that in tribal societies. The exceptions were artisans who learned a trade through apprenticeship and some members of the upper classes who acquired education in schools.

Industrial-Capitalism

The Class Structure.   An industrial-capitalist society of the modern sort can certainly be called a class society. But the nature of class has changed from that found in a feudal or post-feudal society. There is, however, still a distinction between producing and non-producing classes. Perhaps the largest class in capitalist society is the industrial working class who, using their labor, make, transport, or distribute commodities. At the top of an industrial-capitalist society is a small class of owners of factories and of capital called the bourgeoisie. An intermediary class, called the petty bourgeoisie can also be distinguished.

There are, first, those members of the petty bourgeoisie who are professionals such as lawyers, doctors, dentists, and mid-level business managers. Such individuals earn large incomes and thus have a great deal of money. However, the money they have is sometimes just barely enough to support their rather ostentatious lifestyle. Although the petty bourgeoisie usually has enough money left over for investment as *capital*, they still get the bulk of their income from their practise or profession.

The other part of the intermediary group includes lower paid professionals or semi-professionals such as teachers, nurses, social workers, professors, clergy, etc. Such individuals are usually in an occupation with substantial formal educational requirements. Elsewhere such individuals have been identified as a new petty bourgeoisie. However, the income of these individuals is such that they cannot afford a luxurious lifestyle, and the amount they can put aside for investment is either minimal or nil.

Farmers can be viewed as yet a third segment of the petty bourgeoisie. Traditionally, in Canada, this group has been family farmers who at one time formed the majority of the Canadian population. They are considered as part of the petty bourgeoisie since they own their own means of production, and either employ no labor outside of the family, or a small amount of outside labor.

The proletarian class is the largest class within the working population of an industrial-capitalist society. It includes those wage-earners such as skilled and semi-skilled laborers, salespeople, employees of service industries, etc. This is the industrial working class. The members of this class have a lifestyle in which their basic needs are fulfilled though their wants may remain unsatisfied. Proletarians have no reserve of capital.

At the very bottom of the class ladder are those who were described by Marx and Engels as the lumpenproletariat. These are individuals who are not engaged in the productive process in a full-time regular way. The lumpenproletariat includes criminals and prostitutes, many women who are single-parent mothers and who are unable to work, other recipients of welfare or unemployment, and also those at the very bottom of the working class such as some unskilled laborers.

Education and Mobility. A number of observers have emphasized the high degree of mobility in advanced industrial-capitalist countries. The Canadian sociologist S.D. Clark saw very little evidence of social mobility in Canada before World War II. However, since that time, Clark has argued that a "quiet revolution" of upward mobility, largely dependent on the educational system, has taken place. As Clark puts it "the years 1945-1960 witnessed...a great upward socio-economic movement of Canadian people" (1976:59). Clark uses "the farm or working-class boy who put himself through medical college by earning from odd jobs" (Clark 1976:59) as an illustration of this phenomenon.

The problem with Clark's argument is that it places undue emphasis on education, and especially post-secondary education, as a vehicle for upward mobility. Sociologists have regularly used higher education as well as occupational prestige and income in the measurement of "socio-economic status". Indeed, the tradition of stratification analysis has become a rival to the Marxist analysis of classes as defined in terms of the ownership or non-ownership of the means of production.

If we consider the nature of a monopoly industrial-capitalist society, it is unlikely that real mobility is increasing. First, we notice that over time more and more people (currently about 85 percent) have had to be employed by others rather than work for themselves. Yet, as Peter Archibald points out, the majority of people (63.4 percent) would prefer to work on their own (1980:133). We should also bear in mind that the number of capitalist firms has been diminishing—more so in Canada than in the United States (Clement 1977:139). What this means is that the quantity of some of the most desirable positions available has been declining. In addition, James Richardson points out that: "...rates of social mobility have not changed much over this century despite a massive expansion of educational systems." (Richardson 1977) Indeed, education does not appear to have had a significant effect upon the degree of mobility found in different societies. This finding is contrary to what most of us have been taught.

The number of desirable occupations is limited in an industrial-capitalist society. In order to reproduce itself, a capitalist society *must* have unskilled, semiskilled, and skilled workers. It must also have lawyers and doctors, but the need for professionals is not as great. Corporations will always need a few men to fill positions as presidents, chairmen, and vice-presidents. They will also need proportionately more middle and lower level executives. Let us assume that in such companies some people can work their way to the top. (This is of course not always a realistic assumption as capitalist families are still sufficiently in control to give their offspring a clear headstart in the race for power and prestige). The number of individuals who fail to get to the top will nonetheless always be the majority. The Master of Business Administration degree may assure a ticket into the arena of competition but it will not guarantee success. As Richardson points out, not everyone can be upwardly mobile and not everyone should expect to be (1977:422).

Education as Ideology.   The professional class in general and sociologists in particular have always had difficulty in seeing themselves as serving either capitalists or the capitalist system. They discuss the social system without discussing capitalism as a system. Therefore such individuals never fully analyse the real barriers to social mobility. Upward mobility in many educational studies is consequently defined as movement from blue collar to a white collar occupation. But there are many similarities between the two.

In both types of occupations (e.g. an electrician and a teacher) individuals must sell their labor-power to be fed and housed. Neither the electrician nor the teacher has much if any money available for investment as capital. Neither own their means of production, nor do they ordinarily hire the labor-power of others. The only substantial difference between the teacher and the electrician is that one sells labor-power by manipulating other people, and the other by manipulating physical objects. Yet liberal sociologists of education might well argue that a process of mobility had occurred if an electrician's son becomes a teacher, even if the son's income is the same as his father's.

HIGHLIGHT

1. Industrial capitalism has a clearly defined class structure composed of a bourgeoisie, petty bourgeoisie and proletariat.
2. The idea that education leads to social mobility is a myth.
3. In addition to imparting knowledge, the educational system helps legitimize the status quo.
4. The inattention given by academics to the class nature of society results from their own education and experience.

The Triumph of Primary and Secondary Education

Formal mass education at the primary and secondary level is a relatively recent phenomenon. In England such schooling was not available until 1870, and in parts of Canada and the United States, not until the 1840s and 1850s. In Europe, landowners did not feel the need for a literate serf or peasant class. As Bleasdale writes, "Up until the mid-nineteenth century, Mandeville's infamous dictum that the poor had simple needs, none of which included an education, summarized well the prevailing view held by aristocrat and bourgeois alike in class societies" (1978:13).

According to a liberal analysis, class is a relatively unimportant concept, especially in the new industrial society. In the political realm a liberal analysis has led sociologists such as S.M. Lipset to suggest that class based politics no longer exist. Also social contradictions have been resolved by the implementation of the welfare state and the extension of the franchise (Lipset 1963:442). A parallel argument in education theory explains the expansion of education in terms of the democratic ethos and the desire of educators and governments to overcome any remnant of a class society. The expansion of education is seen thus as a logical and rational consequence of the needs of a *democratic* society. After the extension of the franchise, one British aristocrat suggested that, "Now we must educate our masters" implying that the proletariat and peasantry were indeed in control. It may be significant that in England, free and compulsory mass education was implemented when the Church of England began to lose its popularity with the producing classes.

Louis Althusser has suggested that, "In the pre-capitalist historical period...it is absolutely clear that *there was one dominant Ideological*

State apparatus, the Church, which concentrated within it not only the religious functions, but also...a large proportion of the functions of communications and culture" (1969:144). Such ideological state apparatuses, it will be seen in another chapter, functioned to "ensure *subjection to the ruling ideology*" (Althusser 1969:133).

At the very time the church was losing its support in the population, revolutionary sentiments seemed to be on the rise. Formal education, never before considered necessary for the working classes, was now seen as an alternative to the church as an agency of social control. This is clear from the statements of many of the early school promoters.

Take for example, Dr. Sir James Kay-Shuttleworth, who became the secretary of the British Committee of the Privy Council on Education. He wrote in 1832:

> The operative population [his term for the proletariat] constitutes one of the most important elements of society, and when numerically considered, the magnitude of its interests and the extent of its power assumes such vast proportions, that the folly which neglects them is allied to madness. If the higher classes are unwilling to diffuse intelligence among the lower, those exist who are ever ready to take advantage of their ignorance; if they will not seek their confidence, others will excite their distrust; if they will not endeavor to promote domestic comfort, virtue, and knowledge among them, their misery, vice, and prejudice will prove volcanic elements, by whose explosive violence the structure of society may be destroyed (Hurt 1971:22).

Kay-Shuttleworth wrote at a time when ominous signs indicated that a revolution or revolutionary change just might be around the corner. The trade union movement was on the rise, and was still suspect. The "Tolpuddle Martyrs" were a group of landless agricultural laborers in Dorchester, England who were exported to Australia for promoting a union to protect rural workers. The Chartist Movement was growing and loudly demanding voting rights for urban workers. Luddites were smashing machinery in the belief that their jobs were being forfeited to technology. The spirit of the French Revolution with its call for fraternity and equality was still powerful. In view of developments such as these Kay-Shuttleworth suggested that the apathy of workers could no longer be taken for granted:

> laborers sought to extort by fear what they could no longer produce by virtuous exertion. Property seemed their enemy, therefore, they wrapped in one indiscriminating flame the stacks and homesteads of the southern countries, seeking the improvement of their lot by the destruction of capital." The remedy for these evils was to provide "a good secular education to enable them to understand the true causes which determine their physical condition and regulate the distribution of wealth among the several classes of society." This would secure to them "useful knowledge and...guard them against pernicious opinion (Hurt 1971:23).

Many speeches and writings of educators and government people support mass education as a means of control. One of the pioneers, the Reverend Andrew Bell, wrote of the beneficial effects of education, "the improvement in the subordination, and orderly conduct, and general behavior of the children, has been particularly noticed, and must be regarded as infinitely the most valuable part of its character" (Hurt 1971:14). A generation later, a Member of Parliament, R.A. Slaney, suggested to Parliamentarians that "If they did not give the humbler classes of society the means of obtaining a good practical education, in a short time it would be found that those people were not to be ruled by any government which could be found either on this or the other side of the house" (Hurt 1971:21).

Compulsory Education and Unemployment.   Despite these constant warnings from educators about the threat from the lower orders, the upper classes did not always heed the call for the extension of schools. In England it was not until the threat from below was combined with the threat of widespread unemployment among the lower orders that mass education was introduced. The attitude of the upper classes seemed to be that as long as the proletariat was preoccupied with work, the threat identified by school promoters was unreal. But, Musgrove has noted that by the 1860s the economy had a diminishing need for the labor of youthful workers. This situation, Musgrove argued, was the prelude to the introduction of compulsory education between 1870 and 1880. Not only was there a burgeoning population of young people, but advances in technology were displacing the young worker. Young people were no longer central to the economy; they were moving ever more onto the periphery (Musgrove 1965:74).

The consequence of the swelling numbers of young unemployed people was an increase in the number of delinquent youths. Children had been crucial to the work force in the earlier phases of industrialization. But in the mature phase of industrial capitalism, they were excluded from the work force. It was for children such as these that Dr. Barnardo diverted his intended mission to the Chinese. He intended to instruct the vagrant and delinquent children of the streets in useful trades and domestic service. Many of these poor unfortunates ended up in Canada (Bagnell 1980; Parr 1980).

The Canadian Case.   It may appear that what occurred in class-ridden England has no bearing on the experience of Canadians. In Canada, the feudal system had been eliminated and a titled aristocratic class owning vast tracts of land did not exist. But, given that the population was increasing quickly, partly as a result of the influx of anti-English Irish, driven overseas by the Great Famine of the 1840s, and that rebellions had occurred in 1837 and 1838 involving farmers and urban tradesmen, it is hardly surprising that the issue of social control was on the minds of the middle and upper classes.

As far as the promoters of education were concerned, a school system would teach the producing classes the values of the upper classes. Most important among these was a respect for private ownership of property. The schools were intended to inculcate in the pupils a respect for private property and the authority of the state. They were to provide an example of middle and upper class behavior and values for the lower orders to emulate. As Prentice puts it, quoting the Ontario Teachers Association of 1869, "In the hands of the teacher alone was the wand of the enchanter, by which savages were 'transformed into men' (Prentice 1977:132).

Is is clear, then, that a number of factors must enter into an explanation of the introduction of mass education at the lower levels. These are: a) a perceived increase in social unrest among the ranks of the proletariat and a general fear in the middle and upper classes of the consequences of democratic and socialist ideas; b) the emergence of a middle class with an interest in promoting bureaucratic institutions which they could control; c) in Britain, the decreasing reliance on young children as workers in the industrial process; and, d) in Canada, the arrival of many lower class immigrants who because of both their class *and* ethnic background were viewed as dubious citizens by promoters of education.

HIGHLIGHT

1. In Britain, concern with public education as a means of social control corresponded with the decline of religion and an increase in social unrest.
2. In Canada, compulsory education was intended for reasons similar to those advanced in Britain.

The Proletarian University

Over the past eighty years there has been a decline in the number of farmers and others who belong to the old petty bourgeoisie. There has been a simultaneous increase in the number of white collar employees, and an expansion of what elsewhere in this book has been called the new petty bourgeoisie—teachers, state officials, etc. These new occupations in advanced industrial-capitalism require university education. A legal career, which at one time was prepared for by apprenticeship in a lawyer's office, now requires a long and expensive university education. Journalism, which in the past was learned by an apprenticeship, now also requires a university education, often with a journalism specialization. One consequence of this development is that jobs formerly prepared for at the employer's expense, are now paid for by all taxpayers and citizens as a whole.

A related result of these changes has been the expansion and proletari-anization of the university system. In the past, when entry to the university system was restricted to no more than five percent of the population, university graduates normally ended up in petty bourgeois or bourgeois positions. University students were most often the sons and daughters of the wealthy, and the content of courses was often less important than the hidden (or not so hidden) curriculum of learning genteel skills of social intercourse. These social interaction skills were obtained at fraternities and sororities, and in clubs of various sorts. In fact, the formal curriculum was often the least important part of univer-sity to many students and their parents. For females, the purpose of university education was frequently the acquisition of a spouse of a comparable upper or upper middle-class background. And although the university system always included important utilitarian courses, such as medicine or law, there was a toleration, or even encouragement, of courses that were not job oriented such as history, classics, or philosophy.

A similar pattern still exists. Clement (1975) has shown that specific universities are usually chosen by individuals who can be defined as members of an elite. These included the University of Toronto, McGill, and Queens.

In the 1950s and 1960s many new universities were built in Canada. As a consequence, the participation rate in higher education increased dramatically. Some of the increase—though not much—was due to the fact that more farmers and blue collar workers were sending their children to university. Although upon graduation some children of working class families entered the better paid petty bourgeois occupa-tions such as law and medicine, many were destined for programs leading to white collar jobs such as nursing and teaching.

An American author writing in a Canadian journal has described this general process of 'proletarianization' of the university in her article, "The Increasing Stratification of Higher Education: Ideology and Conse-quences". Sharon Mayes comments, in referring to the American con-text, that "as higher education has expanded and diversified, it has become a hierarchical system of institutions. It has stratified into at least three distinct levels: the elite university..., the mass university, and the community colleges" (1977:16). She goes on to differentiate the voca-tional outcomes of the differing higher education systems: "Ivy League and prestigious state universities produce students to fill the upper echelons of business, professions, and academe. The vast majority of mass university students enter white collar bureaucratic and middle-level management positions, and the growing ranks of community college students swell the ranks of skilled and technical labor in indus-try" (Mayes 1977:17).

The mass or proletarian university is of particular significance because of the role it plays in increasing the rate of student participation at the level of higher education. Let us examine further its nature and function.

Those students attending a mass university tend to come from roughly the same background as community college students. This is not typical of past university populations, or of those attending the elite schools. The programs in which the mass university students are enrolled are not of a professional nature. Instead of schools of law, medicine or dentistry, students are found in faculties such as physical education, nursing and education. Thus, there is a high degree of vocationalism present as evidenced both within programs offered, and the number of students found in specifically job-related courses. In sociology, for example, almost half the total enrolment is concentrated in introductory sociology, criminology and social problems.

This orientation of the mass university can be partially attributed to recent economic developments. In a rapidly expanding economy the cultural focus of education is encouraged. During times of retrenchment, a vocational emphasis is established.

Although the trend towards vocationalism has been affected by changing economic conditions, it would be a mistake to see this change as a short-term development. With the decline of the traditional petty bourgeois farmers, the nature of the class system in Canada has changed substantially. The size of the blue-collar working class has declined somewhat over the past few years, and the university system has altered as a result of the expansion of the proportion of the population not directly engaged in producing either commodities or food.

The growth of this segment of the population has resulted in the expansion of higher education. Because the members of this group, who rely on their university credentials to obtain jobs, are so large, it is increasingly more difficult for the university to justify its existence as a centre for the dissemination of knowledge for its own sake.

The movement towards vocationalism is thus a continuing trend that is part of the transformation of the class system. This trend has been the subject of a recent study by Norene Pupo (1978). Pupo examined the development of the University of Waterloo in the 1950s with its emphasis on science and technology and vocationally oriented programs. The establishment of this school must be seen in connection with a 1956 announcement by the Ontario government that it was implementing "a ten year programme of capital assistance to provincial universities and technical institutes, the aim of which was 'to boost the output of engineers and technicians'" (1978:144). Members from the world of corporate business were at the forefront of this movement, in that they advised the government and the public that "efficient and increased production of highly trained people was key to the nation's ability to maintain a competitive position among the industrialized countries of the world" (1978:145).

What characterizes the University of Waterloo is its intense vocational focus and a "co-operative plan" by which students spend their time alternating between study and related work experience. The co-operative plan, originally conceived for such programs as engineering, has been expanded into the arts and social sciences as well.

The graduates of the co-operative program have been well received by business. A Bell Canada executive was quoted as saying that the graduates were "more mature, ready to produce, and less costly to hire" (Pupo 1978:151). It would seem that the program is co-operative not only in the sense that the university is twinned directly with business, but that it produces a more co-operative workforce. As Pupo suggests, "The programme established one more formal link between the university and the socio-economic order" (1978:151).

The Community College.   Another result of the increasing vocationalism of the higher education system has been the development of the community college network. In these schools the vocational function is even clearer than at the university level. Like much else in Canadian society, the community college concept is an American import. (As demonstrated in the chapter on culture and ideology, imitation of the centre by the periphery in the ideological sphere is a common occurrence).

The American community college system began at the turn of the century but was not fully accepted and implemented until the 1960s (Pincus 1978:173). Pincus outlines two sets of goals for the colleges. The first are "public goals" which are linked to the ideas of democracy and egalitarianism. Such goals imply an open door policy for all potential students; the opportunity for a second chance for those who did not do well in high school or who faced other obstacles in the attainment of an education; a comprehensive curriculum so that everyone can find something to their taste; a convenient location so that entrance is not restricted because of geographic distance. A final public goal is defined as 'community orientation'. As Pincus (1978:175) suggests, all these goals "are designed to bring equal opportunity to all students in higher education".

For Pincus, there are other goals which are secondary to the publicly stated objectives. One such unstated goal is for the community colleges to act as a screening agency. Decisions are made concerning who should enter terminal programs and who should be allowed into transfer programs leading to university. To act as a place where students accept and even like their fate on the lower rungs of the class ladder is another unstated aim. In their own limited circulation journals, community college educators will sometimes admit to these aims:

Community colleges may be worth the money if they do nothing more than this: One student came here never having liked to read or write and never having been very good at either. Yet, he wanted to be a lawyer. After some counselling he realized the odds against him were high, so he joined the Air Force. 'Apparently' says the counsellor, 'he's quite happy about it' (Pincus 1978:177).

It should be stressed, however, that coming to terms with one's limitations is not necessarily a bad thing.

Another unstated goal is that of custodial care. The college is "to keep these young people out of the labour market, off the streets and out of trouble" (Pincus 1978:177).

The community college system, according to Pincus, has developed as intended. It is a proletarian alternative to the university. The pressures on universities to expand have been intense. The presence of the community college has taken some of the pressure off by diverting working class students who might otherwise demand entrance to the university. Although the university currently admits students further down the economic ladder than previously, traditional barriers nonetheless remain.

In Canada, as in the United States, community colleges train paraprofessionals rather than professionals. A study on community colleges in British Columbia presents facts even more striking than those revealed by Pincus on the prospects for academic advancement for community college students. In the case of British Columbia, "Almost 40% of college students expected to obtain some sort of university degree." But, it is argued, "expectations are not in line with reality since only about 5% transfer from college to university. Even among academic transfer students only 20% actually transfer, compared to 58% indicating transfer expectations. In other words, the expectations of a large proportion of college students are not being realized" (Dennison et al. 1975:51).

In the typical mass university, there is no difference between the socioeconomic status of those students and community college students. Undoubtedly more students from low income families are now getting to university as compared to, say, twenty years ago. But this finding is largely attributable to the strong vocational emphasis of the proletariat university and is not typical of other (elite) universities.

A more typical finding is reported by Dennison and his associates in their 1971-75 study of British Columbia community colleges. At the colleges, 38 percent of students came from professional or managerial backgrounds. The comparable figure for the universities was 49 percent (1975:40). The community college system in British Columbia is similar to that in Quebec in that terminal, vocational programs are mixed with two year university credit courses (the student completes two years of university material at the college before transferring to the university itself). If the varying programs are broken down further, 56 percent of the community college "vocational" students are recruited from clerical, trade, service, mining, forestry or unskilled backgrounds, as opposed to 31 percent of the university students (Dennison, et al. 1975:40). In the summary of findings, Dennison et al. (1975:154-5) reported that university students typically had parents with higher educational levels, higher incomes, and higher status occupations.

It is time now to summarize some of these findings on higher education. Higher education (or more accurately post-secondary education) is no longer restricted to the scions of the wealthy. But the real nature of change can be found in the creation of many new non-elite universities and non-elite programs which train new white collar employees for their role in the reproduction of the socio-economic order. Elite universities and programs, while they have opened up a bit, still cater to the wealthy. Thus, liberal sociologists of education are mistaken when they suppose that the expansion of post-secondary education has resulted in the dissolution of class barriers to education. Rather, these class barriers are being reproduced within an ever larger and more stratified educational system. Anyone aspiring to upward mobility would find a university education desirable, but such an individual would have to choose both the university and their course of study with care. Even then education cannot guarantee mobility. What is clear is that a university education in nursing, education, or outdoor recreation does not prepare a student for anything other than a position as a white collar employee. A degree in law or business, at the *right* elite university, might be more promising in terms of real upward mobility.

HIGHLIGHT

1. An increase in the number of white collar or petty bourgeois occupations has resulted in an increase in university enrolment and the founding of new universities.
2. This process can be called the proletarianization of the university. While universities formerly emphasized "useless knowledge" such as classics, proletarianization has gone hand in hand with increased vocationalism.
3. Despite proletarianization, the sons and daughters of the wealthy continue to attend elite schools.
4. A disproportionate number of the sons and daughters of working class families end up in vocationally oriented community colleges.
5. As well as having public goals—e.g. egalitarianism—community colleges can also be viewed as having unstated goals.

The Hidden Curriculum

On the surface, schools are concerned with the transmission of knowledge. Beyond this surface level, however, are values and practices taught and encouraged by the schools.

The position of the teacher and the physical arrangement of desks help identify the teacher as the expert and authority. In most fields of knowledge there are widely varying theories and outlooks which are open to individual interpretation by each teacher. Since the student accepts what the teacher presents, a piggy bank theory of education is used to describe this system of learning: the student is seen as the piggy bank accepting the "coins of wisdom" deposited by the teacher. The best teacher is often defined as the one who can deposit the most coins, and ensure their retention.

Because knowledge that is transmitted in primary and secondary schools is so frequently presented as the "common knowledge" of a society, the student is often unaware of the controversies that surround most areas of knowledge. The fact that "common knowledge" is often *not* neutral, detached, or independent from the wider socio-economic order is often perceived most sharply only when there is a change of political regime and a change in the school system and curriculum. Then it becomes clearer that knowledge is a weapon in various political struggles.

An interesting opportunity to observe this process is provided by an examination of the recent efforts by the Quebec Ministry of Education to implement a new *histoire nationale.* According to two critics, this new curriculum "places a heavy emphasis on materialistic economic determinism at the expense of the moral, intellectual and spiritual forces that have shaped our society". It "discounts the role of the individual in history to a point that belies credibility", and it is filled with "anti-English and pro-separatist allusions" (Kelebay and Brooks 1980:33).

In the past, Liberal or Union Nationale governments no doubt sponsored a curriculum with a far different content. Such a content in the case of the Liberal governments was undoubtedly more favorable to the English presence in Quebec, and in both cases more accepting of a capitalist ethos and of the importance of great figures in history. The point being made is not that one approach is wrong or the other is right. It is that both approaches proceed on the assumption of a single version of the truth.

The consequence of emphasizing only one view of reality is that education is not the means to shape a critical individual. Instead it reinforces the belief that knowledge transmitted through education must not be questioned. At Oxford and Cambridge Universities (traditionally oriented to the British upper classes) teaching has relied upon the tutorial system in which a professor meets with his students singly or in pairs. The student presents a short paper almost weekly and is required to defend it before the professor and other student. Another tradition at "Oxbridge" is the debate in which each person is expected to be able to argue either side of any question. Thus, at the elite level, there has been a recognition that truth is difficult to ascertain, and that it may look different to different people. At the mass education level, by way of contrast, education is systematically more authoritarian.

The student who is not encouraged to see different sides of an issue or to question the knowledge he or she receives will tend to make an easier transition to the workplace than might otherwise have been the case. The student is already socialized to deal with a formal bureaucratic system, and to accept authority figures like bosses, superiors, or foremen, who pass on orders. Consequently, both the classroom and the workplace are places which breed alienation. The student/worker must attend the school/workplace, but in neither stituation has that system been built in accordance with individual needs. The workplace has been constructed to maximize profits. The school, to the degree that it conditions individuals to accept authoritarian structures, indirectly works to benefit capitalist owners.

Organization of the School and Society.   In a capitalist society, it is likely that the values of the classroom will in some way mirror the mode of production. In a tribal mode of production, the system of education consists of an alliance between two generations. In a modern classroom, neither the teacher nor the students normally own their classroom. It is usually owned by someone else, usually the State. This situation mirrors the general economic system. For example, the Thunder Bay *Chronicle-Journal* or *Times-News* is produced by a combination of workers including press people, advertising personnel, journalists, editors, managers, and publishers. Whatever control is in the hands of the managers and editors is not their own control, but that delegated from head office and indirectly, Kenneth Thomson, the owner. The same is true of principals and teachers who do not exercise real control, only delegated control.

In a capitalist mode of production, the division of labor and the class system will normally be mirrored by the school. Unlike a tribal society in which everyone participates in the same tasks and all share equal power and resources, in a capitalist society the division of labor is high, and power and resources unequally divided. The same principle is found in the school system. First, there is the system of private schools which cater to the wealthy. (Clement (1977:7) reports 40 percent of the 1972 economic elite attended such institutions although children of the elite account for a miniscule percentage of the total school enrolment.) Second, there are other, and in some cases, less well equipped schools for the rest of the population.

There are other ways in which schools mirror unequal power and resources. Some are set aside for those destined to be manual workers. Non-technical schools frequently offer different courses of study that lead to different jobs. This would not be a bad thing were it not for the fact that a disproportionate number of individuals from working class families, for reasons other than intelligence, often end up in programs that do not make maximum use of their abilities. The process whereby individuals are slotted in categories is referred to as 'tracking.' Further examples of tracking include the distinctions in some high schools in Ontario between those enrolled in four and five year programs and the practice of dividing classes, or groups of classes, in terms of level of attainment. It must be stressed that no judgment is being made on whether or not these and other measures are good or bad. The intent is to demonstrate how certain processes or power-structures found in society in general are also evident in the school.

Transmission of Values. Besides tracking, it can be noted that schools also mirror the wider society by instilling the values of a capitalist mode of production. Bleasdale has suggested that such values include "competition, elitism, authoritarianism, pragmatism, and materialism" (1978:15).

The way in which such values are taught can be more easily observed by taking a close look at a school system which was created to act as a system of cultural replacement for Indian children. The purpose of Shingwauk School was to resocialize Ojibway children and prepare them for an industrial-capitalist mode of production. This school was established in Sault Ste. Marie in 1873 but (in one form or other) lasted until 1971. When reading this account, we might all ask ourselves if the same could not be said for our own school experience.

First, competition was encouraged. It was symbolized by the marking system. The pupils were classified in one of four ways: victor, aspirant, below mark, and lag. The principal stated: "The result of the six examinations alluded to is that out of 85 boys—10 were always victors, 28 victor or aspirant, 29 generally below mark or lag" (Nock 1978:243). One of the Shingwauk boys attended Trinity College School (one of Canada's best known private schools) and wrote back: "I am trying hard to get a prize. I hope the boys at Shingwauk are studying hard too. The boys here are studying till 10 o'clock at night. I think I will be ahead in Latin, for I am always ahead in our form, and the boys are so stupid they can't tell between nouns and adjectives. I am the only one that declined them right this morning" (Nock 1978:244). Regarding a system of marks and prizes in the Sault Ste. Marie school, the principal remarked that "The pupils are thus obliged to keep constantly and steadily at work through the whole year in order to gain prizes" (1978:243).

Values at Shingwauk were taught to make it easier for the children to become good *employees*. One letter from a pupil suggested that, "Politeness often gives people a good situation" (Nock 1978:242). Another such letter read, "Hundreds of men and boys have got into high offices for their honesty. When a man looks out for a boy to work for him, he does not choose a strong and active boy, but an honest boy."

The principal made sure his pupils learned other values that are important to employees such as punctuality and cleanliness. One boy wrote, "And anything we want to do we ought to do it at once and not to be late, and we ought not to be late in the roll call, and we must not get late in school." Another boy wrote about the virtues of tidiness: "Now, when children are sent to school, they are taught to keep themselves tidy, and be like gentlemen and ladies after they leave school" (Nock 1978:242).

Traditionally, such values have also been taught in public and secondary schools, with marks or grades assigned for such matters as deportment, punctuality, tidiness, etc. It is not hard to see that such values are important for *employees* who must become accustomed to pleasing others and be capable of routinized work for long periods of time. Thus, schools have traditionally emphasized bells, buzzers, and punctuality with some form of punishment, detention or suspension of privileges for infractions. The students thus learn ways of behaving that will smooth their path in the world of work.

The ability to handle labor discipline is one of the most important things learned at school. It involves acceptance of routinized tasks and the domination of the clock. In the case of the Indians, the latter was one of the hardest things to teach. Indians worked hard at their hunting and gathering tasks. But it was not the sort of work that demanded attendance at the same spot at the same time daily, and there was a high degree of seasonal variation.

A clock-conscious mentality and the ability to handle labor routinization are learned behavior. This is evident from the absence of these characteristics in tribal societies. Their inculcation can be viewed as an important part of the educational process of industrial-capitalist society.

The Future.   The question may be raised: what does the future hold in store for education and what will be its relation to the socio-economic system? Some indications are aleady available. There will be an increasing switch to a computer based technology in education. However, computer based teaching will be no more free of the constraints of the wider society than was free and compulsory education in the nineteenth century. Jan Mayer has pointed to some further implications of computer based education in an article in *The Canadian Forum*. She suggests that the computerization of learning is a form of mystification because it appears to promote individual control over a person's own learning and appears to add to the range of choices which can be made by an individual. Yet behind this presumed range of choice is an ideology, that of individualism and all it implies. As Mayer suggests: "Individualism... continues to be invoked by the entrenched power interests of late capitalism in the form of the dominant social values" (Mayer 1981:29). According to Mayer, educators have "ignored the potential for ideological manipulation posed by computerized learning" (Mayer 1981:30).

HIGHLIGHT

1. Schools usually attempt to present students with one version of the truth.
2. The clear exception to this trend is elite universities such as Oxford and Cambridge that attempt through various mechanisms to prepare students to handle multiple realities.
3. In various ways the organization of education parallels the organization of society, particularly with regard to power.
4. The values transmitted through the education system help to make students good employees.
5. Computer-based education, the wave of the future, does not provide the student with increased freedom of choice in what he or she learns. All options are embedded in a liberal ideological framework.

Conclusion

The thesis of this chapter is a simple one: each system of education is closely tied to the dominant mode of production. This assumption, known as the correspondence principle, has been rejected by many sociologists of education. Such scholars usually play down the importance of class in our society, or emphasize the industrial nature of our society to the exclusion of its capitalist nature. Others suggest that the capitalist class has lost control because of the triumph of democracy. Such an attitude is voiced by, among others, the French sociologist Raymond Aron. He writes that, "Indirectly, by means of social pluralism and competing political parties, industrial society is nearing the democratic ideal" (Aron 1969:61). A prominent American sociologist, S.M. Lipset, writes that in "western political life... the fundamental political problems of the industrial revolution have been solved" and he points to "this very triumph of the democratic social revolution in the West" (Lipset 1963:442). Another prominent American sociologist, Arnold Rose, suggests that in the United States "power is so complicated... that the top businessmen scarcely understand it, much less control it..." (Rose 1967:490). If such things are true, then the citizen really is sovereign and controls the State and its educational system.

This chapter has illustrated the ways in which education has been tied to the mode of production. The connection has been illustrated in a number of ways. The stratification of the educational system, especially the post-secondary levels, has been shown to correspond to the increased growth of classes or segments of classes that are neither commodity nor food producers. The introduction of free and compulsory formal education has been traced back to changes in industrial technology and to bourgeois fears of working class rebellion. Finally, the form of the curriculum has been shown to be as important as its content in the preparation of pupils for the world of work. Ironically, the survival of relatively "useless" educational programs, such as classics or philosophy, is another indicator of the correspondence principle. Such non-vocational courses were originally introduced for upper class individuals who did not need a profession to carry them through life. As the stratification of the post-secondary system advanced, such courses suffered in terms of enrolments. At the post-secondary level the student body is now drawn from a wider social base than previously—from individuals whose class location necessitates a functional and utilitarian education.

NOTES

[1]From *Power and Privilege* by G. Lenski. Copyright © 1966, Mcgraw-Hill Inc. Used with the permission of McGraw-Hill Book Company.

SUGGESTED READINGS

Canadian Journal of Education, 4:2, 1979, pp. 43-54. Marilyn Assheton-Smith. "John Porter's Sociology: A Theoretical Basis for Canadian Education". An excellent critique of the sociology of education developed by perhaps Canada's best-known and most influential sociologist of the last twenty years. His sociology of education is criticized in many of the same terms used more generally in this chapter.

Schooling in Capitalist America, Samuel Bowles and Herbert Ginitis. New York: Basic Books, 1976. This is one of the most influential Marxist or neo-Marxist works in the field and suggests the importance of the "hidden curriculum".

Sociological Theories of Education, Raymond Murphy. Toronto: McGraw-Hill Ryerson, 1979. Written with the secondary authorship of Ann B. Denis. This book is very useful in presenting much of the European approach to sociology of education from such places as France and Switzerland. There is, also, much material on Canada.

Reading, Writing, and Riches: Education and the Socio-Economic Order in North America, R. W. Nelsen and David A. Nock, eds. Kitchener and Toronto: Between-the-lines, 1978. This book utilizes a materialist approach to analyse Canadian education and compares it to the United States.

The School Promoters: Education and Social Class in Mid-Nineteenth Century Upper Canada, Alison Prentice. Toronto: McClelland and Stewart, 1977. This book is a detailed study of the advent of compulsory public schooling in Canada and describes in depth the motivation of the school promoters.

The Canadian State, Stephen Schecter. Toronto: University of Toronto Press, 1977. "Capitalism, Class and Educational Reform" in Leo Panitch, ed. This is a serious attempt to use a neo-Marxist approach in analysing the development of Canadian education.

CULTURE, IDEOLOGY AND SOCIETY
J. Paul Grayson

Introduction

Cultural Determinism and Materialism. Examinations of the nature and importance of what can loosely be described as ideologies and cultures have been one of the central concerns of social scientists. At one extreme it is possible to identify 'cultural determinists', or 'idealists'. These are individuals who view ideas as the motive force in history and society. In other words, people do things—e.g., change the way they make a living, go to war, make love—in accordance with the ideas they have concerning how, and when, these things should be done. More importantly, the impetus to change ideas, by and large, comes from within the idea systems themselves. Thus, to a large degree, industrial capitalism can be explained in terms of the evolution of Judeo-Christian culture in Western Europe. At the same time, the inability of other parts of the world to advance to industrialism can be explained by their adherence to other sets of ideas or cultures. It is fair to say that until the late 1960s such assumptions were clearly dominant in the social sciences in the Western Hemisphere (Chirot 1977).

An adherence to these assumptions had its advantages. It meant, for example, that when Western social scientists were examining poverty in the Third World and elsewhere, they could point to the cultures of the poor in explanation for this condition. If entire sections of the world were poor, it was their own fault.[1] Accordingly, little time was spent analyzing the operations of, for example, multinational corporations and the impact of these entities on weak states.

The school of thought in sociology that most clearly embraces a form of cultural determinism is called functionalism. According to Abercrombie et al (1980:47), one of the fundamental assumptions of this orientation is that: "Values, norms and meaning do not emerge out of the process of social interaction; they are imposed on the unit act. The actor orients to the situation in terms of norms which already exist and which structure action".

In contrast to cultural determinism or idealism, the perspective defined as 'materialism', as indicated in an earlier chapter, contains the notion that ideas have little independent impact on the course of historical developments or on the way in which people act. Rather, ideas must be seen in relation to other things occurring in society, and particularly in the economy. In essence, in contrast to the idealist perspective, the materialist position rejects the proposition that ideas have an independent existence. Rather, they must be seen as both deriving from, and directing the process whereby, people go about the business of making a living.

This said, it must be stressed that culture or ideology need not be directly 'determined' by the way in which people make a living. Instead, how people make a living—the economy—imposes a set of limiting factors on the culture and type of ideas that are possible within a given context.

To use the example advanced above, in contrast to the cultural determinists, when materialists examine poverty in third world societies, they give primary importance *not* to the cultures of the nations involved, but to the relations, particularly in the economic sphere, between poor and rich societies. They explain poverty in terms of the exploitation of poor nations, via such vehicles as the multinationals, by rich imperialist nations. Any cultural differences that might be found are secondary to— but nonetheless may be factors contributing to—these so-called 'structural' factors.

In this chapter, attention will focus on an examination of culture and ideology in a way consistent with some materialist propositions. Of necessity, such an analysis must start with a brief review of the nature of a mode of production and some other concepts advanced earlier.

Mode of Production.   A mode of production, it will be remembered, consists of the productive forces and relations to the means of production. The productive forces can be divided further into the means of production, labor-power, and general labor. The means of production includes "on the one hand useful materials from natural sources: minerals, coal, petroleum, wood, water, etc.; and on the other hand, the instruments of production: tools, machinery, and—advanced equipment." (Jalee 1977:10). Labor-power, in turn, can be viewed as what human beings do when they actively engage in the transformation of materials into commodities. And general labor, "covers the skill and experience acquired by the workers over generations, the cumulative contributions of scientific and technical innovation, and the modern organization of collective labor" (Jalee 1977:10). It should be noted that particularly in this last definition, the term labor is being used in a highly specialized way. Students frequently have difficulty with this usage as they continue to think of the term as it is commonly used in daily speech.

Classes.   The relations to the means of production, the second major component of a mode of production, are defined in terms of the ownership of the means of production. In some societies and in certain periods of history, those who supply the labor-power also own the materials, tools, etc.—the means of production—with which they work. Such was the case with the medieval artisan. It is also true for the contemporary Canadian farmer. In other instances those who supply the labor-power do not own the means of production. They must therefore work for someone else. As was seen in an earlier chapter, these men and women sell their labor. What they receive in return is usually called a wage or a salary. Examples of individuals who fit these circumstances include the vast majority of Canadian blue-collar and white-collar workers.

Individuals who can be grouped together in terms of whether or not they own their means of production constitute classes. In other words, in contemporary Canadian society, those who own the materials, factories, etc., constitute one class, usually referred to as the bourgeoisie. Those who sell their labor to the bourgeoisie are referred to as the proletariat or working class. As the nature of the exploitative relationship that exists between these classes, and the existence of other classes, has been discussed elsewhere, it will not be elaborated on here; however, it must be remembered that in Canadian society it is also possible to identify what have been called a petty bourgeoisie and a new petty bourgeoisie.

Capitalism. The mode of production that characterizes contemporary Canada, i.e., one in which those who supply the labor do not own the means of production, is called 'capitalist'. Other contemporary societies such as Britain, France, and the United States also have a capitalist mode of production. Nonetheless, a mode of production must be seen in terms of both the *level* attained by its productive forces as well as the *relations* to the means of production. In other words, different levels exist *within* the capitalist and/or other modes of production. For example, Canada a century ago could be characterized as an example of competitive capitalism. Today, to some extent, it typifies what is called advanced capitalism.

Dominant and Subordinate Modes. It is extremely important to recognize that what we usually think of as a society—e.g. Canada, Germany, France—can have more than one mode of production (Foster-Carter 1978). In medieval European societies, for example, it is possible to identify a feudal mode of production and, gradually, the development of a capitalist mode of production within feudal society. In circumstances such as these, the feudal mode of production is described as the dominant mode; capitalism is the subordinate mode. The term 'transitional society' can be used to describe situations in which two or more modes of production co-exist without either being dominant.

Not surprisingly, interactions occur among various modes of production. For example, the feudal mode supplied labor to the capitalist mode, in that those who originally engaged in agricultural production on feudal estates were either driven off, or voluntarily left, their former positions. Consequently, they were available for employment in capitalist enterprises. At the same time, the capitalist mode of production was increasingly able to supply goods for consumption by the feudal aristocracy and to lend them money with which, among other things, nobles could use to finance their wars.

While the development of capitalism in feudal society is a classic example of the co-existence of two modes of production, it is not the only one. In early Canada, for example, European fur trading companies can be viewed as part of a commercial capitalist mode of production. However, up to a point, the relations that existed among Indians who supplied fur to the Europeans were pre-capitalistic. The important point is that once again important transactions or exchanges occurred between different modes of production. While the mode of production engaged in by the Indians rapidly gave way to the capitalist mode of production, a minority of native peoples, particularly in the far North, can still be seen as participating in a pre-capitalistic mode of production (Berger 1977). In many third world societies like India, though, it is possible to identify a relatively large pre-industrial mode of production co-existing with a capitalist one.

The Petty Producers' Mode.   While a number of different modes of production can co-exist in third world societies, it has been argued that in contemporary capitalist societies the range is narrower. Indeed, some have argued that the options are limited to one: the 'petty producers mode of production'. Individuals engaged in this mode own their own means of production and hire little or no labor. Moreover, individuals in this mode do not produce mainly for a market but for themselves. Historically, "the economic agent that typifies this mode of production is the artisan or peasant farmer" (Moniere 1981:34). While only a few can be viewed as currently participating in this mode in Canada, the opposite was true in the past. As was seen in an earlier chapter, the petty producers' mode of production had important implications for ideology, particularly in Quebec.

Surplus Value and Social Control.   It was seen in an earlier chapter that, in a capitalist society, a portion of the labor of the working class, or what was defined as surplus labor, accrues to the owners of the means of production. It was also seen that, in Canada at least, the proportion of surplus labor acquired by the bourgeoisie has increased over time—the amount of time required for the worker to produce enough commodities to pay his/her wages takes up less and less of the day. It is further evident that in Canada the gap between the rich and the poor is getting wider, not narrower. In the face of these observations, the question arises: Why do people continue to work in mines, factories, offices, etc. when they are acquiring less and less of the fruits of their labor? What is it, in essence, that cements the mode of production together?

It should be obvious that questions such as these are not unique to the capitalist mode of production. In feudal times the aristocracy also acquired some of the fruits of the labor of others. But they did it in a different fashion (Poulantzas 1978). Whereas in contemporary Canada the bourgeoisie are able to acquire part of the workers' labor because the bourgeoisie own the means of production, in feudal times the lords did not always own the means of production in the same way that the capitalist owns a factory. As a consequence, they had to rely on political means of obtaining what was produced by the peasant. For example, the peasant might give to the lord a portion of his crop because if he did not, it, and perhaps more, would simply be taken from him. In contemporary capitalist Canada, the bourgeoisie rely on what are regarded as natural market mechanisms to acquire surplus value. The worker has his/her labor to sell, nothing more. The bourgeoisie buys this labor for as little as possible. This is not the best of circumstances for the working class. But if they do not work, they starve.

The Dull Compulsion of Economic Relations.   This possibility is in fact one of the most forceful ties that binds the capitalist mode of production together. Even if he/she is less than enamored with a situation in which others get rich on the basis of his/her labor, the working class person is usually incapable of indulging in the luxury of withdrawing services or seeking employment elsewhere. Given that few have savings that would carry them over an extended period of unemployment, they are unlikely to engage in behavior that would result in their firing. Likewise, for similar reasons, they are unlikely to voluntarily leave a job, independent of its level of undesirability, without alternate employment. This form of social cement has been referred to by Marx as the 'dull compulsion of economic relations'.

The Repressive State Apparatus.   Other mechanisms that ensure the longevity of a mode of production include a set of social practices and institutions collectively referred to as the repressive state apparatus (Althusser 1971). Many of the components of this apparatus are analyzed in more detail in other chapters. Suffice it to say that social practices embodied in law and enforced by the judiciary are part of this apparatus. It must be stressed, however, that under certain circumstances there is less than a consensus concerning the appropriate body of law to be adhered to. Such was the case in the Middle Ages (Tigar and Levy 1977). Later, it will also be shown that in many senses the social practices embodied in law can also be seen as ideology. The quality of law entitling it to a place in the repressive state apparatus is its coercive and class nature. It is coercive because it prohibits certain actions such as theft. It has a class nature in that many laws operate, in our society, to the advantage of the owners of the means of production and to the disadvantage of the working class. All features of the repressive state apparatus share the coercive prerogative and, in many instances, work to the advantage of certain classes.

Using the above criterion for the repressive state apparatus, it is clear that the police are participants in it. Again, it will not be argued that all of their actions are necessarily class biased. Ensuring that speed limits are observed, for example, is to everyone's benefit. On the other hand, there have been too many cases in which, for instance, the RCMP or provincial police have been utilized against striking mine or factory workers, for us to accept that they are neutral in disputes between classes.

In many instances the armed forces can likewise be viewed as part of the repressive state apparatus. This was brought home very forcefully in the FLQ (Front de Liberation de Quebec) crisis in 1970. In this instance the Canadian armed forces, after the kidnapping of a British diplomat by the FLQ, occupied the province of Quebec (Rioux 1978). The justification given by the federal government was that Quebec was in a state of 'apprehended insurrection' and so invoked the War Measures Act. This was undoubtedly inspired in part by the FLQ Manifesto that condemned the Canadian capitalist system of production and demanded change. Whether or not the reader considers state action under these circumstances justified, it must be nonetheless viewed as a form of repression. Such actions on the part of the armed forces are perhaps more commonly associated with other societies, like the 'banana republics' of Central America.

Ideology.   The last factors operative in ensuring the perpetuation of a particular mode of production are ideology, culture, and the ideological state apparatus. It is, however, more difficult to demonstrate the operation of ideology and culture than either the 'dull compulsion of economic relations' or the repressive state apparatus. Difficulties notwithstanding, ideology and culture are necessary components of all contemporary societies and, consequently, require serious consideration.

HIGHLIGHT

1. Explanations of social developments can be divided into those with a cultural or idealist bias and those with a materialist one. The former stress the role of ideas; the latter, while it does not ignore the role of ideas, also emphasizes the importance of economic factors.
2. The capitalist mode of production is one in which a portion of the labor of the working class—surplus labor—is appropriated by the owners of the means of production.
3. The working class tolerates this situation because it must work to live,

and because of the repressive state and ideological apparatuses. In combination, these bind society together.

Ideology and Culture

Definitions.   The appropriate way to begin a discussion of ideology is with a definition. This, however, is more difficult than it may appear. Writers sharing the perspective advanced in this book have often used the concept in different ways. According to Williams (1977:53) they have treated ideology as:

1) a system of beliefs characteristic of a particular class or group;
2) a system of illusory beliefs—false ideas or false consciousness—which can be contrasted with true scientific knowledge;
3) the general process of the production of meanings and ideas.

Independent of how others use the term, Williams believes that ideology should be reserved for a "relatively formal and articulated system of meanings, values, and beliefs, of a kind that can be abstracted as a 'world view' or a 'class outlook'" (1977:109). This definition, while it is more complicated than the one in Chapter 2, is nonetheless consistent with it.

In this chapter, ideology will be treated as a systemized body of beliefs that legitimize the rule of dominant classes and, at the same time, provide a backdrop against which individuals may interpret their everyday lives. Examples that would be included under this definition are liberalism, and fascism. Each are relatively systemized. Each can be identified with, at certain junctures in history, particular classes. Each can provide interpretations for daily occurrences.

Williams takes great pains to distinguish ideology from culture. The latter is viewed as "a 'whole social process', in which men define and shape their whole lives" (1977:108). It includes the process by which meanings are established and communicated as well as the meanings themselves. Paramount among the processes giving rise to meaning and beliefs is the process of earning a living. The way in which people earn their livelihood, however, is contingent on their class. For example, it does not take long, if one is continuously engaged in monotonous repetitive work, to develop a certain set of beliefs about the way the world works and one's place in it. Conversely, if one acquires a fortune as a result of the labor of others, a different set of beliefs and orientations will no doubt develop. When these beliefs and meanings become formal, systematized, and articulate, they become ideology. It is in this way that ideology derives from culture. It is also in this way that ideology acquires its class character. As will be seen later, those in certain classes are able to impose their ideologies on others.

To return to the question of culture, it is clear that culture is not monolithic. Williams divides it into four elements: the archaic, residual, dominant and emergent. These terms do not refer to the content of culture—the content of the meanings, beliefs, etc.—but to the *relations* among different sets of meanings and beliefs.

The Archaic. To elaborate further, the archaic is "that which is wholly recognized as an element in the past, to be observed, to be examined, or even on occasion, to be consciously 'revived', in a deliberately special-ized way" (1977:122). The King Tutankhamen mania that accompanied the exhibition of his treasures in the late seventies is an example of the archaic. So, for example, is the practice sometimes followed by univer-sity students when they dress in medieval garb and have a period dinner. In both instances, what is being celebrated has no meaning outside of a context that is historically remote.

The Residual. The second element, the residual, "has been effec-tively formed in the past, but it is still active in the cultural process, not only and not all as an element in the past, but as an effective element of the present" (1977:122). In many cases, a residual element of culture is associated with a declining class or a declining mode of production. The activities of those who were in the closing of the nineteenth, and early years of the twentieth centuries defined as 'Canadian imperialists', provide a good example of a group that used the past to define the present.

During the period in question, Canadian imperialists did not espouse what we commonly associate with imperialism: the military, political or economic domination of weak by strong states. Rather, the label 'imperi-alists' was used to describe those who in the years 1867-1914 worked for "the closer union of the British Empire through economic and military co-operation and through political changes which would give the dominions influence over imperial policy" (Berger 1970:3). This did not imply that imperialists were prepared to submerge Canadian identity in a large supernational federation. Quite the contrary; involvement in an imperial federation was seen as a necessary condition for the mainte-nance of Canadian nationhood.

Although the movement never reached a true consensus over goals and strategy, the statements of its various leaders and supporters can be viewed as manifestations of imperialist political ideology. Equally impor-tant to ideology was the recognition on the part of some imperialists that if they were to be successful, they would be required to go beyond the political into such matters as art and literature. It was through vehicles such as these that the national consciousness—at least on the part of English-Canadians—was to be achieved. To use the distinctions between ideology and culture outlined above, some Canadian imperialists, via art and particularly literature, were concerned with transforming the every-day processes whereby meanings are produced to ensure that those meanings were consistent with the development of a Canadian nationality. A short-lived literary group called the Canada First Movement perhaps most consciously undertook the task of cultural transformation.

At a more general level the imperialists looked back to the United Empire Loyalists to legitimize their activities. (The conscious use of the past is why, in fact, it is possible to use the imperialists to illustrate the residual element of culture.) It was, after all, through the struggle of these courageous individuals that, for the imperialists, the British hold on Canada became consolidated. It is not surprising, therefore, that the imperialists expressed many of the same conservative values, and held some of the same views, as their ancestors: "they envisaged society as composed of functionally and organically related parts knit together by the impalpable filaments of mutual obligation and history" (Berger 1970:197). Acceptance of these values and beliefs was combined with "a repugnance towards capitalistic values and an abiding suspicion that the ferocious concentration upon material development and the single-minded pursuit of wealth and pleasure were undermining the nation's zest for adventure, respect for authority, and spirit of service and self-sacrifice" (1970:252).

Sentiments such as the above concerning the emerging capitalist industrialists in Canada are not surprising. It was, in fact, the urban based industrial and commercial bourgeoisie who were replacing, in terms of power and influence, the old traditional families. In the words of a contemporary:

> In English-speaking centres the old-time loyalist clan with its official connections, hereditary sentiment and sympathetic touch with English social traditions, has largely passed away or else has experienced the loss of position which so often follows the loss of property or means. Success-ful merchants, well-to-do manufacturers and prosperous professional men have succeeded to its social place and traditions..." (quoted in Berger, 1970:88).

In short, Canadian imperialism was spearheaded by individuals whose class was clearly on the wane. That they should, therefore, attempt to structure the present in terms of a perceived glorious past, or residual element of culture, is understandable. The fact that they failed in their major goal of imperial federation, under the circumstances, was to be expected.

At the same time, some researchers (Grant 1967; Horowitz 1966) have detected a continuity between some of the assumptions held by the imperialists and the introductions of such things as the Canadian Broad-casting Corporation, Trans Canada Airlines (now Air Canada) and a host of other state sponsored policies. The introduction of such measures, so the argument goes, reveals the basic assumption that society is an organism with mutual dependence among the parts—a belief that char-acterized the loyalist-conservative tradition. If there is some truth in this argument it must nonetheless be recognized that a number of other advanced capitalist societies have introduced similar measures.

The Emergent. The emergent refers to the "new meanings and values, new practices, new relationships and kinds of relationships [that] are continually being created" (Williams 1977:122). Whereas residual elements are frequently associated with the presence of a declining class or mode of production in society, the emergent is most often connected with the appearance of a new class or new mode of production. To a substantial degree Canadian and Quebec nationalism in the late nineteen sixties and early seventies, to the extent that it can be associated with the rapid expansion of a new petty bourgeoisie, can be viewed as emergent.

Nationalism itself, of course, is not a new phenomenon in Canada. As was seen when the residual was discussed, imperialists were of the opinion that imperial federation was a way of preserving Canadian nationhood. In different periods of history, however, nationalism may have different class bases.

In the post World War II Canadian context, nationalism has been defined as: "a concern that the political, economic, and cultural affairs of a territorially defined polity be controlled and directed by individuals and/or corporations that are members of that polity, rather than by forces outside it" (Resnick 1977:30). In the 1945-55 period, when a close connection with the United States was widely viewed as the means whereby economic prosperity would be assured, few voices in Canada were expressing nationalist concerns. By the 1956-65 period, however, some of the Canadian financial bourgeoisie were expressing reservations over the magnitude of the American presence. But this was short lived. Between 1966-75 the Canadian banks were themselves capable of competing on a world scale. Consequently, they were not supportive of any suggestions limiting the activities of multinational companies. At the same time, however, nationalism found a base among the new petty bourgeoisie. In other words, the experience of the new petty bourgeoisie during these years was such that it was receptive to an interpretation of their circumstances that included a nationalist component. In this sense, the nationalism was emergent.

In the post war years, there was a dramatic increase in the numbers of teachers, professionals, civil servants, and others who comprise the new petty bourgeoisie. To a large degree, the viability of this class was, and is, contingent upon the continued expansion of the state sector. As Resnick points out with regard to a number of nationalist demands that were being made of the state, "It was the new petty bourgeoisie that stood to be the chief beneficiary of the symbolic investment now called for in 'science policy', 'cultural policy', 'independent foreign policy' and so on" (1977:174).

While the new petty bourgeoisie would have been among the beneficiaries of nationalist policies, there is no doubt that there was cause for
alarm. Most of Canada's manufacturing was controlled by the United
States, as was virtually all of its petrochemical industry. More to the
point, U.S. control was increasing (Levitt, 1970). At the same time, the
Canadian market was, and still is, inundated with American books and
periodicals, films, and television programs (Crean 1976). Likewise, students in primary and secondary schools, educated with, in many
instances, U.S. texts and methods, remained virtually ignorant of their
own society (Hodgetts 1968; Hurtig 1975). At the university level, in
culturally sensitive areas like sociology, departments were dominated by
American citizens and perspectives (Symons 1975). There was, and still
is, cause for alarm.

During the period under discussion, concern was not confined to the
new petty bourgeoisie. Segments of the working class that viewed with
alarm the implications for employment of the actions of U.S. based
multinationals also were advocating, through their unions, the introduction of some nationalist policies. They still do. As pointed out in 1981 to
the Ontario Select Committee on Plant Shutdowns and Employee
Adjustment by Mr. R. Barry, President of the United Electrical, Radio and
Machine Workers Union, The Electrical Workers "remain absolutely
convinced that a branch plant economy which operates at the whim of
decision makers in corporate boardrooms south of the border is not a
healthy economy and has resulted in the exporting of large profits and
hundreds of thousands of jobs to the U.S." (Jan. 1981:7).

It is interesting that in the 1980s many federal state policies, such as
the National Energy Programme, bear a resemblance to measures advocated by nationalist groups in the late sixties and early seventies. It would
appear that once again the adoption of some nationalist measures is seen
as consistent with the interests of some of the Canadian bourgeoisie.

While it was only in the late sixties that in English Canada, nationalism
was embraced by some of the new petty bourgeoisie, in Quebec it had
been adopted earlier. However, whereas in English Canada the concern
was with Americanization, the Québécois were equally concerned with
English Canadian domination. As a consequence, both the targets, and
the strategies of new petty bourgeois nationalists, were different from
those of their English Canadian counterparts (Moniere 1981). More was
said of this in the chapter focussing on Quebec.

It is necessary to stress, however, that in Quebec, nationalism was, and
is, far more deeply rooted in culture than in English Canada. Not only is
there a stronger nationalist tradition, but also, new petty bourgeois
nationalism penetrated more deeply into all aspects of Quebec life than it
did in English Canada. Granted, outside Quebec, many artists and
writers, for example, structured their works around nationalist realities
(e.g., Margaret Atwood and Greg Curnoe), but their impact does not

compare with that of their Québécois colleagues. To quote Marcel Rioux:

> Quebec's creative artists have done much in the past few years to reshape the imaginative life of their society. The creators of songs, poetry, theatre, cinema, music and the plastic and visual arts have helped the Quebecois to obtain a better imaginative grasp of who they are and what their country is (1978:187).

It is clear that emergent nationalism based on the new petty bourgeoisie has made a greater cultural impact on Quebec than on English Canada.

The Dominant.   The dominant element of culture includes the meanings and practices most consistent with the maintenance of existing class relations. For example, the repeated finding that in some capitalist societies many of the unemployed blame themselves rather than socioeconomic forces for their predicament is a set of feelings, or way of viewing the world, that helps perpetuate the status quo. The dominant element, in essence, has qualities that are defined as 'hegemonic':

> Hegemony is . . . not only the articulate upper level of 'ideology', nor are its forms of control only those ordinarily seen as 'manipulation' or 'indoctrination'. It is a whole body of practices and expectations over the whole of living: our senses and assignments of energy, our shaping perceptions of ourselves and our world. It is a lived system of meanings and values . . . It thus contributes a sense of reality for most people in the society, a sense of absolute because of experienced reality beyond which it is very difficult for most members of the society to move, in most areas of their lives. It is, that is to say, in the strongest sense a 'culture', but a culture which has also to be seen as the lived dominance and subordination of particular classes (Williams 1977:110).

In contemporary Canadian society, including, with some modifications, Quebec, the dominant cultural element, the one that is hegemonic, is liberalism.

At the level of political ideology, liberalism "rests on the premise that the individual is more important than the society and that the society does not have the right to limit his or her freedom to pursue happiness as he or she chooses to define it" (Marchak 1981:16). Historically, in Europe, liberalism developed to justify the activities of the bourgeoisie. In other words, the acceptance—grudging or otherwise—by all classes of liberal assumptions, was a pre-condition for the development of capitalism. Without this acceptance, the bourgeoisie could not be assured of the right to buy and sell, enter contracts with whomever they saw fit, and so on.

Although liberalism is not new, it cannot be viewed as the dominant ideology in Canada until the turn of the century. Prior to that date it found expression in the statements of men of affairs (Smith 1978), but its influence was secondary to other considerations. It now permeates not only political philosophy but its assumptions also can be found embedded in formal disciplines such as political science, sociology and economics. Some readers may have already encountered academic liberalism under the guise of political pluralism, the functional theory of stratification, or supply and demand analysis.

Despite the widespread acceptance of liberalism, and its academic manifestations, there is a lot that interpretations based on liberalism cannot deal with. As Marchak points out:

> There is a great deal about society that liberalism fails to explain. There is poverty in the midst of affluence. The liberal ideology fails to take account of it. There is evidence of interference in the political process by privately owned corporations. The liberal ideology cannot explain it. There is a persistent division of the population which the liberal refuses to recognize as a class division but which otherwise is inexplicable. The decisions of large corporations more profoundly affect the lives of citizens than the actions of politcians, yet the liberal ideology provides no understanding of economic power (1981:6).[1]

Ironically, though, it is in part because liberalism does not direct people's attention to these matters that the capitalist mode of production in Canada holds together. In this way liberalism adequately plays the role of deflecting attention from the nature of class domination.

So far, discussion of liberalism has focussed on its ideological dimension. But liberal assumptions can also be seen to permeate the process whereby meanings are established in society, i.e., culture. The particular manifestations liberalism has taken have changed over time. Indeed, some argue that liberalism in what have been defined as its ideological and cultural forms, was, with the initial emergence of the bourgeoisie, a progressive force in history (Lukacs 1963). However, with the development of capitalism, and an increase in the contradictions within capitalism as described in an earlier chapter, liberalism lost its progressive flavor. In advanced capitalist societies the implications of liberalism for both the process whereby meanings are established, as well as the meanings themselves, have been analyzed by Goldmann. He points out that the:

> entire social structure, the global character of inter-human relations, tends to disappear from the consciousness of individuals. Thus the sphere in which their synthesizing actively can be manifested is considerably reduced; and an individualistic, atomized vision of men's relations with other men and with the universe is created. Community, positive values, the hope of transcendence... and all qualitative structures tend to disappear from men's consciousness, yielding to the faculty of understanding... and the quantitatve. Reality loses all transparency and becomes opaque; man becomes limited and disoriented (1976:43).

Although he does not use the term, it is in the ways described by Goldmann that liberalism most reveals its hegemonic properties.

Opposition and Alternatives.   It may be evident from the discussion thus far that in any society it is possible that the residual, emergent and dominant co-exist. (The archaic cannot because it is not part of living culture). The magnitude of the elements, however, can vary. In some societies, e.g., Britain with still a relatively strong tradition of monarchy, the residual can be quite powerful. In others, like the Soviet Union, the state may attempt to repress any manifestations of a residual element of culture. (It might be noted that it has been less than successful in stamping out religion.) In yet other societies, like the United States, the dominant element is virtually all embracive—it overshadows any manifestation of potential residual or emergent elements. This is not to say that the class base, particularly for emergent elements, is absent. Quite the reverse is true. But the dominant, liberal, cultural element results in the control of emergent elements.

Usually, cultural elements other than the dominant which co-exist in a particular society can be viewed as either oppositional to, or as an alternative to, the dominant element. In some circumstances, such as in immediate post-revolutionary France, Russia, or China, manifestations of residual elements of culture, to the degree that they were associated with a repressive class structure, were viewed as oppositional to a potential new order. Most often, the fears of revolutionaries were well founded in this regard. Seldom did a revolution occur without the real prospect of the old rulers attempting to regain their former positions. In other circumstances, such as in contemporary Britain, the residual is regarded as benign.

As for the emergent, there are a number of examples in which it can be viewed as oppositional to the dominant. A familiar one is provided by the assumptions and views of revolutionary workers' parties that grew up in Europe as a response to capitalist industrialization. The view was widespread in many quarters that the inhumane capitalist system of production had to be replaced. Perceptions such as these were frequently countered by the exercise of naked force by the ruling class. An earlier example of the emergent providing opposition to the dominant is found in the development of the bourgeoisie itself. For centuries they were, grudgingly perhaps, prepared to live and work within the framework of feudal culture. Eventually, however, as history shows, the bourgeoisie cast off feudal obligations and assumptions and ushered in a new order in which their culture became dominant.

While in many instances, elements other than the dominant can be defined as oppositional, their threat is frequently neutralized. Such, in part, is the case with the contemporary women's movement. In the mid- to late 1960s, when women were once again, in a collective fashion, starting to question cultural assumptions defining them as inferior, there was, in capitalist society, a general inability to handle their claims. Most frequent, perhaps, was the expression of outrage by those who found no substance to women's contentions. Gradually, however, assumptions of the movement were twisted and absorbed into the dominant element. In advertising, it was found that a projection of a 'liberated' image could sell commodities. At the same time television shows and movies featured 'liberated' heroines. In all but the most superficial of aspects, however, the 'liberated' users of brand 'X', or the 'liberated' leading ladies, engaged in conventional female behavior. As a consequence, the implications of the assumptions of the women's movement were projected to a mass audience in a confused and contradictory way. You could have your cake and eat it too. You could project a liberated image and at the same time do the same old things. An absorption into the dominant element had made some of the claims of the movement less threatening, and perhaps less effective, than they might have been—it also helped sell soap. To put the matter another way, a niche had been carved in the dominant into which the image of the 'liberated' woman could go.

Those elements of culture which are not oppositional to the dominant can, in many instances, be viewed as alternatives to it. It is important, however, to distinguish the truly alternative elements from those that simply co-exist with the dominant. To cite an earlier example, the residual monarchical element in Britain co-exists with the dominant, but it is not seriously viewed as an alternative to it.

The same cannot be said of the residual populism that developed on the Canadian prairies in the early years of the century as an alternative to the dominant liberal element. Based on a petty bourgeoisie (farmers), or a modified petty producers mode of production, in a state of decline, populism embraced various ideologies. One was the idea of 'group government', that would have altered the nature of parliamentary democracy in Canada. The organizational embodiment of these ideologies found expression in the emergence of political parties such as the Progressives and the United Farmers of Alberta. At the level of culture, populism became manifest in newspapers, literature, religion, and in the everyday assumptions in accordance with which people lived out their lives. It is interesting to note that in a sense the Alberta government still draws on the conditions underlying populism to justify its current position regarding oil pricing.

It must be stressed that although populism embodied a rejection of many assumptions embodied in dominant Canadian liberalism, it did not oppose capitalism per se. Rather, it embodied a set of capitalistic assumptions that were more in keeping with the interests of Western farmers. For this reason it would be erroneous to regard it as oppositional rather than alternative.

Phasing.   Often when social scientists deal with culture and ideology they focus on political culture and ideology. They concentrate, that is, on voter attitudes, speeches of politicians, party programs, and so on. So great is the attention to political culture and ideology that it is frequently overlooked that ideology exists in other realms like education, music, art, and literature. In addition, the 'periodization', or pace of development, in the ideology of one medium, such as art, may be different from that manifested in the speeches of, for example, politicians. The inability to recognize this possibility seriously limits the likelihood of fully understanding cultural and ideological dynamics in societies. An example may elucidate this concern.

While it is impossible to specify exact dates, it is possible, as suggested, to identify two dominant cultures and their associated ideologies in English-Canada. The first, that can be identified as toryism, embodied many of the features accepted and defended by individuals such as the Canadian imperialists. Society, it will be remembered, was viewed somewhat as an organism with mutual dependency among the classes. Such ideas remained dominant in society roughly until the turn of the century. At that time liberalism, in both its cultural and ideological manifestations, became dominant. (The fundamental assumption of liberalism, it will be remembered, was that the individual was the basic unit of society.) In establishing this periodization researchers have tended to rely on analyses of culture and ideology in its political manifestations.

An examination of at least one other medium of expression, the English Canadian novel, suggests that the periodization characterizing the political did not necessarily extend to other areas. In the novel, assumptions consistent with liberalism have tended to dominate even during periods in which, at the political level, tory assumptions dominated (Grayson and Grayson 1978a; Grayson 1981).

The explanation, perhaps, is to be found in the class position of those responsible for the expression of the dominant political and literary ideologies. In Canada, those expressing the dominant political ideology have been representatives of, first, a landed 'aristocracy', and later, spokespersons for the commercial and/or industrial bourgeoisie. By way of contrast, writers, in some sense, have been spokespersons for the petty bourgeoisie, and the new petty bourgeoisie. This is not to say that ideologies can always be explained in terms of the class position of those who formulate or express them. But, in the Canadian case, knowledge of class position of the creators of ideology assists in understanding the dynamics of ideology. During the period in which the landed 'aristocracy' dominated the political realm, there was a disjunction between the ideological expressions of the 'aristocracy' and those of the petty bourgeoisie as represented, in this instance, by writers. However, by the time that liberalism became dominant, the ideological expressions of the petty, and now new petty bourgeoisie, were consistent with those of the ruling commercial and industrial bourgeoisie. In essence, in the latter period, other classes greatly assist the bourgeoisie in the fabrication and dissemination of ideology.

The implication of the above is that while it may be possible, at one level such as the political, to point to the dominance of certain assumptions, it is not possible to assume that similar assumptions become manifest in all of the possible avenues of ideological expression. As a consequence, it makes sense to think of the possibility of dominance in each cultural-ideological medium. In some instances, different media, or avenues of expression, are out of phase. Such was the case with political and literary ideology in early English Canada. Under other circumstances, expressions are in phase. Such was the case with political and literary ideology in twentieth century English Canada.

How Ideology Works.   Much has now been said of the difference between culture and ideology, the various ways in which both become manifest, and so on. However, little has been said concerning the way in which ideology works. Although the matter is covered more fully in the chapter on the social psychology of capitalism, it warrants some discussion here.

It can be assumed that individuals must be able to interpret the world in which they live. They must cope with life and death; to, in their own minds, deal with the fact that they have more or less than others with whom they have daily contact; to justify why some must be punished for transgressions of 'accepted' modes of behavior, and so on. It has been the argument of this chapter that the ways in which such matters are handled derive from general assumptions of the culture in which an individual lives and/or the embodiment and systemization of some of these assumptions in ideology.

In some instances, culture and/or ideology develop in accordance with the lived experiences of people as they go about their daily lives—a situation exemplified by a rising class on the historical stage. In essence, people make sense of their lives as they go along. Often, though, assumptions and/or ideologies are more consistent with the interests of classes other than the one to which an individual belongs. In circumstances such as this, ideology frequently is at variance with the lived experience of those in some classes. More importantly, it *ignores* the experience of great numbers of people. In doing so it fails to provide them, at a conceptual level, with the equipment necessary to understand their circumstances and effectively cope with them. Liberalism is a case in point.

The Denial of Class.   As noted above, liberalism rests in the belief that 'the individual is more important than the society and that the society does not have the right to limit his or her freedom to pursue happiness as he or she chooses to define it.' As also noted, a consequence of this assumption is the inability to recognize the role of class in determining peoples' life circumstances. In essence, the reality of class, as experienced by people in their daily lives, is denied in the realm of political ideology. In other words, even if there is an attempt to cope with social ills, the attempts will ignore class, the factor most responsible for creating those ills. As a consequence, the position of the privileged will be maintained. It can be argued that society is not likely to undergo radical change until men and women can recognize class as responsible for structuring their daily experiences, but this matter will not be taken up here. The denial of class, however, is not restricted to the political realm.

Nor, for that matter, is it restricted to particular societies. Several decades ago, Sorokin (1962), in an examination of western societies over several thousand years, argued that in terms of content, the ruling classes were to be found primarily as the subjects of art, sculpture, and so on. In Canada, Lord (1974) demonstrates that, overall, the working-class and their precursors, in both English Canadian and Québécois art, have been virtually absent as subjects from paintings. Instead, in the case of early Quebec art, the focus was on the wealthy. The experience of common people did, however, find expression in religiously inspired 'votive' art— art commissioned by people "who had overcome mortal danger, to commemorate their deliverance, show their devotion and give thanks for their salvation" (Lord 1974:26). Other artists, such as Cornelius Kreighoff, concentrated on the 'common people', but in a way that portrayed them in a happy-go-lucky stereotype. It was not until the work of Joseph Legare (nee 1795) that the experiences of subordinate classes were portrayed in a realistic manner. Legare, however, did not set a trend. In Lord's estimation (1974:179) it was not until the work of Ozias Leduc (nee 1864) that the threads, dropped by Legare, were once again picked up. Even today, Québécois art can be criticized for its tendency to ignore both the working class as subject and the working class experience.

In English Canada, there was little difference. It really was not until the 1920s when Lorne Harris produced a series of paintings dealing with the life of working people that the working class made an effective entrance into the world of the artist. But as with Legare, Harris hardly set a precedent that many were to follow (in fact, Harris soon abandoned this topic and subject matter). The Depression did result in a few artists, like Charles Comfort, attempting to capture the experience of the working class. So did the war. By and large, however, these efforts were, and continue to be, few and far between.

The same can be said with regard to the English Canadian novel. Over the entire course of English Canadian literary history, the working class has been portrayed in few works of fiction. Where they have made an appearance, they have not always been placed in a favorable light (Grayson and Grayson 1978b).

If, instead of concentrating on the class of the subjects in novels, attention focusses on the ideology the works embody, the situation is slightly different. Despite the fact that the vast majority of works suggest an acceptance of the existing class structure, some, particularly around the turn of the century and in recent years, do deal with the implications of a class divided society. In general, however, in both Canadian art and literature, the working class receives little attention. More importantly, the ideology embodied particularly in literature is consistent with the interests of the ruling class (Grayson 1981).

The Denial of Women.   If the position of women in English Canadian literature is examined, a pattern emerges. First, women, as central characters, are under-represented. This holds true even if the novelist is a woman. Second, in the vast majority of works, the ideology underlying the novel is one that takes the subordination of women for granted. Moreover, both patterns date from the appearance of the first Canadian novel in the eighteenth century (Grayson 1983). An examination of values in Canadian magazine fiction has revealed that women receive short shrift in other media as well. Among other things, the authors point to a "negative stereotyping of women" as a common feature of this genre (Zurick and Frizzell 1976:368). Likewise an analysis of local folk songs in Atlantic Canada notes that except in those dealing with love and courtship, "women are seldom mentioned in available songs" (Brunton, et al. 1981:17). By way of contrast, there are many songs that focus on the work experiences and lives of men.

It must be noted that developments such as the above have real consequences. A consistent neglect of women's experience in works of literature and elsewhere contributes to a general insensitivity to women's subordination. It has other effects as well. For example, Gordon (1980) argues that in theatre, after the age of thirty, the number of female roles decreases drastically. Moreover, actresses are often confined to the relationship roles of wives, daughters, mothers and mistresses while men are cast in both 'relationship roles' and 'occupational roles'. Because fewer roles are available for women, they are less likely to economically support themselves through theatrical work.

The situation of the female artist is not much better. Despite the fact that a study of female Canadian artists revealed that 87 percent believed in the existence of a female sensibility in art, evidence suggests that this experience is denied by the art establishment (McInnes-Hayman 1980:9). For example, between 1972 and 1979, "out of 229 [art] jury positions open at the Canada Council (Visual Art), only 28 women were involved" (1980:3). Similarly, few professors of the fine arts are women;

few of the positions of power in cultural institutions are held by women; and so on. The consequence is that, "Many women [artists] expressed a deep feeling of isolation, a poor self concept and a real need to connect with other women artists in a productive way." Moreover, "many wrote that they had experienced discrimination by the Art Establishment, including galleries, government granting agencies and the educational system" (1980:2). In general, it would appear that the exclusion of the female experience cuts across the various media of cultural and/or ideological expression.

HIGHLIGHT

1. Ideology can be viewed as a systemized body of beliefs that legitimize the rule of dominant classes and, at the same time, provide a back-drop against which individuals may interpret their everyday lives. Culture is a whole social process in which men define and shape their whole lives. Cultures and their associated ideologies can be divided into archaic, residual, dominant, and emergent elements.
2. The residual and emergent can exist as either oppositions or alternatives to the dominant. Under certain conditions, oppositions can be neutralized. Under other conditions various elements of culture can co-exist.
3. Ideology is not monolithic. Different media of ideological expression—e.g. the novel and politics—can change at different rates.
4. Ideologies frequently work by deflecting attention from the real nature of domination in society. In Canada, for example, media of ideological expression have consistently ignored class. Women have also received short shrift.

Dissemination

The general cultural meanings and ideologies discussed thus far do not, in some mystical way, simply enter the heads of the newborn, thereafter to direct their interpretations of experiences and monitor their behavior. Rather, both cultural meanings and more systemized ideologies find expression through various social institutions. For example, at one extreme, in Nazi Germany, the state established a ministry to ensure that everyone conformed to prescribed ideology. Transgressors were 're-educated', shot, or worse. In other instances, the state has little if no formal role to play in the dissemination of ideology. Instead, the family and church carry out this role. Such was the case in early Canada. It is fair to say that the state intervenes most in culture and ideology of advanced capitalist societies and in existing communist ones. In other cases, as in some third world nations, the hand of the state is also clearly present. However, social order is most likely to be achieved through direct force rather than through the dissemination of ideologies consistent with the interests of the owners of the means of production.

So sophisticated has the dissemination of ideology become in advanced capitalist societies that many researchers point to the existence of what is termed an 'ideological state apparatus' (Althusser 1971; Poulantzas 1978). This particular concept refers not only to the meanings and ideologies that are disseminated, but also to the institutions and other processes responsible for their dissemination. Depending upon the circumstances, the family, school, church, trade union, or other group may all be viewed as part of the ideological state apparatus. It was perhaps in Nazi Germany that the ideological state apparatus was most complete. However, the ideological state apparatus works to the general advantage of the owners of the means of production, independent of the particular advanced capitalist society in question.

Independent of whether or not researchers choose to work with the specific idea of an ideological state apparatus, all agree that various institutions play roles in the dissemination of cultural meanings and ideologies that are consistent with the interests of, in capitalist society, the owners of the means of production. The process, it is fair to say, may start in the family where the child receives his/her basic orientations toward the world. However, the nature of these orientations, as is clear from the chapter by Smith, depends upon the position of the family in the productive process. It is possible, therefore, that, under certain circumstances, the family may also be instrumental in instilling ideas and ideologies that run counter to those of the dominant class. Whatever the case, in advanced capitalist societies like Canada, participation of the individual in institutions outside of the family will most likely result in a reinforcement of meanings and ideologies consistent with the maintenance of existing class structure.

It must not be assumed that these are the *only* meanings and ideologies encountered. Hopefully, your own experience at university will demonstrate this. In addition, it has been seen earlier that in some societies certain cultural practices and ideologies exist in 'opposition' to the dominant. In many instances, the oppositional is also disseminated through various institutions such as trade unions and/or workers' councils. But in the main, apart from revolutionary circumstances it is a fair comment that in advanced capitalist societies, most institutions give expression to the dominant element of culture and its ideology. In some instances, however, the establishment of institutions with ideological roles to play pre-dates capitalism. Such is the case with the school.

The School.   Although many researchers have focussed on the contemporary role of the school in advanced capitalist society (e.g., Bowles and Gintis 1976) it is perhaps the case that in Canada the class nature of the school is most easily seen if its origins are examined. (A more detailed analysis of the contemporary scene is to be found in the earlier chapter on education.) Fortunately, some good work carried out by social historians enables an examination of the beginnings of the contemporary education system.

Most readers of this book were no doubt raised with the assumption that education was the social vehicle whereby peoples' opportunities were equalized. If you went to school, and worked hard, there were no limits on how far you could go or on what you could achieve. In essence, education was the class equalizer. This belief is part of the dominant ideology in Canada. In reality, this belief does not correspond to the facts. Taking a broad view of secondary educational development, Pike (1980:120) concludes that:

> we are led to suggest...that the expansion of public secondary education probably did not lead to any major equalization of previously existing class differentials in educational opportunity. More specifically, what this suggestion implies is that, although larger percentages of children from all social class backgrounds were receiving some secondary education in 1950 than in 1930 or 1900, the children of the more privileged classes had apparently succeeded in maintaining all or most of their relative advantage within the educational system compared with those from lower-class homes.[2]

Further evidence suggests that even in the 1980s a similar dynamic is equally operative at the post-secondary level.

Seen in proper perspective, this state of affairs is not surprising. In what is now Ontario, for example, the school system was never really intended to equalize opportunity. Rather, when the foundations of the educational system were laid in the nineteenth century, it was assumed that all should attend school for a number of reasons. First, it was assumed that education would have a civilizing effect, particularly on the 'labouring classes'. Second, compulsory education would presumably result in the eradication of offensive and alien ideas from the minds of immigrants. Third, it would instill the virtues of cleanliness, promptness etc. in the working class. Fourth, education would result in a sense of respectability in all. Fifth, and most importantly, it was assumed that education would mitigate the potential of class war. To quote Prentice (1977:120):

> More and more, class friction was to be contained by institutions structured to take the sting out of face-to-face contact between the 'haves' and the 'have nots'. The school promoters saw themselves essentially as the makers of peace. Education would be made free, and all children brought into the schools. This would bind the classes together in a common enterprise and their children in a common history of having been schooled together.[3]

Needless to say, not all welcomed an expanded role for education. They perceived it for what it was: an intrusion of the state into what had hitherto been a private realm. But their arguments were, in the long run, to no avail. Education was too important a matter to leave to the family, the church, the shop, or whatever. Only through a state run school system would it be possible to ensure that the appropriate beliefs, meanings and ideologies would be acquired by all. The institutional embodiments of these assumptions are still with us.

The Church. In many ways the church, like the school, can be viewed as an institutional mechanism whereby meanings and ideologies consistent with the maintenance of societies are disseminated. Indeed, obedience to secular authorities is embodied in Christian teaching. In Canada the religious prescription to render unto Caesar the things that are Caesar's, and unto God the things that are God's, perhaps has most effectively been utilized by the Catholic hierarchy in Quebec (Baum 1980). From apporoximately 1840 to 1960 the Catholic church, as was seen in an earlier chapter, used its religious authority to prop up an often hopelessly corrupt provincial regime which in Canada was unrivalled for its authoritarianism and inattention to the needy. In such a situation it was easy for a foreign based bourgeoisie to realize immense profits through the exploitation of Quebecois labor (Moniere 1981). It was not until the 1960s that the death grip of the church on the province was finally released (Rioux 1978).

An example of the way in which in the nineteenth century the Catholic Church assisted secular authorities in the maintenance of order is provided by Ryerson (1968:184). In 1844, during the construction of the Beauharnois canal, a Report of the Executive Council of Lower Canada reveals that:

> the employment of a Roman Catholic clergyman (at Beauharnois) took place...as a measure of Police and for the preservation through his influence of peace and order on the line of the canal, not for the purpose of furnishing religious instruction to the labourers. It having been deemed inexpedient to station troops along the line of the canal and the large expense which would have attended the establishment of an effective Police force, combined to render the course adopted desirable as economical and effective for the object designed.

Obviously, the Catholic Church has not always been employed in as blatant a fashion as this. Moreover, occasionally it is possible to identify *individuals* who accepted Catholic dogma but nonetheless opposed the status quo. On balance, however, it is fair to say that the Catholic Church per se has aligned itself with propertied interests in Canada.

The Catholic church was not alone in its propogation of religious practices, culture and ideologies consistent with the maintenance of existing class relations. A series of studies have revealed that, historically, particularly the Anglican church has been a propogator of basically conservative ideas consistent with the well-being of the dominant classes. On some occasions this identification has been so close that religious controversies have taken on a distinctly class flavor. In late eighteenth century Nova Scotia, for example, a backwoods religious revivalist movement deriving support from petty commodity producers can, in part, be seen as a reaction to the policies of a Halifax based and Anglican commercial bourgeoisie (Clark 1948). Later, in the 1830s and 1840s, a similar development occurred in Upper Canada (now Ontario). Again, in the 1930s, the conversion of some Albertans to religious sects can be viewed as a manifestation of conflict between classes (Mann 1955).

The thread uniting all of these cases is that the teachings of, particularly, the established churches were more in keeping with the culture and interests of the dominant classes. As a consequence, on some occasions, the 'lower orders' reacted against what amounts to the imposition of a religious culture inconsistent with their daily experience as members of a particular class or as participants in a particular mode of production. It should not be assumed, though, that the reaction was against the idea of private property per se. To use terminology expressed earlier, the contentious religious ideas can be viewed as emergent and alternative to the dominant.

While most religious movements that challenged the religious cultures of existing churches did not consciously call in question capitalist relations of production, there may be, at first glance, one important exception. Around the turn of the century, a number of churchmen were distressed by the misery produced by industry they viewed around them (Allen 1970). They believed that the practices of modern industrial society represented a perversion of true Christian beliefs stressing the brotherhood of man. As a consequence, many clergymen of different denominations joined together in an attempt to consciously introduce reforms into Canadian society which would help alleviate the problems of slums, alcohol, poverty, and so on. They consciously called into question some social practices resulting from the operation of capitalist society, but they did not advocate fundamental changes in the capitalist mode of production. Accordingly, the 'social gospel movement' as it was called, notwithstanding its conscious concern with reform, can also be viewed as emergent and alternative.

The overall conclusion reached from an examination of religious institutions in Canada is that by and large, the religious culture disseminated by the church, to the degree that it explicitly or implicitly reinforces obedience to secular authority, can be viewed as supportive of existing class relations. On some occasions, however, the religious culture of the established churches is challenged by those whose life experiences are inconsistent with this culture. To this extent, conflicts between religious institutions can be viewed as having a class dimension. Usually, however, such disagreements are not manifestations of a conscious attempt to change the nature of capitalist relations of production. Even with the social gospel movement, where there was an appreciation of the fact that many social ills were the product of capitalist relations of production, there was no opposition to private property per se. In essence, in Canada, religious institutions and practices have never been inimical to the capitalist mode of production. Most often, they have supported it. In other societies this has not always been the case.

The Media.   In contemporary Canada, the mass media of communication—TV, movies, radio, newspapers, and magazines—represent important vehicles for the dissemination of cultural assumptions and ideologies. Statistics Canada data reveal that on a yearly basis, individually, Canadians spend thousands of hours watching television, reading newspapers, listening to radio, going to movies, and so on. Unfortunately, insufficient data are available to permit total assessments of the content of these media. However, the information that is available suggests that, by and large, the cultural assumptions and ideologies embodied in the mass media, are, once again, consistent with the maintenance of existing class relations.

Clement (1975) has shown that in Canada, as in other advanced capitalist societies, mass media is big business. Not only does the media, on a yearly basis, realize millions of dollars in profits, but also, enterprises like Power Corporation, a Quebec-based holding company, and individuals like K.C. Irving, a New Brunswick-based multi-millionaire, own much of the Canadian broadcasting and newspaper industries. In essence, those who own and/or control the major economic enterprises in our society also own and/or control, with the exception of the state owned Canadian Broadcasting Corporation, most of the media. In Clement's words, "together the economic and media elite are simply two sides to the same upper class; between them they hold two of the key sources of power—economic and ideological—in Canadian society and form the corporate elite" (1975:325). More specifically, Clement found that "49 percent of the media elite are also members of the executive or hold directorships in one of the 113 dominant corporations in the economic sector and, at the same time, hold one of these positions in one of the dominant media complexes" (1975:325). Given this ownership pattern, it is unlikely that those in the mass media who attempted to disseminate anything but the dominant culture and ideology would be employed for long.

That it is the dominant which is disseminated through the mass media is clear from more than one source. With regard to movies, an American study has probed some of the assumptions underlying Hollywood productions. Given that the major distributors of films in Canada are

American, and that, by far, the greatest number of films viewed by the Canadian public are made in the U.S.A. (Crean 1976), any observations on the American movie are bound to be germane to a study of Canada.

In general, films produced in the 1930s and 1940s, the heyday of American film, can be characterized in the following way:

> a coherent ideological vision of the world is acted out in every Formula movie. The conventions place the emphasis on the individual and argue that anyone can aspire to success. Wealth, status, and power are possible in America, the land of opportunity where the individual is rewarded for virtue. Stereotypical values celebrate Americana in terms of home, motherhood, and community, puritan love and work ethic. All issues are reduced to a good and evil, black and white conflict, a them-and-us identification process where good equals us, the American values and social system (Roffman and Purdy 1981:6).

In the 1950s and 1960s, partly as a result of the increase in power of independent studios, the Formula lost some of its old resilience. But, by and large, American movies continued to uphold the dominant values of 'America the Good'.

This is not to say that all films unequivocally manifested the dominant culture and ideology. Starting in the early 1930s, a series of films, centring on the experience of gangsters, fallen-women, shysters, and so, drew the movie going public's attention to a number of problems. All in all, though, these productions could in no way be viewed as embodying assumptions or ideologies that were oppositional to the dominant culture. Rather, the emphasis was on individualistic solutions to such problems as the Depression. As Roffman and Purdy state, "The explicit social story material of the depression was presented in terms of virtue rewarded, so that any potential criticism was diffused" (1981:11). Therefore, while some movies drew attention to social ills, they at the same time helped neutralize any potential threat to the status quo.

During the Depression, opposition of the movie magnates to the dissemination of radical ideas did not stop with films. When, in 1934, left-leaning Upton Sinclair, a former muckraker, ran for governor of California, Republican movie producer, Louis B. Mayer, organized the other producers against him: "The producers pooled their resources, raised one and a half million dollars (partially by assessing salaries of stars and directors) and made a series of fake newsreels" (Roffman and Purdy 1981:77). Needless to say, the reels were designed to elicit a negative reaction to Sinclair's candidacy. They must have worked. Upton Sinclair lost the election by 250 000 votes.

It might be argued, however, that not all political involvement of the studios was entirely negative. Later in the decade Warner Brothers acquiesced in Roosevelt's New Deal. They produced a series of films consistent with the underlying assumptions of his program of reform. In the war years, via the mechanism of the War Activities Committee, the relations between Roosevelt and Hollywood became even closer. Hollywood was now formally charged with the responsibility of making films to assist the war effort.

Not surprisingly, as a consequence of war, social problem films virtually disappeared. While in an altered form they re-emerged in the early post-war era, the fifties saw their almost complete demise. This development can in large part be attributed to the Communist-baiting activities of the House of Un-American Activities Committee and Senator Joseph McCarthy. It may come as no surprise to learn that actor Ronald Reagan and Walt Disney were two stalwart defenders of efforts to rid Hollywood of anyone seen not to uphold the 'American Way' to the fullest extent.

In contemporary times, Roffman and Purdy (1981:298) point to the existence of films, such as Norma Rae and the China Syndrome, that continue in the tradition of what they call the 'social problem film'. But, they hasten to add, this genre never regained the impetus it developed in the thirties and forties. Even in those years, it must be remembered, such films were a small minority of all productions. In contemporary times, Roffman and Purdy feel that television shows, such as Roots, Holocaust, Lou Grant, and The Defenders are the best examples of the problem film tradition.

(As an aside, it might be mentioned that since 1907, Hollywood has made 575 pictures dealing with Canada (Berton 1975:16). In most, Canada is stereotyped as a snowy, forested wilderness inhabited, by and large, by French-speaking trappers, Indians, and Mounties.)

In general, it appears that the Hollywood movie has been an important vehicle for, in this case, the dissemination of the dominant American culture and its ideologies. True, from time to time, films have drawn attention to some social ills, but they have only suggested individualistic responses to these problems. The consequence has been a neutralization of assumptions in this medium that might otherwise have posed a threat to the dominant cultural element.

The Comic.   Few of us have probably considered Donald Duck and Mickey Mouse as agents of imperialism or that the Disney comic is as laced with ideology as good plum pudding is with rum. In actuality, however, Disney comics, and others like them, can be viewed as part of a world-wide mass media complex that eats away particularly at third world cultures and helps replace them with an alien one. The general process underlying this cultural development is described by Dorfmann and Mattelart, two exiled Chileans:

> Our countries [underdeveloped ones] are exporters of raw materials, and importers of superstructural and cultural goods. To service our 'monoproduct' economies and provide an urban paraphernalia, we send copper, and they send machines to extract copper, and, of course, Coca Cola. Behind the Coca Cola stands a whole structure of expectations and models of

behaviour, and with it, a particular kind of present and future society, and an interpretation of the past. As we import the industrial product conceived, packaged and labelled abroad, and sold to the profit of the rich foreign uncle, at the same time we also import the foreign cultural forms of that society...(1975:98)

As will be seen later in this chapter and has already been noted in the chapter on the capitalist world system, many of the processes described above are operative in Canada.

The charges with regard to the Disney comic may at first seem somewhat unfair. Upon further consideration, however, they develop credibility. The character, Uncle Scrooge, for example, is someone who, because of his wealth and temper, is both feared and held in awe by those with whom he comes in contact. Whether or not this is a desirable state of affairs is a moot point. The fact is that Scrooge is satisfied with this condition and maintains the loyalty of Donald and his nephews. The message, it can be argued, is that independent of their behavior, the propertied have a right to continuous loyalty.

At the other end of the spectrum, Donald, who is frequently unemployed but never seriously in need of life's basics, shuns work like the plague. His unemployment is therefore his own fault. "The socioeconomic basis of unemployment", Dorfmann and Mattelart argue, "is shunted aside in favor of individual psychological explanations, which assume that the causes and consequences of any social phenomenon are rooted in the abnormal elements in individual behaviour" (1975:71). Such assumptions, it will be recalled, are those of the dominant culture of liberalism in Canada. Exposure to this way of experiencing the world is clearly encountered in the comic.

Equally important to Dorfmann and Mattelart is the characterization of obviously non-white residents of the Third World. In stature they are usually "enormous, gigantic, gross, tough, pure raw matter, and pure muscle; but sometimes they can be mere pygmies" (1975:44). In terms of moral qualities they are like children: "Friendly, carefree, naive, trustful and happy. They throw temper tantrums when they are upset" (1975:44). The list could go on. But the point should be obvious: other people are described in a way that makes their subordination seem like the right thing. Every now and then, however, as in the real world, they rebel. Under these circumstances they receive special treatment.

Revolutionaries in general are portrayed as basically self-serving individuals with the gift of deceit. They are often able to dupe otherwise decent people into believing that their proposals will help all. At the same time, the comic trivializes what in the real world are real conflicts involving people:

The war in Vietnam becomes a mere interchange of unconnected and senseless bullets, and a truce becomes a Siesta. 'Wahn Beeg Rhat, yes, Duckburg, no!' cries a guerilla in support of an ambitious (communist) dictator, as he dynamites the Duckburg embassy (Dorfmann and Mattelart, 1975:56).

Just about the only thing that does not change in the characterization of revolutionaries is their implicit country of origin. All revolutionaries in the Western Hemisphere have Castro-like beards. Elsewhere they may have slanted eyes and big front teeth. Whatever the case, the message, is the same: the revolutionary is out for himself.

As with other sectors of the mass media, it is safe to say that the Disney comic disseminates culture and ideology not only in keeping with the class relations in the United States, but also justifies America's now waning world hegemony. The residents of the Third World really are incapable of conducting their own affairs. When in fact they do attempt some national self-determination via revolutionary means, they are treated as self-centred individuals prepared to adopt any means to get their way.

HIGHLIGHT

1. In combination, the ideologies people are exposed to and the means whereby ideologies are disseminated, can be viewed as the ideological state apparatus.
2. Institutions responsible for the dissemination of ideology include: the school, the church, and the mass media.

Metropolis and Hinterland

External Influences.   It would be a mistake to believe that Canada is exempt from the processes of imperialism referred to previously. Indeed, one of the characteristics of Canadian society, and one that has been referred to elsewhere in this book, is that, historically, development has occurred in accordance with external demand for our resources or staple products (Watkins 1980). The European, and then American, demand for fish, fur, timber, wheat, minerals, and oil, in their turn, have had enormous implications for the nature of economic life in Canada. Even in contemporary times raw materials remain Canada's major export (Britton and Gilmour 1978). As a consequence of our heavy reliance on staple exports, and, now, because of our inability to develop indigenously controlled industry, formally or informally, Canada can be viewed as a colony of, in turn, France, Britain and now the United States. To state the problem in very broad terms, some of the major decisions affecting Canadian life, have been, and still are, made *outside* of the country. Societies like Canada, where the shots are called elsewhere, are termed hinterland societies. Societies calling the shots are called metropolitan societies.

The implications of colonialism for cultural life are many and varied. At one end of the spectrum, in order to consolidate his hold, the colonizer attempts to eradicate the culture of the colonized. This process is graphically illustrated by Tunisian born, Albert Memmi. In a discussion of French inspired, colonial education in his country he remarked that:

> The memory which is assigned [the student] is certainly not that of his people. The history which is taught him is not his own. He knows who Colbert or Cromwell was, but he learns nothing about Khaznadar; he knows about Joan of Arc, but not about El Kahena. Everything seems to have taken place out of his country. He and his land are nonentities or exist only with reference to the Gauls, the Franks or the Marne (1965:105).

The implications of colonialism for the types of culture and ideology that developed in Canada are less extreme than those examined by Memmi, but they are nonetheless real.

From the beginning of French settlement in Canada there was an attempt to impose on the colony a European social structure and culture: that of feudalism (Moniere 1981:44). However, conditions in North America were inimical to the successful operation of feudalism and it continued to exist more in symbolic form than anything else. At the same time, it was not really until the abolition of seigneurial debts that the last vestige of the feudal system passed from existence.

While the British conquest changed the imperial centre to which Canada was connected, it did not weaken the nature of the colonial relationship. Indeed, in some senses, the impact of the colonial relationship may have been more obvious than before. Whatever the case, the consequences of the British connection upon culture are obvious.

English Canadians read, as did Americans in the nineteenth century, British literature (Bissell 1976). According to A.J.M. Smith, until the 1950s, literature written in English Canada embodied the spirit of colonialism. Colonialism in literature, according to Smith, "is a spirit that gratefully accepts a place of subordination, that looks elsewhere for its standards of excellence and is content to imitate with a modest and timid conservatism the products of a parent tradition" (1979:213). During the period in question, standards were set in Britain. Today the United States continues to play the same role. In both cases the colonial link influenced the nature of the dominant culture.

The implication of colonialism in the realm of literature is that writers consciously attempt to pour their experience into a mould derived from another society. Unless they are prepared to do this, because the publishers, critics, etc. share colonialist assumptions, their work will not be published. The consequence, however, is the production of literature that is inconsistent with the experience of individuals living in Canadian society. There are those, of course, who doubt that there is anything unique in Canadian culture in general, and in Canadian literature in particular. However, in English Canada, critics and writers, like Northrop Frye and Margaret Atwood, who point to the 'garrison mentality' and 'survival', respectively, as typifying the Canadian literary experience, take exception to this stance. Other critics argue that the colonialism once embodied in Canadian literature is now a thing of the past.

A parallel situation exists in the realm of art in English Canada. There, as in Quebec, during the period of British dominance, artists took their cues from European masters. Thus it was not uncommon to find the Canadian countryside dotted with sheep and the Canadian forest looking like a lush, tropical jungle (Lord 1974). In the realm of landscape painting it was not until the early years of this century that artists known collectively as the Group of Seven began to paint what they saw. No more sheep, no more windmills, no more lush vegetation; instead, pre-Cambrian rock, pine trees, and water.

During the period of British domination it is not surprising that many of those fortunate enough to acquire a university education spent time at Oxford or Cambridge. Even if they remained in Canada, they would have come in contact with professors who were either British, were trained in Britain, or wished they had been. Novelist Hugh MacLennan once remarked that in his youth it was virtually impossible to obtain a Canadian university post unless one was British. After all, how could anyone from a colony be the equal of someone from the imperial centre?

The cultural assumptions Canadians lived their lives in accordance with, and the ideologies they adopted, go well beyond what is evident from a formal study of art, literature, education, and so on. Indeed, the vast majority of Canadians lived without reading literature, or viewing art. Nonetheless, the social structure they participated in, through the reservation of some of the best jobs for foreigners, and the perpetuation of situations in which individuals like the wheat grower who either profited or lost as a consequence of a decision made in Chicago or London, represented colonialism in action. In essence, in one way or another, the daily experiences of Canadians were structured by the colonial relation. It is clear, though, that not many were able to view the situation for what it was. Instead, they continued to examine their lives and experiences through foreign made glasses.

Although it was dealt with more fully in the chapter on Quebec, it should be noted that British domination had important consequences for the culture of French Canada. Basically, as Moniere (1981) points out, the conquest created the conditions whereby the Catholic Church, particularly after 1840, was able to enforce a Catholic orthodoxy on virtually all sectors of Quebec society. The manifestations of this dominance, apart from its implications for the daily lives of the Québécois, were apparent in the realms of art, literature, and education as well as in more obvious sectors such as politics. It was not until approximately 1960 that church dominance in the cultural as well as other areas was finally broken.

In the early years of the twentieth century, it was increasingly evident that the influence of Britain on Canada was waning. Increasingly, British indirect investment was being replaced by American direct investment.

The consequence was the maturation of the branch-plant economy. The cultural implications of this development are many.

In the realm of art and literature, for example, the American metropolis rather than Britain became the place where standards were set. While it was still important to be recognized in London, it was increasingly important to have the American seal of approval for your work. With the development of motion pictures, radio, and later television, American cultural influences became even more pervasive. In his discussion of Hollywood movies, for example, Pierre Berton argues that, in essence, the movies worked against the development of Canadian culture:

> you Canadians, the message keeps telling us, are really just northern versions of Americans: you have no distinctive personality apart from ours, and no distinctive culture, apart from ours. Your identity is our identity. You're quainter, of course, and less sophisticated; but apart from those quirks you're just like US (1975:231).

As a consequence of the underdevelopment of the Canadian film industry (Crean 1976), the difficulties experienced by many Canadian authors in having their works published, the importation of many American radio, and, later, television shows, and the flooding of the Canadian magazine market with U.S. publications, many aspects of Canadian culture have been absorbed by the American variant of the dominant liberal culture. Indeed, today, in English Canada, in many regards it is safe to say that the cultural interpretations English Canadians give to their behavior, and the way in which they experience the world, are very close to those found in the United States.

The truth of this statement is brought home in a number of ways. For example, over a decade ago, Hodgetts (1968) found that in English Canadian Schools, there was a shocking inattention to the study of Canada. While in some schools there may have been an attempt to rectify this situation, the effort was unsuccessful. In 1975 a national study of high school graduates revealed, among other things; "fewer than 30% could identify the BNA Act as Canada's constitution; 71% could not name the capital city of New Brunswick; asked to name any three Canadian authors, 61% were unable to do so; 97% were unable to name even one Canadian playwright" (Hurtig 1975:5). In 1979, a similar study revealed that at the University of Western Ontario, graduating *teachers* were equally ignorant of Canadian circumstances (*Globe and Mail*, March 22, 1979, p. 1). At the university level a 1975 inquiry into, among other disciplines, sociology, revealed that there "is real danger that sociology, and perhaps to a lesser extent, anthropology, as fields of scholarship in Canada will become so oriented to American interests, values, methodologies and research priorities that they can no longer effectively serve the academic and social interests of this country" (Symons 1975:78). It is because of the mechanisms and level of ignorance noted above that the dominant liberal cultural element in Canada must itself, to a large degree, be viewed as a branch-plant culture.

This is not to say that there are no residual or emergent cultural elements and associated ideologies that in Canada challenge the U.S. influenced dominant element. Nor must it be assumed that the impact of U.S. culture is equal across all classes and regions of Canada. It was seen in a former section, for example, that certain developments may lead particularly the new petty bourgeoisie and working classes to increasingly oppose many features of the dominant culture. In addition, Quebec is more clearly resistant to U.S. culture than other regions. Also, it must be recognized that even if American cultural influence were non-existent, an indigenously fostered dominant cultural element would still work to the advantage of the propertied classes. The real danger of the American cultural influence is that it estranges Canadians from an appreciation of the real forces that shape their destinies.

Internal Dynamics.   Just as it is difficult to understand the dominant element of particularly English Canada without reference to other societies, it is difficult to understand what has developed in, say, the Canadian West without reference to Central Canada. Within Canada a replica has developed of the relationship that has characterized Canada's association with France, Britain, and the United States. Some regions have been developed not to the advantage of their indigenous residents, but to the benefit of the members of certain classes living in other regions. This situation has had implications for cultural development.

Most well known, perhaps, is the development of what was described earlier as prairie populism. In the first half of this century, the declining position of prairie farmers made them susceptible to interpretations of events that recognized the complicity of eastern financial and industrial interests in the impoverishment of the farmer. This realization became manifest in political movements and ideologies as well as culture.

Interpretations growing out of the situation of the farmer, i.e. Eastern dominance, are still being used by the Alberta government in its oil pricing disputes with the federal government (Richards and Pratt 1979; Pratt 1981). Moreover, Hiller (1981a) has pointed to the development of a small industry involved in the production and dissemination of cultural objects—buttons, hats, bumper stickers, etc.—which re-affirm the basic opposition of Albertans to what they define as Eastern dominance. Perhaps the most revealing indication that some Canadians in Alberta are re-evaluating some of their assumptions is the recent emergence of Western separatist movements and political parties. It must be noted, however, that should separation ever occur, those likely to profit most are the Alberta-based bourgeoisie and new petty bourgeoisie. Alberta 'nationalism' must, in fact, be viewed as most consistent with the interests of these two classes.

At the other end of the country, Newfoundland, evidence suggests that oil discoveries may fan the development of a provincial conscious-ness similar to that in Alberta (Overton 1979). Although the main beneficiaries of oil developments will be an externally based bourgeoisie (the owners of the oil companies, and so on), some members of the petty bourgeoisie and new petty bourgeoisie, hope to cash in on what they view as a lucrative game. It is, in fact, particularly on the new petty bourgeoisie that a Newfoundland nationalism is based. One of the manifestations of this sentiment is a renewed interest in traditional Newfoundland culture and an attempt to preserve it. In Atlantic Canada in general it has been shown that many local folk songs give expression to the experiences of a 'semi-proletarianized' class of individuals who in their daily lives have felt the consequences of external domination of this region. Many of their folk songs concentrate on activities such as mining or fishing.

In both historically underprivileged Alberta and Newfoundland, it is significant for this discussion that oil-related developments have resulted in a form of provincial 'nationalism' directed, in part, at what is regarded as an exploitative Central Canada. In both instances, moreover, this emergent culture derives in large part from the circumstances of the indigenous new petty bourgeoisie.

It is significant that Quebec nationalism can likewise be associated with the development of the new petty bourgeoisie. It also can be viewed as being in the interests of a petty bourgeoisie. This is discussed in an earlier chapter. For the time being it is sufficient to note that social developments in different parts of the country have the potential to foster distinct elements of culture. However, class relations are at the root of these developments.

HIGHLIGHT

1. Colonial societies usually have some aspects of the ideologies of imperialist society imposed upon them.
2. In Canada, the imperial link had observable consequences in such realms as art and literature. For a long time, attempts to imitate what was happening in Britain or the U.S. inhibited the development of Canadian art and literature.
3. The replacement of Britain by the U.S. as the major external influence on Canada has had consequences for the types of ideologies Canadi-ans are exposed to. Essentially Canadians view what is going on in Canada through U.S. eyes.
4. Within Canada, relationships between the metropolis and hinterland have frequently had cultural and ideological manifestations.

The Intellectuals

It is appropriate to end a chapter devoted to culture and ideology with a discussion of intellectuals. While culture, in the meaning employed over the past few pages, is developed through, among other means, the normal intercourse of everyday life, ideologies can be viewed more as the consequence of systematic thought. Indeed, in many societies, such as our own, entire social strata spend their time in attempts at making sense of the various social and physical events that impinge upon our lives. Some of these people inhabit the universities. Others work for business, the state, or the unions. Some claim to be inspired by divine revelation. Others are on the side of history. Whatever the case, most, in some way or another, can be viewed as contributing to either a process of edification or mystification with regard to the world in which we live.

Partially in recognition of these possibilities, (Gramsci 1978:6) distinguishes between 'organic' and 'traditional' intellectuals. The former are those required by a new class in its efforts to obtain a sense of itself. To use terms developed earlier, they give expression to ideologies of an emergent culture. Such a role was perhaps played by Adam Smith to the extent that he formalized ideas concerning the operation of market forces that enabled the bourgeoisie to define its place in history. The latter are viewed as those linked to established classes. Their role is one of continuing to justify existing relations among classes. Accordingly, they can usually be seen as agents of a dominant or residual culture. Contemporary sociologists who argue that inequality can be justified in terms of the need to motivate individuals to carry out certain social roles can be placed in this category. In more general terms, "the majority of those who could properly be called intellectuals in bourgeois society, not to speak of professional people of one sort or another, lawyers, architects, accountants, doctors, scientists, etc., have been the 'managers of legitimation' of their society" (Miliband 1977:59). They provide the intellectual means to justify the status quo.

It must be stressed that although the role of some people is defined as exclusively 'intellectual', e.g. professors, all work involves an intellectual component. Even the most mundane of tasks requires that the worker, to some degree, conceptualize his/her operation. As Gramsci points out, "All men are intellectuals. . . . but not all men have in society the function of intellectuals" (1978:9).

If the prior distinction between organic and traditional intellectuals is, for the sake of argument, accepted, it is clear that for a particular stage in the development of a mode of production that the ratio of organic to traditional intellectuals varies from one society to the next. For example, both Canada and France—leaving aside, for a moment, Canada's semi-dependent status—are advanced capitalist societies. Both have a large working class. France has large numbers of organic intellectuals who can be viewed as assisting the working class in an assessment of its opinions. Canada has very few such individuals. As Porter has argued, "Neither Canadian newspapers, churches, nor universities have harboured social critics in any large number, and there are some interesting examples of pressure extended on members of these bodies who have become too critical" (1965:494). (One of the consequences of the relative absence of intellectuals associated with the working class is the retardation of overt class politics in English Canada. Even the degree of radicalization in Quebec is a relatively new phenomenon; however, it can clearly be related to the activities of engaged intellectuals.)

Perhaps one of the most obvious examples in English Canada of intellectuals who became 'too critical' is the League for Social Reconstruction (LSR). Spawned by the Depression, the professors and others who constituted this group, "focused on the power of the modern corporation, on its subversion of political democracy while denying economic equality" (Horn 1980:202). The League sought, primarily through the process of education, to alert the Canadian public to options for a better society. To this end it put together a volume, *Social Planning for Canada*, which remained, until the publication thirty years later of John Porter's *The Vertical Mosaic*, the most penetrating analysis of the Canadian power structure ever written. Unfortunately, it was little read.

Not surprisingly, many League supporters were attracted to the left-leaning Co-operative Commonwealth Federation (CCF). Indeed, the Regina Manifesto (1933) was written by a League member. Overall, however, the League fell far short of the attainment of its goals. In the end, "The Second World War and the organizational needs of the CCF... led to the demise of the LSR" (Horn 1980:172).

More recently large numbers of intellectuals were attracted to the Waffle Movement that developed in the ranks of the New Democratic Party in the late 1960s. The political philosophy of this movement combined socialism and nationalism. The former, it was felt, could not be achieved until Canadians dealt with the problem of American domination. The Parti Québécois has also attracted large numbers of intellectuals.

On the other side of the coin, some existing information documents the claim that, in general, Canadian intellectuals, rather than allying themselves with emerging classes, have been staunch defenders of the status quo. An analysis of Canadian historians, for example, reveals them to have been a fairly conservative lot. They can be justly criticized for their failure "to analyze class structure, class conflict, and working-class history" (Berger 1975:236). They have tended to write history in a way consistent with the dominant cultural element. Despite the embodiment of some questioning in their work, English-Canadian novelists can be tarred with the same brush. By and large, ideologies embodied in their work have been consistent with the maintenance of the status quo. In

Quebec more writers now call the class structure of their society into question, but this also is a relatively recent development.

In short, intellectuals give expression to, or formulate ideologies, that may be derived from various elements of culture. European intellectuals who in the past have aligned themselves with the working class gave expression, in many cases, to ideologies associated with an emergent culture. Others have continued to disseminate, and refine, ideology derived from the dominant cultural element. In other words, they have put forward ideas that justify the status quo. In Canada, there has been a paucity of intellectuals who give systematic expression via ideology to the culture of the working class. The exception to this rule is the recent history of Quebec. On the other hand, most Canadian intellectuals can be viewed, both in the past and now, as giving expression to ideologies derived from the dominant cultural element.

HIGHLIGHT

1. Intellectuals have largely been responsible for the formulation and dissemination of ideologies.
2. In Canada, most intellectuals have formulated and disseminated ideologies consistent with the maintenance of the status quo.

Conclusion

As was stated in the Introduction, ideologies and cultures, if we are to make sense of them, must be seen in connection with other things in society. Neither has a totally independent existence. Rather, they are closely connected to the nature of the mode(s) of production found in a society, or to the relations among classes within a particular mode. Because the number of potential modes, and the relations among classes, can vary, it is possible to identify archaic, residual, dominant and emergent elements of culture. The strength of each varies depending upon the society in question.

It must not be assumed that there is a one-to-one relationship between, on the one hand, the mode of production and/or relations among classes, and, on the other, the culture and ideologies that can be detected in a society. A certain amount of variation is possible. Nor must we believe that culture and ideologies are monolithic. Even within, say, the emergent, different avenues of cultural and/or ideological expression may change at different rates. Such a possibility is consistent with the definition of materialism advanced earlier.

Finally, it must be concluded that just as cultures and ideologies must be viewed in connection with modes of production and relations among classes within a society, relations among societies may also have consequences for culture and ideology. Canada is a case in point. Cultural and ideological developments in this country are impossible to understand if they are not seen in conjunction with our historical and contemporary subordination to France, Britain, and the United States. Within Canada, comparable relations among dominant classes located in one part of the country, and subordinate classes located in another part, have also influenced cultural and ideological developments.

NOTES

[1]From *Ideological Perspectives on Canada* by M. Patricia Marchak. Copyright © McGraw-Hill Ryerson Limited, 1981. Reprinted by permission.

[2]From *Power and Change in Canada* by R. Pike. Used by permission of the Canadian publishers, McClelland and Stewart Limited, Toronto.

[3]From *The School Promoters* by A. Prentice. Used by permission of the Canadian publishers, McClelland and Stewart, Limited, Toronto.

SUGGESTED READINGS

Marxism and Literature, Raymond Williams. London: Oxford University Press, 1977. Many of the ideas advanced in this chapter are extensions of what Williams had to say. Students are warned, however, that this is a tough book to read.

Ideological Perspectives on Canada, Patricia Marchak. Toronto: McGraw-Hill Ryerson, 1981. This is both easy to read and provides an overview of some ideological developments in Europe and North America.

Ideologies in Quebec, Denis Monière. Toronto: University of Toronto Press, 1981. This book deservedly won the 1977 Governor General's award for non-fiction in French. It is a must for all serious students of culture and ideology as well as for those interested in Canadian society in general.

Who's Afraid of Canadian Culture, S.M. Crean. Don Mills: General Publishing, 1976. Although published a few years ago, Crean's book remains the best treatment of the institutions that in Canada are responsible for the dissemination of culture and ideology.

The Dominant Ideology Thesis, Nicholas Abercrombie et al. London: George Allen and Unwin Ltd., 1980. This is an excellent attempt to examine Marxist and functionalist approaches to the study of ideology, and to critically examine the role of ideology in advanced capitalist societies.

THE SOCIAL PSYCHOLOGY OF CAPITALISM

Bernd Baldus

Introduction

If we observe the way people select seats in streetcars, buses, or movie theatres, we are likely to find that most of them prefer to remain at some distance from their neighbors. Where seats are not available people will adopt subtle postures to avoid physical contact with strangers. If we give a sample of Canadians pictures of well-dressed, or ordinarily-dressed individuals, and ask them to make a "first impression' judgment, we will probably find that the majority of our subjects have much more positive expectations regarding the intelligence, or the future prospects of attractive or well-dressed people. If we give children in an elementary school a play-problem that can be solved cooperatively or competitively, but arrange it in such a way that cooperation maximizes the returns the children can receive for solving the problem, it is likely that most of them will act competitively. This will happen even though that strategy clearly reduces the number of rewards, such as toys, which they can win."

Behaviors such as these are readily observed in real life or in experimental situations. In fact, they are so common that they become relatively predictable. They are part of our everyday experiences, and we anticipate them—or use them ourselves—when interacting with others. Social scientists generally agree that such structured, relatively stable behavior patterns provide the basic subject matter for their research. But there are at least four different theoretical approaches to the study of such behavior: Sociobiology, Functionalism, Behaviorism, and Marxist theory.

Sociobiological Theory. Sociobiologists see all lasting forms of human behavior as biological adaptations which have come about in the course of human evolution. In its most orthodox form, sociobiology argues that behavioral patterns arose initially as the result of genetic changes. Some of these new patterns turned out to be adaptive. This means that they increased the chances of the individual to survive and to produce more offspring than others who had no such competitive edge in the struggle for survival. Through inheritance, the new behavior would eventually spread through the entire population.

410

Recently, sociobiologists have claimed that this principle is at work not only in the natural selection of genetically based behavior changes, but also in the social selection of cultural innovations. Either process, however, favors only those behaviors which make adaptive sense in a particular environment. All stable and widespread forms of human culture are thus presumed to contribute to the adaptive fitness of human societies. The three earlier examples of structured behavior might thus be seen as indicators of broader adaptive strategies. The seating choices of individuals might be taken as the reflection of a more general territorial behavior. People's willingness to infer status from appearance could be viewed as a recognition of social dominance. And the competitive behavior of the schoolchildren would probably appear as an indication of a wider complex of competitive and aggressive behavior. Territoriality, dominance, competition and aggression found their way into the human gene pool because sometime in the process of human evolution they proved their adaptive value in regulating access to sexual partners or scarce resources.

Functional Theory. Functional theories argue that the roots of all stable social behavior can be found in its functional utility for basic, agreed upon, societal goals and values. In fact, the views of early functionalists were very close to a sociobiological perspective. They saw private property, kinship systems, incest taboos, and the development of economic behavior as cultural responses which functioned to regulate the fulfillment of a number of "basic" or "primary" biological needs such as shelter, sex, or food. The only difference to the sociobiological view is that for functionalists the emergence of such institutional or behavioral responses was seen as a purely cultural, and not a genetic, phenomenon. In contemporary functional theories the reference to biological needs disappears. It is now the consensus on basic societal values that determines which social behavior becomes a stable part of the cultural repertoire of a society.

Functional theories are never very clear about the nature and the origin of such values, or the societal consensus that surrounds them. Nonetheless, we might imagine that in our initial examples of structured social behavior, the value of privacy or individualism in our society might account for the choices of seating. The shared goal of economic growth, on the other hand, might be used to explain the emphasis on competition and achievement in the educational system. The same explanation holds for the willingness to attribute social status to those whose appearance suggests their superior contribution to society's economic objectives.

Behaviorist Theory. On the surface, behaviorist views of the causes of structured social behavior are much less encompassing than the sociobiological or the functionalist perspectives. They simply see all behavior as the result of particular conditions of reinforcement. That is, specific stimuli are viewed as producing specific behavioral outcomes. Behaviorist research starts from the premise that only observable cause-effect connections between stimuli and behavior can be the legitimate subject matter of psychology. As a consequence, only those causes that are observable antecedents of a particular behavior can be used to "explain" that behavior. Certainly, neither adaptive value nor functional utility would be accepted by a behaviorist as possible determinants of human conduct. Neither can be readily investigated empirically.

There is, however, more to the behaviorist view than the collection of isolated and narrow empirical observations of cause-effect relationships. Behaviorism, like sociobiology and functionalism, searches for an underlying principle that explains observed empirical regularities of behavior in more general terms. This principle, in the case of sociobiology, was the adaptive value of a behavior for the biological survival of humankind. In the case of functionalism, the principle was functional utility in the context of shared cultural goals. Behaviorist research is motivated by the search for laws of behavior. Such laws will allow us to *always* predict, from a set of given stimuli, the occurrence of a particular action. The aim is to find, through a number of singular observations of cause-effect relationships, general causal laws which permit us to predict and control human actions.

An Assessment.   Each of these views can tell us something about the origins of social behavior. Few social scientists would, for instance, continue to maintain a strict separation between human and pre-human evolution. Sociobiological research, studies of animal behavior, and psychological work on the behavior of human infants have revealed many traces of our pre-human evolutionary past. Similarly, functional theory has contributed to some extent to our understanding of the relationship between collective goals and the emergence of goal-oriented social processes. Finally, behaviorism has shed a good deal of light on the interaction between environment and human conduct, and the processes of learning through which the latter is shaped. But there are also some major flaws.

No matter how different the three theories are, they have two problem areas in common. First, they assume that all human behavior, regardless of historical and cultural variations, is governed by universally valid laws or can be reduced to ultimate causes. This view has not fared too well over the past decade. The vast amount of empirical data amassed by research in the social sciences has not, as was hoped, revealed the outline of behavioral laws or ultimate determinants. In fact, it had the contrary effect. Human behavior proved to have a degree of complexity and variation which defied any attempt to force it into the mould of general laws. Historical and cross-cultural studies, in particular, have shown that neither functional relevance nor adaptive value can account for the extremely wide range of social behavior and social institutions. Nor can they explain their persistence or change over time. As for behaviorism, some three decades of empirical research have shown many behavioral regularities but have failed to unearth a single behavioral law.

The second problem with these theories is their inability to give proper place to innovation and change. They cannot easily explain the appearance of new, unknown, behavioral patterns in human societies. The problem of dealing with creativity, invention, and social change is perhaps most obvious in functional theories. If one argues that the stability of social behavior and social institutions is proof of their functional necessity for the pursuit of fundamental human values, it becomes very difficult to find any good reason for social change. The same holds true for sociobiology. If structured social behavior owes its stability to the fact that it proved to be adaptively superior and increased the survival chances of humankind, any change would likely be harmful.

Sociobiology concerns itself primarily with the search for invariant patterns of behavior, and for the adaptive reasons that underlie it. Social change that emanates from innovation and human creativity, and which frequently has its roots in the opposition to existing social structures, has little room in the sociobiological perspective.

For behaviorism the problems connected with the presence of innovation and social change have been perhaps most openly acknowledged by B.F. Skinner.

In his book, *Freedom and Dignity*, Skinner attempts to reconcile a notion of human independence with a theory that sees in all human behavior the working of inexorable laws of conditioning. Concepts such as human freedom and human dignity are merely the reflection of an age-old desire of humankind to set itself apart from a universe governed by strict natural processes. From the behaviorist perspective, the search for ways to transcend and change these processes is an illusion. Real freedom can never be more than the acceptance and the intelligent use of the laws of behavior. In spite of Skinner's assurance that this offers humanity a realistic measure of hope, behaviorism remains essentially a closed system. It is one in which a well-meaning optimism regarding the nature of human rationality clashes with a theory whose circular argument about the ubiquity of causal laws leaves little scope for change.

Marxist Theory.   For Marx, there is no hidden agenda or mysterious blueprint that governs human behavior and puts it beyond the individual's control. Human history evolves out of the practical activities of people. It does not come out of some abstract law, purpose or cause. The human involvement in production, the self-construction of humankind through its labor, is the element that takes the evolution of life beyond its animal stage. The gradual development of techniques of food collection and storage, and the invention of tools used in the production of food represent the first step in a history that can be properly called human. They allow people to independently appropriate nature rather than respond to it instinctively.

The process of production carries within it a dual and contradictory potential. On one hand, it provides humankind with the material means for the development of culture. The interaction with nature poses a continuous challenge for the improvement of the techniques of production, and beyond that for human inventiveness and discovery. It provides the raw material for all social change. And to the extent that the development of the forces of production allow people to produce an economic surplus, that is, wealth which exceeds the producers needs for their physical sustenance, it frees the individual from having to concentrate exclusively on the struggle for subsistence. It thereby makes it possible to expand the range of human activity to include the pursuit of desires that are not immediately related to physical survival. These include, for instance, artistic or intellectual objectives. In this sense, production is the most important source of true human freedom; the freedom from physical want, and the challenge for creativity and change.

But the appearance of a material surplus also sets in motion another powerful force. It is the temptation for some to gain control over the surplus produced by others. In its simplest form, this may involve taking away part of the product from the original producer through force, persuasion, deception or some other manner. A more effective way consists in gaining control over the means of production. Where, for instance, access to farmland is essential for peoples' physical survival, exclusive property rights over such land can be used by one group to force another to turn over part of their production to the owners. They do so "in exchange" for their permission to farm. Production thus provides humankind not only with the precondition for its freedom, but also with the tools of domination.

Base and Superstructure. Much of Marx' writing analyzes the effects of domination on human behavior. Domination does not eliminate freedom and creativity altogether. But it harnesses them to its own purposes by exerting a strong selective pressure on human conduct. It discourages those forms of behavior that seem to interfere with, or be of little use to, the prevailing order of domination. And it reinforces those that conserve, stabilize, and support that order. It thus imposes a system of social control on the people in a society which favors behavior that is compatible with the interests of a dominant group. At the same time, it also generates opposition which it can never entirely suppress. Both social control and opposition are reflected in the "superstructure" of cultural and political practices, religious beliefs, ideas, fashions, artistic pursuits, and forms of social organization which correspond to a particular mode of production as its "base".

Marx' concepts of base and superstructure have made an important contribution to our understanding of the historical origins of human behavior and cultural patterns. As a general proposition, they have withstood the test of empirical analysis very well. There are few historians or social scientists who would deny the predominant influence of different modes of production on values and social behavior. But there are two problems. First, the references to the base-superstructure relationship in Marx' work are usually expressed in a general way. The precise nature of the causal link is never clearly outlined. There is, in particular, a great deal of ambiguity about the degree of determinism involved. On the one hand, especially during the time when he was working on *Das Kapital*, Marx employed a language which suggested that the effects of the material and social conditions of production on human culture were in any historical period fixed and invariant.

This view is often embedded in an equally determinist theory of historical development. It sees all societies as moving through the same sequence of successive modes of production in which "the industrially more developed country shows the less developed one the picture of its own future" (Marx and Engels 1968:12). There is little room in this perspective for independent human action, the transcending, creative element in Marx' theory. Such action can, at most, modify, but not alter the inexorable course of historical development.

In this view of the social process Marx came very close to the general law perspective which was common to the theories discussed at the beginning. What it implies for the relationship between base and superstructure is, first, that each mode of production has its own, singular characteristic superstructural forms. Second, all societies will at each stage display the cultural properties typical for the mode of production they have reached.

On the other hand, there are many statements, especially in Marx' more empirical studies, which reveal a more cautious and less deterministic position. Marx stressed the empirical variation of cultural phenomena in different societies, even though their basic mode of production may be the same. In his study of art in ancient Greece he noted, for instance, that the peaks in its development correspond in no clear and direct way to the development of their material base. And he suggested generally that cultural expressions such as philosophy or religion may be so far removed from their economic base that it becomes very difficult to identify the link, even though it exists.

Perhaps because of this ambiguity in Marx' writing, subsequent efforts to elaborate the base-superstructure relationship further have often retained the determinist perspective. They have, as a consequence, interpreted superstructural phenomena as the result of a pervasive conspiratorial presence of a ruling class. Sometimes they assume that the superstructure is a complex mechanism in which all elements are interrelated in the same manner as the parts of a machine.

The second problem with Marx' analysis of base and superstructure lies in the limited empirical evidence he used to illustrate the relationship. Even though he referred to art, philosophy, government, or the judiciary as examples of superstructural phenomena, he rarely discussed their relationship to the conditions of production in any detail. In his writing on the causal connection, Marx concentrated on the ways in which the material conditions of people's existence are represented in, and distorted by, the ideological images through which individuals understand the reality of their lives. But he did not give us many concrete examples of ideologies, or tell us much about the manner in which they develop and spread.

There are two possible reasons for this. One is that Marx' optimistic views about an early collapse of capitalism and its replacement by a communist society also led him to believe that ideological illusions were increasingly loosing their power and would, in fact, come to an end as soon as a communist mode of production would re-establish "transparent and simple relations of men to their labor and the products of their labor". The second reason is that at the time of Marx' writing the institutions of public education or popular literature that subsequently assumed such extraordinary importance in the ideological reconstruction of the social reality of capitalism had barely emerged. Others, such as modern mass media, lay still in the distant future. At his time, Marx had no reason to anticipate the unprecedented growth of technical facilities to create and disseminate ideological imagery.

Forms of Control.   We are now in a position to put together some of Marx' assumptions about the relationship between base and superstructure and use them in an analysis of the social psychology of capitalism. First, we will follow Marx in seeing social behavior as the historical creation of people. It is not the product of laws or ultimate determinants that are beyond their control. Marx had already rejected interpretations of human history as the unfolding of an immanent "spirit" (Hegel), as governed by an "invisible hand" (A. Smith), or as the mechanical reflection of people's material circumstances (Feuerbach).

The development of culture follows no *a priori* logic that directs human action along a predetermined path. Consequently, there is no point in looking for one. Instead, *our analysis of the culture and ideology of capitalist societies will try to understand the process of selection that favors the development of some forms of behavior and discourages or suppresses others.* In order to do so we will pay particular attention to the early decades of Canadian capitalism. It was during this time that the foundations of many of the basic behavioral traditions of our society were laid.

Second, we will agree with Marx that among possible selective factors domination is of particular importance. Other chapters have shown that the benefits one group or class can draw from appropriating the results of the labor of others are tangible and tempting. They are a powerful incentive for the ruling class to secure and strengthen such relations of production. What is more, they also provide that class with the means to take practical measures to maintain their privileged position. This facilitates the emergence of cultural and ideological elements that fit into and support the existing structure of inequality.

This should not lead us to believe that the culture and ideology of a capitalist society is simply the result of the machinations of capitalists themselves. The process of selection is more complicated than that.

Interventive Control.   In order to achieve its objectives a ruling class has two basic choices. The first strategy is called *interventive control*. It includes, broadly speaking, all efforts by the ruling class to purposely modify the beliefs and behavior of others in accordance with its own perceived interests.

Changing behavior through intervention involves one of three processes. First, another person's actions may be modified through the use of direct reinforcements. These are rewards or punishments which are made contingencies of a desired behavior change. In this case, the reinforcement is directly experienced by the individual. Second, a change in behavior can also come about as the result of observational learning. The learner observes the reinforcing consequences of a particular action of another person. This may, for instance, involve seeing someone else rewarded or punished, or seeing others being happy or distressed as a consequence of a particular behavior. In such a process another person may become a "model" whose actions are imitated by the observer. Third, behavior may be encouraged or discouraged by pairing it with what we may call symbolic reinforcers. In this case, the actual reinforcement is neither personally and physically experienced nor observed in a model. Instead, it is represented by a symbol. A picture or a verbal description of the consequences of a behavior, or the morale of a story, are examples here.

The control over the means of production and the surplus derived from it allows the ruling class to use each of them more effectively. The control over greater resources also means control over greater means of direct reinforcement. The consequence is an increased chance of changing the activities of others in a preferred direction.

Domination has a similar impact on observational learning. In all structures of domination the manners and the lifestyle of ruling classes have encouraged imitation by subordinate groups. In fact, they used the conspicuous display of their wealth not infrequently as a deliberate ploy to encourage the acceptance and dissemination of their own culture.

Domination also facilitates control over symbolic rewards. In the pre-capitalist societies of Europe the control by the aristocracy of the church and of artistic production allowed it to invoke the fires of hell and the rewards of heaven as symbols that justified and protected the aristocratic order. Ownership or control of modern mass media allows contemporary ruling classes to create symbolic images of the capitalist order which legitimate it and suggest that there is no realistic alternative to it.

Complementary Control. Interventive control represents purposive and intentional efforts of a person, or a group, to change the behavior of others. But not all the conditions needed to further ruling class interests have to be created through intervention. Some of these interests may already be present in the behavior of subordinate people independent of any prior action by the ruling class. Such conditions offer *complementary* opportunities for the maintenance of domination. Their use constitutes a second strategy for meeting the requirements of rule.

Compared to interventive control, the use of complementary conditions makes for a very different relationship between ruling and dominated groups. First, it is much cheaper. Interventive control invariably involves costs of persuasion or coercion. Actual reinforcements have to be paired with a particular behavior. Even where such reinforcements for desired behavior are symbolic they still involve costs for, say, the printing and the distribution of verbal or visual messages.

Complementary conditions, by contrast, represent a windfall. They can be used in their existing form, without any additional effort beyond finding them. Second, complementary conditions are usually judged by their utility for ruling class interests. This means, for the most part, that those who benefit from these conditions are not really interested in why people act the way they do. Thus, a ruling class can take advantage of complementarity and tolerate at the same time a high level of independence of personal motivations and objectives among subordinate people. Third, the use of complementarity makes social control by the ruling class much less visible. In the case of interventive control the subordinate person is usually aware of the demand to change a behavior. This is so even though the symbolic message which encourages the change may obscure its real reason and its actual beneficiaries. By contrast, complementarity involves the use of an already existing behavior. No change is required. The subordinate group is therefore much less likely to notice that its actions are complementary to the interests of the dominant group. This allows the latter to benefit from the actions of the former while the relationship between the two has the appearance of mutual autonomy and independence.

An example will illustrate these advantages. In the latter half of the

19th century many small Ontario communities were linked by new railroad lines. It was the time of the railway boom; visions of economic progress and access to metropolitan markets made many small towns clamber for the right to have a railroad routed through their area. Tippin (1982) examined the fate of one such line, the Toronto, Grey, and Bruce, which was constructed between 1869 and 1874 and connected Toronto with the southern Georgian Bay and Lake Huron area. Like many similar projects at the time, the construction was initiated and promoted by a group of Toronto speculators. Of the total cost of construction only a small portion was invested by this group. This represents, in our terminology, the expenditure for interventive control: it was used mostly for promotion, and for overcoming some of the initial resistance from communities which felt that the financial burden on the township would be too large. The remaining financing was provided by the provincial government and the local townships along the line. Local contributions in particular were substantial and imposed a heavy debt burden on the often thinly settled areas. But they were given voluntarily, and the vote to subscribe to railway debentures passed in many townships by an enthusiastic majority.

Tippin describes in detail the many different motivations that went into the commitment to financially support the construction of the railroad. These included rivalries between townships, speculation fever among landowners who expect their property values to soar, hopes of farmers to sell their agricultural produce and of new settlers to ship the cordwood from clearing their land, and anticipations of increased trade among local merchants. The expectations grew out of the structural conditions of people in 19th century rural Ontario. The Toronto promoters of the railroad encouraged these local interests, but they did not create them. The catchword of their promotional activities, "progress", served as a vague ideological promise that gained its specific meaning for the people along the railroad line only from their personal experiences, problems, and hopes.

By taking advantage of these complementary conditions, the backers of the Toronto, Grey, and Bruce Railroad were able to carry through their scheme with a remarkably small effort. Their interests were met to a large extent by fortuitous circumstances which arose without any action of their own, but which greatly aided their objectives.

The story of the Toronto, Grey and Bruce Railroad has an appropriate ending. After four years of operation the line went bankrupt in 1878. It is difficult to establish whether this was the result of managerial ineptness, or whether it was the planned final stage of a speculative investment scheme. What is certain is that the costs of the scheme were born by the people along the line who not only saw few of the promised benefits, but lost most of the money they had put into its operation. The financial returns to the Toronto promoters are hidden somewhere in the nebulous financial statements of the company. Judging by the continued prominence of at least some of them they did not fare badly.

Intervention and complementarity are not only used by members of dominant groups. They are the two basic strategies of social action open to any human being. We all employ them all the time. We change our social environment in accordance with our desires or interests just as often as we take advantage or "make the best" of conditions which we have not created. In fact, at any time in our lives the number of social facts that we take as given characteristics—complementary or unfavorable—of our behavior is much greater than those which we actively try to modify. In this sense, our daily lives always involve a substantial measure of opportunism. To say so implies nothing derogatory. It simply means that humans share with all other forms of life an essentially opportunistic approach to their environment. It combines efforts to change that environment with the acceptance of conditions which cannot or need not be controlled. This is true regardless of one's social position.

The control over resources needed by others, and especially over productive property, increases the effectiveness of these strategies. Domination provides the means to change the behavior of others. Those in dominant positions can reward and threaten. They can set the standards for imitation and influence the symbolic reconstruction of the social order. But domination also increases the chances of profiting from complementary opportunities. It turns the appearance of such opportunities from a game of chance into a game with loaded dice. The control over capital makes it not only more likely that opportunities will present themselves more often to those who are in control, but also that the advantage derived from such opportunities is larger. As the old adage goes, it takes money to make money.

HIGHLIGHT

1. Sociobiology, functionalism, and behaviorism are theories that attempt to base explanations for human behavior on natural laws.
2. Marxist theory, in contrast to other theories, assumes that human behavior results from the daily processes associated with making a living. It is not a result of abstract laws.
3. There are two ideas in Marxist thought concerning the relation between ideas and other aspects of society. One theory assumes that ideas are secondary to what goes on in other parts of society, particularly the economy. The other assumes that ideas, under certain circumstances, display a relative autonomy.
4. People do things because they are persuaded or forced to do so—interventive control—or because they are made to want to—complementary control.

INTERVENTIVE CONTROL: THE IDEOLOGICAL TRANSFORMATION OF SOCIAL INEQUALITY

Introduction

Whenever a social group becomes a ruling class, its first efforts to influence other people's behavior usually concentrate on making its own position and interests *appear* compatible with the interests of others, and minimizing demands for a change of the new structure of inequality. Such ends can be accomplished by threatening and intimidating subordinate groups. But it is much more effective to create an image of the ruling class which gives legitimacy to its *characteristics*. This is done by portraying them in a manner that invites admiration and approval, and by making ruling class *goals* appear as the common values and concerns of all members of the society.

Marx described this transformation of a ruling class into an agent of the common good as an elementary part of the legitimation of any structure of rule. As an example he points to the ideological values of reason, justice, equality and fraternity. These had been proclaimed as the "eternal" achievements of the bourgeois revolutions of the eighteenth and nineteenth centuries. They were, however, most compatible with the class interests of the bourgeoisie. He writes that:

> We know now that this empire of reason was nothing more than the idealized empire of the bourgeoisie; that eternal justice became in reality bourgeois justice; that equality amounted to the bourgeois equality before the law; that the bourgeois property was proclaimed as one of the most fundamental rights of man, and that the state of reason, that Rousseau's social contract came into reality and could only come into reality as the bourgeois democratic republic (Marx and Engels 1962:190).

These references by Marx emphasize that the ideological transformation of the position and the goals of a ruling class is not just the result of conspiratorial design. Instead, there is usually a complex interplay between a variety of group interests which are often parallel and complementary to each other. Members of a new ruling class may well be sincere in believing that the advancement of their own interests also furthers the collective good. Other groups, each for their own reasons, may well support them in this view. The early history of the ideologies of Canadian capitalists is a case in point.

They revealed a variety of perspectives and understandings of nineteenth century capitalism. Bliss observes in his study of the views and actions of Canadian businessmen between 1883 and 1911 that, "In general, the evidence presented here suggests a mixed and complex picture of the relationship of business ideology and practice." He adds that "some men in business were extraordinarily money-hungry, others thought profit a by-product of excellence in business. Some beat and kicked their workers, others paid high wages and built baseball diamonds. Some corrupted legislatures, others worked for civil service reform and honest government. Some formed combines and gouged the public, others combined in the literal hope of making a living profit. In personal correspondence the occasional businessman's public rectitude was replaced by private venality. More commonly," he concludes, "the private letters were sprinkled with the same maxims and arguments that were the stuff of the editorials in the business press" (Bliss 1974:136-37).

There were a number of underlying themes in the legitimation of nineteenth century capitalism in Canada. In recent years social historians have argued that Canada, in contrast to the United States, entered capitalist industrialization with a legacy of conservative political values which were rooted as much in the tradition of the British loyalists as in the pre-capitalist social and religious structure of French Canada. Except for the unsuccessful rebellions of 1837 and 1838 this conservatism was not tempered by bourgeois revolutions such as the American War of Independence. As a result, the argument goes, Canadian political values stressed the importance of well-ordered and harmonious social relations rather than individualist effort as a precondition for the pursuit of personal happiness.

There is a good deal of evidence to support this view. Canadian political institutions, for instance, most of which developed in the first half of the nineteenth century, allow for a comparatively greater degree of bureaucratic authority than in the United States. In addition, they leave less recourse for individual participation and appeals than comparable institutions in the United States. But it is also important to see that these different traditions were by no means incompatible. Towards the end of the nineteenth century, the powerful force of the new capitalist order had created legitimating ideas that traveled easily across borders. Their dispersal was facilitated by the growth in literacy and mass communication. Capitalism had become a world system. It had created its own international currency of ideological symbols. In the United States, the egalitarian and individualist views of the Declaration of Independence were used to justify private profit and the resulting inequities. "Lip-service to the catchwords of democracy was inescapable. But there was, on the other hand, nothing to prevent a modification of their meanings. The only limitation was that the change was subtle enough to escape general observation. This is exactly what took place. The traditional terms were drained of their old significance. A new content was injected though it was generally supposed that nothing had happened, because the labels remained unchanged. The conservative exponent of a basically antidemocratic ethos could now bolster up his argument with the language of democracy itself" (McCloskey 1951:16). And if the individualist element in American ideologies was no barrier to conservative interpretations, the conservative tradition in Canada could be readily combined with the portrayal of the new wealth as the deserved result of individual ability and perseverance.

The Legitimation of Capital

If we look at the historical development of the legitimation of capitalist enterprise in Canada we can distinguish several phases. The first of these, up to the late nineteenth century, was characterized by a reliance on personal symbolism. During this period the ideological transformation of Canadian capitalism centred around the idealized portrait of the businessman. It often used actual business or political figures to "explain" their rise to prominence and "success". The picture that emerged was emphatically positive and designed to elicit social approval in its audience.

The goal of private business was to make a "living profit," the equivalent of the living wage of the worker. Profit was a fair compensation for entrepreneurial labor which allowed a comfortable, but by no means extravagant life. Between 1883 and 1911 there were hardly any references to the goal of making money, as such, in the business speeches and publications of the period (Bliss 1974:16). In fact, these pronouncements forcefully disapproved of excessive greed, the "search for Mammon", and extravagance of spending and lifestyle. Profit was the deserved return for the businessman's "service" to his company through his involvement in organizing and financing production, and to society through his contribution to prosperity and economic growth. Behavior based on the lure of profit satisfied the needs of the public for homes, food, clothing and many other goods. Success, thus defined, could be attained by anyone, provided that one first cultivated the proper moral character.

Virtues such as frugality, honesty, perseverance, and above all industry and hard work were essential prerequisites of financial reward and social prominence. People were the makers of their own fate. Individually, success was synonymous with self-improvement. Bliss (1974:32) remarks that "... real success was not necessarily the achievement of wealth. No one who preached the success gospel ever promised that it would inevitably pay off materially. Cultivation of the right qualities was apt to bring a modest competence, but there had never been enough high positions in industry and great rewards to shower upon everyone who strove for them.... In its ultimate implications the success ethic had little or nothing to do with making money, everything to do with the cultivation of moral character." Collectively, the striving for success would lead to *progress*: the moral, scientific and economic improvement of the society as a whole. Private business was the engine that kept it moving.

The Novel as a Factor of Legitimation. Through most of the nineteenth century the portrait of the successful businessman was the most frequently used means of conveying the idea that wealth was the well-deserved result of virtuous life. The image of the poor and the urban working class enter ideology in a slightly different way. Keating, in a study of the working class in English Victorian fiction between 1820 and 1900 finds two major types of characters. The most common is the factory worker who is poor, usually unskilled, and illiterate. His poverty is no fault of his own. He therefore deserves pity and compassion. He shows at least some of the character traits that also characterize the man of success: honesty, industry, moderation and kindness.

Poverty sometimes appears as a trial which puts these virtues to a particularly harsh test. The eventual fate of such "good" working class characters varies. They may be helped by a wealthy patron, or bravely suffer through the hardships of working class life without being corrupted or succumbing to criminal actions, or their death might be used to stir the conscience of the reader (Keating 1971:27). The second most common type of working class character is generally the opposite of the first. He is often a drunkard; he is without discipline or a desire to better himself. He beats and exploits his wife and his children. Generally, he is used to illustrate where a life of poverty leads when there is no individual attempt to change through self-improvement and the building of moral character.

These images described rather realistically the living conditions of a large part of the working class during the 19th century. But they did not portray them as the result of the new capitalist order. Instead, they were related to shortcomings of the poor themselves, and were shown as a condition from which only personal effort could provide an escape.

The ideology of nineteenth century capitalism in Canada was disseminated in school books, newspapers, speeches, business guides, trade journals and popular novels. It was absorbed with a keen interest by a population whose growing literacy enabled many of its members for the first time to expand their knowledge significantly beyond the limited range of everyday experiences. The ideological image confronting them gave a new meaning to these experiences. It added many facets to them which the individual had not, and probably never would see, first hand. It did so in ways which were highly selective and had often little, or nothing to do with reality. But because they were usually the sole source of information, and the same themes were repeated in so many ways, there was little chance that the discrepancy between reality and ideological image would be noticed.

The idealization of "success" in the symbolic figure of the pioneer, the politician, and most of all the business hero, was vague enough to appeal to very different groups in nineteenth century Canadian society. It gave

achievement results from 'hard work' and 'perseverance'. The list of admirable characteristics of the biography figures is rarely tainted by even the mildest critical comment. In the same way, no positive quality disturbs the black picture of the negative characters. The ideological message is that people who are wealthy and successful are hardworking, capable and kind. They achieved their position through industry and perseverance, and therefore deserve it.

The Popular Romance as a Factor of Legitimation.   The same affirmative picture of social inequality, in a very different form, is drawn in romance fiction. It has experienced a phenomenal growth during the past decade. Harlequin Enterprises, one of the publishers of romance fiction, is the only Canadian publishing venture that has entered international markets on a large scale. It sells more than 100 million books per year in North America, and publishes in Holland, the German Federal Republic, France, Israel and other countries. Since they are often treated slightly contemptuously in public discussions, and since readers are often somewhat embarassed to admit their preference for them, it is easy to overlook that books like Harlequin Romance provide many women with an attractive escape from the pressures of their daily lives. Harlequin Enterprises actually markets books in these terms. The women in its advertisements describe them as 'my disappearing act' or 'my passport to a dream'.

Harlequin Romances are about romance. The basic plot involves the relationship between a male hero and female heroine which is temporarily interrupted by their involvement with another partner. The stories always have a happy ending; traditionally, marriage. But there are other themes as well.

The novels draw much of their appeal from the social context in which they are set. This is largely determined by the male hero. He is invariably wealthy and can afford a lifestyle whose details—cars, interiors, house or palace, servants—are constantly described in the books in an ornate language full of superlatives. He owns a 'powerful long-nosed sports car', 'priceless heirlooms in the palazzo', has 'numerous servants', the curtains are of 'priceless lace', and there is a 'fireplace sculptured of black marble'. The occupations of these men also symbolize their success. They are usually doctors, businessmen, or landowners. The latter, often of aristocratic descent, are most common.

Perhaps the most remarkable aspects of the heroes are the personal characteristics attributed to them. The heroes almost always convey an image of superior breeding. Harlequin Romances show wealth not merely as admirable and awe-inspiring, but also see in its male protagonists a quasi-biological predestination to be successful. They have the 'blade-straight nose of a renaissance prince' or a 'regal profile' and exude 'self-confidence' and an 'air of condescension'. By contrast, the heroine has usually a respectable but undistinguished background. She frequently comes from a middle class family. Sometimes, after the early loss of her parents, she receives a small inheritance which gives her a measure of independence. She is usually much younger than the hero and may be a nurse or a secretary.

The eventual marriage means moving into the social class of the male, an important part of the romantic plot. The lower end of the social scale is occupied by chauffeurs, servants, or farmers. Working people are encountered in the frequent rural settings. Though they may be poor, they are happy and content and, in the case of servants, always pleased to oblige. Frequently they are described as "part of the family". Their other common characteristic is their physical coarseness. Though not repulsive, their appearance clearly sets them apart from the hero. This pattern reinforces the impression that success is at least accompanied by, if not rooted in, its corresponding biological properties. Like *Reader's Digest*, Harlequin Romances pair wealth with strongly positive attributes.

Advertising as Legitimation of Capital.   Another example of the symbolic reconstruction of social inequality in a capitalist society is advertising. A study was conducted of one hundred and eleven advertisements which appeared over a two-year period in two Canadian magazines, *Maclean's* and *Chatelaine.* It looked at the estimated age, socio-economic status, emotional state—indicated by facial expressions—and activity of the individuals shown in these advertisements.

It found that there was a strong over-representation of young adults (18-34 years) in both magazines. Fifty four percent of the individuals in *Chatelaine*, and 63 percent of those in *Maclean's* were in this age group. The figure for the Canadian population in the same age group is 30.7 percent. The most under-represented age group were people whose estimated age was 50 years and over. They comprised only 4 percent of the individuals in the advertisements. In reality, 23.4 percent of all Canadians were older than 50 (1981 census estimates, Statistics Canada).

Socio-economic status was estimated on the basis of objects and settings in the advertisements. Individuals shown with a mansion, large, carefully tended residential grounds, or a high-priced automobile were grouped into the high status category. Corresponding indicators were used to identify individuals with medium and low status. High status figures clearly predominated in the advertisements. Between 60 and 70 percent of the individuals in each magazine belonged in this category. Because of the wide range of symbols of high status in the pictures it is difficult to choose a precise income which corresponds with each lifestyle. But it is obvious that the percentage of high-status people in the advertisements exceeds their presence in the Canadian population by a very large margin. By contrast, medium and low status individuals are clearly under-represented. The latter comprised only about 4 percent of the figures in the magazines. They were generally of two types: people in third world countries who were shown in advertisements by Oxfam and other charitable agencies; and people engaged in manual work or wearing work clothing such as overalls. The almost complete absence of working people is all the more remarkable because about 65 percent of all employed Canadians work in clerical, service and manual jobs (*Labor Force Survey*, Statistics Canada, 1982).

If the great majority of the people in the advertisements are young and wealthy, how do they feel, and what do they do? The faces of about 67 percent of the individuals expressed smiles or laughter. About 30 percent appeared serious or indifferent, and only about 3 percent frowned or seemed to be unhappy. But these percentages are somewhat misleading. The "serious" faces, often worn by males, were frequently associated with the "man of destiny" or "tough executive" image. Similarly, frowns and unhappy expressions appeared almost always in a humorous context. Most of the people in the advertisements are shown at parties, in leisure activities such as sports or travel, or buying or using products. Only 18 percent appear in work settings. Most of these are women working in attractive homes or offices. People who are "ordinary" in their appearance, work, and life style, are rarely portrayed, even though they comprise a majority of the population. Advertising carries the implicit suggestion that being ordinary means being deficient in terms of the scale of social desirability it commonly uses (Scott, 1975).

General Applications.   These examples are part of a complex process through which the reality of social inequality in capitalist societies is transformed into an ideological image that is socially acceptable and even attractive. The themes of this ideological reconstruction are surprisingly similar. They hold true for television, magazine advertising, and popular literature. Success, still portrayed as achievable to everyone, is now measured in terms of consumption. The people who are portrayed as successful are frequently anonymous figures. They are less often actual "celebrities", and even more rarely the heroes of business. The latter, it will be remembered, dominated the success stories of the nineteenth century.

The change that the focus on consumption represents is perhaps most obvious in the personages that populate advertisements. They are young, attractive, happy, and display the glamor and satisfaction of wealth. These people, rather than the moral exhortations of the nineteenth century rags-to-riches stories, provide the standards for social desirability and the models for social imitation.

The institution that makes this glamor possible is free enterprise. It assigns specific social positions on the basis of technical and meritocratic rationality. The message is that social hierarchies are technically necessary, and people are assigned to them on the basis of personal merit and ability. On a more general basis, it guarantees success in the form of universal access to consumption. Modern ideological imagery no longer relates success to the virtues of individual businessmen. Instead, it portrays capitalism as the indispensable institutional prerequisite of "prosperity". But it continues to attach positive and legitimating meaning to positions of power and wealth as well as their incumbents.

HIGHLIGHT

1. Ruling class ideologies contain beliefs that social practices, which in reality benefit the ruling class, work to the benefit of all classes.
2. During the early phase of capitalist industrialization, profit, that derived from hard work and initiative, was seen as a legitimate compensation for the individual's engaging in activities that benefited the whole society. The virtues of this type of individual effort were embodied in various media.

Interventive Control: the Making of Work Discipline, Achievement, and Consumption

The Development of a Capitalist Labor Force.   Capitalism not only requires ideological images to justify and legitimate its distributive structure. It also needs to legitimize the development of a new type of labor. Pre-capitalist agricultural work tasks were relatively stable, production technology changed little, and work schedules were relatively flexible. They left the individuals some freedom to organize them as they wished. Social mobility, however, was, for the peasant, virtually non-existent. The ideologies of the time depicted society as a divinely pre-ordained static order of social classes in which the peasant owed loyalty, service and obedience to the lord. Such a belief ensured a steady and reliable flow of peasant labor.

The success of the later capitalist system in securing a sufficient supply of labor was not only the result of the effective manipulation of ideological beliefs in the work force. As in earlier forms of domination, the most important factor was the complete control of the means of production—now industrial capital—by the ruling class. Such complete control was not only the result of private ownership, but also of supportive government action such as the termination of free land grants in Upper Canada in 1827. This measure precluded independent farming for immigrants as an alternative to industrial employment. Thus, an industrial working class was created who had nothing to sell but its labor.

But the availability of labor was not enough for the efficient operation of capitalism. Many laborers in the early Canadian industries came from rural backgrounds in Canada or overseas. As a consequence, they had to become accustomed to an entirely new type of work. It involved long and uninterrupted hours and was rigidly controlled by both supervision and the relentless pace of the machine.

Former agricultural laborers were not the only ones unprepared for, and who resisted, this experience. Resistance came also from those who had emigrated to Canada from Britain and were already familiar with factory work, and from artisans whose skills had been made obsolete by the new industrial system. Especially the latter fought desperately to retain some of their respectability and were among the first to form labor organizations.

The factory owner's answer to the need for a labor force adapted to the rigors of industrial work, and to the fear of the growing proletariat as a source of conflict and instability, was to preach and enforce the value of discipline and order. Inside the factory, this was achieved through a policy of low wages. The imposition of a myriad of rules governing every aspect of the work day, and the imposition of fines and penalties for every infraction also assisted in the process. Workers had to face deductions from their already meagre wages for such things as washing themselves, whistling, being found dirty, putting their tools in the wrong place, or for being sick without being able to find a replacement (Hammond and Hammond 1968:17-8).

Outside the factory, workers faced a wide range of efforts with discipline as the goal. The temperance movement, for example, was designed to rid workers of 'vices' such as drinking, lewd and unruly behavior, and to 'better' the working person's way of life. However, as seen in the previous chapter and in the one on education, the most important assault against the vices of the working class was carried out in the schools.

Advanced Capitalism.   Towards the end of the nineteenth century capitalist production in Canada began to undergo two structural changes. One was the gradual growth of a more complex and differentiated production technology. The other was the rapid growth of administrative bureaucracies in factories as well as in government. These structural changes demanded more adaptable and flexible work values. The earlier task-related discipline that had been such an important theme in the socialization of the working classes and their children gave way to an emphasis on generalized compliance with legitimate authority. Factory owners and their management could rely upon this new disposition in a wide variety of work tasks and occupational positions.

Both Hess and Torney (1967) and Easton and Dennis (1969) have emphasized the general, non-specific form in which children now learn about compliance and authority in elementary schools. Symbols such as the law or the policeman, as well as the confrontation with rules and regulations of the classroom, give children an abstract image of an external authority. It is distinct from close authority figures such as parents or teachers, and is both a necessary and legitimate part of their social environment.

Tapp's (1970) comparative study of children's perception of law and authority in six capitalist countries shows that these images develop quite early. They also show remarkable cross-cultural similarity. Easton and Dennis make the following comment on their findings on children's views of the policeman, one of the earliest figures of external authority: "We can have little doubt that the tail end of the structure of political authority—the policeman—has left a distinct imprint on the mind of the child. Through the policeman the child learns an important lesson about the power of external authority and about the need to accept as obligatory or binding the actions or decisions of others from the broad world beyond the family" (Easton and Dennis 1969:226-7).[1]

Following Orders.   The nature of compliance with authority in contemporary capitalist societies has been demonstrated in a series of well-known studies by Milgram. In his original experiment, Milgram asked a group of randomly selected adults to administer an electric shock of increasing intensity to a 'learner' whenever the latter made a mistake. The 'teachers' believed that they were participating in a study of the effects of punishment on learning. In fact, Milgram wanted to find out how long the participants were willing to follow the orders of the experimenter and give painful and potentially dangerous shocks to another person. The learner was of course an accomplice of Milgram. But the setting was realistic enough—including complaints, screams, and eventually ominous silence—to make the teacher believe that he was indeed punishing the learner for his wrong answers.

Milgram's initial expectation was that few if any people would go up to the maximum shock level of 450 volts. But 62 percent of the participants went through the entire shock range! Many of these showed visible signs of anguish when hearing the reactions of their "victims" from the adjacent room. They nonetheless obeyed the instructions of the experimenter to continue.

In subsequent studies, Milgram varied some of the initial conditions. He found, for instance, that the level of obedience is influenced by the physical distance between teacher and learner. Where the participants were neither able to see nor hear their "victim", almost all went through the entire shock range. Compliance dropped to about 30 percent where the teachers had to force the hand of the learner onto a shock plate.

Closeness of supervision was another factor. Obedience was highest when the participants felt directly supervised by the experimenter. In the most interesting of these variations, Milgram moved the experiment from the university environment to a somewhat run-down commercial building in a downtown area. Even under these circumstances, the nondescript name on the door ("Research Associates"), and the lab coat of the experimenter provided enough symbols of authority to make nearly half of the participants administer the highest shock level. Milgram's study, originally done in the United States, was subsequently replicated in France, Norway, and Germany. In all cases the results were similar.

That people are prepared to follow orders regardless of the consequences was also shown in a survey by Kelman and Lawrence (1972). The study asked a large sample of Americans about their opinions on the My Lai massacre. On March 16, 1968, American troops, under the command of Lieutenant Calley, had killed 500 Vietnamese civilians, mostly women, children and old people. The massacre was unprovoked and quite methodical. There had been no prior fighting in the area. During his trial in 1971, Calley's defense argued that he had acted under orders received from his military superiors. He was sentenced to a prison term and paroled in 1974.

The survey was conducted at the time when the trial received maximum publicity, and the dilemma of receiving a military order that was morally objectionable was widely discussed. Even then, 67 percent of the sample thought that most people would obey orders and shoot in a similar situation. Only 19 percent expected most people to disobey the order. Asked what they would do, 51 percent answered that they would shoot the inhabitants of a village when ordered to do so. Only 35 percent indicated that they would refuse.

These studies suggest that the socialization process in contemporary capitalist societies encourages a generalized readiness to comply. Such a disposition is activated by nothing more than a few anonymous trappings of authority. Unlike the specific, role-related obedience of early capitalism, it constitutes a general functional medium of interchange between superiors and subordinates. Because it lends itself to any application, it is a resource which can be drawn upon, not unlike a bank account, for a wide range of economic or political objectives.

Achievement.   The same degree of generality also characterises the second work-related value that emerges during the latter part of the nineteenth century: achievement. Before that date, the idea of achievement legitimized the rise of the captains of industry and banking. Power and wealth were viewed as the natural result of their hard work and superior ability. With the expansion of occupational structures and the growth of opportunities for mobility, achievement acquired a new meaning.

Addressed to the working population it replaced earlier exhortations not to "ape the rich" and to seek improvement in the pursuit of moral virtues such as modesty, discipline and industry. The increasing encouragement of achievement and mobility in schoolbooks and children's literature around 1900 marks the beginning of modern functional ideological images of capitalist society. Social rank is the reflection of personal effort and ability. All social positions are achievable. Open and unrestrained competition for them assures that the most important positions are filled by the most competent people. Moreover, the reward they receive corresponds to the contribution they make to the well-being of the society.

This popularized image of achievement became the basis for the modern "work ethic". Self-motivated effort and competition became an obligation toward "society" and a pre-condition of social acceptance. Bandura and Perloff (1967) have shown that this work ethic is already well-established in children between seven and ten years of age. Given a choice of claiming a reward at any time during the performance of a task, none of the children did so right away. About half of them completed the entire task before asking to be rewarded. Moreover, their overall performance in this situation was high compared to other reward conditions. The study suggests that for the children work has become a value in itself at an early age. Where rewards can be freely chosen many of them consider it unjust to do so before a task is completed in its entirety.

The competitive aspects of internalized standards of achievement are shown in a study by Nelson and Kagan (1972). They compare competition and co-operation among American, Mexican and Canadian Indian children. The subjects were given a series of tasks which involved two or more partners and were set up in such a way that the children could either compete or co-operate. However, maximum rewards could only be obtained through co-operation. The children were from five to ten years old, and the rewards consisted of toys compatible with their age.

American children competed with each other even where mutual assistance was necessary to obtain toys, and where competitive behavior was clearly contrary to their interests. Their competitiveness was not only irrational. At times it was also punitive. Not content with trying to gain a reward at a partner's expense, they would block opponents. When given a chance, they would take away toys that their opponents had received in previous trials even when they were not allowed to keep them. By contrast, children from rural Mexico co-operated much more frequently and consequently earned significantly more toys than their more competitive American counterparts. A similarly high level of co-operative behavior was also found among Canadian Indian children, and children raised in the communal environment of Israeli Kibbuzim. This comparison suggests at least tentatively that the presence and the strength of internalized competitiveness are culture-specific. It shows further that the socialization process in capitalist societies exposes children to ideological values which encourage competitive behavior at an early age.

The New Consumer.   Nineteenth century capitalists understood very well the importance of encouraging work-values that would ensure the amount and the type of labor needed in industrial employment. It took them much longer to recognize the role of the new proletariat as a market for the products made in the factories. The rapid growth of urban wage-earners who could no longer rely on subsistence farming and had to purchase their livelihood had fuelled the development of capitalist industry from its beginning. But it was by coincidence and not by design that the consumption of urban laborers provided an important market for the goods they produced. Few capitalists fully understood the connection. If anything, the early exhortations of modesty and moral rather than material improvement discouraged any "excessive" spending by the working population. In pre-capitalist Europe, the aristocratic ruling class had viewed consumption by the peasantry as a cost. Both classes drew their livelihood from the same agricultural production. An increase in consumption by the peasants reduced the surplus left for the aristocracy.

This view of consumption carried well into the nineteenth century. Any demand by the worker for an improved standard of living could only mean a demand for higher wages. These could only reduce the profit of the capitalist firm. And even though nineteenth century capitalists in Canada as elsewhere faced periodically large stocks of unsold products, they did not see stimulation of consumption as a way of disposing them. Throughout the period, entrepreneurs saw only two options of improving their profit. They could limit costs, primarily by keeping wages as low as possible. They could also increase sales through price changes. The latter option could lead to ruinous competition. The only strategy directed at manipulating the market was therefore to combine with other competitors to guarantee each a relatively secure share of the sales. Bliss (1974:33-54) gives a good summary of early views of Canadian capitalists on the urgency of reducing competition.

Before 1910, deliberate efforts to increase the *demand* for industrial products did not go beyond publicizing the products themselves. Advertisements in Canadian newspapers or retail catalogues generally contained a description of a single item, its characteristics, and its uses and benefits. These product-portraits were sometimes more, or sometimes less, accurate. But they rarely presented more than a selective positive picture of product properties. Where they tried to influence the feelings of the reader, they did so either through particularly vivid or exaggerated descriptions of the benefits of what they advertised. Or they attempted to encourage brand loyalties through direct comparisons and through claims that only the advertised article was "genuine" and "authentic".

The fundamental change that occurred in this pattern of advertising between 1910 and 1920 coincided with a major technical change in the organization of industrial production: the introduction of assembly-line manufacturing. Initiated by Henry Ford in the assembly of automobiles, it revolutionized the production process. In addition, mass production had a profound effect on market strategies. For one thing, the staggering increase in productivity accomplished through line production made the problem of marketing even more urgent. For another, it brought with it a wave of significantly higher factory wages. The increased buying power of the working population made it obvious that mass production would have to be complemented by an efficient system of mass distribution. Finally, and perhaps most important, assembly-line production became the basis for a new view of labor as well as of consumption. No longer was the individual worker the standard unit in which labor was measured. Instead, "scientific management," as seen in Lowe's chapter, transformed each work process into a series of motions that could be taken apart and recombined at will. And this new technique looked at the psychological component of factory labor as well. Work motivation and work satisfaction could be manipulated in just the same way as the physical work process itself.

Applied to consumption, the same perspective marked the beginning of "scientific" advertising. It was realized that portraying the value of a particular product was no longer sufficient to sell it. Instead, marketing required the knowledge of "human instincts". Such information made it possible to turn the need for a product into desire.

Between 1920 and 1930 the face of advertising changed drastically. It greatly increased in volume. Also, advertisers now made a deliberate attempt to influence the motivations and wants of the buyer. The new psychological methods of advertising turned "the consumer's critical functions away from the product and toward himself" (Ewen 1976:37). Advertisements now became prescriptive and admonishing. They used existing and invented social norms to make the consumer self-conscious of the need to civilize and improve himself through the use of "modern" products. They provoked anxiety by putting everyday behavior into the context of social comparison and social visibility. They raised the spectre of social failure as the result of neglecting to keep up, through consumption, with the norms of "modern living". The Lynds, in their classical study, Middletown, observed that advertisements in the 1920s, unlike those of a generation before, were "concentrating increasingly upon a type of copy aiming to make the reader emotionally uneasy, to bludgeon him with the fact that decent people don't live the way he does . . . This copy points an accusing finger at the stenographer as she reads her motion picture magazine and makes her acutely conscious of her unpolished fingernails . . . and sends the housewife peering anxiously into the mirror to see if her wrinkles look like those that made Mrs. X in the advertisement 'old at thirty-five' because she did not have a Leisure Hour electric washer" (Lynd and Lynd 1929:82).

Contemporary advertising has largely abandoned this moralizing tone. What distinguishes advertisements today from those of the 1920s and 1930s is that they no longer suggest the product as a means of social improvement or of meeting social standards of normalcy or desirability. Instead, advertisements create an identity between reader and product.

Contemporary advertising gives products a meaning that allows the reader to associate with and identify himself in the product. It draws its viewer into the social significance of the product. "Advertisements are selling us something else besides consumer goods: in providing us with a structure in which we, and those goods, are interchangeable, they are selling us ourselves" (Williamson 1978:13).

HIGHLIGHT

1. The transition to early industrial capitalism required the acceptance by workers of values and beliefs such as discipline, frugality, and orderliness.
2. In the twentieth century, beliefs such as the above have been replaced by consumption values. The latter are essential to the continued operation of the capitalist system.
3. Values and beliefs essential to the operation of capitalism are inculcated in children at an early age.

The Effects of Ideologies on Behavior

Perceptions of Inequality.   How effective is the ideological reconstruction of capitalist inequality? Reference has already been made to studies indicating that certain behavioral patterns are established early in life. Two other studies of the perception of social differences by children give us some idea when the influence of capitalist ideology begins, and how it affects the evaluations of social position.

In the first study, 108 children between the ages of five and twelve from the Toronto area were asked to look at the pictures of two men. One was well-dressed. The other was in casual clothing. They were then shown two sets of photos which showed a large house in a high income area of the city and a small house in a working class area. They were also shown an expensive and a somewhat shabby living room interior, a Lincoln Continental and a Volkswagen, and two more photos of a man. Once again, one was carefully dressed, the other was casually attired.

The children were asked to give a short description of the first two men (called Mr. Gordon and Mr. Ellis). They were then told to indicate which man lived in which house, which living room was in which house, which car the two men drove, and which of the last two men they would invite to their house for a party. The purpose of the study was to find out at what age the children began to order the pictures on the basis of the visible social differences which were common to all pictures.

The results showed that by the time they reached Grade 6, almost all the children recognized the social differences between the two men. They allocated houses, living rooms, cars and friends accordingly. The most interesting part of the findings were the verbal comments made by the children, all of which were taped. They showed an increasing tendency to not merely identify, but also to evaluate the people and objects shown in the pictures. The well-dressed man and his life-style received generally favorable comments. Many of the children drew inferences about other aspects of the man—his intelligence, the kind of work he did, the friends he had—for which the pictures contained no information. By contrast, the casually dressed man elicited fewer, more negative, and at times clearly derogatory observations.

In order to investigate such evaluative judgments further, the children were, subsequent to the picture-matching, told four short stories. The stories focussed on minor transgressions, success in school, and being liked by schoolmates. The scenes in the stories were typical of the elementary school environment in which the study took place. After each story, the children were asked whether the boy or the girl in the story was, in their opinion, the son or the daughter of Mr. Gordon or Mr. Ellis.

The choices confirmed the results of the first part of the study. The older the children were, the more likely they were to attribute the transgression and the failure in school to the child of Mr. Ellis. Mr. Gordon's child was seen as well-liked by his classmates. It seemed clear to the children that "good" parents also would have good, well-behaved and intelligent offspring. The children of Mr. Ellis, the less well-dressed man who lived in a small house with a somewhat run-down living-room and who drove an inexpensive car, were considered to be likely to get into trouble. They were also thought to be inclined to fight and swear, and not do very well in school.

What is remarkable about these findings is that the children had only a few visual clues about the social class of the men in the pictures. That was sufficient for many of them to draw far-reaching conclusions about the men's lives. "Mr. Gordon emerged in the comments of Grade 3 and Grade 6 children as a man of 'good manners', 'cheerful', 'nice', 'intelligent', 'happy all the time', 'well-educated', 'polite', with 'good friends', and liked by everybody. Mr. Ellis, on the other hand, looked 'tough', 'rough' and 'lazy' and likely to swear, steal, or drink, and did not care very much about his own affairs and his family" (Baldus 1978:59).

By the time they are ten or eleven years old, most of the children seem to accept symbols of wealth as general indicators of social desirability. People like Mr. Gordon appear to the children as a natural and attractive part of their social environment. The most likely way they have reached that position is by being a "businessman". By the same standards, the children dissociate themselves from Mr. Ellis. In their view, the characteristics of both would also be found in their children. This opinion indirectly reveals a strong belief in the stability and continuity of class differences between people.

A subsequent study investigated in greater detail abstract notions of wealth and poverty prevalent among children between the ages of six and fourteen years. This study asked, first, for drawings of a poor and a rich person. It then asked the children to state some of the reasons why there are rich and poor people. The drawing task left free rein to the children's imaginations. It encouraged the presentation of a bipolar and often over-emphasizing picture, even though many of the drawings contained elements that revealed keen and realistic observations. The main purpose was to find out what symbols the children used in representing wealth and poverty.

The results showed a great deal of similarity, especially in the drawings of the older children. Among the most frequent indicators were facial expressions that suggested moods: a smiling face for the rich figure, and an unhappy face, sometimes crying, for the poor person. This theme was often also emphasized by putting the sun into the drawing of the wealthy individual and occasionally by letting it rain on the poor.

The other large group of symbols which the children used were possessions. Money was usually represented by gold coins or green bills of large denominations. Pictures of poor people almost always showed ragged clothes with holes and patches. By contrast, rich people were dressed elaborately. The drawings of the girls especially went into great detail to suggest fancy and expensive clothing. Girls also frequently depicted jewels: necklaces, rings, and bracelets, studded, most commonly, with "diamonds". Houses of rich people were not only larger, had more windows, and often two garages, but were frequently placed on well-kept and treed streets. They had large front lawns, or were placed in the midst of mountains because, some of the children suggested, "rich people like being isolated from other people". The houses of the poor were usually much smaller, had patched-up roofs and broken windows. Frequently, they displayed other characteristics of low income areas in the city, such as narrow lots or closeness to the street.

Finally, there were cars, especially in the drawings by boys. Usually large cars were used as a symbol of wealth. Sometimes they had a name such as Rolls Royce, or were chauffeur-driven. When commenting on the drawings all children considered the life of a rich person attractive and desirable, and something that many of them wished to have. Their dissociation from the life of a poor person was equally clear, even though it was often tempered by the expression of compassion and the need to help.

The appearance of the same preferences in the comments of the first-graders suggests that the affective disposition towards symbols of wealth and poverty develops even earlier than the cognitive understanding of these concepts. When they are six years old, the children draw only the most rudimentary symbols of wealth, but they definitely know that being rich is a good thing. Hess and Torney observed the same for children's understanding of political symbols, such as flags, high political offices, or concepts such as "freedom" or "communism" (Hess and Torney 1967).

After completing their drawings, the children were asked why some people were rich and others poor. They could first write down any reasons they could think of. Then, they were given a list of reasons to choose from. While the replies of the younger children come close to a random pattern, the children in Grades 6 and 8 identified inheritance and hard work as the main reasons for wealth. As for poverty, they thought most frequently that the poor themselves were to blame—because they "lack common sense" or the "right attitude to life", or because they are "lazy". The children gave other reasons as well. A good job, a business or a good education would guarantee success. No jobs, growing up poor, early death of the main earner in the family, or living in a third world country could result in failure. But by the time they are ten or twelve years old, many children believe in a link between social position and personal responsibility. Critical comments on rich people are almost entirely absent, and only two of the 88 children in the study saw wealth and poverty as interdependent parts of the same distributive order (Baldus 1982).

General Applications.   There is no doubt that the views of social inequality which the children hold will become more complex and more critical as they grow older. Most of them will become aware of the power of big business. Many will realize the importance of connections in getting a job. Many Canadians will express their reservations about business practices and business ethics. They will also question the political influence of large corporations when given a chance to talk about them (Rhinehart and Okraku 1974). But it is also clear that Canadians, to the extent that they obtain their information about the world in which they live from mass media, face a picture of remarkable uniformity. Three broad themes occur particularly frequently.

The first is that free enterprise is the most efficient guarantor of economic prosperity and individual freedom. It is one of the most commonly-used means of justifying pro-business political measures. And in one form or another, the view that their own well-being depends on the well-being of private enterprise is probably shared by a substantial majority of Canadians.

The second theme is the portrayal of wealth as the generalized standard of social success, and the model for social aspirations. Its modern form is perhaps best reflected in the attractive, young, active and glamorous lifestyle of the anonymous figures that populate the world shown in advertisements. The concept of success as status that can be attained through consumption exerts a subtle but powerful influence on people's lives. Just as the children in the study discussed earlier drew wide-ranging inferences from a few visual clues about a person's social position, many adults need to know only that someone is a factory worker or a teacher or office manager to feel quite certain about a variety of personality characteristics of each. Industry, politeness, intelligence and confidence are seen as character traits of the latter two. The worker, on the other hand, is judged in much more negative terms (Davidson, Riesman and Myers 1962). As for personal identity and self-evaluation, Sennett and Cobb (1972) and Rubin (1976) have documented the far-reaching and often destructive consequences of internalized ideological standards of success.

The third major component of the ideological reconstruction of capitalism is the idea that social position is a matter of individual responsibility. The facts, however, suggest otherwise. Recent studies (Jencks 1979; Osberg 1981) agree that ability and effort are just two of a number of factors which affect an individual's social mobility. But they are often much less important than social background, or simply luck. Nonetheless, the myth persists. It affects particularly the public image of the poor.

We saw that as they got older, school children tend to place the responsibility for poverty increasingly on the shoulders of the poor themselves. Feagin (1972) shows the same tendency among adults. About half the people in his survey saw lack of thrift and effort, loose morals and drunkenness, or the lack of ability and talent as the most important causes of poverty. Personal responsibility for poverty was considered much more important than other explanations such as luck, discrimination, failure to provide jobs or being taken advantage of by the rich (Feagin 1972:103). Feagin cites a similar survey done in 1945 which shows that such attitudes towards poverty have remained stable over a long period of time.

HIGHLIGHT

1. Research shows that perceptions of the behavioral correlates of inequality develop in very young children. Usually positive characteristics are attributed to the rich, negative ones to the poor.
2. Numerous studies have verified the idea that reactions to general symbols are established very early in life.

Interventive Control: the Use of Symbolic Values and Boundaries

Political Symbols and Political Decisions.   In addition to explanations of social classes and their relationship with each other, capitalist societies also produce a variety of general ideological values. These are used to legitimate the daily flow of often unforeseen social processes or political decisions. We saw how, during the second half of the nineteenth century, the notion of "progress" was used to gain, at short notice, political and financial backing from local communities for the construction of railroads.

Free enterprise and economic growth are contemporary equivalents of the concept of progess. In today's newspaper commentary, the description of a policy as stimulating economic growth gives that policy a positive meaning. The description of an action as interfering with free enterprise evokes negative connotations. We saw earlier that free enterprise and economic growth have become interchangeable and synonymous. Moreover, they are freely employed to suggest that a particular measure that is favorable to private corporations will benefit the society as a whole.

There are many other, similar symbols. They include general abstract concepts such as "equality" or "freedom", or flags, crests, or anthems. They carry positive affective connotations. These are drawn from their claim to represent values or interests that are shared by most or all members of the society. At the same time, the values are non-specific. They are largely devoid of cognitive content. Because of this vagueness, they provide a reservoir of free-floating and highly adaptable ideological images. Such images can be associated with a wide variety of social and political facts to which they transfer their affective meaning.

Edelmann (1960, 1971) has investigated the use of symbols in the legitimation of day to day political decisions which affect the distribution of resources. He suggests that most of these decisions have a symbolic and a factual aspect. The first of these is highly visible. It usually links a particular piece of legislation with a symbolic value. Thus, changes in taxation and transfer payments are commonly associated with the principle of "fairness" and "social justice", and more specifically with "progressive" and "redistributive" effects that help Canadians with low incomes. Similarly, anti-combine legislation might be passed with the claim that it will protect competition and preserve the free play of market forces. Educational measures may be passed by invoking the principle of equality of opportunity. "Typically, a preamble [to such measures] (which does not pretend to be more than symbolic, even in legal theory) includes strong assurances that the public or the public interest will be protected. And the most widely publicized regulatory provisions always include other nonoperational standards connoting fairness, balance, or equity" (Edelmann 1960:697).

Ironically, Edelmann found an inverse relationship between the visibility of symbols and the significance of the legislation for resource allocations. Those parts of the legislative provisions which were least consequential for the distribution of resources received the highest publicity and were most visibly associated with political symbols. The most significant provisions were least widely publicized (Edelmann 1960:697).

If one examines the factual aspects of such political measures one discovers that their real distributive effects differ substantially from the symbolic promise. Often they directly contradict it. If we take our three examples we find, for instance, that taxation and transfer payments have few if any redistributive consequences. They have not altered the Canadian income distribution which has been remarkably stable over the last three decades (Marchak 1981:23). Detailed calculations indicate that rather than redistributing income from high to low income earners they had the opposite effects: "...the redistributive mechanism of the public sector during the 1960s generated gains to rich Canadians: each rich Canadian family gained three times more than each poor Canadian family and six times more than each Canadian in the lower income class" (Gillespie 1976:433). This trend seems to have continued in the 1970s (Gillespie 1980:41).

As for Canadian anti-combines laws they have, since their first passage in 1889, been singularly ineffective in preventing corporate concentration. In fact, they may have never been intended to stop concentration. Instead they may have been "...meant to inflict the minimum inconvenience on business, consistent with governments' need to convince ordinary citizens that it is against monopoly" (Drummond 1972:101).

Finally, educational institutions have clearly not advanced the goal of equal opportunity. With regard to Ontario universities, for instance, Mehmet concludes, that "the principal net gainers from the university system are the middle and upper income groups at the expense of the lower income groups. In this sense the university system is a large public expenditure programme in which the relatively poor groups tend to subsidize the relatively rich" (Mehmet 1978:45. See also Osenberg 1981:XII).

In view of matters such as the above, Edelmann suggests that such symbolic values are used to placate public opinion and to prevent or reduce social conflict. The latter could arise if the actual consequences of the legislation were known. At the same time, the activation of values conceals the substantive operation of the political system from public scrutiny. It also facilitates actions whose distributive effects strengthen the existing inequality structure.

The Prevention of Change.   The general intent of symbols such as these is to deny or conceal the existence of class divisions. A second category of symbols is used to discourage and prevent significant structural change. The first type of symbol suggested the presence of shared, consensual values and justified a particular political measure by connecting the two. The second type defines the ideological boundaries of the capitalist system by identifying political alternatives to it as socially unacceptable and as detrimental to the collective interest.

The fear of demands for a more equitable distributive order is as old as the bourgeois revolution itself. The French Revolution had already raised the spectre of radical political change that went far beyond what the new capitalist class was willing to tolerate. The threat of such change continued to haunt the bourgeoisie throughout the nineteenth century. What added to their fear was the explosive social situation, the poverty, the rapid growth of an urban proletariat and the apparent breakdown of traditional norms of loyalty and deference.

In Canada, Ryerson's advocacy in 1865 of a public school system as a means of preventing violent social conflict reflected the anxieties of private property owners in Canada. Without the universal disciplining influence of such a system on all young people, there would be "envy, then hatred of the more successful and prosperous classes, then mutual consultations and excitements to revenge their imaginary wrongs, and relieve themselves of their deeply felt but self-inflicted evils; and then among the more daring and least scrupulous portion of such isolated community, the combinations and conspiracies of Fenianism—the employment of brute force to obtain power and wealth, which can only be legitimately obtained by the exercise of virtue, intelligence and industry" (Quoted in Prentice 1977:131).

While nineteenth century capitalists keenly felt the need to defend themselves against threats to their interests, that defense did not yet have a clear focus. Its basic theme was to equate demands for changes in industrial ownership with the prospect of inevitable social disintegration and chaos. But through the nineteenth and early twentieth century no particular group or movement emerged as the prime symbol of such a threat to the social fabric. Jacobins (the radical sans-culottes faction of the French Revolution), Chartists, and Fenians were all accused at various times of plotting to overthrow civilized society. In the latter part of the nineteenth century labor organizations were increasingly suspected of having the same goal. Elson finds in her study of nineteenth century American schoolbooks that by the end of the century these books had clearly come to identify labor organizations with riots and violence, and with doctrines subversive to American institutions (Elson 1964:251). But socialism and communism, the primary boundary symbols of today, had not yet acquired their modern ideological meaning.

With the 1917 revolution in Russia socialism was, for the first time, recognized as a serious danger. Tippin (1974) compared news items and editorials in the *Toronto Daily Star* on Russia, Italy, France and China for four one-year periods (1908, 1912, 1919 and 1923). He found that for the two years after the revolution, reporting and editorial comments on Russia became much more frequent. They also became more negative when compared to reports of other countries. News items on Russia increased from nine in 1908 and eight in 1912, to forty-four in 1919 and sixty-two in 1923. The corresponding figures for France, the country with the next highest news coverage, are: six (1908), twenty-five (1912), twenty-three (1919) and twenty-two (1923). Moreover, by 1923, fifty-one of the sixty-two news items on Russia were negative. This figure is significantly higher than for any of the other countries.

After the revolution, reporting emphasized the destruction of civil liberties (which the *Star* evidently thought to have blossomed under the Tzarist regime), lack of public support, and economic difficulties in the new system. A suggested cause for the latter was the abolition of private enterprise. On May 1, 1923 the *Star* commented, "The Russians are in a hopeless economic muddle, directed by men not knowing what they want, without business attitude, inspired by the maddest dreams... They are drifting to economic ruin unless their course is speedily changed. They must give factory managers complete control without the necessity of consulting Soviets of their own workmen and dozens of government departments." This picture was combined with a variety of suggestions of how the menace of Russian socialism could be fought in Canada. The *Star* admonished Canadians to regard democratic institutions, elections, and Parliament as their own "and not something imposed on them by a governing class" (*Toronto Daily Star*, February 1, 1919). It assured them that "our system is better for the masses of the people than Bolshevism" and that "a keen and genuine interest in social reform is one of the safeguards against Bolshevik propaganda" (*Toronto Daily Star*, August 21, 1919).

Since then, socialism and communism have become the major symbols that delineate the political boundaries of capitalist systems and distinguish unacceptable from acceptable social change. They carry strongly negative affective connotations. Frequently they are used to give meaning to internal and external political movements and events that are deemed to pose a threat to capitalist interests.   The thematic treatment of socialism and communism in contemporary mass media has become largely standardized. Both are portrayed as unworkable, economically inefficient, centrally controlled, lacking popular support, and being maintained only by undemocratic or dictatorial rule. Moreover, they constitute a world-wide subversive danger. It was seen that positive ideological symbols such as progress, success, or free enterprise transform capitalist profit into a general benefit to society. Symbols such as communism interpret challenges to the position of the capitalist ruling class as threats to the well-being of the society as a whole.

Boundary-maintaining symbols are both widely disseminated and effective. Hess and Torney (1967:71) show that American children learn that socialism or Russia are bad at about the same time as they become acquainted with positive system-supportive symbols and are taught that the United States is "the best country in the world". As the children grow older, they learn a more differentiated symbolic vocabulary describing political villains. Terms such as "revolutionary", "radical", "subversive", "trouble-maker", or "communist" may be used synonymously to identify a particular idea or event as being outside the boundary of what is politically tolerated.

Stouffer's study of attitudes of Americans towards communism between 1937 and 1954 provides evidence of the growth of anticommunist beliefs in the United States. In 1937 a majority of Americans wanted to deny basic civil liberties to communists. During the second world war, this percentage decreased as a result of the war-time alliance with the Soviet Union. But by 1954, almost all respondents in Stouffer's large sample had returned to a complete rejection of communism. This was, of course, the time of the McCarthy hearings. The results nonetheless give a vivid illustration of the potential of boundary symbols to immunize people against alternative political ideas.

Among Stouffer's more remarkable findings were that most people interviewed during the survey had little or no knowledge of even basic socialist or communist ideas. This suggests once again that such ideological symbols have a clear affective direction and also encourage the abandonment of critical reason. In this way, it can be quickly attached to any idea that seems to question basic aspects of the capitalist status quo. Thus, environmentalist, anti-nuclear or peace organizations can be labelled "communist-directed", and change-oriented political movements such as the Allende government in Chile or similar groups in Central America can be called "subversive". Unfortunately, capitalist systems have no monopoly on the use of such boundary symbols. Established socialist governments often treat their own political dissidents in similar ways.

Two studies illustrate how boundary symbols change people's perception of a fact to which they have become attached. Hofland and Weiss (1951) found that readers evaluated the same magazine and newspaper articles very differently depending on whether they believed the material came from sources in socialist or in capitalist countries. Communications purportedly taken from Russian newspapers were considered biased and factually incorrect. The same article was considered trustworthy and accurate when readers were told that it was taken from an American source.

In a similar study by Oskamp (1965), participants were asked for their judgment of a number of political actions. These had been carefully selected to represent measures taken by both the American and the Soviet governments in the past. The list contained, for instance, statements such as "The (U.S. or U.S.S.R.) supports regular propoganda broadcasts beamed at nations on the other side of the 'Iron Curtain' "; or "The (U.S. or U.S.S.R.) has put itself on record as favoring general and complete disarmament." Oskamp found that the evaluation of the actions varied considerably depending on which government they were attributed to. "American" actions were viewed positively. "Soviet" measures were judged unfavorably.

The FLQ Crisis.   In Canada, the October crisis of 1970 provided an example of both the use of boundary symbols to label a particular group a public enemy and efforts to mobilize widespread fear and hostility against it. At the time, a small terrorist group calling itself the Front de la Libération du Québèc (F.L.Q.) kidnapped a British trade official and a Quebec government minister. The latter was subsequently killed.

The event was well within the range of a regular police action. The FLQ had been under surveillance for some time. In fact, the RCMP was so well prepared for the event that it was able to send out, during the kidnapping, fake communiques on specially prepared FLQ stationary. The intent was to create the impression that several terrorist cells were involved. Instead of using normal police measures, the federal government invoked the War Measures Act and sent troops to Montreal. Subsequently, five hundred people were arrested. Of these, about thirty were eventually brought to trial. Most were acquitted. The remainder were convicted on charges such as the possession of drugs or traffic offenses. The terrorists directly involved in the kidnapping were given safe conduct to Cuba in exchange for the freedom of the British trade official. They later returned to Quebec and served prison terms.

The transformation of the kidnapping into an incident that was claimed to threaten the boundaries of the Canadian social system must be seen against the background of an increasing concern with the growth of the separatist movement in Quebec. In the April 1970 provincial elections, the Parti Québécois had obtained 24 percent of the vote and 7 seats. Shortly before the election, a well-publicized effort had been made to influence public opinion against the Parti Québécois. Eight Brinks trucks, supposedly filled with corporate securities, left Montreal to demonstrate the flight of capital from Quebec that would follow a separatist victory.

The kidnapping provided a further opportunity to associate the separatist movement with social disorder and radical subversion. This was accomplished by grossly exaggerating the size of the FLQ and by depicting it as a potential danger to all Canadians. Jean Marchand, then federal minister of information, claimed that the FLQ had at least 3000 members. He further claimed that it had enough dynamite to blow up the core of downtown Montreal. The Prime Minister told Canadians that the next target of the FLQ could be "some child . . . or innocent member of your family." These and other statements were given wide publicity in the press.

An opinion poll in November 1970 showed that the transformation of the FLQ action into a threat to the nation had been effective. In total, 89 percent of all Canadians approved the invocation of the War Measures Act, and 68 percent approved of the Prime Minister's handling of the event.

Jill Armstrong (1972) analysed the content of 1043 published and unpublished letters to the editors of four major Canadian newspapers during the crisis. Even though they do not constitute a sample of public opinion, they give us a detailed picture of the effects of the manipulation of boundary symbols. Letters in favor of the government's actions outnumbered those opposed to it by about 4 to 1. Pro-government writers most frequently expressed the need for unity and for closing ranks in the face of crisis. Combined with this was an advocacy of stern and authoritarian measures: "When a man has cancer, it is necessary to treat the growth with radium, harming some innocent tissue in the process" (Quoted in Armstrong 1972:311).

Most of the letters called for strong leadership. More specific measures included calling out troops, the restoration of capital punishment, the use of firing squads or the imposition of censorship. The only criticism of government actions came from those who wanted to see harsher measures: "Why don't you muzzle the press. They are broadcasting to the FLQ every move the forces of law and order are making, thus sabotaging their efforts." "We need a law that makes it compulsory for every Canadian . . . to be fingerprinted and to have a passport . . . to increase the efficiency of our police." "Police (should be) issued open season permits on every known and active sympathizer with subversive causes . . ." (All quotes from Armstrong 1972:313). The targets of the letters were most often the FLQ. Government critics who many letter writers called "bleeding hearts", were also targets. Reds, international conspiracies, radicals and protesters, students, and French Canadians were other groups blamed for the crisis.

The point here is not to judge the actions of either the government or the FLQ. What is important to see is the relative ease with which a criminal act can be transformed into an "apprehended insurrection". In times of real or perceived crisis, there is usually no shortage of groups or ideas which boundary symbols can identify as villains and culprits. Once these symbols are activated and attached to a particular target, their widely socialized but usually latent affective content gains direction. They channel suspicion and hostility towards the target and seem to make many people willing to dispense with elementary civil rights, become intolerant of dissident views, and to lay the fate of the country confidently into the hands of a strong leader.

HIGHLIGHT

1. In contemporary capitalist society, such values as 'free enterprise' and 'economic growth' are frequently used to justify government action.

2. Some values in contemporary capitalist society are used to prevent change. For many individuals, for example, calling a measure socialist or communist is sufficient to guarantee opposition to it.

3. The FLQ 'crisis' in Quebec is an example of the utilization by the state of symbols to oppose groups concerned with change.

Adjustive Behavior and Complementarity

Social Space.   So far we have looked at ways in which the ruling class intervenes in, and modifies the behavior of, subordinate people in such a manner that it serves its interests. Many of these forms of intervention eventually become self-supporting. Control over them shifts from capital owners to governmental agencies or professional groups. In the process, their content and their goals may change substantially.

But the direct intervention by capitalists is not the only reason a particular form of domination leaves its imprint on the behavior of a society. The influence of structures of inequality on people's lives is much more pervasive. It extends far beyond the effects of deliberate efforts by the ruling class to create behavior considered necessary to maintain and reproduce its dominant position. Inequality results in different life chances accruing to people in different social positions. Each position gives its incumbents a socially defined personal space, to use a term suggested by Goffman (1971:28-41).

Individuals control such spaces and can, within them, act with relative autonomy. The limits of such space are determined by such factors as income, formal authority and control, and the informal authority of status. People in managerial positions have, for instance, generally more personal control and autonomy over the work they do than someone on an assembly line. These differences are accompanied by income differentials which provide them with particular consumption and life style options. These are not available to people with a factory or secretarial income.

There are other informal and often very subtle consequences of high status. They may include such things as being given the right to initiate discussions or actions or being deferentially addressed by people of lower rank. These privileges often extend to the receipt of preferential treatment in courts of law. In fact, in some regards, Goffman's concept of personal space is more than a metaphor. Social differences are often reflected in the physical space controlled by an individual. The large executive office, and the desk space in an open plan office allotted to an office worker, symbolize social inequality as much as the different sizes of houses and residential lots in urban areas.

Generally, we may say that the space which a person controls varies directly with his or her position in the inequality structure. The higher the position, the wider a person's range of autonomy. Social inequality, then, imposes differential limitations on people's lives. The more one moves to the lower end of the hierarchy, the more the power or authority of others, the scarcity of resources, and one's low social evaluation restrict and narrow one's existence. These limitations constitute the reality which people encounter from day to day and within which they accommodate their lives.

The many personal ways through which people deal with these restrictions are, for the most part, their own invention. Ideological imagery may broadly guide their efforts. But the practical actions people take to cope with the limits they face are not usually prescribed to them by the ruling class. Instead, people act in original and often highly imaginative ways in attempts to make their lives bearable in an environment that leaves them little control. They similarly endeavor to retain a measure of respect in their own eyes and those of others when their social position does not measure up to the ideological standards of respectability and success.

Learning to Cope.   As discussed in Lowe's chapter, Roy (1959) provides a detailed example of the adjustive behavior of a small group of machine operators that keeps them from "going nuts" in their monotonous and isolated work situation. Roy worked as a participant observer with three other men on punching machines. Such machines cut pieces of varying shapes from sheets of plastic or leather. The work was extremely simple and repetitive, and very boring. Except for the occasional changes in dies, and pick-ups of completed material, the job provided no variation and offered little contact with the rest of the factory. Roy found himself initially adjusting to the tedium of his job by inventing work games. He changed the colors of the material and varied the dies he was using. He set personal short-range production goals and rewarded himself with the cleaning and smoothing out that the cutting block periodically required. By engaging in these games, it was possible for him to gain scope for creativity and self-expression.

Gradually, Roy discovered that similar but more elaborate routines had developed among the three men who had been working for a long time on the other punching machines in the room. One of these routines consisted of what was called "times". These were work interruptions which the men had devised to break up their day. From morning to evening there was peach time, banana time, fish time and Coke time. Each of these times involved some sharing of food which one of the men had brought along. Often 'times' were accompanied by horseplay or pretended theft of a fruit in a standard ritual that was repeated every day. Window time provided another distraction. After some good-natured verbal interplay between two of the older workers, one would "retaliate" by opening the window next to the other's machine. The latter, after long protestations, would eventually close it.

Parallel to these daily rituals were a number of "themes" that were the basis of informal exchanges between the men during their work. The subject of the "professor theme", for instance, was the recent marriage of one of the men's daughters to a college instructor. They listened with admiration to the tales of details of the wedding, and generally of the link of their co-worker to the world of higher learning. The professor connection was a major source of the superior status of the father-in-law in the work group.

These patterned and repeated exchanges were for the men means of making their work more tolerable. They interrupted a monotonous routine, provided some job satisfaction, and gave them some control over their work. But these responses to work were also very much their own. The factory management neither created nor knew about them.

A longer-term adjustment to the contradiction between reality and the dominant ideological norms of social respectability is described by Wadel (1973) in a study of unemployed people in a Newfoundland outport community. In this setting individuals were required to cope with the lack of a regular income and the social stigma of being on welfare. The unemployed, as well as the people in the town, generally accepted the basic precepts of the "work ethic". They believed that individuals should earn their own living and should be held responsible for their economic situation. This view was reflected in comments by townspeople that welfare recipients "don't do nothin' for the money they get" and "don't even look for a job". Some believed that "there'll soon be no difference between what a man gets on welfare and what a man gets for working", and that "there's not much point in workin' when your neighbour can get as much for stayin' home doin' nothin'" (Quoted from Wadel 1973: 110-1).

Wadel gives a very detailed account of the way one of the unemployed men, George, dealt with this social stigma. Being unable to work because of an injured back, he devised a number of strategies for interacting with other people in the community. The fact of being on welfare changed the public perception and evaluation of even very simple activities. It was felt that, "If a workin' man is idlin' around up there, it's a very different matter than if a man on welfare is doin' so. The workin' man is only relaxin' from his work which a hard workin' man deserves; the man on welfare, idlin' around, is remindin' the others that he is idle—not workin', that is" (Quoted from Wadel 1973:85).

The presence of this double standard required George to manage his public identity carefully. He would, for instance, seek out other welfare recipients to talk about such topics as welfare regulations which would have proved embarassing in conversations with employed members of the community. Contacts such as these created solidarity with others whose attributes were similar to his own. At the same time, George also observed the subtle status differences among the welfare recipients. He limited his interaction with people who had been on welfare for a long time and had a low social standing in the community. George used similar caution when dealing with employed members of the town. In conversations with them he would be careful not to reveal the origins of information which came from welfare recipients. He also would reduce his relations with other welfare recipients when employed people in the community disapproved of them.

When looking at these examples of how people adjust to the limitations of their social position, two points need to be emphasized. The first is that adjustive behavior is just as varied as the structural and ideological limitations to which it responds. Some behavior may arise in response to physical conditions over which the individual has little or no control—the dust, the noise, or the monotony of factory work, for example. Equally often it represents an attempt to deal with the gap between the reality of one's own life and the ideological reconstruction of capitalist inequality.

We saw that the promise of equal access to social advancement was an essential component in legitimating private control of industrial capital. It also encouraged achievement-oriented and competitive work attitudes among employees—attitudes that make capital profitable.

For many people the daily experience of the terminal and fixed nature of their social position must be at odds with the symbols of opportunity that surround them. This discrepancy may be subjectively experienced as shame, self-blame, frustration, or deprivation. It may be encountered in a wide scale of social positions. And the ways in which people cope with it may range from the management of information when interacting with others to lowering their aspirations in sour grapes fashion. They may alternately find scapegoats for their frustrations, or find comfort in the world of escape and fantasy projected by mass media. Whatever form it takes, adjustive behavior makes the individual assume at least a part of the personal costs of the structural contradictions of a capitalist system.

Another point is that adjustive behavior is peculiarly two-sided. From the individual's point of view it is intended to alleviate the strains and limitations that inequality creates. Adjustment breaks up a monotonous work day, restores some self-respect, provides a refuge from anxieties, or suggests a substitute for a desired but unattainable goal. But at the same time, and usually without the individual's knowledge, it also makes a complementary contribution to the overall functioning of the capitalist system.

Adjustive behavior helps the individual. But it also reduces the potential of conflict and friction in the system. To the extent that the men at the punching machines relieved the boredom of their job through their "banana-time" antics, they increased their own job satisfaction. They also reduced company turnover in a work situation that few of them would otherwise have endured for a long time. Chinoy makes the same observation in a study of young workers in a Detroit automobile factory. When faced with a reality of non-existent mobility, these workers adjust their dreams of advancement by reducing their career and life aspirations. He argues that such adjustive behavior softens the impact of inequality not only for the workers themselves. "Both self-blame and the defensive rationalizations against self-blame... contribute to the maintenance of both existing economic institutions and the tradition of opportunity itself. To the extent that workers focus blame for their failure to rise above the level of wage labor upon themselves rather than upon the institutions that govern the pursuit of wealth or upon the persons who control those institutions, American society escapes the consequences of its own contradictions" (Chinoy 1955:129).

Wadel makes much the same point. By coping with the stigma of being on welfare, the people in the outport community convert what are potential costs to the larger social systems into personal costs which they carry themselves (Wadel 1973:113).

It is important to keep in mind that the system-supportive consequences of adjustive behavior are generally not known to, and certainly not intended by, those who engage in it. For the individual, such behavior is a rational and often the only possible way for making the limitations of his/her existence more tolerable. Ironically the unintended consequences of such behavior make a complementary contribution to the maintenance of the very structure of inequality which necessitated the adjustive behavior in the first place. An example will illustrate how these complementary features can be deliberately exploited by capitalist business.

In a study of petty theft at the work place, Zeitlin (1971) estimates that a majority of the employees of corporations, including those in managerial positions, engage at some point in their career in some form of theft of company property. The theft may range from taking paper clips or stationary to stealing merchandise or arranging bribes and kickbacks. Especially for lower-paid workers, such actions are primarily a means of supplementing their income. An additional motivation is often the feeling of deserving compensation for low pay, boring work, or long periods of inactivity. But petty theft does more than add the satisfaction of "getting away with it" to an otherwise uninteresting job. Zeitlin points out that the average value of such thefts is relatively small and amounts to something like $1.50 per worker per day. A calculation of costs and benefits may reveal that the company is getting a bargain. By tacitly permitting the continued existence of this illicit source of worker satisfaction, management may avoid costly turnover and strikes. It may even be able to maintain a lower wage level.

In the eyes of the company, controlled employee theft thus becomes a managerial tool that can be used to manipulate employee morale. Zeitlin, who is an "industrial psychologist", suggests a number of measures for fine-tuning this tool. The company must institute a program of "controlled larceny". It is to be carefully concealed from the employee in order to allow him/her to feel that he/she is beating the system. At the same time, the company must determine a tolerable limit for employee theft. It must also devise a signaling system that indicates to individual employees that they have exceeded their quota. Zeitlin provides an example of an organization where such a system is actually functioning. What is, for the employee, a compensation for a frustrating work environment, is used by the company as a low-cost source of "job enrichment". Theft thus becomes a condition that is complementary to corporate interests.

HIGHLIGHT

1. In general, the amount of 'social space' available to an individual is directly related to his/her position in the class structure.
2. Individuals in boring jobs develop informal mechanisms that help them reduce the boredom. Such methods are called adjustive behaviors.
3. Sometimes adjustive behaviors, to the extent that they minimize the possibility of overt conflict, contribute to the perpetuation of social inequality.

Conclusions

The foregoing discussion suggests that the relationship between inequality and social behavior in a capitalist society is not the result of an inexorable base-superstructure mechanism. Nor is it a consequence of a pervasive capitalist presence in all aspects of the social process. Instead, the stability of capitalist systems—and of all forms of inequality for that matter—rests on a complex network of supports. Some supports are based on the active and conscious behavior of capitalists themselves. The huge sums spent on cultivating corporate images in the media, or the direct corporate influence on political decision-making, are two examples. In other cases, patterns of behavior which were originally closely linked to ruling class intervention have become self-supporting. Their persistence is guaranteed by the interests of professional and other middle class groups who benefit from them. And finally, we saw that there are many forms of behavior which are not the consequence of ruling class intervention, but nonetheless make an important complementary contribution to the continued functioning of the capitalist system.

These matters notwithstanding, we should not lose sight of the fact that like any form of inequality, capitalism also generates individual and organized opposition. This eventually leads to significant social change.

Other parts of this book look at such behavior in more detail. No system of social control is so perfect that it can completely prevent the emergence of opposition behavior. But the level of such opposition will to some extent also depend on the success of ideologies and other control measures in creating legitimacy and acceptance for a particular distribution of wealth.

NOTES

[1]From *Children in the Political System*, D. Easton and J. Dennis. © 1980 by the University of Chicago.

SUGGESTED READINGS

Social Psychology as Political Economy, Peter Archibald. Toronto: McGraw-Hill Ryerson Series in Canadian Sociology, 1978. This book differs from conventional social psychology textbooks by putting empirical research into the context of sociological theories. It covers many of the issues discussed in this chapter.

A Living Profit: Studies in the Social History of Canadian Business 1883-1911, Michael Bliss. Toronto: McClelland and Stewart Limited, 1974. An excellent study of the development of business ideologies in Canada.

Television and Human Behavior, George Comstock et al. New York: Columbia University Press, 1978. An extremely useful summary of over 2500 studies of the effects of television on human behavior.

A World of Difference, Heather McHugh. Boston: Houghton Mifflin Co., 1981. This book provides a very good summary of research on gender-roles and gender-specific behavior. It also discusses research on the influence of mass media on such behavior.

The School Promoters: Education and Social Class in Mid-Nineteenth Century Upper Canada, Alison Prentice. Toronto: McClelland and Stewart Limited, 1977. A fine study of the beginnings of public education in Upper Canada and Ontario between about 1800 and 1880. It documents, in particular, the relationship between the social structure of the time, and the values and beliefs which education encouraged.

The Hidden Injuries of Class, Richard Sennett and Jonathan Cobb. New York: Random House Inc., 1973. This book gives a very sensitive analysis of the personal costs of an ideological system centred around the notion of success and achievement.

DEVIANT AND CRIMINAL ACTS

E. J. Bennett
W. G. West

THE NATURE OF DEVIANCE AND CRIME

Introduction

Deviance, in one form or another, has always been a central concern in sociology. Most of us have some interest in the bizarre, the unusual, the different, the off-color, or even the lurid. It is rare indeed when newspaper front pages in their efforts to sell papers do not include incidents of spectacular crime, deception, illusion, etc. It is not surprising, therefore, that deviance courses are usually the second highest-enrolled (after introductory courses) in most sociology departments. Many students take such courses hoping to gain insights into personal problems of their own (e.g., concerning their own sexuality); those of family members or relatives (such as wife battery or alcoholism); or the problems of friends or acquaintances. They may also wish to gain knowledge useful for desired jobs.

On a political level, many public issues are addressed in the study of deviance. Abortion, domestic violence, teen-age sexuality, capital punishment, marijuana laws, off-track gambling, school vandalism, prison riots, court over-crowding, police "dirty-tricks", and homosexual rights are all topics publicly debated and addressed in the sociology of deviance. In addition, much government expenditure in social service programs, welfare, and corrections attempts to deal with deviant behavior. Some knowledge of deviance is crucial to participating publicly as an informed citizen in contemporary society. As in other areas of public debate, however, there are myths about deviance that hinder rational discussion.

In addition to this popular or lay interest, deviance has a central relevance within sociology. Most sociologists define sociology as being centrally concerned with the establishment, continuation, and change of social order. Threats to that order, or aberrations from it, are theoretically interesting for the light they shed on the problem of order. The concern with order, however, has typically been central in more conservative views of society than the one of this text. Marxists in particular have, until recently, all but ignored deviance and law. This chapter will attempt to correct this oversight.

Sociology approaches the study of deviance differently than other disciplines. While sociology concedes that there may be some influence of physiological or biological factors that help account for deviance, it insists that these are always culturally and socially mediated. The argument, for instance, that possession of an extra Y chromosome that is disproportionately found in prison populations explains exceptional male violence, ignores the fact that most inmates are property offenders. They have not been incarcerated for violence. Similarly, although some crimes such as mass murders may be psychologically related, most deviants or criminals are not insane or emotionally disturbed. Rather, they are quite normal in their mental functioning. Durkheim took great pains to argue that even so personal an action as suicide was related to social factors, and hence that it could be studied sociologically (1951).

After offering a number of definitions of deviance, and selecting a legal one as most appropriate for this analysis, we will examine the available factual material regarding delinquency and various kinds of crime. Although some theories developed within mainstream sociology have added to our knowledge and understanding, we will argue that they are fundamentally inadequate. Most crucially, they obscure the fact that most crime is concerned with property and property relations. They fail to integrate the known data about such crime into a wider theory of political economy, specifying crime's connection to production, distribution and consumption.

Definitions.   What exactly is deviance? Consider the following true case from an English experience.

In the year 1884, a yacht was caught in a storm 1600 miles from the nearest land. Its crew of four had to abandon the vessel and put to sea in an open life boat. It contained no water and no food except two small cans of vegetables. For three days there was no other food. On the fourth day the survivors caught a small turtle which was their only food for the next eight days. From then on, until their twentieth day at sea, they had nothing to eat, and only a very small amount of rain water to drink. On the eighteenth day, as their boat was still drifting at sea and was still more than a thousand miles from land, one of the seamen proposed to two of the others that they kill and eat the fourth member. He was a boy of about seventeen who was then in an extremely weakened condition. Although one seaman dissented from this proposal, two days later the boy was killed. The survivors, including the one who had refused to participate in the killing, fed upon the boy's body. On the fourth day after the killing, the survivors were rescued by a passing vessel.

In a similar case, the lifeboat contained both passengers and crew.

Rather than lack of food, difficulty had been occasioned by the unseaworthiness of the lifeboat, a condition compounded by a torrential downpour. To keep the boat from sinking, the members of the crew cast fourteen male passengers overboard. Two women, sisters of one of the male victims, jumped out of the boat to join their brother in death. As a result of this human jettisoning, the boat remained afloat and the survivors were rescued a short time later (Kitsuse 1970).

In the above examples the reader might ponder the question: Who, if anyone, is guilty of criminal homicide? The answer is not an easy one. Clearly, what you might consider deviant under one set of circumstances is excusable under others. It is not surprising, therefore, that sociologists have offered a number of definitions for deviance. Each of them has some strengths, and some drawbacks. The following are some of the most commonly used definitions:

The Statistical Approach.   Some claim deviance consists of any behavior which varies widely from the average or from the typical behavior of members of a society. This definition has some initial attractiveness. It suggests that we might be able to measure deviance objectively, without reference to anyone's personally biased beliefs. By doing head counts, and finding, for example, that very few people murder, a few more commit armed robbery, many more gamble, and even more have violated liquor laws, we could develop a continuum from lesser to serious deviance.

But there are some major difficulties with this approach. It turns out that some behaviors popularly regarded as deviant are committed not just by an aberrant minority at the end of the spectrum, but by the vast majority of people. In self-report questionnaires, for instance, over ninety percent of high school boys report committing delinquent acts. It is the non-delinquent, "goody-goody" youngster who is unusual. He is statistically deviant. When confronted with information such as this, we are forced to recognize that "deviance" has inescapably moral aspects. It refers to what people should not do, even if almost everybody does it.

The Moral Approach.   A second definition claims that deviance is immorality. It is behavior which is wrong. Some sociologists (and many other people) have argued, usually on religious or natural law grounds, that certain behaviors such as murder, incest, treachery, etc., are universally condemned in all societies as wicked and immoral. These actions are deemed evil in themselves. *Mala in se* is the Latin expression. Other acts, such as violations of traffic laws, are regarded as fundamentally culture-bound and vary from society to society. They are dependent upon simple social agreement for defining norms. In Latin such acts are *mala prohibita*.

While reference to moral standards seems essential, and there has been a renewed interest in natural law theories (especially since the holocaust of World War II, in which millions were exterminated legally by a government), this definition also has problems. It is not sufficient to identify behavior as deviant without considering the social context in which it occurs. For example, taking the life of another is not deviant if it is an act of self-defence. The abandonment of an old or weak tribal member whose continued presence threatens the entire group is not comparable to an act of murder. The hanging of a murderer, or the aborting of a fetus is not comparable to genocide. Indeed, taking the life of another is demanded in warfare. When one includes such cultural and situational considerations, it is clear that it is difficult to claim that the act of killing is always deviant.

The Consensus Approach. A third definition states deviance is the violation of the norms and values of a society. This definition is held by structural-functionalists or anomie/strain theorists. Their basic view is that society is held together because people share common values or norms such as honesty and hard work. Deviants violate these values and norms even though they may also adhere to them. Such norms and values are specified for particular statuses. For example, sexual intercourse is permitted within marriage, but is suspect without. Norms and values are also specific to particular roles. Policemen can use violence that is forbidden to the rest of us; and so on.

There are nonetheless some serious problems with this definition. Most modern nation-state societies are quite complicated and diverse. They combine members of different ethnic, religious, and language groups. It is, as a consequence, very difficult to specify common norms and values. We may all advocate respect for human life, but we are clearly divided on the issues of abortion, the justification for nuclear warfare, or corporal punishment in schools. Where is the consensus? It is also very much a "judgment call" as to whether a norm has been broken, or a person is a "real" deviant. Everyone is against child abuse, yet most people are unwilling to outlaw corporal punishment of children. How many slaps constitute violent child abuse? How frequently can spankings be given? If all high school boys are reporting having stolen, how much or how frequently must they have stolen to be "really" delinquent?

The Legal Approach. Deviance may be defined as behavior which any society authoritatively defines as such. In modern societies it is illegal behavior. Even though norms and values may not be shared, and interpreting them may always remain fundamentally a problem, modern societies do in fact authoritatively resolve disputes through law. The legal definition does offer some hope of precision while incorporating specific cultural values into a definition of deviance. Yet ambiguities remain. Disputed legal cases indicate a serious lack of easily interpreted agreement as to what the law means. Overturned decisions and appeals indicate the law is not as clear as one might naively assume. At what point in the legal process can one take the definition to be authoritative? Answers include at the point of arrest, the point of trial, and the point of incarceration.

There is also a serious substantive problem with the legal definition. Are the traffic violations and liquor offences which make up the bulk of lower court cases the events we think of when discussing deviance or "the crime problem"? Using a legal definition may include many morally minor peccadillos. On the other hand, it may leave out some activities which many, or even most, people consider deviant, even though they are quite legal. For instance, sexual relations in private between two consenting adults of the same sex are quite legal. But most Canadians regard homosexuality as deviant. In sum, the legal definition, even if we could agree upon where in the legal process to draw the line, includes some behaviors most people don't regard as really deviant and excludes other behaviors many people do regard as deviant.

The Labelling Approach.   Sociologists who are phenomenologists, ethnomethodologists, or symbolic interactionists have suggested yet another definition. In the words of Howard S. Becker, "Deviant behaviour is behaviour that people so label" (1963:9). Deviance is thus socially constructed in social interaction. This definition recognizes that the circumstances under which people are defined as deviant vary considerably. Moreover, consistent with this definition, the law is seen as only one vehicle whereby deviance is attributed to acts and actors. This approach also considers the possibility that the attribution of deviance is often more socially important than the simple commission of an act. For example, being judged guilty of a crime has in many cases social consequences of deeper import than the crime itself.

The development of this labelling approach during the 1960s coincided with the widespread use of self-report studies. These studies forced researchers to make a clear distinction between 'official' deviants, and unofficially recognized deviance (or deviant behavior). Studies of imprisoned populations, for instance, cannot be taken as representative of the population which commits deviant acts, but only of those caught. Indeed, official statistics may well tell us more about the behavior of the officials (e.g. the police) producing the statistics than those deviants about whom they are ostensibly produced.

Interactionist definitions of deviance may still leave us frustrated, for they insist on leaving for empirical resolution the question of what will be labelled deviant. One can never claim to know in advance, in the abstract, what is deviant. One can only know *post-hoc*. Comparative research becomes difficult if not impossible. The question of who is required to do the labelling is also left unresolved. Can one effectively label oneself? Or is definitive labelling dependent upon an official label? If it is, we return to the problems discussed above under the legalistic definition of deviance.

The Conflict Approach.   While recognizing the cultural variability of deviance, its intertwining with the law, and the ambiguities of labelling, conflict theorists have emphasized that deviance is essentially political and economic. They argue that behavior is labelled deviant when it is deemed by officials to be contrary to the interests of the powerful, especially the dominant economic class.

Not surprisingly, this definition also has its problems. Prohibition of some types of deviance (e.g., murder) is most appropriately described as being in everybody's interest, not to just satisfy the upper class. And some behavior such as forming monopolies or combines in restraint of trade, that would seem to be in the interest of capitalists, is legally prohibited. If strong support for law and order campaigns comes from working class populations, and the latter are the most frequent users of police services, can one really maintain that the law and its agents lack support from among the least powerful, the most exploited? Perhaps this conflict definition is not so much a *definition* of deviance, as an orienting *hypothesis*, which focusses attention on the most important social characteristic of deviance. It is nonetheless a hypothesis needing careful evaluation.

As noted earlier, in this chapter we will use a legal definition of deviance. We will nonetheless remain sensitive to issues raised in other definitions, especially the interactionist one. Unfortunately, limiting the definition in this way will lead to the exclusion of many interesting topics such as mental illness, suicide, aberrant sexuality, and so on.

HIGHLIGHT
1. The study of deviance is a central concern of sociology.
2. There are several different definitions of deviance. The one adopted in this chapter is the legal definition.

Methods

Official Statistics. While the official statistics used regularly in newspaper reports are easily available, and do give some indication of deviance, most contemporary criminologists agree they are not as useful as they initially appear (Taylor 1978; Giffen 1979; cf McDonald 1976). First, their use assumes a particular legal definition of deviance. As mentioned, most cases the courts officially process are minor infractions (e.g., traffic violations), and are of so little moral concern that police usually omit them from many reports. Because official statistics report on events, and to some extent people, after the fact, they aren't particularly good at revealing how deviant or criminal activities are carried out. Because the official agencies gathering the facts are usually also prosecuting deviants, the latter are likely to be somewhat hostile towards them. Consequently, we can only gain a limited amount of knowledge of what types of persons commit deviant acts. Criticisms from a conflict perspective further point out that accepting the official statistics assumes and works within legal definitions extant under the present power structure.

But there are more serious problems around the issues of non-reporting. Deviant behavior is intrinsically behavior which perpetrators generally would like to keep hidden. Furthermore, self-report studies and critiques of legal definitions indicate that even though few persons come to official attention, many if not most of us regularly commit some deviant behavior. Perhaps surprisingly, many victims also fail to report crimes to the police. They regard them as private matters, too minor, or unlikely to be solved anyway. Some victims are unaware they've been duped. Others refuse to recognize themselves as such (e.g. drug purchasers and dealers).

Even when crimes or delinquencies are reported to the police, the police often decide not to record the incident or to lay a charge. This is especially true in juvenile cases. Hackler's (1978) preliminary comparisons of charge rates in various Canadian cities indicate anywhere from 1 percent to 43 percent of juveniles are handled informally without charge. Some persons charged are found not guilty in court. Only a minority of convicted persons are incarcerated. As a result, the criminal justice system can be viewed as a large funnel. Many acts occur in the wider society, but very few persons get to the narrow end of the funnel. Very different official "pictures" of crime emerge depending upon where one slices into this funnel.

Because of these kinds of variations within the official statistics, sociologists have increasingly sought other data collection methods in searching for the truth about deviance.

Self-Report Studies. One alternative methodological approach developed in the last couple of decades is the self-report questionnaire. It asks people whether or not they have committed particular deviant acts, or have been victims (e.g. Evans 1978; Vaz 1979; Leblanc 1975; Linden and Filmore 1980; Hagan et al, 1979; Gomme 1982). Such questionnaires have revealed that almost everybody commits some deviance, even though only some are reported by victims, and less still are officially processed.

Self-report questionnaires have faults. Some persons may not recognize themselves as victims. Some may not know that their activities, such as gambling, are illegal. Some individuals may either hide or exaggerate

FIGURE 1
Sketch Illustrating Attrition In Persons
Through The Criminal Justice Process

This diagram presents a simple yet comprehensve view of the movement of adult and juvenile offenders through the criminal justice system. The rates of attrition shown are for a combination of indictable and summary offences and may be different for specific offences and for different jurisdictions within Canada. The differing widths in the diagram indicate the relative volume of cases still within the system at that stage. Most of the rates were confirmed from more than one source. Even so they are only suggestive since no nation-wide data exist which permit comparison with more precision.

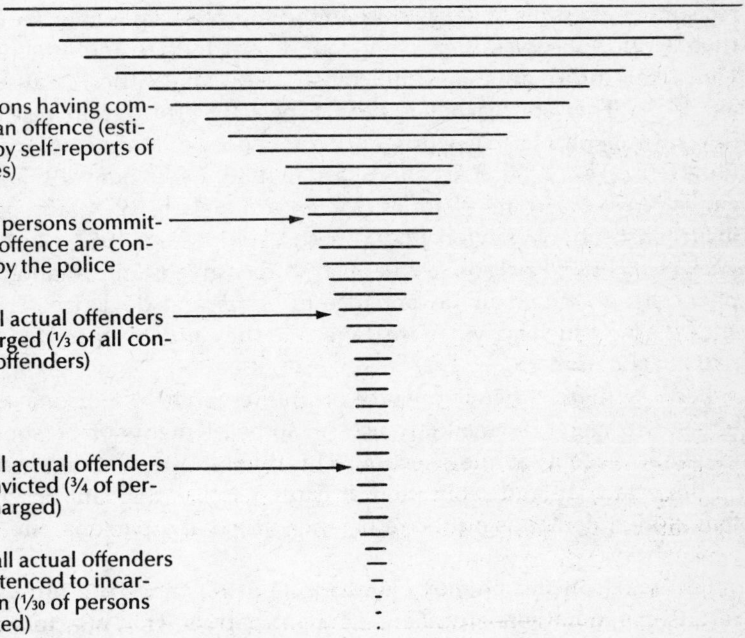

All persons having committed an offence (estimated by self-reports of juveniles)

⅕ of all persons committing an offence are contacted by the police

1⁄15 of all actual offenders are charged (⅓ of all contacted offenders)

1⁄20 of all actual offenders are convicted (¾ of persons charged)

1⁄600 of all actual offenders are sentenced to incarceration (1⁄30 of persons convicted)

- Substantial attrition occurs at each stage, with less than 1% of actual offenders sentenced to prison.

- The major attrition, in terms of number of offenders, occurs early in the process. Large numbers are never contacted by the police and a smaller, but still considerable number are never charged.

- Increased reporting by the public or changes in police ability to identify offenders could result in overload (e.g., delays in trials) for later points in the criminal justice system.

SOURCE: Statistics Canada reports and specific research studies carried out in Ontario and Alberta (Solicitor-General, 1979).

their criminal experiences, although attempts to explore this have not established any systematic patterns of deception (Box 1981). Terms are often not exactly comparable between studies. In addition, the law and respondents may not define terms similarly. Studies asking for self-reports of offences committed have almost always used high school populations. Such populations no doubt differ considerably from adults. The items selected tend to be overweighted towards the minor offences and have usually not revealed high frequencies of crimes committed (Elliot and Ageton 1980).

Participant Observation. Another methodological approach championed by symbolic interactionists has been participant observation. The researcher attempts to get as close to the subjects as possible. He lives in their world, observes their daily round of activities, intensively interviews key informants, and judiciously uses what official statistics are available. This approach has been especially effective in researching deviant subcultures (e.g. Corrigan 1979; Lee 1978; Mann 1961), occupations (e.g. West 1980; Prus and Sharper 1980; Letkemann 1973;), street gangs (West 1979) life histories (Miller and Helwig 1974) and criminal justice institutions (Leyton 1979; Ericson 1981; Mann 1961; Morton and West *et al.* 1980; Erickson 1975). Such studies give us information on the phenomenal or personal experience of crime and deviance. They can show us how such activities are done, and they situate abstract factors in real life situations.

Because there is heavy reliance on the researcher's personal characteristics to gain and maintain access, some elements of personal bias inevitably enters sample selection. This makes representativeness difficult to establish, and replication difficult. Also, participant observation makes high demands on the researcher's time and personal life, and is expensive.

Focussing on the phenomenal aspects of deviance not infrequently results in a morally relativist and idealist analysis. That is, actors, values and culture are depicted as more important than their material conditions. Such studies often see these small worlds as isolated or independent of the wider society. In essence, they lack a sense of totality. Moreover, participant observers and interactionists are often ambivalent about whether or not they are doing causal or descriptive analysis. Even when they attempt causal analysis it is quite limited in its scope (West 1982).

A large part of the reason why all these data collection methods are ultimately unsatisfactory is that they rely upon an empiricist (positivist) conception of social research. Fundamentally, they assume that the social world can be understood by relating regularly recurring events to each other. What is needed, however, is a realist (historical, materialist, political economy) approach which demands analysis which goes beyond the mere examination of surface phenomena.

HIGHLIGHT

1. In addition to official statistics, researchers rely on self-reported questionnaires and participant observation studies for information on deviance.

Myths and Types of Crime

Crime and Ideology. Most of us tend to believe that deviants, delinquents and criminals come from the "wrong side of the tracks". They are poor kids from deprived families, or are undeserving, depraved predators, lying in wait for unsuspecting innocent victims. We also believe that crime is an unusual, antisocial event, although it is growing at an alarmingly increasing rate. Many of us believe that crime is caused by a lack of care for children, a lack of discipline and virtue, irresponsibility, and perhaps poverty. These beliefs are convenient myths.

Perhaps the strongest belief about crime and delinquency is that deviant behavior is rapidly increasing. A recent American survey indicates that annually in 30 percent of all households one family member has been a victim of crime. This figure is actually a decline of 2 percent from 1975. However, official FBI reports indicate an increase in crime of 10 percent over the same period (United States Justice, 1981). The finding is parallelled in official Ontario figures (n.d.) showing a small but steady increase of 5.7 percent in the absolute number of total offences per year from 1973 to 1979. Such an increase, however, would be drastically reduced if only the 15-29 year old crime-prone part of the population were examined. In other words, a large part of the increase in crime is accounted for by a large increase in the number of individuals in the 15-29 age range.

Presumed increases in crime must be examined in the light of other facts as well. McDonald (1976) has shown that the size of police forces correlates more strongly with official crime than causal factors such as poverty. Her earlier work (1969) also indicates that most of the total increases in crime are traffic offences.

From the above cited facts and from other information not reported it is evident that much of the increase in crime rates can be attributed to the baby boom swelling the crime-prone age group, increases in the size of police forces, and increasingly efficient reporting. There may be some actual increase in deviant behavior as well, but police statistics are very poor indicators of whether or not this is happening. Comparison of self-report figures for juvenile delinquency over the last two decades indicates very little change. The exceptions to this rule are drug and alcohol use.

There is a myth that delinquency and crime are committed by males. Female deviation is assumed to be sexually oriented. Self-report studies of juveniles do indicate somewhat more male than female offences, but the ratio, about 2 or 3:1, is far smaller than in the official statistics. The latter are approximately 5 or 10:1. Furthermore, even when charged, females are generally charged for the same kinds of offences as males. Property crimes predominate, violent offences are rare, and sexual offences are a very small proportion of the total (Ontario Government 1981). There is, however, some sex-role stereotyping in actual behavior. Males are prominent in aggressive or violent offences such as armed robbery, car theft, etc. Female theft is often shoplifting, a form of non-violent activity that fits a conventional stereotype concerning female behavior (Hoffman-Bustamonte 1973).

Juvenile and adult female offenders are selectively processed in the justice system. Particular attention is given to any aberrant sexual behavior. The system also shows comparative leniency for economic offences by females. Criminological theories of female deviance that justified the above practices have been condemned recently as being blatantly sexist. Such theories explained behavior such as female prostitution and even shoplifting in terms of female sexual needs. However, when it came to males, both of these activities were seen as economically motivated (Klein 1973).

There are further myths that crime is an urban affair, whereas rural settings promote health and conformity. Ontario figures reveal robbery, prostitution, and gaming and betting are more likely in large cities. Large thefts and drug usage also are somewhat more prominent in large urban centres. However, the overall crime rate is slightly higher in small towns and villages than in small or large cities (Ontario Government 1981). This finding is even more remarkable as there are proportionately more police in large centres.

The belief that ethnic minorities cause more crime is also popular. However, at least one Canadian study indicates higher rates of juvenile delinquency for native-born Canadian youngsters than for the foreign-born (Byles 1969). Certainly native Canadian Indians have traditionally been over-represented in jails and prisons. But their incarceration usually results from the inability to pay fines for minor offences, such as drinking.

Having dealt with some general myths about crime and delinquency, let us examine some specific types of activities.

Delinquency.   Polls reveal that crime and delinquency rank third after inflation and unemployment as issues of concern to Canadians. In addition, public opinion polls (e.g. Livingstone and Hart 1979, 1980) indicate that the Ontario public is more concerned about student discipline than any other educational matter. Frequently lack of discipline is blamed on family breakup and poverety-stricken and uncaring parents.

Historical research suggests that youthful delinquency in general has always existed, but it has become of particular concern in the last couple of centuries. Although it is very difficult to interpret the longitudinal historical statistics available from police and court records in any meaningful way as indicating more delinquent behavior, it is generally agreed (Tepperman 1977) that there has been a long-term increase in *official* crime and delinquency over the past century. And these official data consistently indicate that the young figure disproportionately in misdemeanors. Regarding this age factor, the official data are corroborated by self-report studies over the last couple of decades (reviewed in Greenberg 1977; West 1975), which indicate that almost all youngsters commit delinquent acts. It would seem that the young really are more deviant than the rest of us. However, better evidence is needed to firmly establish this fact.

Perhaps surprisingly, the self-report studies fairly consistently report very little, if any, social class differences in delinquent acts. Middle-class youngsters are almost as likely as working-class ones to be deviant, although they are considerably less likely to be formally arrested, charged, found delinquent in court or removed from home to a training school or similar facility.

Studies show that youngsters in official care—such as reform schools—are inordinately from broken homes. But self-report studies repeatedly find no relation between single parent homes and delinquent behavior. Unhappiness, weak attachment to parents, or family conflict are far better predictors (Hirschi, 1969; Nye, 1958).

Although girls are gaining on boys in terms of misbehavior, males still predominate in the self-report data. This is particularly true for more serious offences such as those involving personal violence, breaking and entering, and so on. Overall, sex and school failure are the strongest correlates of crime/delinquency in self-report studies (West 1975; 1979).

It is interesting to examine the types of offences the young are involved in. Most delinquent acts consist of property crimes (theft, vandalism, etc.). Another major category consists of "status" offences, acts which are deemed illegal only for juveniles. They include running away from home, truancy, use of alcohol, etc. These activities result in about 10-25 percent of all official charges. Traditionally an astounding sixty-five to seventy-five percent of incarcerated female juveniles have been locked up for status offences for which adults can't even be charged!

Most delinquent episodes are, in fact, of a minor, nuisance nature. The majority of those found delinquent in court do not go on to have adult criminal records. Delinquent actions by the young may be more frequent than by adults, but they are less violent. Moreover, the property loss involved in delinquent acts by the young is relatively low.

Clearly, youngsters given official attention by the police and courts constitute a rather peculiar subset of all those who commit delinquent acts. Working class youngsters, from broken homes, from ethnic minority groups, from "defiant" adolescent subcultural groups, who are individually insubordinate, or (if a girl) sexually precocious, are singled out for attention. Coming from a broken home is probably more decisive as a ticket to training school than commission of all but the most extreme delinquent acts (cf. Leyton 1979).

Property Crime. The vast majority of official criminal incidents concern property crime. Some ²/₃ of the violations of the Criminal Code of Canada reported by Statistics Canada are property offences. The overall property crime rates are some 40 times greater than for violent crimes.

Ordinary Street Property Crime. The most frequent incidents of property crime consist of ordinary theft, breaking and entering and motor vehicle theft. Such activities as shoplifting, house burglary, pickpocketing, etc. are included within these categories. Males seem to engage in this activity much more than females, and the peak ages for commission occur somewhat earlier than for violent crime. They are highest in the middle to late teens and decline rapidly through the twenties. Although self-report studies of delinquents indicate very little difference between social classes, as adults the least educated and those in the least prestigious occupations are most frequently convicted (Boydell and Bell-Rowbotham 1972).

Sutherland's early work (1937) popularized the idea that some thieves operate as professionals. They make a regular business of stealing. They plan acts carefully, and utilize technical skills and methods in carrying out their tasks. In general such thieves are migratory, live in a congenial subcultural world, and are able to "fix" or "patch" cases to avoid conviction upon detection. Safe-cracking, shoplifting, confidence games, picking pockets, and forgery number among the specialties.

Letkemann's (1973) intensive interview study of imprisoned hold-up men and safe-crackers in Canada updates and replicates Sutherland's work. But Klein (1974) quite appropriately questions the whole notion of identifying major thieves as professional. He argues that they are not highly educated, specialized, or similar in other major ways to other professionals. Hence they are better seen as skilled craftsmen.

The vast majority of "real crooks" would seem to be less-than-professional "serious" thieves (West 1979b). They make a concerted business of stealing, organize their activities occupationally, have specialized methods of theft, and sophisticated networks for distribution of "hot goods". Unlike professionals, they do not possess high technical skills (e.g. safe cracking), are non-migratory, can't "patch" cases, and are not very successful. Such thieves focus their activities on shoplifting, commercial and residential burglary, "clouting" (or stealing goods in transit), and auto theft. They develop a number of direct consumer buyers. These are individuals who will use the stolen goods themselves. In addition, they rely upon "fences" to receive and redistribute their merchandise. Although the profit from single theft episodes may be quite small (perhaps a few dollars for stolen shirts or ties), such thieves are able to net on average $100 to $150 per week. This is roughly equal to the after tax take-home pay for many regular unskilled jobs. However, the hours are fewer and the work more exciting.

To carry out their work, such thieves must rely on others. They must be careful to distinguish those who assist them from those who might "fink" or "burn" them. They therefore expose themselves as little as possible, and try to ensure only trustworthy persons know them and their activities. Trusted people are those who: 1) experience direct personal gain from the theft activities (e.g., a customer); 2) must maintain personal ties through the maintenance of a community reputation as trustworthy; 3) are vulnerable to retaliatory violence if trust is betrayed; and 4) hold an ideological viewpoint supportive of theft (West 1981).

Although they may collectively cause considerable property loss and operate within a supportive community or subculture, such thieves lead a rather precarious and short-term career (West 1980). They seem to be recruited mainly from the ranks of seriously unemployed working class youth who have dropped out of school. Growing up in a working class community where theft is common helps them acquire the requisite skills and contacts essential to their 'occupation'. Recruitment and training take place through informal peer groups. Inevitably, however, apprehension and arrest occur since numerous scores are needed to earn a living profit.

After a couple of arrests, long prison sentences become a possibility. If the thief has any possible self-defined "good" job in the regular employment sector, and/or a spouse to whom he is attached, he is then highly likely to retire from pursuing theft or indeed other crime as an occupation. However, he may still dabble in it occasionally, or purchase hot goods from younger thieves. Nevertheless, the enduring economic disadvantages of young, uneducated, working class, males will continue to make a couple of years in such an occupation comparatively attractive. The predominance of working class people in official police statistics probably reflects in part the activities of these serious, though non-professional thieves who are inordinately drawn from working class areas. Official statistics aside, it must be remembered that self-reported studies of juveniles indicate a fairly equal spread of petty theft across all classes.

Blue and White Collar Theft. Although most of the official police or court incidents of property crime would seem to fall in the above categories of ordinary, or petty/amateur theft, this kind of crime does not constitute the most serious *economic* threat to property. Most of the dollar loss suffered through crime comes from elsewhere. The United States government's crime commission (1967) estimated that approximately

$600 000 000 was lost in ordinary theft. Half that much, some $282 000 000, was lost in embezzlement and forgery. Usually, embezzlement involves white collar workers and forgery involves one's employer. Twice as much $1 350 000 000, was lost in fraud, and a further $1 400 000 000 was lost in unreported commercial theft, i.e. either shoplifting or employee theft. In short, more money is lost through the betrayal of trust either between worker and entrepreneur, between entrepreneurs, or between entrepreneurs and customers than is lost in ordinary "predatory" theft.

Mars argues (1973:1978) that a number of low income, low skilled jobs encourage what is called "fiddling". Whereas pilfering cargo by longshoremen on the St. John's docks requires a tight-knit group and co-operation between signalmen operating the hoists, laborers in the hold, and store-room managers, other situations, such as those in which a restaurant waitress fiddles, can be done with more ad hoc arrangements. These may be individually negotiated between cook and waiter, or between waiter and cashier.

Such blue collar theft is of growing public concern to businesses. Some estimates claim that perhaps 5-7 percent of the domestic product is transferred through such activities. Such theft provides an ideological function in that it allows blame for lack of profits to be placed on disloyal workers. It also allows the introduction of private policing within industry (Henry 1978; Ditton 1977).

More than half the police in Canada are now private police. They are necessary not only to provide security in establishments such as apartment complexes and shopping centres, but they also provide continuous on-the-spot surveillance of workers (Shearing and Stenning 1980). Normandeau (1971) found in studying theft in large department stores in Montreal that half the dossiers of private, in-house investigations involved employees, half involved shoppers. Whereas the mean loss per shopper involved $3 worth of goods, the mean loss per employee averaged $40. The mean loss per executive was a stunning $900. As a result, although the incidents of minor theft by low level employees and shoppers were more numerous, the actual dollar loss was greater from executive crime. If early American research is indicative (Cressey, 1953), such embezzlement takes place in situations where trusted employees feel they have an unshareable problem, become aware of the possibilities of embezzlement, and are able to articulate a rationalization for their activities. They may, for example, say that they were only borrowing the funds, and that they intended to pay them back.

Analyses such as the above ignore the extent to which such workplace crime can be seen as working-class resistance to employer exploitation of surplus value created in the production process (Scraton and South 1981). Indeed, it is only in the last couple of centuries, since the capitalist mode of production has become dominant, that employees have not been entitled in most economic activities to appropriate a share of the goods produced. It is still common in a number of jobs to skim "perks" off the top. Scraton and South argue that decontextualizing such deviance from work relations and class struggle within a historically evolving relationship of worker and employer allows the mixing up of working and upper-class fiddling. In fact they are quite different in terms of amounts garnered, and in responses taken.

The few employee thieves caught and prosecuted in law courts become defined as the "worst offenders". They are the rotten apples who may corrupt the rest of the work force. In actuality, however, the majority of employees engage in such pursuits. The response of capitalists to the situation is to incorporate work-crime into a system of discipline and control in the growing area of private justice. Such private justice is not strictly under the control of the judiciary or popularly elected democratic parliaments which make laws supposedly to express the will of the people. Rather, it is directly under the control of the capitalist enterprise which hires private security forces to police employees.

Organized Crime. A third type of activity which seeks illegally to acquire material goods is organized crime. Relatively minor acts of delinquency and infrequent violent crimes make newspapers' headlines. Ordinary working-class, and occasionally white collar, thieves occupy much police time. The publicity given these acts notwithstanding, far more dollars are gained illicitly in organized crime. Whereas individual motivations and peculiarities may account for some of the former types of crime, social organization accounts for far more of the latter.

Organized crime is primarily a business operation. Profit making is its goal. Not surprisingly, organized crime strives to limit its competition. The products of organized crime are illegal goods and services. To operate, it needs corruption, both on the part of individual customers who collude in the exchange of such goods and services, and on the part of officials, who either ignore such transactions, or even encourage them. It is estimated that some 15 percent of American electoral campaign funds come from criminal sources (McCaghy, 1976). Finally, illegal violence is occasionally necessary to enforce contracts for illegal goods and services. At its highest stage, organized crime even provides its own mock government and courts to decide jurisdictional disputes and sanction misbehavior.

There are four main types of revenue sources for organized crime. First, and most important, is the supplying of illegal goods and services: gambling, loan sharking, selling narcotics, bootlegging liquor, and prostitution and pornography are the main areas. It is on the basis of these activities that organized crime is built. A second source of revenue is the distribution and sale of stolen goods. Protection racketeering and extortion, both of which are based on a potential recourse to violence, are a third type of activity. Finally, much organized crime money now finds its way into legitimate business. Real estate, construction, retail chains, etc., can all provide investment opportunities to "launder" illicitly obtained capital.

Contemporary organized crime has seen its highest and perhaps most spectacular development in the United States, especially in large cities. Historically, various ethnic group organizations provided needed services and protection to their members. Such services were necessary as the United States offered few government services to assist the needy. Over time, however, many such organizations progressively engaged in illegal activities. Municipal corruption allowed such groups to provide a sort of informal welfare system (Merton 1938). Prohibition in 1920 encouraged even greater organization and provided fabulous riches for delivering illegal booze. The Canadian Bronfman family owes much of its wealth to prohibition (Newman 1975:334). Since prohibition, organized crime has managed to continue diversifying and providing new goods and services.

Drug trafficking can be examined as an example of how organized crime works (Commission on the Non-Medical Use of Drugs, 1973). Medically, any substance other than food that by its chemical nature alters structures or functions in living organisms is considered a drug. One should note how general this definition is, and how it in fact makes only an arbitrary distinction between drugs and other substances, like food, which are taken into the body. Legal drugs are by far used most. They range from aspirin and coffee to tranquilizers and more powerful stimulants. Medically, abuse of legally prescribed tranquilizers, stimulants, and alcohol are the major drug problems.

It is estimated that over 5.5 million dollars worth of Valium is consumed in Canada through more than a million prescriptions per year. Over 80 percent of Canadians over age fifteen use alcohol regularly. About 3.5 billion dollars were spent on alcohol and governments derived about 1.6 billion dollars of revenue from such sales in 1975. It is estimated that in Canada, there are about 500 000 alcoholics compared to only some 20 000 heroin addicts. Alcohol use is very frequently connected with violent crime (Ryan 1978). Most experts agree that alcohol abuse is our biggest drug problem.

Yet most public attention to "the drug problem" focusses on narcotics. After the Vancouver race riots of 1907, some Chinese-Canadian opium merchants' request for government compensation outraged the special investigator, William Lyon Mackenzie King. In 1908, King succeeded in having the Narcotics Control Act passed on a wave of moral indignation and panic that centred on the belief that depraved oriental dope fiends were seducing Canadian youth into the white slave trade (Cook 1969).

The Act prohibited the non-medical use of opium, cannabis, and their synthetics. It also provided fines and prison terms of up to seven years for possession of illegal drugs and up to life imprisonment for trafficking. Importing drugs had a minimum sentence of seven years. The Act criminalized behavior which had previously been legal. It also led to considerable enforcement problems. Because drug use is a "victimless" crime, there is not usually any complainant. Consequently, police are forced into using rather unusual measures in apprehending criminals. They can search any place other than a dwelling without a warrant if they have reasonable grounds for suspecting that drug use is occurring. In order to gain sufficient evidence for conviction they can entrap sellers and users by encouraging them to commit offences. If a person is found in court to be in possession of illicit substances, the burden of proof shifts to the accused to prove he or she is not guilty of trafficking.

Marijuana is far more frequently used than heroin. It grows locally in Canada, but is bulky to transport. Consequently, its production and distribution is not particularly attractive to organized crime. In addition, although users may become habituated, it is not physically addictive in the sense that it does not create severe withdrawal symptoms and cravings for further doses. A short period of regular heroin use, however, usually does produce physiological addiction. As a result, there is a "fixed" or "inelastic" demand for heroin that cannot be supplied by local production of poppies, the plant from which heroin is derived.

Interestingly, even the official police figures fail to substantiate some of the popular myths about heroin users. One of the occupational groups that uses it most, for instance, is medical doctors. Known prostitutes compose only 4 percent of addicts. Although there are marked physical effects of the drug, the average dosage does not prevent the user from performing the tasks associated with most jobs. Surprisingly, the most effective known "cure" from heroin addiction is aging. Around mid-life, most heroin addicts "burn out" and cease using the drug voluntarily. Substitute drugs such as methadone have turned out to be as addictive and more debilitating than heroin itself. In 1979 an average "habit" cost about $150/day or $50 000 a year. The ability to meet this expense requires a professional income, or forces users to resort to crime.

The importation of heroin is prohibited. However, the steady and substantial local demand provides an extremely attractive opportunity to organized criminal entrepreneurs. Poppies grown by Third World farmers in Turkey or South East Asia produce more profit than legitimate crops such as grain. Furthermore, the Turkish farmer in 1971 netted about $25-$33 on the black market for a kilogram of opium compared to only $10 if it was sold for medical purposes. After refinement in French laboratories, importation through Montreal, and further "cutting" or dilution, the initial kilogram could be sold on Canadian streets for about a quarter million dollars! By dividing tasks such as financing, transporting, distributing, storing, enforcing, and street sales, organized criminals are able to avoid arrest. The really dangerous and visible aspects of the drug trade are delegated to expendable couriers and street pushers, many of whom are addicts.

The consequences of this underground economy are enormous.

Because of their addiction and the consequent demand, consumers provide a captive market willing to pay "any price". The potentially enormous profits make the legal risks attractive to organized crime. At the same time, the grossly inflated street price forces almost all addicts to engage in criminal behavior in order to feed their addiction. Consequently, it must be acknowledged that indirectly government policy has helped to create an enormous criminal drug problem. It is also true that there is considerable disrespect for the law as witnessed by some 40 000 arrests for possession of marijuana per year. Most people now regard the use of this drug as a relatively harmless, victimless offence. Nonetheless, the police work required to apprehend users is costly, shady and dangerous. In seventy-five years of "enforcement" the drug problem has certainly not been solved.

Corporate Crime. The most serious operating problem for organized crime is that the services it delivers or the goods that it sells are illegal. Hence, individuals offering them may become subject to criminal prosecution. If, however, legal goods or services are being offered, detection or recognition that a crime is occurring becomes most unlikely, even if the conditions of sale are illegal. Robbery with a fountain pen is far less noticeable than robbery with a gun. Illegally overpriced items are indistinguishable from legitimate sales.

Corporate crime consists of illegal activities, usually by high status individuals, on behalf of their company's interests. It is distinguished from white collar crime which involves acts by persons simply in their own interest and from organized crime in that the corporation involved is itself quite legitimate. It provides goods and services which are not illegal. Corporate crime consists of acts which are socially injurious, with penalties and victims. Some types of corporate crime such as fraud are directly prohibited in the Criminal Code of Canada while most are proscribed by other statutes like The Combines Investigation Act. Examples of corporate crime include misrepresentative advertising, price fixing, fraud, fee splitting and kick-backs, failure to maintain safety regulations, and somewhat ambiguously, monopolies in restraint of trade.

The United States Senate Judicial Subcommittee on Antitrust and Monopolies estimated in 1973 that 30 percent of spending, or $174-231 billon per year, results in "no product value" (McCaghy 1976:205). Some $9 billion was lost annually on bogus auto repairs, $45 billion on monopoly price fixing, and $14 billion on deceptive labelling. This compares with similar estimates of $4.8 billion for inventory shrinkage (shoplifting, employee pilfering, fraud) and $1.6 billion for the major crimes of robbery, burglary, and larceny-theft. While extremely difficult to fully substantiate, the evidence available even from official records strongly suggests that far more dollar loss is incurred from corporate crime than from the street crime we normally think of as "the crime problem".

The history of the Combines Investigation Act illustrates the difficulty of enforcing laws against corporate crime. As argued elsewhere in this text, Canadian industry has from the beginning looked upon this land as a source of profit and wealth. Corporations such as the Hudson's Bay Company, The Grand Trunk Railway, the Galt/Canada Land Co., The NorthWest Company, the Canadian Pacific Railway, etc., have all sought government permission to limit market competition and establish monopoly conditions in order to make their investments "profitable". This practice contrasts rather sharply with the traditional British reluctance to allow labor unions for fear they would unduly restrict trade.

The National Policy of 1879 encouraged Canadian combinations and large firms. It also encouraged establishment of foreign branch plant operations. Small business at the mercy of competition from large and/or foreign firms pressed government for legislation preventing monopolies. Such pressure was finally successful in influencing the passing of the Combines Act in 1889. However, an unfriendly Senate, sympathetic to big business, managed to thwart the intent of the bill by inserting "wild card" terms such as "unlawful", "undue", or "unreasonable" to qualify the prohibition of restraint of trade. There was no specific enforcement agency, and individual complainants found themselves at a severe disadvantage against corporate legal might.

Increasing public concern about the cost of living, price scandals during and after World Wars I and II, and during the depression forced various improvements to the Act. Such changes have usually been short-lived. The present Combines Investigation Act was passed in 1960. In 1976, the first stage of a revision prohibiting double ticketing of goods for sale, pyramid selling, and misleading advertising was passed. The second stage has been much more controversial, and has not yet been passed. It would establish a new board to investigate complaints, but would allow mergers if they resulted in greater efficiency. It would, however, provide no criminal penalties for transgressions. As Irving Brecher, Chairman of McGill University's Economics Department states:

> Canadian merger law was once grossly inadequate; thanks largely to simplistic court interpretation, that law is now a farce. We are...in great need of stronger provisions on collusion and monopolization, more effective enforcement procedures, and an expert board or tribunal applying a civil-law approach to structural problems. Despite the inroads of direct government control, Canada's private sector remains big enough to provide significant coverage for competition policy (Brecher 1982).[1]

Like most countries, Canada is now dominated by multinational corporations. These are in many ways beyond control of our local national government. If such governments do not accede to corporate wishes, multinationals threaten to withdraw and relocate in more favorable circumstances. Such actions in effect constitute a strike by capital. Huge legal departments are part of such corporations. They lobby with government to provide cover and protection for their company's operations.

Basically, monopoly conditions have been seen as good for Canada, as they allow improvement in our international marketing position and, coincidentally, raise prices at home.

Corporate criminal activities are very difficult to police. As mentioned above, these illegal acts are committed by 'respectable' citizens going about what appears to be their ordinary business of producing and selling legitimate goods and services. There are no obvious broken windows to investigate, complaints from victims, or bodies found. Citizens who have been duped by false advertising or bilked by fixed prices seldom realize they are victims. As a consequence, they seldom make complaints.

Enforcement of the law is in the hands of officials who usually need considerable co-operation from the organizations they police. Records must be examined, market conditions compared, and premises inspected. There is usually much warning, during which time evidence can be altered or "corrected". Even when wrong-doing is discovered, inspectors typically warn violators.

From 1931 to 1965, The Ontario Securities Commission regulation of stocks, market pricing, and competition resulted in one prosecution! In 1972, there were only 15 charges made against 17 000 industrial employers. Their fines averaged $50-$60. Between 1968 and 1977, there were only 12 convictions under the Ontario Environmental Protection Act. Most of these were against pulp and paper companies and resulted in fines averaging $812 for water pollution, and $1400 for air pollution. Under the Federal Combines Investigation Act, between 1965 and 1977, 346 cases of misleading advertising resulted in 269 convictions. The average fines were $350. Only one person has ever been jailed under the section of the Act dealing with advertising. Between 1889 and 1977, there have been 96 charges brought under the merger and monopoly clauses of the same Act. Of these 70 percent resulted in orders of prohibition preventing mergers, and fines averaged $1248. The statutes are notoriously poorly worded. Even when K.C. Irving owned all the newspapers and private radio and television outlets in New Brunswick, and a provincial court convicted his company of having a monopoly, the Supreme Court overturned the conviction. The estimated cost to the taxpayer was $1 000 000 for prosecuting the case.

Corporate crime is in many ways the worst criminal behavior (Goff and Reasons, 1978). The gains are enormous and of far more dollar value than for any other type of crime. It is extremely difficult to detect, as few victims define themselves as such, and investigations must then rely upon securing information from official agencies. Most crucial, however, is the ambiguity and subtlety of corporate crime. It occupies a grey area by offering legitimate goods and services in ways that are marginally illegal. Such activities are often described in statutes other than the Criminal Code. They are proscribed by laws with enormous loopholes written in poor legal language. As a consequence conviction is very difficult.

Major corporations have far more expert and expensive legal help at their command than the prosecuting agencies. Even if conviction is obtained, the penalties incurred (usually fines or simply orders to desist) are small. The enforcement agencies usually see themselves playing an "educative" role as much as being policemen, and, in view of the aforementioned difficulties, are usually willing to enter into accomodative settlements. The major media sources of information to the public on this situation are sometimes owned by the very corporate violators themselves and often dependent upon their advertising revenue. As a consequence, we do not read or hear a great deal about corporate crime. Politicians find it difficult to encourage vigorous prosecution. They too rely upon campaign donations from corporate sources. They are also continually cowed by threats from business to relocate. Moreover, politicians often have personal ties with corporate directors. They are fellow members of the Canadian elite.

Violence.   The reader may object at this point that although economic crime is costly and frequent, it is certainly not as serious as personal violence. When asked, most people identify violent acts as the most deviant, citing murder, rape or other violent sexual assault. There are regular editorial cries for more police protection and harsher sentences for crimes such as these. Recent Gallup polls indicate that 60 percent of Canadians think the death penalty should be restored for murderers. Only 20 percent favor continued abolition of capital punishment.

Although it is a serious matter, violent crime is relatively rare. The official police rate is 106.8 per 100 000 population. For property crimes the rate is 4109.5 per 100 000. Nonetheless, the absolute figures for violent crime are considerable. In 1977, according to official police statistics in Canada, there were 624 murders, 1886 rapes, 2070 woundings, and 19 491 robberies (Solicitor General, 1979). Furthermore, self-reported victimology studies reveal that only about 33 percent of assaults, twenty-five percent of robberies, and 30 percent of rapes experienced by citizens are brought to police attention. The official data on violent offenders are thus suspect, and likely underestimate the true rate of crime.

Violent offenders who are apprehended tend to be much like those arrested and/or convicted of petty property crime. They are male, uneducated, and working class. They are, however, somewhat older than thieves and are in their late teens or early twenties. The characteristics of this type of offender as revealed in official statistics are comparable to those of individuals who in self-reported studies indicate that they have committed similar crimes (Byles 1969). Nonetheless, a detailed examination of a few offences will serve to raise further questions.

Rape. Few crimes raise such moral outrage as rape. The present Canadian legislation forbids sexual intercourse with a female who is not one's wife without her consent. Courts have generally held that complaint must be made at the first reasonable opportunity, and that there must be some independent corroboration by a witness or physical signs such as torn clothing, bruises, etc. Since legislative changes in 1975, the victim's character (e.g., whether she was previously chaste, etc.) is not necessarily an issue. Before it can be introduced, the judge must rule that evidence related to the victim's character is materially relevant. He must also give the victim advance warning about the nature of possible questioning (Mcteer, 1978). It is nonetheless true that in many rape cases, intercourse is conceded to have occurred, and the conviction depends on proving lack of consent. This usually involves considerable questioning of the victim, who may feel herself as much on trial as the accused. Feminists in particular have thus pressed for further legislative change, perhaps redefining rape as aggravated sexual assault. A change such as this would make it possible to consider males as potential victims. It would also allow a wife to refuse consent, and would reduce the potential for publicity of rape cases.

Because of the low report rates we really know very little about rape (McCaghy, 1976). In American victimology studies, only about twenty-five to fifty percent of victims reported rape to the police. Only eighty percent of these were considered genuine and about half of these were cleared by arrest of a suspect. Only about one-third of such charges resulted in convictions. As a result, under 10 percent of rapes experienced by women produce a convicted offender upon whom research could be done. In Canada, in 1975, out of 2843 rape incidents reported to the police, only 152 persons were sent to penitentiary.

What indepth research is available raises some surprising facts. Only 25 percent of the official rape cases resulted in physical injury. Some force, however, was used in almost all the cases. Almost all rapes are intraracial, i.e. between members of the same racial group. About half are by complete strangers, but the rest are by acquaintances, close friends or relatives. One suspects that these figures would be considerably higher if unconvicted and unreported cases were added. Alcohol is a factor in from one-third to one-half the cases. The usual age for victims is 19, although rapes occur involving females from infancy to old age. Three quarters of officially convicted rapists had planned their attacks.

The women's movement has endeavored to increase public awareness about rape, to provide easier means for rape victims to come forward, and has pressed for changes in the statutes. Largely because of feminist activities, we now know that there is far more sexual assault than previously believed. We also know that a great many women are subject to various degrees of coercive sexual activity, often by men they know and have trusted. The women's movement has also been instrumental in exposing how cultural values enshrined in popular mythology often encourage rape (e.g. the female as a possession of the male; the myth of women "needing", "desiring" or "deserving" rape, etc.). Furthermore, rape, and other sexual offences, theoretically challenge the general analysis we have been developing by suggesting that economistic explanations are not adequate for understanding all kinds of crime. The existence of non-economic crime suggests that our notions of political economy must be considerably widened to take account of gender.

Murder. Compared with other crimes, murders are extremely difficult to hide. In almost all cases, someone notices the victim is missing quite soon and about 80-90 percent of murders known to the police are solved. As a consequence, data on offenders are available. Males in their twenties or thirties, who are relatively uneducated, and in low occupational strata form the majority of murderers (Boydell and Bell-Rowbotham 1972). But the popular image of danger from hulking, strange, desperate men in dark alleys or bushes, lying in wait for innocent victims, is quite misleading. In Canada, it is still the case that most murders involve relatives, friends, lovers, neighbors, and acquaintances.

The most popular methods of murder consist of shooting or beating. In addition, it is noteworthy that most murders seem to occur "spontaneously", often over rather trivial precipitating disagreements, quarrels, spats, or arguments. In a considerable percentage of murders (some 20 percent in American studies), the eventual victim is quite clearly the decisive instigator. The victim may be the first to throw a knife, for instance, and the murderer then retaliates. Some studies also indicate that well over half of our homicides involve the use of alcohol (Reed et al, 1978).

All of this suggests, in general, that murder is a very unusual criminal act, not only in its horrendous consequences, but also in its usually non-rational, uncalculated, spontaneous, and hence unpredictable nature. For these reasons most murderers are not deterred through "rational" policies. Various studies have shown, for instance, that capital punishment makes little difference in a country's murder rate, and that murderers are the most easily rehabilitated of all criminals (Fattah 1973). Murders would also seem, like rape, to pose a problem to simplistic economistic explanations of crime. How can interpersonal violence between intimates be explained? But we must note that most violent deaths are not officially considered murders. Suicide, automobile deaths, and "other accidents" are far more prevalent.

Corporate Assaults. Reasons et al (1981) argue in their book *Assault on the Worker*, that workers are killed by industrial accidents at a rate of three times the rate for murder. Such deaths are class-related. Being a fisherman, lumberman, or miner, is far more likely to cause death on the job than being a salesperson, a banker or even a policeman. Furthermore, according to International Labour Organization data, Canadian work fatality rates are among the highest in the industrialized world. Some estimates claim that, for the United States, about a third of job injuries are due to illegal working conditions, and another quarter are due to unsafe, although legal, conditions. Reasons et al suggest that work-related injuries far outnumber criminal assaults as well. In almost all these cases, the worker is blamed for being careless.

State Assaults and Killings. Modern states claim the exclusive legitimate use of force within their territories. Neither deviants nor dissenters have easy recourse to using state-sanctioned force. Whenever these "outsiders" use force it will be condemned by the authorities as a threat to civilization and society. When the authorities resort to the same behavior themselves, they can claim that their violence is legitimate. More will be said of this in the chapter by Lee.

In terms of threat to human life, modern states have become extremely violent. Many Canadians were among the millions killed in World War II. While some $30 billion were spent in 1979 on development aid for impoverished countries, some $450 billion were spent on armaments (Ross, 1981). A modern tank costs about a million dollars and a jet fighter costs about $20 million. One half of one year's global arms spending would pay for all the farm equipment needed to approach food self-sufficiency for low income countries by 1990 (Webster, 1981). Present NATO plans concede that some *40 million* Britons (of 54 million total) would die should they suffer a nuclear attack. If a one megaton bomb exploded at ground level in Detroit, it is estimated that a quarter million people would die and a half million would be injured (Radical Statistics Nuclear Disarmament Group, 1982:49; 61). These estimates of potential state violence make the effects of contemporary crime in "murder city" look rather small.

It must be recognized that these enormous, carefully calculated plans and monstrously huge expenditures to kill other humans are carried out not by those normally deemed criminals, but by the respected and acknowledged leaders of our societies. Many such individuals have used law and order platforms to gain election. Perhaps because governments make the law, they have been less than effective in outlawing and controlling their own violence.

HIGHLIGHT

1. Myths surrounding deviance assume that crime is on the increase, that crime is basically a male phenomenon, that it occurs mainly in large cities, and that immigrants have higher rates of crime than the native born.
2. Male gender and school failure are among the highest correlates of delinquent behavior.
3. Although property crimes account for two-thirds of the violations of the Criminal Code, the number of professional thieves are few.

4. Far more money is lost through white collar and corporate crime than through other forms of theft.
5. The operation of organized crime involves more money than individual crime.
6. In many ways, organized crime is conducted in ways comparable to major business.
7. In Canada, acts of violence when compared with other crimes are relatively few. They are, nonetheless, very serious matters.
8. State violence, e.g. murder, is a form of violence that is frequently overlooked when violence in general is analysed.

Conclusion

The chapter began by indicating that it is difficult to define what deviance means. What is deviant under some circumstances may be regarded as perfectly acceptable under others. Viewing deviance in other ways, such as in terms of statistics, may assist in coming to terms with some aspects of this quandry. At the same time such approaches create as many problems as they solve. For this and for a number of other reasons deviance in this chapter was initially defined in terms of what the law defines as aberrant and subject to sanction.

Having adopted this definition it was seen that the most sensational crimes—murder, armed robbery, etc.—are not the most common. (Petty property crimes head the list.) Nor do sensational crimes involve the most money. This distinction is reserved for white-collar and corporate crime.

Whereas the perpetrators of sensational crimes and, to a far lesser extent, petty property crimes, are under most circumstances prosecuted to the full extent of the law, 'white-collar' and corporate criminals receive far more lenient treatment. Even if the latter are caught and convicted, their penalties are relatively light. In view of this and other evidence presented in the chapter, it is clear that the type of criminal activity an individual is likely to engage in, and the probability of apprehension, trial and conviction, are clearly related to the criminal's position in the class structure and, by definition, role in the mode of production.

NOTES

[1]From *Choices*, © Feb. 1982. The Institute for Research on Public Policy, Montreal.

SUGGESTED READINGS

The Great Stumble Forward: The Prevention of Youthful Crime, J. Hackler. Toronto: Butterworths, 1978. This book is a good introduction to Canadian juvenile justice.

Criminal Justice in Canada, J. Griffiths Klein, K. and S. Verdun-Jones. Toronto: Butterworths, 1980. An overview of the justice system is presented in a way that can be understood by the non-specialist.

Assault on the Worker, C. Reasons. Toronto: Butterworths, 1981. This book gives a detailed treatment of corporate violence against employees. It is a must for those interested in the hidden dynamics of capitalism.

Crime in Canadian Society, R. S. Silverman and J. J. Teevan, eds. Toronto: Butterworths, 1980, (2nd ed.). A collection of various papers on theory, methods, and substantive studies of crime of various levels of sophistication comprise this volume.

Crime Control, L. Tepperman. Toronto: McGraw-Hill, 1977. The focus here is on the Canadian justice system. It is especially good as a source of statistics.

Crime and Delinquency in Canada, E. Vaz and A. Lodhi, eds. Toronto: Prentice-Hall, 1980. This volume is a varied collection of articles on delinquency and crime.

CONTROLLING SOCIETY

John Alan Lee

Introduction

Critics of social science often insist that "You can't predict human behavior. Human beings are too varied, and besides, they have free will. There's no telling what people will do next."

But we can predict a great deal of human behavior, and we do so all the time. It would be impossible to invite a guest for dinner, drive on a highway, or attend a university class, if the behavior of people around you was generally unpredictable. In short, our daily lives depend on *social order.*

Disputes between members of society are also an everyday event. Thus, if social order is to be maintained, disputes must be resolved before they get "out of control." *Social control* is essential for social order.

Talking is probably the most universal means of settling disputes (Roberts 1976:69). In simple societies, talking was often enough to control deviant behavior. Expressions of shame, ridicule, disgust, ostracism and excommunication were powerful means of control within communities where members knew each other and felt accountable to each other. Verbal social control developed into elaborate rituals such as the Eskimo *nith* song. In this disputants confronted each other before a community assembly, and sang mocking songs improvised for the occasion (Roberts 1979:59).

Modern urban societies cannot rely on talking for social control, for we live in "nations of strangers" where we feel accountable to few people around us. Turk (1976) suggests that it is fear of strangers (and the possible unpredictability of their behavior) which compels us to rely so heavily on *law* as social control. (Of course talking is still the major ingredient of legal processes!)

The behavior of strangers remains reasonably predictable in modern society because each new citizen, from a very early age, is socialized into respect for the law and obedience to rules. Kindergarten, for example, may be viewed as a kind of "boot camp". Here children strange to each other learn within a few months to follow rules and obey school *authorities.*

The rules of law are more than habit or moral norms. Max Weber (1954:2) argued that three features distinguish law from other norms of behavior: a) an external guarantee of enforcement (rather than mere conscience or the desire to please someone); b) ultimate resort to coercive force if necessary; and c) the presence of a *specialized staff* assigned to enforce and coerce. As babies we learned to obey our parents because they were personally important to us for love and nourishment. But in school we learned to obey a stranger, because he or she was an authority, the teacher. Later we learned to obey other strangers in authority, such as the police.

Weber did not overlook the fact that most of the time we obey the rules without the actual presence and coercion of an authority. It is not necessary to have a cop beside every stop sign. The possibility of coercion by the specialized staff is usually enough.

But the temptation to ignore the formal rules is present in all of us, especially when there seems to be much to gain, and little to lose. The risk of unpleasant consequences for cheating is high in an invigilated examination. But the temptation to plagiarize in an essay is a great test of self-enforcement of the rules. In fact, probably there is not a single reader of this sentence who has not violated some Canadian law. The focus of this chapter will be on the ways in which these laws come into being, whose interests they serve, how they are enforced, and how they affect people who transgress them.

The Law and Consensus

Though the best socialized members of society still break a law occasionally, most of us have been conditioned to feel considerable anxiety when we do so. The result is subsequent guilt even if we are not caught. We tend to assume that everyone else feels the same anxiety and generally prefers to obey the law. Thus it appears that law is based on *social consensus.*

Laws which obviously do not enjoy social consensus seem to prove this point. Where a law is notoriously out of sympathy with public opinion or taste, it becomes almost impossible to enforce. The list of examples includes prohibition of alcohol, various drug laws, tax laws and gambling laws (such as anti-lottery laws prior to their recent legalization). These examples, as well as an apparently universal desire to generally obey the law, seem to confirm that law is viewed as simply a codified form of basic human morality.

The Law Reform Commission of Canada put the matter this way (Goode 1978:401):

> Crimes are not just forbidden, they are also wrong. In truth, the criminal law is fundamentally a moral system....criminal law simply underlines our general notions of right and wrong.

Surveys across societies as varied as Iran, Indonesia, Italy and the United States seem to confirm that there is a world-wide consensus supporting the laws against a variety of "predatory crimes" (Wilson 1975:xx). These include murder, assault, theft and fraud (Newman 1976). But Newman also found *dissensus* about other illegal actions of a less predatory nature, especially moral offences and "victimless crimes." Even within a society such as Canada, there is great disagreement about the laws on homosexuality, abortion, and the use of marijuana. This possibility was identified in the previous chapter.

Even the authorities responsible for enforcing the rules may disagree with them. Judge Anthony Charlton told the press that he was handing out his *one thousandth* absolute discharge for possession of marijuana: "This is sort of an anniversary for me. I can't for the life of me discover any [real harm in marijuana]...it doesn't hurt anybody much. The people who look ridiculous are the lawyers and judges...they are from the same club." (*Toronto Star*, October 17, 1980). The judge probably knew that there are judges and lawyers who use marijuana (including those responsible for sentencing other users!). He may also have known that such high-status users rarely get charged for this legal violation.

It seems that "general notions of right and wrong" are not a satisfactory explanation of how various behaviors become unlawful. Even on issues of extremely harmful predatory crime there is disagreement. For example, the Law Reform Commission chooses murder to prove its point: "Whether or not the accused is familiar with the actual language of the criminal code...is quite irrelevant. He knows it is wrong to kill" (Goode 1978:401). But *when* is it wrong to kill? As shown in the last chapter there are times when it is patriotic and heroic to kill. Also, there are times when the state kills, but its citizens may not call it murder. They call it capital punishment.

The Image of Lawbreaker

When asked to imagine someone committing a crime, many students report seeing a young male in the act of hurting or robbing another person, or both. A female is only rarely reported. Significantly, older men also are infrequently reported. Most important of all, few students see a "white collar" or "corporate" crime in process. Our typical image of a crime is a predatory one-on-one situation, but as the previous chapter demonstrated, the crimes which cause the greatest social harm and cost are those committed by older men in business suits.

When people imagine crimes they usually concentrate on crimes which are in fashion and are getting high media attention. Almost never will an individual imagine a crime which was once a crime, but is no longer. From day to day we assume that "the law is the law, and must be obeyed whether we like it or not".

A slavish obedience for law overlooks the fact that the law is a social product. It is made by humans and frequently changed by humans. Frank Drea was for some years Minister of Corrections for Ontario—the top man in charge of the province's places and means for punishing people who break the law. But at one time Mr. Drea worked as a reporter. His assignment for a TV program called W-5 was to enter drug stores (in 1967) while secretly filmed, and attempt to buy male prophylactics over the counter. At the time, such sales were against the law. W-5 broadcast the film to demonstrate how stupid this law was. It invited the police to lay charges against the druggists involved. Nothing came of it at the time, but three years later the law was abolished.

There is obviously nothing sacred about The Law, though many Canadians seem to believe there is. For example, Ontario lowered its legal drinking age to 18 then raised it to 19. It has even happened that behavior which was illegal for citizens at one time, was *encouraged* by official state agencies at another. Legalization of lotteries is an example. Sometimes one need only cross an imaginary line, from one province to another, or even one county to another, to turn a legal action into an unlawful one.

Who defines what is unlawful in our society? The answer is extremely complex. Legislators approve the laws defining crimes, but they often act on, and rubber-stamp, the advice of career civil servants. Judges decide if a particular action is a crime as defined by law, but judges vary a great deal in their reading of the law. Police who see an action in progress may see a crime and make an arrest. They may also see a crime but ignore it, or not see a crime where another constable would see one.

The media play an important role in defining unlawful acts. Page one of Canada's largest daily, *The Toronto Star*, featured two headlines on October 31, 1981:

U.S. 'LIED' ON RIVER POISON, REPORT SAYS
THE TERROR IN THE NIGHT: BURGLARY BOOM

The river poison story reported that public officials had deliberately, over many years, covered up the dumping of millions of gallons of toxic waste in waters from which thirty million people draw their drinking water. Tens of millions of dollars of state funds (taxpayers' money) would be required to clean up the mess. But nowhere was it suggested that the officials committed a crime. Note the delicate quotation marks around 'lied.'

The burglary story—which ignored the statistics that over the whole year there was little change in thefts in the city—focussed on a recent series of sensational break-ins, such as that of a hockey star's home. Burglary was called a nightmare, a horror, really scary, traumatizing. The media have been demonstrated to be a powerful means to convert a novel crime, which does not represent any particular change in criminal patterns, into a "crime wave" (Hall et al 1978).

Myths and the Law

The task of explaining how certain actions become unlawful is further complicated by a veritable minefield of myths surrounding the enforcement of law in our society. Myths are not mere illusion or falsehood. They are significant beliefs about what is important or sacred in a society. They are "the very fibre of the legal system" (Arnold 1975:49). Whenever the "staff" enforcing a law try to explain their actions, they cite myths. Myths are used to justify enforcing the rules when the offender tries to argue that the enforcement is unjustified (Fuller 1975:81). We cannot examine these myths in detail here. We can merely note a few.

1. The myth of rationality.   It is believed that the law is a rational system of ideas which can be understood and applied to actions:

> The ideal relationship between the rule and decision is "clearcut": the facts lead the judge to the appropriate rule in the repertoire, which in turn indicates the decision. Rule determines outcome (Roberts 1979:20).

For example, the posted speed limit is 100 km/h. You were clocked at 120 km/h by a radar trap. The fine or jail term is assessed on a graduated basis for each km/h over the limit. But imagine a situation where the highway sign reads "No speeding," but indicates no speed limit. You are stopped by a pursuing police car and told you were driving too fast. You must appear in court. Here a judge will decide *how much too fast*, and then decide what the penalty will be. Perhaps the policeman will testify that your speed was "too fast" for your car, but safe enough for some other car, or too fast in terms of the amount of traffic on the road, or whatever.

This may sound irrational—even crazy? Yet there are many laws in the Criminal Code of Canada (C.C.C.) which fit this model. Section 159 makes punishable the publication of obscene matter, or exhibition of a disgusting object. Section 157 punishes gross indecency. Section 179 punishes people who keep places "to which resort is had for the purpose of acts of indecency." The Canadian law limits, and once forbade, abortion, unless necessary for the "health" of the mother. The law forbids "sexual immorality and similar vice" to juveniles. And so forth. In none of these cases does the law set a "speed limit."

The police and/or a crown attorney decide that a particular book on the newsstand is obscene. They may first warn the shopkeeper to take it off the stands, or be charged. Or they may swoop down without warning and seize not only the book in question, but any other material, including the accounts and business records of the offender.

Months later, by which time the vendor may have been driven out of business by such tactics, the case comes to court. There, a judge, and sometimes a jury, must decide if the material exhibited to them is obscene, indecent, disgusting, or whatever. Experts may be called to discuss "community standards", even though they may all agree that there is no single, widely agreed community standard about such material. Eventually the material may be condemned as "too fast" for society. It may be destroyed, the vendor fined, etc.

The extreme examples of such clearly irrational and arbitrary law are almost amusing. In 1982 a high court in Canada found that a parking lot could be a bawdy house. Meanwhile another court dismissed charges of prostitution on the grounds that a prostitute must be shown to be *persistent* in her/his soliciting. The judge found the woman in question "no more persistent than the usual seller of poppies on Remembrance Day" (*Globe and Mail*, December 31, 1981).

It is a myth—but one which most Canadians believe and need to believe—that the law is a rational set of rules which define actions as crimes, or not crimes. The actuality is closer to the discussion among three referees as to what constitutes a foul ball:
First referee: I calls them the way I sees them.
Second referee: I calls them the way they are.
Third referee: They ain't nothin' til I calls them.

2. Myth of equality before the law. While this myth enjoys considerable token expression in the courts and the media, it may be more easily debunked than the myth of rational law.

Most Canadians probably feel the law *should* be blind to race and religion. Whether or not it is, is hotly debated among sociologists. But what about *age*? Elderly people are often let off easily by police and courts. At the same time, juveniles are made examples. We might also ask: what about sex, and sexual orientation? Should women receive the same treatment from the criminal justice system as men, for every offence? Should gay and non-gay always be treated equally?

3. Myths about policing. These myths range from the silly to the pernicious. At the silly end there is the myth, now rapidly dying in Canada, that cops must be *tall males*. For many years, various police commissions have insisted on height requirements which have effectively excluded certain minority ethnic groups. Yet much tougher cities (New York, Chicago, Los Angeles) had demonstrated that short cops could do as well. While the height myth is largely debunked, there are still few women, black, oriental or native Indian constables.

At the pernicious end is the myth that police work is a very dangerous occupation. This myth is still extravagantly celebrated in the press and by police forces, who send representatives by the hundreds to any police funeral (Posner 1978). Yet the statistics are that police work is a less dangerous occupation than that of fireman, miner, or construction worker (Sykes and Clark 1975:585). Indeed, many constables report that they chose the occupation for its *security*. Police are rarely laid off in times of unemployment (Vincent 1979).

Also dangerously misleading is the myth that the police are all that prevents crime from turning society into a jungle. We will return to this "thin blue line" myth later.

4. The myth of crime waves.   How much crime is there at any given time in Canada? How long is a piece of string? (Ditton 1979:21). The amount of crime cannot be a fixed figure because, as discussed in detail in the chapter by Bennett and West, crime depends on how many actions are reported, charged, convicted. Any notion of a "wave" of crime is likely to involve more than a change in actual 'offences'. It will probably involve a change in police behavior (including the number of police— MacDonald 1976) as well as possible changes in law that may define something as crime which was formerly legal. Prohibition of alcohol is the classic example.

5. The myth of a day in court.   "Tell it to the judge, you'll have your day in court." Not necessarily. It will surprise many Canadians to learn that only about one tenth of those who are found guilty and sentenced, are actually *tried* (with hearing of evidence, witnesses, cross-examination and so forth). The bulk of the sentences passed follow after *plea bargaining*. This is discussed in detail later. Without plea bargaining, the courts would collapse in a few weeks from total overload. The police, by laying multiple charges, assure that most offenders will bargain. (Ericson 1980).

6. Other myths.   We have certainly not exhausted the minefield. There is the old chestnut that you are "innocent until proved guilty." It does not fit very well with the fact that from 40 to 50 percent of the inmates of city jails at any time have not yet been found guilty. They are simply being held for trial. Then there is the myth about a "jury of one's peers." Aside from the fact that few offenders actually face a jury, and even fewer, a jury of one's social peers, as Strick (1977:79) asks, would you refer a life-and-death decision to twelve strangers who have never met before, have no expertise, and remain unaccountable for the consequences of their decision? For example, would you submit the question of whether to have surgery, or even repair your car, to such a decision-making process?

Still other myths cannot be spared our limited attention—for example, "legal fictions." One of the greatest of such fictions for many centuries was the principle in English law that a woman might appear before a court as an *offender*, for "pain and penalty", but was not a *person* before the courts. For example, she could not seek her rights under a contract. Only in 1927 did women become persons at law in Canada.

HIGHLIGHT

1. It is difficult to find one element that all laws have in common.
2. In our society, a number of myths surround law and its enforcement. They include ideas that: a) law is a rational system of ideas; b) that all citizens are equal before the law; c) that police work is more dangerous than other professions; and, d) that everyone has the right to— and gets—a fair trial.

History of the Legal Process

In attempting to understand how behavior becomes unlawful, some sociologists argue that the history of social control is irrelevant. Turk (1969:51) argues that, "How authorities came to be authorities is irrelevant; it is sufficient that a social structure built out of authority relations exists...". Others, including the author, consider some knowledge of the historical origins of social structures essential to understanding their workings. Obviously such a history cannot be more than superficially summarized here.

Emergence of Criminal Law.   In feudal times, the central "state", to the extent that it existed at all, took rather little interest in most wrongdoing. It left most offenders to local civil procedures and the church. Social control relied mainly on local custom enforced by local authorities (Bloch 1961).

As modern nations emerged, legal control of the population became an important political instrument of central governments in their competition with local powers. In England, William the Conqueror appointed judges to travel on circuits. They held sittings (assizes) to hear the most politically significant cases in each district. Back in London, the judges compared cases and exchanged decisions. They thus worked toward a single standard of justice throughout the island kingdom. Thus emerged an English "common law."

Local traditions had been largely oral. Then a written, systematic *code* of state-enforced criminal law was developed. Henry II (1154-89) assigned judges to produce a written legal code which could be enforced everywhere in the kingdom. This led to a need for literate interpreters of the code. Previously, the offended person had prosecuted his own case before the judge. Now a need for lawyers who understood the code began to push the victim onto the sidelines.

Under the old local, tribal justice, the offended person received a large share of any fine levied against the accused. Now, as the state bureaucracy took a greater role, it also demanded a share in the revenues produced by justice. From 1176, the state began taking the whole fine. It left the victim with no financial compensation—a situation still largely in effect today.

Property Rights as the Basis of Law.   In feudal Europe, few people owned land or resources outright. Instead, various people enjoyed different rights of use, according to the rights exercised by their ancestors. One man might have had the right to farm certain land. Another had the right to hunt on it. A third had the right to gather firewood on it. Each carried on the tradition of his father. But the enclosure of common lands, the rise of cities, and the development of modern industrial capitalism brought the need for "freehold" property rights. According to these, one person had complete control of a piece of property, including mineral rights, right of way, and other property rights (Pearson 1981:98-117).

Thus, as we will note in more detail later, the major purpose of law became that of protecting property rather than ancestral tradition. The two forms of law are still profoundly in conflict today in Canada in the contest of native Indian *aboriginal rights* versus the freehold property rights of those who have purchased land in former Indian territories.

Law as Ritual.   There had always been a certain degree of magic and ritual in criminal justice—for example, the trial by ordeal, in which God was expected to spare the innocent from the fire or from drowning. But the emergence of a new state-administered criminal process that focussed on protecting the property rights of the new bourgeois class against the ancestral claims of peasants and workers, produced an urgent need for law to keep the "dangerous class" in their place. Grand ritual was a major ingredient of social control of the masses in religion and the monarchy. It was natural to extend the power of ritual to the courtroom. The assizes of circuit justice became elaborate annual events, with formal processions in robes and wigs, lengthy public addresses, county balls, and elaborately ritual public executions. Many of these formalities are still part of "British"—and Canadian—justice.

An important function of legal ritual was the insistence on technical exactitude—the letter of the law. Documents had to be exactly correct. Every 'jot and title of the law' had to be correctly carried out. It is still possible to have a traffic ticket cancelled, for example, simply because the constable misspelled your name, or got the date wrong, even though the charge was correct and you do not deny it.

This rigid insistence on technicalities of the law gave the impression to the lower classes that the Law was impartial. Technical precision gave the illusion of treating everyone alike, according to the exact *rules* of law.

Adversary Justice.   In England the criminal justice system developed in quite a different direction than on the continent. At one time both used the *inquisitorial* system, in which the judge was an active participant in the trial. His goal was the establishment of *truth.* The judge might ask questions, be present during torture, and take sides on the matter in dispute. This system is still widely used in Europe and countries formerly colonized by the continental nations. But in England, and later in British colonies (and thus also in the modern United States), the role of judge changed over the centuries into that of neutral arbitrator. He was to oversee a contest between the two sides but was not to show bias.

In this *adversary system*, the theory is that truth is most likely to emerge if the prosecution and defence each wholeheartedly argue their own side of the case. Thus a good defence lawyer puts up as hard a fight (the theory goes) for a client who is guilty, as for one who is innocent. Anything the client tells his lawyer about whether he "really did it" is private, *privileged* information, which the lawyer does not have to tell the court.

The adversary system has its defenders and its critics. This author has been entertained by high-priced criminal lawyers who boast over dinner about the number of clients they "got off," even knowing that the clients were guilty. The adversary system, for example, leads defence lawyers in rape trials to attempt to shatter the credibility of the victim, so that the defence lawyer's client may go free. That is the lawyer's job. It is the job of the prosecution to find the evidence to convict. It is symptomatic of the degree to which the legal profession takes the adversary system for granted (as a "good thing"), that most law schools and texts devote very little time to discussion of the system and its inquisitorial alternatives (Strick 1977).

The Proliferation of Statute Law.   Prior to the nineteenth century, the larger part of English common law was drawn from tradition and precedent. The law was "case law," systematically codified and commented on by great jurists such as Blackstone. With the increasing power and activity of parliament, and the rapid pace of technological change, more and more law was created by legislated *statute.* Though it is still true that "ignorance of the law is no excuse," it is unlikely that Canada's most expert legal minds are aware of all the unlawful acts it is now possible to commit. There are more than 40 000 of them! (Mohr 1979).

When speed is required, statute law responds much more quickly than case law. For example, striking workers in "essential" public service can be legislated back to work in a single day. Statute law can create a crime where none existed before in the moral tradition of the society. For example, it had long been a major sin to engage in a homosexual act in England, and a military offence in certain cases. But it was not a crime until a statute made it one in 1885. Oddly enough, it became a crime only for men. It is said that Queen Victoria refused to sign any legislation criminalizing lesbian acts because she could not believe women capable of such things.

Origins of the Canadian Criminal Code.   In the late nineteenth century a prominent English jurist, Sir James Fitzjames Stephen, published a comprehensive codification of English laws. He hoped it would become the model penal code of England. It never did. But the new nation of Canada adopted it as our Criminal Code. This adoption was extremely significant, because English legal tradition was long divided on a central question: Should the law legislate private moral behavior, or "should the state stay out of the bedrooms of the nation?"

On the side of non-intervention were such prominent English legal theorists as John Stuart Mill. There was also the experience of the Napoleonic Code. It tends to avoid legislating private morality. This may have been one reason why English legal thought in the nineteenth century tended to go against Mill, and favor state presence in the bedroom. The 1885 law on homosexuality was only one example.

Sir Stephen was firmly in the interventionist camp. Consequently, the code which became Canada's Criminal Code takes the state very often into the private, moral lives of citizens. During the twentieth century a moral-interventionist interpretation of Canadian law was further reinforced by American legal change brought about by Anthony Comstock. He was a moral entrepreneur who crusaded for legislation against obscenity, sexual indecency, nudity, birth control information, etc.

Rise of the Modern Prison System.   In feudal Europe, people usually had little real property. Thus, most punishments were directed against their bodies. Whipping, branding, public confinement in the stock or pillory, amputations, torture, slavery in the galleys or transportation to the colony were typical penalties. Prisons were limited to confining important felons until a judge arrived on circuit, holding debtors until creditors were satisfied, and putting away such political prisoners as were too dangerous to let loose but too important to execute.

With the rise of modern industrial society, the denial of personal freedom became a more potent punishment. It replaced direct assault on the felon's body (Foucault 1977). Canada in the early nineteenth century used much the same methods of punishment as England—branding, whipping, even transportation (92 of the rebels in 1837 were shipped to Tasmania). But in 1835 our first penitentiary was opened at Kingston, and prison became the usual punishment for serious offenders against the law. Transportation, in the form of deportation, remained a penalty for some, especially minority groups (such as the Chinese) and alleged "political subversives."

HIGHLIGHT

1. Law can be divided into its criminal and civil components. The former describes laws the transgression of which is an offence against the state; the latter describes laws the transgression of which is an offence against an individual, corporation, etc.
2. In capitalist society, the major role of law is the protection of private property.
3. The ritualistic features of the Canadian justice system—the wearing of court room robes, etc.—have medieval roots.
4. Systems of justice can be divided into inquisitorial or adversarial forms. In an inquisition the judge is an active participant in the trial. In an adversarial trial he hears arguments put forward by prosecution and defence and restricts his own role in questioning.
5. Common-law derives from precedents established in previous law cases. Statutory law is decreed by an arm of the state.
6. The long-term denial of personal freedom (jailing) as a punishment for crime is a relatively recent innovation. By and large, it is a product of the industrial revolution.

The Apparatus of Social Control

Armed with some historical perspective on our legal system, and a readiness to cut our way through the mythology of law, we may now turn to an examination of some of the specific social structures and mechanisms by which law is used to control Canadian society. Again, we obviously cannot exhaust the subject. So we will focus mainly on the police, lawyers, judges, and prisons.

Any effective analysis must begin with a theoretical framework. There are several different possible approaches to the structure of our legal system. In one, the system can be summed up like this:

Law

Legitimation of Power

Authority

This view holds that we live under "a government of laws, not men." The Law is considered primary and supreme. Law makes society possible. Without law, society would collapse into a "war of all against all." As two Canadian legal scholars put it (Bala and Clark 1981:14):

> We have laws...to preserve order....[A] world without laws would be a world of anarchy and would cause the destruction of society as we know it.

This approach sees law as providing a set of rules for behavior in society. These rules justify the intervention of the specialized staff of enforcers. Law *legitimates* the enforcer's use of coercive force. Thus, law turns force or *power* into *authority*.

Max Weber was the first to clearly distinguish between power and authority. He defined power as the ability to achieve your will over another person, even against that person's resistance. Ultimately, state power "comes down the barrel of a gun," in the famous words of Mao Tse Tung. But because of our socialization to obey orders coming from people with a legitimate right to give orders (teachers, police, etc.) it is not frequently necessary for the enforcing staff to resort to physical force (such as guns). As long as the enforcers are acting according to the laws (the rules), we are likely to legitimate their actions. We obey even when we don't want to.

There is an alternative way of looking at the structure:

Power
Law
Legitimation
Authority

One difficulty with Weber's definition of power is that it implies that power exists only when there is some resistance to overcome. But often subordinates are willing to obey an order which is really against their best interests, *without resisting*, because they have been misled into thinking that obedience is in their best interest. (This type of behavior has been analysed in the chapters on culture and ideology and social psychology.) Slaves can be persuaded to go into battle on the side of their master-owners, as the American Confederacy proved. (There is a memorable scene in *Gone with the Wind* in which a black battalion marches through Atlanta. It is a Confederate battalion). Workers can be persuaded to oppose trade unions. Consumers can be persuaded to prefer inferior (but well-advertised) goods. Students can be persuaded to attend classes which teach them nothing they need or want to know, merely to get a degree.

The shortcoming in Weber's definition of power can be mended by redefining power (Baldus 1975). Power is the ability to maintain, in favor of the powerholder, a disproportionate division of scarce and desired resources in a society. Power, for example, is the ability of a small minority of whites to control most of the wealth of South Africa, including the labor of several times as many blacks. Power is the ability of men, slightly in the minority in our population, to control much more than their proportion of status, income, property, and other desired resources, to the disadvantage of women. (Men even get a larger share of time, including conversational time (Henley 1977). Power is the ability of about one thousand Canadians each year to earn more than $100 000 yet pay no income tax. Meanwhile, many Canadians earning only $15 000 must pay every penny of tax due. Power, in the university classroom, is control over the resource most desired by the students: marks.

If power is defined as the ability to maintain a disproportionately favorable share of resources, then LAW becomes one of the methods for doing so. Power sets up the rules of the game so as to justify and legitimate the unfair division of resources. Those with power make the laws. In turn, laws legitimate their power into authority. The powerful do not have to violate the rules of the game (commit crimes) to keep their control of resources. They have already set up the rules to that very purpose. As we have seen (in the previous chapter), the rules of the economic game in Canada make it criminal for less powerful citizens to attempt to acquire more resources without "working for them". At the same time, they facilitate corporate gain without working for it (for example, through high interest rates).

An Explanation From Civil Law

Most Canadian students have been intensively socialized long before arriving in university to believe that law comes first. It legitimates power into authority. As a consequence, it will be difficult to understand, much less accept, the alternative model. The apparatus of civil law may help.

Canadian law may be roughly divided into criminal law and civil law. Civil law is law governing disputes between citizens in which the state does not take a position as an offended party. In criminal law, the state, since late feudal times, has become almost exclusively the offended party. It pushes the personal victim to the side as spectator (Christie 1980). In criminal law, the state *charges* the offender, and exacts a penalty. In civil law, the offended party *sues* the offender, for damages. Examples of civil legal actions include breach of contract, wrongful dismissal, trespassing, negligence, divorce, estate disputes, and so forth.

While civil law is certainly not insignificant in controlling society, criminal law is clearly the type of law most important for social control. This chapter therefore concentrates on criminal law. You may recall that most of the crime studied in the last chapter also falls under criminal law. But most students will have some experience with civil law. Does your experience give validity to the argument that civil law is generally of most use to those with property rather than those without? Does it seem reasonable to argue that mortgage law is of greater benefit to those with money to lend, than those needing to borrow? The power to foreclose a mortgage is much greater in impact than the right, if any, to obtain a mortgage.

Many students—perhaps most in your class—are generally prepared to recognize that in civil law, power (control of the scarce resource of property) comes first. It uses the law to its advantage to maintain a disproportionate division of property. This is not surprising. In civil law, many great "liberal thinkers" have argued that civil law *should* protect property. John Locke observed that "government has no other end but the preservation of property." Thomas Jefferson agreed when drafting the Declaration of Independence to assure property rights. John A. Macdonald argued the need for a Senate patterned on the English House of Lords, rather than democratically elected "because the wealthy are always fewer than the poor."

The rationale of the property holder is clear enough. The civil law enables him to maintain control of more than his proportionate share of property in the society, without having to use force. This end is achieved by socializing those with little or no property to believe in the rule of law. Those without property will not seize it from the property-holders because of belief in the "legal rights of property." For example, a tenant behind in the rent, or a mortgagee about to be foreclosed, may well resent being thrown "into the street". But the law is on the side of the owner. His threat to use force is regarded as legitimate. He is therefore obeyed, without force having to be used.

This agreement saves much expense and trouble in calling on the services of the bailiff, sheriff, local police, and so on. It also reduces the probability of a general resentment building up and spreading among other tenants, homeowners, and farmers going bankrupt. Property owners can use power, legitimated by law, to establish their rightful authority to control their property without resorting to force. The power of property comes first, and uses law. If this argument seems reasonable in civil law, it will be easier to accept in criminal law.

Explaining Law: Ideal Versus Material Culture

Theories which place law first, followed by legitimation of power into authority, usually explain the social origins of law in terms of ideas and culture. The question "How did this law come about?" is answered in terms of emerging ideas. (*The Idea of Law* by Lloyd is an example). A modern law may be explained by tracing its precursors all the way back to Roman times.

Structural-functionalists take the analysis further by looking for basic, universal features of social control. For example, almost any society, ancient or modern, simple or industrial, will have some form of *trial procedure* by which an accused person is brought to 'justice.' The existence of laws will be explained in terms of the manner in which the given culture has defined such basic institutions as 'trial,' 'accused,' 'judge,' and other legal components. Structural-functionalists generally take for granted that deviant behavior exists in every society, as a means of reinforcing obedience to the norms (Durkheim 1964 ; Merton 1957).

In the mid-twentieth century sociologists began to take a new approach to social control. It is known as the "labelling perspective" (Schur, 1971 and 1974). This approach examined what the structural-functionalist took for granted. It asked how a given society came to choose particular acts and persons to label as deviant. It concluded that deviance and crime, like beauty, are in the eye of the beholder.

A further analysis is developed by the approach called *conflict theory.* Conflict theorists are interested in the struggle between groups and classes in society. In the case of law, they analyse the struggle to pin deviant and criminal labels on each other. Law expresses the will of the winners in such struggles. Law becomes a weapon (Turk 1976) and "power determines legality" (Reasons and Rich 1978:166).

Within a broad conflict approach there are a variety of possible points of emphasis. One of these is materialism, arising from the historical materialism of Marxism. The materialist focusses on a particular kind of conflict and struggle in society: the relationship of various classes to the means of production. From this "class struggle" the materialist expects to find the political decision-making processes by which victorious social classes manage to pin deviant and criminal labels on subordinate class behavior. Thus, criminology is a particular application of the general materialist study of class struggle (Taylor Walton and Young 1973).

For example, materialist conflict theorists will find the explanation for laws on vagrancy, or trespassing, or poaching, not in ancient Roman or feudal ideas of law as such, but in the conflict of social classes over resources and the power to control them, at various stages in our history (Chambliss 1964). As a result of his studies on the struggle of German peasants to maintain their feudal woodcutting rights against the efforts of the new bourgeoisie to establish freehold property rights on land, Karl Marx concluded that the notion that law makes society possible was quite wrong. He turned the notion upside down:

> Society is not based on law, that is a legal fiction. Law is based on society...
> The Code Napoleon, which I have in my hand, did not produce modern bourgeois society. Bourgeois society, as it arose in the eighteenth century and developed in the nineteenth, merely finds its legal expression in the Code. As soon as [the law] no longer corresponds to social relationships, it is no more than the paper it is written on (cited in Taylor Walton and Young 1973:56).

Canadians generally have a difficult time understanding, much less accepting, a materialist explanation of law. The reason is that we witness so little obvious and harsh class struggle. In a society such as South Africa, where a small minority of whites rule over a majority of blacks, it is more apparent that law does not create authority. Authority comes when the powerful use law as a weapon to legitimate their actions. All the weapons of law, the police, the courts and prisons, are openly used in South Africa to protect white privilege and keep blacks in their ghettos. Law is used to deny blacks the right to travel, vote, or marry freely. It is much less likely that a black South African will believe that the law is "based on general notions of right and wrong."

There are comparable situations for certain groups in Canada. If you are a native Indian your reaction to Canada's new constitution is not likely to be so enthusiastic as English-speaking Canadians'. You know that part of the federal-provincial deal making the constitution possible was the exclusion of aboriginal rights.

If you have ever gone on strike, or lived with someone on strike, you may have realized that the weapons of law are much more commonly used against workers and for property-owners in Canada, than the reverse. The law is a weapon of the powerful to keep subordinate classes in place. It is less likely to be used on sections of the powerful itself. For example, the Ontario government did not hesitate to legislate hospital workers back to work and put their union leader in jail, but refused to take similar action against a doctors' strike.

Other kinds of experience can make Canadians more aware that the powerful do not have power because of the Law, but rather, the powerful use the Law to keep their power. Among such disenchanting experiences are: being busted for carrying a marijuana cigarette (joint), attending a gay club, supporting an unpopular political party or movement, or even protesting to save the whales or end acid rain. But such experiences only involve a relatively small number of Canadians. Moreover, it is rare that real political struggle will come out in the open in Canada on the scale of black-white struggle in South Africa. However, such events have occurred. One of them, which allowed journalists and the public to witness and record the willingness of the powerful to use the weapons of law, the police and the army to defend the powerful, was the October Crisis of 1970. At that time, the spokesmen of power in Canada made it quite clear that they were willing to use these weapons to protect themselves, and to go very far to do so.

Crime In Every Society?

Those who prefer explanations of the origin of law based on ideal culture and social functions generally tend to view human nature as easily corrupted and probably fundamentally flawed. Human nature is considered greedy, selfish, moved by territorial imperatives and lust for power. Law is necessary to tame human nature and make society possible. Without law we would quickly revert to "the jungle."

Materialists, Marxists and humanists, generally take the opposite approach. Human nature is seen as basically good, or at least neutral. The greed and selfishness and violence of life is explained by the suffering and oppression of people by certain forms of social order.

When people are exploited, both the exploiters and the exploited are corrupted.

Some Marxists and conflict theorists take their optimism about human nature to an extreme. They argue that if a truly free and non-oppressive social order were achieved, there would be no crime. Quinney, for example, argues that "Crime is an index of the extent to which the ruling class must coerce the rest of the population" (1977). The author would agree that there would probably be less crime in a society where everyone had a fair share of the scarce and desired resources such as food, shelter, free time, privacy, etc. But there is very little evidence indeed that any society will be entirely free of crime. Even simple communal societies on paradisical tropical islands occasionally witnessed theft and murder.

What is more important in the materialist insight is the recognition that the impetus for unlawful behavior comes from the deprivations of human nature, not the depravation. A great deal of the crime in our society is the product of efforts of those with more than their fair share of scarce and desired resources to hold on to their advantage. The weapon of law is one of the most effective in this struggle.

Sometimes history provides us with a clear and unambivalent example of the way in which law is used as a weapon of power. Two groups will be struggling for power in society—those now holding it and those wanting it. The subordinate group will be labelled as criminal, terrorist, subversive, or revolutionary. The ruling group will be lawful, legitimate, or the legal government. Its acts will be constitutional, supportive of 'our way of life,' and so forth.

Following an upheaval, the sides change. The former terrorists and subversives become the legitimate authorities. The previously lawful group become the criminals, put on trial. Within the past few years history has afforded examples in Iran, several Latin American countries, and Poland where former Communist officials recently (1981) were tried for corruption by leaders of a military coup.

Once in power, the formerly unlawful group seeks to rapidly legitimate its new powers. This will make it possible to win the obedience of the mass of citizens without using naked force like curfews, military law, troops in the streets, secret police, etc. The new powerful use law to give their power the appearance of lawful *authority*. They perhaps accomplish this end through carefully staged elections, a new national assembly, or a new constitution.

Since such upheavals are rare in western liberal democracies, we have fewer unambivalent examples of the use of the law by the powerful to legitimate their control of society. But from time to time, the veils of legal mythology are briefly drawn back, and we witness an example of law being manipulated by power. Revelations such as Watergate in the United States are the most famous examples. But in the daily press we can often find lesser examples. We will limit ourselves here to some examples of the way in which power is used in the police, courts, and prisons.

HIGHLIGHT

1. There are two basic sets of assumptions concerning the nature of law. The first includes the notion that law is preeminent and is necessary for the maintenance of society to everyone's advantage. The second includes the notion that law is created by, and exercised in, the interests of the powerful.
2. Power is the ability to maintain, in favor of the power holder, a disproportionate division of scarce and desired resources in a society.
3. Those who believe that law is pre-eminent find its roots in systems of legal ideas and practices. Those who see law as the creation of the powerful find its roots in social structures. The former are idealists; the latter materialists.

Power, Law, and the Police

It is essential to understand that the police often decide when, where, and on whom to enforce the law. Only a small proportion of all the behavior which might potentially be labelled crime, is ever formally charged. Naturally the people involved in 'victimless crime' do not ask the police to lay charges. The extent to which sex, gambling, drugs etc. result in criminal charges depends a great deal on how active the police are in investigating such crime, posing as suppliers or users, entrapping, and so forth.

Even when a complaint about crime is brought to the police, or police witness a crime in progress, they do not necessarily lay charges. An example concerning male prophylactics was cited earlier. The classic statement on police discretion is that of the Presidential Commission on Law Enforcement (1967:106):

> Police should openly acknowledge that, quite properly, they do not arrest all, or even most, offenders they know of. Among the factors accounting for this exercise of discretion are the volume of offences and the limited resources of the police, the ambiguity of and the public desire for the nonenforcement of many statutes, the reluctance of victims to complain, and, most important, an entirely proper conviction by police that the invocation of criminal sanctions is too drastic a response to many offences.

Even if a citizen is arrested and charged, higher levels of the police and the crown prosecution may decide to proceed no further, and the charges are 'dropped.' Constables may file reports of crimes for detectives to investigate. The latter may merely file and forget (Ericson 1981:9ff).

If such discretion were equally applied to all social classes, minorities, and groups in society, there would be little evidence to support a materialist-conflict argument about police power. But the evidence is clear that police discretion is not used equally with rich and poor, black and white, Anglo-Saxon and native Indian, gay and non-gay, young and old, protestor and non-protestor.

The police do not see a single public which they must serve and protect. Rather, they divide the public into sections—the VIPs (very important people), decent respectable people, the helpless, and the "scum" (Westley 1970). Some members of the public are much more deserving than others, in police eyes. Some sections of the public are fair game for unfavorable discretion (harassment). They are viewed as "police property" (Cray 1972). At various times, such groups have included ethnic minorities—Black, Chinese, Italian, Jewish, etc.,—beatniks and hippies, drug users, radical women, militant gays, striking trade unionists, and members of various political groups. They have also included the down-and-out, winos, hustlers, etc.

Whenever such target groups become troublesome, and especially if they become militant and uppity, police increasingly apply discretionary power to control these groups and keep them in their place. Such control may include deliberate provocation. Thereafter, citizens can be charged with "refusing to obey a police order," "obstructing police" or even "assault on a police officer." From time to time, the police go too far. Such activity results in an uproar in the media, and, eventually, to a judicial inquiry or royal commission. Several such commissions have reported on police harassment in Canada. These independent inquiries are rare windows into the police world (see the Morand report 1976 as an example).

The attitude of the powerful toward police use of law as a weapon of harassment has been clearly established. The police must do what is "necessary" in pursuit of their duties. Sometimes necessity is taken to surprising extremes. For example, when Toronto police were under great pressure to find someone to charge in a certain murder, two detectives decided to fabricate an affidavit in order to trick their favorite suspect into confessing. The trick failed. But the suspect was charged anyway. He was eventually acquitted. During the trial the police trick came out, and eventually the detectives were charged with fraud. But one crown prosecutor refused to disapprove of the trick: "Tricks and stratagems by police officers are recognized as legitimate tools." The trick was called "nothing but an imaginative tool" at the detectives' trial. They were eventually found guilty, but given an *absolute discharge. (Toronto Star*, May 23, 1980).

A more sensational example still, involved the RCMP investigation of alleged separatist groups in Quebec. At a time when public spokesmen of the separatists were calling for the use of non-violent, legal means to bring about their goals, the RCMP were busy manufacturing "communiques" from a fake "cell" of the FLQ. These communiques, pretending to come from the 'true radicals', condemned the public spokesmen as selling out the revolution, and called for violent methods. To date, no RCMP member has been tried, or even charged, for these strange activities. In other cases revealed at the McDonald royal commission inquiry into RCMP crimes, it was disclosed that Mounties had stolen dynamite, burned a barn, kidnapped people, broken and entered on more than 400 occasions, and in other strange ways used their police discretion as a necessary and imaginative tool.

Less outrageous, but no less horrendous for the victim, are the occasions when police entrap individual citizens into crimes which they might not otherwise commit. For example, Solicitor General Robert Kaplan has admitted that the police have no lawful right to pose as drug pushers. He nonetheless feels that such action is necessary to catch drug users. Police constables are also assigned to dangle their genitals temptingly in men's washrooms in the hope of eliciting an approach of a possible homosexual. The police may even reconstruct parts of a washroom to facilitate such entrapment (Lee 1978:128).

It may be felt that such examples of police abuse of their discretionary powers are cases of corruption, of "bad apples" in the police department, rogue cops, or bent bobbies. The evidence is otherwise. The police do not often allow social scientists to get inside the police operations to find out what is actually going on. When they do allow it, they are usually enraged by the results that are revealed by the participant observer. Such was the case with Ericson (1980). He has produced one of Canada's rare and candid inside views of an urban police force at work and was roundly denounced by the police afterward. One of the most revealing sections of Ericson's study is the personally observed report of constables arriving at the scene of an alleged "assault" of a bar bouncer by a customer. The customer had to be taken to the hospital while the bouncer was hardly scratched. But the police knew the bouncer, and charged the customer. Later, Ericson observed the police coaching the bouncer on how to state the facts in his report on what happened (Ericson 1980:113).

As we noted in redefining Weber's concept of power to take into account the frequent absence of resistance by the subordinate group, many citizens not only know, but approve of, the discriminatory use of police discretion. They feel that "the cops have to do what's necessary" and the victims "probably got what they deserved." During the daily revelations of unlawful RCMP activity from 1977 to 1980, many citizens wrote to the newspapers supporting the Mounties, not the Royal Commission Inquiry. One Canadian wrote:

> It gives us a warm, cosy feeling to know that our country is in such capable hands as the RCMP (*Toronto Star*, Nov. 4th, 1977).

More idealistic Canadians might have imagined that our country was in the hands of its elected government, not its police forces.

Growth Of Police Forces

Canada's police chiefs often complain about the lack of funds and manpower to do their job, especially when the media whip up a 'crime wave.' Such shortages are largely fictional. First, they are relative to the current priorities of the force in question. The Toronto police force told women's groups that it lacked personnel to patrol streets at night (and women should therefore stay at home), and explained to business associations that it could not provide foot patrols on main streets to reduce break-ins. Nevertheless it found the money and manpower to plan and execute massive raids on "gay baths." More than 250 constables were involved in these raids, which resulted in the largest mass arrests in Canada since the 1970 crisis. Yet there had been no complaints against the baths. They had operated quietly for eighteen years.

Likewise, the RCMP—responsible for police work in eight provinces and over 200 municipalities—uses the claim of shortages when renegotiating its police contracts with provinces. But it has found no lack of personnel and funds to produce a list of more than 800 000 Canadians observed and filed as possible security risks. The list includes leaders and members of public organizations as diverse as the Farmers Union, the Native Indian Brotherhood, the New Democratic Party, the Canadian Union of Public Employees, the Parti Québécois, and the Canadian Association of University Teachers (Mann and Lee 1979:178).

But even given their priorities, the Canadian police forces are hardly underconstabled or underfunded. They have grown faster than both the rate of population and the inflation rate in the past two decades. Canada had only 47 police per 100 000 population in 1901. Today there are more than 100 police per 100 000 (Tepperman 1977:48).

The RCMP, our major police force in most of Canada, cost Canadians $550 million in 1978, a growth of 150 percent over the 1971 figure. Inflation had increased only 65 percent in the same period. From 1971 to 1978 Canada's population grew by 6 percent, from 21.6 to 23 million. The RCMP grew from 13 500 to 19 000 members, a growth rate of 41 percent. These are not stacked statistics. If we choose a different base year the results are the same. For example, from 1961 to 1967 the Canadian population grew by 26 percent. The Mounties expanded 153 percent—a ratio of six times the population growth. Far from being short of manpower, ex-members of the RCMP indicate that the Mounties are overstaffed. They rely on drug busts, anti-labor activities and harassment of various political and social movements to keep themselves busy (Mann and Lee 1979). Likewise, Ericson found that a major problem for the Toronto area police force he investigated was looking busy (Ericson 1981).

Furthermore, it is important to remember that increases in manpower and funding alone do not fully express the vast increase in power of modern police forces. Technology has made one constable today worth several a few decades ago. The constable with two-way radio in communication with radio dispatchers, and access to instant computer data on a cross-country sytem, brings impressive resources to the constable's encounter with a citizen. Finally, statistics on growth of public police forces ignore the impact of private and ancillary forces. Much former police work, such as tagging parked cars, is now done by other services. In addition, the private police forces of major corporations now rival those of some cities. General Motors, for example, has more than 4000 of its own police (O'Toole 1978).

The Push For More Police Power

In recent years, Canadian police leaders have abandoned their traditional political "neutrality". Conflict theorists would argue that it never existed in more than appearance anyway. Thus it is easier to see that the police understand how to use the law as a weapon more so than formerly. Among the publicly admitted goals of police today are more punitive laws, more control over 'immoral' behavior which is not presently illegal (such as more power to control 'pornography' especially in modern technological forms such as videotape), and more power to contain social groups whose goals are disapproved by police. A recent Toronto example was the drafting of an Emergency Power by-law which would have allowed the police, during a proclaimed "emergency," to swoop down on looters and rioters. It also allowed them to deal with those involved in "activities related to social unrest, subversive activity, and organized activism" (*Toronto Star*, February 7, 1980). Many groups indeed could fall within such broad parameters. Only a combined outcry by public groups and the press prevented this draft from becoming law.

Police enthusiasm for greater power to control society is periodically revealed in an excess of zeal such as the raid on a Niagara nightclub (*Toronto Star*, September 8, 1979). Fifty police surrounded the club, body-searched the patrons and came up with all of six ounces of marijuana, the alleged justification for the raid. A judicial inquiry later reprimanded the police, but only verbally.

Naturally the sociologist seeks an explanation for the police thirst for greater power. *There is no evidence that the police attract more "authoritarian" personalities than other occupations, or that police constables are just nastier people* (Skolnick 1966, Niederhoffer 1967; McNamara 1967). *The explanation is in the social structure of police work, not the personality of constables.*

The majority of policemen and women are recruited from working-class and lower middle-class social backgrounds. It is not an occupation attractive to the upper levels of society, or the especially well educated (Preiss and Ehrlich 1966; Bayley and Mendelsohn 1969). On the job, constables soon learn that they must use their discretion differently with VIPs than with the "scum" or the helpless (including those who call on the police to solve problems which police feel they should be able to solve for themselves, such as trouble with neighbors). Constables soon learn that they are "dirty workers". They are expected to look after people like winos, transients, vandals, strikers, etc. who are problems for the powerful and respectable in society.

It is deeply frustrating to have to do the dirty work for powerful people, but not be allowed to join the powerful and enjoy their privileges. Even the chief of police of a major city cannot expect to be in the same lofty social class or enjoy the same lifestyle as top businessmen and political leaders. Ordinary constables find themselves called upon to harass striking workers. At the same time they are themselves often treated oppressively by their superiors, and denied the right to strike. In this case, exceptions illustrate the rule.

Recently the constables of Halifax went on strike. They had the experience of watching RCMP constables cross their picket lines and take over their jobs. As a result, the eyes of some Halifax constables were opened. They may be less willing to act harshly against other striking workers in future. This is a major reason why most police are not allowed to form regular unions or strike in Canada.

Likewise it was Mounties disenchanted by the rigid discipline of the RCMP who first blew the whistle on RCMP crimes (Ramsay, 1978; Mann and Lee 1979). Members of police forces, including urban police and the RCMP, are often allowed fewer civil rights than ordinary citizens. They must obey orders as if in a military organization. Military-style discipline is taken to extremes to teach unquestioning obedience to superiors. In 1981 a Toronto police constable was punished for allowing his moustache to grow an eighth of an inch too long, and another for eating a pear in public (*Toronto Star*, April 25, 1982).

Frustrated by denial of the privileges and lifestyle of the people whose dirty-work he or she carries out, the police constable often turns the resulting aggression on those sections of the public who provide likely targets. Constables demand more than civility from such targets. They demand meek deference. Anyone who acts the "wise guy" is likely to get hurt. As a former Toronto policeman put it:

> You could ask a kid who was loitering what he was doing and he would say "I don't even have to tell you my name." He was right, he didn't. But it was hard on a cop. . . . It wasn't surprising to me that some policemen would take that kid into an alley and slap him in the mouth. I didn't condone it, but it worked (*Toronto Star*, October 26, 1974).

The combination of resentment of dirty work, authoritarian organization, and aggression directed towards likely police targets, is especially destructive when the police resort to 'deadly force'—use of their guns.

Police in Canada kill several times as many citizens in the course of duty as police are killed by civilians. More significantly, the civilian is much more likely to get killed if a member of a target group. Tagaki (1979) found that a disproportionate number of blacks and native Indians were killed by police. Yet even when a civilian is shot in the back while fleeing, and thus obviously not in self-defence by the constable, the constable is often not even charged. If charged, he or she is rarely punished (Lee 1982).

In summary, there is ample evidence if we care to look for it, that police do not get their power from the "rule of law". Rather, they use law as an expression of power, especially on behalf of more powerful groups in society. This conclusion is by no means limited to Marxists or materialists. For example, the structural-functionalist sociologists who have studied police, have sometimes recognized, in the words of Westley (1969:13):

> The police function is to support and enforce the interests of the dominant
> political, social and economic interests of the town, and only incidentally
> to enforce the law.

Berkley, not a Marxist or conflict theorist, concludes that "the police, more than any other institution, exhibit an antagonism, both in concept and practice, to some of the basic precepts of a democratic society" (1969:1). The conclusions of a Canadian non-Marxist sociologist will be discussed later.

HIGHLIGHT

1. The police exercise a considerable amount of discretion in their apprehension of suspected wrongdoers and in their decisions concerning whether or not to lay charges.
2. The discretionary power of the police is not always exercised in an equal fashion. Working class people, minorities, gays, etc. receive harsher treatment at police hands than others.
3. Police forces have grown, faster than the population. The growth has been accompanied by demands for increased police powers.
4. The explanation for demands for an increase in police power should not be sought in the personalities of individual police officers but in the social structure.
5. In general, the power of the police is exercised more in the interests of the powerful than the weak in our society.

The Role Of The Courts

"First you'll need a good lawyer." Most modern court procedure—to say nothing of case law—is so complex that few Canadians could successfully argue their own case. Individuals may begin with the illusion that their lawyer will argue their case with as much zeal and concern as they would. They may be surprised when their lawyer explains that many of the "facts" they consider vitally important will not count for much in court, and that some of the arguments they might want to make could do them more harm than good. "If you say that they'll hang you!". As the proverb has it, what happens in court is law, not justice. How the case fits the precedents, especially any recent and relevant decisions, matters more than the details.

As an experienced "expert witness' when a sociologist's testimony is wanted, I could continue to be amazed, if such things amazed me any longer, at the procrastinating, disorganized, lackadaisical attitude of many lawyers. Many seem to wait to the last minute to begin preparing a case. They always give the explanation of having too many other cases to ever catch up. At the early appearances of the client in court, the lawyer may not show up at all. He/she sends a student apprentice instead. The distress and anxiety of the clients is painful to see.

The theory is that when the trial begins in earnest, the equivalent of Clarence Darrow or Edward Greenspan will be there, ready to defend without qualification, guilty or not. As Edward Greenspan, one of Canada's most famous and successful criminal lawyers put it (1980):

> An advocate in the discharge of his duty knows but one person in all the world, and that person is his client. To save that client by all means and expedients, and at all hazards and costs to other persons...is his first and only duty...

The theory of the adversary system is that the defence lawyer "has a professional obligation to place obstacles in the path of truth" if the truth will go against you (Strick 1977:15). A lawyer cannot lie to the court. But he does not have to tell the court that his client is lying. Character assassination of hostile witnesses, trick questions in cross-examination, and dramatic flights of oratory, are all legitimate.

If the client is still found guilty the lawyer's job is, theoretically, to get the least penalty. "Taking the pre-sentence reporter to lunch" so that his recommendations to the judge are softened may help "more than discovering a 1952 precedent where a like offender got a fine instead of five years in jail" (Greenspan 1980:265).

The result of processes such as the above is the mythology of the defence lawyer, as portrayed by great defence lawyers, as well as the television and press. Canada's top lawyers are "high rollers" (*Macleans*, Sept 17, 1979). "Make your one phone call count by retaining one of Canada's top ten" advised *Canadian Magazine* (July 19, 1975). Hire the "radical among the pinstripes (*Globe and Mail*, March 28, 1981). Retain the "Gladiator of the courts," a Vancouver lawyer, who defended 63 clients charged with murder and only two were hanged" (*Globe and Mail*, October 24, 1981). Success as a defence lawyer comes big. Toronto's

Clayton Ruby asked the city for $1500 a day. "I didn't ask for a raise...I told them...I'm not an employee I'm a lawyer" (March 27, 1980). Greenspan, at 35 "has it all" including "the live-in help tucked away in one wing of the house" (*Macleans*, Sept. 17, 1979).

Plea Bargaining

Few Canadians can afford Canada's top ten defence lawyers, or even the top hundred. The lower the client's social class, the more likely his lawyer will suggest that he plead guilty to a lesser charge in plea bargaining. It works like this.

The police are rated effective according to the proportion of arrests which lead to convictions. Thus police will lay several charges. Some are more serious than others. The practice is so obvious and pervasive it has even been condemned by outspoken judges (Judge Vanek, *Toronto Sun*, Jan 25, 1975). It has other advantages for the police which assure its continued use. It enables them to:

> [Charge] everyone possible with everything possible as a means of maxim-
> izing the chances for convictions, to stamp a more major "criminal"
> identity on the accused,...as justification for future surveillance, and to
> maximize their productive appearances within the police organization
> (Ericson 1981:171).

In order to process their clients, lawyers like to stay on reasonably good terms with the police. This means pleasing the police by encouraging a proportion of clients to plead guilty to something. "Good counsel will plead his people guilty" (A detective to Ericson 1981:193). In a survey of 724 defendants, Blumberg (1967) found that it was the *defence* lawyer who made the first suggestion of a guilty plea in most cases.

The client is not present during actual plea bargaining. He/she is told the "deal" later. He/she can take it or leave it. But the police are often present. Ericson (1981:196) had the opportunity to tape-record a reveal-ing bargaining session between a defence lawyer, the crown prosecutor, and the detective who laid the charges. The crown agrees: "OK. So the robbery is now going to be a theft over." (That is, a lesser charge of theft over $200 will replace the charge of armed robbery.) Crown and defence agree in advance to keep it out of court that there was a weapon involved (See *Globe and Mail*, October 25, 1974). The deal is that the client will plead guilty to theft. This stance will save the crown and the court time and trouble in proving their case, to say nothing of the time and effort of the detective in collecting the necessary evidence.

The police present may even suggest what sentence they would like to see so that the crown may be guided accordingly in demanding sentence from the judge. The client sees and hears none of the bargaining. In addition, there is no record kept, unless a rare sociologist happens to be doing a study! In court, the client goes through the charade of pleading guilty "without any promises having been made."

Thus, in about 85 to 90 percent of all cases (varying with the legal jurisdiction and level of court), the client never gets a trial, with evidence, witnesses, cross-examination. The "trial" goes on without him, and without a court recorder, in a deal behind closed doors. In the United States it is fairly common for the judge also to be involved in the plea bargaining. In Canada high courts frown on this. In 1982 the Ontario Court of Appeal rapped a Supreme Court judge for participating in a three-hour "haggling session" with the crown and defence lawyers (*Globe and Mail*, April 27, 1982).

The extremes of plea bargaining demonstrate what a myth the "advocate. . . . who knows but one person in the world" is for most clients. In a 1980 case in Buffalo, the accused accepted a bargain and pleaded guilty to manslaughter. The irony is that the man supposedly killed was alive at the time, and the court knew it (*Buffalo Courier*, Dec. 5, 1980)! The judge refused to explain how he could accept such a deal, but the defence lawyer explained: "The offer the district attorney made was the only one available, so we took it."

Perhaps the most extreme case in Canada in recent years involved three friends who returned from a Jamaica holiday with three pounds of marijuana. They were caught at customs and charged with importing. For this offence the law requires the judge to give a *minimum seven year* sentence. However, the crown's case was weak on evidence, so the prosecution offered one of the three friends a deal. Plead guilty to mere *possession* of marijuana, with a light sentence assured. In exchange, testify against the other two collaborators. She agreed. The other two friends then, through their lawyers, asked the crown for the same deal. They would plead guilty to possession, thus saving the crown the trouble of going to trial.

But the prosecutor decided to make a lesson of the pair, and went to trial. Despite an appeal to a high court, the two unfortunates were sentenced to seven years and ten years (*Globe and Mail*, May 14, 1980; October 17, 1981). Ironically, major newspaper editors slammed this outrage of "justice" not for the excessive sentence or for the dealing of justice, but because it was 'unfair' to offer different deals to participants in the same crime.

Those from a lower class background are most likely to plead guilty, without even retaining a lawyer. In a study of use of lawyers, 76 percent of upper class respondents had used a lawyer at least once, 64 percent of the upper middle class had done so, but only 52 percent of the lower middle class, and only 36 percent of the lower class (Aubert 1969). These figures are the exact opposite of the proportion of each social class likely to be found in prison (Friedland 1975:28). A Canadian study found upper class accused three times as likely to contact a lawyer as the lowest class (Friedland *ibid*).

A costly lawyer helps because he has more credibility with the judge (Greenspan 1980). He is also likely to work a better deal with the prosecutor (Tepperman 1977:164). The lowest class are most likely to be persuaded to plead guilty, not only because they cannot afford top lawyers, but also because even when they do retain a lawyer, the lawyer is likely to realize that collecting his fee won't be easy. Thus a minimum of time and effort should be invested in the case. By pleading "hopeless cases" guilty, lawyers save their pull with the judges and crown prosecutors for clients who can afford an extended court battle....and the lawyer's fees.

Police Witnesses In Court

Most readers will be aware that the testimony of a police constable counts for more in court than that of a citizen. But few may realize the extent to which police are willing to lie in court. Police are especially ready to lie to cover for fellow officers (Wesley 1970; Barker and Roebuck 1973:15). "I thought I had an obligation to cover for buddy officers by lying," a Toronto policeman explained. (*Toronto Star*, Sept. 23, 1978). "You lie, first to survive, then, as fear and guilt blunt conscience, to get ahead..." reported former Mountie Jack Ramsay (1978:92). You lie to 'cover your ass' admits former cop-turned-sociologist Niederhoffer (1975:6). "Police lying is the most pervasive of all abuses," concludes Chevigny (1969:141). And the most corrosive to any hope of justice, concluded Judge Morand who found that police lied to his inquiry (Morand, 1976). Vincent (1979:105) quotes a Windsor policeman's attempt to justify frustration leading to perjury:

> We're just a bunch of frustrated blue knights. No matter how hard you work, crime still seems to pay, and they get the good-looking dolls...

Judges understand police frustration, and are reluctant to accuse a police witness of perjury, or even express doubt about police testimony. Few judges want the reputation of copbasher. At best, they will suggest that the officer might possibly be mistaken.

The rules of law in Canada encourage the police to use unlawful means to achieve their ends. Contrary to the myth created by American television among Canadian viewers, police evidence obtained by illegal methods is quite admissible in Canadian courts. "If evidence is deemed by the court to be relevant,...a judge cannot reject it...even if it is obtained by the authorities through fraud, deceit, or even physical violence" (Queen vs. Wray, Supreme Court of Canada, 1970, 4.C.C.C.C. 1).

Not until April 17, 1982, when the new Charter of Rights became law, but is yet to survive its tests in court, did Canadian police have to warn suspects of their legal right to retain a lawyer and to say nothing. It will be several years before the courts make it clear whether illegal evidence is now "inadmissable" in Canadian courts. But in any event, American sociologists have found that court decisions requiring the police to advise suspects of their rights, and preventing police from introducing illegally obtained evidence in court, have not significantly affected police methods or success (Ericson 1981:218ff).

A pessimistic analysis of the role of police in using law as a weapon of power—including getting away with whatever unlawful methods they find 'necessary'—leads some observers to the conclusion that there is little likelihood of reforming the system. The police will "always innovate in response to change in the rules. . . . Our analysis is that the law does not rule. Rather detectives use law and other rules to control the process" (Ericson 1981:219).

Monarchs in the Palace of Justice

Most citizens in modern constitutional democracies are under the impression that the divine right of kings vanished long ago. Not so. It merely moved from the royal palace to the palace of justice. The modern high court judge rules like a king. "May I approach the bench, your lordship?" "With all due respect, your lordship. . ." Even in lower courts a magistrate may order a mere observer or witness held for the day, simply for talking out of order. Five Toronto women were sentenced to three days in jail for refusing to stand when a judge left court for lunch (*Toronto Star*, Feb. 14, 1976).

The judge is historically a representative of the king, though few now travel on "circuit" to hold their "assizes." The judge still sits elevated above all, bewigged and robed (in higher courts). No one may argue with a judge. He and he alone, or very rarely she, rules the courtroom. In Canada a judge or magistrate may summarily sentence anyone to prison for up to ninety days for contempt of court (C.C.C. 636:2). Until 1969, the sentence could be up to two years!

Even a federal cabinet minister may be called before a judge because he has unwisely criticised a judge's findings. Consumer Affairs Minister, Andre Ouellet, was so disgusted that a judge had found certain corporations not guilty of price fixing that he called the judgment "silly. . . a complete shock. . . a disgrace." Faced with the prospect of prison, he was grateful for the opportunity to merely apologize in court.

The power of "contempt of court" extends far beyond stifling the opposition to the judge on the bench (Roberts 1979:22). It is used as a device for preventing public discussion of controversial actions by the powerful. Newspaper and other media controversy is suppressed on the grounds that "this matter is now before the courts."

Through the ritual and formality of courtroom procedure we are mystified into believing that judges are merely administrators and interpreters of law; that law is above all, and the judge merely a servant of the law (Becker and Murray 1971:xix). But the judge is much more like a ruler than a mere interpreter. He/she decides what evidence will be admitted, what witnesses will be heard, perhaps even what lawyers will speak to the court. The judge also decides whether media coverage will be allowed, and whether objections to the proceedings by either side will be allowed or overruled. The judges rulings are final, and non-negotiable.

Certainly lower court rulings may be appealed to higher courts. But the process ends with the Supreme Court. Here the judges have imperial power indeed. In any event, appeals to the rulings and decisions of lower court judges do not involve retrying the case. The Supreme Court does not hear the evidence and witnesses all over again. It merely hears legal presentations by the two sides...usually for a matter of less than an hour...then goes away to read the precedents. (*The Brethren*, Woodward and Armstrong 1979 is highly recommended for an inside view of [American] Supreme Court processes).

The judge's power comes first, and law is generally a weapon and resource used by power. Hogarth (1971:366) found that Canadian law "offers little guidance or control over magistrates' behavior....Those who found the law restrictive, resorted to a number of devices which enabled them to achieve their objectives without fear of [successful appeal in a higher court]. Among these devices were informal agreements with crown prosecutors and postponement of cases until conditions changed."

Judges in Canada are careful to hide their power behind a mystique of robe and ritual built on elaborate secrecy. It is rare indeed for the public to catch a glimpse of judges at work. It is rarer still to see judges in conflict with each other. Yet the present secrecy is not considered sufficient. The former chief justice of Ontario has called for rules preventing any witness before the Judicial Council from ever disclosing their testimony outside Council (*Globe and Mail*, May 3, 1979). The Council wants to expand its control to include more administrative features and budgetary power (*Globe and Mail*, October 2, 1981).

Above all, the mystique persuades us that judges are "above politics." This myth persists despite studies showing that the former political attachment of a judge is often a better predictor of his/her decisions in cases, than the facts of the case (Hogarth, 1971; Nagel 1962). In the United States the mystique that judges are above politics is more difficult to maintain. Many lower level judges are elected. However, high courts are appointed, and lower court judges, once elected, tend to stay in for life.

In Canada, it is more obvious that tomorrow's judges are probably yesterday's politicians, especially retired or failed politicians. A Liberal Member of Parliament, H. Chappell, explained the process:

> Someone who wants to become a judge puts his name forward to an MP, either directly or through a friend. Then the person seeks support by way of letters, personal interviews...There are exceptions; there are well known leaders of the bar where a request comes to them directly, but I would say they do not exceed, counting both the high court and the county court judges, more than about 5% (*Globe and Mail*, October 12, 1971).

Judges are expected to be grateful to the party that appointed them. A member of an opposition party may be offered an appointment to the bench if he will resign his seat in Parliament, and open it to a by-election at a time propitious to the ruling party. As for the Supreme Court itself, it is well known to be divided between "left wing" and "right wing" (*Globe and Mail*, June 6, 1981). The left wing, of course, is never far from centre.

Equal Justice For All

As we noted earlier, one of the central myths of law is that it applies equally to every citizen. Justice is portrayed as being blind to the special privileges of any race or creed. The capacity of legal institutions to twist words so as to serve *power* on the one hand, and give the illusion of legitimacy on the other, is nowhere better illustrated than in the myth of equality of law.

The best opportunity for a Canadian to see this word-twisting is to visit a trial on a *bawdy house* charge. There have been a number of such trials in recent years in Edmonton, Hamilton, Toronto, Montreal and other centres. A 'bawdy house' is a place to which resort is had for the purposes of prostitution or for the purpose of acts of indecency. The latter is a perfect example of the "too fast" crime with no speed limit posted. Whether a particular act is indecent (for example, three consenting adults having 'group sex') is determined by the court assessing whether it is offensive to Contemporary Canadian Community Standards (CCCS). But what is the specific CCCS applicable in, say, Regina, concerning two married couples swapping partners in a sex club?

The judge must decide. Contrary to another myth, this offence cannot be taken to a jury. The judge will often be assisted by both crown and defence calling *expert witnesses*, such as sociologists, psychologists and even psychiartists to testify as to what acts would or would not offend the morals of the Contemporary Canadian Community. It is CCCS which is the issue, not the local morality of Regina. The Canadian legal establishment urgently wants to maintain the myth that the law applies equally to all citizens of Canada, and does not vary from one community to another.

A Canadian community is obviously a fiction. Canada is perhaps made up of many local communities. There is no factual sense in which Quebec and British Columbia, Toronto and Fredericton, native Indians and Hamilton steelworkers can be said to belong to one community. A high court has called CCCS "sociologically naive" but a necessary "legal fiction". As an experienced expert witness at such trials, the author has observed everyone—defence, crown and judge—all agree that there is no such thing as CCCS. But everyone is required to pretend there is, because the law requires that this legal fiction exist. So it does, in the reality that people are fined and sent to jail for offending it. Only a few hundred Canadians suffer each year from this fiction. However, their suffering is no fiction.

Many millions of Americans suffered for decades from an American legal fiction, perhaps history's most infamous example of the twisting of words to make law meet the needs of established power: the legal doctrine of separate but equal. The American civil war had ostensibly ended the inferior status of American blacks. But by the end of the nineteenth century the former white establishment was fully restored to power in the South. As a result, an all-white Supreme Court, appointed by an all-white government, ruled that blacks and whites did not have to go to the same schools. If equal schools were provided for each race, such schools could be separate—one for blacks, another for whites. It was not until 1957 that political realities of power in America forced another Supreme Court to strike down this doctrine. It ruled that separate facilities were not equal treatment of American citizens. But for sixty years the powers-that-be used legal fiction to achieve their political goals.

In Canada, a major fiction in law is that our native Indian peoples are nations in their own right who signed treaties with the Canadian nation represented by the Queen. In those treaties, Indians accepted the defence of law and order in their nations by Canadian troops, the RCMP. Thus an American wild west scenario, where the only good Indian was a dead Indian, was not repeated in Canada.

But over the years, the situation has changed. Today the proportion of native Indians imprisoned in the four western provinces far exceed their proportion in the overall population (Nettler 1978:144). Natives form a median proportion of two thirds of the total western prison population.

The efforts of the legal establishment to maintain the fiction that Canadian law is blind to race are aided, in this case (as in the case of American blacks: Williams 1980) by the efforts of some sociologists. For example, Hagan (1974) argues that "when legal variables are held constant, differences in sentences [between white and native defendants] are minimal." Bienvenue and Latif (1975) found that native

Indians were greatly overrepresented in 6000 sentences in Winnipeg courts, but argue that no discrimination existed. They suggest that Indians land in jail proportionately more often than whites because Indians prefer to go to jail. They consider it "a shared experience, a chance to rest . . . get better food and meet old friends." Native Indians do not find this line of reasoning very amusing.

Few sociologists are willing to argue that ability to get bail has nothing to do with social class. There is something too obvious about the fact that ability to raise money from property increases with ownership of property. What many readers will not realize is that despite bail reform in Canada—which police have bitterly opposed, arguing that criminals are allowed back on the street to commit more crimes—the fact is that at any given time, between 40 and 50 percent of the inmates of city jails are not serving their time. They are waiting for trial. Though mythologically innocent until proven guilty, they are already in prison.

A study conducted by the Ontario Ministry of Corrections in 1979 found that of 23 369 defendants held in custody for trial over that year, 17 000 were eventually sentenced to *no prison term* when they came to trial. They were either found not guilty, or sentenced only to a fine. But all of these people had also, already, served prison terms. "There's no reason why most of those people could not have been out on bail while awaiting trial," the Minister concluded (*Globe and Mail*, April 11, 1980). Ironically, the minister's argument was not based on fair play before the law, but monetary concern: "Even if a third had been released on bail, that's a phenomenal . . . saving to taxpayers, at $50 per person per day [to keep them in jail]."

Waiting for trial in jail or being out on bail makes a considerable difference, not merely to one's freedom of action and freedom from anxiety of confinement, but also a difference in *the outcome of the trial.* Friedland (1969) found in a study of Toronto trials that the accused out on bail can continue to work. As a consequence they can afford a better lawyer. In addition, they have an opportunity to shop around for a lawyer suitable to their case. The defendant can also personally recruit helpful witnesses and assemble relevant information for his lawyer.

The defendant out on bail is also more resistant to the seductions of plea bargaining. This is why. Suppose an accused has already spent the average of about five months in jail before coming to trial. (The average is high because of backlog in large urban courts). The crown offers his lawyer a deal. "We'll drop the major charge if you will persuade your client to plead guilty to the lesser charge. We'll ask for a sentence of three months in jail, with time already served in jail to be counted. Your client can walk into court on the day of trial, plead guilty, and walk out a free man."

If the lawyer is one of the sort whose names are frequently passed about by word of mouth among jailmates, rather than a higher-priced but more effective counsel, and if he values and wants to preserve a good relationship with the crown, jail personnel, and the courts by saving everyone the time of going to trial, gathering evidence, taking police witnesses from their jobs to appear in court, etc., he is very likely to persuade his client to take the deal. What can the client lose? If he insists on going to trial he may wait several more months as the crown asks for remands to continue gathering evidence and prepare its case. Then he is going to trial on the *major* charge, with a sentence of perhaps a year or more. So he will still have time left to serve. Moreover, many trials are not finished in one day. Nonetheless they cannot necessarily be put over for continuation the next day. Some other case has already been booked in. The judge must look at his calendar to find his next open day. It may be two weeks to a month away. The trial is put over, and the client continues to wait—still unconvicted—in his jail cell. Finally, it has been found that clients who appear in court looking well, refreshed, at ease—in short, 'normal'—are more likely to impress the judge than those who arrive in court from a jail cell (Tepperman 1977:162). Thus, in many respects, being out on bail is a great advantage, but one which is directly related to property ownership and social class.

It is generally agreed among judges that those accused who insist on putting the state to the trouble and expense of a trial should, if found guilty, receive a stiffer penalty than if they had pleaded guilty and saved all the trouble. In addition, those in jail who turn down a bargain and insist on trial are 20 percent more likely to be found guilty than those on bail who turn down the same bargain (Friedland 1969:112).

If social class makes the law less than equal for the accused, what about the other side of the bench? What are the chances that Canadian judges will have social backgrounds in proportion to the population in each social class? Not very good. Eighty percent of the judges in an Ontario study came from the professional, managerial and wealthy classes (Hogarth 1971; Tepperman 1977). But well under a third of the population are in these classes.

The Courts as Growth Industry

Like the police apparatus of social control, the court system is steadily growing in Canada. In Ontario, the case load has grown from 2.8 million per year in the 1970s to almost four million cases per year. Of course two thirds of this load are non-serious provincial offences—traffic, driving, liquor, and so forth. The majority of these cases are pled guilty through paperwork. But the court load also continued to burgeon, and the provinces have been unwilling to finance expansion of courtrooms and members of the bench at the same pace.

The powers-that-be are less interested in paying for more courts than more police or, as we shall see, for more prisons. It is police and prison more than court which act to keep the subordinate classes in their place. The courts are more important for a facade of legitimacy than for real control. In cases of "emergency power" they are dispensed with altogether. During periods of "military law" when power comes out from behind the facade of law, military tribunals and rapid execution replace the slower process of justice. In Canada, when the War Measures Act is proclaimed, as in 1970, police may arrest and jail and may hold suspects without charge and without appearing before a judge to fix a date for trial, for up to ninety days.

Immense increases in the case load on one hand, and reluctance to finance judges and courtrooms on the other, have inevitably led to a lengthy backlog of cases in larger Canadian centres. It may now take many months, and even several years, for a case to come to trial. A judge cited to the press a case which took four and a half years (*Toronto Star*, June 29, 1981): "In the meantime, [the accused] went to university and got a degree and was working."

The judges must work a lot harder too, to keep up with the load. In Toronto, in 1970, the average caseload per judge per year was 900 cases. This figure represents a considerable number of lives to be affected by the judge's decision each day in court. But in 1979 the average caseload per judge has risen to 3000 a year. (*Toronto Star*, March 16, 1979). How much attention can a judge pay to more than ten accused per day in court? Some judges have even developed a vestige of class consciousness, and gone "on strike". They have refused to set more trial dates until more judges were appointed (*Globe and Mail*, June 29, 1981)!

Alice in Court

During the trial of the knave of hearts for stealing the tarts in Alice in Wonderland, we are told that the execution comes first, then the trial, then the charges. Cressey (1980:63) suggests similar follies in Canadian court: "Consider the possibility that the judge first decides what the sentence shall be, then picks an offence consistent with that decision, then finds the defendant guilty of it." An example might be a college student accused of theft of a school trophy. The judge finds the accused a likeable and decent young man, and decides the offence must have been a prank. A few days in jail will be enough to teach the student a lesson. The usual sentence for the actual offence, breaking and entering, would be much too harsh. The judge looks for an offence which will produce the desired sentence, and settles on public mischief.

Examples are manifold in Canadian law. Cabinet members, we have learned in recent years, do not forge documents, they "sign another man's name." Mounties do not break and enter, they "fail to obtain a search warrant" (Mann and Lee 1979:83). The wealthy do not steal, but they may "unlawfully evade taxes." When caught, they are rarely sentenced for fraud or misappropriation of funds. Instead they are often quietly offered the opportunity to make restitution. A lawyer for the Department of Revenue explained that the department was interested in getting its money, not turning respectable people into criminals (*Globe and Mail*, May 19, 1976). Fewer than 20 percent of those found guilty in court of tax fraud and similar offences get prison sentences, though the average offence leading to conviction involves about $200 000. The average car theft or burglary involves far less loss. However, 90 percent of those convicted go to prison, for an average term of 52 months (Centre for Criminal Research, 1975).

Allan Fotheringham (*Maclean's Magazine*, April 7, 1980) discussed the fate of Clarence Campbell, president of the National Hockey League. He had been convicted of bribing a senator for a government franchise in airport shops. The transaction involved 5000 shares at $1 each which were later sold for $20 each, a tidy profit. Campbell was sentenced to one day—five hours—in jail, and a $25 000 fine. The NHL had already covered the fine by providing Campbell with $50 000 for his legal expenses. Fotheringham compares the fate of Jean Parrot, president of the postal workers' union. He defied a government back-to-work order during a postal strike. Though the judge found him "an honest and dedicated man" he sent him to jail for two months.

Being the knave of hearts, compared to the king of hearts, is important before the court! Tepperman found that the lower social classes were far more likely to be convicted during the Great Depression years than higher social classes. Conviction rates of the latter changed very little in those hard times (1977:176). Frankel (1972) found that among 502 persons convicted of income tax fraud, generally a crime of the well-to-do, only 19 percent were sent to prison, with an average term of three months. But among 3791 persons convicted of auto theft, 63 percent got prison, with an average of seven months. Delinquency rates are also well known to vary according to the social class of the area in which the youths are picked up by police (Chambliss 1973).

Any reading of the daily papers will underline the inequality of law. "Crimes pays handsomely for Watergate authors." After serving comfortable sentences in special federal prisons with minimum security, swimming pools, golf courses and private bedrooms, the Watergate convicts are accumulating millions of dollars in lecture fees and royalties (*Toronto Star*, June 24, 1977). At the other end of the scale, people who have already served their time, but have no money or friends outside to help them get official action, may remain in prison *after their sentence*, against their will, because of bureaucratic bungling.

Even the superintendent of Toronto's east detention centre (jail) sympathized in the press with an inmate who went on a hunger strike to get out, after his sentence was complete. The bureaucratic problem was a rule that the convict had to be transferred back to the jail where he was originally confined, for release. Personnel and transportation to move him were not available. Of course it was unthinkable to free him and ask him to take a bus back. Better still, telex the release information from one jail to the other!

The police who have served the interests of the powerful may never come to trial. "Extortion charges against Mounties stayed again" (*Globe and Mail*, October 20, 1981). "Attorney General Roy McMurtry believes activities in which the men involved were wrong but has decided it would not be in the public interest to allow the two RCMP officers to be charged." (In the *public* interest?)

Tepperman (1977:159) concludes from his study of crime control in Canada: "the evidence suggests that whatever discretion is available will be used in ways ultimately damaging to poor people." Ericson cites McBarnet (1979:39):

> Legality requires equality; the law discriminates against the homeless and jobless. Legality requires that officials be governed by law; the law is based on post hoc decisions. Legality requires that each case be judged on its facts; the law makes previous convictions grounds for defining behaviour as an offence. Legality requires incriminating evidence as a basis for arrest and search; the law allows arrest and search in order to establish it.

The situation has not changed much from 1822, when Edward Livingston, a penal official, wrote (Inciardia 1980:36):

> Everywhere, with but few exceptions, the interest of the many has been.... sacrificed to the power of the few. Everywhere penal laws have been framed to support this power.

His observation was confirmed by the President's Commission on Law Enforcement (1976:pp. C:151):

> The poor are arrested more often, convicted more often, sentenced more harshly, rehabilitated less successfully....

HIGHLIGHT

1. Informal relations among police, lawyers and judges are frequently more important in determining the outcome of a case than its merits.
2. Plea bargaining is a process whereby defendants agree to plead guilty to a lesser charge. The prosecution is thereby not required to present a potentially costly case on the basis of possibly dubious evidence. And the court can process more offenders in a shorter time. The defendants, if they are innocent, are the losers in the process.
3. The lower classes more than others are likely to plea bargain. Usually, they are unable to raise bail, or hire the best lawyers.
4. Through their ability to find individuals in contempt of court, judges can rule courtrooms in dictatorial fashion.
5. There has been a drastic increase in the case load of judges in recent years.

6. The working class receives harsher treatment in the courts—in terms of sentences, etc.—than the other classes.

Prison, the Lawless Jungle

It is profoundly ironic that when citizens break the law, we condemn them to live in our most lawless environment, the penitentiary.

Canadians should be deeply ashamed of our prisons, we are told by our members of Parliament. A committee of seventeen MPs representing all political parties toured our prisons. It interviewed administrators, guards and inmates. It concluded *unanimously* (*Hansard*, June 7, 1977):

> A crisis exists in the Canadian penitentiary system. It can only be met by immediate...large scale reforms. It is imperative that the Solicitor General act...as a matter of utmost urgency.

The unanimous report found some cells not fit for animals. It condemned systematic harassment of prisoners, including "waking prisoners at night, delay or adulteration of meals, locking up ten minutes before the end of a movie or sporting event on television, delay in summoning an inmate when a visitor arrives, cutting shower time, insulting denials of equipment." Prisoners were found to have been hog-tied, beaten, and tear-gassed in their cells.

Harassment of this kind is unpleasant, sometimes even cruel, but it does not make prison a lawless jungle. What does, is the fear of death or severe wounding by fellow inmates.

The greatest irony of all is that the lives most at stake in the penitentiary are those of former law enforcement officials. For their own protection they must almost always be held in solitary confinement, away from possible harm by other criminals whom they helped to send to prison.

At Archambault penitentiary, following six murders of prisoners in six months, guards told reporters "they knew who did [the murders] but the prisoners who witnessed the slayings refuse to testify. "Small wonder, if the witnesses must point the finger, but go on living in the same prison. Warden Lemarier explained: "I can't blame an inmate who won't talk. If he did, and somehow he wasn't killed here, he would eventually be killed on the outside."

Our local prisons are no more admirable than the penitentiaries. When Toronto's old Don jail was closed in 1978, it had been condemned as a firetrap by twenty grand juries. The Toronto Humane Society was looking for new quarters for its dog pound, and asked a contractor to estimate the cost of renovating the jailhouse, which the government was willing to sell. The estimate to make the jailhouse *fit for dogs* was seven million dollars. Because the old jail was terribly overcrowded, two new detention centres were built on the outskirts of Toronto. In 1983 these new centres, plus the new Don jail downtown, are so overcrowded that two or three prisoners are sleeping on the floors of cells designed for one. The guards are threatening to strike because of the increased danger to their lives from an inevitable outbreak of violence or prison riot.

Canada has one of the highest rates of imprisonment per capita in the western world (Grosman 1980). Our system is also one of the most expensive per prisoner, despite the misery and overcrowding.

There is one staff person in our penitentiary system for every inmate. "Canada is the only country in the world, the entire world, that employs more personnel in its system than it has inmates." (Minutes of parliamentary subcommittee on the penitentiary system, Dec. 7, 1976:52. At the time there were 9429 staff for 9374 inmates). It cost the Canadian public $17 515 per prisoner per year in 1976, not including the capital cost of buildings. The current 1982 cost including buildings is estimated at about $30 000 per inmate per year.

Jails cost almost as much. Jobson (1980) found that the annual cost per prisoner bed was $16 257, again not allowing for capital costs. A typical prisoner guilty of break and enter (193 in his sample) cost the taxpayer $3163 while serving his sentence. But the average break-and-enter caused a loss of only $300 to the homeowner affected, plus an average of $50 in damage. Most break and enter is by amateur criminals usually under twenty-one (Jobson 1980:81). Most home-owners, 80 percent, would rather have had restitution of their loss than prison for the thief. This would certainly have been cheaper for the taxpayer too.

Canadian prisons and penitentiaries are operated by ministries euphemistically titled "Correctional." Guards are correctional officers. But few indeed are the inmates whose lives are corrected by a prison sentence. The rate of recidivism in our prisons is never less than 60 percent and often tops 80 percent. The United Church general council concluded (August 1977):

> Our prisons are clogged to a surfeit, not because Canada is a more crime-ridden society than any other, but because we resort to prison far too often for crimes which do not warrant a prison term... Our prison sentences are among the most severe in the western industrialized countries...

It is reasonably safe to say that there is not a scholar left in Canada in the field of penology who argues that our prisons rehabilitate prisoners.

What, then, is the role of prisons in the social control apparatus of our society? Again, it can be argued that historical origins are an important source of insight. When prison became a major form of punishment for lawbreakers in the nineteenth century, it was modelled on the older *workhouse.* This was an institution dating from Elizabethan times, in which the poor and unemployed were confined and forced to labor, usually on contract at cheap rates to local manufacturers and merchants. The first North American modern penitentiary at Auburn, New York, was directly modelled on the British workhouse (Greenberg 1981).

The intention was to compel penitence in the inmate for having become idle and mischievous by teaching him the value of labor. Prison rather than hanging was by no means a humanitarian improvement as some later romantic historians have claimed. It was a means of getting some production out of the no-goods and do-nothings of society (Tagaki 1981). Industrialists were often able to arrange cheap labor through the pen system (Greenberg 1981). However, the rise of modern trade unions brought demands for an end to this unfair competition. The unions were sometimes supported by manufacturers unfortunate enough not to be located near a penitentiary, and thus suffering from unfair competition from companies who had this advantage.

The Canadian public is sometimes persuaded to think that our penitentiaries are teaching inmates useful trades they can work at when they are freed. But the previously noted parliamentary committee found that the trades program in the pens is a farce. The tools and equipment are obsolete compared to what the worker would be expected to use outside. More importantly, the certificates of training awarded for completion of prison trades training are not even recognized by the Canadian government's own Manpower offices, much less by employers, as evidence of skills in these trades (McNeil 1978:109).

If prisons do not reform criminals, perhaps they at least deter citizens from committing crimes and thus risking unpleasant prison terms. There is little evidence, as witnessed by the recidivism rate, that prison deters those who have already committed crimes and gone to prison. In many other cases, there is little evidence that prison deters the *first* crime. The most serious crimes (murder, manslaughter) are usually one-in-a-lifetime crimes directed at someone the killer already knew. In the case of property crimes, increases in the crime rates during periods of recession and unemployment suggest that economic policies might be a more effective deterrent.

Another role of prison is simple retribution: an eye for an eye. But prison is a more productive method in modern society for punishing people than putting out their eye, cutting off the hand, as is still done with thieves in some Islamic countries, branding, or otherwise assaulting the criminal's body. Prison produces work for law-abiding citizens. It is often the only important industry in small towns where most of our penitentiaries are located. It employs large numbers of poorly educated, relatively unskilled labor as guards, clerks, etc.

War is not an entirely bad thing for profit-making corporations. This is true even of those on the defeated side, as the corporations of Germany and Japan have demonstrated. Could crime, and the continued war on crime, be at least partly a good thing of the owners and controllers of property who control our society through police, courts, prisons and law?

There's an old saying that war is "a rich man's war but a poor man's fight." Is this true of the war on crime? The statistics seem to confirm this.

Prison, like war, does not recruit proportionately from all social classes, or levels of education, or racial background. Neither the Canadian penitentiary service nor provincial corrections ministries keep records on the social class of inmates. But they do record education, which is some indicator of class. Forty three percent of inmates in provincial prisons in 1978 had a grade eight education or less (Correctional Institution Statistics, Canada). In federal penitentiaries in the same year, 34 percent had grade eight or less. Only 4 percent had even one year of college. These figures suggest that it is the lowest social classes who are most often in prison.

Native Indians form about 8 percent of our population, but form 40 percent to 60 percent, depending on the province, of our prison and jail populations. They are also more harshly treated: "In 1976, 54 percent of all native inmates were held in maximum security as against 31 percent of non-natives" (Parliament subcommittee, Minutes of March 1, 1977:29).

The original concept of penitentiary as a place where the idle and mischievous might learn the value of labor has now been totally reversed. The law Reform Commission has reported that about half of all prisoners in Canadian prisons are there because they cannot pay their fine (*Working Paper 11*, 6). But while there, they are unable to work off the fine to the state, much less work in a useful way to improve their own rehabilitation. Still fewer produce wealth for the community and for restitution to their victims. On the contrary, while a breadwinner—and most prisoners are males—is serving time, the state—we, the taxpayers— must keep him. At the same time, we must often support his family as well. As a result of loss of his working income, they frequently go on welfare (Goldfarb 1975:57).

The major portion of prisoners in Canadian prisons are there for offences against property. They are not violent. They could as easily be working off their fines and paying restitution in the community. Two thirds of all admissions to Canadian penitentiaries in 1978 were between 18 and 29 years of age. Half ($^2/_3$ under age 17) were convicted of break and entry, or robbery (Correctional Institution Statistics, Canada, 1978).

Fewer than 700 of the 4695 males and only 29 of the 131 women were imprisoned for a crime of violence—i.e. murder, manslaughter, attempted murder, rape, kidnapping, wounding, assault. In comparison, ten percent of admissions were for narcotics convictions; surely the most obvious crime for which prison is a pointless punishment. It is well known that most prisoners can continue to obtain drugs while in prison.

Among prisoners over thirty, the most common cause of admission is revocation of parole. Prisoners let out early because of good behavior are not free men. They have "permission to be slightly free" (MacNaughton-Smith 1976) They are "puppets on a string" (Chief Justice Bora Laskin, in Mitchell vs. The Queen, 24 C C C 2d:245). The parole board can revoke parole at any time, and has not been required to give any reason, though an appeal under the 1982 Charter of Rights may change this.

Applying for parole is a very uncertain risk. Even if he gets it the prisoner is not necessarily better off. On parole his sentence is still in effect. It hangs over him and at any time a parole officer may decide to return him to prison. While out, the paroled inmate is forbidden to change jobs, drive a car, drink alcohol, marry, or even see personal friends without clearance from the parole officer. If returned to prison he must begin to serve his sentence where he left off. As a consequence he may actually be a free man at a later calendar date than if he had simply stayed in prison.

The prison system may provide employment for many small-town unskilled workers. But it corrupts their humane instincts. The Parliamentary subcommittee report is replete with instances of cruel, malicious and just plain mean behavior by guards. They have used clubs, shackles, dogs and tear gas. At the same time, guards were found to have arranged a system of booking off work "sick" so that other guards were called in on overtime. By returning the favor for each other the net result is considerable overtime for everyone. In 1976, Millhaven guard salaries totalled five million dollars. But overtime the same year added another two million. Some guards worked 1800 hours of overtime (See the Morand inquiry for examples of guard behavior in city jails).

Prison is a lawless jungle likely to produce more, and much more bitter, criminals. It is lawless not only because of the threat of physical violence, but because prisoners are denied the fundamental human rights available to free citizens. Courts have generally refused to allow prisoner appeals against decisions of guards and wardens, on the legal fiction that when a man goes to prison he loses the status of citizen. Prisoners must resort to hunger strikes and riots to get attention for their grievances. Citizens outside our prisons who dedicate their lives to efforts to improve the lot of prisoners, such as a 64-year old Vancouver grandmother, Claire Culhane, are actually barred from visiting prison. They are labelled by guards and administration as troublemakers (Culhane 1979). Wardens in our prisons can condemn prisoners to unlimited solitary punishment without giving reasons, allowing a hearing or an appeal. Reforms in prisons are particularly opposed by the guards' unions.

The Goal of the War On Crime

The system of control of Canadian society is such that it fits the model of a system best suited to *produce a steady supply of criminals* (Reiman 1979). The obvious question is: "What use is a steady supply of criminals to the powerful (the 'ruling class') in Canadian society?"

The stimulation of employment for guards, clerks etc. to staff the prisons, even to the extent of 10 000 full time jobs, can hardly justify such a model. The construction of new prisons, a current growth industry in Canada with about $300 million planned in new construction (*Globe and Mail*, Jan. 19, 1979), might double that number of jobs, and building also produces considerable profit for major construction corporations. But it still seems an insufficient explanation.

Reiman's answer (1979) is that the ruling class maintains a war on crime because of its effect on the middle class. (Elsewhere in this book this class has included the petty bourgeoisie, new petty bourgeoisie, etc.) The crime war persuades the middle class that the people they have to fear most, are those below them in society, not those above. Lower class crime is controlled by police action, courts and prisons. Middle class crime, so-called white collar crime, is often dealt with through more civil and polite means. For example, Mounties in the corporate investigation section arrive at the suspect's office in business suits, not uniforms. Restitution is often permitted, with formal charges, court and jail held in reserve.

As for the ruling class, since they make the rules of the game, they don't usually have to break them to get what they want. When members of the ruling class do break the rules, as seen in the previous chapter, the violation is often on a corporate rather than individual scale. While the corporation may be found guilty, the executives are rarely sent to jail.

Exceptions are often cited by sociologists opposed to this argument, such as the General Electric executives in the United States, or the executives in the Hamilton dredging case in Canada. These exceptions prove the rule, since they are so rare. In any event, the people involved managed to stay out of jail on appeal for a very long time. They then serve very short sentences in relative prison comfort. They do not have to mix with the "common criminal element". Their lives in prison are far less at risk of violence than the ordinary inmate's.

Much of the "crime" of the upper and upper middle classes is not even the sort likely to be processed and punished under the criminal code. It consists of offences against the many regulatory agencies of modern society. Examples of such agencies include the Canadian Wheat Board, the Canadian Radio-Telecommunications Commission, the Air Transport Board, Labour Relations boards and Workmen's Compensation Boards. These agencies are all part of the social control apparatus of the modern state. However, their procedures do not usually involve armed men (police) hailing offenders before courtroom monarchs and sending them to lawless jungles.

The more polite methods of regulatory agencies do not indicate that less is at stake in society. The lives of several hundred people at one time ride on the decision of an Air Transport inspector to allow a pilot and plane into the air, or to allow an industrial process (safety regulation), or to refuse to cover a typical industrial injury, eg. asbestos-related lung diseases. There are many offenders under these regulations and agencies. Their actions have caused at least as much harm and grief to Canadian citizens as a burglar or mugger.

The most recent example is the inquiry into the air transport industry under Judge Charles Dubin. It disclosed that a cosy relationship between the board's inspectors and the industry's management allowed many unsafe planes to fly. Worse, when crashes took place, the board's inspectors were found to have deliberately destroyed evidence which would have shown their malfeasance (*Toronto Star*, October 23, 1981). Other contemporary examples come from the agencies supposed to be regulating environmental problems caused by industry such as air pollution, or acid rain.

When officials of such agencies are caught red-handed they are almost never criminalized. Often they are not even fired. Transport Minister Jean-Luc Pepin announced after the Dubin report that no inspectors who covered up crashes caused by faulty inspections would lose their jobs. "The minister could see no point in dwelling on past mistakes and old horror stories. But he promised that his officials would be much more stringent about maintaining proper safety standards in Canadian skies" (*Toronto Star*, Oct. 24, 1981). How many police constables, judges or prison wardens would accept that sort of assurance "to do better next time" from common criminals?

Decarceration, the Latest Twist in the Game

If Reiman's thesis is supportable, that a steady rate of criminalization of the lower social classes is used by the ruling class to keep the middle classes more worried about what lower class criminals might do to them than what executive and corporate crime does to them, (the student is referred to Reiman, 1979 for a detailed account), then what about the recent trend to "decarceration." In recent years it has become popular for state social control to discuss and to some extent implement a closing down of traditional incarceration. This is true not only in prisons but also in mental institutions. The inmates are 'returned to the community'—for example in group homes, half-way houses, community restitution work, 'diversion programs,' etc.

Does the current popularity of decarceration suggest that Reiman is entirely wrong, or that the ruling class currently has more criminals than it needs to keep the middle classes in line? Or is there a third explanation? Scull (1977) has argued a third explanation.

Decarceration achieves as good an impact on middle class perceptions as putting people in prison does. But the cost to the state is less. The possibility of an ex-convict half-way house being located in a quiet, respectable, middle-class neighborhood is enough to stir up a storm of protest, stereotypes of criminals, and baseless fears. Decarceration is an effective program for using the people who have already been labelled as social garbage as a form of social dynamite.

HIGHLIGHT

1. Numerous commissions have found many Canadian prisons unfit for human habitation and have revealed that guards often mete out cruel and harsh treatment.
2. Quite often, guards are unable to maintain "law and order" inside the prison.
3. Prison terms seldom result in rehabilitation of the incarcerated.
4. Some theorists suggest that the main role of the penitentiary system and all that it implies is to have the "middle class" believe that their enemies are criminals from the working class.
5. Decarceration—group homes, parole, etc.—has the same effect on the middle class as the prison system. It leads them to believe that their real enemies are the working class.

Conclusion

The Coming Obsolescence of Crime.   There is no reason to believe that the present model of irrational laws, arbitrary enforcement, revolving door prisonization, fiction-ridden courtrooms, and violence-ridden prisons will continue to serve the interests of the powerful. Technology is providing new methods of social control. They will very probably replace the reliable criminalization of a section of the lower classes as a technique for controlling any possible unrest among the middle classes. This method, the Reiman model, has only a relatively short pedigree in human history. It dates largely from the early days of the "industrial revolution" which gave birth to the modern middle classes and the modern state. Prior to that time a very different kind of ruling class, the feudal nobility, used quite different methods of social control.

The prospect for the future is one of elaborate electronic social control. The ruling class, through state agencies, may replace prison with "hundreds of tiny theatres of punishment" (Foucault 1978:297). Tiny electronic implants in the skulls of criminals will be in radio communication with central computer control stations in each community. These implants will be capable of informing the controller about what the wearer is doing. If the action is not approved, the controller will be able to push a button and send a sharp pain pulsing out of the implant into the body. Orders to 'cease and desist' unlawful action will no longer be paper documents but instant enforcements. The technology for such a model of social control is already invented. It will be supplemented by other forms of population surveillance, such as television monitors.

These too are already in existence, and in use in some industries and in our post office.

It will not be necessary to watch all citizens on monitors, or implant electronic devices in more than a fraction of the population. The rest of us, fearfully aware of those who have been made an example, will conform to the orders we receive from the "authorities" rather than risk becoming implanted. Bentham's "moral calculus" will take on a new meaning, as each free citizen carefully weighs each action. What do I have to lose by resisting? What do I have to gain by conforming?"

SUGGESTED READINGS

Making Crime, Richard Ericson. Toronto: Butterworth, 1980. A sociologist accompanies police detectives on their daily rounds, and concludes that the real product of police work, using the enabling power of law, is the definition of behavior as crime.

Crime and Capitalism, Readings in Marxist Criminology, David Greenberg, editor. Palo Alto, California: Mayfield Publishing, 1981. A wide assortment of readings, historical and modern, from several different academic disiplines.

The RCMP Versus the People, Edward Mann and John Alan Lee. Don Mills: General Publishing, 1979. Two sociologists draw on interviews with ex-Mounties and secret RCMP documents to analyse the social causation of the RCMP wrongdoings investigated by the McDonald Commission.

Cruel and Unusual, Gerard Neil and Sharon Vance. Montreal: Deneau and Greenberg, 1978. Two journalists accompanied the tour of Canadian penitentiaries by the House of Commons all-party sub-committee in 1977, and combine their own experiences with the official report.

Sociology of Law, a Conflict Perspective, Charles Reasons and Robert Rich. Toronto: Butterworth, 1978. A Canadian collection of readings for the student wanting a more advanced sociology text on law and social control.

The Rich Get Richer and the Poor Get Prison, Jeffrey Reiman. New York: Wiley, 1979. A deliberately provocative analysis of ideology and class struggle in the American "criminal justice system."

Doing Sociology

RESEARCH AND WRITING IN THE SOCIAL SCIENCES

John R. Hofley
Roz Usiskin

Introduction

When a student in introductory sociology picks up the textbook, he or she will find usually a chapter on "research methods". A chapter discussing how sociology is a "science" and therefore quite different from English or History is also a possibility.

The very phrase "research methods", as used in most texts, connotes a set of steps, procedures, or techniques whereby a scientist can demonstrate the "truth" or "falseness" of a hypothesis. (For example, the higher the parental income, the more likely a person will attend university.) The student is often told what a scientist does, how a scientist tests hypotheses about relationships, how probabilistic statistics are used, and how to present data in tables. Indeed this general equation of "method" with statistics is quite common.

This fact aside, it is evident that many students enrol in the social sciences, especially sociology and political science, to avoid statistics or anything that resembles mathematics. The single chapter on research in a sociology text is seen as simply a slight hurdle. It is one that can safely be avoided without hurting one's final grade too much.

While it is important that people who will eventually end up doing or evaluating research learn statistics, computer languages and other techniques of the social sciences, it is more appropriate, we believe, to learn these at a second or third year level. They should come after a person has some solid grounding in the substance and theory of sociology. Why then, is this chapter included in this volume? The answer will be given shortly.

The previous chapters share certain ideas about what sociology is about, and the processes through which we can understand and change society. For example, it has been assumed that sociology needs to focus its analysis on a "macro" level. That is, it must strive towards an understanding and explanation of total societies. It should not simply dwell on "micro" phenomenon such as interaction between two or three people.

It must be stressed, however, that individual behavior is *not* totally determined by external social forces which are usually examined at the macro level. Social phenomena are made by humans. But for any single person, social relations—such as the class of which a person is a member—have an existence apart from his or her activity (Keat and Urry 1975:193). They nonetheless limit the nature and range of activity that can be engaged in. The unemployed worker, for example, cannot always choose to take a room at the Ritz.

In view of these considerations, it is important to write a sociology text that recognizes simultaneously the importance of ideas, individual meanings, and the extent to which ideas are embedded in a complex set of determinate social relations. The reason, as seen in the chapter by Grayson, is that ideas do not exist in a social vacuum. Nor do they, by themselves, change people.

In our view, research and method are terms that properly refer to the *processes* by which social scientists search for explanations of social phenomena. They also enable us to confront social reality and ourselves. Simply put, we use research to answer the questions: what, where, who, when and why? In answer to the earlier question as to why this chapter is included in this book, it can simply be stated that the chapter is to make the reader conscious of what the research process involves.

We will examine research as a process and the importance of these questions by focussing on three topics:
(1) What is research?
(2) Positivism and Realism as two approaches to the study of social phenomena.
(3) Social Science research as ideology.

HIGHLIGHT
1. The sociological method involves more than a mere knowledge of statistics.
2. Sociologists can be described as carrying out their analyses at either "macro" or "micro" levels.
3. Research shall be seen as a process in which the questions—what, where, who, when, and why—are asked.

THE RESEARCH PROCESS

What is Research?

The term research is quite commonly used by both scientists and non-scientists, by professors and students. When you were in high school, and had a term paper to complete, perhaps you often did "research" by reading relevant sections in an encyclopedia. If you took biology, chemistry, or physics, you learned how to do "research" on a problem by completing laboratory assignments. Or, perhaps your employer has asked you to do "research" on a particular topic before a decision is made on a course of action.

If you play a sport and want to improve your skills, you may do "research". You read books on the sport written by professionals. You may also watch good players and how they perform. While watching a T.V. news or public affairs program, you may hear the reporter discuss the "research" done for the report. Newspaper journalists do "research" for their articles.

The list of examples is limitless. You can even do "research" on the person(s) with whom you would like to date. We may well ask, then, what is common to all these examples of "doing research"?

We think there are six common characteristics: (1) Researeh begins by asking a question. (2) We assess what we know and do not know. (3) Assumptions are important to research. (4) Values and Research go together. (5) Research must be systematic and empirical. (6) Research generates new knowledge.

1. Research begins by asking a question.   Who was Shakespeare? Who is ELO? What is the relationship between heat and light? Why is Prime Minister Trudeau interested in the North-South dialogue? What is the North-South dialogue? Who is that person in my class? What is he/she like?

Sociologists do research by asking questions also. Each preceding chapter in this text was guided by one or more questions. In the chapter by Grayson on culture, ideology and society, for example, the question guiding the analysis was: What is the relation between modes of thought and expression, and the class structure? Earlier, Veltmeyer asked the question: What is Canada's position in the capitalist world system?

Some questions are concerned with *acquiring information* that can be found in a variety of sources (see References). For example: "How many people over 65 live in Canada?"

Other types of questions are more complex and require someone or some group to do research guided by a given question or set of questions. For example, in John Porter's *The Vertical Mosaic*, he asked, "What is the relationship between class, power and ethnicity in Canada?" He spent twelve years of his life on the answer!

Questions can also be asked that cannot be answered by the sociologist because they cannot be directly tested in the real world. For example, "Is there a God?", "Is there life after death?" While the sociologist cannot answer these specific questions, nonetheless he/she may be interested in questions about how such beliefs influence the behavior of people. For example, "Do people who profess a belief in God behave differently in a time of crisis from those who are atheist?" These types of questions can be answered.

The importance attached to various questions may or may not be shared by other sociologists. They are influenced by a variety of factors such as our personal values and interests. They are also influenced by the interests of colleagues and/or friends, our social and economic background, the concerns of our Ph.D. advisor, the availability of research grants, and the theoretical perspective we adopt in our approach to an understanding of society. Later in the chapter, we will compare two different theoretical approaches on the research of society.

2. What we know and do not know. Sometimes when we ask a question, we do so on a topic about which we are completely ignorant or have very little knowledge. For example, the odds are that very few of us knew much about the Falkland Islands until April of 1982. In this month the news broke that Argentina had occupied the islands and that Great Britain was sending troops there. Perhaps, as a consequence of this event, we began to ask a number of questions. However, for a person trained in the history of South America, on relationships between Argentina and Great Britain, or on relationships between colonial and Third World countries, the questions asked would be influenced by a body of knowledge accumulated over time. Thus, the type and quality of questions we ask will be partly a function of what knowledge we possess.

By reading and listening to the media, for example, it would be easy to come to the conclusion that divorce is increasing rapidly. We may also believe that this is a new event in world history. However, the sociologist interested in the study of the family and divorce can call upon a body of knowledge accumulated by archaeologists, anthropologists, historians and other sociologists. It will likely demonstrate that our original assumption is false. Divorce is quite common in countless pre-industrial societies. The question, then, about rising divorce rates needs to be reworked and asked in a different way. Sociologists, like all other scholars, build their research upon the work of others. It is imperative that we admit our lack of knowledge if good research is to be done.

3. The importance of assumptions. The research questions we ask are also affected by certain assumptions we make about the nature of the human race, knowledge (what philosophers call epistemology), and the nature of society. As Berlin remarked in 1971 (Cumming 1973:502):

> The ideas of every philosopher concerned with human affairs in the end rest on his conception of what man is and can be. To understand such thinkers, it is [more] important to grasp this central notion or image, which may be implicit . . . than even the most forceful arguments with which they defend their views.

The three greatest nineteenth century thinkers in sociology, Karl Marx, Max Weber, and Emile Durkheim, wrestled with this question of "Who is Man?" Their answers profoundly affected their work (Yankelovich 1973).

The question of human nature remains important for two reasons. First, grasping a writer's assumptions concerning human nature is essential for an understanding of a writer's analysis of the nature of society. For example, if you believe that we are by nature aggressive, selfish and competitive, then Adam Smith's depiction of capitalism as a mode of production compatible with human nature makes complete sense. Therefore, the inequality we see around us in Canadian society remains unfortunate but understandable. It is a "natural" outcome of our competitive natures.

However if, like Marx, you were to believe that our natures are produced and reproduced by a given mode of production and that capitalism *produces* aggressiveness, selfishness and competitiveness, then you would "see" the inequality in Canadian society as a consequence of capitalist relationships. It is not due to our inherent nature.

Second, a person's assumptions can and often do "blind" one to alternative questions and explanations of a given social phenomenon. Indeed, as we have seen in Cuneo's chapter, much of Marx's work on "class", "surplus value" etc. demonstrates that the political economists of the eighteenth and nineteenth centuries were blinded by their assumptions concerning man as an economic animal.

Doing sociological research requires each of us to explore our own and one another's assumptions. Such an exploration will help us discover why many times we talk "past one another" rather than "to one another." Max Weber summed up this possibility in a letter he wrote to his wife after attending a convention in 1908 (Weber 1975:393):

> The participants ought to have handed one another terminological diction-
> aries first. As it was, they usually talked past one another. . . . , basically no
> one wanted to learn from anyone else and each one thought he was
> already standing on the throne of the one Absolute Truth.[1]

Our assumptions are closely linked to the next characteristic common to all research, our personal and social values.

4. Values and research.   An important question that has plagued the social sciences since the nineteenth century revolves around the extent to which the social scientist's values bias research. During the nineteenth century when sociology arose, the physical and natural sciences were making great strides. Sociologists such as Comte, Spencer and Durkheim argued that sociology could be a science modelled along the lines of the physical sciences. This view became known as "positivism." It stimulated a range of debates that continue to this day. One of the central debates revolved around the place of values in research and the extent to which personal values make "objectivity" in the social sciences impossible.

The issue stems, in part, from the fact that the subject matter of the social sciences is neither "material" nor "natural" as in the physical or biological sciences. Humans do not act as robots, nor as animals guided by genetic codes. We think, act, and react.

Researchers also think, act and react. We often do so in accordance with our personal values. Does it automatically follow, then, that my research will be biased? If I personally do not believe in marriage, does it mean that any research that I would do on marriage would be suspect? Can a married person understand and do research on celibacy? Can a non-athlete do research on athletics? These types of questions are endless.

With some exceptions, sociologists of the last century felt that the answer was "yes". The model of the physical sciences was appropriate. In the late nineteenth century the great German sociologist, Max Weber, was at the centre of the controversy as to the possibility of a "value-free" sociology. His most important statement on the subject was published in 1904 in the journal *Archiv* of which he was editor. In an article entitled "Objectivity in Social Science and Social Policy," (Weber 1949) he tried to state clearly the role of the journal, and the type of papers he would consider appropriate for a scholarly, scientific journal.

To Weber, sociology was the study of human action, i.e. behavior that is goal oriented. The goals we have and the means we use to attain those goals are influenced by our values. Therefore, as scientists, we must accept the validity of values, especially those values that influence the individual's choice of means appropriate to his/her end(s).

This is not the same thing as judging the validity of such values in the sense of goodness, badness, or being right or wrong. For example, if a person is interested in studying the question "What factors influence people's selection of spouses?" and chooses to research this by interviewing a random sample of people, he/she will discover that people will tell them about the sort of values they have and want in a mate. The person's own values may not coincide with the respondents'. It does not matter.

If a follow-up study of the couples is done five or ten years from the time of their marriages, it may be found that a number of the couples have divorced. Some may say that they made a "wrong" or "bad" decision. Again, the sociologist listens, but need not share the judgment.

Weber argued that researchers must make a clear distinction between *value-relevance* and *value-judgment*. The sociologist does utilize values. Karl Marx, for example, was passionately devoted to equality of the human condition. He consequently fought against oppression and exploitation. All knowledge of social reality is, in a sense, knowledge from a particular point of view. We *subjectively* pick out what we want to study.

This situation is not unique to sociology. A biologist may study water-mites because of a personal fascination. A chemist may study acid rain because of a personal concern over the pollution of our natural resources. Thus, no science, including sociology, is absolutely free from value presuppositions. Moreover, no science can prove its fundamental value to the person who rejects these presuppositions.

Compare the debates between "evolutionists" and "creationists" or, currently, "right to lifers" and "pro-abortionists". The strong differences arise out of different value presuppositions.

While arguing for the place of values in the *selection* of research topics, Weber thought that value-judgments had no place in science. How can this be? How can we do research that can be seen as valid despite our own values? These questions bring us to the next characteristic common to good research. It is systematic and empirical.

5. Research must be systematic and empirical. We have already touched upon this characteristic when we discussed the importance of what we know and do not know. All research begins with a question, perhaps influenced by some personal value. However, good research does not proceed in a random fashion. It needs to be systematic.

This, in sociology, is easy to say, but the *practice* of doing research varies enormously. Conventional introductory or methodology text books often present to the reader a set of steps that researchers either follow or should follow (see Forcese & Richer 1973; Hagedorn 1980; Li 1981; Teevan 1982; Westhues 1982). For example, Hagedorn and Hedly (Hagedorn 1980:39), delineate ten stages of social research:

1. Select the problem.
2. Review previous research on the problem.
3. State the hypotheses (predict what you will find).
4. Construct indicators for all variables in the hypotheses (operational definition).
5. Set up the research design.
6. Select the appropriate sample or population.
7. Decide upon data collection method(s).
8. Collect the data.
9. Analyze the data.
10. Interpret the data (write the research report).

These steps are systematic and can be followed in attempting to answer certain types of questions. For example: "What is the relationship between education and income?" They cannot be followed so easily if one is interested in, say, questions about the relationships between a husband and wife, or about the development of capitalism in Canada during the nineteenth century. Different questions require different research procedures.

However, regardless of the nature of the questions asked, all sociological research needs to be "tested" empirically. What do we mean by this? Do the "facts" exist out there in the social world and all that is necessary is for us to collect them? Our answer is "No". The social world, including the historical world, must be "interrogated by minds *trained* in a discipline of attentive disbelief" (Thompson 1978:28.29).

For research to be systematic and empirical the researcher must be willing to enter into a living relation with the real world, with real people (Sartre 1968:72). The questions asked must be genuine, not rhetorical. They must put our theory, or ideas about the way things happen, to work (see Thompson, 1978, 111). This requires patience, and a willingness to admit that one's preconceived answer to a question may be quite wrong. As Berger and Kellner (1981:67) have recently remarked:

> Objectivity....is the quality of the interpretive process itself, not....a quality of 'the facts out there.'

Research in the social sciences, then, is not merely the use of certain techniques such as interviews, questionnaires, and statistical manipulations. It is nonetheless important to know these. Rather, research is the *process* through which we gather evidence to support or reject a given point of view. The evidence gathered and interpreted leads us to the sixth and last characteristic common to all research.

6. Research generates new knowledge. The purpose of all research is to answer questions. If we know something, for example, who the Prime Minister of Canada is in 1983, we do not need to ask a question. Usually we ask questions in order to acquire new knowledge.

This knowledge needs to be shared. Hence the importance of writing our research results and publishing them. Publishing also enables others to critically evaluate our questions and the evidence we have accumulated. The assessment can be either positive or negative.

Such new knowledge feeds back to the earlier research steps. It may alter the questions we originally asked. It may force us to re-examine the body of knowledge we received. It may encourage us to think through our assumptions and values.

While most sociologists would agree that the above characteristics are common to all good research, a casual glance at research studies done would soon convince the reader that sociologists disagree a lot on what the important questions are, their assumptions, values, etc.

We often begin with different assumptions about not only the nature of research, but of social reality itself. As the noted historian, E.P. Thompson remarks:

> The problem is to find a model for the social process which allows an autonomy to social consciousness within a context which, in the final analysis, has always been determined by social being (1978:291).

In the following pages we will acquaint the reader with positivism and realism, two quite different approaches to the study of phenomena. Through this discussion, we hope to demonstrate that "method" can *never* be divorced from theory.

HIGHLIGHT

1. There are six basic steps in the research process. Nonetheless, it would be difficult to get sociologists to agree on what should be researched, and the way in which it should be researched.
2. The research procedures frequently referred to in introductory texts, usually survey analysis, have many applications. However, they are not appropriate for all sociological problems.
3. The method used by the researcher is dictated by the type of question asked.

Positivism and Realism

Until the 1970s, most North American sociology was dominated by a view of theory and method called positivism. For the positivist, sociological theory is made up of general statements (propositions) "whose truth or falsity can be assessed by means of systematic observation and experiment" (Keat and Urry 1975:13). This is usually done by either demonstrating that a relationship is "false" (for example, that there is no correlation between the number of births and storks in a given geographical area), or "true" (for example, that the higher the income of one's parents, the higher the probability that he/she will attend university).

This positivist tradition was established by the founder of sociology, August Comte. It was built upon the idealist philosophical tradition, especially that of Hume, Kant, and more recently Popper. It was practised by such classical sociologists as Durkheim and, to a lesser extent, Weber. In a real sense the struggle for the legitimacy of sociology as a discipline that was fought out in the universities of Europe and North America in the late nineteenth and early twentieth centuries was won by scholars who adopted a positivist stance towards the study of human societies.

What, then, exactly is positivism? What are its strengths and weaknesses? How does it view the relationship between theory and method?

Positivism, like most "isms", is not a neat, homogeneous, clearcut body of thought. Positivists do not always agree with one another. However, until the late 1960s and early 1970s much of North American sociology had been dominated by schools of thought such as structural-functionalism, symbolic interactionism, exchange theory, dramaturgy, and systematic model building. These, more or less, subscribed to a form of positivism (cf. Hindess 1977:16).

There are three main arguments that run through all these different forms of positivism:

(1) For sociology to be a science, it must be primarily interested in prediction and the discovery of regular patterns between social phenomena. Positivists tend to argue that the "facts" are out there in the real world, and that to be "objective" means that we grasp those facts and base predictions on them.

There are a number of examples of this approach. Let us briefly examine just one, the study of "class" or social status in Canada and the United States from a positivist tradition.

Class, in contrast to the perspective adopted in this book, is often seen as a *descriptive* term of certain types of inequalities between persons or aggregates of individuals. It is based on measures such as income, education and occupation. It is relatively easy to notice that Canadians differ on one or more of these factors. The positivist sociologist accumulates the evidence in order to make comparisons, for example, between one nation and another or between different regions of Canada. The accumulation of such evidence, it could be argued, might enhance our capacity to predict future inequalities.

In our view, the best example of this approach can be found in the work of Bernard Blishen and his colleagues. Over the years they have developed a socio-economic index of occupations in Canada (Blishen, 1967; Blishen and McRoberts, 1976; Blishen and Carroll, 1978). This index eventually became a combination of three factors—occupational prestige scores, education and income. There is no doubt that such an index can be a useful research tool (see Pineo, 1981, 620). However, it tells us almost nothing about how these inequalities came into being, or how they are perpetuated over time. Nor does it indicate to what extent they can be reduced or eliminated.

Positivism tends to downplay the interpretive process and the importance of one's theoretical framework in influencing what facts we see or do not see out there. As Berger and Kellner recently remarked (1981:129):

> The basic fault of every form of positivism in the social sciences is the belief that the act of interpretation can be circumvented.

Though the act of interpretation is crucial to any research, we must be careful that by interpretation, we do not simply mean finding out what people intend by a particular act. The so-called 'interpretive' or 'action' theory approach, first articulated by Weber and later by American sociologists such as G.H. Mead and Talcott Parsons, fails "to acknowledge the fact that meaning is always produced, it is never simply expressed (Williams 1977:166)."

(2) The foundation upon which prediction must be based is observation of events in the external world. As we will see shortly, this approach tends to ignore the possibility that the world we "see" is profoundly influenced by the ideas we already have of it. Moreover, good research

must *risk and test* the possibility that our own pre-conceived views of a particular social phenomenon may be wrong. Worse still, they may "blind" us to what is really there.

(3) An analysis of the "parts" of a society (for example, individuals, dyads, occupations, political parties) will enable us to grasp the "totality" of a society. Hence, many research studies go into great detail about, say, the relationship between a husband and wife within the home. They nonetheless fail to examine this relationship within the broader context of the couple's social situation, i.e. their work, children, and resource networks (cf. Cohen 1968:11-5).

An important consequence of these points is that sociological research done by positivists tends to examine social behavior and societies as if they were static, fixed entities. Much of the work is mired in details and techniques. It loses sight of the sociological question with which it began. The techniques become "ends" in themselves, rather than tools to assist in the research process. Thus, much of positivistic research tends to lose sight of the six characteristics of research discussed earlier. We think this is no accident, but endemic to the positivist approach.

Realists, on the other hand, while sharing with the positivists a conception of sociology as a systematic and empirically based process, approach research in three quite different ways. Before delineating these major differences, it is important to emphasize, as we did with positivism, that a "realist" approach to sociology contains within it a fairly wide, disparate set of scholars. Most would be classified as "political economists" and/or "Marxists".

Since our purpose in this chapter is to acquaint the reader with what we see as broad, general differences in approach to research, we are ignoring the details of differences within positivism and realism. (Some of the differences among the 'realist' authors of this book should be apparent by now.) This does not mean that these differences are silly or unimportant. It means that, at present, they are best left for further study. Let us turn, then, to an examination of how "realists" would approach research.

1. Prediction is not equivalent to an explanation, though it is by no means irrelevant. As Keat and Urry (1975:31) point out:

> The realist view of explanation can be conveniently summarized in the claim that answers to "why-questions" (i.e., requests for causal explanations) require answers to "how", and "what" questions.

An example will help clarify this statement. Given Wayne Gretzky's accomplishments in 1980-81, most hockey observers, and Gretzky himself, predicted that he would score more points in 1981-82. In February/March of 1982, as he began to break scoring records and neared the 100 goals and 200 points, much discussion took place. It did not focus on the predictability of his performance, but around the questions of

"How?" and "why?" i.e. explanation. Positivists fail to "distinguish between providing the grounds [Gretzky's feats in the W.H.A. and first two years in N.H.L.] for expecting that an event will occur, and explaining why it does occur" (Keat and Urry, 1975:13).

To continue the example, it has been suggested that Gretzky has the capacity to "see" all ten players on the ice at any given moment. He knows not only where they are but where they will be. Hence his anticipation is amazing and perhaps the reason for his accomplishments. These are the answers to the how and why questions: therefore, they provide the realist explanation of Gretzky's abilities.

Sociologists want to discover regular patterns, or facts, between social phenomena. However, the observation and announcement of such relationships, such facts, are simply the first steps in any research analysis. They tell us virtually nothing about "how", "why", "what". Such information, while useful, is not explanatory. As Marvin Harris has recently remarked, "Facts are always unreliable without theories that guide their collection and that distinguish between superficial and significant appearances" (1979:7).

Unfortunately, much of the empirical work done in sociology still stops at the descriptive level. However, as Keat and Urry (1975:32) point out:

> For the realist, the primary purpose of scientific theories is to enable us to give causal explanations of observable phenomena, and of the regular relations that exist between them. Further, such explanations must make reference to the underlying structures and mechanisms which are involved in the causal processes. It is these structures and mechanisms which it is the task of theories to describe.

The search for "underlying structures and mechanisms which are involved in the causal process" brings us to the second argument realists would make against the positivists and their stress that prediction comes from observing phenomena in the external world.

2. The causes of or reasons for, a given phenomenon are not necessarily readily apparent to either the persons acting or the sociologists. Research done from a realist perspective begins with a premise that there is a distinction between the level of appearances and the underlying social reality which produces those appearances (Wright 1979:11). Any analysis that remains at the level of appearances cannot explain what it describes or predicts.

One of the best proponents of a "realist" approach to research was Karl Marx. As E.P. Thompson remarks (1978:152):

> Marx's most extraordinary accomplishment was to infer—'read'—'decode'—the only—partly visible structure of rules, by which human relations were mediated by money: capital.

Similarly, Jean-Paul Sartre emphasized in his *Search for a Method* (1968:25):

> Marx was convinced that the facts are never isolated from appearances, that if they come into being together, it is always within the higher unity of a whole, that they are bound to each other by internal relations, and that the presence of one profoundly modifies the nature of the other.[2]

Research must begin with observation. It must also seek out causal explanations. However, as indicated we must also realize that the "reality" of a given phenonenon or society may decide the subjects of the research and/or the researcher.

For example, we live in a very male dominated world. The structure of this dominance or patriarchy, as shown in the chapter by Smith, influences how we see men and women. It also influences how we see and evaluate paid work and housework, and how we see pornography.

The reality at the level of appearances often gets in the way of our grasping the underlying causal mechanism. "To explain...is to strip reality of the appearances covering it like a veil, in order to see the bare reality itself" (Nidditch 1968:3). We must recognize that, "it is not the subject who deceives himself, but reality which deceives him" (Godelier 1972:337).

We are not suggesting that the sociologist should deny peoples' experiences in doing research. Experience is valid, but what intrigues the social scientist is that experiences occur within determined limits. As Thompson (1978:7) puts it:

> The farmer 'knows' his seasons, the sailor 'knows' his seas, but both may remain mystified about kingship and cosmology.

The sociologist wants to grasp the limits, the determinations of people's experiences. The sociologist wants to, and needs to, study both the sailor and cosmology, both the Western farmer and the regional economic inequalities that may affect his experiences.

3. Realists, following Marx, argue that elements can only be understood in relation to one another (Keat and Urry 1975:99) and that these relations can be explained only when we grasp the underlying structures of the total society. Realism is an attempt to "show in what determinate ways each activity was related to the other, the logic of this process and the rationality of causation" (Thompson 1978:70). It is *not* an approach that throws the individual out as a mere actor responding to situations in a completely deterministic way.

All sociologists must deal with the issue of subject/object distinctions and their interrelationships. They must deal with, for example, the *relationship* between the individual farmer and the nature of agriculture in an industrial, capitalist society, or the individual case of rape and the prevalence of both violence and misogyny in our culture. By way of contrast, we noted earlier that positivists tend to concentrate their research on studying *elements* that make up a particular whole.

It is nonetheless true that some positivists, following Durkheim, encourage us to choose between an individualistic and holistic approach to social phenomena (cf. Cronin 1978-79:96). For some, one of the greatest sociologists in American history was Talcott Parsons of Harvard. He wrote a number of influential works, one of which was on the family. He developed a model of the family by focusing on the elements that make up a nuclear family: mother, father, son and daughter. He articulated the roles of each person in the family. The role of the mother was called 'expressive'. That of the father was termed 'instrumental'. He also linked the family into a more complex model of institutions (polity, economy, education, etc.).

Parsons knew the family was undergoing some change. But he tended to minimize the analysis of change and stress the tendency of systems, like the family, to adapt and achieve some sort of equilibrium with the other institutions.

Even though Parson's analysis was holistic, it was static, and non-historical. It treated individuals, and even the family, as if they were "things". Moreover, as the Armstrongs point out, an "analysis such as Parsons' does not account for the existence of these different systems, for changes in them, for the dominance of some ideas over others, or for the variety of beliefs which exists within our culture" (1978:113).

There is nothing inherently illegitimate about isolating individuals, parents or families for analysis. At the same time we must not "allow ourselves to be deluded by our own procedures into supposing these systems [that we isolate for analysis] to be distinct" (Thompson 1978:110) and isolated from other aspects of society.

It is clear that for realists the study of any social phenomenon must always be done by research into social processes in their totality. This research and emphasis on the totality, on "macro" characteristics, does not reduce human action to some external forces such as God, abstracted Nature, human nature, instinct or animal inheritance.

At the very centre of a realist approach "is an extraordinary emphasis on human creativity and self-creation" (Williams 1977:206).

An approach based on such assumptions, can never be set down neatly in a series of steps, or in a number of techniques. It can be learned only through apprenticeship, i.e., the doing of research with the above three realist principles in mind. This is clearly antithetical to the self-assuredness of the research steps by Hagedorn referred to earlier.

The doing of research does not take place in a social vacuum, however. Often social science research is used by governments, corporations, various social agencies, volunteer groups and unions. Frequently, it is carried out to support a given political or economic viewpoint. Thus, research can be used as an ideological weapon and, consequently, we need to be sensitive to the dangers of research as ideology.

HIGHLIGHT

1. The positive approach rests on the assumption that the social sciences are like the physical sciences. As a consequence, positivists are concerned with getting the "facts," they are less interested in interpreting human behavior. Their research tends to be non-theoretical and ahistorical. They are more concerned with technique than with theory.

2. The realist approach is premised on the belief that "facts" have no meaning in themselves. Meaning associated with facts derives from the theory which the researcher uses to approach the questions. In addition, the task of social science is to examine the structures that give rise to the facts. Quite frequently such structures are not obvious to either the researcher or the people being studied.

Research and Ideology

Much of the social science research sponsored in Canada is supported either by governments at various levels or by large corporations. A rough estimate is that about 85 percent of such research is what we call "tied" or "contract" research. It is undertaken by a social scientist on behalf of a "sponsor" who provides not only the funds but the question, assumptions, and values. In addition, there is, in Canada, a strong undercurrent of belief that methods of research are neutral. Sociological findings are, as a result, merely the compilation of "facts."

Social researchers, particularly those who approach research from a realist perspective, are beginning to see two possible consequences of this situation: (1) Research is or can be used as both an *apologetic* for the governing groups in Canada and as a *rationale* for controlling dissidents within our population. (2) Research can *justify or legitimize* certain types of social changes in Canadian society.

Research done with positivist principles in mind, i.e. modelled after the physical and natural sciences, is particularly vulnerable to ignoring these dangers. As one of Weber's proponents, Rickman, argued:

> To model the social sciences entirely on the physical sciences is, I believe, intellectually misguided, scientifically sterile and morally dangerous. It is misguided because it ignores or misconstrues familiar cognitive processes, sterile because it does not yield the knowledge we need, and dangerous because it fosters the conception of man as something else in the world which can be manipulated (1967:131).

Research and research results can be used as weapons to influence the way we think about events. It can also affect our actions and reactions to given changes. This means that you and I have, and will continue to have, a number of difficult value decisions to make about our research and whom it will serve. This is called *praxis*, a Greek word meaning "doing" or "acting." We may choose between values but we cannot choose to be without values (cf. Thompson 1978:347).

HIGHLIGHT

1. Research in the social sciences is often supported by government and/or corporations. Consequently it may be used to legitimize the existing social structure and/or as a mechanism of social control.

Conclusion

As we have seen throughout this book, sociology is a discipline that engages us in a critical appraisal of Canadian society. We do our research and writing within a capitalist society. Thus, our choice of values and of the questions we ask to guide our research will be "ultimately restricted by the very nature and structure of bourgeois economic reasoning" (Green 1977:8).

There are numerous examples of the ways in which sociologists in Canada have not seen the extent to which our research simply assumes bourgeois values. The two best examples are our conceptions of class and our analysis of women.

Only recently have Canadian scholars, working from a realist perspective, begun to critically examine the extent to which our research on class and women has been "ideological." Usually, such research focused on the level of appearances. It thereby served to perpetuate existing inequalities between classes and between men and women.

We are not suggesting that non-realist research cannot be critical. It can. Nor are we suggesting that previous researchers in Canada who studied class, for example, were in favor of the status quo. They weren't. However, as we have tried to suggest throughout this chapter, good research needs to get beyond the level of appearances. It needs to struggle with social reality. It needs to engage one's own and society's assumptions and values. Such an approach to research is not easy. Research and writing in the social sciences is an intellectually demanding task; a task that involves values, our feelings, and our emotions.

NOTES

[1]From Max Weber: A Biography by Marianne Weber, Copyright © 1975 John Wiley and Sons, Inc. Reprinted by permission of John Wiley & Sons, Inc.

[2]From Search for a Method by Jean-Paul Sartre, translated by Hazel E. Barnes, Copyright © 1968. Reprinted by permission of Alfred A. Knopf, Inc.

APPENDIX

In Canada there are a number of excellent sources of information available to the sociologist. Some of these are listed below. A good number of these materials should be available in your library.

RESEARCH RESOURCES

Archives

Public Archives of Canada
395 Wellington Street, Ottawa, Ontario

> Government records, newspapers, photographs, maps, drawings, paintings, prints, film and sound recordings, machine readable records.

Provincial Archives—in each provincial capital

> Contains newspapers, map and picture collections, and public records relating to the history of the province.

Census Tract Series

By Statistics Canada

> Reports in Census Tract Series presents basic population, housing, household, family and labor force characteristics for statistical areas (i.e. census tracts) within each of 29 larger rural centres and census metropolitan areas. Two reports are being issued for each tracted centre—one providing distributions of 100 percent data ("A" Series) and the other containing classifications of sample data ("B" Series). Each report contains an index map outlining the locations of the census tracts for that particular area.

User Services Division
Statistics Canada, January, 1981

Data Banks and Research Centres

Canadian Plains Research Centre
(University of Regina, Regina, Saskatchewan)
Canadian Plains Bulletin—official newsletter of the Research Centre. Bulletin is published quarterly.

Centre for Community Studies
University of Toronto, Toronto, Ontario

Centre for Resource Studies (C.R.S.)
Queen's University, Kingston, Ontario
Room 642, Goodwin Hall.

C.R.S. Perspectives—published by Centre for Resource Studies Appears 3-4 times a year and contains brief articles and reviews in the mineral policy field, as well as information about C.R.S. activities and publications.

Dialog Information Retrieval Service, from Dialog Information Services, Inc.—has been operative since 1972. Now, it has more than 130 data bases available, containing more than 45,000,000 records. Records, or units of information can range from a directory-type listing of specific manufacturing plants to a citation with bibliographic information and an abstract referencing a journal, conference paper, or other original sources. Generally, this Dialog Information Retrieval Service is now available at all University libraries. These services generally entail a nominal fee.

Institute for Behavioral Research
York University, Toronto, Ontario.
Newsletter provides current research projects.

Population and Research Laboratory
University of Alberta, Edmonton, Alberta.
Deals with demographic, economic questions. Also migration and mobility studies for the city of Edmonton, Alberta.

Research Centre for Ethnic Studies
University of Calgary, 2920–24th Avenue, N.W., Calgary, Alberta.

Sociology Research
Research Newsletter
Department of Sociology
University of Manitoba, Winnipeg, Manitoba.

Employment, Unemployment and Labour Income

Part of *Statistics Canada* Series.

Several examples have been chosen to indicate the wide variety of information available to the researcher.

1. *Annual Report of the Minister of Supply and Services Canada Under the Corporations and Labour Unions Return Act, Part II.*
   Annual, Bilingual. First Issue–1970.

   Contains statistical summaries and analysis of labour union activity in Canada including organization and structure of the unions, male and female union membership, geographical location and industry of local unions, affiliations and union financial activity. Also included is the extent of the affiliation of organized labour in Canada with International Unions.

2. *Corporation and Labour Unions Return Act.*
   Division of Statistics Canada. See Wallace Clement, *The Canadian Corporate Elite*, McClelland and Stewart, Ltd., 1975, pp. 396-433, for an explanation.

3. *Historical Labour Force Statistics—Actual Data Seasonal Factors, Seasonally Adjusted Date.*
   Annual, Bilingual. First Issue, 1953-1966.

4. *Labour Force Information*
   Monthly. Bilingual. First Issue, 1946.

5. *The Labour Force*
   Monthly. Bilingual. First Issue, 1945.

   Presents adjusted and unadjusted estimates of labour force, employment and unemployment, with unemployment and participation rates analyzed by selecting geographic, demographic and occupational variables.

Selected Sociological Journals

General

> American Journal of Sociology
> American Sociological Review
> British Journal of Sociology
> Canadian Dimensions
> Canadian Journal of Sociology
> Canadian Journal of Political and Social Thought
> Canadian Review of Social History
> Canadian Review of Sociology and Anthropology
> Labour/Le Travailleur
> Pacific Sociological Review
> Public Opinion Quarterly
> Recherches Sociographiques
> Social Forces
> Social Problems
> Sociological Analysis
> Sociological Inquiry
> Sociological Quarterly
> Sociologie et Societies
> Sociology
> Sociology and Social Research
> Studies in Political Economy. A Socialist Review

Topical Sociological Journals

> Canadian Ethnic Studies
> Comparative Studies in Society and History

Criminology
Demography
International Migration Reviews
Journal of Comparative Family Studies
Journal of Marriage and The Family
Phylon
Population Studies
Rural Sociology
Signs-Journal of Women in Culture And Society
Sociology of Education
Technocracy Digest

Statistics Canada

User Advisory Series
Statistics Canada, Ottawa, Ontario, K1A 0T6
Statistics Canada Catalogue in French and English
Prior to 1971 called Dominion Bureau of Statistics

–National Income and Expenditures Accounts
 found in every quarter Statistics Canada

–Historical Catalogue (for pre-1960)
 –all publications from 1918-1960

Historical Catalogue–1973-74. Catalogue (for the period 1960-74)
                     –and all subsequent catalogues
                     –plus the 1968 catalogue which contains the 1956
                      quinquennial census

The Canadian Statistical Review (cat. nos. 11-003E and 11-003F)
–published monthly, summarizes the major current economic indicators

Perspective Canada II (cat. nos. 11-503E and 11-508F)
–contains over 200 tables, 145 charts and a brief text on such basic social
 issues as health, education, work and cultural diversity.

The Canada Year Book (cat. nos. 11-402E and 11-402F)
–is issued biennially as an authoritative reference work on Canada's
 physical and natural resources, social and economic conditions,
 governments, industry, finances and legal system.

Canada Handbook (cat. nos. 11-403E and 11-403F)
–is issued biennially, provides information on the *present* conditions and
 recent development in Canada. i.e.–physical environment
                     –the people and their heritage
                     –the economy
                     –government structure and services

The Market Research Handbook (cat. no. 63-224)
–provides a convenient source of information and reference for those engaged in analyzing Canadian markets.

The Statistics Canada Daily (cat. nos. 11-001E and 11-001F)
–published every business day—with summary information of statistical findings, announcements of reports, reference papers and other releases.

Informat (cat. nos. 11-002E and 11-002F)
–a weekly digest highlighting major Statistics Canada reports, reference papers and other releases.

New Surveys (cat. no. 110006)
–a quarterly production
new surveys and major revisions to existing surveys carried out by Statistics Canada and other federal government departments.

Statistics Canada Annual Report (cat. no. 110201)
–information on bureau activities, plus a detailed review of each division in the previous fiscal year.

To order Publications:
  Publications Distribution
  Statistics Canada
  OTTAWA, Ontario
  K1A 0T6
  Telephone: (613) 922 3151

Data Available Via Computer
  CANSIM (Canadian Socio-Economic Information Management System)
  CANSIM is Statistics Canada's Computerized database.
  Two Types: 1) Time series data—changes over a period of time
              2) Cross-classified data—relationships between differ-
                 ent phenomena at a given point in time.
Information obtainable on a broad range of socio-economic subjects.

i.e. System of National Accounts
  Price and Price Indexes
  Labour
  Manufacturing and Primary Industries (including Full, Power and
      Mining)
  Capital and Finance, Construction, Merchandising and Services
  External Trade
  Transportation
  Agriculture and Food
  Population Estimates and Projections
  Health and Welfare

CANSIM is housed at Datacrown Inc.
May be obtained from:
    CANSIM
    Statistics Canada
    Ottawa, Ontario
    K1A 0Z8

Microfilm and Microfiche Included
    Ex 1976 Census of Population and Housing
    All 1976 Census of Agriculture Tabulations
    All current serial publications of the External Trade Division

Can be obtained from
    Micromedia Limited
    5th Floor
    144 Front Street West
    Toronto, Ontario
    M5J 1G2
    Telephone: (416) 593 4211

Bibliography of Papers and Reports in the Census International Series
    covers work in the period 1965-75.

A Bibliography of Canadian Demography, Technical Paper No. 5 (1966)
    Central Inquiries
    Statistics Canada
    Ottawa, Ontario   Updates to this bibliography will be issued as
    K1A 0T6   required.

Perspective Canada III (English and French editions)

Printing and Publishing
Supply and Services Canada
Ottawa, Ontario
K1A 0S9
–deals with population, work, crime and justice, family, income and
consumption, the Indians and Metis of Canada, health social security in
Canada, urban profiles, education, leisure, environment, the use of
energy, general perceptions on the quality of life.

L'age de la Retraite (Retirement Age) 1978—revised 1979

–published by Health and Welfare, Canada.
Brief presented to the Special Senate Committee on Retirement Age
Policies by the Minister of National Health and Welfare.

Reference Canada (English and French)

Selected Economic and Social Statistics
Statistics Canada

–includes the Basic Resource—People (Pop. 1961-81) (Add 000)
  The Working Life—Over the Years
  Selected Statistics—Canada, Provinces and Territories
  Languages of the land (Population by Mother Tongue, 1976 Census)
  The Economy—Then and Now
  Price Changes in the Consumer Basket

Migration Estimates From Tax Records: 1976-77 to 1978-79. La Migration Estimee A Partrir Des Rapports D'impot: 1976-77 A 1978-79.

Available in each province, i.e. Manitoba Census Divisions
Administrative Data Development Staff
Statistics Canada

Family Allowance Data (Program F55) Donnes Des Allocations Familiales (Programme F55)

–data on children from Family Allowance Records
–data can be obtained for any area specified by a grouping of postal
  codes, for June and December of each year
–requests for further information and for data should be directed to Mr.
  Russ Page, CANSIM Division of Statistics Canada.

Experimental Income Tax Data Profiles For Census Divisions and Provinces, 1976-1979

Information:
Nelson Ropustas
Administrative Data Development Staff
Statistics Canada
Jean Talon Building, 5A2
Tunney's Pasture
OTTAWA, Ontario
K1A 0T6
Telephone (613) 995 5172

SUGGESTED READINGS

Objectivity in Social Science, Frank Cunningham. Toronto: University of Toronto Press, 1973. A very good overview of the problems of values and of the issues surrounding the question of whether or not the social sciences can be "objective" in their research.

Social Theory as Science, Russell Keat and John Urry. London: Routledge and Kegan Paul, 1975. A first class presentation by a philosopher and a sociologist of the different approaches to the relationship between theory and method. The first part of the book deals with positivism and realism. The second part is a realist critique built upon Marx of some of the major theorists in sociology—Comte, Spencer, Durkheim, Marx, Weber, and Berger.

Social Research Methods: An Introduction, Peter S. Li. Toronto: Butterworth and Company, 1981. A new, concise text on research methods. It follows the standard approach of most methods texts, i.e., it discusses the relationship between theory and method, hypotheses, testing, tables, and different types of research techniques such as surveys, questionnaires and interviews.

The Philosophy of the Social Sciences, Vernon Pratt. London: Methuen Publications Ltd., 1978. An excellent, short introduction to the issues of human nature, causality, values, etc. in the social sciences. Pratt is a philosopher. The book is written in a straightforward style that compares and contrasts at least two different philosophical answers to each question.

Understanding and the Human Studies, H. P. Rickman. London: Heinemann Educational Books, 1967. An excellent introduction to the interpretive approach to sociology. It presents the reader with a sound analysis of Dilthey, Rickert and Weber. An appreciation of Weber is essential for a thorough understanding of contemporary sociology.

The Poverty of Theory, E. P. Thompson. New York: Monthly Review Press, 1978. A number of essays by an eminent British, Marxist historian. The first is a strong attack on the French structuralist Marxist, Louis Althusser. It highlights the importance of research being systematic and empirical and not the pursuit of a dogmatic theory. The second essays highlight some of the strong differences of approach taken by scholars who call themselves "Marxists."

REFERENCES

Abercrombie, Nicholas et al. *The Dominant Ideology Thesis.* London: Allen & Unwin Inc., 1980.

Acker, Joan. "Issues in the Sociological Study of Women's Work." In *Women Working*, ed. Ann H. Stromberg and Shirley Harkness. Palo Alto: Mayfield Publishing Co., 1978.

Acker, Joan and Van Houten, Donald R. "Differential Recruitment and Control: the Sex Structuring of Organizations." *Administrative Science Quarterly* 19:152-63, 1974.

Alavi, Hamza. "Peasants and Revolution." In *The Sociologist Register*, ed. Ralph Miliband and John Saville. New York: Monthly Review Press, 1965.

Albrow, Martin. *Bureaucracy.* London: Macmillan Publishing Co., 1970.

Alexander, David. *The Decay of Trade: An Economic History of the Newfoundland Saltfish Trade, 1935-1965.* St. John's: Institute of Social and Economic Research, 1977.

Allen, Richard. *The Social Passion.* Toronto: University of Toronto Press, 1971.

Althusser, Louis. *Lenin and Philosophy and Other Essays.* New York: Monthly Review Press, 1969 and London: New Left Books, 1971.

———. *For Marx.* Translated by Ben Brewster. New York: Vintage Books, 1970.

Amin, Samir. *Accumulation on a World Scale: A Critique of the Theory of Underdevelopment.* Translated by Brian Pearce. New York: Monthly Review Press, 1974.

———. *Unequal Development: An Essay on the Social Formations of Peripheral Capitalism.* New York: Monthly Review Press, 1976.

———. *Imperialism and Unequal Development.* New York: Monthly Review Press, 1977.

———. *Class and Nation, Historically and in the Current Crisis.* New York: Monthly Review Press, 1980.

———. "The Class Structure of the Contemporary Imperialist System." *Monthly Review* 31:8, 1980a.

———. "The World Crisis of the 1980's." *Monthly Review* 33:2, 1981.

Anderson, Nels. *The Hobo: The Sociology of the Homeless Man.* Chicago: University of Chicago Press, 1923.

Anderson, Perry. *Passages from Antiquity to Feudalism.* London: New Left Books, 1974.

Andren, Gunnar et al. *Rhetoric and Ideology in Advertising.* Stockholm: LiberForlag, 1978.

Anthony, Donna. "The Contribution of Nova Scotia Capital to Regional Underdevelopment, 1890-1915." Bachelor's thesis, Acadia University, Wolfville, NS, 1979.

Anthony, P.D. *The Ideology of Work.* London: Tavistock, 1977.

Antler, S.D. "Colonial Exploitation and Economic Stagnation in Nineteenth Century Newfoundland." Ph.D. dissertation, University of Connecticut, 1975.

Archibald, Bruce. "Atlantic Regional Underdevelopment and Socialism." In *Essays on the Left*, ed. L. LaPierre et al. Toronto: McClelland and Stewart Ltd., 1971.

Archibald, W. Peter. *Social Psychology as Political Economy.* Toronto: McGraw-Hill Ryerson Ltd., 1978.

Armstrong, Hugh and Armstrong, Pat. "The Segregated Participation of Women in the Canadian Labour Force." *Canadian Review of Sociology and Anthropology* 12(4):270-84, 1975.

Armstrong, Jill. "Canadians in Crisis." *Canadian Review of Sociology and Anthropology* 9(4):299-324, 1972.

Armstrong, Pat and Armstrong, Hugh. *The Double Ghetto: Canadian Women and Their Segregated Work.* Toronto: McClelland and Stewart Ltd., 1978.

Arnold, T. "Law as Symbolism." In *Sociology of Law*, ed. V. Aubert. London: Penguin Books, 1975.

Aron, Raymond. *Progress and Disillusion: The Dialectics of Modern Society.* New York: Mentor Books, 1969.

Ashenfelter, Orley and Johnston, George E. "Bargaining Theory, Trade Unions and Industrial Strike Activity." *American Economic Review* 59:35-49, 1969.

Aubert, Vilhem. *Sociology of Law.* London: Penguin Books, 1975.

Averitt, Robert. *The Dual Economy.* New York: Norton Press, 1968.

Avery, Donald. *'Dangerous Foreigners': European Immigrant Workers and Labor Radicalism in Canada, 1896-1932.* Toronto: McClelland and Stewart Ltd., 1979.

Bagnell, Kenneth. *The Little Immigrants.* Toronto: Macmillan of Canada, 1980.

Bain, George S. *Union Growth and Public Policy in Canada.* Ottawa: Labour Canada, 1978.

Bala, N.C. and Clarke, K.L. *The Child and the Law.* Toronto: McGraw-Hill Ryerson Ltd., 1981.

Baldus, Bernd. "The Study of Power." *Canadian Journal of Sociology* 2:179-201, 1975.

Baldus, Bernd and Tribe, Verna. "The Development of Perceptions and Evaluations of Social Inequality Among Public School Children." *Canadian Review of Sociology and Anthropology* 15,1:50-60, 1978.

Balibar, Etienne. "The Basic Concepts of Historical Materialism." In *Reading Capital*, ed. Louis Althusser and Etienne Balibar. Translated by Ben Brewster. London: NLB, 1970.

Bandura, A. and Perloff, B. "Relative Efficacy of Self-monitored and Externally Imposed Reinforcement Systems." *Journal of Personality and Social Psychology* 7:111-16, 1967.

Baran, Paul. *The Political Economy of Growth.* London: Penguin Books, 1957.

Barbash, Jack. "Collective Bargaining and the Theory of Conflict." *Relations Industrielles/Industrial Relations* 34:646-59, 1979.

Barker, Thomas and Roebuck, Julian. *A Typology of Police Corruption.* Springfield, IL: Charles C. Thomas, 1973.

Barnes, Harry E. "Leonard Trelawney Hobhouse: Evolutionary Philosophy in the Service of Democracy and Social Reform." In *An Introduction to the History of Sociology*, ed. Harry Elmer Barnes. Chicago: University of Chicago Press, 1948.

Barnet, Richard and Muller, Ronald. *Global Reach, The Power of the MNCs.* New York: Simon and Schuster, 1974.

Baum, Gregory. *Catholics and Canadian Socialism.* Toronto: James Lorimer, 1980.

Bayley, Charles M. "The Social Structure of the Italian and Ukrainian Immigrant Communities in Montreal." Master's thesis, McGill University, Montreal, 1939.

Bayley, David and Mendelsohn. *Minorities and the Police.* New York: Free Press, 1969.

Becker, H.S. *Outsiders.* New York: Free Press, 1963.

Becker, T.L. and Murray, V.G. *Government Lawlessness in America.* New York: Oxford Press, 1971.

Beckhart, B. H. *The Banking System of Canada.* New York: Holt, Rinehart and Winston, 1971.

Bell, Daniel. *The Coming of Post-Industrial Society.* New York: Basic Books, 1973.

Bell, David and Tepperman, Lorne. *The Roots of Disunity: A Look at Canadian Political Culture.* Toronto: McClelland and Stewart Ltd., 1979.

Bendix, Rinehard. *Work and Authority in Industry.* Berkeley: University of California Press, 1974.

Bercuson, David J. *Confrontation at Winnipeg: Labor, Industrial Relations, and the General Strike.* Montreal: McGill-Queen's University Press, 1974.

————. "Through the Looking Glass of Culture: An Essay on the New Labor History and Working-class Culture in Recent Canadian Historical Writing." *Labor/Le Travailleur* 7 (Spring):95-112, 1981.

Berger, Carl. *The Sense of Power.* Toronto: University of Toronto Press, 1970.

————. *The Writing of Canadian History: Aspects of English Canadian Historical Writing: 1900 to 1970.* Toronto: Oxford University Press, 1976.

Berger, Peter and Kellner, Hansfried. *Sociology Reinterpreted.* New York: Anchor Books, 1981.

Berger, Thomas. *Northern Frontier, Northern Homeland.* Ottawa: Supply and Services Canada, 1977.

Bergeron, Leandre. *The History of Quebec: A Patriotes Handbook.* Toronto: NC Press, 1971.

Berkley, George. *The Democratic Policeman.* Boston: Beacon Press, 1969.

Berle, Adolf A.,Jr. and Gardiner, C. Means. *The Modern Corporation and Private Property.* New York: Macmillan Publishing Co., 1933.

Berton, Pierre. *Hollywood's Canada.* Toronto: McClelland and Stewart Ltd., 1975.

Bertram, G.W. "Economic Growth in Canadian Industry, 1870-1915." In *Approaches to Canadian History*, ed. W.T. Easterbrook and M.H. Watkins. Toronto: McClelland and Stewart Ltd., 1967.

Bienvenue, R. and LaTif, A.H. "Arrests, Dispositions and Recidivism." In *Crime in Canadian Society*, ed. R.A. Silverman and J.J. Teevan. Toronto: Butterworth & Co. (Canada) Ltd., 1975.

Bird, Pat. *Of Dust and Time and Dreams and Agonies.* Toronto: The Canadian News Synthesis Project, 1975.

Blau, Peter M. *The Dynamics of Bureaucracy.* 2d ed., rev. Chicago: University of Chicago Press, 1963.

Blauner, Robert. *Alienation and Freedom: The Factory Worker and His Industry.* Chicago: University of Chicago Press, 1964.

Bleasdale, Graham. "Towards a Political Economy of Capitalist Educational Values." In *Reading, Writing and Riches*, ed. R.W. Nelsen and D.A. Nock. Kitchener: Between-the-Lines, 1978.

Blishen, Bernard R. "A Socio-Economic Index for Occupations in Canada." *Canadian Review of Sociology and Anthropology* 4:41-57, 1967.

Blishen, Bernard R. and Carroll, William K. "Sex Differences in a Socio-Economic Index for Occupations in Canada." *Canadian Review of Sociology and Anthropology* 15(3):352-71, 1978.

Blishen, Bernard R. and McRoberts, Hugh. "A Revised Socioeconomic Index for Occupations in Canada." *Canadian Review of Sociology and Anthropology* 13(1):71-79, 1981.

Bliss, Michael. *A Living Profit.* Toronto: McClelland and Stewart Ltd., 1974.

Bloch, Marc. *Feudal Society.* Chicago: University of Chicago Press, 1961.

Block, Fred. "The Ruling Class does not Rule: Notes on the Marxist Theory of the State." *Socialist Revolution* 33:6-28, 1977.

Blumberg, A. "The Practice of Law as Confidence Game." *Law and Society Review* 1:15-39, 1967.

Blumberg, Philip. *The Megacorporation in American Society: the Scope of Corporation Power.* Englewood Cliffs: Prentice-Hall Inc., 1975.

Bossen, Marianne. *Employment in Chartered Banks, 1969-1975.* Advisory Council on the Status of Women and the Canadian Banker's Association, 1976.

Bottomore, Tom B. *Karl Marx. Selected Writings in Sociology and Social Philosophy.* (1956). New York: McGraw-Hill Book Co., 1964.

Bourgault, Pierre. *Innovation and the Structure of Canadian Industry.* Ottawa: Science Council of Canada, 1972.

Bowles, Samuel and Gintis, Herbert. *Schooling in Capitalist America. Education Reform and the Contradictions of Economic Life.* New York: Basic Books, 1976.

Box, S. *Deviance, Reality and Society.* New York: Holt, Rinehart & Winston, 1981.

Boyd, Monica. "Sex Differences in the Canadian Occupational Attainment Process." *Canadian Review of Sociology and Anthropology* 19(1):1-28, 1982.

Boydell, C. and Bell-Rowbotham, B. "Crime in Canada." In *Deviance and Societal Reaction in Canada*, ed. C. Boydell et al. Toronto: Holt, Rinehart & Winston, 1972.

Bradwin, Edwin. *The Bunkhouse Man: A Study of Work and Pay in the Camps of Canada, 1903-1914.* (1928). Toronto: University of Toronto Press, 1972.

Braverman, Harry. *Labor and Monopoly Capital: The Degredation of Work in the Twentieth Century.* New York: Monthly Review Press, 1974.

Brewer, Anthony. *Marxist Theory of Imperialism: A Critical Survey.* London: Routledge & Kegan Paul, 1980.

Britton, John and Gilmour, James. *The Weakest Link.* Ottawa: Science Council of Canada, 1978.

Brown, J.A.C. *The Social Psychology of Industry.* London: Penguin Books, 1954.

Brown, Robert Craig and Cook, Ramsay. *Canada 1896-1921: A Nation Transformed.* Toronto: McClelland and Stewart Ltd., 1974.

Bruntun, R. et al. "Uneven Underdevelopment and Song: Expressions of Popular Class Culture in Atlantic Canada." Mimeographed, 1981.

Bukharin, N. *Imperialism and World Economy.* London: Merliss, 1972a.

———. *Imperialism and the Accumulation of Capital,* ed. K. Tarbuck. London: Atlen Lane, 1972b.

Bullock, Christopher J. "The 'Futility of Changeless Change': The Worth Report, Progressivism and Canadian Education." In *Reading, Writing and Riches*, ed. R.W. Nelsen and D.A. Nock. Kitchener: Between-the-Lines, 1978.

Bumsted, J.M. "The Origins of the Land Question on Prince Edward Island, 1767-1805." *Acadiensis* XI:1, 1981.

Burawoy, Michael. *Manufacturing Consent: Changes in the Labor Process Under Monopoly Capitalism.* Chicago: University of Chicago Press, 1979.

Burgess, Ernest W. "The Growth of the City: An Introduction to a Research Project." In *The City*, ed. R. Park et al. Chicago: University of Chicago Press, 1925.

Burnet, Jean. *Next Year Country.* Toronto: University of Toronto Press, 1951.

Burstein, M. et al. *Canadian Work Values: Findings of a Work Ethic Survey and a Job Satisfaction Survey.* Ottawa: Information Canada, 1975.

Byles, J. *Alienation, Deviance and Control.* Toronto: Ministry of Education, 1969.

Cain, Sydney. *The History of the Foundation of the London School of Economics and Political Science.* London: G. Bell and Sons Ltd., 1963.

Campbell, Kenneth. "Regional Disparity and Interregional Exchange Imbalance." In *Modernization and the Canadian State*, ed. Daniel Glenday et al. Toronto: Macmillan of Canada, 1978.

Canada. *Corporations and Labor Unions Returns Act.* Report for 1977. Part II - Labour Unions. Ottawa: Statistics Canada, 1979.

Canada. *Perspective Canada II.* Ottawa: Statistics Canada, 1977.

Canada. *Perspective Canada III.* Ottawa: Statistics Canada, 1980.

Carchedi, Guglielmo. "The Economic Identification of the State Employees." *Social Praxis* 3(1-2):93-120, 1976.

Carey, Alex. "The Hawthorne Studies: A Radical Criticism." *American Sociological Review* 32:403-16, 1967.

Carey, James T. *Sociology and Public Affairs: The Chicago School.* Beverly Hills: Sage Publications, 1975.

Carey, Patricia. "Farm Wives: The Forgotten Women." *Canadian Women's Studies*:4-5, 1978.

Carroll, William K.; Fox, John; and Ornstein, Michael. "The Network of Directorate Interlocks among the Largest Canadian Firms." *Canadian Review of Sociology and Anthropology* 19(1):44-69, 1982.

Centre for Crime Research. "The Iron Fist and the Velvet Glove." Berkeley, CA, 1975.

Centre for World Development Education. *Cartoon Sheets.* London: CWDE, 1980.

Chambliss, William. "A Sociological Analysis of the Law of Vagrancy." *Social Problems* 12:61-77, 1964.

————. "The Saints and the Roughnecks." *Society*(1973): 24-31.

Chandler, Alfred D., Jr. *The Visible Hand; The Managerial Revolution In American Business.* Cambridge: Harvard University Press, 1977.

Chevigny, Paul. *Police Power.* New York: Pantheon Press, 1969.

Chilcote, Ronald and Edelstern, Joel, eds. *Latin America: The Struggle with Dependence and Beyond.* Cambridge: Schernkman Publishing, 1974.

Chinoy, Ely. *Automobile Workers and the American Dream.* Boston: Beacon Press, 1955.

Chirot, Daniel. *Social Change in the Twentieth Century.* Don Mills: Longman Canada, 1977.

Chodos, Robert. *The C.P.R.: A Century of Corporate Welfare.* Toronto: James Lorimer, 1973.

————.*The Caribbean Connection.* Toronto: James Lorimer, 1977.

Christie, Nels. "Conflicts as Property." *British Journal of Criminology* 17:1-15, 1977.

Clairmont, Donald H.; Macdonald, Martha; and Wein, Fred C. "A Segmentation Approach to Poverty and Low-wage Work in the Maritimes." In *Structured Inequality in Canada*, ed. John Harp and John R. Hofley. Toronto: Prentice-Hall Canada Inc., 1980.

Clark, S.D. *The Canadian Manufacturer's Association: A Study in Collective Bargaining and Political Pressure.* Toronto: University of Toronto Press, 1939.

————. *The Social Development of Canada: An Introductory Study with Select Documents.* Toronto: University of Toronto Press, 1942.

————. *Church and Sect in Canada.* Toronto: University of Toronto Press, 1948.

————. *Movements of Political Protest in Canada, 1640-1840.* Toronto: University of Toronto Press, 1959.

————. *The Developing Canadian Community.* Toronto: University of Toronto Press, 1962 and 1968.

————. *The Suburban Society.* Toronto: University of Toronto Press, 1966.

————. *The New Urban Poor.* Toronto: McGraw-Hill Ryerson, 1978.

————. "Economic Expansion and the Moral Order." *Canadian Journal of Economics and Political Science* 4:203-25, 1940.

Clark, S.D., ed. *Canadian Society in Historical Perspective.* Toronto: McGraw-Hill Ryerson, 1976.

Clarke, Phyllis. "Canada: Colony? Hinterland? Imperial Power?" Paper presented at Annual Conference, Committee on Socialist Studies, June 1, 1973.

Clarke, Simon et al, eds. *One-Dimensional Marxism: Althusser and the Politics of Culture.* London: Allison and Busby, 1980.

Clement, Wallace. *The Canadian Corporate Elite: An Analysis of Economic Power.* Toronto: McClelland and Stewart Ltd., 1975.

————. *Continental Corporate Power: Economical Linkages Between Canada and the United States.* Toronto: McClelland and Stewart Ltd., 1977.

————. *Hardrock Mining: Industrial Relations and Technological Changes at Inco.* Toronto: McClelland and Stewart Ltd., 1981.

————. "A Political Economy of Regionalism in Canada." In *Modernization and the Canadian State*, ed. D. Glenday et al. Toronto: Macmillan of Canada, 1978.

————. "Uneven Development: Some Implications of Continental Capitalism for Canada." In *Economy, Class and Social Reality: Issues in Contemporary Canadian Society*, ed. John Allan Fry. Toronto: Butterworth & Co., 1979.

————. "Searching for Equality: The Sociology of John Porter." *Canadian Journal of Political and Social Theory* 4:2, 1980.

Clement, Wallace and Drache, Daniel. *A Practical Guide to Canadian Political Economy.* Toronto: James Lorimer, 1978.

Cohen, Percy S. *Modern Social Theory.* London: Heinemann Educational Books, 1968.

Cohen, Robin; Gutkind, Peter; and Brazier, Phyllis. *Peasants and Proletarians; The Struggles of Third World Workers.* New York: Monthly Review Press, 1979.

Commission on the Non-Medical Use of Drugs. *Final Report* (LeDain Commission). Ottawa: Information Canada, 1973.

Comstock, George et al. *Television and Human Behavior.* New York: Columbia University Press, 1978.

Connelly, Patricia. *Last Hired, First Fired: Women and the Canadian Work Force.* Toronto: Women's Press, 1978.

Conway, J.F. "From Petitions to Politics: the Agitation for Redress of Prairie Agrarian Grievances, 1830-1930." Paper read to the annual meeting of the Canadian Sociology and Anthropology Association, University of New Brunswick, 1977.

———. "The Place of the Prairie West in Confederation." Paper read to the annual meeting of the Canadian Sociology and Anthropology Association, University of New Brunswick, 1977a.

Cook, Ramsay and Mitchinson, Wendy, eds. *The Proper Sphere: Women's Place in Canadian Society.* Toronto: Oxford Unviersity Press, 1976.

Cook, S. "Canadian Narcotics Legislation." *Canadian Review of Sociology and Anthropology* 6:31-46, 1969.

Cordell, Arthur. *The Multinational Firm, Foreign Direct Investment and the Canadian Science Policy.* Ottawa: The Science Council of Canada, 1971.

Corrigan, Paul. *Schooling the Smash Street Kids.* London: Macmillan Publishing Co., 1979.

Coulson, Margaret A. and Riddell, Carol. *Approaching Sociology.* London: Routledge and Kegan Paul, 1980.

Craig, Glen H. "The Means and Modes of Living on the Pioneer Fringe of Land Settlement, with Special Reference to the Peace River Area." Master's thesis, McGill University, Montreal, 1933.

Craven, Paul. *'An Impartial Umpire': Industrial Relations and the Canadian State, 1900-1911.* Toronto: University of Toronto Press, 1980.

Cray, Ed. *The Enemy in the Streets.* New York: Anchor Books, 1972.

Crean, S.M. *Who's Afraid of Canadian Culture.* Toronto: General Publishers, 1976.

Creighton, Donald. *Harold Adams Innis: Portrait of a Scholar.* Toronto: University of Toronto Press, 1957.

Cressey, D. *Other Peoples Money.* Glencoe, IL.: Free Press, 1953.

———. "Sentencing: Legislative Rule versus Judicial Discretion." In *New Directions in Sentencing,* ed. Brian Grosman. Toronto: Butterworth & Co., 1980.

Crispo, John and Arthurs, H. "Industrial Unrest in Canada: A Diagnosis of Recent Experience." *Relations Industrielles/Industrial Relations* 23(2):237-64, 1968.

Cronin, James. "Creating a Marxist Historiography: The Contribution of Hobsbawm." *Radical History Review* 19:87-109, 1979.

Cross, Michael, ed. "The Working Man In The Nineteenth Century." Excerpts from *Travels Through the Canadas, 1807,* ed., George Heriot. Toronto: Oxford University Press, 1974.

Cross, Suzanne D. "The Neglected Majority: the Changing Role of Women in 19th Century Montreal." In *The Neglected Majority: Essays in Canadian Women's History,* ed., S.M. Trofimenkoff and A. Prentice. Toronto: McClelland and Stewart Ltd., 1977.

Culhane, Clare. *Barred from Prison.* Vancouver: Pulp Press, 1979.

Cumming, Robert D. "Is Man Still Man?" *Social Research* 40:481-510, 1973.

Cuneo, Carl J. "Class Exploitation in Canada." *Canadian Review of Sociology and Anthropology* 15(3):284-300, 1978a.

———. "A Class Perspective on Regionalism." In *Modernization and the Canadian State,* ed. Daniel Glenday et al. Toronto: Macmillan, 1978b.

———. "Class Contradictions in Canada's International Setting." *Canadian Review of Sociology and Anthropology* 16(1):1-20, 1979a.

———. "State, Class and Reserve Labour: The Case of the 1941 Canadian Unemployment Insurance Act." *Canadian Review of Sociology and Anthropology* 16(2):147-70, 1979b.

————. "Class, Stratification and Mobility." In *Sociology*, ed. R. Hagedorn et al. Toronto: Holt, Rinehart and Winston, 1980a.

————. "State Mediation of Class Contradictions in Canadian Unemployment Insurance, 1930-35." *Studies in Political Economy* 3:37-65 (Spring), 1980b.

————. "Surplus Labour in Staple Commodities During Merchant and Early Industrial Capitalism." *Studies in Political Economy* 7:61-87, 1982a.

————. "Class Struggle and Measurement of the Rate of Surplus Value." *Canadian Review of Sociology and Anthropology* 19(3):377-425, 1982b.

Cunningham, Frank. *Objectivity in Social Science.* Toronto: University of Toronto Press, 1973.

Dale, R.R. and Griffith, S. "The Influence of the Home." In *Family, Class and Education: A Reader*, ed. Maurice Craft. London: Longmans Publishers Inc., 1970.

Darroch, Gordon. "Another Look of Ethnicity, Stratification and Social Mobility in Canada." *Canadian Journal of Sociology* 4:1-25, 1979.

Davidson, Basil. *The African Slave Trade: Precolonial History, 1450-1850.* Boston: Atlantic-Little Brown, 1961.

Davidson, Helen H.; Riessman, Frank; and Myers, Edna. "Personality Characteristics Attributed to the Worker." *Journal of Social Psychology* 57:155-60, 1962.

Davis, K. and Moore, W.E. "Some Principles of Stratification." *American Sociological Review* 10, 1945.

Dawson, Carl A. *The City as an Organism with Special Reference to Montreal.* Montreal: McGill University Publications, Series XIII, No. 10, 1926.

————. *Group Settlement: Ethnic Communities in Western Canada.* Toronto: The Macmillan Company of Canada Limited, 1936.

Dawson, Carl A. and Gettys, Warner E. *An Introduction to Sociology.* New York: The Ronald Press Company, 1929.

Dawson, Carl A. and Munchie, R.W. *The Settlement of the Peace River Country: A Study of a Pioneer Area.* Toronto: The Macmillan Company of Canada Limited, 1934.

Dawson, Carl A. and Younge, Eva. R. *Pioneering in the Prairie Provinces: The Social Side of the Settlement Process.* Toronto: The Macmillan Company of Canada Limited, 1940 and 1947.

Deane, P. and Cole, N. A. *British Economic Growth, 1688-1959.* New York: Cambridge University Press, 1967.

Dennison, John D. *The Impact of Community Colleges: A Study of the College Concept in British Columbia.* Vancouver: B.C. Research, 1975.

Devereaux, M.S. and Rechnitzer, Edith. *Higher Education - Hired? Sex Differences in Employment Characteristics of 1976 Post Secondary Graduates.* Ottawa: Statistics Canada and Labour Canada, Women's Bureau, 1980.

Ditton, J. *Part-time Crime: An Ethnography of Fiddling and Pilferage.* London: Macmillan Publishing Co., 1977.

Doeringer, Peter B. and Piore, Michael J. *Internal Labor Markets and Manpower Analysis.* Lexington, MA: D.C. Heath & Co., 1971.

Dorfman, A. and Mattelart, A. *How to Read Donald Duck.* New York: International Publishers, 1975.

Dos Santos, Theotonia. "The Crisis of Development Theory and the Problem of Dependence in Latin America." In *Underdevelopment and Development*, ed. H. Bernstein. London: Penguin Books, 1973.

Douglas, Jack. *Investigative Social Research.* Beverly Hills: Sage Publications, 1976.

Drache, Daniel. "The Canadian Bourgeoisie and Its National Consciousness." In *Close the 49th Parallel etc.: The Americanization of Canada*, ed. Ian Lumsden. Toronto: University of Toronto Press, 1970.

————. "What passes for Canadian History?" *Canadian Dimension* 8:38-41, 1972.

————. "Staple-ization: A Theory of Canadian Capitalist Development." In *Imperialism, Nationalism, and Canada.* Cambridge: Massachusetts Institute of Technology, 1977.

————. "Rediscovering Canadian Political Economy." In *A Practical Guide to Canadian Political Economy*, eds. Wallace Clement and Daniel Drache. Toronto: James Lorimer, 1978.

Drache, Daniel, ed. *Quebec - Only the Beginning; The Manifestos of the Common Front.* Toronto: New Press, 1972a.

Dray, William. *Philosophy of History.* Englewood Cliffs: Prentice-Hall Inc., 1964.

Dray, William, ed. *Philosophical Analysis and History.* New York: Harper and Row Publishers, Inc., 1966.

Drummond, Ian M. *The Canadian Economy: Structure and Development.* Georgetown: Irwin-Dorsey Ltd., 1972.

Dunlop, John T. et al. "Industrialism and Industrial Man Reconsidered." Final Report of the Inter-University Study of Labor Problems in Economic Development, Princeton, NJ, 1975.

Durkheim, Emile. *Suicide.* New York: Free Press, 1951.

————. *The Division of Labour.* New York: Free Press, 1964.

Easton, David and Dennis, Jack. *Children in the Political System.* New York: McGraw-Hill Inc., 1969.

Eckberg, Douglas L. and Hill, Lester, Jr. "The Paradigm Concept and Sociology: A Critical Review." *American Sociological Review* 44:6, 1979.

Edelman, Murray. "Symbols and Political Quiescence." *American Political Science Review* 54:695-704, 1960.

————. *Politics and Symbolic Action.* Chicago: Markham, 1971.

Edwards, Richard C. *Contested Terrain: The Transformation of the Workplace in the Twentieth Century.* New York: Basic Books, 1979.

————. "The Social Relations of Production in the Firm and Labor Market Structure." In *Labor Market Segmentation*, ed. Richard C. Edwards, Michael Reich and David M. Gordon. Lexington, MA: D.C. Heath, 1975.

Elliott, D. and Ageton, S. "Reconciling Race and Class Differences in Self-reported and Official Estimates of Delinquency." *American Sociological Review* 45, 1980.

Elson, Ruth M. *Guardians of Tradition.* Lincoln: University of Nebraska Press, 1964.

Emmanuel, Arghiri. *Unequal Exchange. A Study of the Imperialism of Trade.* Translated by Brian Pearce. London: New Left Books, 1972.

Engels, Frederick. *The Peasant War In Germany.* Moscow: Progress Publishers, 1969a.

————. *The Origin of the Family, Private Property, and the State,* ed. Eleanor Leacock. New York: International Publishers, 1972.

————. "Introduction." In *The Class Struggles in France, 1848-50*, ed. Karl Marx. New York: International Publishers, 1969.

————. "Speech at the Graveside of Karl Marx." In *The Marx-Engels Reader*, ed. Robert C. Tucker. New York: W.W. Norton, 1972a.

————. "Preface to the Third German Edition." In *The Eighteenth Brumaire of Louis Bonaparte*, ed. Karl Marx. New York: International Publishers, 1972b.

Epp, Abram. "Cooperation Among Capitalists: The Canadian Merger Movement." Ph.D. dissertation, Johns Hopkins University, Boston, 1973.

Erickson, P.G. "Legalistic and Traditional Role Expectations for Defence Counsel in Juvenile Court." *Canadian Journal of Criminology* 19:78-85, 1975.

Ericson, Richard. *Making Crime.* Toronto: Butterworth & Co., 1981.

————. *Reproducing Order.* Toronto: University of Toronto Press, 1982.

Esland, Geoff and Salaman, Graeme, eds. *The Politics of Work and Occupations.* Toronto: University of Toronto Press, 1980.

Etzioni, Amitai. *A Comparative Analysis of Complex Organizations,* 2d rev. ed. New York: Free Press, 1975.

Etzioni, A. and Etzioni, E., eds. *Social Change.* New York: Basic Books, 1964.

Evans, J. "Canadian Vicimization Surveys." Ottawa: Solicitor-General, 1978.

Ewen, Stuart. *Captains of Consciousness.* New York: McGraw-Hill Inc., 1976.

Fage, T. D. *An Introduction to the History of West Africa.* New York: Cambridge University Press, 1964.

Fattah, E. *A Study of the Effects of Capital Punishment with Specific Reference to the Canadian Situation.* Ottawa: Information Canada, 1973.

Faunce, William A. and Form, William H., eds. *Comparative Perspectives on Industrial Society.* Boston: Little, Brown and Co., 1969.

Feagin, Joe H. "God Helps Those Who Help Themselves." *Psychology Today* (November):103, 1972.

Feldberg, Roslyn L. and Nakano Glen, Evelyn. "Male and Female: Job Versus Gender Models in the Sociology of Work." *Social Problems* 26:524-38, 1979.

Ferrer, Aldo. *The Argentine Economy.* Los Angeles: University of California Press, 1967.

Finkle, T. and Gable, R., eds. *Political Development and Social Change.* New York: John Wiley & Sons, 1971.

Fitt, Yann et al. *The World Economic Crisis.* London: Zed Press, 1980.

Flood, Maxwell. "The Growth of the Non-Institutional Response in the Canadian Industrial Sector." *Relations Industrielles/Industrial Relations* 27:603-15, 1972.

Forbes, Ernest R. *The Maritime Rights Movement, 1919-1927: A Study in Canadian Regionalism.* Montreal: McGill-Queen's University Press, 1979.

————. "In Search of a Post-Confederation Maritime Historiography." *Acadiensis* VIII:1 (Autumn), 1978.

Forcese, Dennis P. and Richer, Stephen. *Social Research Methods.* Englewood Cliffs: Prentice-Hall Inc., 1973.

Foster-Carter, Aidan. "The Modes of Production Controversy." *New Left Review* (1978):107.

Foucault, Michel. *Discipline and Punish: Birth of the Prison.* New York: Pantheon Books Inc., 1977.

Fowke, Vernon C. *Canadian Agricultural Policy: The Historical Pattern.* Toronto: University of Toronto Press, 1947.

————. *The National Policy and the Wheat Economy.* Toronto: University of Toronto Press, 1957.

Fox, Bonnie, ed. *Hidden in the Household: Women's Domestic Labour under Capitalism.* Toronto: Women's Press, 1980.

Frank, Andre Gunder. *Capitalism and Underdevelopment in Latin America: Historical Studies of Chile and Brazil.* New York: Monthly Review Press, 1967.

————. *Latin America: Underdevelopment or Revolution, Essays on the Development of Underdevelopment and the Immediate Enemy.* New York: Monthly Review Press, 1969.

————. *Sociology of Development and Underdevelopment of Sociology.* London: Pluto Press, 1971.

————. *World Accumulation, 1492-1789.* New York: Monthly Review Press, 1978.

————. *Dependent Accumulation and Underdevelopment.* New York: Monthly Review Press, 1979.

————. *Reflections on the World Economic Crisis.* New York: Monthly Review Press, 1981.

————. "The Development of Underdevelopment." *Monthly Review* 17:9, 1966.

Franke, Richard Herbert and Kaul, James D. "The Hawthorne Experiments: First Statistical Interpretation." *American Sociological Review* 43:623-43, 1978.

Frankel, Marvin. *Criminal Sentences: Law without Order.* New York: Hill and Wang, 1972.

Freedman, Marcia. *Labor Markets: Segments and Shelters.* Montclair, NJ: Allanheld, Osmun and Co., 1976.

Freeman, Richard B. and Medoff, James L. "The Two Faces of Unionism." *The Public Interest* 57:69-93, 1979.

Friedland, Martin. *Detention before Trial.* Toronto: University of Toronto Press, 1969.

————. *Access to the Law.* Toronto: Methuen Publications, 1975.

Friedman, Andrew L. *Industry and Labor: Class Struggle at Work and Monopoly Capitalism.* London: Macmillan Publishing Co., 1977.

Friedricks, Robert W. *A Sociology of Sociology.* New York: Free Press, 1970.

Froebel, F.; Heinrichs, J.; and Kreye, O. *The New International Division of Labor.* London: Cambridge University Press, 1980.

Fromm, Erich. *Marx's Concept of Man.* New York: Frederick Ungar, 1961.

Frost, James D. "Principles of Interest." Master's thesis, Queen's University, Kingston, 1978.

Fuller, L. *The Morality of Law.* New York: Yale University Press, 1975.

Galbraith, John Kenneth. *The New Industrial State.* 2d ed. New York: Houghton Mifflin, 1971.

Gamble, Andrew and Walton, Paul. *Capitalism in Crisis: Inflation and the State.* London: Macmillan Publishing Co., 1976.

Giddens, Anthony. *Capitalism and Modern Social Theory.* London: Cambridge University Press, 1971.

Giffen, P.J. "Official Rates of Crime and Delinquency." In *Crime and Delinquency in Canada*, ed. E. Vaz and A. Lodhi. Toronto: Prentice-Hall Canada Inc., 1979.

Gillespie, W.I. "On Redistribution of Income in Canada." *Canadian Tax Journal.* (July/August):419-50, 1976.

————. "Taxes, Expenditures, and the Redistribution of Income in Canada, 1951-1977." *Reflections on Canadian Incomes.* Ottawa: Economic Council of Canada 27-50, 1980.

Girvan, Norman. *Corporate Imperialism: Conflict and Expropriation.* New York: Monthly Review Press, 1978.

————. "Managing the International Capitalist Economy." In *Trilateralism*, ed. Holly Sklar. Montreal: Black Rose Books, 1980.

Glenn, Norval and Werner, David. "Some Trends in the Social Origins of American Sociologists." *Sociologist* 4:291-302, 1969.

Godelier, Maurice. "Structure and Contradiction in Capital." In *Ideology in Social Science*, ed. R. Blackburn. Glasgow: Fontana/Collins, 1972.

Goff, C. and Reasons, C. *Corporate Crime in Canada.* Toronto: Prentice-Hall Canada Inc., 1978.

Goffman, Erving. *Asylums.* Garden City: Doubleday, 1961.

————. *Relations in Public.* New York: Harper and Row, 1971.

Goldfarb, Ronald. *Jails.* New York: Anchor Press, 1975.

Goldmann, Lucien. *The Human Sciences and Philosophy.* London: Jonathan Cape, 1969.

————.*Cultural Creation.* Saint Louis: Telos Press, 1976.

Gomme, I.M. "A Multivariate Analysis of Self-Reported Delinquency among Students." Ph.D. dissertation, Ontario Institute for Studies in Education, Toronto, 1982.

Gonick, Cy. *Out of Work.* Toronto: James Lorimer, 1978.

Goode, M.R. "The Law Reform Commission of Canada." *Canadian Bar Review*, September 1976.

Gordon, David M. *Theories of Poverty and Under-Employment: Orthodox, Radical, and Dual Labor Market Perspectives.* Lexington, MA: D.C. Heath, 1972.

Gough, Ian. *The Political Economy of the Welfare State.* London: Macmillan Publishing Co., 1979.

————. "Marx's Theory of Productive and Unproductive Labour." *New Left Review* 76:47-72, 1972.

Gramsci, Antonio. *Selections from the Prison Notebooks.* New York: International Publishers, 1971 and 1978.

Grant, George. *Lament for a Nation: The Defeat of Canadian Nationalism.* Toronto: McClelland and Stewart Ltd., 1967.

Grayson, J. Paul. "The English Canadian Novel and the Class Structure." *Canadian Journal of Sociology* 6:3, 1981.

————. "Male Hegemony and the English Canadian Novel." *Canadian Review of Sociology and Anthropology* 20:1, 1983.

Grayson, J. Paul and Grayson, Linda. "Class and Ideologies of Class in the English and Canadian Novel." *Canadian Review of Sociology and Anthropology* 15:3, 1978a.

Grayson, J. Paul and Grayson, Linda. "The Canadian Literary Elite, A Socio-historical Perspective." *The Canadian Journal of Sociology* 3:3, 1978b.

Grayson, J. Paul and Magill, Dennis William. "One Step Forward, Two Steps Sideways: Sociology and Anthropology in Canada." Report prepared for the Canadian Sociology and Anthropology Association, 1981.

Green, Francis. "The Myth of Objectivity in Positive Economics." In *Economics: An Anti-Text*, ed. Francis Green and Pelter Nore. London: The Macmillan Press, 1977.

Greenberg, David. *Crime and Capitalism.* Palo Alto: Mayfield Publishing Co., 1981.

————. "Age Structure and Delinquency." *Contemporary* 1:189-223, 1977.

Greenglass, Esther, E. *A World of Difference.* Toronto: John Wiley & Sons, 1982.

Greenspan, Edward. "The Role of the Defence Lawyer in Sentencing." In *New Directions in Sentencing*, ed. Brian Grosman. Toronto: Butterworth & Co., 1980.

Guest, Dennis. *The Emergence of Social Security in Canada.* Vancouver: University of British Columbia Press, 1980.

Gurstein, Michael. "From a Colonial Canadian Sociology to a Sociology of Canada's Colonization." Paper read to the Canadian Sociology and Anthropology Association, McGill University, Montreal, 1972.

Guttsman, W.L. "Aristocracy and the Middle Class in the British Political Elite 1886-1916." *British Journal of Sociology* 5:12-32, 1954.

Haber, Samuel. *Efficiency and Uplift: Scientific Management in the Progressive Era: 1980-1920.* Chicago: University of Chicago Press, 1964.

Hackler, J. *The Prevention of Youthful Crime: The Great Stumble Forward.* Toronto: Methuen Publications, 1978.

Hagan, John. "Criminal Justice in a Canadian Province." Doctoral thesis, University of Alberta, Edmonton, 1974.

Hagan, J.; Simpson, J.H.; and Gillis, A.R. "The Sexual Stratification of Social Control." *British Journal of Sociology* 30:25-38, 1979.

Hagedorn, Robert, ed. *Sociology.* Toronto: Holt, Rinehart & Winston, 1980.

Hall, Stuart et al. *Policing the Crisis.* London: Macmillan Publishing Co., 1978.

Hammond, J.L. and Hammond, Barbara. *The Town Labourer.* Garden City, NJ: Doubleday, 1968.

Hammond, Philip E., ed. *Sociologists at Work: Essays on the Craft of Social Research.* New York: Basic Books, 1964.

Harre, R. and Secord, P.F. *The Explanation of Social Behaviour.* Oxford: Basil Blackwell, 1972.

Harris, José. *William Beveridge: A Biography.* London: Oxford University Press, 1977.

Harris, Marvin. *Cultural Materialism.* New York: Random House, 1979.

Harrison, Deborah. *The Limits of Liberalism: The Making of Canadian Sociology.* Montreal: Black Rose Books, 1981.

Heap, James L. *Everybody's Canada: The Vertical Mosaic Reviewed and Re-examined.* Toronto: Burns and MacEachern Limited, 1974.

Heer, Frederich. *The Medieval World.* New York: New American Library, 1962.

Heilbroner, Robert L. *Marxism: For and Against.* New York: W.W. Norton and Co., 1980.

Henley, Nancy. *Body Politics.* New York: Prentice-Hall Inc., 1977.

Henry, S. *The Hidden Economy.* London: Martin Robertson, 1978.

Heron, Craig. "Hamilton's Metal Workers in the Early Twentieth Century." *Labor/Le Travailleur* 6(Autumn):7-48, 1980.

Heron, Craig and Palmer, Bryan. "Through the prism of the strike: industrial conflict in southern Ontario, 1910-14." *Canadian Historical Review* 58:423-58, 1977.

Hess, R.D. and Torney, J.V. *The Development of Political Attitudes in Children.* Chicago: Aldine Publishing Co., 1967.

Hiller, Harry H. *Society and Change: S.D. Clark and the Development of Canadian Sociology*. Toronto: University of Toronto Press, 1981.
————. "The Canadian Sociology Movement." *Canadian Journal of Sociology* 4 (Spring), 1979.
————. "Humour and Hostility: An Analysis of Novelty Items in the Recent Wave of Western Separatism." Paper presented at the Annual Meetings of the Canadian Sociology and Anthropology Association, 1981a.
Hilton, Rodney, ed. *The Transition from Feudalism to Capitalism*. London: New Left Books, 1976.
Hindess, Barry. *The Use of Official Statistics in Sociology*. London: The Macmillan Press, 1973.
————. *Philosophy and Methodology in the Social Sciences*. Sussex: The Harvester Press, 1977.
Hindess, Barry and Hirst, Paul Q. *Pre-Capitalist Modes of Production*. London: Routledge and Kegan Paul, 1975.
Hirsh, T. *Causes of Delinquency*. Berkeley: University of California Press, 1969.
Hirst, Paul. *On Law and Ideology*. Atlantic Highlands, NJ: Humanities Press, 1979.
Hobsbawn, E.J. *Industry and Empire*. London: Penguin Books, 1969.
————. "Karl Marx's Contribution to Historiography." In *Ideology in Social Science*, ed. R. Blackburn. Glasgow: Fontana/Collins, 1972.
Hoffman-Bustamonte, J. "Female Criminology." *Issues in Criminology* 8:117-36, 1973.
Hofstadter, Richard. *The Progressive Historians*. New York: Knopf, 1968.
Hogarth, John. *Sentencing as a Human Process*. Toronto: University of Toronto Press, 1971.
Hoggetts, A.B. *What Culture? What Heritage?* Toronto: Ontario Institute for Studies in Education, 1968.
Homans, George C. *The Human Group*. New York: Harcourt, Brace and World, 1950.
Horn, D.B. *A Short History of the University of Edinburgh 1556-1889*. Edinburgh: Edinburgh University Press, 1967.
Horn, Michael. *The League for Social Reconstruction: Intellectual Origins of the Democratic Left in Canada 1930-1942*. Toronto: University of Toronto Press, 1980.
Horowitz, Gad. "Conservatism, Liberalism, and Socialism in Canada. An Interpretation." In *Canadian Labour in Politics*, ed. G. Horowitz. Toronto: University of Toronto Press, 1966.
House, J.D. "Big Oil and Small Communities in Coastal Labrador: the Local Dynamics of Dependency." *Canadian Review of Sociology and Anthropology* 18:433-52, 1981.
Hovland, C.I. and Weiss, W. "The Influence of Source Credibility on Communications Effectiveness." *Public Opinion Quarterly* 15:635-50, 1951.
Hughes, Everett C. *French Canada in Transition*. Chicago: University of Chicago Press, 1943.
Hughes, H. Stuart. *Consciousness and Society*. New York: Vintage, 1958.
Hunter, Jean I. "The French Invasion of the Eastern Townships: A Regional Study." Master's thesis, McGill University, Montreal, 1939.
Hurt, John. *Education in Evolution*. London: Paladin, 1971.
Hurtig, Mel. *Never Heard of Them...They Must be Canadian*. Toronto: Canada Books, 1975.
Hutcheson, John. *Dominance and Dependence*. Toronto: McClelland and Stewart Ltd., 1978.
————. "Special Issue: Imperialism and the State?" *Insurgent Sociologist* VII:II, 1977.
Huxley, Christopher. "The State, Collective Bargaining and the Shape of Strikes in Canada." *Canadian Journal of Sociology* 4:223-39, 1979.
Hyman, Richard. *Industrial Relations: A Marxist Introduction*. London: Macmillan Publishing Co., 1975.

————. "Trade Unions, Control and Resistance." In *The Politics of Work and Occupations*, ed. Geoff Esland and Graeme Salaman. Toronto: University of Toronto Press, 1980.

Hyman, Richard and Brough, Ian. *Social Values and Industrial Relations*. Oxford: Blackwell, 1975.

Hymer, Stephen. "Robinson Crusoe and the Secret of Primitive Accumulation." *Monthly Review* 4 (September), 1971.

Inciardi, James. *Radical Criminology: the Coming Crisis*. Beverly Hills: Sage Publications, 1980.

Innis, Harold A. *A History of the Canadian Pacific Railway*. London: P. S. King, 1923.

————. *Settlement and the Mining Frontier*. Toronto: The Macmillan Company of Canada Limited, 1936.

————. *Empire and Communications*. Oxford: Clarendon Press, 1950.

————. *The Bias of Communication*. Toronto: University of Toronto Press, 1951.

————. *The Fur Trade in Canada: An Introduction to Canadian Economic History*. Toronto: University of Toronto Press, 1956, 1970, 1975.

————. *Essays in Canadian Economic History*. Toronto: University of Toronto Press, 1956a and 1973.

————. *The Cod Fisheries: The History of an International Economy*. Toronto: University of Toronto Press, 1978.

————. "The Work of Thorstein Veblen." In *Essays in Canadian Economic History*, ed. Mary Q. Innis. Toronto: University of Toronto Press, 1929a.

————. "The Teaching of Economic History of Canada." In op. cit., 1929b.

Irving, J. A. *The Social Credit Movement in Alberta*. Toronto: University of Toronto Press, 1959.

Jalée, Pierre. *The Pillage of the Third World*. New York: Monthly Review Press, 1968.

————. *Imperialism in the Seventies*. New York: Joseph Okpaku Publ. Co., 1972.

————. *How Capitalism Works*. New York: Monthly Review Press, 1977.

Jamieson, Stuart M. *Times of Trouble: Labour and Industrial Conflict in Canada, 1900-66*. Task Force on Labour Relations Study 22. Ottawa: Information Canada, 1968 and Queen's Printer, 1971.

Jay, Martin. *The Dialectical Imagination*. London: Hienemann Educational Books, 1973.

Jencks, Christopher. *Who Gets Ahead? The Determinants of Economic Success in America*. New York: Basic Books, 1979.

Jencks, Christopher et al. *Inequality*. New York: Basic Books, 1972.

Jobson, K. "Reforming Sentencing Laws: A Canadian Perspective." In *New Directions in Sentencing*, ed. Brian Grosman. Toronto: Butterworth & Co., 1980.

Johnson, Leo A. *History of the County of Ontario 1615-1875*. Whitby: The Corporation of the County of Ontario, 1973.

————. "The Development of Class in Canada in the Twentieth Century." In *Structured Inequality in Canada*, ed. John Harp and John R. Hofley. Toronto: Prentice-Hall Canada Inc., 1980.

————. *Poverty in Wealth*. 2d ed. rev. Toronto: New Hogtown Press, 1977.

————. "The Political Economy of Ontario Women in the Nineteenth Century." In *Women at Work: Ontario, 1850-1930*, ed. Janice Acton et al. Toronto: Canadian Women's Educational Press, 1974.

Johnson, Terry. "Work and Power." In *The Politics of Work and Occupations*, ed. Geoff Esland and Graeme Salaman. Toronto: University of Toronto Press, 1980.

Kalbach, W. and McVey, W. *The Demographic Basis of Canadian Society*. Toronto: McGraw-Hill Ryerson Ltd., 1971.

Kanter, Rosabeth Moss. *Men and Women of the Corporation*. New York: Basic Books, 1977.

Kay, Geoffrey. *Development and Underdevelopment*. New York: St. Martin's Press, 1975.

Kealey, Gregory, ed. *Canada Investigates Industrialism*. Toronto: University of Toronto Press, 1973.

————. *Toronto Workers Respond to Industrial Capitalism, 1867-1892.* Toronto: University of Toronto Press, 1980.

————. "Labour and Working-class History in Canada: Prospects in the 1980s." *Labor/Le Travailleur* 7:67-94, 1981.

Keat, Russell and Urry, John. *Social Theory as Science.* London: Routledge and Kegan Paul, 1975.

Keating, P.J. *The Working Classes in Victorian Fiction.* London: Routledge and Kegan Paul, 1971.

Kelebay, Y. and Brooks, William. "The Case Against the New 'Histoire Nationale'". *Teaching History* 23:32-33, 1980.

Kelman, H.C. and Lawrence, L.H. "Violent Man: American Responses to the Trial of Lt. William L. Calley." *Psychology Today* (June):41-81, 1972.

Kerr, Clark et al. *Industrialism and Industrial Man: The Problems of Labor and Management In Economic Growth.* Cambridge: Harvard University Press, 1980.

Kessler-Harris, Alice. "Stratifying by Sex: Understanding the History of Working Women." In *Labor Market Segmentation*, ed. Richard Edwards et al. Lexington: D.C. Heath, 1975.

Kitsuse, J.I. Class notes. Law and Criminology Course, Northwestern University, 1970.

Klein, D. "The Etiology of Female Crime." *Issues in Criminology* 8:3-30, 1973.

Klein, J. "Professional Theft: The Utility of a Concept." *Canadian Journal of Criminology and Corrections* 16:133-44, 1974.

Klinck, Carl F. et al. *Literary History of Canada.* Toronto: University of Toronto Press, 1976.

Knight, Rolf. *Work Camps and Company Towns in Canada and the U.S.; An Annotated Bibliography.* Vancouver: New Start Books, 1975.

Knuttila, K. Murray and McCrorie, James N. "National Policy and Canadian Agrarian Development: a Reassessment." *Canadian Review of Sociology and Anthropology* 17:263-72, 1980.

Kohl, Seena B. *Working Together: Women and Family in Southwestern Saskatchewan.* Toronto: Holt, Rinehart & Winston of Canada Ltd., 1976.

Kolakowski, Leszek. *Main Currents of Marxism.* Oxford: Clarendon Press, 1978.

Kuhn, Thomas S. *The Structure of Scientific Revolutions*, 2d ed. Chicago: University of Chicago Press, 1970a.

————. "Reflections on My Critics." In *Criticism and the Growth of Knowledge*, ed. A. Musgrave. Cambridge: Cambridge University Press, 1970b.

————. "Second Thoughts on Paradigms." In *The Essential Tension*, ed. T.S. Kuhn. Chicago: University of Chicago Press, 1977.

Labour Canada. *1978-1979 Women in the Labor Force.* Part I, Participation. Ottawa: Women's Bureau, Labour Canada, 1980a.

————. *Women in the Labor Force, 1977 Edition.* Part II, Earnings of Men and Women. Ottawa: Women's Bureau, Labour Canada, 1980b.

————. *Women in the Labor Force: Facts and Figures.* Part III, Miscellaneous. Ottawa: Women's Bureau, Labour Canada, 1980c.

Landes, David. *The Unbound Prometheus: Technological Change and Industrial Development in Western Europe from 1750 to the Present.* Cambridge: Cambridge University Press, 1969.

Laslett, Peter. *The World We Have Lost.* London: Methuen and Co. Ltd., 1965.

Laxer, Robert, ed. *Canada Ltd.* Toronto : McClelland & Stewart Ltd., 1973.

————. *Canada's Unions.* Toronto: James Lorimer, 1976.

Laxer, T. and Laxer, R. *The Liberal Idea of Canada.* Toronto: James Lorimer, 1977.

Lazonick, William. "The Subjection of Labour to Capital: the Rise of the Capitalist System." *Review of Radical Economics* 10:1, 1974.

Leblanc, M. "Upper Class Versus Working Class Delinquency." In *Crime in Canadian Society*, ed. R.A. Silverman and J.J. Teevan, 1st. ed. Toronto: Butterworth & Co., 1975.

Lebowitz, Michael A. "The General and the Specific in Marx's Theory of Crisis." *Studies in Political Economy: A Socialist Review* 7:5-25, 1982.

Lee, John Alan. *Getting Sex.* Don Mills: General Publishing, 1978.

————. "Structural Aspects of Police Deviance." In *Organizational Police Deviance*, ed. C.D. Shearing. Toronto: Butterworth & Co., 1981.

Lee, Richard B. "What Hunters Do for a Living." In *Man the Hunter*, ed. Richard B. Lee and Irven Devore. Chicago: Aldine, 1968.

Lenin, V.I. *The State and Revolution.* Peking: Foreign Languages Press, 1965.

————. *Imperialism, the Highest Stage of Capitalism.* Peking: Foreign Languages Press, 1973 (and 1965).

Lenski, G. *Power and Privilege.* New York: McGraw-Hill Book Co., 1966.

Lenski, G. and Lenski, J. *Human Societies.* Toronto: McGraw-Hill Ryerson Ltd., 1971.

Letkemann, P. *Crime As Work.* Toronto: Prentice-Hall Canada Inc., 1973.

Levitt, Kari. *Silent Surrender: The Multinational Corporation in Canada.* Toronto: The Macmillan Company of Canada Limited, 1970.

Lewis, David. *Louder Voices: The Corporate Welfare Bums.* Toronto: James, Lewis and Samuel, 1972.

Lewis, James N., "The Human Ecology of the St. John River Valley," Master's thesis, McGill University, Montreal, 1939.

Leyton, E. *The Myth of Delinquency.* Toronto: McClelland and Stewart Ltd., 1979.

Li, Peter S. *Social Research Methods: An Introduction.* Toronto: Butterworth & Co., 1981.

Linden, E. and Filmore, K. "A Comparative Study of Delinquent Involvement." In *Crime in Canadian Society*, ed., R.A. Silverman and J.J. Teevan. Toronto: Butterworth & Co., 1980.

Lipset, S.M. *Political Man: The Social Bases of Politics.* Garden City: Anchor Books, 1963.

Livingstone, D.W. and Hart, D. *Public Attitudes Towards Education in Ontario.* Toronto: OISE Press, 1979 and 1980.

Lloyd, D. *The Idea of Law.* London: Pelican Books, 1974.

Lodahl, Janice; Gordon, Beyer; and Gordon, Gerald. "The Structure of Scientific Fields and the Functioning of University Graduate Departments." *American Sociological Review* 37:1, 1972.

Logan, H.A. *Trade Unions in Canada: Their Development and Functioning.* Toronto: The Macmillan Company of Canada Ltd., 1948.

Lord, Barry. *The History of Painting in Canada.* Toronto: N.C. Press, 1974.

Lowe, Graham S. "The Rise of Modern Management in Canada." *Canadian Dimensions* 14:32-38, 1979.

————. "Women, Work and the Office: the Feminization of Clerical Occupations in Canada, 1901-1931." *Canadian Journal of Sociology* 5:361-81, 1980a.

————. Bank Unionization in Canada: A Preliminary Analysis. Research Monograph Series, Centre for Industrial Relations. Toronto: University of Toronto Press, 1980b.

Lowenthal, Leo. *Literature, Popular Culture, and Society.* Englewood Cliffs: Prentice-Hall Inc., 1961.

Lucas, Rex A. *Minetown, Milltown, Railtown: Life in Canadian Communities of Single Industry.* Toronto: University of Toronto Press, 1971.

Lukacs, George. *The Meaning of Contemporary Realism.* London: Merlin Press, 1963.

Lumsden, Ian. *Close the 49th Parallel.* Toronto: University of Toronto Press, 1970.

Lundy, Katherina L.P. and Warme, Barbara D., eds. *Work in the Canadian Context: Continuity Despite Change.* Toronto: Butterworth & Co., 1981.

Luxemburg, Rosa. *The Accumulation of Capital.* London: Routledge & Kegan Paul, 1951.

Lynd, Robert S. and Lynd, Helen M. *Middletown.* New York: Harcourt, Brace and World, 1929.

Macdonald, L.R. "Merchants Against Industry: an Idea and its Origins." *Canadian Historical Review* 56(3):263-81, 1975.

MacGuigan, M. *Report of the Subcommittee on the Penitentiary System in Canada.* Ottawa: Supply and Services Canada, 1977.

MacIntyre, Alasdair. "A Mistake About Causality in Social Science." In *Philosophy, Politics and Society*, ed. Peter Laslett and W.G. Runciman. New York: Barnes and Noble Books, 1969.

Mackintosh, William A. "Economic Factors in Canadian History." *Canadian Historical Review* IV:1, 1923.

MacNaughton-Smith, P. *Permission to be Slightly Free.* Ottawa: Law Reform Commission, 1976.

Macpherson, C. B. *Democracy in Alberta.* Toronto: University of Toronto Press, 1953.

————. *The Political Theory of Possessive Individualism.* New York: Oxford University Press, 1962.

Madden, Janice Fanning. *The Economics of Sex Discrimination.* Lexington: Lexington Books, 1973.

Magdoff, Harry. *The Age of Imperialism.* New York: Monthly Review Press, 1969.

Mallory, J.R. *Social Credit and the Federal Power in Canada.* Toronto: University of Toronto Press, 1954.

Mamchur, Stephen W. "The Economic and Social Adjustment of Slavic Immigrants in Canada with Especial Reference to the Ukrainians in Montreal." Master's thesis, McGill University, Montreal, 1934.

Mandel, Ernest. *Marxist Economic Theory.* New York: Monthly Review Press, 1970.

————. *Europe vs. America: Contradictions of Imperialism.* New York: Monthly Review Press, 1970a.

————. *Late Capitalism.* Translated by Joris De Bres. London: New Left Books, 1975.

————. *The Second Slump: A Marxist Analysis of Recession in the Seventies.* Translated by Jon Rothschild. London: New Left Books, 1978.

————. *Long Waves of Capitalist Development, The Marxist Interpretation.* Cambridge: Cambridge University Press, 1980.

Mann, Edward and Lee, John Alan. *The RCMP versus the People.* Don Mills: General Publishing, 1979.

Mann, Michael. *Consciousness and Action Among the Western Working Class.* London: Macmillan Publishing Co., 1973.

Mann, W. E. *Sect, Cult and Church in Alberta.* Toronto: University of Toronto Press, 1955.

————. *Society Behind Bars.* Toronto: Social Science Press, 1961.

Mannix, Daniel and Cowley, Malcolm. *Black Cargoes: A History of the Atlantic Slave Trade, 1518-1865.* New York: Viking Press, 1962.

Mantoux, Paul. *The Industrial Revolution in the Eighteenth Century.* London: Methuen Publications, 1964, and Chicago: University of Chicago Press, 1983. (© 1961 by Jonathan Cape Ltd. and © 1983 by The University of Chicago.)

Marchak, Patricia. *In Whose Interests.* Toronto: McClelland and Stewart Ltd., 1979.

————. *Ideological Perspectives on Canada.* Toronto: McGraw-Hill Ryerson Ltd., 1981.

————. "Labor in a Staples Economy." *Studies in Political Economy* 2:7-35, 1979a.

Marglin, Stephen A. "What do Bosses do? The Origins and Functions of Hierarchy in Capitalist Production." In *The Division of Labor*, ed. Andre Gorz. New York: Humanities Press, 1976.

Mars, G. "Chance, Painters and the Fiddle." In *The Sociology of the Workplace*, ed. M. Warner. London: Allen and Unwin, 1973.

Mars, G. and Henry, S. "Crime at Work." *Sociology* 92:245-63, 1978.

Marsden, Lorna R. and Harvey, Edward B. *Fragile Federation: Social Change in Canada.* Toronto: McGraw-Hill Ryerson Ltd., 1979.

Marsh, Leonard C. *Canadians In and Out of Work: A Survey of Economic Classes and their Relation to the Labour Market.* Toronto: Oxford University Press, 1940.

————. "Report on Social Security for Canada 1943." Reprint of the 1943 edition published by the King's Printer, with a new introduction. Toronto: University of Toronto Press, 1975.

Marx, Karl. *The Communist Manifesto.* Chicago: Henry Regnery, 1954.

————. *Capital,* Vol. II Moscow: Progress, 1956.

————. *Capital,* Vol. III. Moscow: Progress, 1959.

————. *Economic and Philosophical Manuscripts of 1844.* Moscow: Foreign Languages Publishing House, 1961.

————. *Theories of Surplus Value.* Moscow: Progress, 1963a.

————. *The Poverty of Philosophy.* New York: International Publishers, 1963b.

————. *Capital. I. The Process of Capitalist Production.* New York: International Publishers, 1967a.

————. *Capital. II. The Process of Circulation of Capital.* New York: International Publishers, 1967b.

————. *Capital. III. The Process of Capitalist Production as a Whole.* New York: International Publishers, 1967c.

————. *Das Kapital.* 1867. Berlin: Dietz Verlag, 1968.

————. *The Class Struggles in France, 1848-50.* New York: International Publishers, 1969.

————. *Critique of Hegel's "Philosophy of Right."* 1843. Cambridge: Cambridge University Press, 1970.

————. *A Contribution to the Critique of Political Economy.* Moscow: Progress, 1970a.

————. *The Civil War in France.* Peking: Foreign Languages Press, 1970b.

————. *The Eighteenth Brumaire of Louis Bonaparte.* New York: International Publishers, 1972.

————. *Grundrisse. Foundations of the Critique of Political Economy.* Translated with a foreword by Martin Nicolaus. London: Penguin Books, 1973.

————. *The Revolutions of 1848.* London: Penguin Books, 1973a.

————. *Surveys from Exile.* London: Penguin Books, 1973b.

————. *The First International and After.* London: Penguin Books, 1975.

————. *Capital: Volume I.* London: Penguin Books, 1976.

————. *Capital. I. A Critique of Political Economy.* Translated by Ben Fowkes. New York: Random House Inc., 1977.

————. *Capital: Volume II.* London: Penguin Books, 1978.

————. *Capital: Volume III.* London: Penguin Books, 1981.

————. "Economic and Philosophic Manuscripts. (1844)" In *Writings of the Young Marx on Philosophy and Society,* ed., trans. Lloyd D. Easton and Kurt H. Guddat. Garden City, NY: Anchor Books, 1967.

Marx, Karl and Engels, Frederick. *The German Ideology, 1846.* Edited with an introduction by R. Pascal. New York: International Publishers, 1947 and 1970.

————. *Selected Correspondence.* Moscow: Foreign Languages Publishing House, 1953.

————. *Selected Correspondence.* Moscow: Progress, 1955.

————. *Werke, Vol. 20.* (1878.) Berlin: Dietz Verlag: 1962.

Masters, D. C. *The Winnipeg General Strike.* Toronto: University of Toronto Press, 1950.

Mayer, Jan. "Educations, Computers and Dominance." *The Canadian Forum* 713:29-30, 1981.

Mayes, Sharon S. "The Increasing Stratification of Higher Education: Ideology and Consequences." *The Journal of Educational Thought* 11:1,16-27, 1977.

Mayo, Elton. *The Social Problems of an Industrial Civilization.* Cambridge: Harvard University Press, 1945.

McBarnet, D. "Arrest: the Legal Context of Policing." In *The British Police,* ed. S. Holdaway. London: Edward Arnold, 1979.

McCaghy, C. *Deviant Behavior: Crime, Conflict and Interest Groups.* New York: Macmillan Inc., 1976.

McCann, L.D. "Staples and the New Industrialism in the Growth of Post-Confederation Halifax." *Acadiensis* III:2, 1979.

————. "The Mercantile-Industrial Transition in the Metal Towns of Pictou County, 1857-1931." *Acadiensis* X:2, 1981.

McCaul, Marilyn and Michnick, Debbie. "A Content Analysis of Biographies in Reader's Digest." Mimeographed. Toronto: University of Toronto Press, 1975.

McCloskey, Robert G. *American Conservatism in the Age of Enterprise 1865-1910.* 1951. New York: Harper and Row Publishers, Inc., 1964.

McClung, Nellie. *Clearing in the West: My Own Story.* Toronto: Thomas Allen Ltd., 1964.

————. *In Times Like These.* Toronto: University of Toronto Press, 1972.

McDonald, Lynn. *The Sociology of Law and Order.* London: Faber, 1976 and Toronto: Methuen Publications, 1979.

————. "Crime and Punishment in Canada." *Canadian Review of Sociology and Anthropology* 6:212-36, 1969.

McInnes-Hayman, Sasha. Contemporary Canadian Women Artists—A Survey. Unpublished manuscript. London: Womanspirit Art Research and Resource Center, 1980.

McKenzie, Roderick D. "The Ecological Approach to the Study of the Human Community." In *The City*, ed. R. Park et al. Chicago: University of Chicago Press, 1925.

McLeod, Hugh. "The de-Christianisation of the Working Class in Western Europe. (1850-1900)." *Social Compass* 27:191-214, 1980.

McNally, David. "Staple Theory as Commodity Fetishism: Marx, Innis, and Canadian Political Economy." *Studies in Political Economy: A Socialist Review* 6 (Autumn), 1981.

McNamara, J.H. "Uncertainties in Police Work." In *The Police*, ed. D.J. Bordus. New York: John Wiley and Sons. 1967.

McNeil, Gerard and Vance, Sharon. *Cruel and Unusual.* Ottawa: Deneau and Greenberg, 1978.

McTeer, M. "Rape and the Canadian Legal Process." In *Violence in Canada*, ed. M.A. Beyer-Gammon. Toronto: Methuen Publications, 1978.

Mehmet, O. "Who Benefits from the Ontario University System?" Occasional Paper No. 7. Toronto: Ontario Economic Council, 1978.

Meltz, Noah M. *Manpower in Canada; Historical Statistics of the Canadian Labor Force.* Ottawa: Queen's Printer, 1969.

Memmi, Alberta. *The Colonizer and the Colonized.* Boston: Beacon Press, 1965.

Menzies, Heather. *Women and the Chip: Case Studies of the Effects of Informatics on Employment in Canada.* Montreal: Institute for Research on Public Policy, 1981.

Merton, R.K. *Social Theory and Social Structure.* New York: Free Press, 1957 and 1968.

————. "Social Structure and Anomie." *American Sociological Review* 3:672-82, 1938.

————. "Bureaucratic Structure and Personality." In *Reader in Bureaucracy*, ed. Robert K. Merton et al. New York: Free Press, 1952.

Milgram, Stanley. "Some Conditions of Obedience and Disobedience to Authority." In *The Logic of Social Hierarchies*, ed. E.O. Lautmann et al. Chicago: Markham, 1965.

Miliband, Ralph. "Marx and the State." In *Socialist Register*, ed. Ralph Miliband and John Saville. New York: Monthly Review Press, 1965.

————. *The State in Capitalist Society.* London: Quartet Books, 1973.

————. *Marxism and Politics.* Oxford: Oxford University Press, 1977.

Miller, B. and Helwig, D. *A Book About Billie.* Ottawa: Oberon Press, 1974.

Mills, C. Wright. *White Collar: The American Middle Classes.* New York: Oxford University Press, 1956.

————. *The Sociological Imagination.* New York: Oxford University Press, 1959.

————. *The Marxists.* New York: Dell Books, 1962.

Mohr, J.W. "New directions in Sentencing." Paper presented to International Conference on New Directions in Sentencing, May 1979, Saskatoon, Saskatchewan.

Moniere, Denis. *Ideologies in Quebec.* Toronto: University of Toronto Press, 1981.

Moore, Kristin A. and Sawhill, Isabell V. "Implications of Women's Employment for

Home." In *Women Working: Theories and Facts in Perspective*, ed. A.H. Stromberg and S. Harkess. Palo Alto: Mayfield Publishing Co., 1978.

Moore, Steve and Wells, Debi. *Imperialism and the National Question in Canada.* Toronto: Moore, 1975.

Morand, Justice Donald R. *Royal Commission into Metro Toronto Police Practices.* Ottawa: Queen's Printer, 1976.

Morton, Desmond and Copp, Terry. *Working People: An Illustrated History of Canadian Labour.* Ottawa: Deneau and Greenberg, 1980.

Morton, M.E. and West, W.G. *Research Evaluation of the Frontenac Diversion Programme.* Ottawa: Solicitor-General, 1980.

Morton, W. L. *The Progressive Party in Canada.* Toronto: University of Toronto Press, 1950.

Moyes, Adrian. *One in Ten: Disability and the Very Poor.* Birmingham: Third World Publications, 1981.

Müller, Ronald. "The Multinational Corporation and the Underdevelopment of the Third World." In *The Political Economy of Development and Underdevelopment*, ed. C.K. Wilber. New York: Random House, 1973.

Muñoz, Heraldo. *From Dependency to Development.* Boulder: Westview Press, 1981.

Musgrove, Frank. *Youth and the Social Order.* Bloomington: Indiana University Press, 1965.

————. *School and the Social Order.* Toronto: John Wiley and Sons, 1979.

Myers, Gustavus. *The History of Canadian Wealth.* Toronto: James Lewis & Samuel, 1972.

Nagel, S. "The Tipped Scales of American Justice." In *Critical Issues in the Study of Crime*, ed. S. Dinitz and W. Reckless. Boston: Little Brown, 1968.

National Film Board. "Cree Hunters of Mistassini."

Navarro, Vicente. *Class Struggle, the State and Medicine.* London: Martin Robinson, 1978.

Naylor, Tom. *The History of Canadian Business 1867-1914, vols. I and II.* Toronto: James Lorimer, 1975.

————. "The Rise and Fall of the Third Commercial Empire of the St. Lawrence." In *Capitalism and the National Question*, ed. G. Teeple. Toronto: University of Toronto Press, 1972.

————. "Dominion of Capital: Canada and International Investment." In *Class State, Ideology and Change*, ed. P. Grayson. Toronto: Holt, Rinehart & Winston of Canada Ltd., 1980.

Nelsen, R.W. "The Education-as-autonomous Argument and Pluralism: the Sociologies of Burton R. Clark, David Riesman, and Christopher Jencks." In *Reading, Writing and Riches: Education and the Socio-Economic Order in North America*, ed. R.W. Nelsen and D.A. Nock. Kitchener: Between-the-Lines, 1978.

Nelson, Daniel. *Frederick W. Taylor and the Rise of Scientific Management.* Madison: University of Wisconsin Press, 1980.

Nelson, L.L. and Kagan, S. "The Star-Spangled Scramble." *Psychology Today* (September):53, 1972.

Nettler, G. *Explaining Crime.* Toronto: McGraw-Hill Ryerson Ltd., 1978.

Neufeld, E. P. *The Financial System of Canada: Its Growth and Development.* Toronto: Macmillan of Canada, 1972.

Newbigin, Marion. *Canada: The Great River, The Lands, and the Men.* London: Christophers, 1926.

Newfarmer, Richard and Muller, Willard. U.S., Congress, Senate, Subcommittee on Multinational Corporations in Brazil and Mexico: Structural Sources of Economic and Noneconomic Power, 94th Cong., 9th sess., 1975.

Newman, G. *Comparative Deviance.* New York: Elsevier, 1976.

Newman, P. *The Canadian Establishment.* Toronto: McClelland & Stewart Ltd., 1975.

Niederhoffer, Arthur. *Behind the Shield: the Police in Urban Society.* New York: Doubleday, 1969.

Niederhoffer, Arthur and Blumberg, A.S. *The Ambivalent Force: Perspectives on the Police.* Waltham, MA: Ginn and Company, 1970.

Nightingale, Donald V. *Workplace Democracy: An Inquiry into Employee Participation in Canadian Work Organizations.* Toronto: University of Toronto Press, 1982.

Niosi, Jorge. *The Economy of Canada: Who Controls It.* Montreal: Black Rose Books, 1978.

————. *Canadian Capitalism.* Montreal: Black Rose Books, 1981.

Nock, David. A. "A White Man's Burden: A Portrait of E.F. Wilson, Missionary in Ontario, 1868-1885." Master's thesis, Carleton University, Ottawa, 1973.

————. "The Initimate Connection: Links between the Political and Economic Systems in Canadian Federal Politics." Ph.D. dissertation, University of Alberta, Edmonton, 1976.

————. "The Social Effects of Missionary Education: a Victorian Case Study." In *Reading, Writing and Riches*, ed. R.W. Nelsen and D.A. Nock. Kitchener: Between-the-Lines, 1978.

Normandeau, A. "Quelques Faits Sur le Vol Dans Les Grands Magasins." *Canadian Journal of Criminology and Corrections* 13:251-65, 1971.

Nye, F.I. *Family Relations and Delinquent Behavior.* New York: John Wiley & Sons, 1958.

O'Connor, James. *The Fiscal Crisis of the State.* New York: St. Martin's Press, 1973.

————. "Productive and Unproductive Labour." *Politics and Society.* 5(3):297-336, 1975.

O'Hearn, Michael. "The Canadianization Sociology Debate in English Canada, 1972-1976." In Grayson and Magill, 1981.

Ollman, Bertell. "Marx's Use of 'Class.'" *American Journal of Sociology* 73(5):573-80, 1968.

Olson, Paul. "Laboring to Learn: How Working Theory Gets Down to Classrooms and Kids." *Interchange* 12:2, 1981.

Ommer, Rosemary. "All the Fish of the Post: Perrty Resource Rights and Development in a Nineteenth Century Inshore Fishery." *Acadiensis* X:2, 1981.

Ontario. Provincial Secretariat for Justice. *Crime in Ontario.* Toronto: Justice, n.d.

Ontario Select Committee on Plant Shutdowns and Employee Adjustment. *Preceedings, 1980-81.* Toronto: Queen's Park, 1981.

Ornstein, Michael. "The Occupational Mobility of Men in Ontario." *Canadian Review of Sociology and Anthropology* 18(2):183-215, 1981.

Osberg, Lars. *Economic Inequality in Canada.* Toronto: Butterworth & Co., 1981.

Oskamp, S. "Attitudes Toward U.S. and Russian Actions—A Double Standard." *Psychological Reports* 16:43-46, 1965.

Ostenso, Martha. *Wild Geese.* Toronto: McClelland & Stewart Ltd., 1967.

Ostry, Sylvia and Zaidi, Mahmood A. *Labor Economics in Canada,* 2d ed. Toronto: Macmillan of Canada, 1972.

Ouellet, Fernand. *Lower Canada 1791-1840: Social Change and Nationalism.* Toronto: McClelland & Stewart Ltd., 1980.

Overton, James. "Towards a Critical Analysis of Neo-nationalism in Newfoundland." In *Underdevelopment and Social Movements in Atlantic Canada*, ed. R. Brym and J. Sacouman. Toronto: New Hogtown Press, 1979.

Palmer, Bryan. *A Culture in Conflict: Skilled Workers and Industrial Capitalism in Hamilton, Ontario 1860-1914.* Montreal: McGill- Queen's University Press, 1979.

————. "Class, Conception and Conflict: the Thrust for Efficiency, Managerial Views of Labor and the Working Class Rebellion, 1903-22." *Radical Review of Political Economics* 7:31-49, 1975.

Parr, Joy. *Labouring Children.* Montreal: McGill-Queen's University Press, 1980.

Pattison, J.C. *Financial Markets and Foreign Ownership.* Toronto: Ontario Economic Council, 1978.

Pearson, G. "Goths and Vandals, Crime in History." In *Crime and Capitalism*, ed. David Greenberg. Palo Alto: Mayfield Publishing Co., 1981.

Pentland, H. Claire. *Labor and Capital in Canada, 1650-1860.* Toronto: James Lorimer, 1981.

————. "The Development of a Capitalistic Labour Market in Canada." *Canadian Journal of Economics and Political Science* 25, 1959.

————. "Labour and the Development of Industrial Capitalism in Canada." Ph.D. dissertation, University of Toronto, 1960.

————. "The Canadian Industrial Relations System: Some Formative Factors." *Labor/Le Travailleur* 4:9-23, 1979.

Perrow, Charles. *Complex Organizations: A Critical Essay.* Glenview: Scott, Foresman & Co., 1972.

Petchesky, Rosalind. "At Hard Labour, Penal Confinement and Production in Nineteenth Century America." In *Crime and Capitalism*, ed. David Greenberg. Palo Alto: Mayfield Publishing Co., 1981.

Petras, James. *Politics and Social Structure in Latin America.* New York: Monthly Review Press, 1970.

————. *Critical Perspectives on Imperialism and Social Class in the Third World.* New York: Monthly Review Press, 1978.

Phillips, Paul. *Regional Disparities.* Toronto: James Lorimer & Company, 1978a.

————. "Vernon C. Fowke and the Hinterland Perspective." *Canadian Journal of Political and Social Theory* 2:73-96, 1978b.

Pike, Robert M. "Education, Class and Power in Canada." In *Power and Change in Canada*, ed. Richard J. Ossenberg. Toronto: McClelland & Stewart Ltd., 1980.

Pincus, Fred. "Tracking in Community Colleges." In *Reading, Writing and Riches*, ed. R.W. Nelsen and D.A. Nock. Kitchener: Between-the-Lines. 1978.

Pineo, Peter C. "Prestige and Mobility: the Two National Surveys." *Canadian Review of Sociology and Anthropology* 18:5, 615-62, 1981.

Pollard, Sidney. *The Genesis of Modern Management.* London: Penguin Books, 1968.

Pomfret, John. *The Economic Development of Canada.* Toronto: Methuen Publications, 1981.

Pöntinen, Seppo and Husitalo, Hannu. "Socioeconomic Background and Income." *Acta Sociologica* 18(4):322-29, 1975.

Porter, John. *The Vertical Mosaic: An Analysis of Social Class and Power in Canada.* Toronto: University of Toronto Press, 1965.

————. *Stations and Callings: Making it Through the School System.* Toronto: Methuen Publications, 1982.

————. "Ethnic Pluralism in Canadian Perspective." In *Ethnicity: Theory and Experience*, ed. N. Glazer and D. P. Moynihan. Cambridge: Harvard University Press, 1975.

————. "Research Biography of a Macrosociological Study: The Vertical Mosaic." In *The Measure of Canadian Society: Education, Equality and Opportunity*, ed. John Porter. Toronto: Gage Publishing Limited, 1979a.

————. "Prologue." In op.cit., 1979b.

Porter, John; Porter, Marion R.; and Blishen, Bernard R. *Does Money Matter? Prospects for Higher Education in Ontario.* Toronto: Macmillan of Canada Limited, 1973.

Posner, Michael. "Law and Order on the March." *Macleans* October 2:26-30, 1978.

Poulantzas, Nicos. *Classes in Contemporary Capitalism.* London: New Left Review, 1974 and London: Verso, 1978.

Pratt, Larry. *The Tar Sands: Syncrude and the Politics of Oil.* Toronto: McClelland & Stewart Ltd., 1976.

Pratt, Vernon. *The Philosophy of the Social Sciences.* London: Methuen Publications, 1978.

Preiss, J.J. and Ehrlich, H.J. *An Examination of Role Theory: the Case of the State Police.* Lincoln: University of Nebraska Press, 1968.

Prentice, Alison. *The School Promoters: Education and Social Class in Mid-Nineteenth Century Upper Canada.* Toronto: McClelland & Stewart Ltd., 1977.

Preston, Richard A., ed. *Perspectives on Revolution and Evolution.* Durham: Duke University Press, 1979.

Prus, R. and Sharper, C.R.D. *Road Hustler*. Toronto: Gage Publishing Limited, 1980.

Pupo, Norene. "The Postwar University in Canada and the Need for Skilled Labour: the Waterloo Example." In *Reading, Writing and Riches*, ed., R.W. Nelsen and D.A. Nock. Kitchener: Between-the-Lines, 1978.

Quinney, Richard. *Critique of Legal Order*. Boston: Little Brown, 1974.

Radical Statistics Nuclear Disarmament Group. *The Nuclear Numbers Game*. London: Radical Statistics, 1982.

Radice, H., ed. *International Firms and Modern Imperialism*. London: Penguin Books, 1976.

Ramsay, Jack. "My Case Against the RCMP." In *Decency and Deviance*, J. Haas and B. Shaffir. Toronto: McClelland & Stewart Ltd., 1978.

Reasons, C. et al. *Assault on the Worker*. Toronto: Butterworth & Co., 1981.

Reed, P.; Blesznyski, T.; and Gaucher, R. "Homicide in Canada." In *Violence in Canada*, ed. M.A. Beyer-Gammon. Toronto: Methuen Publications, 1978.

Reiman, J.H. *The Rich get Richer and the Poor get Prison*. New York: John Wiley & Sons, 1979.

Resnick, Philip. *The Land of Cain: Class and Nationalism in English Canada 1945-1975.* Vancouver: New Star Books, 1977 and 1979.

Reynold, Lloyd G. "The Occupational Adjustment of the British Immigrant in Montreal." Master's thesis, McGill University, Montreal, 1933.

Richards, John and Pratt, Larry. *Prairie Capitalism: Power and Influence in the New West*. Toronto: McClelland & Stewart Ltd., 1979.

Richardson, James. "Education and Social Mobility: Changing Conceptions of the Role of the Educational Systems." *Canadian Journal of Sociology* 2:417-733, 1977.

Rickman, H.P. *Understanding and the Human Studies*. London: Heinemann Educational Books, 1967.

Riesman, David. *Thorstein Veblen: A Critical Interpretation*. New York: Charles Scribner's Sons, 1953.

Rinehart, James W. *The Tyranny of Work*. Don Mills: Longman Canada, 1975.

Rinehart, James W. and Okraku, Ishmael O. "A Study of Class Consciousness." *Canadian Review of Sociology and Anthropology* 11:197-213, 1974.

Rioux, Marcel. *Quebec in Question*. Toronto: James Lorimer, 1978.

Ritzer, George. *Sociology: A Multi-Paradigm Science*. Boston: Allyn and Bacon, 1975.

Roberts, Simon. *Order and Dispute: An Introduction to Legal Anthropology*. London: Penguin Books, 1979.

Roberts, Wayne. "Patterson Takes It." *Canadian Dimension* 15(Aug-Sept):4-6, 1981.

Roethlisberger, F.J. and Dickson, W.J. *Management and the Worker*. Cambridge: Harvard University Press, 1939.

Roffman, Peter and Purdy, Jim. *The Hollywood Social Problem Film*. Bloomington: Indiana University Press, 1981.

Rose, Arnold. *The Power Structure: Political Process in American Society*. New York: Oxford University Press, 1967.

Rosenbluth, Gideon. *Concentration in Canadian Manufacturing Industries*. Princeton: Princeton University Press, 1957.

Ross, O. "North-south: a Summit to Narrow a Global Gap." *Globe and Mail*, Toronto, October 19, 1981.

Rowthorn, Robert and Hymer, Stephen. *International Big Business*. New York: Cambridge University Press, 1971.

Roy, Donald F. "Quota Restriction and Goldbricking in a Machine Shop." *American Journal of Sociology* 57:427-42, 1952.

————. "Work Satisfaction and Social Reward in Quota Achievement and Analysis of Piecework Incentive." *American Sociological Review* 18:507-14, 1953.

————. "Efficiency and the Fix: Informal Intergroup Relations in a Piecework Machine Shop." *American Journal of Sociology* 60:255-66, 1954.

————. "'Banana Time': Job Satisfaction and Informal Interaction." *Human Organization* 18:158-68, 1958.

Rubin, Lillian B. *Worlds of Pain.* New York: Basic Books, 1976.

Runciman, W.G. *Sociology in its Place.* Oxford: Cambridge University Press, 1970.

Ryan, S. "Canada's Alcohol Appetite: 500 Billion Gallons a Year." *Kingston Whig Standard*, May 3, 1978.

Ryerson, Stanley. *Unequal Union.* Toronto: Progress Books, 1968.

————. *The Foundings of Canada: Beginnings to 1815.* Toronto: Progress Books, 1972.

————. "Who's Looking After Business." *This Magazine* 10(Nov.-Dec.):4-6, 1976.

Sacouman, R. James. "Semi-proletarianization and Rural Underdevelopment in the Maritimes." *Canadian Review of Sociology and Anthropology* 17:232-45, 1980.

————. "The 'Peripheral' Maritimes and Canada-wide Marxist Political Economy." *Studies in Political Economy: a Socialist Review* 6:135-60, 1981.

Safarian, A.E. *Foreign Ownership of Canadian Industry.* Toronto: McGraw-Hill Ryerson Ltd., 1966.

Sangster, Joan. "The 1907 Bell Telephone Strike: Organizing Women Workers." *Labour: Journal of Canadian Labour Studies* 3:109-30, 1978.

Sartre, Jean-Paul. *Search for a Method.* New York: Vintage Books, 1968.

Schecter, Stephen. "Capitalism, Class and Educational Reform in Canada." In *The Canadian State*, ed. Leo Panitch. Toronto: University of Toronto Press, 1977.

Schur, Edwin. *Labelling Deviant Behavior.* New York: Harper & Row Publishers, Inc., 1971.

————. *Victimless Crimes.* New York: Prentice-Hall Inc., 1974.

Schwartz, Jesse, ed. *The Subtle Anatomy of Capitalism.* Santa Monica: Goodyear, 1977.

Scott, Bruce D. "Social Norms and Value in Magazine Advertising." Mimeographed. Toronto: University of Toronto, 1975.

Scraton, P. and South, N. "Capitalist Discipline, Private Justice and the Hidden Economy." Occasional Papers in Crime and Deviance. Middlesex Polytechnic, U.K., 1981.

Scull, A. *Decarceration.* New York: Prentice-Hall Inc., 1977.

Seidel, Judith. "The Development and Social Adjustment of the Jewish Community in Montreal." Master's thesis, McGill University, Montreal, 1939.

Sennett, Richard and Cobb, Jonathan. *The Hidden Injuries of Class.* New York: Random House, 1973.

Shearing, C.D. *Organizational Police Deviance.* Toronto: Butterworth & Co., 1981.

Shearing, C. and Stenning. P. "Private Justice: the Privatization of Social Control under Capitalism." Paper read at American Society of Criminology, Washington, 1981.

Sheridan, Richard. "The Plantation Revolution and the Industrial Revolution, 1625-1775." *Caribbean Studies* 9:3, 1969.

Shoup, Lawrence and Minter, William. *Imperial Brain Trust.* New York: Monthly Review Press, 1977.

Silver, Arthur. "French Canada and the Prairie Frontier." *The Canadian Historical Review* L (March), 1969.

Simey, T. S. and Simey, M. B. *Charles Booth: Social Scientist.* London: Oxford University Press, 1960.

Skinner, B.F. *Beyond Freedom and Dignity.* New York: Bantam Books, 1971.

Sklar, Holly, ed. *Trilateralism.* Montreal: Black Rose Books, 1980.

Skolnick, Jerome. *Justice Without Trial.* New York: John Wiley & Sons, 1966.

Smith, A.J.M. "Evolution and Revolution as Aspects of English-Canadian and American Literature." In *Perspectives on Revolution and Evolution*, ed. R.A. Preston. Durham: Duke University Press, 1979.

Smith, Adam. *The Wealth of Nations.* Chicago: University of Chicago Press, 1976 (originally published in 1776).

————. *An Inquiry into the Nature and Courses of the Wealth of Nations.* Oxford: Clarendon Press, 1976.

Smith, Allan. "The Myth of the Selfmade Man in English Canada." *Canadian Historical Review* 59(2), 1978.

Smith, Dorothy E. "The Experienced World as Problematic: A Feminist Method." Paper presented at the Sorokin Lecture, University of Saskatchewan, 1981.

Smith, Douglas. "The Determinants of Strike Activity in Canada." *Relations Industrielles/Industrial Relations* 27:663-78, 1972.

————. "The Impact of Inflation on Strike Activity in Canada." *Relations Industrielles/Industrial Relations* 31:139-45, 1976.

Smith, Joan. *Social Issues and the Social Order: The Contradications of Capitalism.* Cambridge: Winthrop Publishers, Inc., 1981.

Smith, Michael R. "The Effects of Strikes on Workers: a Critical Analysis." *Canadian Journal of Sociology* 3:457-72, 1978.

Smucker, Joseph. "Ideology and Authority." *Canadian Journal of Sociology* 2,3:263-82, 1977.

————. *Industrialization in Canada.* Toronto: Prentice-Hall Canada Inc., 1980.

Snider, L. "Does the Legal Order Reflect the Power Structure." Ph.D. dissertation, University of Toronto, 1977.

Snyder, David. "Early North American Strikes: A Reinterpretation." *Industrial and Labour Relations Review* 30(3):325-41, 1977.

Solicitor-General. *Selected Trends in Canadian Criminal Justice.* Ottawa, 1979.

Sorokin, Pitirim. *Social and Cultural Dynamics, I.* New York: The Bedminister Press, 1962.

Souza, Herbert. "Notes on World Capital." *Latin American Research Unit* (LARU) 11:2, 1978.

Stanbury, W.T. *Business Interests and the Reform of Canadian Competition Policy 1971-1975.* Toronto: Methuen Publications, 1977.

Starks, Richard. *Industry in Decline.* Toronto: James Lorimer, 1978.

Statistics Canada. *Perspective Canada.* Ottawa: Supply and Services, 1974.

————. *Perspective Canada II.* Ottawa: Supply and Services, 1977.

————. *The Distribution of Income and Wealth in Canada 1977.* Ottawa, 1979.

————. *Canada Year Book, 1980-81.* Ottawa: Supply and Services, 1981.

Stevenson, Garth. *Unfulfilled Union: Canadian Federalism and National Unity.* Toronto: Gage Publishing Limited, 1982.

Stevenson, Paul. "Accumulation in the World Economy and the International Division of Labour." *Canadian Review of Sociology and Anthropology* 17:3, 1980.

Stone, Katherine. "The Origins of Job Structures in the Steel Industry." *Review of Radical Political Economics* 6:113-73, 1974.

Stone, Lawrence. *The Family, Sex and Marriage in England 1500-1800.* London: Penguin Books, 1979.

Strick, Anne. *Injustice for All.* London: Penguin Books, 1977.

Sutherland, E. *The Professional Thief.* Chicago: University of Chicago Press, 1937.

Svalastoga, Karre and Rishj, Tom. "Social Mobility: the Western Europe Model." *Acta Sociologica* 9(3):175-82, 1966.

Swainson, Donald. "Regionalism and the Social Scientists." *Acadiensis* 10:143-53, 1980.

Swartz, Donald. "New Forms of Worker Participation: a Critique of Quality of Working Life." *Studies in Political Economy* 5:55-78, 1981.

Sykes, Richard and Clark, John. "A Theory of Deference Exchange in Police-Civilian Encounters." *American Journal of Sociology* 81:584-600, 1975.

Symons, T.H.B. *To Know Ourselves: The Report of the Commission on Canadian Studies.* Ottawa: Association of Universities and Colleges of Canada, 1975.

Szymanski, Al. *The Logic of Imperialism.* New York: Praeger Publishers, 1981.

————. "Capital Accumulation on a World Scale and the Necessity of Imperialism." *The Insurgent Sociologist* VII: 35-53, 1977.

Tagaki, Paul. "Death by Police Intervention." In *A Community Concern: Police Use of Deadly Force*, issued by United States Department of Justice. Washington: Govt. Printing Office, 1979.

Tapp, June L. "A Child's Garden of Law and Order." *Psychology Today* 4, 7:29-31, 62, 64, 1970.

Tawney, R. H. *Religion and the Rise of Capitalism.* New York: Mentor, 1947.

Taylor, Frederick W. *Shop Management.* New York: Harper & Row, Publishers Inc., 1919.

————. *Scientific Management.* New York: Harper & Row, Publishers Inc., 1947.

————. "What is Scientific Management?" *Industrial Canada* (April):1224-25, 1913.

Taylor, I. "The Sociology of Law and Order." *Canadian Journal of Sociology* 3:263-69, 1978.

Taylor, Ian; Walton, Paul; and Young, Jock. *The New Criminology.* London: Routledge and Kegan Paul, 1973.

Taylor, Peter J. "Geographical Scales Within the World-economy Approach." *Review* 5:3-11, 1981.

Teeple, Gary, ed. *Capitalism and the National Question.* Toronto: University of Toronto Press, 1972.

Teevan, James, ed. *Introduction to Sociology: A Canadian Focus.* Toronto: Prentice-Hall Canada Inc., 1982.

Tegaki, Paul. "The Walnut Street Jail." In *Crime and Capitalism*, ed. David Greenberg. Palo Alto: Mayfield Publishing Co., 1981.

Tepperman, Lorne. *Crime Control.* Toronto: McGraw-Hill Ryerson Ltd., 1977.

Tepperman, Lorne and Smith, David. "Changes in the Canadian Business and Legal Elites, 1860-1960." Mimeographed. Toronto: University of Toronto, 1974.

Terkel, Studs. *Working.* New York: Pantheon Press, 1972.

Therbron, Göran. *What Does the Ruling Class Do When It Rules?* London: New Left Books, 1978.

Thomas, Dylan. "A Few Words of a Kind." *Dylon Thomas Reciting*, Vol III. Caedmon Records, n.d.

Thomas, L. G. *The Liberal Party in Alberta.* Toronto: University of Toronto Press, 1959.

Thomas, William I. and Znaniecki, Florian. *The Polish Peasant in Poland and America.* New York: Alfred A. Knopf Inc., 1918.

Thompson, E.P. *The Poverty of Theory.* New York: Monthly Review Press, 1978.

Tigar, Michael and Levy, Madeleine. *Law and the Rise of Capitalism.* New York: Monthly Review Press, 1977.

Tippen, David. "Socialization Processes in Media of Communication: The Creation of Boundaries of Behavior." Mimeographed. Toronto: University of Toronto, 1974.

————. "The Social Bases of Ontario Railroad Ideology, 1840-1890." Ph.D dissertation, University of Toronto, 1983.

Tugendhart, Christopher. *The Multinationals.* London: Eyre and Spottiiworde, 1971.

Turk, Austin. *Criminality and the Legal Order.* Chicago: Rand McNally, 1969.

————. "Law as a Weapon in Social Conflict." *Social Problems* 23:276-91, 1976.

Turnbull, Colin M. *The Forest People.* New York: Simon and Schuster, 1962.

Turrittin, Anton H. "Social Mobility in Canada: a Comparison of the Provincial Studies and Some Methodological Questions." *Canadian Review of Sociology and Anthropology*, special publication on aspects of Canadian society:163-86, 1974.

Tuttle, Harry G. "Frontier Religious Organization with Special Reference to the Peace River Area." Master's thesis, McGill University, Montreal, 1931.

United Nations. *Yearbook of National Account Statistics.* New York: Department of Economics, 1967.

————. *Multinational Corporations in World Development.* New York: Department of Economics, 1973.

————. *Yearbook of Industrial Statistics.* New York: Department of Economics, 1977.

————. *UNESCO Yearbook.* New York: UNESCO, 1978.

————. *Statistical Yearbook.* New York: Department of Economics, 1978a.

————. *Multinational Corporations in World Development.* New York: U.N. Department of Economics and Social Affairs, 1978b.

United States. President's Commission on Law Enforcement and the Administration of Justice. *Task Force Report: Crime and its Impact - An Assessment.* Washington, D.C.: U.S. Government Printing Office, 1967.

United States Department of Commerce. *Sources and Uses of Funds of Majority-Owned Foreign Affiliates of U.S. Companies: 1966-76.* Bureau of Economic Analysis Staff Paper. Washington: Govt. Printing Office, 1979a.

United States Department of Justice. *A Community Concern: Police Use of Deadly Force.* Washington: Govt. Printing Office, 1979b.

Vallee, Frank G. "Obituary: John Porter (1921-1979)." *Society* 4:1, 1980.

Van Kirk, Sylvia. "The Impact of the White Woman on Fur Trade Society." In *The Neglected Majority*, ed. Susan Mann Trofimenkoff and Alison Prentice. Toronto: McClelland & Stewart Ltd., 1977.

Vaz, E. "Juvenile Delinquency in the Middle Class Youth Culture." In *Crime and Delinquency in Canada*, ed. E. Vaz and A. Lodhi. Toronto: Prentice-Hall Canada Inc., 1979.

Veltmeyer, Henry. "The Capitalist Underdevelopment of Atlantic Canada." In *Underdevelopment and Social Movements in Atlantic Canada*, ed. R. Brym and J. Sacouman. Toronto: New Hogtown Press, 1979.

Vernon, Raymond. *Sovereignty at Bay: The Multinational Spread of U.S. Enterprises.* New York: Basic Books, 1971.

Vigier, Jean-Pierre. "The Crisis and the Third World War." In *The World Economic Crisis*, ed. Yann Fitt et al. London: Zed Press, 1980.

Vincent, C.L. *Policeman.* Toronto: Gage Publishing Limited, 1979.

Vipond, Mary. "The Images of Women in Mass Circulation Magazines in the 1920s." In *The Neglected Majority*, ed. Susan Mann Trofimenkoff and Alison Prentice. Toronto: McClelland & Stewart Ltd., 1977.

Wadel, Cato. *Now, Whose Fault is That?* St. John's: Memorial University of Newfoundland, Institute of Social and Economic Research, 1973.

Wallerstain, Immanuel. *The Modern World System.* New York: Academic Press, 1974.

Warren, Bill. *Imperialism—Pioneer of Capitalism.* London: Versa, 1980.

Watkins, Mel. "The Staple Theory of Economic Growth." *Canadian Journal of Economics and Political Science* 29:2, 1963.

————. "A Staple Theory of Economic Growth." In *Approaches to Canadian Economic History*, ed. W.T. Easterbrook and M.H. Watkins. Toronto: McClelland & Stewart Ltd., 1967.

————. *The Dene Nations: The Colony Within.* Toronto: University of Toronto Press, 1977a.

————. "The Staple Theory Revisited." *Journal of Canadian Studies* 12:5 (Winter), 1977b.

Watson, Tony J. *Sociology, Work and Industry.* London: Routledge and Kegan Paul, 1980.

Weber, Marianne. *Max Weber: A Biography.* New York: John Wiley & Sons, 1975.

Weber, Max. *Law in Economy and Society.* Cambridge: Harvard University Press, 1954.

————. *From Max Weber: Essays in Sociology*, ed. and Trans., H.H. Gerth and C. Wright Mills. New York: Oxford University Press, 1958.

————. *The Theory of Social and Economic Organization.* New York: Free Press, 1964.

————. *Economy and Society*, ed. G. Roth and C. Wittich. 3 vols. New York: Bedminister Press, 1968.

————. *The Methodology of the Social Sciences.* Glencoe, IL: The Free Press, 1979.

Webster, N. "Swords not Ploughshares." *Globe and Mail*, Toronto, October 31, 1981.

Wells, Miriam J. "Alienation, Work Structure, and the Quality of Life: Can Co-operatives Make a Difference?" *Social Problems* 28:548-62, 1981.

West, W.G. "Adolescent Deviance and the School." *Interchange* 6, 1975.

————. "Adolescent Autonomy, Education and Delinquency." In *Schools, Pupils and Deviance*, ed. L. Barton and R. Meighan. Nafferton: Nafferton Educational Publishing, 1979.

————. "Serious Thieves." In *Crime and Delinquency in Canada*, ed., E. Vaz and A. Lodhi. Toronto: Prentice-Hall Canada Inc., 1979a.

————. "The Short Term Careers of Serious Thieves." In *Crime in Canadian Society*, ed., R.A. Silverman and J.J. Teevan, 2nd ed. Toronto: Butterworth & Co., 1980.

————. "Trust among Serious Thieves." *Crime et/and Justice*, 7/8, 3/4, 1981.

————. "The Possibility of British Neo-Marxist Educational Ethnography." Paper read at International Sociological Association Meetings, Mexico City, 1982.

Westhues, Kenneth. *First Sociology*. New York: McGraw-Hill Inc., 1982.

Westley, William. *Violence and the Police*. Boston: MIT Press, 1970.

White, Julie. *Women and Unions*. Report for the Canadian Advisory Council on the Status of Women. Ottawa: Supply and Services Canada, 1980.

White, Terrance H. "The Relative Importance of Work as a Factor in Life Satisfaction." *Relations Industrielles/Industrial Relations* 36:179-91, 1981.

Whitely, W.H. "The Social Composition of the British House of Commons, 1868-1885." *Historical Papers*. The Canadian Historical Association :171-85, 1970.

Wilensky, Harold. "Women's Work: Economic Growth, Ideology, Structure." *Relations Industrielles/Industrial Relations* 7:235-48, 1968.

Wilensky, Jeanne L. and Wilensky, Harold L. "Personal Counselling: The Hawthorne Case." *American Journal of Sociology* 57:265-80, 1951.

Williams, Eric. *Capitalism and Slavery*. New York: Capricorn Books, 1966.

Williams, F.P. "Conflict Theory and Differential Processing." In *Radical Criminology: the Coming Crisis*, ed. James Inciardi. Beverly Hills: Sage Publications, 1980.

Williams, Glen. "Canada: The Case of the Wealthiest Colony." *This Magazine* 10:1 (February-March), 1976.

Williams, Raymond. *Marxism and Literature*. Oxford: Oxford University Press, 1977.

Williams, Rick. "Inshore Fishermen, Unionization, and the Struggle against Underdevelopment Today." In *Underdevelopment and Social Movements in Atlantic Canada*, ed. R. Brym and J. Sacouman. Toronto: New Hogtown Press, 1979.

Williamson, Judith. *Decoding Advertisements*. London: Boyars, 1978.

Wilson, James Q. *Thinking About Crime*. New York: Basic Books, 1975.

Winch, Peter. *The Idea of a Social Science*. London: Routledge and Kegan Paul, 1958.

Wirth, Louis. *The Ghetto*. Chicago: University of Chicago Press, 1928.

Woodruff, William. *Impact of Western Man: A Study of Europes' Role in the World Economy, 1750-1960*. New York: St. Martin's Press, 1967.

Woodward, Bob and Armstrong, Scott. *The Brethren*. New York: Simon and Schuster, 1979.

World Bank. *World Development Report*. New York: Oxford University Press, 1978.

Worrell, Peter. "Educational Selection in Northwestern Ontario." Master's thesis, Department of Sociology, Lakehead University, Thunder Bay, 1980.

Wright, Erik Olin. *The Politics of Punishment*. New York: Harper and Row, 1973.

————. *Class, Crisis and the State*. London: Verso, 1979.

————. "Class Boundaries in Advanced Capitalist Societies." *New Left Review* 98:3-41, 1976.

————. "Alternative Perspectives in Marxist Theory of Accumulation and Crisis." In Schwartz, 1977.

Wynn, Graeme. *Timber Colony*. Toronto: University of Toronto Press, 1981.

Yankelovich, Daniel. "The Ideas of Human Nature." *Social Research* 40:407-28, 1973.

Younge, Eva R. "Social Organization on the Pioneer Fringe, with Special Reference to the Peace River Area." Master's thesis, McGill University, Montreal, 1933.

Zeitlin, Irving M. *Marxism: A Re-examination.* New York: Van Nostrand Reinhold, 1967.

Zeitlin, Lawrence A. "A Little Larceny Can Do a Lot for Employee Moral." *Psychology Today,* June:22-26, 64, 1971.

Zimbardo, Philip. "The Pathology of Imprisonment." *Society* 9:4-8, 1972.

Zorbaugh, Harvey W. *The Gold Coast and the Slum.* Chicago: The University of Chicago Press, 1929.

Zurciek, Elia, and Frizzell, Alan. "Values in Canadian Magazine Fiction." *Journal of Popular Culture* 10, 1976.

Zwelling, Marc. *The Strikebreakers: The Report of the Strike Breaking Committee of the Ontario Federation of Labor and the Labor Council of Metropolitan Toronto.* Toronto: Ontario Federation of Labour and Labour Council of Metropolitan Toronto, 1972.

INDEX

Abercrombie, 372, 409
Absolutism, 183-4, 186
Abstract quantity, 50
Accommodation, 8
Achievement, 433-4
Acker, 283, 294
Act of Union, 1840, 192-6
Adjustive behavior, 450, 452-4
Advanced capitalism, 374
Advanced capitalist societies, 381
Adversary system, 492, 508
Advertising, 428
Age of industry, 106
Ageton, 464
Agribusiness, 325
Agriculture, 237, 240, 266, 277
Aitken, 132-3, 180
Alberta, 404-5
Albrow, 288
Alcohol, 478
Alexander, 160
Alienation, 263-4, 367
Alienation of culture, 313-4
Allen, 395
Alternative element of culture, 385
Alternative religious ideas, 395
Alternatives, 391
Althusser, 45-6, 58, 176, 357-8, 376, 392
American Federation of Labor, 337
Amin, 76, 112-3, 124, 140, 145, 168, 254, 257
Anderson, 5, 258
Anglican church, 395
Anomie/strain theorists, 459
Anthony, 109, 262, 309
Archaic element of culture, 379
Archibald, 81, 164, 356, 455
Aristocracy, 376, 387, 435
Armstrong, J., 448
Armstrong, H., 257, 282, 344, 543
Armstrong, P., 257, 282, 344, 543
Arnold, 487
Aron, 370
Art, 379, 402

Arthurs, 39
Ashenfelter, 43
Assheton-Smith, 371
Assimilation, 8-9, 186-7, 191-2, 210
Assumptions, 537
Atwood, 382
Aubert, 510
Authoritarian personalities, 505
Authoritarianism, 366-8, 394
Authority, 231, 235, 247, 286, 288, 494
Automation, 308
Autonomous development, 250
Autonomy, 420, 449
Averitt, 227
Avery, 284

Babbage, 287
Bagnell, 359
Bail, 516-7, 520
Bain, 305
Bala, 494
Baldus, 44, 438, 440, 495
Bandura, 434
Bank Wiring Observation Room study, 293
Banking, 255
Bankruptcies, 248
Baran, 81
Barbash, 299
Barker, 511
Barnes, 19
Base, 415
Base-superstructure, 454
Baum, 394
Bawdy house, 514
Bayley, 7, 505
Becker, 460, 513
Behaviorism, 410, 412-3, 420
Behaviorist theory, 411
Bell, 165-6, 258, 266
Bell-Rowbotham, 468, 479
Bendix, 289